The Public International Law Study Guide for Students

Exercises and Answers

Cristina Verones and Sébastien Rosselet

HART PUBLISHING

OXFORD AND PORTLAND, OREGON
2013

Published in the United Kingdom by Hart Publishing Ltd
16C Worcester Place, Oxford, OX1 2JW
Telephone: +44 (0)1865 517530
Fax: +44 (0)1865 510710
E-mail: mail@hartpub.co.uk
Website: http://www.hartpub.co.uk

Published in North America (US and Canada) by
Hart Publishing
c/o International Specialized Book Services
920 NE 58th Avenue, Suite 300
Portland, OR 97213-3786
USA
Tel: +1 503 287 3093 or toll-free: (1) 800 944 6190
Fax: +1 503 280 8832
E-mail: orders@isbs.com
Website: http://www.isbs.com

British Library Cataloguing in Publication Data

Data Available

ISBN: 978-1-84946-454-3

Typeset by Forewords, Oxon
Printed and bound in Great Britain by
TJ International Ltd, Padstow

FSC
www.fsc.org
MIX
Paper from responsible sources
FSC® C013056

THE PUBLIC INTERNATIONAL LAW STUDY GUIDE FOR STUDENTS

A sound understanding of public international law is indispensable for any lawyer, whether working in an international or domestic context. It is therefore important that students have a thorough theoretical understanding of international law issues, and are able to apply the relevant international legal rules to a given set of facts, so as to arrive at a legally coherent conclusion. This practical aspect of learning international law is often neglected in favour of more theoretical aspects—which is where this book comes in. The book offers a series of hypothetical practical cases in public international law, including some of its specialised branches, such as international human rights law and international criminal law. It challenges students to practise and familiarise themselves with the methodology and to write solutions to practical international legal questions. The book is in two parts: Part I contains practical (exam-like) questions, while Part II contains the solutions. The practical questions in Part I are organised by subject, such as treaty law or State responsibility. One chapter is dedicated to more complex 'interconnected' cases, where students are asked to tackle problems that span multiple potential cases and topics.

Contents

Introduction and General Presentation

1. Objectives

This exercise book has been created in order to help students to improve their capacities to solve (hypothetical) practical cases in public international law. In their professional careers students will often be asked to determine the law applicable to a particular set of facts, the relevant rules that can be invoked, to apply these rules to the facts and finally to come to a legally motivated conclusion in the case at hand.

Due to their experience, the authors have observed that the level of students is not homogeneous in this regard. The legal syllogism, which is the basis of legal reasoning, is too often not satisfactorily applied. Therefore, the authors considered it to be important to prepare an exercise book, allowing the students to practice the resolution of practical cases and to acquire familiarity with the methodology and the writing of such case solutions.

It is important to stress that the solutions in this book are *suggestions* and that other solutions or arguments can be possible. Nevertheless, the solution proposed for every case in the exercise book should allow the student to compare his/her own solution with the suggested example solution and if necessary to correct his/her methodology, reasoning and writing. Where possible, alternative approaches and solutions or complementary elements are indicated in square brackets and in italics.

The objective of this exercise book is to enable the student to understand by him/herself the legal logic for the resolution of cases and to apply it to different sets of facts and practical cases. The goal of the exercise book is *not* to be a theoretical complement to or even a replacement of a general course of public international law. Even if theoretical elements will be dealt with in the resolution of the cases in order to clarify the law, it is up to each user of this exercise book to previously acquire the necessary knowledge of public international law in order to be able to understand the cases and their solutions.

A sound background in public international law is key also for all other more specialised branches of international law, such as human rights or humanitarian law, since basic principles of public international law are also applicable there. Thus, in order to give students an insight into some of the specialised subjects of international law, some additional cases have been added in the last chapter of this book. It should, however, be emphasised that these cases serve the purpose of an introduction or as a 'glimpse' of specialised subjects in relation to public international law and are in no way sufficient for students wishing to specialise in these branches. For reasons of space only a few specialised subjects have been chosen, mainly because of their importance in today's international legal sphere and their connection to the issues of public international law dealt with elsewhere in this book. The following topics have been selected:

international humanitarian law (IHL), human rights law (HRL), international criminal law (ICL), international refugee law (IRL) and international environmental law (IEL). Since we will be dealing under a public international law perspective with the law of use of force, we considered it appropriate to include some cases on the actual 'law of armed conflict'—that is IHL. The importance of human rights law hardly needs to be stressed today, since this is a specialised branch that has managed to have a clear influence on many other branches. Thus, human rights are also a recurrent theme in public international law as such, not least, for example, in diplomatic protection issues. If we are dealing with subjects such as IHL and HRL, it is clear that international criminal law should also be dealt with. After all, this branch of law, which has known an impressive development since World War II, deals with the most horrible crimes, which plague both IHL but evidently also HRL. Additionally, we thought it appropriate to include a few cases on IRL. IRL can be seen as a branch of law closely tied to armed conflict (among other things) and thus simultaneously to both issues of PIL, IHL and HRL. Last but not least we have decided to include also IEL in this series of specialised subjects. IEL is probably one of the youngest of the specialised law branches, having started to develop only in the 1970s. However, since then it has undergone incredible development and is today rightly considered as a fundamental topic. As with HRL, issues of environmental law are closely connected to other branches such as HRL itself, but also IHL.

The subjects dealt with in this exercise book have been chosen due to their indispensable character for every international lawyer. Furthermore, the authors have only chosen subjects that can be dealt with by practical cases. Nevertheless, certain specific problems of PIL, which are not specifically the main subject of the cases, might arise in the solutions. For example, the legal value of United Nations General Assembly Resolutions or the customary nature of certain international obligations might have to be dealt with.

It should be noted that in an exam-like setting students having previously studied PIL (or one of the specialised branches for the last chapter) should be able to solve the smaller cases (generally Chapters 1–6 and Chapter 8) in about one hour per question, while they should allow about three hours per case for the interconnected cases in Chapter 7. Of course, there is no obligation on the part of the student to solve these cases under time pressure. Rather, it is important for exercise purposes to work on and present a thorough reasoning rather than just a few bullet points as an answer, since in law a proper and convincing reasoning is crucial. Nevertheless, since time pressure is an issue in most exams, it might be appropriate as a way of training to solve at least a few cases in the time indicated above.

2. User's guide

In this part you will find information on the general structure of the book (part A), as well as explanations and tips on how to use it (part B).

A. General structure

The book is divided into two big parts, each containing several chapters.

Part I is composed of the practical cases. Chapters 1–6 contain a series of small cases on different subjects of PIL, such as treaty law and diplomatic protection. Each of these cases will deal with one or two specific problems. The number of small cases varies according to the subject. Chapter 7 is then composed of several interconnected cases, following the model of exams. The legal problems raised in these cases vary and test the student's ability to identify the relevant legal problems within a set of facts dealing with different topics of public international law. In addition, Chapters 1–6 follow a uniform structure for all the subjects. At the beginning of each chapter, the book proposes first a 'general plan' on how to solve the legal problems associated with this subject. The plan is followed by a series of small cases and, finally, additional readings will be proposed at the end of the chapter, allowing students to deepen their knowledge of the subject if they wish to do so. At the end in Chapter 8 a few cases on specialised issues of international law are proposed, to give students the opportunity to deal with some issues of public international law in specialised settings and to give them an idea about these other branches.

Part II of the book contains all the solutions of the cases proposed in Part I, split into the same chapter structure to enable the student easily to find the solution she/he is looking for. *It is very important to stress that the solutions are only suggestions.* They should under no circumstances be considered as being the only possible answer. Depending on the arguments made, other solutions might be perfectly valid. As indicated above, where possible, alternative solutions and additional elements are provided in square brackets and italics. The goal of this part is to give *examples* of how to solve such cases and to show the reasoning behind and the writing of practical cases in (public) international law. Furthermore, it should be noted that the solutions proposed are rather extensive, with detailed explanations and—where appropriate—different possibilities. The idea is not that students would have to be as detailed in their own answers, but rather it was thought important to present the reasoning as clearly as possible to allow students to grasp fully the suggested line of argument.

B. Tips on how to use this book

In order to be able to solve practical cases, a good grounding in public international law, but also in other international law branches, is essential. This exercise book can therefore under no circumstances be considered to be a replacement for a course of public international law or other subjects.

The authors suggest that the user first has a look at and gets familiar with the general plans on how to solve the various legal issues proposed at the beginning of every chapter (Chapters 1–6). This will enable the student to understand the logic and the different steps within the reasoning in relation to each of the subjects proposed. Therefore, it is important to understand the general structure of these plans, since these will determine the steps within the reasoning in order to solve a practical case.

In order fully to understand the method and benefit most from the exercises, it is advised to solve the case for a first time without previously looking at the suggested solution proposed in Part II. When working on the answer, it is highly recommended to have the relevant treaties applicable in the case close at hand, in order to check for relevant provisions. It is not expected that students know the treaties by heart; in fact it is more important that students know how to use and apply a treaty's provisions. The student's first solution can then be compared to the suggested solution proposed by the authors and will show the strong and weak points in the student's reasoning, as well as parts that should still be worked on.

Finally, if the solution of the student is too different from the proposed solution, it is advised that the student deepens her/his knowledge of the subject, among other things by having recourse to the additional readings proposed at the end of each chapter. Once the subject is better understood, the student can then rewrite her/his first solution to improve her/his reasoning and writing abilities.

3. Methodology

At the beginning, it is important to read the whole case (including any 'nota bene' parts at the end) carefully. Afterwards, the legal problems and issues have to be identified in order to structure your legal arguments. The questions asked at the end of each case will help you determine the relevant legal problems to be dealt with in this case. It is important to stress here that you should *only answer the question asked*, regardless of the fact that other legal issues might be present in the case as well.

It is highly advisable to make a plan of your solution of the case. This allows you to verify if the structure of the solution is logical and correct and if you have forgotten any elements. Once the plan has been made, the writing stage starts.

First of all, you should identify the relevant legal *issue* or issues in the case. For example, is there a problem in relation to a treaty, or is the issue rather use of force? You should not simply rewrite the entire case, but determine the legal issues that need to be solved in function of the questions asked.

Once you have identified the issues that need to be determined, you have to set out the *law that is applicable* specifically to your issues. It is necessary to cite and explain the 'relevant law'. It is thus necessary that the relevant treaties and other necessary documents such as General Assembly resolutions are available for checking. Yet, the relevant law includes not only treaty and customary law, but where necessary also case law, articles by leading academics or commentaries to treaties.

Afterwards, you have to *apply the law to the facts* of your case. This is the reasoning part of your solution and you should clearly indicate why, or why not, you consider that this rule is applicable to this situation. It is essential to find evidence in the facts of the case to support all of your conclusions.

Finally, never forget to *conclude* on all the issues, even if this means writing several intermediary conclusions (after each issue).

The following is a schema proposed for the successful resolution of cases:

Question asked:

1. Applicable law in general (eg Vienna Convention on the Law of Treaties)
2. Issue 1 (eg invalidity of the treaty on basis of Article 46 VCLT)
   (a) set out the relevant legal facts for issue 1
   (b) set out, explain and develop the applicable law to issue 1, where necessary complemented with case law and academic writing
   (c) application of the law of issue 1 to the facts of issue 1
   (d) conclusion of issue 1
3. Issue 2 (eg termination of the treaty based on Article 60 VCLT)
   (a) set out the relevant legal facts for issue 2

(b) set out, explain and develop the applicable law to issue 2, where necessary complemented with case law and academic writing
(c) application of the law of issue 2 to the facts of issue 2
(d) conclusion of issue 2
4. Issue x
Etc
5. General conclusion on the question asked

Repeat this schema for all the different questions asked.

It is of course possible to vary this structure, for example by first explaining the applicable law (letter b) and then setting out the relevant legal facts (letter a). However, it should be kept in mind that the application of the law to the facts and the conclusion cannot change their respective places in this general structure.

It should be pointed out that one question often raises several different issues. Sometimes, depending on the subject, it is necessary first to solve some preliminary questions before continuing with the analysis. For example, for the question whether or not the use of self-defence was legitimate or not, it has first to be analysed whether the conditions underlying the exercise of self-defence are fulfilled. This is the reason why the schema proposed above sets out several issues for only one question.

In these cases where there are several issues to be solved for one question, it is important to structure your answer well and to separate the different problems. Your reader has to be able to follow your reasoning as well as possible. Thus, also the order in which you deal with the different issues should be logic and coherent.

4. Some advice on how to deal with practical cases

The authors thought it helpful to provide some advice on how to approach and write practical cases. In fact, there are several small elements which have to be kept in mind in order to minimise errors and to gain time when writing the solution.

How to start with a practical case

When you start with a practical case, read it *carefully* and *in its entirety* for a first time and also have a close look at the questions asked. Afterwards, read the case a second time, in order to identify the relevant (legal) facts that you need to solve the legal questions asked.

Legal syllogism when many conditions have to be examined

Practical cases, and especially interconnected cases, often contain a large number of relevant facts and conditions to be examined. Such a complex structure can lead to the situation where certain conditions are forgotten and are not dealt with in the application of the law to the facts. When there are many conditions to be analysed, it is advisable to use the general plan for each specific issue and not to mix the analysis of different conditions. It will thus also be easier for the reader to follow your reasoning and to avoid errors and to forget certain conditions.

For example: when dealing with legitimate self-defence under Article 51 of the United Nations Charter, a series of conditions have to be dealt with; each condition needs to be accompanied by a development and analysis of the relevant law. Thus, instead of writing one long paragraph and mixing the different conditions, it is advisable to deal with each condition one after the other. So, in our example, start by developing the notion of armed attack. Then, apply the relevant law in relation to this condition to the facts of your case. After that, make a conclusion on this condition of the occurrence of an armed attack. Proceed to the following conditions, one by one.

Answer the question asked

It is indispensable to reply to the question asked in the case. Not doing so, but also going beyond what the question asked, will not satisfy the requirements. Therefore, there needs to be a certain parallel between the question and the conclusion, including all the issues that have been identified. In fact, this parallel is easy to verify, since it is enough to take your conclusion and confront it to the question asked. If your conclusion is an answer to the question, then the parallel is respected.

Arguments invoked by the parties

The facts of the cases often mention the different arguments made by the different parties in the case in support of their position or in questioning the others' position. These arguments are frequently crucial and offer lines of reasoning or issues to be dealt with in your solution. Furthermore, often one of the arguments is well founded and will thus indicate important elements for your answer. It is therefore sensible to address the different arguments made by the parties well, since they can serve as a guide in your solution.

Chronology of events

The potential problem of the chronology of events usually occurs in the interconnected cases. If you have time, it is often useful to write down the different events in chronological order on a time line. This allows you to visualise better the chain of events, which can be important when the order of the different actions is crucial for the analysis of one question.

For example, concerning counter-measures, it is necessary to show that an internationally wrongful act has previously occurred. Establishing a chronological order of the events allows you to determine whether or not this condition is fulfilled. It should, however, be stressed that the chronology should not necessarily figure in your final solution, but is rather just an auxiliary means to synthesise and visualise a complex series of events.

Argumentation

In reality it is, of course, always possible to look for new facts and elements that are relevant to a particular case. However, the cases in this exercise book give you all the necessary elements in order to solve the questions asked. The difficulty rather resides with the identification of these important elements, which will support your arguments. It is therefore not necessary to make a hypothesis going beyond the circumstances that are contained in the facts given in the cases.

There is, however, an exception to this general rule. It might happen that a case deliberately does not clarify a point or does not contain elements allowing you to decide a question. In these situations, you should thus deal with and analyse all *reasonable* possibilities. For example, if it is important for the answer whether State A is a party to treaty X (which is not customary), but it is not indicated whether State A is a party to this treaty, then you should analyse the situation where State A *is* a party to treaty X and the situation where State A *is not* a party to treaty X.

It is often not necessary to make very big and complicated arguments. It is preferable to write and argue in a clear and concise style. This method will give your argumentation more force and will demonstrate your facility with the matter. It is also useful to keep in mind that the cases have often been written with a solution in mind. Thus, in general, the difficulty lies rather with the identification of the relevant legal facts for a particular argument, than with the way of arguing as such. This rule applies, of course, only to cases which have been written for exercising and teaching purposes. The reality is very different.

5. Acknowledgments

First, we warmly thank Professor Robert Kolb for all his support and encouragement. Furthermore, we would like to thank also Professor Paola Gaeta and Professor Giovanni Distefano for their encouragement, and Professor Andrew Clapham for giving us the opportunity to test parts of this exercise book in his class at the Geneva Academy of International Humanitarian Law and Human Rights.

In addition, we would like to sincerely thank the following persons for their critical proof-reading and comments on our cases and solutions: Céline Bauloz, Dr Christophe Golay, Tom Haeck, Antoine Kabore, Dr Sandra Krähenmann, Dr Maria Ludwiczak, Géraldine Ruiz, Dr Damien Scalia, Katja Schöberl, Deborah Stotz, Ivona Truscan, Pauline Vanseymortier, and Nara Weigel.

Without them, this book would not have been possible. All errors remain of course our own.

6. Feedback

The authors are very happy to receive from students suggestions, comments, questions and general feedback regarding content, form or any other issue in relation to the exercise book.

Please feel free to write to Cristina Verones (cristina.verones@geneva-academy.ch) or Sébastien Rosselet (sebastien.rosselet@geneva-academy.ch).

General recommended reading

The following books allow students to read more about general international law, without any particular focus on a specific topic. Most books deal with all subjects (and more) covered in this exercise book. Books marked with a star (*) are not classical textbooks, but present either international law through the cases or case law as such.

Ian Brownlie, *Principles of Public International Law*, 7th edn (Oxford, Oxford University Press, 2008).

Givoanni Distefano and Gionata Buzzini, *Bréviaire de jurisprudence internationale: les fondamentaux du droit international public*, 2nd edn (Brussels, Bruylant, 2010).*

Malcom Evans (ed), *International Law*, 2nd edn (Oxford, Oxford University Press, 2006).

Jörg Paul Müller and Luzius Wildhaber (with the participation of Robert Kolb and Andrea Binder), *Praxis des Völkerrechts*, 3rd edn (Berne, Stämpfli Verlag AG, 2001).*

Quoc Dinh Nguyen, Patrick Daillier and Alain, Pellet, *Droit international public*, 7th edn (Paris, LGDJ, 2002).

Malcom Shaw, *International Law*, 6th edn (Cambridge, Cambridge University Press, 2008).

Andreas Ziegler, *Introduction au droit international public* (Bern, Stämpfli Verlag AG, 2011).

Part I

CASES

Chapter 1

Subjects of Public International Law: States and International Organisations

General plan: how to solve cases relating to subjects of international law

The State

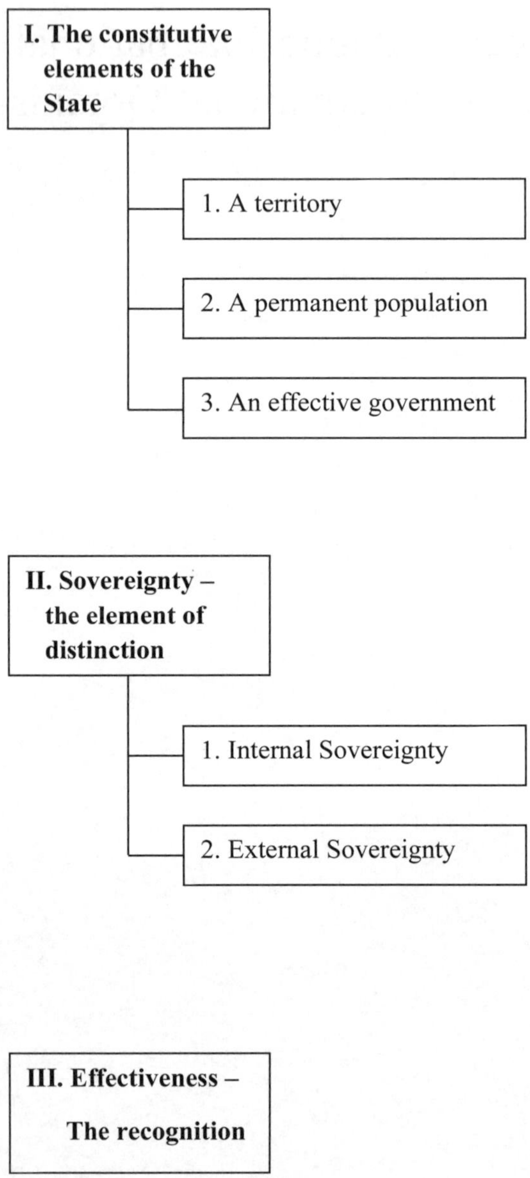

Figure 1. The State.

The International Organisation

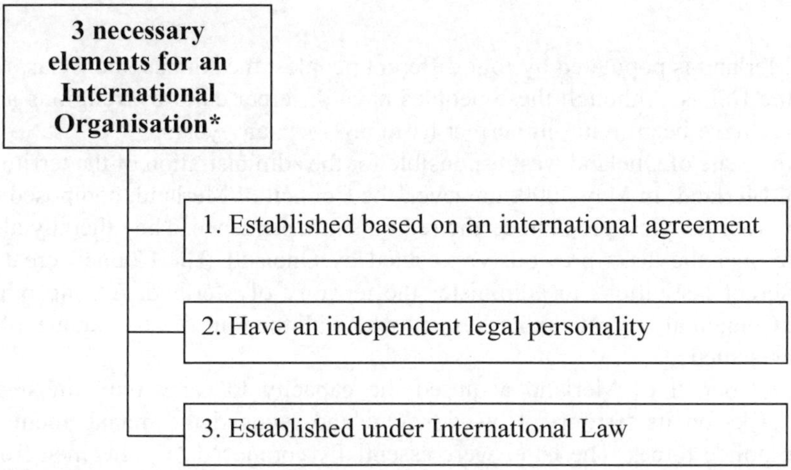

Figure 2. The international organisation.

*Based on the following definitions: 'The term "international organisation" means a collectivity of States established by treaty, with a constitution and common organs, having a personality distinct from that of its member-States, and being a subject of international law with treaty-making capacity' (Special Rapporteur G Fitzmaurice, Yearbook of the International Law Commission 1956, Vol II, 108); 'For the purposes of the present draft articles [ie the draft articles on the Responsibility of International Organisations], the term "international organisation" refers to an organisation established by a treaty or other instrument governed by international law and possessing its own international legal personality. International organisations may include as members, in addition to States, other entities'. (International Law Commission, Report of the 55th session (2003), UN Doc A/58/10, 38). Also see H Schermers and N Blokker, *International Institutional Law: Unity within Diversity*, 5th edn (Leiden, Martinus Nijhoff Publishers, 2011) 21–36, which establish basically the same three criteria.

The State and its constitutive elements

Case 1.1

The region of Merland is populated by four different peoples: the Alphas, the Betas, the Gammas and the Deltas. Although these peoples have different cultures, religions and ways of life they have been living in perfect harmony for many years.

Until 2000 the State of Oneland was responsible for the administration of the territory of the region of Merland. In May 2000, however, the Council of Merland, composed of the heads of the four peoples, proclaimed the region's independence. They thereby also decided to take over the tasks previously executed by Oneland. The Council created a series of different institutions to administer the territory of Merland. Among other institutions the Council also created a Parliament where all the four Merlandian peoples are equally represented.

In 2002, the Council of Merland acquired the capacity to carry out almost all administrative tasks on its territory. However, Oneland retained the management of the Merlandian police forces. The latter were essentially composed of policemen from Oneland. At the end of 2003, Merland signed a treaty with Oneland on the withdrawal of the Onelandian police forces. The treaty established, among other things, that the police forces from Oneland would no longer exercise their support function in relation to the police of Merland after 30 April 2004. This was meticulously respected, and from 1 May 2004 onwards, the Council of Merland had its own police forces.

At the same time, during 2003, Merland became a party to several international conventions and signed different bilateral treaties, especially of a commercial nature, with various States. At the end of 2004, the majority of the international community had recognised Merland as an independent State.

Can we say that Merland is a State according to international law? If yes, from when on?

International organisations

Case 1.2

Abbreviation used
IFPO = International Fund for the Protection of Orchids

The International Fund for the Protection of Orchids (IFPO) has been established recently. The founding members are 24 States with large and varied populations of orchids and the Orchid Society—a well-known international organisation. They decided to create the IFPO in order to improve research on but also the protection of various orchid species. To set up the IFPO the founding members concluded an international treaty. The treaty starts by saying: 'The International Fund for the Protection of Orchids (IFPO) is thereby established. It is open to all States interested in the research and protection of orchids as well as to intergovernmental or scientific organisations active in that field' (Article 1). Article 3 establishes that the IFPO should be headed by a

Director, which, together with the permanent Secretariat set up under Article 4, should be responsible for the good functioning of the IFPO. Article 5 then provides that 'In performing their tasks attributed to them under the present treaty, the Director as well as the Secretariat shall under no circumstances seek or receive instruction from governments or other organisations or authorities.' After this, a detailed explanation of the tasks of the IFPO follows. Towards the end, Article 37 declares that the permanent seat of the IFPO was to be Monocot, a city in a particular orchid-rich State. Article 38, just before the final provisions, provides that 'The IFPO shall have international legal personality as well as the necessary legal capacity to carry out all its functions and realise its purposes wherever it is active.'

Orchid clubs all over the world have welcomed the creation of the IFPO and various specialised newspapers have written long articles about 'the newest member in the family of international organisations'. However, other journalists have questioned whether the IFPO is really an international organisation, 'since it is not called an "organisation" but a "fund", thereby clearly indicating that it was not the intention of the founders to create an international organisation as such'.

You are a well-known specialist in international law. Some journalists approach you and ask you to clarify the debate on whether or not the IFPO is an international organisation under international law.

Case 1.3

Abbreviations used

ODE = Organisation for the Defence of the Environment
TODE = Treaty on the Organisation for the Defence of the Environment

The region of Vertarea is composed of twenty States. These States have always supported very bold environmental policies and have often been precursors concerning the protection of the natural environment.

In 2005, the States of Vertarea met for an international conference. They decided to work together in the noble cause of protecting the natural environment. Therefore, they created the Organisation for the Defence of the Environment (ODE). Established based on a multilateral treaty (the TODE) ratified by all twenty States of Vertarea, the goal of the ODE was to seek common solutions in environmental matters, in clean energy policies, and in the protection of plant and animal species in the region of Vertarea. The ODE had three main organs: the Main Secretariat, the Assembly of State Parties and the Decision-making Council.

After four years of research and development in environmental protection, the ODE decided through its Secretariat to send a certain number of its agents to different States of the international community in order to investigate their respective environmental policies. The goal of these investigations was to show that it was necessary to adopt a common global line in the matter of environmental protection.

One agent, Ecoloboy, was sent to the State of Hydrocarbu, which implemented very opaque energy policies. It was very difficult to collect information on this topic and several local journalists, who subsequently disappeared mysteriously, had only been able to find various parties apparently trading in nuclear waste for large sums of money.

In addition, a very powerful nuclear and oil lobby existed in Hydrocarbu, which in fact made up the government of this State. Thus, the arrival of an agent of the ODE was highly unpopular with the government.

After a few days in Hydrocarbu, Ecoloboy was about to discover what was hidden behind the energy policies of this State. However, he was murdered before he was able to contact the Secretariat of the ODE.

Outraged by this crime, the Decision-making Council and the Assembly of State Parties decided to present an international claim against Hycdrocarbu in order to obtain reparations for the damage suffered by the loss of the ODE's agent Ecoloboy.

Hydrocarbu replied by saying that the ODE was only a small regional association of States and could not be equal to a State. In addition, according to Hydrocarbu, the ODE could not present any claim against Hydrocarbu, since this State was not a member of this organisation.

You are an eminent international lawyer and legal advisor to the Decision-making Council. The Council asks you to write a legal opinion on the following question: 'Is the ODE entitled to present an international claim against Hydrocarbu in order to obtain reparation for the damages suffered by the organisation?'

Nota bene

— According to Article 87 paragraph 1 of the TODE: 'The Organisation enjoys full legal personality and has especially the capacity: (i) to contract; (ii) to acquire movable goods and to dispose of them; (iii) to bring claims in justice.'

In order to reply to the question you are only asked to pronounce yourself on the legal personality of the ODE.

Recommended reading on subjects of public international law

Articles

Guido Aquaviva, 'Subjects of International Law: A Power-Based Analysis' (2005) 38 *Vanderbilt Journal of Transnational Law* 345.

Georges Berlia, 'Admission d'un Etat aux Nations Unies' (1948) 52 *Revue Générale de Droit International Public* 481.

Mark Janis, 'Individuals as Subjects of International Law', (1984) 17 *Cornell International Law Journal* 61.

Books

Andrew Clapham, *Human Rights Obligations of Non-State Actors* (Oxford, Oxford University Press, 2006).

Hent Kalmo and Quentin Skinner (eds), *Sovereignty in Fragments: the Past, Present and Future of a Contested Concept* (Cambridge, Cambridge University Press, 2010).

Henry Schermers and Nils Blokker, *International Institutional Law: Unity Within Diversity*, 5th edn (Leiden, Martinus Nijhoff Publishers, 2011).

Chapter 2

Diplomatic Protection

General plan to solve diplomatic protection cases, based on the ILC's Draft Articles on Diplomatic Protection from 2006

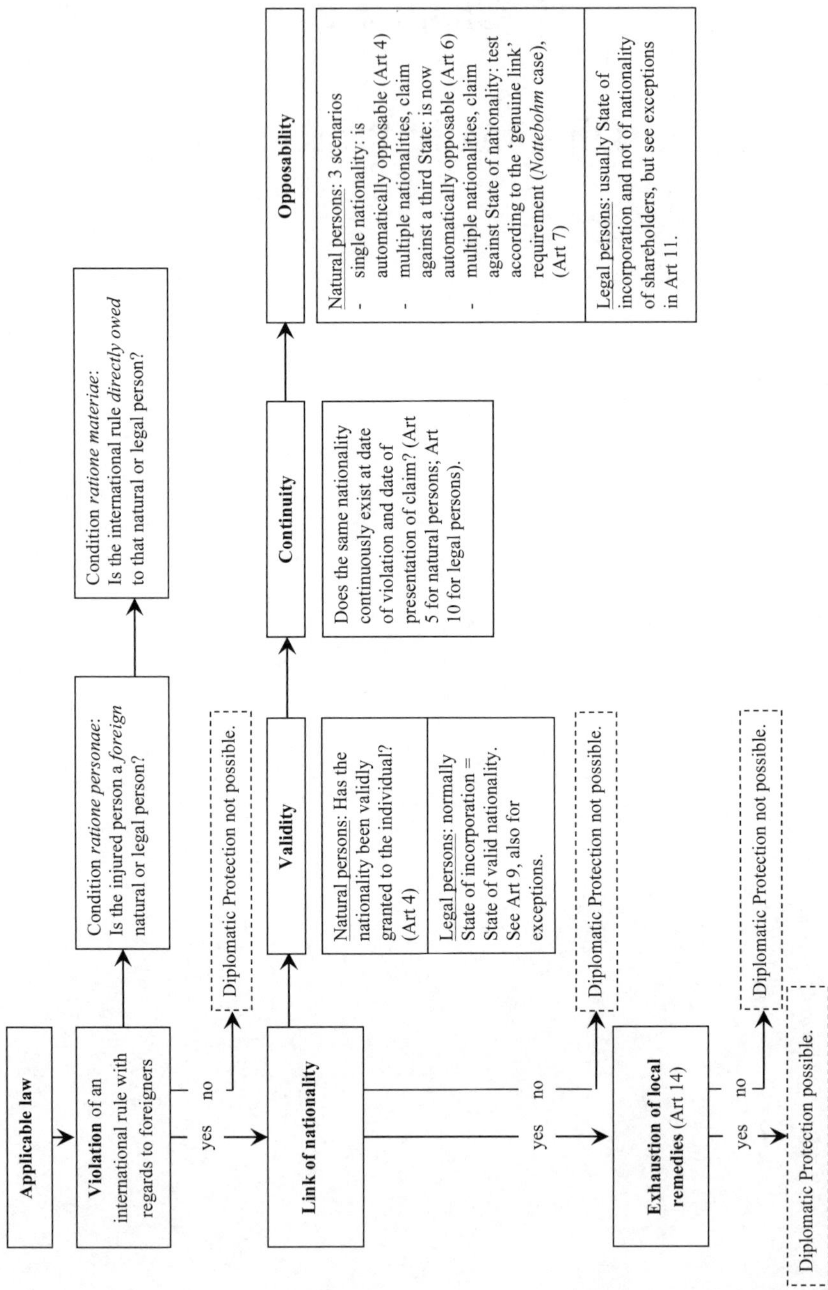

Figure 3. Diplomatic protection.

Case 2.1

Oscar Lai is a national of the State of Saoseo. He was born and has lived most of his life in Saoseo, but after high school he left his home to study at the prestigious national university of the State of Alzasca.

During his studies in Alzasca Oscar becomes politically interested and joins the Green Party of Alzasca as a volunteer. The Green Party organises various demonstrations against the government, especially against their energy and environmental politics. During one of these peaceful protests, the police start to beat and randomly arrest protesters. Oscar Lai is also arrested and put in jail. For several days he is not informed why he is imprisoned, nor does he have the right to make phone calls. On the fourth day, three police officers interrogate Oscar, still without explaining the charges against him. When they find that Oscar is not capable of giving the expected answer, the policemen violently beat him, breaking several of his ribs. After two weeks Oscar is finally released and can contact his family in Saoseo. His family has not been informed about his whereabouts despite repeated requests to the authorities of Alzasca.

A friend of Oscar advises him to start proceedings against Alzasca for his mistreatment and for violations of his human rights. Oscar does this, but the courts in Alzasca, including the High Court, all reject his case for different but equally obscure reasons. Oscar wants to get justice and again on the advice of his friend asks the Embassy of Saoseo in Alzasca whether Saoseo would be ready to exercise diplomatic protection on his behalf.

You are working for the Embassy of Saoseo in Alzasca. The Ambassador, who has never been confronted with a similar case, asks you whether in your opinion Saoseo could exercise diplomatic protection on behalf of Oscar Lai or not.

Nota bene

— Both States are parties to the International Covenant on Civil and Political Rights (ICCPR) as well as to the Convention on Torture and Other Cruel, Inhuman or Degrading Treatment or Punishment (CAT).

Case 2.2

Lily Fenix was born in Behem in 1960. The national law of this State provides that every person born in its territory automatically acquires Behemese nationality. The parents of Lily are originally from Mantiko, a State that transmits its nationality according to the *jus sanguinis* rule. Therefore, little Lily is a national both of Mantiko and of Behem.

Lily Fenix receives all her education in Behem, but when she is 25 years old she meets Ricardo Dahu from Thoris, whom she marries. When Ricardo moves back to Thoris, Lily follows him in 1986. Lily quickly finds work in a bank in the capital and Ricardo works in a security company. Lily frequently goes back to Behem during her holidays to visit friends and family. Furthermore, she is still executing her civic duties in Behem. Sometimes she also visits more distant aunts and uncles in Mantiko, but since she has never lived there she cannot vote in this country.

After 15 years in Thoris, Lily submits an application to be granted Thorisian nationality. This request is, however, rejected.

In 2006, after having lived in Thoris for 20 years, Ricardo suddenly disappears. Two days later, the Thoris police appear at the house of the couple in order to arrest Ricardo. Finding that he has already left, the police arrest Lily. She is informed that her husband has been involved in various large-scale criminal activities and that she is suspected of being his accomplice. Lily is flabbergasted. She had no idea in what activities her husband was involved. Finally, after long weeks of interrogation, the police have to accept that Lily indeed does not know anything. However, instead of releasing her from prison they keep her in custody, hoping to get more information about Ricardo or at best to lure him back to Thoris. However, Ricardo, who has fled to Adda—a State that does not have any extradition treaty with Thoris—makes no attempt to return and help his wife.

Finally, Lily is released in 2010 without having been formally charged with anything.

Lily is indignant about the way she has been treated and decides to take her case to court. However, the courts in Thoris up to the Supreme Court reject her case, saying that fighting criminal activities was more important than her human rights.

Lily is desperate and tells her story to one of her relatives in Mantiko, who works at the Ministry of Foreign Affairs of Mantiko. A few days later, Mantiko writes an official note of protest concerning the mistreatment of one of its nationals to the government of Thoris, saying that they are ready to exercise diplomatic protection on behalf of Lily Fenix.

However, Thoris replies that this would be impossible for several reasons. First, there was no violation of international law in that case; second, only Behem and certainly not Mantiko could exercise diplomatic protection on behalf of Lily Fenix, since she had never lived in Mantiko; and third, in any event diplomatic protection by any State would not be possible since the only real links of Lily Fenix to any State were to Thoris, since she has been living and working there since 1986.

You are a legal adviser to the Ministry of Foreign Affairs of Mantiko. You are asked to assess whether Mantiko can exercise diplomatic protection on behalf of Lily Fenix and to reply to all the arguments made by Thoris.

Nota bene

— Thoris, Mantiko and Behem are all parties to the International Covenant on Civil and Political Rights (ICCPR), as well as the European Convention on Human Rights (ECHR).

Case 2.3

Mr Mischa Dom is a national of Etzel. He was born in Etzel and received his education there. After his studies he moved to Toissa and started to work there for an international organisation. He fell in love with Lena, a young woman from Toissa, and the couple married in 1998. According to the national law of Toissa, their nationality is also attained through marriage. Therefore, since his wife Lena is a Toissian national, Mischa Dom also receives Toissian nationality, though without losing his former Etzelian nationality. The Doms continue to live and work in Toissa, in whose capital they buy a house. In the beginning, the couple often spend their holidays in Etzel, but after the parents of Mischa passed away in 2004, they went back to Etzel only twice.

In 2008, Mischa Dom launches his own newspaper. The newspaper, which compared to other newspapers in Toissa contains more reliable information but also more open criticism towards the governing elite, is a huge success. Encouraged by this achievement, the articles written by Mischa Dom become bolder and even more outspoken. He criticises the lethargy and corruption of the government, but also presents proof for the rampant nepotism among the governing elite. Unhappy with this criticism, the governmental authorities start to radically censor the newspaper, but Mischa Dom most of the time finds ways to get his opinion known nevertheless. In mid-2009 the police arrest Mischa Dom on his way to work and put him in jail. When he does not come home in the evening, his wife suspects that he might have been arrested and contacts the responsible authorities. However, the authorities are apparently unable or unwilling to tell her whether or not Mischa Dom has been arrested or where he is. After three days in detention, Mischa Dom is released without having been informed about the reasons why he was detained in the first place. Before he leaves, the police commander recommends him that he stops writing his articles, since otherwise he would have to face 'serious consequences'.

Mischa Dom is not ready to accept this treatment and starts proceedings in court. However, all instances right up to the highest court in Toissa reject his claim (which in Mischa Dom's opinion shows that the judiciary is not independent and is in the pocket of the politicians). Thus, in early 2011 there are no other national legal procedures available to Mischa Dom.

You are a legal adviser to the government of Etzel, which has observed the authoritarian tendencies in neighbouring Toissa with concern. After Mischa Dom's case has become public, it decides to exercise diplomatic protection on his behalf. You are now asked to assess whether or not Etzel can exercise diplomatic protection for the benefit of Mischa Dom.

Nota bene

— Toissa is a party to the International Covenant on Civil and Political Rights (ICCPR).

Case 2.4

Abbreviation used
BI = Beverages Inc

Beverages Inc (BI) is a large company active in the market of soft drinks. It was founded in the State of Kala, where it is still incorporated today and where its headquarters is located. However, BI has subsidiaries and production facilities in more than 47 countries around the world, including one in Sico. In this country BI has three large production facilities for their lemon, raspberry and watermelon flavoured drinks, respectively. BI has been present in Sico for roughly ten years and so far has never had any problems.

However, after a recent change of government, the situation for BI worsens. The new president has a rather hostile attitude towards all foreign firms and especially against those 'that only produce junk and render our population sick and fat'. One of the president's officially declared enemies is BI and their soft drink production. After a few weeks of tension, BI is forcibly expropriated by Sico and its production facilities are dismantled. No compensation is paid and the president of Sico publicly declares that no compensation will ever be paid to these 'enemies of public health'. The manager of BI, as well as the government of Kala, vehemently protest but the government of Sico does not change its mind. The manager of BI brings the case to court in Sico, but there he is told that since BI was a foreign company it could under no circumstances bring a claim in a court in Sico. This statement is repeated to him by various credible sources afterwards. Outraged, the manager contacts the authorities of Kala and asks for help.

You are a legal adviser to the government of Kala and you are asked to explain to the president whether Kala could exercise diplomatic protection on behalf of BI against Sico.

Nota bene

—Both Kala and Sico are parties to the European Convention on Human Rights (ECHR) and all its protocols.

Case 2.5

Abbreviations used
CPE = Council for the Protection of the Environment
UN = United Nations

On 23 September 2005 the UN General Assembly created a new subsidiary organ, the Council for the Protection of the Environment (CPE). This new organ had among other things the task of making enquiries in the territory of different UN Member States concerning their respective practice in environmental matters.

On 2 July 2009 Mr Fleurrose, an expert of the CPE and a national of Tulipland, was mandated by the CPE to make investigations on two oil companies owned by the State of Brutland. Among other things the expert had to verify the conditions of extraction and security for the environment in their different oil refineries. Thus, Mr Fleurrose travelled to Brutland and investigated for almost a month.

On 7 August 2009 Mr Fleurrose gave in his official capacity as an expert of the CPE an interview to the national television of Brutland. In this interview he affirmed that the two oil companies were not acting in conformity with international environmental rules on the operation of oil refineries. The two companies reacted outraged to these 'false and defamatory declarations', which had caused their stock values to collapse.

Therefore, the two companies decided to bring Mr Fleurrose to justice for defamation in the national courts of Brutland and require that he pay for the damages suffered.

Mr Fleurrose was arrested and put in remand, at the disposal of the attorney general of Brutland. Following this incident, the legal advisor to the United Nations orally asked the permanent representative of Brutland to the United Nations to inform the relevant competent court in Brutland that the expert of the CPE—Mr Fleurrose—enjoyed immunity from jurisdiction for the acts executed during his mission and that consequently he could not be judged by or referred to the national courts of Brutland.

The authorities of Brutland, however, replied that giving interviews and defaming State companies was not part of the expert's mission. Therefore, the immunity from jurisdiction was not applicable to the statements made by Mr Fleurrose during the interview on 7 August 2009.

During his imprisonment, Mr Fleurrose was repeatedly tortured, which finally made him change his conclusion on the two oil companies.

In its resolution 91/273 from 10 August 2009 the UN General Assembly asked the International Court of Justice to '1. Give an advisory opinion on the question whether the Convention on the Privileges and Immunities of the United Nations of 13 February 1946 is applicable to the expert of the CPE, Mr Fleurrose; and 2. Invite the authorities of Brutland to free Mr Fleurrose as soon as possible and to refrain from any act of torture or pressure against him.'

At the same time, Tulipland decided to hold Brutland internationally responsible for the torture of Mr Fleurrose by the authorities of Brutland. Furthermore, Tulipland asked the legal advisor to the United Nations to refrain from introducing a case against Brutland for the acts committed against Mr Fleurrose, since only the State of nationality would be competent to introduce such a case. As a national of Tulipland, Mr Fleurrose had to have the possibility to benefit from the protection of his State of nationality.

You are a young lawyer working for the legal advisor to the United Nations in New York. You are asked to write a legal opinion on the question asked by the General Assembly in its resolution 91/273. Furthermore, you are also asked to solve the question whether Tulipland can exercise its diplomatic protection on behalf of Mr Fleurrose, excluding the protection granted under the Convention on the Privileges and Immunities of the United Nations of 13 February 1946.

Nota bene

- —Brutland acceded to the Convention on the Privileges and Immunities of the United Nations of 13 February 1946 on 8 August 1957.
- —All States are original members of the United Nations.

Recommended reading on diplomatic protection

Articles

Richard Lillich, 'The Diplomatic Protection of Nationals Abroad: An Elementary Principle of International Law Under Attack' (1975) 69 *American Journal of International Law* 359.

Enrico Milano, 'Diplomatic Protection and Human Rights before the International Court of Justice: Re-fashioning Tradition?' (2004) 35 *Netherlands Yearbook of International Law* 85.

Alain Pellet, 'Le projet d'articles de la CDI sur la protection diplomatique: une codification pour (presque) rien', in Marcelo Kohen (ed), *Promotion de la justice, des droits de l'homme et du règlement des conflits par le droit international: Liber amicorum Lucius Caflisch* (Leiden, Martinus Nijhoff, 2007) 1133–1155.

Vasileios Pergantis, 'Towards a "Humanization" of Diplomatic Protection?' (2006) 66 *Heidelberg Journal of International Law* 351.

Annemarieke Künzli, 'Exercising Diplomatic Protection: The Fine Line Between Litigation, Demarches and Consular Assistance' (2006) 66 *Heidelberg Journal of International Law* 321.

Annemarieke Vermeer-Künzli, 'As If: The Legal Fiction in Diplomatic Protection', (2007) 18 *European Journal of International Law* 37.

Annemarieke Vermeer-Künzli, 'Restricting Discretion: Judicial Review of Diplomatic Protection', (2006) 75 *Nordic Journal of International Law* 279.

Eric Wyler, 'La protection diplomatique: la concurrence des réclamations', in Société française pour le droit international, *Les compétences de l'Etat en droit international: Colloque de Rennes* (Paris, Pedone, 2006), 239–262.

Books

Chittharanjan F Amerasinghe, *Diplomatic Protection* (Oxford, Oxford University Press, 2008).

John Dugard, *Reports of the Special Rapporteur Mr John Dugard to the International Law Commission* (available on the International Law Commission's website).

Jean-François Flauss (ed), *La protection diplomatique: Mutations contemporaines et pratiques nationales: Actes de la fournée d'études du 30 mars 2001 organisée à la mémoire de Georges Perrin* (Brussels, Bruylant/Nemesis, 2003).

Thomas Jürgens, *Diplomatischer Schutz und Staatenlose* (Berlin, Duncker & Humboldt, 1987).

Sébastien Touzé, *La protection des droits des nationaux à l'étranger: Recherches sur la protection diplomatique* (Paris, A Pedone, 2007).

Chapter 3

Treaty Law

General plan to solve treaty law cases based on the Vienna Convention on the Law of Treaties 1969

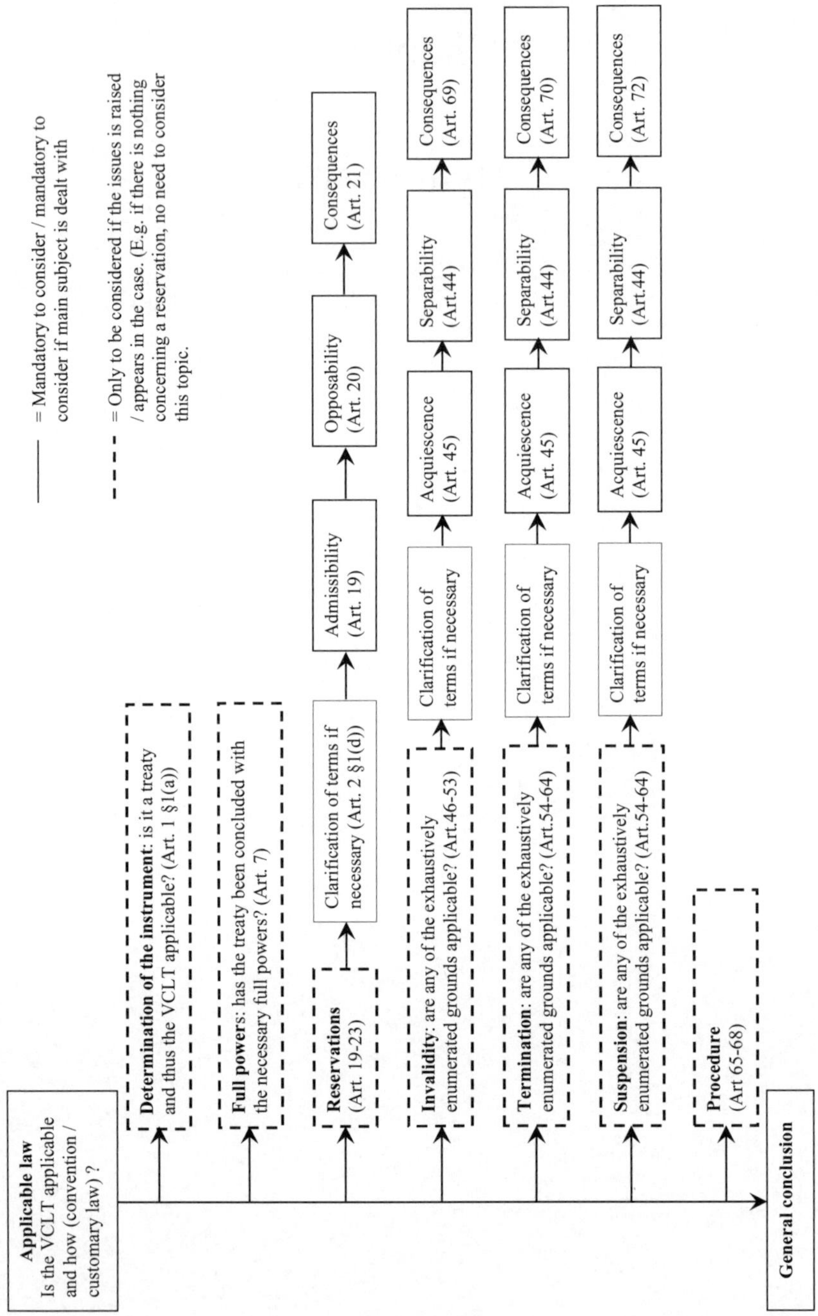

Figure 4. Treaty law.

Applicability of the Vienna Convention on the Law of Treaties (VCLT)

Case 3.1

Abbreviations used
FEE = Treaty on Friendship and Economic Exchange
TEOS = Treaty on the Exchange of Oil Against Sugar
VCLT = Vienna Convention on the Law of Treaties

(a) State A has ratified the VCLT on the 25 May 1978, while State B has acceded to the VCLT on 13 October 1985. The two States conclude a treaty of Friendship and Economic Exchange (FEE) on 5 June 1988. The FEE enters into force 30 days later, on 5 July 1988.

Is the VCLT applicable to this treaty?

(b) State O has ratified the VCLT on 3 February 1973 and State X has ratified this convention on 19 April 1970. A few years later, on 8 August 1977, they conclude together a treaty on the free movement of nationals between their two countries.
Is the VCLT applicable to this treaty?

(c) States L and C conclude on 31 May 2010 a treaty on the exchange of oil against sugar (TEOS). The TEOS enters into force according to its Article 17 45 days after its conclusion. While L has ratified the VCLT on 14 April 1983, C has never become a party to it.

Is the VCLT applicable to this treaty?

(d) State F has been a party to the VCLT since 3 September 1995, while State M has ratified the VCLT on 10 March 2009. On the 15 March 2009, M and F conclude a treaty on the common use and regulation of transboundary water sources, which is called the Water Treaty.

Is the VCLT applicable to this treaty?

(e) Five States, T, S, K, N and E, conclude on 25 July 2007 a treaty on disarmament. State T has ratified the VCLT on 5 May 1972, State S has ratified the VCLT on 16 September 1998, K has done so on 7 December 1990, E has ratified the VCLT on 29 November 1979, while N has never ratified the VCLT.

Is the VCLT applicable to this treaty?

Reservations

Case 3.2

Abbreviation used
TOCAS = Treaty on the Co-operation Against Smugglers

The States of Apro, Tuor, Fenis and the Republic of Bibiton are all located around the Bay of Balcun. Faced with an increase in smuggling of various goods as well as drug trafficking across the Bay of Balcun, the four States therefore concluded a treaty in order to improve co-operation among their police forces and coastguards to be better prepared to counter the often violent smugglers. The Treaty on the Co-operation Against Smugglers (TOCAS) was concluded after long weeks of negotiations on 5 August 2008.

The treaty provides in its preamble that 'co-operation in order to combat smuggling is considered to be crucial'. The TOCAS not only foresees closer co-operation and joint education programmes between the police forces as well as the coastguards of the four States, but also exchange of information. In order to facilitate this exchange, Article 44 of the treaty States that reports on the activities of each police force will be exchanged on a weekly basis. In addition, Article 45 foresees that in order to establish good personal relations, meetings between the heads of the police forces will take place every month. Furthermore, Article 57 of the TOCAS provides that 'Common patrols of the police as well as coast guards of the contracting parties shall be organised on a regular basis. Due to the often dangerous nature of the smugglers, these patrols will take place by airplanes.'

Apro and Fenis ratify the TOCAS without making any reservation. Tuor deposits with its instrument of ratification the following reservation: 'Tuor considers that despite the danger, common patrols by ship will be much more effective than by airplanes. As a consequence, Tuor reserves the right to carry out the common patrols by ship and not airplane.' The Republic of Bibiton informs the other States that it attaches to its instrument of ratification an interpretative declaration stating that 'Due to high costs of travel, the Republic of Bibiton will interpret the TOCAS only as containing an obligation for a regular exchange of reports but not meetings between the police forces.'

Apro and the Republic of Bibiton remain silent. Tuor publicly announces that it 'accepts the Republic of Bibiton's interpretative declaration'. Fenis, on the other hand, circulates the following observation: 'Fenis strongly opposes the reservations of Tuor and the Republic of Bibiton since after weeks of negotiation the TOCAS is a carefully equilibrated instrument which should not be changed anymore. This declaration, however, does not preclude the entry into force of the TOCAS between Fenis and all parties to the TOCAS.'

Assess the nature of the two statements made by Tuor and the Republic of Bibiton together with their respective instruments of ratification of the TOCAS, as well as all the relevant consequences for the application of the TOCAS between all the parties.

Nota bene

—The TOCAS is silent on the matter of reservations.
—All four States are parties to the Vienna Convention on the Law of Treaties since its entry into force.

Case 3.3

Abbreviation used
CJT = Convention on Joint Telecommunication

Six States, Aleta, Carmon, Vignar, Oskam, Rayte and Tamra, conclude a treaty on telecommunication services on 3 March 2009. The treaty, called the Convention on Joint Telecommunication (CJT), provides for the establishment of a common telecommunication network, to which all national telecommunication suppliers will contribute. In Article 7, the CJT lists, each in a different paragraph, over 20 frequencies that will henceforth be used for telecommunication purposes. After a number of further technical provisions, Article 15 contains a dispute settlement clause and reads as follows:

Article 15: Dispute settlement

1. In the event of a dispute among the parties relating to the interpretation or application of the present convention, the State Parties to the dispute shall consult each other in order to find solutions to the dispute.
2. If within 6 months no solution is found either party to the dispute may:
   (a) Bring the dispute to the International Court of Justice, provided that both or all parties to the dispute have at that time accepted the jurisdiction of the International Court of Justice in respect to such disputes;
   (b) Request to establish an arbitral tribunal to solve the dispute.

Carmon, Rayte, Tamra and Aleta deposited their respective instruments of ratification in May 2009. Upon ratification at the end of May 2009, Vignar makes the following written reservation: 'The Government of the State of Vignar formulates a reservation to paragraph 2 of Article 15, meaning that Vignar does not consider itself bound by both of the dispute settlement procedures provided for in paragraph 2 of Article 15.'

In addition, Oskam attaches a reservation to its instrument of ratification which it deposits at the beginning of June 2009, saying that 'The Government of the State of Oskam reserves the right to prohibit the use of the frequency listed in paragraph 5 of Article 7 (1,920.5 MHz) for telecommunication purposes, since this frequency is traditionally reserved for emergency situations of the Oskamian air force.'

While Aleta remains silent on these two communications, the other States (Carmon, Rayte, Tamra and also Oskam) vehemently protest against the reservation made by Vignar, which they consider not to be acceptable. Concerning the reservation made by Oskam, only Rayte reacts, saying that it strongly objects to such late changes of negotiated frequencies as a matter of principle since Oskam could have said earlier that it had a problem with that particular frequency instead of now 'destroying' the treaty. As a consequence 'mutual trust between the parties is severely hampered and Rayte does not see itself fit to enter into treaty relations with Oskam under these circumstances'.

Determine the nature as well as the effects of both reservations made by Vignar and Oskam in respect to and between all States as of today.

Nota bene

—All States are parties to the Vienna Convention on the Law of Treaties since its entry into force.
—Article 18 of the CJT States: 'Reservations made to Articles 14, 15 and 21 are prohibited.'

Competence to conclude treaties

Case 3.4

Abbreviations used
OPNE = Organisation for the Protection of the Natural Environment
TEMT = Treaty on the Exchange of Military Technology
TPIF = Treaty on the Increased Protection of Marine Animal and Plant Species against Industrial Fishing

(a) After several days of intensive negotiations, the President of Warland and the President of Peaceland signed the Treaty on the Exchange of Military Technology (TEMT). The TEMT was signed on 4 April 2011 and, according to its Article 34, entered into force 30 days after its signature by the two presidents. This treaty does not contain any special procedure concerning its authentication. However, during the negotiations, the two parties agreed that a simple signature would be enough to conclude the TEMT.

Has this treaty been validly concluded (ie is the intent of the respective States to be bound by the treaty validly expressed)?

(b) On the occasion of an international conference on the protection of the maritime fauna and flora organised by the intergovernmental Organisation for the Protection of the Natural Environment (OPNE), States concluded a Treaty on the increased Protection of marine animal and plant species against Industrial Fishing (TPIF). Among the participants to this conference that signed the TPIF were also the permanent representative of Souchiland to the OPNE and the leader of the Green Party of the State of Cyanoland. Due to its interest in protecting the environment and its motivation always to increase further the protection and preservation of the ecosystems of the planet, Cyanoland has been sending the leader of its national Green Party to represent it in these kinds of conferences for years, though without ever granting him formal accreditation. Furthermore, the other States always wanted to preserve this practice, since the Cyanoland Green Party is very up to date concerning all problems related to the natural environment and is therefore able to stimulate very productive debates.

Has the TPIF been validly concluded by Souchiland and Cyanoland (ie is the intent of the respective States to be bound by the treaty validly expressed)?

'Pathologies' of treaties: invalidity, termination and suspension

Case 3.5

Abbreviations used
MFA = Minister of Foreign Affairs
MLT = Military Liquidation Treaty

Fedeland is a federal State composed of 15 cantons. The Federal Constitution of Fedeland provides that 'the federal government is competent to conclude international treaties dealing with military or economic questions' (Article 46 Federal Constitution). Article 47 of this Constitution States that 'the cantons have the competence to conclude international treaties with other sovereign States in matters not falling within the competence of the federal government'.

Fedeland has long had excellent relations with Natioland. The two States have concluded numerous treaties on a wide range of issues, from environmental protection to the supply of military equipment. Furthermore, the Minister of Foreign Affairs (MFA) of Fedeland has been a very good friend of the MFA of Natioland for years.

1 June 2010 was a very important date for Fedeland. On this date, Fedeland decided to declare its international neutrality and to abolish its army. Consequently, it completely closed down all its military facilities. Oportunor, one of the cantons of Fedeland, found that the opportunity was too good too miss and decided to sell all the military equipment located in the barracks on its territory to Natioland. Therefore, Oportunor contacted Natioland and proposed to conclude an international treaty on the sale of this equipment for unbeatable prices.

Natioland, a State which was engaged militarily in a number of conflicts around the world, could not refuse such an offer. The Military Liquidation Treaty (MLT) was concluded between this State and Oportunor on 15 July 2010.

At the beginning of August 2010, the federal government of Fedeland learnt about the existence of the MLT and was outraged by the behavior of both Oprotunor but also of Natioland. The MFA of Fedeland immediately wrote a sharp diplomatic note, in which he required the immediate termination of the MLT and the restitution of the military equipment with the shortest delay possible. He based his request on the argument that this treaty had been concluded in violation of the supreme internal law of Fedeland and that Oportunor did not have the capacity to conclude such treaties.

However, the MFA of Natioland replied by saying that it was uncontested in international law that a State could not invoke its internal law in order to revoke its international commitments. Furthermore, he added that it was not the task of States to be familiar with the internal law of all the other States. Consequently, Natioland refused to accept the request made by Fedeland.

You are a young lawyer who just started to work at the Ministry of Foreign Affairs of Fedeland. The MFA, exasperated by the treason of his old friend, asks you to write a legal opinion on the matter. He would like to know whether the MLT has been validly concluded.

Nota bene

—Fedeland and Natioland are both parties to the Vienna Convention on the Law of Treaties since its entry into force.

Case 3.6

Abbreviation used
ACUA = Agreement on the Cetaca, its Use and Apportionment

The mighty River Cetaca flows through four States until, after several hundred kilometers, it finally reaches the sea in the State of Larida. In the 1970s, the four riparian States, Patello, Glossida, Arapam and Larida, decide to conclude a treaty on the use of the Cetaca, mainly for fisheries and navigational purposes, but especially also on some border issues.

In order to prepare for the diplomatic conference, it is decided that detailed maps of the watercourse have to be drawn. The national cartographic services of Glossida and Arapam are jointly mandated to prepare these maps. Larida and Patello are very poor and do not have the necessary financial as well as human resources and know-how to undertake such a huge task as to chart an entire river hundreds of kilometers long. Furthermore, Patello has at that time serious internal problems and is fighting an internal group of rebels, which takes up most of its attention and resources. Finally, the Agreement on the Cetaca, its Use and Apportionment (ACUA) is concluded on 30 July 1979 and enters into force six months later.

Based on the maps provided by Glossida and Arapam, it is clear that the source of the Cetaca, which is to be found in the jungle of the very remote and hardly accessible mountain region between Glossida and Patello, lies on the right of a mountain ridge and therefore on the territory of Glossida. Impressed by the detailed maps, Patello declares after the conclusion that it had been those 'amazingly accurate maps' that had finally convinced Patello to sign the ACUA and accept the borderlines established within it.

Only a few years later, Glossida presents plans to build a huge dam for energy production close to the source of the Cetaca, which is according to the experts the only place where it is possible to realise this project. According to the plans, the dam would retain so much water that the rest of the river flowing through the three other States would become not much more than a trickle. Arapam seems to be unconcerned, but Larida and Patello start to protest. Unfortunately, this situation is not regulated by the ACUA and Glossida responds that it can do whatever it wants on its territory, including building a dam. It reiterates that the ACUA clearly shows that the source of the Cetaca lies on its territory.

But then, in 1982 a scientific expedition from Patello exploring the jungle in the border region by chance discovers that the maps prepared by Glossida and Arapam do not match reality. The source, and therefore also the planned dam (for which a few preparatory measures have already been taken), actually lie on the left of the mountain ridge and hence in Patello's territory. As soon as the government of Patello is informed about this, it vehemently protests and the President declares that it is clear that the source of the river belongs to Patello and not Glossida and that 'under these circumstances Patello considers the ACUA, which is based on wrong maps, to be terminated'.

A few weeks later several investigative journalists in Glossida publish secret documents, which show that at the time of the preparation of the maps, the government of Glossida was already aware that the only possibility to build a dam would be close to the source of the Cetaca. According to the secret documents, Glossida persuaded Arapam to prepare the maps to its, ie Glossida's, advantage and had promised Arapam cheap electricity in return. The governments of Patello and Larida both react outraged at this 'malicious deception' and Patello adds that as a consequence it 'considers the whole ACUA to be dead'.

You are a legal adviser in the office of the President of Patello. You are asked to analyse the situation and to write an objective legal opinion as to its solution, as well as all the eventual consequences.

Nota bene

— All four States are parties to the Vienna Convention on the Law of Treaties since its entry into force.
— The ACUA has been concluded for an undetermined time and does not contain any denunciation clauses.

Case 3.7

Abbreviations used
AEPOR = Agreement on the Exploitation and Production of Oil Resources
MFA = Ministers of Foreign Affairs

Large oil resources are located in the territory of the State of Suhmiland. However, Suhmiland possesses neither the necessary infrastructure for the exploitation of these resources, nor the necessary financial means to acquire this infrastructure. However, Suhmiland's neighbour, Tyraland, has a great deal of experience in oil extraction and all things related to the oil industry. Since Tyraland was in the middle of a significant financial crisis, it seized the golden opportunity and offered to help Suhmiland with oil extraction and production, in exchange for a certain percentage of the extracted crude oil.

The Ministers of Foreign Affairs (MFAs) of the two States consequently meet in Tyraland in June 2008 to discuss the collaboration. The Agreement on the Exploitation and Production of Oil Resources (AEPOR) has, among other things, to clarify the percentage of crude oil allocated to each party. This quickly becomes the main point of discussion. The MFA of Tyraland, Mr Blackgold, argues that in the light of the fact that without the help of Tyraland the oil resources of Suhmiland would remain unexploited, Tyraland should receive 75 per cent of the extracted crude oil. The MFA of Suhmiland, Mr Walter, on the other hand considers that since the oil resources were located on the territory of his country, the percentage of extracted crude oil allocated to Tyraland should not exceed 35 per cent.

After five days of fierce disputes concerning the percentage of crude oil to be allocated to each State, Mr Blackgold decides to speed things up and to disregard the usual niceties of diplomacy. He instructs Mr Hics, his daunting secret-service agent, to convince Mr Walter to sign the AEPOR with 90 per cent of the extracted crude oil allocated to Tyraland. Mr Blackgold thinks as he is using his best agent on this, this seems like an opportunity to increase the percentage. This would only be beneficial for his country and furthermore would allow him secretly to keep a little oil for himself.

Mr Hics, an expert in 'persuasion', visits Mr Walter in the latter's hotel room. Accompanied by his 357 Magnum he 'asks' Mr Walter to sign the AEPOR allocating 90 per cent of the extracted crude oil to Tyraland. Feeling the cold barrel of the gun on his temple, the poor MFA is aware that any fight or discussion would be in vain and thus signs the agreement.

Back in Suhmiland with a copy of the AEPOR, Mr Walter is not very well received by his colleagues in the government. It is only then that he finally explains Mr Blackgold's concept of diplomacy.

Outraged, the government of Suhmiland ask you, a specialist in international law, whether the treaty between Suhmiland and Tyraland has been validly concluded.

Nota bene

— Both States are parties to the Vienna Convention on the Law of Treaties since its entry into force.
— The AEPOR is an international bilateral treaty which has been concluded in simplified form (ie the treaty entered into force with the signatures of the two MFAs) .

Case 3.8

Abbreviation used
AT = Art Treaty

The famous painter Pablo Trebol was a national of Litemonte but lived and worked practically all his live in Fappa. As a consequence, the National Museum of Fappa is the proud owner of the biggest collection of Trebol's artworks in the world. Nevertheless, Litemonte is also very proud of its most famous son. Litemonte plans to organise a big exposition of Trebol's work on the occasion of the 100th anniversary of his death. Unfortunately, only 12 early paintings by Pablo Trebol can be found in Litemonte itself, clearly not enough for such a huge undertaking as the planned exhibition. Since the exhibition is a matter of national pride, the government of Litemonte decides to negotiate with the government of Fappa in order to borrow some of the paintings and statues from the National Museum of Fappa. Fappa agrees to lend to Litemonte 30 of Trebol's finest paintings for five years in exchange of considerable financial support by Litemonte of Fappa's world-famous Academy of Fine Art Conservation and Restoration. The payments are to be made in five instalments over the five years, the first part of the amount being due three weeks after the entry into force of the treaty. The two States quickly agree and conclude a treaty (the Art Treaty, AT) in simplified form on 14 September 2006. The AT enters into force on the same day.

However, about one week later tragedy strikes Fappa. An earthquake destroys parts of the capital city, where the National Museum is located. As a consequence of the earthquake several fires break out, including in the National Museum. Even though the fire brigade intervenes as quickly as possible it takes a long time to bring the fire under control. Once the flames have finally died down, it becomes apparent that a large number of paintings, including all works by Trebol that the National Museum owned, have been burnt beyond repair. Both Fappa but also Litemonte are shocked and saddened by this cultural loss.

After a few weeks, at the end of October 2006, the government of Fappa notes that the deadline has passed and that Litemonte has not paid the first instalment agreed on in the AT—to be paid three weeks after the entry into force of the AT—to the Academy of Fine Art Conservation and Restoration. Fappa contacts Litemonte and insists on the payment. Litemonte declares that of course it will not pay as it did not get what was agreed on in return; moreover, Litemonte takes the opportunity to declare that it considers the treaty to have ended.

You are a well-known specialist in international law. The government of Litemonte contacts you to clarify the legal situation concerning the treaty and to help to resolve the problem peacefully based on law.

Nota bene

—Litemonte is a party to the Vienna Convention on the Law of Treaties since its entry into force.
—Fappa ratified the Vienna Convention on the Law of Treaties on 5 January 1999.
—The AT is limited to five years.

Case 3.9

Abbreviations used
MFA = Minister of Foreign Affairs
TCB = Treaty on the Construction of the Bigpower Dam

Nucland, a coastal State facing the ocean, possesses several nuclear power stations which provide electricity to the whole territory of the State. When the Ecological Party took power, the energy policy of Nucland changed. The new government declared that although nuclear power was certainly an important source of electricity, it also brought many risks. Therefore, it decided that it no longer wanted to base national electricity production exclusively on nuclear power, but wanted to use another, less risky source for this production.

Candleland, a neighbouring State of Nucland, however, had an outdated energy policy, which would soon no longer suffice to cover all the needs of the population. It was therefore necessary to find a way to produce energy in a lasting way. After having learnt that they both wanted to modernise their energy production, Nucland and Candleland discussed the possibility of using the River Ziwari, marking the border between the two States, for energy production. They agreed to work together in order to construct a hydroelectric dam on this river.

Therefore, Nucland and Candleland concluded on 13 May 2009 a treaty on the construction, financing and administration of the Bigpower dam (TCB, Treaty on the Construction of the Bigpower Dam). In accordance with its Article 104, the TCB entered into force on 1 September 2009.

The TCB provided among other things that the costs of construction and administration were to be split 50–50 between the two States. Nucland was in addition charged to work out all the parts relating to the construction of the project, while Candleland had to develop a plan for the administration of the dam, particularly concerning the distribution of electricity.

The Bigpower dam was one of the boldest projects that had ever been undertaken in the region. The construction was planned to last for about seven years. The total budget was huge, but perfectly realistic, amounting to 85 billion kreuz (the national currency of Nucland) per year.

The construction works started in the beginning of 2010 and advanced well. However, a terrible catastrophe was to disrupt the good progress made. On the morning of 17 November 2010, an earthquake shook Nucland, which was located close to a very important submarine fault. As a consequence, a huge tsunami hit the coast of Nucland. The wave was approximately 15 meters high and penetrated about 30 km inland. Nucland suffered highly significant material damage to its territory and a great number of people lost their lives. Winter in Nucland was about to begin and a quarter of the population was without shelter and heating. Confronted with this exceptional catastrophe, the re-establishment of electricity and heating became priorities for the government of Nucland. Therefore, it decided to concentrate all its efforts on the rapid restoration of its nuclear power plants.

In addition, due to this tragedy the budget of Nucland had to be reviewed. Nucland quickly realised that it would no longer be able to pay its part of the financing of the Bigpower dam project. In fact, its leading economic advisors all warned the government that if Nucland continued to finance this project, the State risked going bankrupt.

Via diplomatic post, the Minister of Foreign Affairs (MFA) of Nucland informed his counterpart in Candleland on 25 November 2010 that Nucland intended to terminate the TCB from 1 February onwards. The reason was that due to the recent natural catastrophe which had hit Nucland, it was completely impossible for his State to continue to finance the construction of the dam. The MFA of Nucland asked his counterpart to understand that in such a situation assisting the victims and the necessity to provide them with heating and shelter against the approaching winter had priority over any other obligation and that he could not wait until the dam was finally finished and operational, which was foreseen only in the beginning of 2017. Therefore, it was necessary that Nucland repair some of its nuclear power plants, which had also been affected by the recent catastrophe, in order to remedy as fast as possible the lack of electricity in the country. Since it was not able to finance the construction of the dam and the reparation of its nuclear power plants at the same time, Nucland had to decide in favour of the latter in order to protect its population.

Candleland replied by saying that it fully understood the difficult situation of Nucland. Nevertheless, it contested whether Nucland could terminate the TCB. In its opinion, since the dam had not been affected by the earthquake, construction had to go on. It argued that Candleland also had to make sure that its population had sufficient energy and that it was not able to finance the remaining construction of the dam on its own. Furthermore, it reminded Nucland that according to the rule *pacta sunt servanda* a State is obliged to respect its international commitments. In addition, the simple fact that the execution of the treaty had become more difficult by the circumstances in question could not be seen as satisfying the conditions to terminate the treaty.

You are a well-known international lawyer and are mandated by Nucland. It asks you whether, according to the Vienna Convention on the Law of Treaties, it can terminate the TCB from 1 February 2011 onwards.

Nota bene

—Both Nucland and Candleland are parties to the Vienna Convention on the Law of Treaties since its entry into force.

Case 3.10

Abbreviation used
PoD = Pact on Disarmament

A number of international and internal armed conflicts raged worldwide a few years ago, causing heavy casualties and environmental destruction. The general agreement in the international community is that one major way to prevent further conflicts, and especially also to reduce their damage, is disarmament. Therefore, the State of Tellus, the State of Unda, the Republic of Ignis and the State of Aura meet to conclude a disarmament treaty. After long and cumbersome negotiations the Pact on Disarmament (PoD) is concluded on 4 March 2004. It enters into force five months later on 4 August 2004, after all four parties have deposited their instrument of ratification.

Article 1 of the PoD declares that the main aim of the Pact is 'to reduce the presence of dangerous weapons and therefore improve peaceful mutual relations based on trust'. Article 3 obliges all Member States to disclose the current number of their nuclear, biological and chemical weapons. These numbers shall, according to this Article 3, be controlled by independent international inspectors. Furthermore, Article 5 provides in paragraph 1 that the parties to the pact agree to reduce their current respective arsenals of nuclear weapons disclosed under Article 3 by at least half within two years after the entry into force of the PoD and that no increase would be allowed under any circumstances. The following Articles 6 and 7 establish the same as Article 5, for biological and chemical weapons, respectively. Article 11 provides that every State party has the obligation to allow independent international inspectors to have access to their territory and weapon storage facilities at any time 'in order to ensure control and a timely fulfilment of the present obligations'.

First, everything seems to be going well. However, in the beginning of 2005 journalists report that Unda has been constructing and secretly testing new biological and chemical weapons. Following public outcry, the independent international inspectors named under the PoD demand Unda give them access to their territory as well as weapon storage facilities. Unda refuses, saying that these are just malicious rumours and that it would not allow 'these inspectors to poke their nose into matters within the sovereignty of Unda'. In the following months there is more and more credible evidence that Unda has indeed been increasing its arsenal of biological and chemical weapons. Tellus and the Republic of Ignis call upon Unda to 'come to reason and give the inspectors access'. But they add that more time should be given to Unda to 'get itself together'. Aura on the other hand is outraged and wants to take concrete steps.

You are a legal adviser to the cabinet of the Prime Minister of Aura. You are asked to give your opinion as to which concrete steps Aura can take 'in conformity with international treaty law' in the current situation.

Nota bene

—Tellus and Unda have signed the Vienna Convention on the Law of Treaties on the same day, namely on 15 February 1997.
—The Republic of Ignis has been a party to the Vienna Convention on the Law of Treaties since its entry into force.
—Aura has ratified the Vienna Convention on the Law of Treaties on 29 May 1985.
—The PoD has been concluded for an undetermined time and without any provision relating to termination or withdrawal.

Recommended reading on treaty law

Articles

Winfried Lang, 'Les règles d'interprétation codifiées par la Convention de Vienne sur le droit des traités et les divers types de traités' (1973) 24 *Österreichische Zeitschrift für öffentliches Recht* 114.

Santiago Torres Bernárdez, 'Interpretation of Treaties by the International Court of Justice Following the Adoption of the 1969 Vienna Convention on the Law of Treaties', in Gerhard Hafner et al (eds), *Liber Amicorum Professor Ignaz Seidl-Hohenveldern in Honour of his 80th Birthday* (The Hague, Kluwer Law International,1998) 721–748.

Bert EW Vierdag, 'The Law Governing Treaty Relations between Parties to the Vienna Convention on the Law of Treaties and States not Party to the Convention' (1982) 76 *American Journal of International Law* 779.

Books

Enzo Cannizzaro (ed), *The Law of Treaties beyond the Vienna Convention* (Oxford, Oxford University Press, 2011).

Olivier Corten, *Les Conventions de Vienne sur le droit des traités: commentaire article par article* (Brussels, Bruylant, 2006).

Malgosia Fitzmaurice, Olufemi Elias, Panos Merkouris (eds), *Treaty Interpretation and the Vienna Convention on the Law of Treaties: 30 years on* (Leiden, Martinus Nijhoff Publishers, 2010).

Duncan Hollis, *The Oxford Guide to Treaties* (Oxford, Oxford University Press, 2012).

Mustafa Kamil Yasseen, *L'interprétation des traités d'après la Convention de Vienne sur le droit des traités* (Recueil des Cours, Vol 151, 1976).

Alexander Orakhelashvili and Sarah Williams (eds), *40 Years of the Vienna Convention on the Law of Treaties* (London, British Institute of International and Comparative Law, 2010).

Ian Sinclair, *The Vienna Convention on the Law of Treaties* (Manchester, Manchester University Press, 1984).

Mark Villiger, *Commentary on the 1969 Vienna Convention on the Law of Treaties* (Leiden, Martinus Nijhoff Publishers, 2009).

Mark Villiger, *Customary International Law and Treaties: A Study of their Interactions and Interrelations with Special Consideration of the 1969 Vienna Convention on the Law of Treaties* (Dordrecht, Martinus Nijhoff Publishers, 1985).

Chapter 4

Responsibility of States for Internationally Wrongful Acts

General plan to solve State responsibility cases based on the ILC Articles on Responsibility of States for Internationally Wrongful Acts (2001) (SRA)

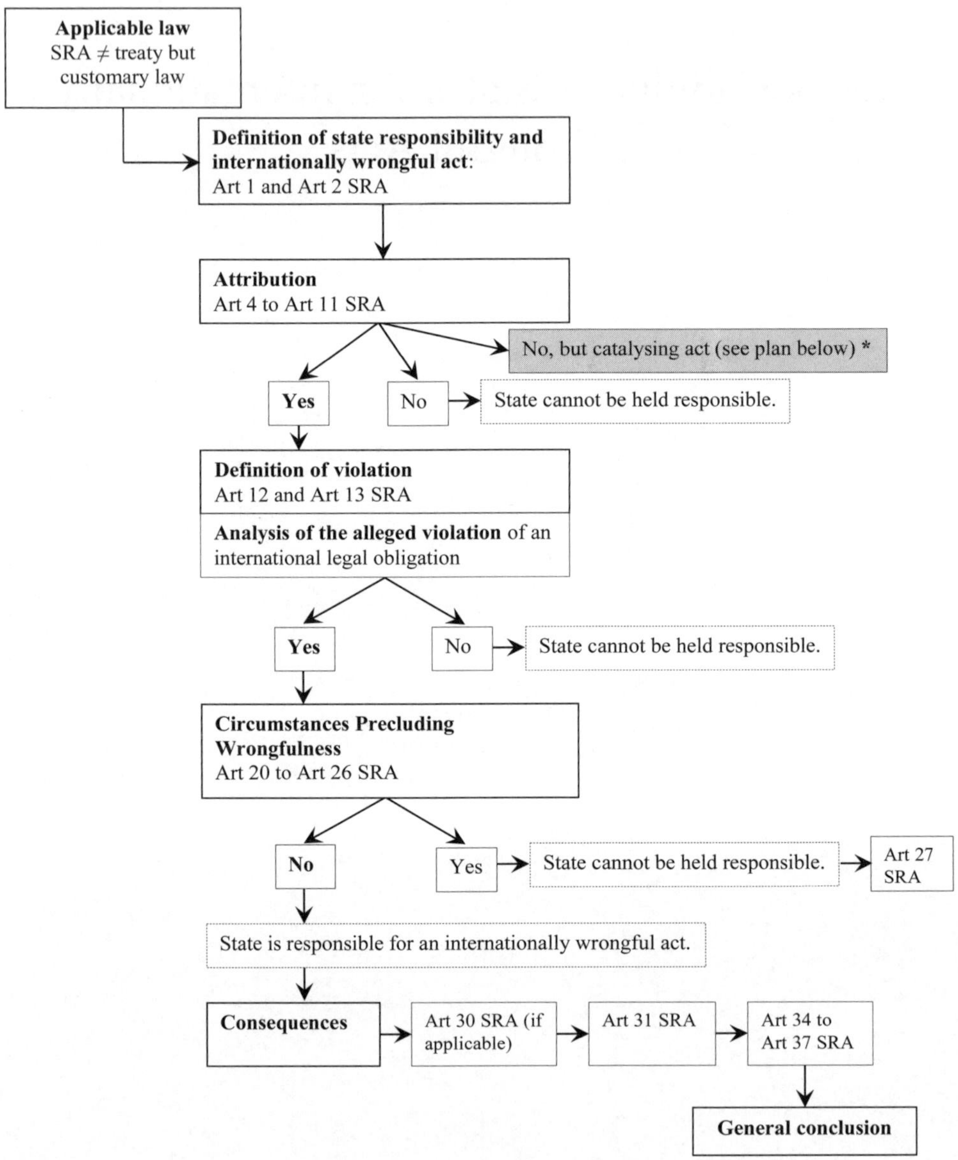

Figure 5. State responsibility.

Catalysing act

A **'catalysing act'** is found in the following situation: the act in question cannot be attributed to the State in question (i.e. no attribution under Art. 4 to 11 SRA). However, the act ***reveals*** an act or omission attributable to the State (most often it is an omission).

For example: State A is not responsible for the attack on the Embassy of State B, but the facts surrounding the attack show that State A did not take all necessary measures to protect the Embassy, as would have been its obligation under international law.

Thus, under a catalysing act attributable to it, the State in question is responsible for its *own* conduct (act or omission) and *not* for the original act in question (e.g. the attack on the Embassy).

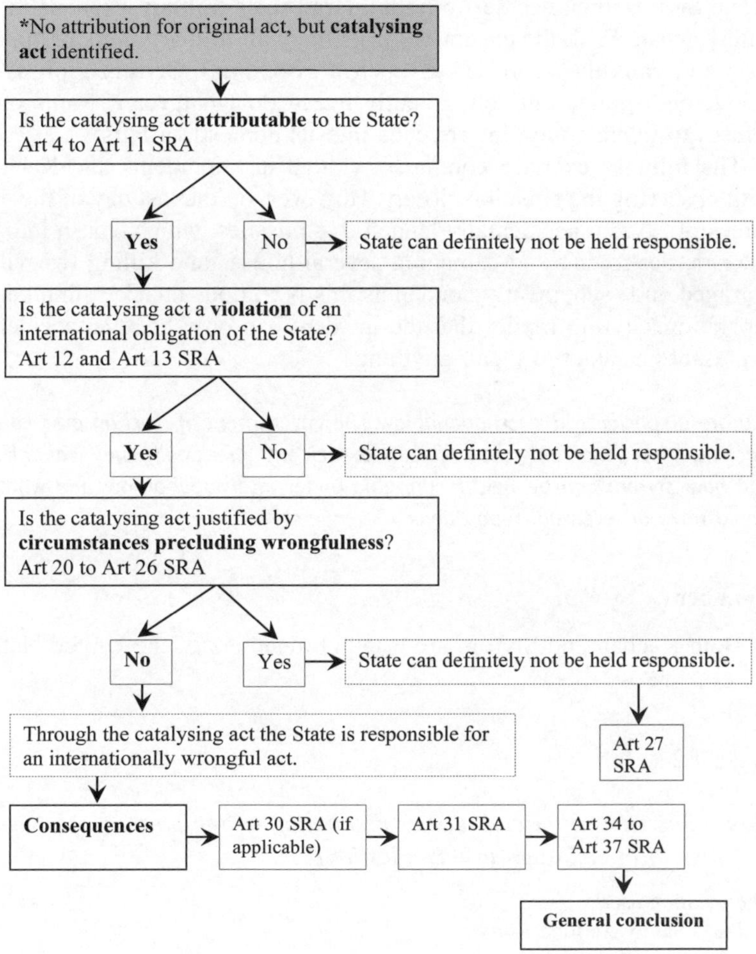

Figure 6. Catalysing act.

Attribution and violation of an international obligation

Note: The following six cases (4.1–4.6) are limited to issues of attribution and the violation of an international obligation. Thus, questions of circumstances precluding wrongfulness – otherwise mandatory – do not have to be analysed.

Case 4.1

Relations between Styrom and the Kingdom of Kachan have been tense for several years. Styrom then decides to hold a large-scale military exercise in the border region with Kachan. With the exception of its navy all military units participate. Kachan protests and calls the exercise 'an open provocation'. Styrom replies that it is after all a sovereign State, and consequently it can do whatever it wants on its territory and refuses to tolerate any 'interference into its domestic affairs'.

The military exercise continues without any incidents and Kachan contents itself with observing the situation closely. However, on the last day of the exercise the armed forces of Styrom accidentally launch five missiles, which smash into a small village in Kachan, destroying and damaging several houses and killing two villagers. Kachan is outraged and 'vehemently condemns this perfidious attack', simultaneously asking for reparation. Styrom replies that the incident had only been an accident and that thus it could not be asked to repair anything.

You are a specialist in international law. The government of Kachan asks you to advise it on the legal situation concerning the unfortunate incident. Specifically, they would like to know whether and how Styrom can be held responsible under international law and what consequences this would have on eventual reparations.

Nota bene

—Both Kachan and Styrom are original members of the United Nations.

Case 4.2

(Note: questions of circumstances precluding wrongfulness—otherwise mandatory—do not have to be analysed in this question)

Abbreviation used
SAFE = Safety As First End

Allenda is a State that is currently facing some economic difficulties. Therefore, the government has had to impose some radical budget cuts. Since experts have calculated that outsourcing police functions would be cheaper than maintaining the current Allendian police, the government of Allenda recently dismissed the entire police force with the exception of the section for criminal investigations. Instead, several private security firms are mandated by a governmental decree having the force of law to 'maintain law and public order' in the areas assigned to them. Under this decree, the private security firm Safety As First End (SAFE) is responsible for law and public order in the capital of Allenda, Yema.

For several months, there are no problems. However, things change after the Soccer World Cup Final between Allenda and Pomal. Allenda loses because of a penalty which is granted to Pomal in consequence of a very dubious foul against Pomal's striker, Eduardo. As is visible in the television replay, the action was actually not a foul at all, but Eduardo had deliberately—and very convincingly—made it look like one. The public in Allenda, a soccer-loving nation, is scandalised and very angry with Pomal. After the end of the game, many Allenda fans continue to linger in Yema, trying to forget their defeat. At the same time, the Ambassador of Pomal in Allenda and some of his diplomats joyfully leave their embassy where they had watched the game together. A group of Allenda supporters sees them leave the embassy wearing the national colours of Pomal and singing Pomal's national anthem. Furious, this group starts to attack and beat the Ambassador and his diplomats. A patrol of three SAFE members passes by but instead of intervening, they just silently watch, even though, as later investigations will show, they have clearly recognised the Ambassador and diplomats. In the end, the Ambassador and the other diplomats have to be transported to the hospital with multiple injuries.

Pomal vehemently protests against this treatment of its diplomats and asks for reparation. However, Allenda responds by claiming that it is in no way responsible for what had happened to them, since it was 'a group of rightfully disappointed fans of Allenda's national soccer team' which was responsible for this incident. Allenda adds that it is a well-established principle in international law that States are never responsible for the actions of private individuals.

You are a legal adviser to the government of Pomal. The Prime Minister asks you whether Allenda's statements are correct and whether there was really no possibility under international law to hold Allenda responsible for the mistreatment of Pomal's diplomats.

Nota bene

- Both States are original members of the United Nations.
- Both States are parties to the Vienna Convention on Diplomatic Relations from 1961.

Case 4.3

(Note: questions of circumstances precluding wrongfulness—otherwise mandatory—do not have to be analysed in this question)

Abbreviation used
SPP = Service for the Protection of Personalities

Gideon and Tristan have worked for almost twenty years for the Service for the Protection of Personalities (SPP) of the State of Monailand. Among other things the SPP is charged with protecting foreign Ambassadors when they travel in the territory of Monailand. It is not really the salary that motivates these men to work for the SPP but rather their desire to protect leading personalities and VIPs.

However, for several years now our two main characters have lost this commendable motivation and are fed up with their miserable salary in light of the danger of their profession. Therefore, they decide to prepare a big coup in order to grant themselves a decent retirement which they feel they fully deserve after their hard work at the SPP. They tell themselves that there is a lot of money to make with all the high-level personalities they were dealing with.

In the morning of the 14 May 2010 Gideon and Tristan start their service at the SPP as usual, putting on their uniform and taking their weapons. They had received an order to drive the wife of the Ambassador from Petroland, Madam Diamgold, to the airport, where she had to take an airplane to return to her country. After picking up Madam Diamgold the two accomplices drive in the direction of the airport. But Madam Diamgold never catches her airplane. Gideon and Tristan lock her up in the latter's garage and ask the Ambassador to pay a ransom of several millions if he wishes to see his wife alive again.

The two accomplices are convinced that their plan has been very well prepared. However, they have not taken into account the exceptional insight of the secret service of Petroland which does not take long to identify them as the responsible persons. A rescue operation is quickly mounted and at the end of the afternoon the Petroland secret service surround the garage. Seeing that their original plan is going to fail, the two agents of the SPP try to flee by threatening to kill the wife of the Ambassador if they are not allowed to escape. Shots are exchanged and in a clumsy movement Tristan shoots Madame Diamgold, injuring her fatally.

After a few days, the Minister of Foreign Affairs of Petroland writes a diplomatic note to his colleague in Monailand, claiming that Monailand is entirely responsible for the abduction of Madam Diamgold, which clearly amounts to a violation of a body of century-old rules. He also asks Monailand for full reparation for the injury suffered. Monailand replies by saying that it cannot be held responsible for this abduction, since it had served a purely private goal. It adds that it is impossible to hold a State responsible for acts of its agents which had clearly exceeded their competences.

After this reply of Monailand, the Minister of Foreign Affairs of Petroland asks you whether Monailand can be held responsible for the acts of the two agents of the SPP.

Nota bene

— Monailand and Petroland are both parties to the Vienna Convention on Diplomatic Relations from 1961 since its entry into force.

Case 4.4

(Note: questions of circumstances precluding wrongfulness—otherwise mandatory—do not have to be analysed in this question)

Abbreviation used
EC = Equalisation Committee

The State of Mata and its neighbour, the State of Corle, gained their independence at the same time in 1973. However, since then the two States have developed very differently. Mata has been economically successful, not least because several oil fields were found on its territory and due to its development of an excellent industry for technical high-precision instruments. At the same time, Corle has remained poor and rather underdeveloped. Over the years, the relations between the two States worsened, especially also because Corle considers that Mata has treated it unfairly and that Mata should have helped Corle in their economic development since they 'became independent as brothers and should now treat each other as brothers as well'.

Then, one day a hitherto unknown group calling itself the Equalisation Committee (EC) attacks Mata, killing several border guards of Mata as well as some civilians who happen to be present at the border between Corle and Mata. The group breaks into a factory for high-precision instruments, stealing the secret construction plans of some of these instruments. On their way back the EC injurs and also kills some policemen who have been dispatched to arrest the group. A few days later, the EC forcibly enters the territorial waters of Mata and attacks and robs a ship which just has left the port of Mata.

After a public outcry in Mata and investigations by the secret service of Mata, the following facts become known.

The EC is a group which has been created secretly on the order of the current President of Corle, Mr Leon. The EC does not have any official status and does not appear in any of the officially available documents or laws of the State. However, it has been trained as well as equipped by military officers of Corle. The confidential documents obtained by the secret service of Mata also show that it was the President himself who had ordered the EC to 'go and get the secrets of the production of some high precision instruments of Mata, no matter what the cost', in order to 'catch up economically with them'. However, there is no evidence at all to prove that the President or any other State official also ordered the attack on the ship in the territorial waters of Mata.

You are a well-known specialist in public international law. The government of Mata asks for help, since they are unsure how to deal with this situation under international law. They ask you whether—and if yes, how and with what consequences—they can hold the State of Corle responsible for the 'cowardly attacks', as the President of Mata puts it.

Nota bene

— Both States have been members of the United Nations since their independence.

Case 4.5

(Note: questions of circumstances precluding wrongfulness – otherwise mandatory – do not have to be analysed in this question)

Unluckland is a large coastal State. Its capital, Fastcity, is the best example for the country's economic and industrial success. The entire State apparatus is located in this city, which also constitutes the nerve centre of the State, on the national as well as on the international level. In addition, most of the embassies and consulates are also located there. Yet, this is by far not the nicest region in the country.

Nicetown is located 1,500 km to the south of the capital at the foot of the terrible volcano Mentor, which has, however, been dormant for almost four centuries now. This little town is visited every year by numerous tourists from all over the world. They climb the 'beast' and from the top of the volcano admire the splendid view of beautiful bays with turquoise water. Waïkiland, a small island State, has set up its consulate in this little paradise.

In the morning of the 4 April 2010 a terrible earthquake shook the small town. Some minutes later, a gigantic volcanic eruption occurred and tons of red-hot lava flowed down the sides of Mentor towards Nicetown. Thanks to the particular geographical situation, the lava split into two enormous streams, encircling the town and finally flowing into the bay. The earthquake, on the other hand, hit Nicetown more seriously, damaging houses and roads. Electricity was cut off and all lines of communication were completely broken. Furthermore, there were a large number of victims, including in the police forces and emergency services. Confronted with this shortage of available means, the inhabitants of Nicetown organised themselves and decided to manage some aspects of the rescue activities, such as distributing food and water but also providing for security, for example against looters.

A small group of Nicetownians was making surveillance rounds in the various neighbourhoods of the devastated town. They surprised several looters and decided to arrest them. Unfortunately, the police station had been completely destroyed by the catastrophe. Noticing that the Waïkiland consulate building was surprisingly still intact, this group of Nicetownians decided to seize the building and to transform the basement into a detention centre for looters. Therefore, they expelled the consul and his wife, as well as all the administrative and technical personnel of the consulate.

This situation persisted for more than two weeks, until the central authorities were finally able to reach Nicetown. In fact, it had been impossible to reach Nicetown by land or sea before, since the lava formed a wall around the town. In addition, the ashes that the volcano launched into the sky had made it impossible for helicopters to land.

After the catastrophe, Waïkiland addressed a diplomatic note to Unluckland, in which it complained about the absolutely scandalous seizing of its consulate building. Even if it understood the tragedy with which the little town of Nicetown had been hit, this did not give anyone the right to expel the consular personnel and seize the building in order to transform it into a detention centre. Therefore, Waïkiland requested reparation for the injury suffered. Unluckland replied by saying that since it could not reach the place and since all lines of communication with the town were disrupted, it could not be held responsible for what had happened there. Furthermore, those people were private people acting without the knowledge of the State; and it is a well-accepted principle in international law that a State cannot be held responsible for actions of simple private parties.

You are a well-known international lawyer in the Ministry of Foreign Affairs of Waïkiland. You are asked to defend the position of Waïkiland, according to which the act of seizing of the consulate can be attributed to Unluckland and constitutes a possible violation of international law.

Case 4.6

(Note: questions of circumstances precluding wrongfulness—otherwise mandatory—do not have to be analysed in this question)

There have been tensions between the States of Tiranoc and Saphery for several years, mainly due to the totally different political and economic systems and convictions of the two States. In Tiranoc, Saphery is viewed as a greedy and corrupt country, while the common understanding on Tiranoc in Saphery is that they are somewhat backward looking and slow. However, so far relations have remained peaceful.

Then, one day a group of students from the main University of Tiranoc starts to protest in front of the embassy of Saphery against the 'inhuman capitalistic system of Saphery'. Soon, more and more students join the protests. All of a sudden the students tear down the gates and storm the embassy (which happens to be empty at that time) without any opposition from the police. The students also start to search for and destroy the embassy archives. The students declare that they will remain and occupy the embassy as long as Saphery does not change its politics with regards to 'their economic exploitation of humans and Mother Nature alike'.

Saphery furiously protests at this violation of its embassy and asks Tiranoc to chase the students away and to punish them appropriately. However, the President of Tiranoc publicly declares that the government of Tiranoc 'is proud of the courage and initiative shown by the students', and that they 'support their fight against economic exploitation of the weakest'. Furthermore, he adds that the State will send food and water to the students occupying the embassy so that 'they can keep up their good work, which is wholeheartedly supported by the government of Tiranoc and which has to be understood as part of the official policy of Tiranoc vis-à-vis greedy capitalist States such as Saphery'. However, it should be noted that at the same time the President strongly condemns the destruction of the embassy archives. Saphery immediately sends an urgent note of protest to Tiranoc, stating that it holds Tiranoc responsible for this 'blatant violation of international law'. But the government of Tiranoc only laughs at this and replies that apparently Saphery needs some lessons in international law, since it is absolutely clear that actions of private individuals—such as the students—could never and under no circumstance be attributed to a State.

The President of Saphery is confused and rather desperate. He asks you—a legal adviser to the government and specialist in international law—whether Tiranoc is right with its assertion. The President wants to know if Tiranoc can be held responsible; if yes, how and what for exactly.

Nota bene

—Both Saphery and Tiranoc are original members of the United Nations.
—Both States are also parties to the Vienna Convention on Diplomatic Relations from 1961.

Circumstances precluding wrongfulness

Note: the focus of the next four cases (cases 4.7–4.10) is on the circumstances precluding wrongfulness. The solution of these cases also requires a full analysis of attribution and the violation of an international obligation.

Case 4.7

Abbreviation used
MPT = Military Passage Treaty

The State of Alindor lies on a large, scenic bay. Particular geographical and political constellations have, however, resulted in the strait between the bay and the open sea being exclusively controlled by the State of Jemm. While commercial ships have been allowed to pass through the straits for years, the navy of Alindor has so far not been allowed passage due to concerns by Jemm over sovereignty (since the ships would have to pass through Jemm's territorial waters). The well-equipped and highly organised Alindor navy has therefore for years only been training in the bay.

Recently, in 2010, the presidents of Alindor and Jemm met in the context of the annual General Assembly meeting of the United Nations. Alongside some other subjects, the issue of the access of Alindor's navy to the open sea was raised. The presidents agreed to conclude a treaty on the topic. A few months later this treaty, the so-called Military Passage Treaty (MPT), was concluded, allowing the passage of warships of Alindor's navy. The MPT provides that warships of Alindor are allowed to pass through the territorial waters of Jemm for the purpose of military exercises in the open sea, after prior notification to the Ministry of Defence of Jemm at least 12 hours before the passage. The treaty was duly ratified by the parliaments of both countries, as is required in their constitutions, and entered into force at the end of 2010.

In January 2011 a new President was elected in Jemm, since the term of the previous one had come to an end.

In March 2011 the Ministry of Defence of Alindor notified its counterpart in Jemm that three warships of the navy of Alindor would pass through the strait the next day (in 24 hours) to participate in an exercise of the regional defence organisation on the high seas.

However, shortly after the warships have passed through the strait the next day, the new President of Jemm vehemently protests and declares that he is 'deeply disappointed, because so far Alindor has always respected international law and the territorial integrity of Jemm'. He strongly condemns the passage of the warships as a serious violation of international law and demands financial reparation.

You are the legal adviser to the Minister of Defence of Alindor, who has to explain the situation to the President in a few hours. He is rather confused about the situation and asks you to make a legal analysis of the issue of the passage of the three warships in order to clarify whether Alindor is responsible for any breach of international law.

Nota bene

—Both Alindor and Jemm are original members of the United Nations.
—Both States are furthermore parties to the Vienna Convention on the Law of Treaties since its entry into force.

Case 4.8

Abbreviations used
ICJ = International Court of Justice
TOFT = Treaty on the Over Flight of Territories

Airstate is a neighbouring State of Spaceland, located on the eastern side of the latter. For a long time Airstate has wanted to open its market of commercial and tourist flights towards the west. However, without the authorisation of Spaceland, it cannot fly over the latter's territory, consequently obliging commercial flights to make lengthy detours and to charge very high prices.

After negotiations with Spaceland, the two States concluded a treaty on the 12 September 1974 which authorised the free flight of aircrafts over their respective territories. Both States benefited from this treaty: the commercial flights from Airstate could finally transit through the territory of Spaceland towards the west, and were therefore able to charge much lower prices, and Spaceland was able to do the same towards the east.

The Treaty on the Over Flight of Territories (TOFT) provided in its Article 4 that 'the aircrafts of Airstate transporting passengers are allowed to fly freely over the territory of Spaceland'. The same right for the aircrafts from Spaceland was accorded to them on the territory of Airstate in Article 5 TOFT. According to Article 2 TOFT 'the present treaty applies only to commercial passenger flights'.

In February 2010, a conflict erupted between Airstate and the State of Moonland. Moonland, on whose territory the conflict takes place, is located in the west of Airstate. Wanting to bring its troops as fast as possible to the territory of Moonland, Airstate organised military flights to transport troops. These had to fly over the territory of Spaceland. Spaceland, who was on good terms with Moonland and wished to remain neutral in the conflict between Airstate and Moonland, called upon Airstate to stop the military flights over Spacelandian territory. It added that these flights constituted a clear violation of the TOFT.

Airstate replied that such flights had already taken place twice in the past, without any complaint from Spaceland. Therefore, it considered that the TOFT could be read in a broader manner, incorporating also military transport flights. Spaceland reacted by saying that these two previous military flights could not be seen as relevant precedents since these flights had brought humanitarian assistance to the State of Shakeland, which had been hit by a natural catastrophe, and thus had nothing to do with an armed conflict. Furthermore, two precedents would in any event not be enough to establish a relevant practice and to enlarge the interpretation of the TOFT. Consequently, Spaceland considered these military flights over its territory as a violation of the TOFT and of its international sovereignty. It further declared that should these acts continue, it would use its airforce to divert all Airstatian flights and would close its airspace to all flights from Airstate.

However, Airstate, very sure that it was acting within its rights, continued to transport its troops by military flights over the territory of Spaceland. Consequently, Spaceland activated the measures it had threatened, namely closure of its airspace to all flights from Airstate and the diversion of planes from Airstate.

As a reaction, Airstate seized the International Court of Justice (ICJ) which was competent to hear the case based on a compromissory clause contained in Article 57 TOFT. Airstate asked the ICJ to declare that Spaceland had violated the TOFT and to decide on appropriate reparations. The ICJ declared itself competent on 23 April 2010. Spaceland continued to prohibit all Airstatian flights from overflying its territory.

You are one of the most brilliant lawyers at the ICJ. You are asked to give a legal opinion on whether Spaceland has violated the TOFT and to determine whether Spaceland is responsible for an internationally wrongful act.

Case 4.9

On 27 March 2011 a military ship flying the flag of the State of Apteno violently hit hidden rocks in the high seas, not very far from the coast of the State of Eudyp. The ship was mainly carrying oil and kerosene to one of Apteno's aircraft carriers.

After the incident, a lot of the oil and kerosene in the ship spills into the sea, while the crew is rescued. Winds and sea currents cause the oil to flow in the direction of the coast of Eudyp. Just off the coast of Eudyp there is a small island belonging to this State. A rare species of penguin is located on this island. In fact, the colony of penguins located on this island make up 80 per cent of the worldwide population of these penguins, which already figure on the red list for species in danger of extinction. Furthermore, the waters around the island are one of the most important breeding grounds for lobster, very important for the local fishing industry in Eudyp.

The outflow of oil from the stranded war ship continues unhindered and now there is also the danger that the ship will break in two, releasing even more oil into the ocean. This danger and the pollution increase by the hour and urgent measures are needed. An emergency expert meeting comes to the conclusion that the only possibility to stop the outflow of oil immediately would be to close the hole in the ship violently and to trap the oil under water, for example by causing explosions on and in the ship.

A few hours after this public announcement by the expert group, still nothing has happened and Apteno, as the owner and flag State of the ship, has neither taken any position nor taken any measures. Therefore, three military airplanes from Eudyp take to the sky and bomb the stranded ship. As the experts predicted, the ship indeed sinks and the outflow of oil is stopped immediately.

While everyone seems to be relieved by this successful operation, Apteno violently protests. It says that such an armed attack on one of its military ships is to be seen as an attack on Apteno itself, which is absolutely unacceptable and against the most fundamental principles in international law. Apteno insists that 'Eudyp – and Eudyp alone – is entirely responsible for this wrongful act' and demands excuses as well as financial compensation.

You are a well-known specialist in international law. The government of Eudyp contacts you and asks you to make an objective determination of the situation in order to clarify whether Eudyp really is responsible and what the consequences would be.

Nota bene

—Both States are members of the United Nations.

Case 4.10

Mecanoland is a coastal State with a rather outdated military fleet. Therefore, it decided ten years ago to build a fleet of nuclear-powered submarines. After several years of research and development it finally managed to construct its first prototype.

Commander Luck, Mecanoland's most highly decorated and experienced military officer, was charged with testing the submarine and its crew of 125 men under combat conditions. The submarine set sail on 1 May 2010 and proceeded to the designated testing zone on the high seas. The tests were planned to last between six and seven months, during which the crew had to perform all sorts of manoeuvres, in particular to test the capacities of the nuclear engine.

After five months of intensive manoeuvres, Commander Luck considered the mission to be a success. He proudly declared to his crew that in his opinion the construction of this submarine had enabled Mecanoland to achieve a major step defending its coast. He decided to finish the mission and ordered the ship to set sail for home.

However, a few days into the return journey a thundering noise started to come from the engine room and the lights of the control panel started to blink like a Christmas tree. The alarm sounded incessantly and the crew soon started to panic. A leak was detected in the reactor, and it was possible that this could cause the whole submarine to become contaminated.

Thanks to his experience, Commander Luck remained calm and tried to find a solution. While examining his maps, he quickly became aware that the submarine would not be able to reach its home port in Mecanoland. In fact, the damage to the engine was so serious that there was a risk the whole submarine might explode if it was not promptly repaired. Therefore, Commander Luck decided to call at the closest port possible in order to save the submarine, which was supposed to become the pride of the submarine fleet of Mecanoland. According to his maps, the submarine was currently located several miles away from the port of Orchycity, capital of the island of Paradiland. Due to its exceptional flora and fauna, this small island with 800,000 inhabitants is registered as a UNESCO World Heritage site. The majority of the people live in the capital.

Since the radio system of the submarine was completely out of order, it was not possible to ask the authorities of Paradiland for their permission to enter its territorial waters. Nevertheless, Commander Luck proceeded towards the port of Orchycity. He and his crew were, however, not very well received when they resurfaced in the middle of the splendid port. For security reasons, the Paradilandian authorities were obliged to evacuate the entire port district.

The reactor leak was finally repaired and explosion averted. After the repair had been effected, Paradiland towed the submarine into international waters. There, a tugboat from Mecanoland took over and brought the boat back home.

After some days, the Minister of Foreign Affairs from Paradiland wrote a diplomatic note to his colleague in Mecanoland indicating that he judged the intrusion of a military submarine into its territorial waters inadmissible and that Paradiland considered this act as a serious violation of international law. Therefore, Paradiland requested reparation for all the injuries suffered.

You are a well-known international lawyer, mandated by Mecanoland. This State has asked you to write an objective legal opinion on the question as to whether Mecanoland has engaged its international responsibility by the intrusion of its submarine into the port of Orchycity.

Nota bene

— Thanks to the quick thinking of Commander Luck, the radioactivity on the island of Paradiland did not increase and the entire ecosystem remained untouched by this incident.

Recommended reading on State responsibility

Articles

James Crawford and Simon Olleson, 'The Continuing Debate on a UN Convention on State Responsibility' (2005) 54 *International and Comparative Law Quarterly* 959.

Christian Dominicé, 'The International Responsibility of States for Breach of Multilateral Obligations' (1999) 10 *European Journal of International Law* 353.

Pierre-Marie Dupuy et al, 'Assessing the Work of the International Law Commission on State Responsibility: Symposium' (2002) 13 *European Journal of International Law* 1053.

Eduardo Jiménez de Aréchaga, 'International Responsibility of States for Acts of the Judiciary', in Wolfgang Friedman, Louis Henkin and Oliver Lissitzyn (eds), *Transnational Law in a Changing Society: Essays in Honour of Philip C. Jessup* (New York, Columbia University Press, 1972) 171–187.

Matti Koskenniemi, 'Solidarity Measures: State Responsibility as a New International Order?' (2001) 72 *British Yearbook of International Law* 337.

Brigitte Stern, 'La responsabilité internationale des Etats: perspectives récentes' (2003) 7 *Cursos Euromediterráneos Bancaja de derecho internacional* 645.

Books

Ian Brownlie, *System of the Law of Nations: State Responsibility, Part I* (Oxford, Oxford University Press, 1983).

James Crawford, *The International Law Commission's Articles on State Responsibility: Introduction, Text and Commentaries* (Cambridge, Cambridge University Press, 2002).

James Crawford, *Les articles de la CDI sur la responsabilité de l'Etat pour fait internationalement illicite: introduction, texte et commentaires* (Paris, A Pedone, 2003).

Pierre-Maire Dupuy (ed), *Obligations multilatérales, droit impératif et responsabilité internationale des Etats: colloque international de Florence, 7 et 8 décembre 2001* (Paris, A Pedone, 2003).

Nina Jørgensen, *The Responsibility of States for International Crimes* (Oxford, Oxford University Press, 2003).

Maurizio Ragazzi (ed), *International Responsibility Today: Essays in Memory of Oscar Schachter* (Leiden, Martinus Nijhoff, 2005).

Chapter 5

International Dispute Settlement: The International Court of Justice

General plan to solve questions related to the competence of the International Court of Justice to judge *contentious* cases

Applicable law

Jurisdictional issues

Personal jurisdiction (jurisdiction *ratione personae*)
Article 34 ICJ Statute, Article35 ICJ Statute
+ Article 93 §1 UN Charter

Raised ex officio by ICJ

↓

Subject matter jurisdiction (jurisdiction *ratione materiae*)
Article 38 ICJ Statute
Definition of a legal dispute under international law
(*Mavrommatis Palestine Concessions* case)

Raised ex officio by ICJ

↓

Consensual jurisdiction (jurisdiction *ratione consensus*)
Article 36 ICJ Statute
4 possibilities
1) special agreement
2) optional cause declaration
3) compromissory clause in a treaty
4) *forum prorogatum*

Not raised ex officio by ICJ

Admissibility issues

For example:

- Case has become moot
- Case is of purely hypothetical nature
- Lack of interest of claimant State in subject matter
- Legal interest of a third State
- …

——— = Mandatory to consider in an exam

\- - - - = Only to be considered if the issues is raised

Figure 7. ICJ contentious cases.

General plan to solve questions related to the competence of the International Court of Justice to pronounce upon *advisory opinions*

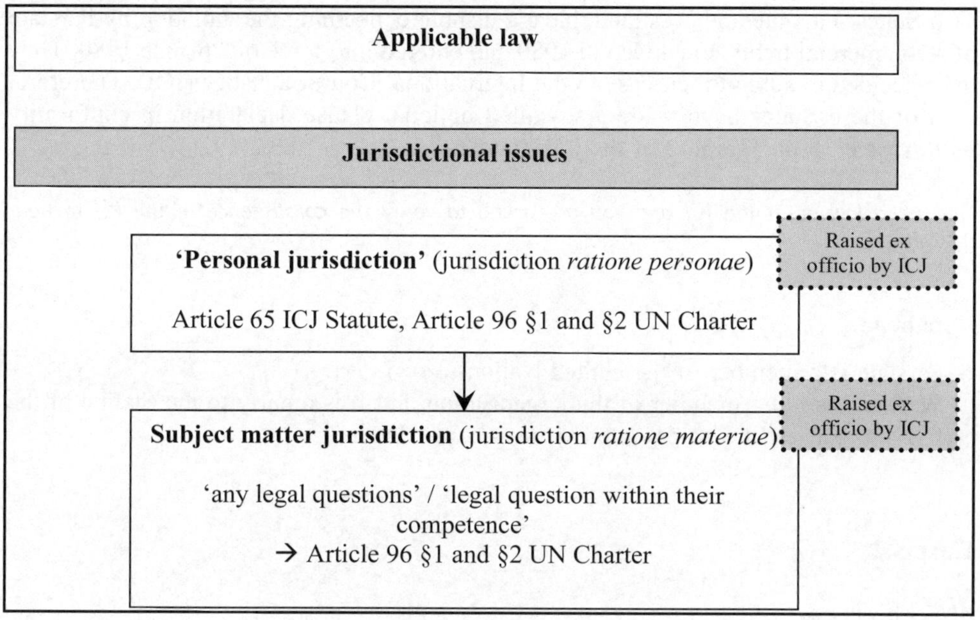

Figure 8. ICJ advisory opinions.

Issues of personal jurisdiction

Case 5.1

Abbreviation used
ICJ = International Court of Justice

Two States, Farstate and Westland, have a dispute concerning the violation by Farstate of a commercial treaty concluded in 1980 and entered into force on 26 June 1980. They have decided to submit their case to the International Court of Justice (ICJ). Therefore, both of these States have made a so-called optional clause declaration in conformity with Article 36 paragraph 2 of the ICJ Statute.

You are a lawyer at the ICJ and you are asked to verify the competence of the ICJ to hear this dispute.

Nota bene

—Farstate is a member of the United Nations.
—Westland is not a member of this organisation, but it is a party to the Statute of the ICJ and participates to pay the expenses of the latter.

Case 5.2

Abbreviation used
ICJ = International Court of Justice

Cany is a company mainly active in the food and beverage sector. It is registered in Ekto, but is doing business in many different countries, among others also in Tirup. Tirup is governed by an authoritarian regime, but so far Cany has never had any problems. But then, practically overnight, the government of Tirup expropriates Cany and seizes most of its production facilities and movable goods. The head of Cany vehemently protests and starts legal proceedings to get its property back. However, the legal steps taken lead to nothing since the judiciary of Tirup is highly corrupt and under the influence of the government.

The head of Cany then reads in a newspaper a short notice about the International Court of Justice (ICJ), which he has never heard of before. He immediately decides to bring his case against Tirup to this international court to get a decision of an independent judiciary.

You are the assistant to the registrar of the ICJ. The registrar gives you the application written by the head of Cany and asks you to assess this situation in order to determine the jurisdiction of the ICJ.

Nota bene

—Both Tirup and Ekto are parties to the Charter of the United Nations.

— Tirup has made an optional clause declaration under Article 36 paragraph 2 of the ICJ Statute without any reservation.
— Ekto has also made such an optional clause declaration without any reservation.

Forms of consent: reservations to optional clause declarations

Case 5.3

Abbreviations used
ICJ = International Court of Justice
TOE = Treaty on Oil Exports

The State of Skir is a small oil-producing country. On 22 July 2004 it concluded a treaty, the so-called Treaty on Oil Exports (TOE), with Reggo. Under the TOE, Skir commits itself to export every year 2 million barrels of oil at a very favourable price to Reggo. All the oil that Reggo imports in addition to these 2 million barrels will be charged at the prevailing market price. Payments are to be made in the national currency of Reggo, which is seen as a very stable currency. This is an important point for Skir, since it constantly has problems and shortages in its foreign exchange reserves.

In 2008, Reggo does not pay for the oil that it bought in addition to the 2 million barrels. After repeated requests from Skir, Reggo finally pays, but only a part of the sum and in addition in the local currency of Skir and not that of Reggo. Skir protests and insists that payments under the TOE have to be made in the national currency of Reggo. However, Reggo replies that this is only the case for the first 2 million barrels they imported but not for the rest. Skir is convinced that the TOE cannot be read like this, but Reggo insists on its own point of view.

As a consequence, on 1 May 2009 Skir starts proceedings against Reggo in the International Court of Justice (ICJ). As basis of jurisdiction, Skir invokes the optional clause declarations made by both States in accordance with Article 36 paragraph 2 of the ICJ Statute. Reggo has made an optional clause declaration in 1957, without attaching any reservation to it. Skir, on the other hand, has submitted its optional clause declaration in 1986 with the following reservation: 'Skir excludes from the jurisdiction of the Court all matters relating to oil, oil extraction, oil exports or oil products.' In its reply, Reggo contests the competence of the ICJ to deal with the case by invoking Skir's reservation. The government of Skir reacts in outrage, declaring that this was their own reservation and that it could under no circumstances be used against them.

You are an independent legal expert. Some journalists who follow the case between Skir and Reggo ask you to explain them whether on the basis of the facts presented above the ICJ has or has not jurisdiction to hear the case.

Nota bene

— Both States are original members of the United Nations.

Case 5.4

Abbreviations used
ICJ = International Court of Justice
FISH = Formulation of International Safeguards for Herrings

Concerned by the overfishing of herrings in the ocean, several States conclude a treaty for the protection of this species, called the treaty on the Formulation of International Safeguards for Herrings (FISH). The treaty, among other things, establishes quotas of herrings each State party is allowed to catch per season on the high seas.

Two States, Scombria and Clupe, both rather big fishing nations, are also parties to the FISH. There are rumours that Scombria regularly catches more herrings than its allocated quota allows.

One day, a vessel from the navy of Clupe, the *Poseidon*, stops a large fishing ship, the *Raptor*, flying the flag of Scombria on the high seas. The *Raptor* is returning home from two days fishing at sea. The officers of the *Poseidon* declare to the captain of the *Raptor* that they have—by order of their government of Clupe—to check whether or not the *Raptor* has caught too many herrings. The captain of the *Raptor* refuses, in consequence of which the soldiers on board the *Poseidon* forcibly board his ship. They discover that with this latest catch the *Raptor* has indeed been catching more herring than Scombira's quota established under the FISH allowed.

After both the *Poseidon* and the *Raptor* have regained their respective home States and reported what has happened, both governments publicly protest and accuse the other of violations of international law: the government of Clupe vehemently denounces the alleged violation of the FISH by Scombria by exceeding its seasonal herring quota, while the government of Scombria vigorously condemns the interception and forcible boarding of the *Raptor* by the *Poseidon*.

Estimating that 'only justice can now solve the situation and re-establish the previous trustful relations between Clupe and Scombria', the government of Clupe brings the dispute(s) between itself and Scombria to the International Court of Justice (ICJ). Although Scombria has not yet submitted any documents to the ICJ in response, it publicly declares that it welcomes this step and that it is ready to 'defend itself in front of international justice'.

You work for the government of Clupe as a legal adviser. After having brought the case to the ICJ, the President of Clupe asks you to assess objectively whether or not in your opinion the ICJ will be competent to deal with the disputes in question based on the optional clauses made by both States.

Nota bene

- Both States are original members of the United Nations.
- Clupe has made an optional clause declaration under Article 36 paragraph 2 of the ICJ Statute, attaching to it the following reservation: 'Clupe excludes from the jurisdiction of the International Court of Justice all matters falling within the issue of fisheries.'
- Scombria has also made an optional clause declaration with the following reserva-

tion: 'Scombira excludes from the jurisdiction of the International Court of Justice any issue touching upon its textile production and exports.'

Case 5.5

Abbreviation used
ICJ = International Court of Justice

Several years ago, two States Melusina and Karabo concluded a commercial treaty, which among other things also foresees that nationals of either State no longer need a visa to travel to the other State. This system has worked very well for many years. However, two years ago, Karabo suddenly declared that every foreigner, including nationals from Melusina needed a visa to cross into Karabo. While Melusina first thinks that this statement was simply a mistake made by the government spokesperson, it soon discovers that Karabo is serious when several Melusian nationals are not allowed to enter Karabo without a visa.

Melusina writes a diplomatic note to Karabo, politely indicating that there was a commercial treaty between the two of them, stipulating that their respective nationals would not need visas to go to the other State. Karabo replies that in today's insecure world every State has to protect itself against terrorists seeking entry to its territory. For Karabo, one possibility of protection was to impose visa requirements. Furthermore, Karabo adds that immigration issues were part of the reserved domain of every State, and thus protected by the principles of equal sovereignty of States and non-intervention in internal affairs, it could do what it wanted.

Melusina does not agree with Karabo at all. Because Karabo is an important job market for Melusian nationals, it seeks to negotiate with Karabo. However, Karabo reveals itself as not being very co-operative and the talks soon end.

Melusina, not being satisfied with the current situation, decides to bring the dispute to the International Court of Justice (ICJ) in spring 2011. After having been informed about the introduction of the case, Karabo contests the jurisdiction of the ICJ in the present case by referring to the reservation attached to its own optional clause declaration.

You are working for the ICJ and are asked to analyse whether the ICJ is competent to hear the case in question.

Nota bene

- Both Karabo and Melusina are members of the United Nations.
- Karabo has made an optional clause declaration under Article 36 paragraph 2 of the ICJ Statute in 1951. It attached the following reservation to the declaration: 'Karabo excludes from the jurisdiction of the Court all matters falling essentially within the domestic jurisdiction of Karabo, as determined by Karabo.'
- Melusina has made an optional clause declaration under Article 36 paragraph 2 of the ICJ Statute in 1975. It attached no reservation which is relevant to this case.

Other forms of consent

Case 5.6

Abbreviation used
TUW = Treaty on the Use of the Waterflo

The River Waterflo flows through the territories of two States, Defland and Attaland. The river has its source in the first State and ends its long journey in the biggest lake in the second State, called Biglake. In order to regulate the use of the river between the two States, Defland and Attaland concluded a Treaty on the Use of the Waterflo (TUW) on 21 June 1934. In accordance with its Article 74, the TUW entered into force 30 days after its date of conclusion.

Article 48 TUW deals with the settlement of disputes. This provision provides: 'In case of a dispute between the contracting States on the applicability or interpretation of the present treaty, the International Court of Justice will be competent to hear the case.'

On 24 May 2010 Defland decided to build a dam on the Waterflo in order to use parts of its water for the irrigation of its agricultural production. Attaland considered this to be a manifest violation of the TUW, and therefore decided to bring the case to the International Court of Justice (ICJ).

You are a well-known international lawyer working for Attaland. Your Minster of Foreign Affairs asks you to write a legal opinion to clarify the question whether or not the ICJ is competent to hear the case.

Nota bene

— Attaland and Defland are both parties to the UN Charter since its entry into force.

Case 5.7

Abbreviations used
ICJ = International Court of Justice
TEST = Treaty on the Exchange of Sugar against Tin
VCLT = Vienna Convention on the Law of Treaties

The States of Hanchez and Bonnat concluded a commercial treaty, the Treaty on the Exchange of Sugar against Tin (TEST). The TEST has been applied between the parties without any problem for years.

However, recently Hanchez has argued that the treaty should be terminated since Bonnat delivered less sugar than agreed. This, in the opinion of Hanchez, constituted a material breach of the TEST, which could thus be terminated according to Article 60 of the Vienna Convention on the Law of Treaties (VCLT).

Bonnat publicly contests this, saying that first of all they did deliver enough sugar; second, Hanchez should have informed them that they think sugar was missing before announcing the termination of the TEST; and third, Bonnat expresses its firm conviction that in any event Article 60 of the VCLT would not be fulfilled and could thus not be applied.

After a hectic exchange of diplomatic notes, which does not, however, contribute to the resolution of the dispute, Hanchez decides to bring the case to the International Court of Justice (ICJ).

Its ambassador in The Hague transmits all the necessary documents to the Court on 8 November 2010.

After Bonnat has been informed of the case brought against it, the President holds a press conference. He declares that Bonnat strongly believes in the importance of international justice as deployed by the ICJ. The President says that he can only but reiterate the arguments made previously, adding that Bonnat is convinced that their position is the correct one, which will also be recognised by the ICJ.

A journalist from Hanchez wants to write an article on the development of the dispute between Hanchez and Bonnat. Since he is not quite sure about the legal implications, he asks you—an independent legal expert in public international law—to explain if in your opinion the ICJ is competent to deal with the case.

Nota bene

— Both Hanchez and Bonnat are original members of the United Nations.
— Hanchez has made an optional clause declaration under Article 36 paragraph 2 of the Statute of the ICJ with no reservation relevant for this case.
— Bonnat has never made an optional clause declaration.

Case 5.8

Abbreviation used
ICJ = International Court of Justice

The two States Nemesis and Titania have been living peacefully side-by-side for many years, despite the fact that a large part of their common border is still undefined. In practice the border has slowly been established over the years, but there was never any legally binding agreement on it. In 2009 a small field of diamonds is discovered in the border region. Each State claims that these diamonds are located on its territory. Negotiations between the parties are unsuccessful.

Therefore, in June 2010 Nemesis brings the case to the International Court of Justice (ICJ), together with a document stating the following:

> Article 1: Hereby the parties to this agreement request the International Court of Justice to decide:
>
> (a) how the border between Nemesis and Titania in the region of the newly discovered diamond mine shall be drawn; and
> (b) what law is applicable to this exercise.
>
> Article 2: The two parties shall present to the Court all documents which they consider useful for the solution of the case, including ancient maps.

Article 3: The present agreement shall enter into force on the day of signature thereof.

The agreement, as transmitted to the Court, has duly been signed on 31 May 2010 in the capital of Nemesis by the presidents of Titania and Nemesis.

A journalist asks you—an expert in international law—to explain whether you consider that the ICJ would be competent to hear the case between Nemesis and Titania.

Nota bene

—Both Nemesis and Titania are members of the United Nations.
—Nemesis has made an optional clause declaration under Article 36 paragraph 2 of the ICJ Statute, without any relevant reservation.
—Titania has never made an optional clause declaration.

Issues of admissibility

Case 5.9

Abbreviations used
BT = Boundary Treaty
ICJ = International Court of Justice

The island of Husvik is composed of three States, Boja, Lesta and Nyfor. On 26 February 1984 these three States concluded a treaty, the so-called Boundary Treaty (BT), to settle their territorial as well as maritime boundaries.

After a few years tensions between Boja and Lesta are increasing. Lesta accuses Boja of repeatedly violating the maritime boundaries between those two States with its fishing fleet. Boja flatly denies these allegations but ominously adds that in any event Lesta was not using the sea at all so that it would not harm anyone if Boja sometimes used a little more of it. Recurring offers to negotiate made by Lesta are all either ignored or turned down by Boja. The tensions become so serious that Lesta decides to bring the border dispute with Boja to the International Court of Justice (ICJ). Lesta files the case on 4 October 1999 and Boja is informed of the instigation of proceedings a few days later. Boja replies to the ICJ, contesting first of all the jurisdiction of the Court to deal with the case at hand. It also adds that it would be impossible to have a case only between Boja and Lesta, since the dispute concerned essentially the BT, to which Nyfor was also a party. Thus, in the opinion of Boja, a dispute without the presence of Nyfor before the ICJ would in any event not be possible and thus the ICJ should declare itself not competent to hear the case.

You are working for the ICJ and are asked by the registrar to make a determination whether or not the ICJ has jurisdiction in this case and to address all the relevant arguments made by the parties.

Nota bene

— All three States are original members of the United Nations.
— The BT in its Article 77 provides: 'Any dispute concerning the interpretation or application of the present treaty can be brought to the International Court of Justice by any party to the treaty, on condition that previous negotiations have failed.'

Advisory opinions

Case 5.10

Abbreviations used
TWOOS = Treaty on the World Organisation for Outer Space
UN = United Nations
WOOS = World Organisation for Outer Space

With the development of manned flights to outer space, the international community decided that it was necessary to strengthen international co-operation in areas such as the exploration and use of outer space and celestial bodies. In fact, the rapidly rising costs were hindering scientific advancement in these areas. Therefore, States decided to create an intergovernmental organisation charged with the exploration and use of outer space. Since outer space was thought to belong to the entire human population, it was deemed important that all States participated in this noble cause. This would also allow the costs of the flights to outer space to be divided between all States parties to this organisation.

In this context, the Treaty on the World Organisation for Outer Space (TWOOS) was concluded on 10 January 2011 between more than 130 States. According to its Article 78, the TWOOS entered into force on 1 June 2011. The newly created organisation, called the WOOS, was, as a specialised organisation, an integral part of the system of the United Nations. On 7 June 2011, the UN General Assembly adopted resolution 95/504 in which it authorised the WOOS to request advisory opinions of the International Court of Justice (ICJ) on all legal questions arising within the scope of its competences, with the exception of questions concerning the reciprocal relations between the WOOS and the UN or other specialised institutions.

According to its founding Charter, the WOOS had among other things the aim of reinforcing co-operation between States in matters related to the exploration of outer space. Furthermore, it had the competence to independently undertake missions of manned flights to outer space for scientific purposes.

In its initial stages of operation, a number of questions arose concerning the functioning of the WOOS. The General Assembly of the WOOS adopted on 14 August 2011 a resolution in which it requested the ICJ to give an advisory opinion on the following question: 'In the case where space shuttles are launched by the WOOS from the territory of a State which is a party to the Outer Space Treaty from 27 January 1967 and a member of the present Organisation, is Article VII of the Outer Space Treaty applicable to this State in a case where it has only made available its territory for such a launch or is this Article applicable to the WOOS in the event where damages are caused to another State as a result of this launch?'

After having received this request from the WOOS, the registrar of the ICJ asks you to write a legal opinion to determine whether or not the Court is competent to give such an advisory opinion.

Nota bene

— The Outer Space Treaty mentioned in the WOOS resolution refers to the Treaty on Principles Governing the Activities of States in the Exploration and Use of Outer Space, including the Moon and Other Celestial Bodies of 27 January 1967.
— Article VII of this treaty provides the following: 'Each State Party to the Treaty that launches or procures the launching of an object into outer space, including the Moon and other celestial bodies, and each State Party from whose territory or facility an object is launched, is internationally liable for damage to another State Party to the Treaty or to its natural or juridical persons by such object or its component parts on the Earth, in air space or in outer space, including the Moon and other celestial bodies.'

Recommended reading on the International Court of Justice

Articles

Dapo Akande, 'The Competence of International Organisations and the Advisory Jurisdiction of the International Court of Justice' (1998) 9 *European Journal of International Law* 437.
Charles Brower, 'Process, Practice and Procedure of the International Court of Justice' (1998) 92 *Proceedings of the Annual Meeting—American Society of International Law* 278.
Christine Gray, 'The Use and Abuse of the International Court of Justice: Cases concerning the Use of Force After Nicaragua' (2003) 14 *European Journal of International Law* 867.
Richard Plender, 'Rules of Procedure in the International Court and the European Court' (1991) 2(2) *European Journal of International Law* 1.

Books

Stanimir Alexandrov, *Reservations in Unilateral Declarations Accepting the Compulsory Jurisdiction of the International Court of Justice* (Dordrecht, Martinus Nijhoff, 1995).
Mohamed Sameh Amr, *The Role of the International Court of Justice as the Principal Judicial Organ of the United Nations* (The Hague, Kluwer Law International, 2003).
Herbert Briggs, *Reservations to the Acceptance of Compulsory Jurisdiction of the International Court of Justice* (Recueil des Cours, Vol 93, 1958).
John Collier and Vaughan Lowe, *The Settlement of Disputes in International Law—Institutions and Procedures* (Oxford, Oxford University Press, 2009).
Duncan French, *International Law and Dispute Settlement: New Problems and Techniques* (Oxford, Hart Publishing, 2010).

JP Gardner and Chanaka Wickermasinghe (eds), *The International Court of Justice: Process, Practice and Procedure* (London, British Institute of International and Comparative Law, 1997).

Edvard Hambro, *The Jurisdiction of the International Court of Justice* (Recueil des Cours, Vol 76, 1950).

Silvia Lucht, *Der Internationale Gerichtshof—Zwischen Recht und Politik* (Munich, Herbert Utz Verlag, 2011).

John Graham Merrills, *International Dispute Settlement*, 5th edn (Cambridge, Cambridge University Press, 2011).

Shabtai Rosenne, with the assistance of Yaël Roney, *The Law and Practice of the International Court 1920–2005*, 4th edn (Leiden, Martinus Nijhoff Publishers, 2006).

Shabtai Rosenne, *The World Court: What It Is and How It Works* (Leiden, AW Sythoff, 1962).

Andreas Zimmermann, Christian Tomuschat and Karin Oellers-Frahm (eds), *The Statute of the International Court of Justice: A Commentary* (Oxford, Oxford University Press, 2006).

Chapter 6

Use of Force

General plan to solve cases on the use or threat of use of force

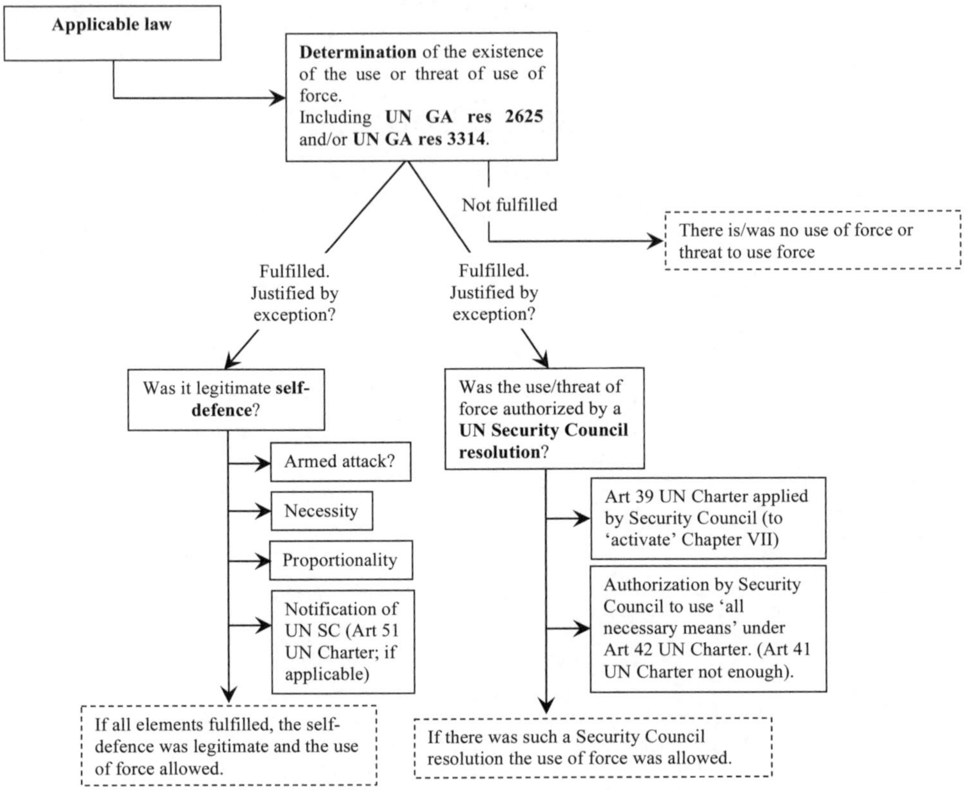

Figure 9. Use of force.

Article 2, paragraph 4 of the UN Charter

Case 6.1

There have been tensions between Assuria and Lyreco for years, especially since Lyreco claimed that parts of the territory of Assuria rightfully belong to Lyreco. However, lately the situation seems to be getting more serious. The president of Lyreco, Mr Prid, States in a television broadcast that Assuria is a State 'not worthy of its own existence' and that Assurians should be prepared for 'the day when the glorious Lyreco takes over their miserable country'. The next day, several ministers of the government of Lyreco make similar statements. Assuria publicly condemns this 'verbal attack' and asks for explanations. Lyreco, however, remains silent. A few weeks later, Lyreco's army gathers close to the border of Assuria. It even makes attempts to advance to the border, but does not cross it. Alarmed, Assuria calls upon Lyreco to withdraw its army. After a few more days of the army's threatening presence, Lyreco withdraws most of its soldiers, but leaves a large battalion behind. The battalion continues to set up its position alongside the border with Assuria.

At the same time, it becomes known that there exists a group of citizens from Lyreco, called the Xerox, which—following their government's position—have developed a deep hatred of Assuria. Xerox has organised arms and its leader publicly States that since the government of Lyreco is not doing anything to 'destroy that ridiculous Assurian State', it—the Xerox—would soon take steps to regain what in its eyes is Lyreco's rightful territory. The Xerox leader adds that soon they will start by planting some bombs at strategic places in Assuria. Following a public outcry by the international community, the government of Lyreco declares that the Xerox is composed of emancipated citizens whom Lyreco cannot tell what or what not to do. Besides, Lyreco's President Prid adds that in fact the government essentially agrees with the policies and measures proposed by the Xerox.

You are a legal adviser of the government of Ache, a neighbouring country of Lyreco and Assuria. Ache is deeply disturbed about the developments in these two countries. It would like to know how the acts should in your opinion be legally qualified under the United Nations Charter, especially under its Article 2 paragraph 4.

Nota bene

—Both Lyreco and Assuria are members of the United Nations.

Case 6.2

Abbreviation used
MTL = Movement against Tyranny and for Liberty

Armeland and Missland are two neighbouring States, whose mutual relations are not very stable. Nevertheless, there has never been an armed conflict between them.

The government of Missland is very authoritarian, and its president, supported by his large force of secret police, rules the country with an iron fist.

The politics of Missland is often criticised, both internally and externally. However, Misslandian protesters are usually silenced very quickly. Nevertheless, small groups organise themselves in order to overthrow this tyrannical government. However, in Missland the surveillance of the population is much too tight to try to do anything from within this State.

After a while, the small groups gather and form into one larger group, the so-called Movement against Tyranny and for Liberty (MTL). Their common goal is to carry out targeted attacks on the administrative and military infrastructure of Missland in order to overthrow the present government. Their base is located on the territory of Armeland. This State was aware of their presence, but did not take any steps against them.

The MLT trains for almost six months and plans various terrorist attacks on the territory of Missland. Then, on 6 September 2009, the MLT launches attacks on four different targets: the building of the Ministry of Defence, the central police station of the Misslandian secret police, the secondary residence of the President (failing to kill him only by a fraction of an inch), and an administrative building located in the heart of the capital of Missland. The operation is a great 'success' and kills 150 members of the authorities of Missland.

Outraged, the President of Missland declares that these acts constituted an attack against his State, and an unforgiveable violation of the most fundamental rule of the UN Charter. Publicly, he accuses Armeland of being responsible for these attacks and requests reparation for the injuries suffered. Some hours later, Armeland makes a declaration in order to reply to the allegations made by the President of Missland. In this declaration, it points out that it was impossible for Armeland to have violated the UN Charter with these acts, since they were perpetrated by a group of purely private individuals. Therefore, their acts could not be attributed to Armeland. As a consequence, it does not hold itself liable for any reparation for the damages suffered by Missland.

You are working for the legal service of the Secretary General of the United Nations. You are asked to examine the behaviour of Armeland in the light of the UN Charter.

Nota bene

—The two States are original members of the United Nations.

Article 51 of the UN Charter

Case 6.3

Worried, the State of Endo observes the situation in its neighbouring State, Preg. There, the newly elected government is taking increasingly harsher tones with its neighbours. Furthermore, it has told its army 'to be prepared to take action soon'. Repeated offers and requests for negotiations are turned down. However, nothing else happens and the situation is tense but peaceful for weeks.

But then during the night of 6/7 May 2010 Preg attacks Endo, not only by using ground forces but also by launching hundreds of missiles. Endo had feared such an attack but, according to its President, had no legal possibility to prevent this. Nevertheless it had already put its own army on red alert, and is therefore able to respond very quickly. After giving the order to attack Preg's army as well as the installations launching the missiles from within Preg, the President of Endo calls the representative of Teny at the United Nations, currently the President of the United Nations Security Council. The President of Endo informs him of the situation and Endo's actions and asks him to pass on the information to the Security Council, which is kept up to date in the following days. Endo's army succeeds in pushing the Pregian army back into its own territory within a few days. Furthermore, Endo's air force mounts a series of targeted airstrikes and manages to destroy most of Preg's missile installations.

After this incident, a controversy breaks out in Endo, which is normally a very peaceful country. Some prominent intellectuals accuse the President of Endo of first having done nothing and then having blatantly violated the Charter of the United Nations, and especially its non-use of force provision, by authorising and even ordering the use of force against a neighbouring country.

You are an independent and well-known specialist in international law. The President of Endo contacts you to ask you for an assessment of whether or not his actions were, as he assumed, in conformity with the United Nations Charter and general international law.

Nota bene

— Both Endo and Preg are original members of the United Nations.

Case 6.4

In the region of Oriland, which comprises four States (Bouland, Packland, Warnland and Tareland), there are numerous political as well as religious tensions. On several occasions, a wider conflict has only just been avoided. In fact, Tareland is quite isolated relative to the three other States, which share the same political values as well as the same religion. Furthermore, Tareland incessantly claims ownership over a mineral-rich part of Warnland, called Aeragold.

On 1 December 2009 Tareland forcefully repressed an anti-government demonstration. Several nationals of Warnland were killed or imprisoned during this repression. Following this incident, the tensions between Tareland and Warnland grew. Warnland mobilized all its troops and stationed them at the border. Tareland, sensing an attack against its territorial integrity, did the same.

On 4 January 2010, Warnland started a vast military operation against the military sites of Tareland and penetrated with several battalions of tanks into the territory of the latter. The aim of the operation was to take the capital of Tareland and to overthrow the government. Tareland replied immediately by bombarding the backlines of the Warnlandian army located close to the Tarelandian–Warnlandian border. The goal was to cut the supply lines of the advanced Warnladian army and to push this army back over the border to Warnland.

On 10 January 2010, the government of Tareland saw that its troops were winning over the troops of Warnland and decided to strike a hard blow and to concentrate its forces in order to take over the region of Aeragold. After a blitz operation, the army of Tareland completely controlled the region of Aeragold on 11 January 2010. Since Warnland was unable to confront the army of Tareland on its own, it asked Bouland and Packland for help.

You are a well-known international lawyer and a specialist on all questions dealing with the use of force. Before deciding on a potential intervention in the conflict between Tareland and Warnland, the Minister of Foreign Affairs of Bouland asks you for a legal opinion concerning the use of force of Tareland against Warnland. In particular, he would like to know if the attack on the region of Aeragold was legal under international law such as the rules contained in the UN Charter.

Nota bene

— All States of the region of Oriland are original members of the United Nations, except Tareland.

Case 6.5

Abbreviation used
MFS = Movement for a Free Spartland

The region of Combateland has for about twenty years been the scene of much tension, especially between two States, Spartland and Vikiland. These two States have engaged in a long-running battle over a region rich in diamonds, called Diamsberg, located in the High Peaks mountains.

Spartland, the owner of the legal rights of Diamsberg, has always claimed sovereignty over this part of the High Peaks. Furthermore, almost the entire international community recognises that Diamsberg belongs to Spartland. However, Vikiland has always disputed the legal value of Spartland's rights and continues to assert that Diamsberg is an integral part of its territory.

In this context, Spartland a few years ago set up several military installations at the border between the region of Diamsberg and the part of the High Peaks belonging to Vikiland. Among other things Spartland also constructed an airport, from which military airplanes charged with the surveillance of the region regularly take off. Several ammunition and fuel depots are also located close to this airport. Furthermore, there exist in addition three surveillance locations for ground forces, where also tanks are stationed.

This Spartlandian infrastructure constitutes the first line of defence of the region of Diamsberg against any potential invasion coming from Vikiland. It has been deployed in a strategic manner in order to guarantee the sovereignty of Spartland over the region.

Being aware of the economic potential of Diamsberg, Vikiland decided to launch an attack against the military infrastructure mentioned above. Yet, it did not want to act directly itself.

The Movement for a Free Spartland (MFS) has been using the Vikilandian part of the High Peaks for its training and to conduct armed operations against the government of Spartland. The MFS is a group which never held political power and which, ten years ago, turned to military action to gain its ends, ie the overthrow of the government of Spartland. Vikiland was completely aware of the presence of the MFS on its territory.

An emissary of the government of Vikiland was sent to make a deal with this rebel group. He asked it to attack the Spartlandian military infrastructure mentioned above in order to open the way for the Vikilandian army, which would take Diamsberg after the attack. In return, Vikiland promised to finance and arm the MFS and to give it a percentage of the profits made in the various diamond mines in Diamsberg. Seeing an opportunity to finance their future military acts, the rebels accepted the offer.

In order to prepare the attack, Vikiland armed, financed and trained the MFS for several months. Three senior officials of the army and four agents of the secret service of Vikiland were in charge to ensure that the operation would go smoothly. On the morning of 17 October 2008, the attack on the various Spartlandian military installations was launched. The MFS managed to take two of the three locations for ground forces and to destroy three ammunition and fuel depots. Violent fighting took place around the military airport, which was still in the hands of Spartland.

Additional Spartlandian troops were deployed to the region of Diamsberg. Meanwhile, the secret service of Spartland discovered that it was actually Vikiland which was behind this attack. Seeing that the Vikilandian troops had concentrated at the border between Vikiland and Spartland, Spartland decided to react and thus on 28 October 2008 launched several missiles on the territory of Vikiland. It was planned that this would be accompanied by heavy bombing of the Vikilandian part of the High Peaks.

In order to plan the operation of 28 October 2008, the Minister of Defence of Spartland asks you to write a legal opinion on the legality of this operation in the light of the rules contained in the UN Charter. In fact, the Minister would like to have judicial guarantees as to the legality of the action before launching such an attack against Vikiland.

Nota bene

— Both Vikiland and Spartland are original members of the United Nations.

Chapter VII of the UN Charter

Case 6.6

For a few months, the United Nations Security Council has been closely observing the situation in the State of Haida. In Haida, the human rights of the ethnic minority Cesto are systematically violated, ranging from expropriation to arbitrary arrest and torture. Furthermore, the government of Haida has recently threatened several of its smaller neighbours with military invasion, and there have been at least three reported border incidents between armed forces of Haida and border guards or soldiers of other countries. The Security Council as well as the General Assembly of the United Nations have repeatedly called upon Haida to respect international law and to refrain from threats and the actual use of force, as well as from any human rights violations. However, no change in Haida's behaviour can be observed.

After a further border incident, the Security Council declares that the situation is 'a threat to the peace in the whole region' and adopts the following resolution:

> The Security Council,
>
> *Recalling* its previous relevant resolutions,
>
> …
>
> *Acting* under Chapter VII of the Charter of the United Nations, and taking measures under its Article 41,
>
> 1. *Condemns* the use of force by Haida both against its neighbours as well as against its own population in whatever form,
> 2. *Requests* Haida to immediately stop any threat or use of force,
> 3. *Decides* that:
>   (a) all Member States shall interrupt their economic relations with Haida by preventing the direct or indirect supply of goods listed in Annex I;[1]
>   (b) all Member States shall take measures to enforce the interruption of postal relations;
>   (c) all Member States shall enforce a travel ban on the persons listed in Annex II.
> 4. *Calls upon* all Member States to report to the Security Council within thirty days of the adoption of this resolution on the steps they have taken with a view to implementing effectively the provisions of paragraph 3 above;
> 5. *Decides* to remain actively seized of the matter.

Ayent, one of the neighbours of Haida and its main provider of stamps, immediately interrupts its delivery of stamps as well as the exportation of replacement parts for certain oil pumps to Haida. In addition, it instructs its border guards that henceforth all people coming from Haida would have to be checked in order to make sure that no one falling under the travel ban could pass.

Fearing violent protests from Haida, the government of Ayent asks you—a specialist in international law—to make sure that all the measures taken by them are completely legal and in conformity with international law.

Nota bene

- —Both Ayent and Haida are members of the United Nations.
- —In 1980 Ayent and Haida concluded a bilateral treaty on the free movement of persons, effectively removing all controls of persons at their common border.

[1] This Annex includes different forms of weapons but also technologies for the extraction of oil and valuable minerals.

Case 6.7

Exasperated by fifty years of a dictatorial regime that violates their most fundamental human rights more often than not, the population of Tyraland decided to rise up against their President. The revolutionary movement quickly attracted a large part of the population and called on the President to step down.

However, the military decided to put down the rebellion and attacked the civilians protesting against the regime. As a consequence, a civil war erupted throughout almost the entire territory of Tyraland.

The United Nations Security Council met in an emergency session in order to discuss the questions of Tyraland. On this occasion the Council adopted its resolution 1945, the relevant parts of which read as follows:

> *The Security Council,*
>
> *alarmed* by the situation taking place in the territory of Tyraland;
>
> *proclaims* that no individual should see its most fundamental rights violated by tyrannical regimes;
>
> *concerned* about the destiny of the Tyralandian population;
>
> *convinced* that this conflict can destabilize the whole region;
>
> *acting in conformity with Chapter VII of the Charter of the United Nations,*
>
> (1) *decides* that the conflict taking place on the territory of Tyraland constitutes a danger to international peace and security,
> (2) *asks* the Government of Tyraland to find a peaceful solution to the conflict,
> (3) *asks* the Government of Tyraland to stop the bombing of its own civilian population.

Anxieuland, a neighbouring State of Tyraland, was concerned about a potential overflow of the conflict onto its territory. It was also worried about the situation of its many nationals working in Tyraland. After several requests to the Security Council, Anxieuland decided to take action. It intervened militarily in Tyraland in order to protect its own nationals and to stop the cruelties committed by Tyraland against its own civilian population.

The next day, the United Nations Security Council adopted a new resolution, resolution 1946. In this resolution it authorised States to take all necessary means to end the brutality committed by Tyraland against its civilian population.

You are a legal adviser in the Ministry of Foreign Affairs of Tyraland. You are asked to write a legal opinion on the legality of the use of force of Anxieuland against Tyraland in the light of the UN Charter.

Nota bene

— Tyraland and Anxieuland are both original members of the United Nations.

Recommended reading on the use of force

Articles

Andrea Bianchi, 'The International Regulation of the Use of Force: The Politics of Interpretive Method' (2009) 22 *Leiden Journal of International Law* 651.

Ian Brownlie, 'International Law and the Use of Force by States Revisited' (2001) 21 *Australian Yearbook of International Law* 21.

Olivier Corten and Pierre Klein, 'Action humanitaire et Chapitre VII: la redéfinition du mandat et des moyens d'action des Forces des Nations Unies' (1993) 39 *Annuaire français de droit international* 105.

Oscar Schachter, 'The Right of States to Use Armed Force' (1984) 82 *Michigan Law Review* 1620.

Linos-Alexander Sicilianos, 'L'autorisation par le Conseil de sécurité de recourir à la force: une tentative d'évaluation' (2002) 106 *Revue générale de droit international public* 5.

Raphaël Van Steenberghe, 'Self-defence in response to attacks by non-State actors in the light of recent State practice' (2010) 23 *Leiden Journal of International Law* 183.

Books

Anthony Arend and Robert Beck, *International Law and the Use of Force*, 2nd edn (London, Routledge, 2011).

Belatchew Asrat, *Prohibition of Force under the United Nations Charter: A Study of Article 2(4)* (Uppsala, Iustus Förlag, 1991).

Ian Brownlie, *International Law and the Use of Force by States* (Oxford, Clarendon Press, 2002).

Erika De Wet, *Chapter VII Powers of the United Nations Security Council* (Oxford, Hart Publishing, 2004).

Yoram Dinstein, *War, Aggression and Self Defence*, 4th edn (Cambridge, Cambridge University Press, 2005).

Judith Gardam, *Necessity, Proportionality and the Use of Force by States*, 3rd edn (Cambridge, Cambridge University Press, 2009).

Vera Gowlland-Debbas (ed), *United Nations Sanctions and International Law* (The Hague, Kluwer Law International, 2001).

Belinda Helmke, *Under attack: Challenges to the Rules Governing the International Use of Force* (Farnham, Ashgate, 2010).

Robert Kolb, *Ius contra bellum: Le droit international relatif au maintien de la paix: Précis*, 2nd edn (Basel, Helbing & Lichtenhahn, 2009).

Noam Lubell, *Extraterritorial Use of Force Against Non-State Actors* (Oxford, Oxford University Press, 2010).

Chapter 7

Interconnected Cases

Case 7.1

Abbreviations used
ELF = Enemy Listeners and Fighters
ICJ = International Court of Justice
PAC = Protocol Against Criminals
VCLT = Vienna Convention on the Law of Treaties

The four States of Naggaroth, Sindar, Valinor and Arda are located in the south of the region of Gondolin. Generally, these four States are on good terms with each other. However, drug trafficking as well as other criminal activities are growing in the area. To deal with this problem, the governments of Naggaroth, Sindar, Valinor and Arda organise in 2002 a meeting in Valinor between the ambassadors of the four countries. The ambassadors are all officially given full powers, in order to facilitate decision-making. After several days of intensive debate, the four present the outcome of their discussions to the public: the Protocol Against Criminals (PAC).

The negotiations were not easy and Arda in particular opposed the conclusion of the PAC on several grounds, before suddenly changing its mind and signing the Protocol. This happened after the ambassador of Arda had received a fax from the office of the President of Arda, telling him that it would be appropriate to sign now.

The Protocol aims to improve co-operation especially in combating the widespread drug trafficking, but also other criminal activities such as smuggling of goods and persons. Therefore, Article 24 of the PAC provides that the police and border guard patrols of all four countries should have direct contact via radio or mobile phone whenever they are on duty in order to facilitate the pursuit of suspected criminals. However, Article 25 paragraph 1 PAC makes clear that the police forces and border guards of one country are not allowed to cross the border into another country, unless there is a real danger that their inaction subsequent to a criminal crossing the border would lead to a serious threat to the life or limb of an innocent person or the irreparable destruction of a very valuable good and there was no patrol of that other country in a reasonable distance to take over the case. Paragraph 2 of the same Article further specifies that regardless of the seriousness of the situation, military forces are excluded from border crossing at all times. Article 31 of the PAC holds that in order to co-ordinate the search and interception of criminals effectively, the heads of the different police and border patrol departments of the four States should exchange regular reports but also meet at least every three months in person.

Finally, Article 56 of the PAC provides that: 'In case of a dispute between the parties as to the application or interpretation of the present Protocol, two parties jointly can bring any case against any other of the parties to the International Court of Justice.'

When signing the Protocol in a ceremony on 4 June 2002, the ambassador of Sindar declares that his government wished to make two interpretative declarations. In the first declaration, Sindar States that:

> Since this is a treaty on criminal activities and since the International Court of Justice (ICJ) is not a criminal court, Sindar does not regard it as a good option to submit disputes to the ICJ. Therefore, Sindar will consider Article 56 as not binding on itself.

In the second declaration Sindar writes the following:

> Sindar is fully conscious of the necessity of a regular exchange of information for better co-operation. However, it sees this need already fulfilled with the exchange of reports as provided for in Article 31 of the PAC without the need of organising expensive and useless meetings. Hence, Sindar is going to read Article 31 PAC as only containing the proposition of exchanging information via reports.

Valinor reacts to this by saying that it did consider the meetings between the heads of the police forces as an important element of co-operation and hence would object to the interpretation just given by Sindar. The other two States, Arda and Naggaroth, do not comment at all.

Many years later, in late 2009, an incident shakes the relationship between Sindar and Arda. Mr Malekith, originally from Naggaroth but having lived for years in Arda, is accused by Sindar of being the boss of a large drug-trafficking ring. However, there is no reliable evidence to prove this and after having questioned him thoroughly the Arda police are forced to free him without having found any grounds for accusation. Sindar is outraged, considering that Arda is treating Mr Malekith too softly. It decides to take matters into its own hands. In its vast and impenetrable forests Sindar has been building up a highly trained group of spies, the ELF (Enemy Listeners and Fighters) 'because who knows when it could become useful to find out more about your enemies'. The spies are mainly members of a former criminal gang, and even though they do not belong to the official secret services of the country, they are secretly trained and equipped by some of the best members of the official secret services. The President of Sindar himself calls the head of the ELF and orders him to go to Arda with his group and get Mr Malekith 'no matter what'. The group successfully manages to kidnap Mr Malekith, but on their way back they are stopped by a border patrol from Arda, which wants to know what kind of strange package they are carrying. The ELF, remembering the order given by the president, start to shoot their way out, in the process wounding two of the frontier-gurads, but finally escaping with Mr Malekith to Sindar.

As if this irritation between Arda and Sindar were not already enough, secret documents from the Foreign Ministry of Sindar are leaked to the public, indicating that the fax received in 2002 by the ambassador of Arda which made him sign the PAC was in fact sent by the Ministry of Foreign Affairs of Sindar, rather than the Ministry of Foreign Affairs of Arda. The ambassador of Arda indicates, when asked, that at the time he had no reason to doubt the authenticity of the document, since it presented all the necessary official signs, albeit these were somewhat reduced in clarity due to the poor quality of the fax print-out. The President of Arda immediately writes to the President of Sindar, indicating that Arda saw the PAC as being invalidated since 'the foundation of mutual trust indispensable for the respect of every treaty has been eroded by the revelations of this scandalous practice'. Sindar replies by saying that this statement by Arda was completely inappropriate since everyone knew that only treaties could be invalidated but that the PAC was in fact—as the name suggested—only a Protocol. Furthermore, they claimed that there was no ground of invalidity in any event, even if one would admit the application of the Vienna Convention on the Law of Treaties to something like this Protocol.

The government of Arda is outraged by this reaction. They decide to have the various disputes with Sindar solved once and for all by the International Court of Justice (ICJ). On 12 March 2010 Arda brings a case to the ICJ based both on the PAC and the optional clauses made by both countries. As soon as Sindar is informed about this, they immediately contest the jurisdiction of the ICJ on both grounds relied on by Arda.

You are a lawyer at the Foreign Ministry of Arda and are asked to help clarify a few matters:

1. *How does the PAC apply between the parties (especially also before 2009) and is Arda right to argue for its invalidity?*
2. *Has Sindar engaged its international responsibility by kidnapping Mr Malekith?*
3. *Is the ICJ competent to deal with the dispute(s) and if yes on which basis?*

Nota bene

- —Arda and Valinor are parties to the Vienna Convention on the Law of Treaties (VCLT) since its entry into force.
- —Sindar has ratified the VCLT on 30 April 1987.
- —Naggaroth has ratified the VCLT on 6 June 2004.
- —The PAC is a treaty concluded in simplified form and enters into force on the day of signature.
- —Article 67 of PAC provides that: 'At the time of signature any State may make reservations to articles in this Protocol other than Articles 1, 2, 13 and 56.'
- —All four States are founding members of the United Nations.
- —Arda has made an optional clause declaration under Article 36 of the Statute of the ICJ without any reservation.
- —Sindar has made an optional clause declaration under Article 36 of the Statute of the ICJ on condition of reciprocity and adding the following: 'Sindar recognises the jurisdiction of the Court for all disputes except for disputes involving a multilateral treaty where not all parties are involved and present in the case before the Court.'

Case 7.2

Abbreviations used
ICJ = International Court of Justice
MFS = Movement for Freedom in Silla
NCS = National Cartography Service of Silla
TEMR = Treaty on the Exploitation of Maritime Resources

The three States of Silla, Munkus and Aspara are neighbours and all border the Ocean of Tantomile, which is rich in fish, minerals and, it is presumed, also oil. Since the abundant fish stocks, in particular, do not know borders, the three States decide to conclude a treaty to regulate the use of all the natural resources of the Ocean of Tantomile, but also to define exactly each State's territorial sea and the adjacent Exclusive Economic Zone (EEZ), which is seen as very important by the three States, especially with regard to potential oil and mineral sources. Therefore, on 25 June 1973 the three States conclude the Treaty on the Exploitation of Maritime Resources (TEMR).

Since Munkus and Aspara are both rather poor and do not have the necessary human and financial resources to draw a map of the Ocean of Tantomile including all the islands, this task is left to the National Cartography Service of Silla (NCS). Based on the map produced by the NCS, and of course taking into account all the islands belonging to one of the three parties, the three States negotiate the boundaries of their respective territorial seas.

Apart from the provisions fixing those boundaries and regulating in detail the ways and means of exploiting the natural resources of the Ocean of Tantomile, the TEMR also makes some provisions on the protection of some rare species of maritime wildlife.

With its ratification document Munkus also circulates to the other parties the following declaration: 'The President of Munkus declares the TEMR ratified under the condition that shearwaters (*a type of seabird*) are included on the list of protected species under Article 37 of the TEMR.' Shearwaters are the official national birds of Munkus, but during the negotiations Munkus did not succeed in getting them included on the protected list since experts generally do not consider them to be threatened. Aspara does not react to this declaration, while Silla says that it does not agree to include this seabird, since it was made crystal clear during negotiations that this was neither a threatened nor a rare species. The TEMR enters into force between the parties on 1 November 1973.

A few years later, in 1976, a group of scientific researchers from Aspara and Silla discovers that there is in fact a mistake in the maps of the Ocean of Tantomile prepared by the NCS. One of the islands belonging to Munkus is located further to the west than it has been mapped. Changing the border to reflect this would reduce Silla's territorial sea by several square kilometers while at the same time enlarging the territorial sea of Munkus. The NCS publicly apologises, indicating that an internal investigation has shown that one of the cartographers at the time had apparently mixed up two islands. Several newspapers in all three countries report the discovery of the scientists, and speculate about a renegotiation of the TEMR. However, the three governments remain silent.

Then, in 1997 a small oil field is discovered in the Ocean of Tantomile, located exactly in the area which now belongs to Silla, but which would have been part of

Munkus's territory had there been no mistake. The government of Munkus immediately sends a letter to both Silla and Aspara, saying that it considered the TEMR to be terminated with immediate effects because the boundaries of the territorial sea were based on incorrect maps prepared by Silla, which was intolerable, undermining the trust in the treaty and depriving Munkus of its rightful ownership of the newly discovered oil field. As a further argument Munkus stated that in any event the TEMR was not in force between Silla and Munkus since back in 1973 Silla had objected to Munkus's reservation, which results 'as everyone knows' in no treaty between the parties at all. Silla and Aspara both protest and seriously contest Munkus's interpretation of the several (legal) facts.

As if the resentment especially between Silla and Munkus were not already enough, recent events add to the tension. For a few years a radical political group, the so-called Movement for Freedom in Silla (MFS), has been engaged in fierce though peaceful opposition to the government of Silla. However, recently this group has officially endorsed armed attacks and has hence transformed into a rebel group, claiming authority over a part of the territory of Silla. In order to prepare fully for their big attack, a large group of supporters of the MFS retreated to the mountainous border region and established camp in Munkus. The secret services of Munkus, as well as the army, closely observe the actions of the MFS on their territory. They even manage to infiltrate the MFS and have thus access to very valuable first-hand information. As a consequence, the government of Munkus learns that the MFS is planning to attack undefended villages in Silla and at the same time to sabotage the oil extraction facilities of that country. The secret service of Munkus even manages to find out the exact date when that operation is supposed to take place. However, the government of Munkus decides not to take any measures, since after all 'the problems of Silla with the MFS are their own problems and have nothing to do with us'. It also does not inform Silla or pass on any information. Thus, the rebel attack takes Silla completely by surprise. A large number of civilians are massacred and about two-thirds of all oil extraction facilities are completely destroyed, resulting in a huge negative impact on the economy of Silla. The government of Silla is outraged, accusing Munkus of being responsible for the attacks of the MFS (which retreated back to Munkus after the operation, without being bothered by the forces of order of Munkus). Munkus reacts offended, saying that it has nothing to do with the MFS at all and that therefore it could also not be responsible for anything connected to them.

The government of Silla is furious and decides to bring the pending disputes between the two States to the International Court of Justice (ICJ). It introduces its case on the TEMR and the issue of State responsibility on 22 July 2010. On 15 August 2010 Munkus replies by saying that it could only reiterate what it had said before, namely that the MFS is a private party and not connected to Munkus and that even first-year law students (but apparently not Silla) would know that States are not responsible for the acts of private parties. Furthermore, on the TEMR issue, Munkus declares that the newly discovered oil field is clearly located in what is their rightful territorial sea and that Silla has no right to insist on an old treaty which had clearly drawn the boundary lines incorrectly.

You are a lawyer at the Foreign Ministry of Silla. The Minister asks you to write an objective opinion thereby clarifying several of the issues opposing Silla and Munkus.

1. *Is the TEMR (still) in force between the parties, and especially also between Silla and Munkus? Address all the legal arguments made by the parties.*
2. *Can Munkus be held responsible for an internationally wrongful act? If yes, what are the consequences?*
3. *Is the ICJ competent to deal with the disputes submitted to it? Analyse all the possible jurisdictional bases.*

Nota bene

—Silla, Munkus and Aspara are all members to the VCLT since its entry into force.
—All three States are original members of the United Nations.
—The TEMR in its Article 68 provides that: 'Reservations cannot be made to Articles 1 to 17 and Articles 25 to 30.'
—The TEMR has been concluded for an undetermined time and does not contain any clause of denunciation or termination.
—Silla has not made an optional clause declaration under the ICJ Statute. But it has made an optional clause declaration under the Statute of the Permanent Court of International Justice and has never revoked it since. The optional clause declaration does not contain any reservation.
—Munkus has made an optional clause declaration under the ICJ Statute with the following reservation: 'Munkus excludes from the jurisdiction of the International Court of Justice matters which essentially fall within the domestic jurisdiction and domestic law of Munkus.'

Case 7.3

Abbreviations used
ICJ = International Court of Justice
MOILEX = Memorandum on Oil Extraction

The democratic government of the State of Coru has been toppled by a military coup in 1950. In the aftermath, the leader of the coup, Carl Eberhard, establishes a dictatorship. Although not all States in the international community recognise his government, he rules the country for over 40 years in a strict but peaceful and stable manner. During this time Coru concludes a number of international treaties with other States. With the State of Ottis for example, Coru adopts and signs in 1976 a Memorandum on Oil Extraction (MOILEX). The MOILEX foresees that Coru grants several companies from Ottis the right to look for and extract oil in Coru's territorial waters.

These companies indeed find a lot of oil and are very successful. Since the formulation of the MOILEX is rather unbalanced, Coru does not profit as much as Ottis from its own oil richness. In addition, in the beginning of the 1990s, scientific research shows that the oil extraction has potentially negative consequences on the marine environment, which should, according to the experts, be further observed.

In 1994, Carl Eberhard dies unexpectedly. After several weeks of uncertainty the ruling elite decides to hold democratic elections and a few months later a new democratic government is elected. As one of his first official actions the democratic President Frank Neil declares that the MOILEX 'which is responsible for the heavy pollution of our sea' was considered to be terminated. He claims that such an unbalanced memorandum should never have been concluded in the first place and that this conclusion was only possible because the government at that time was a dictatorship. Therefore, the MOILEX had to be considered terminated, since 'circumstances have fundamentally changed and a new democratic government is in force'. Furthermore, President Neil pronounces his deep doubts as to whether the MOILEX was a treaty at all, 'since it is clearly called a "memorandum" and not a "treaty" or "agreement"', he says. Ottis vehemently protests, saying that the MOILEX was certainly a treaty and holds that it is fully entitled to execute the MOILEX as it was concluded. It proposes negotiations, which are, however, rejected by Coru.

Frustrated, the government of Ottis decides to change its approach. It knows that there exists in Coru a group of followers of the late dictator Eberhard, who are unhappy with the return to democracy. Agents of the Ottis secret service contact this group, known as the Carlists. Since the Carlists do not shy away from using force to achieve their goal of overturning the government of Frank Neil, the agents from Ottis offer them weapons, financial support and training. The Carlists gladly accept, without, however, completely understanding why Ottis is offering them its help.

After a few months of training the government of Ottis, through its agents, orders the Carlists to mine the ports closest to the oil platforms in the territorial sea which once had belonged to companies from Ottis. The ports are the only way in which the extracted oil can be brought ashore and later sold. With this action Ottis wants to make sure that 'if we cannot benefit from the oil that is rightfully ours, then Coru too should not benefit from it'. The Carlists do as they are told and successfully mine the ports, causing three ships to sink (though fortunately the crews are saved). After this incident, Ottis withdraws its agents from Coru. However, as the only link to the Carlists, Ottis maintains its monthly payments and weapon deliveries to this group. A few weeks later, the Carlists decide to attack a power station, completely destroying the facility and killing five people working there. While attacks by the Carlists continue, the secret service of Coru finally manages to present evidence that Ottis is somehow involved in the activities of this group.

President Neil from Coru is outraged. He publicly States that Ottis has been responsible for all acts of the Carlists and that his government is asking for full reparation for the physical and moral damage done. Ottis, on the other hand, flatly denies all the allegations and its President remarks that States such as Coru that themselves violate international law are not in a position to accuse others. In response to Coru's demands, Ottis declares that it has no intention whatsoever in engaging in any negotiations with Coru, regardless of the subject or the problem.

Having decided that the situation cannot go on like this, President Neil from Coru elects to bring the cases concerning the MOILEX and the State responsibility issue standing between itself and Ottis to the International Court of Justice (ICJ). As a basis of jurisdiction Coru invokes an old regional dispute-settlement treaty, concluded in 1949, but which is, however, still in force (see below). As expected, the government of Ottis contests that the ICJ is competent to hear any of the disputes between the two States, saying, among other things, that it was impossible to use a treaty older than the disputes themselves as a basis of jurisdiction.

You are an independent expert in international law. Some journalists contact you for a legal opinion about the facts and disputes between Coru and Ottis, since the situation is rather confusing for them. In particular, they ask you to answer the following questions, thereby addressing all the relevant arguments made by the parties:

1. *Is the MOILEX a treaty, and if yes, can it be terminated on the grounds presented by Coru?*
2. *Is President Neil right to say that Ottis is responsible for all acts of the Carlists, and if yes, what are the consequences?*
3. *Is the ICJ competent to deal with the dispute(s) in issue?*

Nota bene

—Both Coru and Ottis are parties to the Vienna Convention on the Law of Treaties since its entry into force.

—The MOILEX has been concluded in a simplified form and entered into force on the day of its signature by the Presidents of both States, as is provided in Article 57 of the MOILEX.

—The MOILEX has been concluded for an undetermined time and does not contain a clause of denunciation.

—Both Coru and Ottis are original members of the United Nations.

—The regional dispute-settlement treaty concluded in 1949 between twelve States (among them Ottis and Coru) provides in its Article 6: '§ 1: All disputes between States party to the present treaty shall be brought to arbitration by a common agreement of the parties to the dispute; § 2: Alternatively, disputes between States party to the present treaty may be brought to the International Court of Justice by a unilateral act, provided that previous negotiations have failed.'

Case 7.4

Abbreviations used

AMR = Agreement on Movement and Residence
ICJ = International Court of Justice

On 4 March 1995 four States, Jada, Chardun, Ruvi and Barat, conclude the so-called Agreement on Movement and Residence (AMR). The purpose of the AMR is to establish the free movement and residence for all nationals of the four States within the territory of these four States in order to stimulate economic growth and trade in the region. According to the treaty, nationals of any one of those four States no longer require a visa to enter any of the other three countries; a simple identity card is enough. Furthermore, Article 15 of the AMR States that: 'Any national of the High Contracting Parties can take up lawful residence anywhere in the territory of the High Contracting Parties without prior consent or approval of the relevant national authorities.' Article 16 of the AMR adds that 'All nationals of the High Contracting Parties have in the territory of the other High Contracting Parties the same rights as the respective nationals concerning purchase and selling of property, including houses, apartments and villas.'

After its signature on 4 March 1995 the AMR is ratified by presidential decrees of all four countries, which are deposited with Jada. According to its Article 74, the AMR entered into force one month after the last deposit and was thus in force from 12 July 1995 onwards. However, a few weeks later, the Foreign Minister of Jada suddenly remembers that unlike in Jada, and as far as he remembers unlike in Chardun and Barat, a presidential decree is not enough in Ruvi in order for that State to validly express consent to be bound by a treaty. Upon request, the Foreign Minister of Ruvi confirms a few days later that the Ruvian constitution indeed provides in its Article 42 that 'All international treaties have to be approved and ratified by the Parliament, except for treaties dealing exclusively with commodity exchanges.' The Minister adds that there had apparently been a mistake in the internal classification of the AMR: it had been put under 'commodity exchange treaties', 'probably due to its purpose of stimulating the economy', as the Minister says. Therefore, it had only been sent for ratification to the President and not the Parliament. However, the Minister adds that meanwhile the Parliament had been informed and consultations between the government and the Parliament had taken place. Since the parliamentary summer break was only a few days away and both the government and the Parliament of Ruvi considered the AMR to be of utmost importance, the Parliament together with the government decided that it was not necessary to pursue the ratification further. Therefore, even though the ratification of the Parliament was missing, Ruvi could be considered to be fully bound by the AMR. Satisfied, Jada transmits this explanation to all States party to the AMR.

For the next ten years the relations between the four States are peaceful, the economies are thriving and the AMR proves to be a very successful treaty. However, in 2005 a very conservative political party gains power in Ruvi. The party is very sceptical, if not to say hostile, towards foreigners in general. In 2008, the government adopts a new law, prohibiting all foreigners from buying houses. Only a few days later, the High Court of Ruvi hands down a judgment in that matter, which has considerable influence. The case involved a dispute between a national from Chardun and a national from Ruvi. The national from Chardun had bought a house from the national from Ruvi and now accused him of fraud since the house, which he had been assured would be newly renovated, was in a very bad condition. The national from Chardun now felt that he had significantly overpaid for the house and wanted his money back, which the national from Ruvi, however, refused.

The High Court of Ruvi declares purchase of property by foreigners to be illegal and that all foreign-owned property should be expropriated. It added that, in any event, foreigners could not just come to Ruvi and decide where they wanted to live. The judges, under the lead of their president, Toni Dalia, based their argument on two main points. First, they said that seeing that the government had adopted a new law affecting all foreigners it was apparent that Ruvi no longer considers itself bound by the AMR. This was a perfectly valid internal political decision, with the consequence that there would no longer be any favourable treatment for nationals of Jada, Chardun and Barat. The judges added that this decision had to be respected and there was nothing national judges could do should their government wish to act contrary to an international treaty, since after all 'it is not us judges who sign a treaty'. Secondly, the judges State that in any event the AMR was to be considered as invalid since in 1995 it had been concluded in violation of the constitution of Ruvi, the most important law of the nation.

Jada, Chardun and Barat protest vehemently, saying that this was a blatant violation of international law which was not acceptable and which was going against the most fundamental principles of international treaty relations, namely *pacta sunt servanda*. They request Ruvi to respect the AMR and to stop its violation of international law; otherwise they would hold it responsible. Ruvi, however, says that it could not be held responsible: first, it was its right to pass laws in its territory; and second, it was only acting in conformity with the judgment of the High Court of Ruvi, which—as all national courts—could under no circumstances be responsible under international law and thus also Ruvi could not be responsible.

Jada, tired of the disputes on the applicability of the AMR and the eventual State responsibility of Ruvi, decides to submit the case to the International Court of Justice (ICJ). On 28 May 2009 its ambassador to The Hague submits the necessary documents to the Court. Thereby, Jada bases itself on Article 85 of the AMR, which States that 'All disputes on the interpretation or application of the present treaty can be brought to the International Court of Justice by unilateral application.'

Ruvi contests that the ICJ is competent on that basis. As a further bar it adds that since the AMR concerned not only Jada and Ruvi, the case was not admissible as long as Chardun and Barat were not parties to the proceedings before the Court, 'since it is also their interest which is at stake'. Consequently, Ruvi concludes that the ICJ is not competent to deal with the case.

You are a legal adviser in the Ministry of Foreign Affairs of Jada. The Foreign Minister in person asks you to write an objective legal opinion to answer a few questions. He gives you the following questions.

1. *Is the AMR still in force between the four States?*
2. *Can Ruvi be held responsible for violation(s) of international law? If yes, how and what are the consequences? Please analyse all the potential possibilities.*
3. *Is the ICJ competent to deal with the dispute?*

Nota bene

— All four States are original members of the United Nations.
— Jada and Chardun are parties to the Vienna Convention on the Law of Treaties since its entry into force.
— Ruvi has ratified the Vienna Convention on the Law of Treaties on 7 July 1993.
— Barat has ratified the Vienna Convention on the Law of Treaties on 9 September 1985.
— The AMR has been concluded for an undetermined time and does not contain any clause of denunciation or withdrawal.
— Jada has made an optional clause declaration under Article 36 paragraph 2 of the ICJ Statute, without any reservation relevant for our case.
— Ruvi, Chardun and Barat have not made optional clause declarations.

Case 7.5

Abbreviations used
APT = Agricultural Products Treaty
ICJ = International Court of Justice

The Kingdom of Pulica is blessed with very fertile soil of mainly volcanic origin. Everything that the farmers of Pulica sow seems to grow. Therefore, Pulica is able to export large quantities of wheat, sugar as well as other foodstuffs.

In 2003 the Kingdom of Pulica concluded a treaty with the States of Conyza and of Sambu, the Agricultural Products Treaty (APT). Under the very short APT, Pulica engages itself to deliver every year 25 tons of wheat as well as 20 tons of sugar to both States for the next 30 years. Article 3 APT provides that Conyza and Sambu will pay according to market prices, unless the market price is higher than US$4,000 per ton sugar or US$420 per ton wheat, under which circumstances Conyza and Samub would be charged US$4,000 per ton sugar and US$420 per ton wheat. Article 9 APT States: 'Every dispute as to the interpretation or application of the APT can be brought to the International Court of Justice by any of the Parties in order to achieve a peaceful solution.' In Article 10 the ATP adds: 'Should the concerned High Contracting Parties so agree, disputes can be brought to arbitration for peaceful settlement. In these cases, Article 10 takes precedence over Article 9 of the present treaty.'

When ratifying the APT, Pulica attaches the following reservation to its instrument of ratification: 'The Kingdom of Pulica considers arbitration as a more convenient method to settle disputes peacefully between the High Contracting Parties. Seeing that under the ATP arbitration would take precedence over the jurisdiction of the International Court of Justice, the Kingdom of Pulica declares that it does not consider itself bound by Article 9 of the ATP.' Conyza replies that it does not have a problem with this and hence accepts Pulica's reservation. However, Sambu protests, saying that dispute settlement provisions in all treaties had always to be considered to be among the most important provisions and thus Sambu objected to any reservation made to Article 9 ATP, stressing, however, at the same time that it was looking forward to the execution of the ATP between the parties.

The first few years the APT is executed in a very successful manner. However, since 2008 the market prices for wheat and sugar are often higher than the ceiling of US$4,000 per ton sugar and US$420 US per ton wheat agreed to in the APT. Pulica is unhappy with this situation and reflects on how it could get out of the treaty. Conyza and Sambu are obviously not ready to renegotiate a treaty that is so beneficial for them.

In 2009 chance seems to come to the aid of Pulica. A heavy earthquake shakes Pulica in the night of 8/9 April 2009. As a consequence, the volcano Gali, which had been dormant for over a century, erupts, destroying most Pulican sugar and wheat production. The remaining production is barely enough to cover Pulica's own need. The positive aspect in the tragedy is that, according to experts, the soil will be even more fertile in two to three years. Meanwhile, however, Pulica sees the opportunity to be rid of the APT. It declares that due to the destruction of the majority of its wheat and sugar production the APT could no longer be executed and would therefore be terminated. Sambu vehemently protests and insists that the APT is still in force, while Conyza does not say anything.

Pulica, annoyed by the fact that getting out of the APT seems to be more complicated than anticipated, decides to divert public and governmental attention in Sambu from the treaty issue. Conyza is a neighbour of Sambu, while Pulica does not have a common border with Sambu. On 15 May 2009 the army of Conyza attacks Sambu. It destroys several border villages, but immediately retreats when finally the army of Sambu advances. Sambu, which had been completely taken by surprise, is shocked, that Conyza, with whom they had had peaceful relations for centuries, attacked it for no apparent reason. Pulica's hidden goal has been achieved, since the only subject discussed now is the attack, and the APT is apparently completely forgotten. The government of Sambu, however, suspects that something is wrong and mandates its secret service to find out what lies behind this attack.

It is widely known that Conyza has long been dependent on Pulica both economically and politically. Therefore, the government of Pulica exerted enormous influence on the government on Conyza, which by some is seen as a mere puppet of Pulica. Reliable investigations by the secret service of Sambu reveal that the government of Pulica has indeed basically ordered the government of Conyza to carry out the attack to divert public attention, in exchange for economic favours. Sambu is irritated. By invoking State responsibility, it accuses both Conyza and Pulica of breaching international law. While Conyza does not say anything as usual, Pulica first denies having anything to do with the attack. As evidence of its involvement becomes too incriminating, Pulica declares that it had not been the army of Pulica that was attacking Sambu, nor was Pulica involved in the attack as such in any other way. Therefore, it was impossible that Pulica could be responsible for anything.

Sambu is exasperated and decides to bring the various disputes to the International Court of Justice (ICJ) on 9 June 2009. It brings the case against both Pulica and Conyza. It invokes the compromissory clause in the APT as well as optional clause declarations as a basis of jurisdiction. As soon as it is informed that a case has been introduced against it before the ICJ, Pulica furiously contests the jurisdiction of the Court. Concerning the optional clause declarations as basis of jurisdiction it is especially indignant, since it had so far not known that Sambu had made an optional clause declaration and had only become aware of that through the documents transmitted by the registrar of the ICJ. Indeed, Sambu had deposited its optional clause declaration with the Secretary General of the United Nations only three days before bringing the case to the ICJ, ie on 6 June 2009. Pulica contends that since it had not been informed about this beforehand, this was an invalid basis of jurisdiction and therefore the ICJ would not be competent to hear the case. Conyza, as usual, does not say anything.

You are an independent expert in international law. A journalist from Sambu who is covering the disputes surrounding the three States asks you whether you could answer a few questions to clarify the legal matters for him:

1. *How does the APT apply between all the respective parties and is it still in force between them?*
2. *Is someone, and if yes, who, internationally responsible for the attack on Sambu? Please explain all the potential responsibilities of all parties involved. In case responsibility is found, what are the consequences?*
3. *Is the ICJ competent to hear the case and if yes, what is the basis of jurisdiction? Please provide all the potential possibilities.*

Nota bene

- —Sambu, Pulica and Conyza are all members of the United Nations.
- —Sambu has ratified the Vienna Convention on the Law of Treaties on 27 November 1997.
- —Conyza has ratified the Vienna Convention on the Law of Treaties on 19 July 2001.
- —Pulica has signed the Vienna Convention on the Law of Treaties on 8 October 1999.
- —The ATP is silent on the matters of reservations.
- —Pulica has made an optional clause declaration under Article 36 paragraph 2 of the ICJ Statute. A reservation is attached to the declaration, saying that 'Pulica excludes from the jurisdiction of the International Court of Justice all disputes having to do with international fisheries.'
- —Sambu has made an optional clause declaration under Article 36 paragraph 2 of the ICJ Statute and has deposited it with the Secretary General on 6 June 2009.
- —Conyza has made an optional clause declaration under Article 36 paragraph 2 of the ICJ Statute with no reservation.

Case 7.6

Abbreviations used

ICJ = International Court of Justice
MET = Military Exercise Treaty

The States of Farfa and Mollugo are neighbours. Farfa has a thriving economy, which is mainly based on the invention and production of military equipment and weapons. Farfa is generally a peaceful State, which has nevertheless a very large and well-trained army. The problem Farfa's army often faces is that this State's territory is rather small, making it impossible to conduct certain military exercises. Mollugo, on the other hand, has a very large territory, but is rather poor.

Therefore, the government of Farfa conceives the idea of a bilateral treaty allowing Farfa to use part of the territory of Mollugo for military exercises. It invites Mollugo to send a representative for negotiations. Mollugo, though rather sceptical about this idea, nevertheless sends its Minister of Foreign Affairs, Mr P. Lucidum. Negotiations between Mr Lucidum and his counterpart from Farfa are difficult, mainly because Mollugo is only willing to allow Farfa's military to exercise in its territory if the latter pays large sums of money and engages in know-how transfers to allow Mollugo to build up its own production of military material. Farfa considers the conditions to be too demanding, but since it desperately wants more space to train its army, negotiations proceed. Then, on 16 September 2010 Mr Lucidum suddenly signs the so-called Military Exercise Treaty (MET) with far less in return of what Mollugo had previously been asking. Mr Lucidum is even ready to conclude the MET in simplified form, whereby signature is automatically taken also as ratification. Therefore, the MET enters into force on the same day, on 16 September 2010.

Back home, Mr Lucidum is not very well received. On 17 September 2010 the President of Mollugo declares that in fact Mollugo was not bound by the MET, since the full powers of Mr Lucidum had been restricted by a governmental decree. Under this decree he was allowed to adopt a treaty, but not to ratify it. Therefore, the MET had to be considered as still not ratified by Mollugo. Farfa reacts in astonishment, saying that it had not been aware of this restriction, since it had never been communicated. Consequently, in Farfa's opinion Mollugo is bound by the MET. Investigations in the Ministry of Foreign Affairs of Mollugo indeed show that the governmental decree had never been forwarded to Farfa, nor had Mr Lucidum told anyone about this restriction (since he considered this to be a disgrace).

On 18 September 2010, the first airplanes of the air force of Farfa fly over the territory of Mollugo for an exercise. In the coming days Farfa penetrates the territory of Mollugo with another five exercises of the air force, three exercises of the navy and ten exercises of ground troops. Unsure of what to do, Mollugo only repeatedly expresses its discontent.

About one month later, Mr Lucidum finally breaks his silence and confesses to the Vice-Foreign Minister, a good friend of his, what really had happened during the negotiations in Farfa. In the beginning, Mr Lucidum had obviously defended the position of Mollugo. However, the representative of Farfa had soon started to offer him personally more and more money if he signed the MET on Farfa's conditions. Finally, in the evening of the 15 September 2010, he had offered him so much money, plus a villa at a fashionable seaside resort in Farfa, that Mr Luciudm could not resist and signed the MET the next day. Shocked, the Vice-Foreign Minister informs the government. The President of Mollugo is furious, fires Mr Lucidum and publicly States that the MET was terminated and that any further exercise of the army of Farfa would violate international law.

Farfa however, denies that the MET can be terminated because of 'such a minor issue' and continues to penetrate Mollugo's territory during its exercises. Mollugo vehemently protests, but does not dare to take any military measures, since it knows that its military is hopelessly inferior to the highly trained forces of Farfa.

Seeking a peaceful solution to its various problems, Mollugo decides to bring a case to the International Court of Justice (ICJ) on 15 December 2010, basing itself on the compromissory clause of the MET. As soon as Farfa is informed, its President contests the jurisdiction of the Court by saying: 'As everyone knows the ICJ is part of the machinery of the United Nations. Therefore, only members of the United Nations can be brought in front of the ICJ. However, since Farfa is not a member of this Organisation the honourable Court is not competent to hear that case.'

You are a legal adviser to the Ministry of Foreign Affairs of Mollugo. The President is rather confused about all the international law issues and asks you to write an objective legal opinion, answering the following questions.

1. *Is the MET in force between the two States? Address all the arguments made by the Parties.*
2. *Can Farfa be held responsible for a violation of international law due to its military exercises, and if yes, what are the consequences?*
3. *Is the ICJ competent to hear the case, and if yes, what is/are the basis of jurisdiction?*

Nota bene

—Mollugo is a party to the Vienna Convention on the Law of Treaties since its entry into force.

— Farfa has ratified the Vienna Convention on the Law of Treaties on 8 July 1999.
— Mollugo is an original member of the United Nations.
— Farfa is not a member of the United Nations. However, in 1950 the Security Council of the United Nations accepted Farfa's request to become a party to the Statute of the International Court of Justice, and set the necessary (financial) conditions, which have all been fulfilled by Farfa.
— The MET in its Article 44 provides that: 'Disputes concerning the interpretation or application of the present treaty shall be brought to the International Court of Justice by any of the Parties.'

Case 7.7

Mr Alfred Mill is a national of the State of Acero. He was born there and has always lived in Acero. At the age of 19 years he went to the university in the capital of Acero to study international relations. One of his classmates there was Ms Elisa Montana, a national from Betula, who has decided to leave her native country to study international relations at the prestigious university in the capital of Acero. Alfred Mill and Elisa Montana are mutually attracted to each other, and after one semester they have fallen deeply in love.

After their successful graduation, Alfred Mill and Elisa Montana get married in Acero. According to the laws of Acero, Elisa Montana-Mill automatically acquires the nationality of her husband from Acero, though without losing her former nationality. Betula also allows the possession of multiple nationalities. The couple establishes itself in Acero and starts a family there. Both find positions in an international organisation, where they work for the next 25 years and raise their two children. They regularly visit friends and family of Elisa in Betula.

In 2005, when their kids are already grown up and have left home, Elisa Montana-Mill receives a very tempting offer for a leading position in a large international organisation headquartered in the neighbouring State of Carpinus. After some deliberations, she decides to accept the offer and moves to Carpinus. Her husband Alfred accompanies her, and quickly finds a position in a State company of Carpinus—Calumniari—which has just invented a new way to produce aluminium.

According to the national law of Carpinus, foreigners can, after residing for three years in the same city, pass a test in order to acquire the nationality of Carpinus. Alfred Mill decides to take this test after having spent three and a half years in Carpinus, since being a national of that State is beneficial if one works for one of its State companies. Alfred passes the test with flying colours and thus acquires the nationality of Carpinus. His wife is not interested in taking the test, and consequently does not become a national of that State.

Throughout their time in Carpinus, the couple frequently travels back to Acero, where both their children live. In addition, since Elisa Montana-Mill's position is limited to six years in office, the couple has kept their house in Acero and plans to move back there once her contract expires.

After four years in Carpinus, Alfred Mill is suddenly arrested and put into jail. He is accused of spying for the government of Acero, allegations which are neither true, nor for which the police of Carpinus has clear evidence. The only evidence the police have is a declaration by a former subordinate of Alfred Mill at Calumniari. Alfred Mill is repeatedly tortured by the police to force him to reveal who else is a spy in the company and what information he has given to the government of Acero so far. Since Alfred Mill is not a spy at all, he cannot answer the questions, angering the policemen in charge.

Meanwhile, Elisa Montana-Mill is very worried, since she does not know where her husband is. One day, she is arrested on her way to work. She is not informed why she is arrested, but the police officers beat and torture her and ask her where 'the information had been taken to'. Elisa Montana-Mill has no idea what they are talking about, which does not, however, seem to impress her tormentors. With bruises all over her body and in a fragile psychical condition, she is finally released after two weeks in custody, still without knowing why she had been arrested. Even worse, she still has no information concerning the whereabouts of her husband. About seven months later Elisa Montana-Mill receives a phone call from an anonymous source, telling her that her husband Alfred had been admitted to a hospital in the city centre. Elisa Montana-Mill rushes to the hospital, where she finds her husband in very bad health. However, he can be released after two weeks in hospital.

Shocked by the recent events, the Mills decide to bring their case to justice to elucidate what actually has happened but also to get justice. However, there seems to be a wall of silence and all the courts reject their claim on flimsy grounds without even seriously considering it. The Supreme Court, the highest judicial instance in Carpinus, despite the Mills' well-documented injuries, even tells them that 'in Carpinus court cases could not be based purely on fantasies'.

The Mills are frustrated but more determined than ever to get redress for what happened. Remembering their international law courses during their studies in international relations, they ask the government of Acero through its ambassador in Carpinus whether it would be willing to exercise diplomatic protection on their behalf. The government of Acero indeed decides to protect Mr Alfred Mill and Ms Elisa Montana-Mill and informs the authorities of Carpinus accordingly. However, Carpinus only laughs, saying that Acero would in any event not be able to exercise diplomatic protection: concerning Alfred this was not possible since he was also a national of Carpinus and it was well known that diplomatic protection could never be exercised against the State of the nationality of the respective person. As for Elisa Montana-Mill, her first and therefore real nationality was that of Betula and hence Acero could not take any action on her behalf.

Meanwhile, the story of the Mills has been widely publicised. The State of Betula, which is actively engaged in the fight against torture in the world, is outraged to learn that one of its nationals has been tortured. Betula considers that Carpinus has violated international law and publicly declares that it is determined to hold Carpinus responsible for this breach. It calls on Carpinus to stop torture in its prisons altogether, but since Carpinus does not react at all after several weeks, Betula declares that in order to induce Carpinus to stop its abhorrent practice of torture by the police, it would suspend the operation of a bilateral commercial treaty between itself and Carpinus. Carpinus, for whom the commercial treaty is of the utmost economic importance, protests, saying that suspending the treaty is an illegal act which could under no circumstances be taken by Betula. However, Betula insists that it is its right to suspend such a treaty in order to force Carpinus to change its behaviour. However, Betula offers Carpinus negotiations to find a solution, an offer that is, however, turned down by Carpinus, which claims that it 'does not negotiate with States like Betula'.

A few weeks later, Carpinus, put under pressure by both Acero and Betula, feels treated unfairly. Finally it first tries to negotiate with Betula to solve their dispute surrounding the State responsibility issue. However, long weeks of negotiations do not lead to any solution of the dispute. This is when Betula proposes to have recourse to arbitration. Carpinus accepts, but eight months after this decision the arbitral tribunal still has not been created. This is mainly due to the fact that Carpinus insists on including among its arbitrators a former general, who is himself an alleged torturer. Betula is unable to accept this and therefore the situation concerning arbitration is blocked.

This is the situation when Carpinus, in 2011, decides to bring cases against Acero and Betula to the International Court of Justice (ICJ) to clarify that these two States were actually violating international law.

When Acero and Betula are informed of the cases brought against them by Carpinus, they immediately welcome this step and without delay provide arguments why—in their opinion—and how Carpinus violated international law in their respective cases.

Due to the introduction of the cases to the ICJ, the media have taken up the disputes in several articles. One journalist plans to write a legally well-founded article to clarify several points. This journalist contacts you—a specialist in international law—and asks you whether you could help him by answering the following questions.

1. *Can Acero exercise diplomatic protection on behalf of Mr Alfred Mill and Ms Elisa Montana-Mill?*
2. *Is Carpinus responsible for an international wrongful act as alleged by Betula and is the action of suspending a commercial treaty taken by Betula in conformity with international law?*
3. *Is the ICJ competent to hear the disputes between Carpinus and Acero and Carpinus and Betula? Please explain all the possible basis for jurisdiction.*

Nota bene

- —Carpinus is a party to the Convention Against Torture and Other Cruel, Inhuman or Degrading Treatment or Punishment (CAT) and the International Covenant on Civil and Political Rights (ICCPR) since 1990. It has not made any reservation to these treaties.
- —Betula is also a party to the CAT and the ICCPR since 1993, while Acero is only a party to the ICCPR since 1977. They have both not made any reservation to these treaties.
- —Article 30 paragraph 1 of the CAT provides: 'Any dispute between two or more States Parties concerning the interpretation or application of this Convention which cannot be settled through negotiations shall, at the request of one of them, be submitted to arbitration. If within six months from the date of the request for arbitration the Parties are unable to agree on the organisation of the arbitration, any one of

those Parties may refer the dispute to the International Court of Justice by request in conformity with the Statute of the Court.'

—All three States are original members of the United Nations.
—Acero has made an optional clause declaration under Article 36 paragraph 2 of the ICJ Statute and has not attached any reservation to it.
—Betula has not made any optional clause declaration.
—Carpinus has made an optional clause declaration under Article 36 paragraph 2 of the ICJ Statute and has attached the following reservation: 'Carpinus excludes from the jurisdiction of the International Court of Justice all the disputes in which Carpinus's police, military or other security organ is involved.'

Case 7.8

Abbreviations used

APMF = Agreement on the Protection of Migratory Fish
FF = Friends of the Fishes
ICJ = International Court of Justice

The region of Hucho is very rich in fish. Most of the fish there belong to migratory species, which move between the five States of the region, Salmo, Perca, Esox, Tinca and Lampetra. One of the migratory species, *Piscarius pusillus*, which is also called 'tiny fish', is especially important. *Piscarius pusillus* is vital for the livelihood of many other fish, not only because it serves them as food, but also because it has an unprecedented ability to filter water and thereby clean it from all kinds of residues. At the same time tiny fish is considered to be a delicacy for human consumption and is therefore heavily fished. However, the five States of the region of Hucho soon note that the decrease in the number of tiny fish has severe adverse consequences also on the other fish species and the whole aquatic ecosystem in the region. Therefore, Salmo, Perca, Esox, Tinca and Lampetra decide to conclude a treaty for the protection of migratory fish species, and especially for the *Piscarius pusillus*.

The treaty, the Agreement on the Protection of Migratory Fish (APMF), is concluded on 6 February 2002 and enters into force on 2 March 2002. It States in its preamble that the purpose of the treaty is the protection of migratory fish, especially *Piscarius pusillus*, in order to safeguard the aquatic ecosystems in the region of Hucho. Article 5 APMF specifies that 'Catching *Piscarius pusillus*, also called the "tiny fish", is prohibited at all times, except as further provided in the following Articles.' Article 6 APMF establishes a committee of scientific experts, composed by experts appointed by participating States. According to Article 7 APMF, this committee has the task of monitoring the situation of *Piscarius pusillus*. Article 7 continues as follows: 'If the committee unanimously decides that the stock of 'tiny fish' is sufficiently large to allow the catch of this species without endangering the stability of the ecosystem, the committee shall fix fishing quotas for *Piscarius pusillus* for each participating State.' The APMF then contains some additional provisions concerning the protection of other migratory fish species, none of which is, however, so rigorously protected as the tiny fish, but also none of which is as vital to the ecosystem as *Piscaurius pusillus*.

For five years the APMF is scrupulously respected and the stock of tiny fish slowly increases. However, the scientific committee has so far never allowed the fishing of tiny fish, since the situation is still precarious and it is deemed by the committee that it would take an additional five–ten years to re-establish the situation in so as to allow the catch of this fish again. However, in May 2008 Esox secretly starts fishing for *Piscarius pusillus* again, which happen at this time of the year to transit mostly through the territorial waters of Esox.

At first, the other States do not notice anything. However, a few months later the scientific committee sounds the alarm due to the dramatically reduced stock of tiny fish in the region of Hucho. It is soon clear that the fish must have disappeared in the territory of Esox. Esox first denies all the allegations, but under the crushing weight of evidence it finally admits that it 'might have taken one or two fishes'. The other four State parties to the APMF are furious, requesting Esox to stop fishing immediately. Even though Esox pledges to come back into compliance with the APMF, observations of the fish stocks show that it is not living up to its promise. In January 2009 the scientific committee declares that *Piscarius pusillus* is again on the brink of extinction and that the aquatic ecosystem has sustained serious damage.

Salmo, Perca, Tinca and Lampetra convene an emergency meeting, not inviting Esox which is seen as 'responsible for the whole misery'. After the meeting, the President of Salmo, speaking for all four States, declares that they consider the APMF to be terminated by reason of its breach by Esox, since 'when there is no longer any fish you also do not need a treaty for their protection'. He announces that the four States plan instead to adopt a new treaty on fish protection but also fish breeding, to try to raise enough *Piscairus pusillus* to replace the natural stock and restore equilibrium to the ecosystem. Esox, offended that it had not been invited to the meeting, declares that it is impossible to terminate a treaty of this nature without all the parties involved, especially also because the APMF did not contain any provisions for termination or withdrawal.

Salmo decides after the emergency meeting to do its utmost on its own to protect the remaining tiny fish but also other fish species. It passes a law that prohibits fishing in all internal waters of Salmo. So far, ensuring enforcement of prohibitions on fishing in certain waters had been the task of the police. However, under the new law there are so many lakes and rivers to be controlled that the police would simply be overburdened. Therefore, the government of Salmo by an addition to the internal law on fisheries mandates the Friends of the Fishes (FF) with the task of monitoring the waters and punishing anyone fishing there. The FF is a nature conservation organisation, mainly active, as the name suggests, in the protection of fishes. It has already built an extensive network of observers, which can now be used to monitor the rivers and lakes. Even though the law giving the FF the task of ensuring respect for fishing prohibitions so far exercised by the police grants the FF wide-ranging powers, it specifies that the FF is not allowed to use physical force during the exercise of its duties and especially is under no circumstances authorised to carry a weapon. Should its observers encounter difficulties, they are under an obligation to call the police to enact any kind of physical enforcement.

The population in Salmo is not very happy that they are no longer allowed to fish, and numerous people try to circumvent the prohibition. Among them is also the ambassador of Esox in Salmo. He and his chauffeur are great fishing fans and so they regularly try to fish early in the morning. However, since the FF is very vigilant, they are caught every time and sent back home. Over the time, the notorious ambassador of Esox is known by every member of the FF.

One morning, the ambassador and his chauffeur try again to fish in a very remote lake. However, the FF is present again and the two members of the FF patrol tell them to stop and go home. However, the ambassador for the first time refuses to obey and simply continues fishing. A heated dispute erupts between the FF patrol and the ambassador, during which one member of the patrol beats the ambassador and finally pulls a gun and shoots him, wounding him severely. The chauffeur flees and immediately informs the government of Esox of what has happened. Esox vehemently protests in a diplomatic note to the government of Salmo and asks for reparation for the wrong done. Salmo replies that, first, the FF is a private organisation and not a State organ; and second, that it had expressly prohibited the FF from carrying weapons and thus it was not its fault if one of the FF staff nevertheless did. Thus, in Salmo's opinion, it was impossible to ask for any kind of reparation since it was not responsible.

Yet, because Esox insists on its position, Salmo decides to bring the case to the International Court of Justice (ICJ), but to include also the still pending dispute concerning the APMF in its application. It bases itself on the two optional clause declarations made by itself and Esox. As soon as Esox is informed about the case brought against it by Salmo, it contests that the ICJ has jurisdiction and declares that it would invoke the reservation to the optional clause declaration made by Salmo. Salmo replies saying that this was impossible, since no State could invoke the reservation of another State and thus, since it had not invoked its own reservation itself, the ICJ would be competent to deal with the case.

You are a legal adviser to the Ministry of Foreign Affairs of Lampetra. The Minister closely observes the disputes between Esox and Salmo and now asks you to write an objective legal opinion on the following points, addressing all the relevant arguments made by the parties:

1. *Is the APMF still in force between the parties or not?*
2. *Is Salmo responsible for an internationally wrongful act as is claimed by Esox, and if yes, what are the consequences?*
3. *Is the ICJ competent to hear the disputes between Salmo and Esox?*

Nota bene

- —Perca and Tinca are parties to the Vienna Convention on the Law of Treaties (VCLT) since its entry into force.
- —Lampetra has deposited its instrument of ratification of the VCLT on 6 August 1985.
- —Salmo has deposited its instrument of ratification of the VCLT on 15 March 2000.
- —Esox has deposited its instrument of ratification of the VCLT on 30 January 2002.
- —The APMF has been concluded for an undetermined time and does not contain any provisions on withdrawal or denunciation.
- —All five States are parties to the Vienna Convention on Diplomatic Relations.
- —All States except Perca are members of the United Nations.
- —Esox has made an optional clause declaration under Article 36 paragraph 2 of the ICJ Statute with no reservation attached.
- —Salmo has made an optional clause declaration under Article 36 paragraph 2 of the ICJ Statute with the following reservation attached: 'Salmo does not recognise the jurisdiction of the International Court of Justice for disputes involving the matter of fisheries.'

Case 7.9

Abbreviations used

ERCT = Emission Reduction and Compensation Treaty
ICJ = International Court of Justice
UN = United Nations

Worried by global warming and determined to take at least some action against climate change, four States Astat, Tellur, Niob and Osmium meet in order to conclude a treaty on the compensation for and reduction of CO_2 and other greenhouse gas emissions. After long negotiations the Emission Reduction and Compensation Treaty (ERCT) is concluded on 28 October 2009. According to its Article 58, it enters into force 30 days after the deposit of the last instrument of ratification of the four parties to the Secretary General of the United Nations, who is the depository of the treaty.

The aim of the ERCT, as stated in its preamble, is to reduce overall CO_2 and other greenhouse gases in the atmosphere, essentially with the help of a comprehensive emission compensation and reduction scheme, to be established as the heart of the treaty. Article 4 ERCT establishes the compensation and reduction scheme. Article 5 ERCT specifies the precise functioning of the scheme and the way in which the compensations as well as the achieved reductions should be calculated. The calculation method is based on accepted scientific evidence on the emission of greenhouse gases from certain activities and products. Under Article 11 ERCT, every State party pledges to reduce their greenhouse gas emissions by a specified amount, which will be verified periodically. According to the ERCT, States are free to adopt measures to reduce and compensate their emissions, but Article 15 ERCT lists as examples reforestation, use of solar power plants or restrictions on the use of cars and other means of transport burning fossil energy. Lastly, Article 62 ERCT provides that 'Disputes as to the interpretation or application of the present treaty can be brought to the International Court of Justice by any of the State Parties.'

Even though it generally supports the idea of reducing greenhouse gases, Niob was at the beginning very sceptical concerning the conclusion of the ERCT. Its main concern was that the ERCT will just be another climate treaty with no clear impact. However, seeing the precise calculation scheme for compensation and reduction proposed under Article 5 of the treaty, Niob is convinced that this treaty 'will be different, because it is based on clear and just calculations' and therefore signs the treaty.

The last instrument of ratification, the one from Tellur, is deposited with the Secretary General of the United Nations on 27 November 2009. It is accompanied by two reservations. The first reservation reads: 'For internal political and economic reasons Tellur does not consider itself bound by Article 5 of the ERCT.' The second reservation reads: 'Considering arbitration a more appropriate means of settling international disputes, Tellur does not consider itself bound by Article 62 of the ERCT.' Upon communication of the reservations to the other State parties, Niob objects to both of them, saying that Tellur was 'totally destroying the treaty'. Consequently, Niob adds, it would prefer not to have anything to do with Tellur anymore in relation to the treaty. Astat also objects to both reservations, though without going as far as Niob. On the contrary, Astat States that it considers the ERCT to be a very important treaty and did not object to its entry into force between itself and Tellur. Osmium, on the other hand, accepts the reservations made by Tellur.

In June 2010 a paper is published in the renowned journal *Science*. In this paper, scientists convincingly show that the method so far widely used to calculate compensation and achieve greenhouse gas reduction contains a scientific error. The error comes from the fact that the effects of bio energies are not properly taken into account, 'leading to a serious error in the calculated results', as the scientists write. The error can be fixed by a new calculation method presented in the paper. A few days after this publication, the President of Niob declares that based on the paper in *Science*, the ERCT had to be invalidated. Surprised, the three other State parties deny that invalidity would be possible in this case.

Meanwhile, the tense relationship between Niob and Tellur gets worse. The two States share a river, which is the main means of irrigation for the farmers in both countries. However, Tellur, which is located upstream on the river, started to retain more and more water, severely reducing the water flowing to Niob. The government of Niob officially protests but nothing changes. In August 2010, at the height of a long period of draught which has caused the river almost to dry up, leaving the farmers in Niob virtually without water, hundreds of protesters from Niob cross the border to Tellur. They march towards the nearest dam, with the declared purpose of tearing it down 'to allow the water to flow freely again'. Yet, Tellur is not ready to just stand by and watch and sends its army. The army is quickly able to push the unarmed protesters back over the border, but following a secret order of the government, it does not stop there but invades Niob. The soldiers from Tellur attack and plunder villages, apparently aiming in particular at destroying goods and machines used for farming. Shocked, the government of Niob first calls on Tellur to stop, then seeing no reaction, it calls on the UN Security Council to take action and announces that meanwhile it will mobilise its own army, which is after a few days able to drive the army of Tellur back over the border into Tellur. Since then, the two armies are facing each other across the border, but without any further incident. Both governments accuse the other of breaching international law, but at the same time both also claim to have acted only in legitimate self-defence when they had ordered their armies to act.

Eventually, Niob decides to bring its disputes with Tellur on the alleged invalidity of the ERCT and the State responsibility question to the International Court of Justice (ICJ), based on the compromissory clause contained in the ERCT. Tellur, as could have been expected, contests that the ICJ is competent to deal with the case 'on principle'.

At the same time, Astat introduces a case against Niob to the ICJ, in order to clarify whether or not the ERCT was really invalid. Astat invokes the compromissory clause of the ERCT as basis of consent to the ICJ's jurisdiction. Now it is Niob that contests on several grounds that the ICJ is competent in this particular case to hear the dispute.

You are an independent legal expert in Niob. The government asks you to help clarify certain questions and therefore to write an objective legal opinion. In particular, the government asks you to address the following questions, thereby taking into account all the relevant arguments of the parties:

1. *How does the ERCT apply between all the parties after the reservations made by Tellur and is the ERCT still in force between the parties?*
2. *Did Tellur and/or Niob breach international law and engage their international responsibility by the actions of their armies? If yes, what are the consequences?*

3. Is the ICJ competent to hear the disputes between Niob and Tellur, and Niob and Astat, respectively? Please provide all possible bases of jurisdiction.

Nota bene

—Niob, Tellur and Osmium are parties to the Vienna Convention on the Law of Treaties (VCLT) since its entry into force.
—Astat has ratified the VCLT on 7 January 1999.
—The ERCT is silent on the matter of reservations.
—All four States are members of the United Nations.
—None of the four States has made an optional clause declaration under Article 36 paragraph 2 of the ICJ Statute.

Case 7.10

Abbreviations used
CREP = Convention on Rare Earth Production
ICJ = International Court of Justice

In the territory of Erebos large deposits of rare earth elements are discovered. Rare earths are used in a multitude of technologies, ranging from computers to LCD screens, electric motors and electric lighting. Rare earths are not exactly 'rare', but since they are often dispersed and found in low concentrations, they are expensive to mine and consequently rather precious. Erebos is a poor country, which does not have the necessary technology and know-how to benefit from the recent discovery of rare earths. Therefore, it concludes a treaty with Zelos who, having rare earths itself, has extensive experience in the matter. The Convention on Rare Earth Production (CREP) foresees that Zelos would deliver all the necessary technical material to extract the rare earths. Moreover, the CREP States that the extraction of the rare earths is to be placed entirely in the hands of Zelos, but that it would at the same time educate some mining specialists from Erebos in the handling of the necessary techniques. The treaty is signed by the respective Foreign Ministers in 1985 and ratified by exchange of letters. It entered into force in February 1986. The Convention is, however, never registered with the Secretary General of the United Nations.

Ten years later in January 1996, the autobiography of the former Foreign Minister of Zelos, Mr Ate, reveals that the most difficult point during the negotiations of the CREP had been the attribution of the percentages of the gain made by the sale of the mined rare earths. While Zelos had requested at least 50% of the profit, Erebos was only ready to accord a maximum of 45% to Zelos. Mr Ate boasts that he himself had managed to hack into the computer of the President of Erebos at that time and to send to the Foreign Minister of Erebos involved in the negotiations an encoded e-mail apparently from the President himself. In this e-mail, the "President of Erebos" ordered his Foreign Minister to accept the demand of Zelos and grant it 50% of the profit made. Amazed, but seeing that this was an official e-mail from the account of the President, and in addition used not to questioning his President whose opinion could change rather quickly, the Foreign Minister of Erebos had accepted the 50% for Zelos and had signed the treaty. These revelations make the headlines of all the big newspapers. However, the two governments do not comment.

Then, on 4 March 1998 an incident puts a strain on the otherwise peaceful relations between Erebos and Zelos. On this day, a warship from Zelos is surprised by a heavy storm during an exercise on the high seas. The captain tries to reach their home port in Zelos but the wind and waves are too strong and there is no possibility for the ship to reach the safety of their port. Unfortunately, the ship hits rocks hidden below the waters and is severely damaged. Since the current and the wind lead towards the territorial waters of Erebos, the captain of the warship first transmits an 'SOS' to the authorities of Erebos and then asks for permission to enter the nearest port. After a long silence, the responsible authorities, however, deny them access to their territorial waters and order them to proceed. The captain implores them, explaining that the ship is already starting to sink and that they do not have much time to reach safety. Nevertheless, the authorities of Erebos remain firm. The captain of the ship, worried about the 120 sailors and other personnel under his command decides to disregard the prohibition and to enter the territorial waters of Erebos. He manages to reach the nearest port just before the ship sinks. Fortunately, the crew manages to take to the lifeboats and there is no loss of life.

The government of Erebos is outraged and vehemently denounces this 'violation of our territorial sovereignty by a foreign military ship'. The government of Zelos offers its apologies in a diplomatic note sent the next day, but points out that the circumstances had forced the captain to act like this. Erebos, however, seems to be deaf for apologies and stubbornly asks for financial reparations for the wrong done.

Zelos, angered by the attitude of Erebos 'that only seems to want money', suddenly declares that it considers the CREP to have been invalid since its beginning, since it had not been ratified in accordance with Article 189 of the constitution of Zelos. Erebos is first taken aback, but contests that the internal law of a State could be a ground for invalidating a treaty. Nevertheless, Erebos adds, the CREP was invalid on a different ground, namely based on the 'malicious behaviour of Mr Ate, former Foreign Minister of Zelos, during the negotiations over the CREP'. This in turn is challenged by Zelos.

Zelos is aware that the situation cannot go on like this. Therefore, on 1 August 1998, its ambassador in The Hague transmits the necessary documents to the International Court of Justice (ICJ) and asks the Court to decide on the legality of the action of the warship of Zelos during the storm, as well as on the applicability of the CREP.

However, one day later, the Minister of Foreign Affairs of Erebos contests the jurisdiction of the ICJ. He says that the CREP is non-existent—and thus cannot constitute the basis of the ICJ's jurisdiction—since it had not been validly concluded in 1985. Moreover, the CREP was also non-existent because it had never been registered with the Secretary General of the United Nations.

You are a legal advisor to the ICJ. You are asked to write a legal opinion on the present case, addressing all the relevant arguments made by both parties. In particular, you are asked to answer the following questions:

1. *Is the CREP still in force between the two parties?*
2. *Is the international responsibility of Zelos engaged by the incident of the 4 March 1998, and if yes, what are the consequences?*

3. What are the legal possibilities to settle the various disputes between the two States?

Nota bene

—Erebos and Zelos are founding members of the United Nations.
—Erebos has signed the Vienna Convention on the Law of Treaties (VCLT) on 31 May 1981.
—Zelos has ratified the VCLT on 5 November 1980.
—Article 189 of the constitution of Zelos provides that 'Peace treaties as well as treaties or agreements concerning the cessation or annexation of territory have to be ratified or approved by the Parliament of Zelos.'
—Article 22 of the CREP reads as follows: 'All disputes between the High Contracting Parties concerning the interpretation or application of the present convention shall be submitted to an arbitral tribunal upon request of one of the two parties, unless the competence of the International Court of Justice to hear the case can be established on another basis. In this situation the International Court of Justice will have precedence.'
—Zelos has made an optional clause declaration under Article 36 paragraph 2 of the ICJ Statute without any relevant reservation.
—Erebos has not made an optional clause declaration.

Case 7.11

Abbreviations used
ICJ = International Court of Justice
MST = Military Stationing Treaty
UN = United Nations

The State of Amino is composed of different regions. Most of them are peaceful and on good terms with the central government of Amino. However, the region Carboxy has been fighting for its independence for decades. Carboxy has enjoyed considerable competences, eg in provision of education and health, and acts almost completely independently from the central government in Amino. The population of Carboxy, about 150,000 people, is mainly composed of a particular linguistic group, which exists nowhere else in Amino.

On 7 July 1997 the Governor of Carboxy declares the independence of the region of Carboxy from Amino. The regional government declares itself as the new government of the sovereign State of Carboxy and creates a new Parliament as well as a new High Court. Amino vehemently protests, saying that there was no way Carboxy could declare itself independent on its own and added that it still considered Carboxy as an integral part of its territory.

Over the years, Carboxy builds up its own governmental apparatus including their own police force which effectively establish law and order in the region. In fact, they are so efficient that in 1999 Amino withdraws its police force 'in order to save money'. Carboxy also further extends its competences and acts independently from Amino in security, tax and economic policy matters, and handles all administrative matters on its own. Amino protests at every expansion of competence, but does not take any concrete steps to regain its influence in the region.

Carboxy greatly benefits from the fact that in 1999 gold and coal are discovered on its territory. The extraction and exportation of gold and coal allows the government of Carboxy to amass a considerable fortune, which is used to pay the salaries of public officials as well as for their various governmental programmes.

In 2000, Carboxy starts to forge economic relations with neighbouring as well as other States. Political exchanges and meetings soon follow these economic and commercial treaties. In December 2009, about 65 States of the international community have recognised Carboxy as an independent State. Despite the urging of some States, however, Carboxy has not yet applied for membership in the United Nations.

In December 2009 Carboxy concludes with its direct neighbour Leucin a treaty on the stationing of Leucin's military troops on the territory of Carboxy. The so-called Military Stationing Treaty (MST) is signed on 2 December 2009 and ratified by the Parliaments of Leucin and Carboxy on 17 December 2009. According to its Article 86 the MST enters into force on 15 January 2010. On this day, Leucin starts to move a considerable part of its ground troops and air force to the new military base in Carboxy. Amino, not aware of the MST, vehemently protests and qualifies this act as a clear violation of its territorial sovereignty since Carboxy is still an integral part of its territory. Informed about the MST, the President of Amino declares that Carboxy has no right to conclude such treaties since it is not a State and that thus the MST was void. He further requests that the troops of Leucin immediately leave Amino's territory. Now, however, it is Carboxy's turn to protest. The President of Carboxy affirms that Carboxy has been independent since 1997 and that every sovereign State has the right to conclude whatever international treaty it likes and thus also to offer itself as a host for the military base of another State. The President of Leucin—who was in 1999 the first State to recognise Carboxy's independence—publicly supports the statements made by Carboxy and says that Amino finally has to accept reality, namely the independence of Carboxy.

At this point, however, the President of Amino is outraged. He is not ready to 'tolerate any foreign army on Amino's territory' and decides to bring the case to the International Court of Justice (ICJ).

On 25 March 2010 Amino's ambassador in The Hague transmits to the ICJ all the relevant material to bring Leucin before the Court for the 'violation of international law and of Amino's territory by erecting there an unauthorized military basis'. It bases the jurisdiction of the Court on the optional clause declarations made by both parties. The registrar of the Court informs Leucin about the case brought against it on 27 March 2010. In a public reaction on 29 March 2010 Leucin contests the jurisdiction of the Court. It first says that there is no valid basis of consent existing since it would invoke the reservation that Amino had attached to its optional clause declaration (see below) and that consequently the ICJ would have to declare itself not competent because of the involvement of the UN Charter in the case. Furthermore, Leucin argues that the Court should declare the case as inadmissible since the legal interests of Carboxy were directly affected and thus the ICJ could not deal with the case. Amino contradicts these statements made by Leucin by saying that first of all a State could under no circumstances invoke the reservation made by another State since these were 'personalised reservations, only applicable for the benefit of the State that originally has made them'. Secondly, it says that the legal interests of Carboxy do not matter at all on the international level since this entity was not a State but only a region of Amino, entirely under Amino's sovereignty. Besides, Amino adds that a clear indication that Carboxy was not a State was its small population of only 150,000 people, clearly too few to constitute a State.

You are a lawyer at the ICJ. The registrar asks you to write a legal opinion on the following questions.

1. *Is Carboxy according to international law an independent State or not? Address all the arguments made by the parties.*
2. *Did Leucin violate international law by establishing a military base in Carboxy, and if yes, what are the consequences? Argue on the basis of the ILC Articles on Responsibility of States for Internationally Wrongful Act and address all the relevant arguments made by the parties.*
3. *Is the ICJ competent to hear the case between Amino and Leucin?*

Nota bene

— Amino and Leucin are original members of the United Nations.
— The constitution of Amino provides that regions of the country can under no circumstances conclude international treaties, but that such treaties will always be concluded by the central government in Amino.
— Leucin has made an optional clause declaration on the basis of Article 36 paragraph 2 ICJ Statute without any relevant reservation.
— Amino has made an optional clause declaration based on Article 36 paragraph 2 ICJ Statute with the following reservation: 'Amino declares that it does not recognise the competence of the Court to deal with disputes involving the interpretation or application of multilateral treaties where not all State parties to this treaty are parties to the dispute before the Court.'

Chapter 8

Specialised Branches of International Law

International human rights law

(*The following cases deal with international human rights law, thereby mainly focusing on the European Convention on Human Rights*).

Case 8.1

The situation between the States Tredor and Kata has been more than just strained for the past 75 years, mainly due to an ongoing territorial dispute between these two nations. Kata has been claiming territorial sovereignty over the region of Mirscha, a region rich in precious metals and which formally belongs to Tredor. In fact, when these two States gained their independence, the former colonial power had arbitrarily drawn the borderline between them, attributing the region Mirscha to Tredor, despite the fact that Kata had possessed this region throughout the whole period of colonial rule and even before.

Kata decided to recapture Mirscha, which was 'rightfully theirs'. Thus, on 17 May 2012 Kata launched an aerial offensive against Tredor in the region of Mirscha. Kata's air force bombarded the military positions of Tredor in this region non-stop for a month. These bombardments also caused a certain number of victims among the civilian population.

By 17 June 2012, the military forces of Tredor had been completely destroyed. Kata hence decided to send its ground troops into Mirscha in order to establish control in the region. Soon after, on 28 June 2012, Mirscha was completely controlled by Kata's army.

Fearful for its control in the region, the government of Kata decided that no citizen from Tredor was to be allowed to remain in the region and ordered the military to conduct a large operation of forced expulsions. During this operation, Tredorian citizens who did not want to leave were either imprisoned or killed.

This tragedy continued until 15 November 2012. On 10 October 2012, horrified by these massive violations of fundamental human rights, the United Nations Security

Council adopted a resolution on the basis of Chapter VII of the UN Charter, in which it authorised States to take 'all necessary means' to protect the Tredorian population and to oblige Kata's army to retreat from the region of Mirscha. Based on this resolution, a coalition of States intervened militarily and was able to force Kata's army to withdraw from Mirscha, thereby effectively ending six months of atrocities.

Some family members of victims of these atrocities decided to bring a complaint against Kata over the violations of human rights. Since the claimants did not receive satisfaction before national tribunals, they decided to bring their case to the European Court of Human Rights.

You are a former lawyer at the European Court of Human Rights. The claimants ask you to provide them with an objective legal opinion on the jurisdiction ratione loci (territorial jurisdiction) of the European Court of Human Rights in relation to (a) the cases concerning the victims killed in the bombardments from 17 May to 17 June 2012, and (b) the expulsions, summary executions and imprisonment of Tredorian citizens by Kata's army in the region of Mirscha in the period from 28 June to 15 November 2012.

Nota bene

- —Kata is a European State and is a party to the European Convention for the Protection of Human Rights and Fundamental Freedoms of 4 November 1950 since its entry into force.
- —Tredor is not a European State and is not a party to the European Convention for the Protection of Human Rights and Fundamental Freedoms of 4 November 1950.

Case 8.2

Abbreviations used

ATL 2012 = Anti-Terrorist Law 2012
ECHR = European Convention for the Protection of Human Rights and Fundamental Freedoms of 4 November 1950
ECtHR = European Court on Human Rights

The State Scissorland has had to face a rise in terrorist attacks ever since a separatist group called MalikaLibre declared that it wanted to separate the region Malika from Scissorland and to make it into an independent State. The government of Scissorland had serious problems fighting against the MalikaLibre, especially also because its legal arsenal did not allow it to take effective steps against this terrorist group.

Confronted with a growing number of increasingly murderous attacks, the population of Scissorland was seized by a climate of terror. The population as well as the authorities knew that the MalikaLibre was able to perpetrate an attack at any time, any place and against any person. They had demonstrated their abilities several times in the past, leading to more than 300 deaths in a few months.

In these circumstances, after having declared a State of emergency, the parliament of Scissorland adopted on 14 August 2012 an emergency rule, the so-called Anti-Terrorist Law 2012 (ATL 2012). Article 2 of this law provides: 'The present law authorises derogations from fundamental human rights, in conformity with Article 15 of the European Convention for the Protection of Human Rights and Fundamental Freedoms of 4 November 1950.' The ATL 2012 further sets out in its Article 3 that 'the police and other competent authorities of the State of Scissorland are authorised to use all necessary means in order to obtain information on activities related to the MalikaLibre'. Article 4 of the ATL 2012 stipulates that a person can be kept in administrative detention for 40 days without justification. The ATL 2012 does not provide for any judicial guarantees for the persons detained thereunder, particularly in relation to the right to counsel and habeas corpus. Finally, the ATL 2012 does not contain any time limit.

Empowered by this new law, the police of Scissorland started a veritable manhunt against the members of the MalikaLibre. Following some tip-offs, the police on 10 September 2012 arrested Mr Alfred Pasnette. Based on Article 4 ATL 2012, he was placed in administrative detention. In particular, Mr Alfred Pasnette was suspected of providing detonators to the members of the MalikaLibre. During his detention, the police questioned Mr Alfred Pasnette on his relations and links to the terrorist group. In these interrogation sessions, the police repeatedly made use of techniques such as waterboarding, reverse hanging (also called 'Palestinian hanging') and sleep deprivation. After 38 days of detention and interrogation, the police had not been able to establish any link between Mr Alfred Pasnette and the MalikaLibre. Consequently, Mr Alfred Pasnette was released.

However, Mr Alfred Pasnette has been deeply marked by his detention and will no longer be able to lead a normal life. Therefore, he decided to bring a complaint concerning his treatment in detention against the government of Scissorland. Unfortunately, all the tribunals in Scissorland concluded that Mr Alfred Pasnette's fundamental human rights had not been violated, since the police had acted on the basis of the ATL 2012.

Dissatisfied with these decisions, Mr Alfred Pasnette decides to bring his case to the European Court on Human Rights (ECtHR). He claims that Scissorland violated the prohibition on torture contained in Article 3 of the European Convention on Human Rights (ECHR), as well as his right to liberty under Article 5 ECHR. Scissorland strongly rejects these allegations and declares that it has not violated any fundamental human rights since with the ATL 2012 the government of Scissorland has derogated from certain rights contained in the ECHR, in conformity with Article 15 of this convention.

You are a judge at the ECtHR. In preparation of the judgment of the ECtHR, you are asked to take position on the allegations made by Mr Alfred Pasnette.

Nota bene

- Scissorland is a party to the European Convention for the Protection of Human Rights and Fundamental Freedoms of 4 November 1950 since its entry into force.
- Scissorland had informed the Secretary General of the Council of Europe about the adoption of ATL 2012. It had pointed out that this law was necessary, since it had to face an unprecedented wave of terrorist attacks on its territory, which could not effectively by countered with its current legal instruments and that this terrorist menace had already caused too much bloodshed among its citizens.

Case 8.3

On 14 January 2012, a very large demonstration against the latest drastic austerity measures adopted by the government three days earlier in order to fight the astronomic public debt took place in Nowdstate. Nowdstate was used to this sort of manifestation, which was not the first of its kind. Very violent thugs often took part in these manifestations.

Concerning the demonstration of 14 January 2012, the police had received the order to shoot— using real ammunition—at any protester who exhibited dangerous behaviour towards other persons or goods. In addition, the anti-riot squad had been deployed as reinforcement and was present with trucks equipped with water cannons.

When the police started to approach, the demonstration turned violent very quickly. Some participants in the demo, while chanting slogans against government policies, threw glass bottles and stones at the police. A group of thugs destroyed several shops and cars, and was also throwing bottles and stones at the police. The latter first intervened by using the water cannons. However, this was not sufficient and only a small number of protestors scattered. The police thus decided to open fire on the remaining protestors.

During this forceful intervention, a teenager named Guy Badkopf was shot in the head by police sergeant Ted Shooter and died on the spot. Ted Shooter, a very experienced police officer and former army sharpshooter, had believed that Badkopf was about to throw a bottle at him, while in reality it was only an empty soda can, which Badkopf had wanted to toss on the ground.

Guy Badkopf's parents impatiently waited for an investigation into the events of 14 January 2012, especially in relation to the death of their son and the intervention of Sergeant Shooter. However, after a sketchy inquiry, the competent authorities closed the case.

Outraged, Guy Badkopf's parents turned to the superior authorities to complain about the lack of diligence and impartiality of the police of Nowdstate. Yet, despite all their efforts, their requests met with no response. Therefore, they decided to bring the case concerning the violation of the right to life of their son to the European Court on Human Rights.

You are the legal counsel of the parents of Guy Badkopf and you have to present the case in front of the European Court on Human Rights. You therefore have to establish the violation of the right to life allegedly committed by Nowdstate by causing the death of Guy Badkopf during the demonstration of 14 January 2012.

Nota bene

—Nowdstate is a party to the European Convention for the Protection of Human Rights and Fundamental Freedoms of 4 November 1950 since its entry into force.

Recommended reading on international human rights law

Articles

Fionnuala Ni Aolin, 'The Evolving Jurisprudence of the European Convention Concerning the Right to Life', (2001) 19 *Netherlands Quarterly of Human Rights* 21.

Despina Chatzivassiliou, 'The Guarantees of Judicial Control with Respect to Deprivation of Liberty under Article 5 of the European Convention on Human Rights: on Overview of the Strasbourg Case-Law, (2004) 4 *ERA-Forum: scripta iuris europaei* 499.

Louise Doswald-Beck, 'What does the Prohibition of "Torture or Inhuman or Degrading Treatment or Punishment" Mean?', (1978) 25 *Netherlands International Law Review* 24.

Michael Duttwiler, 'Authority, Control and Jurisdiction in the Extraterritorial Application of the European Convention on Human Rights', (2012) 30 *Netherlands Quarterly of Human Rights* 137.

Kara Irwin, 'Prospects for Justice: the Procedural Aspect of the Right to Life under the European Convention on Human Rights and its Applications to Investigations of Northern Ireland's Bloody Sunday', (1999) 22 *Fordham International Law Journal* 1822.

Rick Lawson, 'Life After Bankovic: on the Extraterritorial Application of the European Convention on Human Rights', in Fons Coomans and Menno Kamminga (eds), *Extraterritorial Application of Human Rights Treaties* (Antwerp, Intersentia, 2004) 83–123.

Jan-Peter Loof, 'Crisis Situations, Counter Terrorism and Derogation from the European Convention on Human Rights', in Antoine Buyse (ed), *Margins of Conflict: the ECHR Transitions to and from an Armed Conflict* (Antwerp, Intersentia, 2011) 35–56.

Raffaella Nigro, 'The Notion of "Jurisdiction" in Article 1: Future Scenarios for the Extra-Territorial Application of the European Convention on Human Rights', (2010) 20 *Italian Yearbook of International Law* 11.

Richard Stone, 'Deprivation of Liberty: the Scope of Article 5 of the European Convention on Human Rights', (2012) 12 *European Human Rights Law Review*, 46.

Books

Louise Doswald-Beck, *Human Rights in Times of Conflict and Terrorism* (Oxford, Oxford University Press, 2011).

Alistair Mowbray, *Cases, Materials and Commentary on the European Convention on Human Rights*, 3rd edn (Oxford, Oxford University Press, 2012).

International refugee law

Case 8.4

Abbreviation used
YSL = Young Socialist League

Pascal DeGray is a national of Apoka, but he has been living and working in the neighbouring State of Luren for about two years. Despite living abroad, Pascal is still very interested in the political developments in his home country, where he used to be a leader of the Young Socialist League (YSL), a party active in the opposition. Worried, he notes that the government of Apoka is suppressing the YSL more and more.

He is especially concerned because his younger brother, Tom DeGray, and one of their cousins, Ben Nolin, are very much involved in the YSL's work as activists.

A few months ago, the government of Apoka started arbitrarily to arrest and detain politically active persons from all opposition parties, including the YSL. Initially, the detained persons are released again after a few days. Recently, however, several activists have disappeared and there are reliable reports from human rights groups that detained political activists are being systematically tortured and sometimes even killed. One evening, when Tom and Ben arrive at their flat, they notice that the door is open and that the place has been searched. Their neighbours tell them that the police have been looking for them. Tom and Ben—seriously afraid after what has happened to several of their colleagues from the YSL—decide to flee. Unfortunately, they are separated during their flight. Ben finally arrives in Luren, while Tom escapes to Desor, another neighbouring State of Apoka. The next morning, both Tom and Ben apply for refugee status in the respective State.

At the same time, Pascal reads in the newspaper that there had been a serious crackdown by the police in Apoka on current but also former members of the YSL, all of whom have been imprisoned. He is very afraid and decides that it would be safer for him if he applies for asylum in Luren.

As a specialist in international refugee law, please determine whether Pascal, Tom and Ben are refugees in the countries where they applied for asylum.

Nota bene

- Luren is a party to the 1951 Convention and the 1967 Protocol Relating to the Status of Refugees, but is not party to any regional refugee law convention.
- Desor is not a party to the 1951 Convention and the 1967 Protocol Relating to the Status of Refugees but has a national law provision on refugee status, essentially replicating the refugee definition found in the Cartagena Protocol.
- Ben is a national of Apoka, but also a national of Conda.
- Tom and Pascal are only nationals of Apoka.

Case 8.5

Abbreviation used
UNHCR = Office of the United Nations High Commissioner for Refugees

The State of Essa became independent in 1948. Since then, the Shasta have officially become a religious minority in that country. In 1962, the military took power in Essa and created a dictatorial regime, which started to oppress the Shasta, who were seen as 'unworthy' due to their different religion but also darker skin. In 1982 the government of Essa passed a new 'citizenship legislation', which effectively made all the Shasta stateless. Today, the Shasta are not allowed to own land; any land they once owned has been confiscated. Also, the Shasta are not allowed to go to school without special permission by the government, which leads to an illiteracy right of over 80% among the members of this religious minority. Further restrictions and limitations apply to them concerning free movement and marriage. The security forces often arrest members of the Shasta without reason, and frequently mistreat or even torture them during detention.

Faced with these living conditions, many Shasta decide to leave Essa and seek refuge in the neighbouring State of Naret. The government of Naret is not at all happy with the presence of the Shasta in their territory and tries to force them to return 'voluntarily' to Essa by imposing difficult living conditions. Recently, the government of Naret has started to expel members of the Shasta (mostly those without status) to Essa, because they fear a further mass influx after the next elections in Essa.

You are a well-known specialist in international refugee law. A journalist, wanting to write about the expulsion of the Shasta, contacts you and asks you to give him an answer on the following question: is the expulsion of the Shasta from Naret legal under international treaty and customary law?

Nota bene

—Naret is not a party to the 1951 Convention or the 1967 Protocol relating to the Status of Refugees.
—However, Naret is a party to the UN Convention against Torture and other Cruel, Inhuman or Degrading Treatment or Punishment and the International Covenant on Civil and Political Rights.
—The Shasta living in Naret have been recognised as refugees by the UNHCR. Naret does not conduct its own refugee status determinations, but has given the UNHCR the power to make refugee status determinations in its territory, and usually accepts their decisions – also in relation to the Shasta.

Case 8.6

Roberto Linea has been living as a refugee in Ometry for the last seven years. He is originally a national from Calculu, belonging to the ethnic minority of the Bool. The dictatorial regime in power in Calculu at that time severely persecuted all ethnic minorities. Roberto had never been imprisoned or tortured himself, but he was frequently threatened and harassed by the police. Finally, with more and more members of the Bool imprisoned, Roberto decided to flee. He reached Ometry, where he applied for refugee status, which was promptly granted to him. Upon noticing that Roberto had left Calculu and sought asylum in a foreign country, the authorities of Calculu revoked his nationality, rendering him stateless. This was a standard procedure in Calculu: everyone not 'happy enough to stay here but seeking refuge elsewhere' will lose their Calculuan nationality.

Now, seven years later, the situation is very different. The dictatorial regime has been toppled three years ago and a new democratic government is in place in Calculu. All ethnic groups living there are represented in the government according to their population size. Many new laws have been passed, including several bills to strengthen the protection of human rights. While there were some security problems in the beginning, the country has now been stable and peaceful for roughly two years. Moreover, 'to make the wrong done good', the authorities of Calculu have restored the nationality of Calculu to everyone who had previously lost it and who was interested in reacquiring it. Roberto was among those who took advantage of this offer and thereby ended his statelessness. Last year, he travelled to Calculu a few times to visit friends and family that had returned there.

A few days ago Roberto received a letter from the immigration authorities of Ometry, where he is still a refugee. The letter informs him that the authorities had thoroughly assessed his situation and had come to the conclusion that there were no longer any reasons to consider him a refugee. They hereby wished to inform Roberto Linea that they were ending his refugee status, asking him to leave Ometry within 90 days, as any other legal alien. Roberto was indignant about this letter. He replied that under the 1951 Convention it is impossible just to end his refugee status, which was an unlimited status bestowed on him. Sending him back to the country he once fled from would thus effectively violate the *non-refoulement* provision in Article 33 of the 1951 Convention relating to the Status of Refugees.

You are a specialist in international refugee law working in the immigration authority of Ometry. Your boss asks you to clarify whether it is true that refugee status can never be ended under the 1951 Convention and to assess Roberto Linea's situation.

Nota bene

— Ometry is a party to the 1951 Convention and the 1967 Protocol relating to the Status of Refugees as well as the UN Convention against Torture and other Cruel, Inhuman or Degrading Treatment or Punishment.

Recommended reading on international refugee law

It should be pointed out that UNCHR guidelines and other UNHCR documents and publications are especially important for the subject of international refugee law. It is furthermore recommended to have recourse to *Refworld*, the leading online source for information on refugees and refugee law.

Articles

Erika Feller, 'Asylum, Migration and Refugee Protection: Realities, Myths and the Promise of Things to Come', (2006) 18 *International Journal of Refugee Law* 509.

Ivor Jackson, 'The 1951 Convention Relating to the Status of Refugees: A Universal Basis for Protection', (1991) 3 *International Journal of Refugee Law* 403.

Ninette Kelley, 'International Refugee Protection Challenges and Opportunities', (2007) 19 *International Journal of Refugee Law* 401.

Books

Vincent Chetail (ed), *La Convention de Genève du 28 juillet 1951 relative au statut des réfugiés 50 ans après: bilan et perspectives* (Brussels, Bruylant, 2001).

Erika Feller, Volker Türk and Frances Nicholson (eds), *Refugee Protection in International Law: UNHCR's Global Consultation on International Protection* (Cambridge, Cambridge University Press, 2003).

Thomas Gammeltoft-Hansen, *Access to Asylum: International Refugee Law and the Globalisation of Migration Control* (Cambridge, Cambridge University Press, 2011).

Guy Goodwin-Gill and Jane McAdam, *The Refugee in International Law*, 3rd edn (Oxford, Oxford University Press, 2007).

James Hathaway, *The Rights of Refugees under International Law* (Cambridge, Cambridge University Press, 2005).

Hélène Lambert (ed), *International Refugee Law*, Surrey, Ashgate, 2010.

Caroline Lantero, *Le droit des réfugiés: entre droits de l'homme et gestion de l'immigration* (Bruxelles, Bruylant, 2010).

Frances Nicholson and Patrick Twomey (eds), *Refugee Rights and Realities: Evolving International Concepts and Regimes* (Cambridge, Cambridge University Press, 1999).

UNHCR, *The State of the World's Refugees 2012: In Search of Solidarity* (Oxford, Oxford University Press, 2012).

International humanitarian law

(Note: the following cases deal with the qualification of an armed conflict. This qualification is the first indispensable step to be taken in any analysis involving international humanitarian law, since it will determine the applicable law as such: international humanitarian law in relation to international armed conflict, non-international armed conflict or none of the two. The proposed cases aim at allowing the student to deal with and analyse the law for different types of conflicts).

Case 8.7

Abbreviation used

DoL = Defenders of Liberty

A dictatorial regime has been governing the State of Nounabe with an iron fist for the past 35 years. Despite repeated protests from the international community, the Security Council of the United Nations has never been able to adopt a resolution against the Nounabian regime. This was mainly due to the fact that Nounabe had a powerful ally among the members of the Security Council, who systematically used its veto power against all proposed resolutions targeting Nounabe. It was well known that this powerful member of the Security Council had important economic interests in Nounabe and therefore did not wish the situation there to change.

The Nounabian regime continuously oppressed the population and kept all the wealth of the country for the benefit of the President and his regime alone. In light of this situation, a group called the Defenders of Liberty (DoL) decided to rebel against the regime, and in 2010 began a series of sporadic attacks aimed at destabilising the regime.

However, due to a lack of financial as well as military means, the DoL was not able to affect seriously the politics of the Nounabian president and his regime. Nevertheless, the DoL became generally known to the international community.

The State of Gagea, which was horrified at the oppression of the Nounabian population by their own State, and had repeatedly pushed for the adoption of a Security Council resolution on the critical situation in Nounabe, decided to support the DoL. From November 2010 onwards, Gagea provided the DoL with an impressive amount and variety of weapons. Furthermore, Gagea also supported the DoL financially.

Subsequently, the DoL gained in importance and developed into a veritable, highly structured paramilitary group. Fairly quickly, the DoL was able to control a small region of Nounabe's territory. Fighting between the DoL and the armed forces of Nounabe increased in magnitude, and by the end of February 2011 this had resulted in almost 3,000 casualties, both from the civilian population as well as the army of Nounabe.

In light of this development, Gagea decided to tighten its link with the DoL, and in March 2011 began also to give the DoL strategic military advice. Finally, in June 2011 officers and agents from the Gagean secret service began to support the DoL leader in the planning and execution of all the armed activities of the group.

Despite this substantial support by Gagea, however, it was not possible to topple the government of Nounabe. Therefore, on 14 November 2011, Gagea sent its troops proper into Nounabe.

Since then, a significant armed conflict has engulfed the entire territory of Nounabe, with the DoL and the Gagean army both involved in fighting against Nounabe's armed forces.

You are working at the Legal Division of the ICRC. You are asked to determine whether international humanitarian law is applicable to the situation in Nounabe's territory and since when (starting from 2010 until today). You are also asked to establish which legal instruments are applicable.

Nota bene

—Nounabe and Gagea are both parties to the four Geneva Conventions of 12 August 1949.
—Only Gagea is a party to Additional Protocol I of 8 June 1977 to the four Geneva Conventions of 12 August 1949.
—Only Nounabe is a party to Additional Protocol II of 8 June 1977 to the four Geneva Conventions of 12 August 1949.

Case 8.8

Since 1 June 2012 an armed conflict has been raging between the States of Kaolea and Kurki. Due to territorial claims from both sides, the armies of these States have been clashing very violently all along their common border. On 27 September 2012, the army of Kaolea decided to launch a substantial offensive, involving both infantry troops and the air force. Furthermore, it planned to strengthen one of its infantry battalions with a paramilitary group called the TousseKaos. The latter was a very well structured group placed under the command of the army of Kaolea, even though they were actually independent of the army. In fact, the fighters from the TousseKaos were easily recognisable when they went into combat: all of them wore red and yellow brassards on both arms, and, in addition, the distinctive sign of the TousseKaos—two crossed guns forming an 'x' in front of a phoenix—was embroidered on their jackets.

At 6 am on 27 September 2012, the Kaoleanian offensive started and its troops rapidly advanced on the territory of Kurki. The front line saw very intensive combat and both the infantry troops from Kaolea and the TousseKaos soon faced trouble from the redoubtable defence and accurate shooting mounted by the army of Kurki. Feeling that the advantage was slowly turning in favour of the latter, the commander of the Kaoleanian infantry troops requested aerial support.

Thus, two fighter planes as well as two bombers took off and rapidly arrived at the scene of combat. Unfortunately for them, however, the air defences of Kurki were formidable. The two fighter planes as well as one of the bombers were literally pulverised in the air, while the second bomber was also shot down, though the crew was able to bail out successfully.

The commander of the infantry troops of Kaolea received the order to go to the aid of the pilots of the second bomber. During this rescue operation, soldiers of the Kurkian army wounded ten soldiers and three officers from Kaolea. Finally, these thirteen wounded as well as the entire bomber crew were captured and hauled off by soldiers from Kurki.

At the end of the day, the army of Kaolea was no longer able to withstand the Kurkian counter-offensive, and had to retreat rapidly. The operation cost Kaolea dear: 48 soldiers dead and 34 persons, including members of the TousseKaos, hauled off by the army of Kurki. In fact, this ignominious defeat was a veritable turnaround for Kaolea.

Boris Fourtout and Alex Sniffpuliz, two journalists from a well-known daily newspaper, decided to write an article on the conditions of imprisonment of soldiers detained by the Kurkian army. After having successfully smuggled themselves across the border to Kurki, they contacted one of the prison guards at Paradisjail, one of the military detention centres in Kurki.

Despite the information provided by the guardian, they decided that they needed more material to write a good article. Boris Fourtout convinced Alex Sniffpuliz to creep up close to the prison during the night, in order to take pictures with a telephoto lens. During the night of 3–4 October 2012, the two journalists thus took up position a few hundred meters away from the barbed wire surrounding the prison and started to take pictures.

However, they were surprised in this endeavour by the military police and brought to Paradisjail for questioning. Alex and Boris incessantly repeated that they were journalists and could thus not be arrested. Despite their assurances, they were brutally tortured, the army of Kurki being convinced that they were mercenaries in the service of Kaolea.

After four days of vicious interrogation, using unspeakable techniques such as waterboarding, burns with cigarettes and other atrocities, the commander of the prison accused Alex and Boris of espionage against the State of Kurki. Consequently, the two journalists were imprisoned for an undetermined time, without any possibility of having the lawfulness of their detention verified.

You are a legal adviser to the armed forces of Kurki. The Chief Commander of the army of Kurki asks you to determine the status of the captured Kaoleans, ie the thirteen wounded soldiers and the crew of the bomber, as well as the members of the TousseKaos.

In addition, he also asks you to ascertain the status of Boris Fourtout and Alex Sniffpuliz, and if the conditions of their interrogation as well as their detention were legal in light of the applicable rules of international humanitarian law.

Nota bene

— Both Kurki and Kaolea are parties to the four Geneva Conventions of 12 August 1949 as well as all the additional protocols since their entry into force.

Case 8.9

An armed conflict between the State of Pescade and the State of Mourna—an island in the northern Pacific—has arisen, taking place exclusively on the latter's territory. The Pescadian army, not directly present on the territory of Mourna, launches its attacks from its aircraft carriers located on the high seas.

The Pescadian air force bombards the island of Mourna every day. At 4 am on 14 June 2012, two fighter planes take off with the mission to bombard a specific building located in the middle of a residential neighbourhood in the capital of Mourna. According to the information from the Pescadian secret service, the Mournian army are using this building to produce new types of weapons and ammunition.

Despite being equipped with extremely precise missiles, the two fighter planes miss their target. A school is completely destroyed, as well as one wing of a hospital. While the destruction of the school does not cause any victims due to the early hour of the attack, almost 40 people die in the attack on the hospital.

You are a legal adviser of the army of Mourna. You are asked to determine all the potential violations of international humanitarian law committed by the air force of Pescade during its conduct of hostilities on 14 June 2012.

Nota bene

— Pescade and Mourna are both parties to the Geneva Conventions of 12 August 1949 as well as Additional Protocol I of 8 June 1977 to these Conventions.

Recommended reading on international humanitarian law

Articles

Alexandre Balguy-Gallois, 'The Protection of Journalists and News Media Personnel in Armed Conflict', (2004) 86 *International Review of the Red Cross* 37.

Ryan Goodman, 'The Detention of Civilians in Armed Conflict', (2009) 103 *American Journal of International Law* 48.
Jean-François Quéguiner, 'Precautions under the Law Governing the Conduct of Hostilities', (2006) 88 *International Review of the Red Cross* 793.
Michael Schmitt, 'Precision Attack and International Humanitarian Law', (2005) 87 *International Review of the Red Cross* 445.
Sylvain Vité, 'Typology of Armed Conflicts in International Humanitarian Law: Legal Concepts and Actual Situations', (2009) 91 *International Review of the Red Cross* 69.

Books

Emily Crawford, *The Treatment of Combatants and Insurgents under the Law of Armed Conflict* (Oxford, Oxford University Press, 2010).
Eric David, *Principes de droit des conflits armés*, 4th edn (Bruxelles, Bruylant, 2008).
Nils Melzer, *Targeted Killing in International Law* (Oxford, Oxford University Press, 2008).
Jean Pictet, *Geneva Convention for the Amelioration of the Condition of Wounded and Sick in Armed Forces in the Field: Commentary* (Geneva, International Committee of the Red Cross, 1952).
Claude Pilloud, Yves Sandoz, Christophe Swinarski, Bruno Zimmerman (eds), *Commentary on the Additional Protocols of 8 June 1977 to the Geneva Conventions of 12 August 1949*, (Geneva, International Committee of the Red Cross / Dordrecht, Martinus Nijhoff Publishers, 1987).
Marco Sassolí, Antoine Bouvier and Anne Quintin, *How Does Law Protect in War?*, Vol I, 3rd edn (Geneva, International Committee of the Red Cross, 2011).
Oscar Uhler and Henri Coursier, *Geneva Convention Relative to the Protection of Civilian Persons in Time of War: Commentary* (Geneva, International Committee of the Red Cross, 1958).

International criminal law

Case 8.10

A very brutal international armed conflict is presently taking place between the States of Falcon and Tyton. Numerous war crimes and potentially also crimes against humanity are being committed by the armies and in the territories of both parties. Falcon, having a rather small army compared to Tyton, is relying heavily on voluntary foreign nationals for their combat operations. These foreign nationals form their own battalions under the command of officers of the Falcon army. One of the larger battalions is made up of soldiers from Columbi. Columbi is a State with huge economic problems, which leads citizens of that State to search for work elsewhere. There are several reports that those foreign battalions are also actively involved in the commission of atrocities.

Columbi is a State that strongly believes in the power of international law. The government is horrified to learn that potentially some of its nationals have committed war crimes or crimes against humanity.

You are an independent expert on international criminal law. The President of Columbi contacts you in order to get your advice. He wants to know what possibilities Columbi has under international law to bring all those perpetrators involved in 'those absolutely horrid crimes' to justice.

He stresses that he wants to get advice under international law, since 'Columbi had nothing to do with the conflict as such' and is furthermore short on financial resources, preventing any successful prosecution in Columbi. The President is, however, a little bit worried to offend other States and thus stresses that he would not like to enter into subjects related to State responsibility.

Nota bene

—Columbi has been a party to the Rome Statute of the International Criminal Court since its entry into force.
—Falcon has been a party to the Rome Statue of the International Criminal Court since its entry into force.
—Tyton is not a party to the Rome Statute of the International Criminal Court.

Case 8.11

Abbreviation used
PoWs = Prisoners of War

A long-lasting international armed conflict is taking place between Neit and Painal. Both sides have established numerous camps for prisoners of war (PoWs).

In the camps established by Neit, PoWs are not able to buy tobacco in the camp kiosks, since Neit has a very strict non-smoking policy applied throughout the whole country. The prices for other goods that can be bought at the camp kiosk, such as soap, writing and reading materials including newspapers and some foodstuff (eg chocolate), are slightly above market prices. Furthermore, the authorities from Neit also compel PoWs to fight for them, since Neit is currently short on soldiers and the authorities consider that the PoWs 'can also do some real work for all the food they eat'.

For all these reasons, Painal publicly accuses Neit, and especially also the authorities and soldiers in charge of the PoW camps, of committing war crimes.

You are a specialist in international criminal law. A journalist contacts you and asks you to assess and explain whether Painal's allegations that Neit is committing war crimes is correct.

Nota bene

—Both Neit and Painal are parties to the four Geneva Conventions from 1949.

Case 8.12

The States of Pomacan and Centrostan are neighbours. Pomacan previously was a part of Centrostan and became only independent in the 1970s. Centrostan formally accepted the independence, but has since then had a tendency to intervene in political matters in Pomacan, a fact that considerably angers the government of the latter. Due to this and also to some economic rivalry, relations have been very tense between the two parties for years. About a year ago, these tensions finally erupted into a fully fledged, very brutal international armed conflict. Centrostan has now invaded Pomacan and is advancing rapidly towards the country's capital. The armed forces of Centrostan attack not only military objects, but systematically attack undefended villages with no military presence at all.

During one of the above-mentioned attacks on a village, some Centrostan soldiers capture a group of five fleeing civilians. Two of these civilians happen to be nationals from Centrostan living in Pomacan. Because they are tired of fighting, the soldiers decide to take a break and to 'amuse' themselves a bit with the captured civilians. They burn them with cigarettes, stab them with knifes and repeatedly give them electric shocks with their tasers. All five civilians are severely wounded in the process.

You are working for the office of the prosecutor of Centrostan, which has the task of investigating alleged international crimes committed by or against nationals of Centrostan, on or outside the territory of Centrostan. Your boss asks you to make an objective determination whether the acts of the soldiers mentioned above can qualify as crimes against humanity.

Nota bene

— Centrostan has a national law on crimes against humanity. The definition of crimes against humanity contained therein is word for word exactly the same as the definition found in the Rome Statute of the International Criminal Court.

Recommended reading on International Criminal Law

Articles

Yoram Dinstein, 'International Criminal Law', (1985) 20 *Israel Law Review* 206.

Paola Gaeta, 'International Criminal Law' in Basak Çali (ed), *International Law for International Relations* (Oxford, Oxford University Press, 2010) 258–280.

Robert Cryer, 'International Criminal Law' in Malcom Evans (ed), *International Law*, 3rd edn (Oxford, Oxford University Press, 2010) 752–783.

Books

Ilias Bantekas, *International Criminal Law*, 4th edn (Oxford, Hart Publishing, 2010).

Cherif Bassiouni, *Introduction to International Criminal Law* (Ardsley NY, Transnational Publishers Inc, 2003).

Antonio Cassese, Guido Acquaviva, Mary Fan and Alex Whiting, *International Criminal Law: Cases and Commentaries* (Oxford, Oxford University Press, 2011).

Antonio Cassese, *International Criminal Law*, 2nd edn (Oxford, Oxford University Press, 2008).

Antonio Cassese, Paola Gaeta and John RWD Jones (eds), *The Rome Statute of the International Criminal Court: A Commentary* (Oxford, Oxford University Press, 2002).

Robert Cryer, Håkan Friman, Darryl Robinson and Elizabeth Wilmshurst, *An Introduction to International Criminal Law and Procedure* (Cambridge, Cambridge University Press, 2010).

Robert Kolb and Damien Scalia, *Droit international penal: précis*, 2nd edn (Basel, Helbling Lichtenhahn, 2012).

Gerhard Werle, *Principles of International Criminal Law*, 2nd edn (The Hague, TMC Asser Press, 2009).

International environmental law

Case 8.13

Abbreviation used
GHGs = greenhouse gases

Ceotu is a State that is actively engaged in the fight against global warming. Therefore, it has established its own research centre, where scientists regularly measure the concentration of greenhouse gases (GHGs) in Ceotu's atmosphere. In June 2010, these scientists noticed that the general level of GHGs found in the atmosphere had noticeably increased. After the scientists had publicly reported their findings, the government of Ceotu decided that something needed to be done. Despite repeated inquiries, the scientists are not, however, sure of the reason for this increase. Ceotu suspects a number of other States are responsible for the increase. They especially think of Othree, a neighbouring State which has struggled with its reduction goals in the beginning, but is now generally complying. In Othree's territory a couple of new factories have been constructed in the past year, which—according to Ceotu–'can only be bad for the environment'. This allegation is not, however, supported by scientific facts.

You are one of the legal advisers to the government of Ceotu and a specialist in international law. The President of Ceotu asks you in August 2010 to write a short memo on whether it would be possible to bring a case against Othree under the State Responsibility Articles. If yes, he asks you to describe all the necessary steps. If not, he asks you to analyse theoretically the situation where Article 2 of the State Responsibility Articles would be satisfied.

Nota bene

— Both Ceotu and Othree are members to the United Nations Framework Convention on Climate Change (UNFCCC) and the Kyoto Protocol. Furthermore, they both belong to the so-called Annex I countries having fixed reduction goals for GHGs under the Kyoto Protocol.

Case 8.14

Abbreviations used
Montreal Protocol = Montreal Protocol on Substances that Deplete the Ozone Layer
CFCs = chlorofluorocarbons

The Montreal Protocol on Substances that Deplete the Ozone Layer (Montreal Protocol) mandates a phasing out of the production as well as the consumption of a large number of ozone-depleting substances, including chlorofluorocarbons (CFCs). Thus, State parties have an obligation no longer to produce or consume these substances.

Argonia is a small country surrounded by two other States, Bismu and Chloland. Argonia has been very efficient in complying with the Montreal Protocol. This is mainly due to the fact that even though highly developed, Argonia does not produce its own CFCs. Furthermore, due to its high scientific standards it was relatively easy for this State to replace CFCs with other less harmful chemicals. However, credible scientific evidence (corroborated by information from Argonia's efficient secret service) shows that both Bismu and Chloland are still using as well as producing large amounts of CFCs.

The Minister for the Environment of Argonia finally decides to take action and sends a letter to the Secretariat of the Vienna Convention for the Protection of the Ozone Layer, informing it about the non-compliance of Bismu and Chloland. The letter is accompanied with the latest scientific evidence.

The President of Argonia hears about this letter and is suddenly afraid that this action was not in conformity with international law. He therefore contacts you, a specialist in international environmental law who is well acquainted with the working of the Montreal Protocol. He asks you whether the action taken by the Minister for the Environment was legal under international treaty law and what the possible consequences would be under the Montreal Protocol.

Nota bene

— Both Argonia and Bismu are parties to the Montreal Protocol and the Vienna Convention for the Protection of the Ozone Layer.
— Chloland is not a party to the Montreal Protocol and the Vienna Convention for the Protection of the Ozone Layer.
— Argonia, Bismu and Chloland are parties to the Vienna Convention on the Law of Treaties since its entry into force.

Recommended reading on international environmental law

Articles

Laurence Boisson de Chazournes, 'La mise en œuvre du droit international dans le domaine de la protection de l'environnement: enjeux et défis' (1995) 99 *Revue Générale de Droit International Public* 37.

Jutta Brunnée, 'Of Sense and Sensibility; Reflections on International Liability Regimes as Tools for Environmental Protection' (2004) 53 *International and Comparative Law Quarterly* 351.

Peter Grabosky, 'Green Markets: Environmental Regulation by the Private Sector'(1994) 16 *Law & Policy* 419.

Kal Raustiala, 'The "Participatory Revolution" in International Environmental Law' (1997) 21 *Harvard Environmental Law Review* 537.

Nicholas Robinson, 'Enforcing Environmental Norms: Diplomatic and Judicial Approaches' (2003) 26 *Hastings International and Comparative Law Review* 387.

Jorge Viñuales, 'Foreign Investment and the Environment in International Law: An Ambiguous Relationship' (2009) 80 *British Yearbook of International Law* 244.

Books

Patricia Birnie, Alan Boyle, and Catherine Redgwell, *International Law and the Environment*, 3rd edn (Oxford, Oxford University Press, 2009).

Daniel Bodansky, Jutta Brunnée and Ellen Hey (eds), *The Oxford Handbook of International Environmental Law* (Oxford, Oxford University Press, 2007).

Lakshman Guruswamy with Kevin Doran, *International Environmental Law in a Nutshell*, 3rd edn (St Paul MN, Thomson West, 2007).
Elisa Morgera, *Corporate Accountability in International Environmental Law*, (Oxford, Oxford University Press, 2009).
Philippe Sands, *Principles of International Environmental Law*, 2nd edn (Cambridge, Cambridge University Press, 2003).
Tullio Treves et al (eds), *Non-Compliance Procedures and Mechanisms and the Effectiveness of International Environmental Agreements* (The Hague, TMC Asser Press, 2009).
Edith Brown Weiss and Harold Jacobson (eds), *Engaging Countries—Strengthening Compliance with International Environmental Accords* (Cambridge MA, MIT Press, 1998).

Part II

SUGGESTED SOLUTIONS

Chapter 1

SUGGESTED SOLUTIONS
Subjects of Public International Law: States and International Organisations

SUGGESTED SOLUTIONS
The State and its constitutive elements

Suggested Solution—Case 1.1

1. Applicable law

There is no legally binding definition of a State. However, the most widely accepted definition of a State can be found in the Montevideo Convention on the Rights and Duties of States from 1933. This Convention is not universally legally binding since it has been concluded only among some Latin American States. Nevertheless, the definition of a State contained in its first Article is usually used to define States. Hence, we will also use it here.

According to Article 1 of the Montevideo Convention, there are four elements any entity has to have in order to be a State:

1. A permanent population (though the size of the population does not matter—in particular there is no minimum established. Otherwise, States with very small populations, such as Tuvalu, which has some 10,000 inhabitants, could never qualify as States).
2. A defined territory (however, the fact that some of its borders might still be disputed or the size of the territory are not relevant for this criterion).
3. A government (this is usually equated to the necessity of an entity to have internal sovereignty and control over its whole territory).
4. Capacity to enter into relations with other States (this is often termed external sovereignty).

It is useful to look at all four elements to see whether (and from when on) Merland can be considered to be a State.

2. Permanent Population

This criterion does not pose any problem. The four peoples live there and together constitute the permanent population. As noted above, the size (of which there is no indication) or the character (mixed here between four peoples) does not matter.

3. Defined territory

This criterion also does not seem to be problematic. What is known as 'Merland' clearly occupies a certain physical territory.

4. Government

On one hand, this requirement clearly means to have some governing organs such as a Parliament, but in addition, as stated above, the need to have a government is often equated with internal sovereignty, ie in order to be a State the entity should have control over its whole territory. (*It has to be admitted that in practice this criterion is not always respected and some have been called and recognised as States even before they actually controlled their territory*).

The Council of Merland created a number of institutions including a Parliament in 2000 and seems itself to be acting as a government. However, just having institutions is not enough. These institutions also need to be capable of acting and fulfilling governmental tasks. We know from the facts that Merland was able to handle almost all administrative tasks in 2002. This is an important step towards fulfilling the criterion of 'government'. Yet, as explained above, this third criterion is broader than just having executive, legislative and judiciary organs. It is also necessary that this government can actually control its own territory to the exclusion of other States (as was stated by Arbitrator Max Huber in the *Island of Palmas case*; Arbitral Tribunal, Award, *Island of Palmas case* (Netherlands, USA), 1928, at 838). Only then can it be said to be internally sovereign. However, we know that until the end of April 2004 the police forces were still from Oneland and not from Merland. Thus, it cannot be argued that Merland was actually internally sovereign before that date, since foreign police forces were responsible for 'law and order' and control in the territory. Only from May 2004 after the withdrawal of the police forces of the foreign State Oneland did Merland start to contol its territory by itself. The third criterion is thus only fulfilled from that date onwards.

5. Capacity to enter into legal relations with other States

Arguably, this is the most political of all the criteria. Recognition is crucial to fulfil this criterion, but recognition by other States is largely a political process. If no State recognises the entity in question as an equal to enter into treaty relations with each other, this entity cannot be considered to be a State (since it would then not be capable of entering into legal relations with other States). It is thereby difficult to say how many

States need to have recognised a new State. There is no absolute number, but it can be argued that today with over 190 States it has to be a good portion of them.

Merland became a party to several international conventions during 2003. In most cases only States can become parties to such conventions (unless the treaty specifically provides that other international actors such as international organisations can also become parties). Furthermore, Merland has also concluded a series of bilateral (commercial) treaties, thereby clearly indicating that others do recognise it as an equal partner. Thus, as can be seen by its various treaty relations established in 2003, Merland clearly is able to enter into legal relations with other States. Moreover, at the end of 2004 the majority of the international community had officially recognised Merland as an independent State. Thus, also this last element in order to be a State is fulfilled by Merland.

6. Conclusion

As established above, Merland clearly is a State today according to international law. We now have to determine from when on it can be considered to be a State.

Since the criteria of population and territory are not controversial here, the two other criteria will determine from when on Merland can be recognised as a State. It has to be pointed out that it might be difficult to establish the exact moment in practice since the creation of a new State is more often than not a subtle transition. However, as argued under the third element above, in order to be a State, the entity in question needs internal sovereignty. Since this can only be seen as fulfilled from 1 May 2004 onwards we can argue that Merland is a State under international law from 1 May 2004 onwards. We do not know how many States have recognised Merland at this moment. However, we do know that Merland has already entered into numerous treaty relations at this point in time. Since as pointed out above the number of other States recognising the new State is not fixed, we can say that the fact that Merland became a party to various international treaties is proof enough that it actually can enter into foreign legal relations, thereby fulfilling the fourth criterion.

Thus, following the arguments made above, Merland can be considered to be a State at the latest from 1 May 2004 onwards.

SUGGESTED SOLUTIONS
International Organisations

Suggested Solution—Case 1.2

Abbreviations used
IFPO = International Fund for the Protection of Orchids
ILC = International Law Commission

1. Applicable law

First of all it has to be recognised that there is no universally accepted definition of an international organisation. International organisations can thus present a wide variety of characteristics.

Nevertheless, while there are different definitions possible there seem to be three main criteria which we can identify from different approaches to define an international organisation.[1]

The three criteria in order to be an international organisation can be said to be the following:

1. The organisation needs to be established based on an international agreement.
2. The organisation needs to have an independent legal personality.
3. The organisation needs to be established under international law.

2. Establishment based on an international agreement

There seems to be general agreement on this point. Both scholars as well as the International Law Commission have included this element (in the ILC definition from 2003 it is noted that an international organisation needs to be established by 'treaty or other instrument', and Special Rapporteur Fitzmaurice talks about establishment by treaty as well). It is also necessary to note here that the denomination of the international agreement does not matter (see Article 2 paragraph 1(a) of the Vienna Convention on the Law of Treaties)—whether it is called 'agreement', 'treaty' or even 'charter' is irrelevant. Furthermore, we can also note that it is not important who is among the founding members of the organisation. The only requirement is that it is based on an international treaty, but as is well known international organisations can also enter into treaty relations either with other international organisations or with States (see the Vienna Convention on the Law of Treaties between States and International Organisa-

[1] See the following definitions: 'The term "international organization" means a collectivity of States established by treaty, with a constitution and common organs, having a personality distinct from that of its member-States, and being a subject of international law with treaty-making capacity' (Special Rapporteur Gerald Fitzmaurice, *Yearbook of the International Law Commission 1956*, Vol II, 108); 'For the purposes of the present draft articles [ie the draft articles on the Responsibility of International Organisations], the term "international organisation" refers to an organisation established by a treaty or other instrument governed by international law and possessing its own international legal personality. International organisations may include as members, in addition to States, other entities' (International Law Commission, Report of the 55th session (2003), UN Doc A/58/10, 38). Also see Schermers and Blokker, *International Institutional Law* (Martinus Nijhoff, Leiden, 2003) 21–36, which establish basically the same three criteria that will be analysed above.

tions or between International Organisations). It is thus irrelevant for qualification as an international organisation that among the founding members were not only States but also international organisations.

In our case, there is no doubt that the IFPO has been established by an international treaty, concluded by 24 States and an international organisation called the Orchid Society. In particular, the fact that the Orchid Society was among the founders does not preclude the IFPO from being an international organisation itself.

3. Independent legal personality *(see also next exercise)*

In order for an international organisation to perform its functions, it is necessary that it has its own legal personality (this has been confirmed by the International Court of Justice in its *Reparations of Injuries* Advisory Opinion (ICJ, Advisory Opinion *Reparations of Injuries Suffered in the Service of the United Nations*, 1949, 177–180)). This necessary requirement has been acknowledged in most descriptions or definitions as well. In that sense, Special Rapporteur Fitzmaurice mentions that international organisations need to have 'a personality distinct from that of its member-States', and the ILC definition from 2003 says that an international organisation is an organisation 'possessing its own international legal personality'.

If this requirement it not explicitly mentioned in the founding treaty, as is for example the case of the United Nations, it is admittedly not always easy to test (as can be seen, for example, by the lengths to which the International Court of Justice went in its Advisory Opinion mentioned above). However, in our case this does not pose a problem, since Article 38 of the treaty establishing the IFPO clearly States that this organisation is endowed with international legal personality.

[*Some authors, eg Schermers and Blokker, add to this second requirement that an international organisation needs to have at least one organ with a will of its own, which is independent of its members. This is, however, not a generally accepted criterion. Even if we would add this as a further condition to be fulfilled, the IFPO could still be seen as an international organisation. Article 3 creates the position (or 'organ') of the Director of the IFPO, while Article 4 sets up a permanent Secretariat. More importantly, however, Article 5 of the treaty establishing the IFPO provides that both organs previously established should 'under no circumstances' seek or receive instructions from governments but also other organisations. Therefore, it seems to be clear that the IFPO is endowed with more than one organ which has a will independent from that of the members.*]

4. Establishment under international law

If one looks at the various definitions, this point is also recurrent. The importance here is to make sure that the organisation is not established under national law, but really under international law. Normally, however, international treaties are always concluded under international law (which is in fact even part of the definition of a 'treaty' to be found in the Vienna Convention on the Law of Treaties). Hence, as long as no facts expressly indicate the contrary, we can reasonably assume that a treaty concluded between different States (and especially such a large number as 24 States as in our case) is concluded under international law and that consequently the organisation in question is indeed established under international law.

Furthermore, nothing in our case lets us suspect that the treaty establishing the IFPO was concluded under national law. Hence, the third requirement seems also be fulfilled in relation to the IFPO.

Other elements such as the name of the organisation ('fund' instead of 'organisation') are not relevant at all as to whether an entity is an international organisation. In that sense we can make an analogy to treaty law, where the denomination of the legally binding instrument does not matter either, as mentioned above. The important point is that the entity fulfils the elements analysed above. Furthermore, the type of members an organisation has is also not determinative, as can be seen in the ICL definition from 2003, which recognises that as well as States other entities can also be members of international organisations. Thus, the fact that the IFPO is open not only to States but also 'intergovernmental and scientific organisations active in that field' does not prevent the IFPO from being an international organisation.

5. Conclusion

In conclusion, we can say that there is no doubt that the IFPO fulfils all the necessary criteria in order to be an international organisation. [*However, we would like to stress again that this determination has been done based on the widest commonly accepted characteristics, but it has to be kept in mind that until now there is no universally accepted legal definition of an international organisation.*]

Suggested Solution—Case 1.3

Abbreviations used

ICJ	= International Court of Justice
IO	= International organisation
ODE	= Organisation for the Defence of the Environment
TODE	= Treaty on the Organisation for the Defence of the Environment
UN	= United Nations
VCLT	= Vienna Convention on the Law of Treaties

1. Applicable law

The (international) legal personality of the IO is essential for the performance of the functions of the organisation. If the organisation has no legal personality it cannot, for example, conclude treaties or bring court cases.

Today, most founding instruments of IOs contain a clause explicitly stating whether or not the organisation in question has legal personality (see eg the Rome Statute establishing the International Criminal Court, which States in Article 4 paragraph 1 that 'the Court shall have international legal personality'). Where this is not the case, as for example in the UN Charter, interpretations are necessary, which can be seen by the long analysis made by the ICJ in its *Reparations of Injuries* Advisory Opinion (ICJ, Advisory Opinion, *Reparations of Injuries Suffered in the Service of the United Nations*, 1949, 177–180).

There, the ICJ held, among other things, that the UN needed to have international legal personality in order to carry out its functions. Without this personality, the UN could not act in the fulfilment of its tasks, which could not have been the intention of the founders. Therefore, the UN was deemed to have international legal personality. The ICJ, however, also stressed that acknowledging the international legal personality of an IO was not the same as saying that this organisation is a State (or even a 'super-State'), nor does it mean that the IO necessarily has the same powers as a State.

2. Application to the ODE

In our case, we can first of all observe that Article 87 paragraph 1 of the Treaty establishing the ODE provides that the organisation has full legal personality. Furthermore, the same Article adds that the ODE under its legal personality also has the right to bring claims in justice. In that sense, it seems clear that the ODE is entitled to bring international claims against States.

The first argument made by Hydrocarbu, that the ODE could not be equal to or assimilated to a State, has to be rejected. As seen above, acknowledging the legal personality of an IO (explicitly in the founding treaty or implicitly later on) does not mean that the IO is 'equal' to a State. It does not have the same functions. The IO only has the necessary international legal personality to carry out its functions and is thus necessarily limited in comparison with a State.

3. Possibility of claims against non-members?

Yet, the difficulty, which is also detected by Hydrocarbu in its second argument, lies in the fact that Hydrocarbu is not a member of the ODE. We have therefore to assess whether it is possible for the ODE to bring an international claim against a State not party to its founding treaty. This is not to put in doubt our previous conclusion that the ODE has an international legal personality, but we have to assess whether this international legal personality extends to all States or is limited to the States that have ratified the TODE.

In the *Reparations of Injuries* Advisory Opinion (ICJ, Advisory Opinion, *Reparations of Injuries Suffered in the Service of the United Nations*, 1949, 185), the ICJ answered the same question in the affirmative based on the following reasons. The Court held that 50 States—the founding States of the UN—were a 'vast majority of the international community', which were able in accordance with international law to bring into being an entity having so-called *objective* international legal personality. This means that the legal personality was existing for all States and not just for the UN Member States.

However, it is highly questionable whether a similar argument can be made today. First of all, it is well recognised that in general treaties are not binding on third States without their consent (Article 34 VCLT) and especially if they impose an obligation on a third State, this State expressly has to accept this in writing (Article 35 VCLT). In our case, no such written acceptance exists.

In addition, the international community has grown considerably since the creation of the UN. While in 1949 50 States might have constituted the 'vast majority of the international community', the same clearly cannot be said about 20 States in 2005. Therefore, the number of State parties to the TODE is not important enough to argue that they could have established an international organisation with international legal personality binding on all States.

4. Conclusion

We can conclude that the ODE has international legal personality based on its own founding treaty. Nevertheless, it cannot bring an international claim against Hydrocarbu, since this State is not a party to the TODE and the number of 20 States is not significant enough to establish that they can create an organisation with an international legal personality binding on all members and non-members alike.

Chapter 2

SUGGESTED SOLUTIONS
Diplomatic Protection

Suggested Solution—Case 2.1

Abbreviations used

CAT	=	Convention on Torture and Other Cruel, Inhuman or Degrading Treatment or Punishment
ICCPR	=	International Covenant on Civil and Political Rights
ICJ	=	International Court of Justice
ILC	=	International Law Commission
PCIJ	=	Permanent Court of International Justice

1. Applicable law

There is no legally binding convention on the issues of diplomatic protection. However, it is widely recognised that the Draft Articles on Diplomatic Protection, adopted by the International Law Commission in 2006 (hereinafter the Draft Articles), reflect to a large extent customary international law. The ILC working group on Diplomatic Protection did not only expressly base themselves on customary law when elaborating the Draft Articles,[1] but in addition the International Court of Justice (ICJ) has confirmed at least parts of the Draft Articles as customary law (see eg the *Diallo* case (ICJ, Judgment on Preliminary Objections, *Ahamdou Sadio Diallo* (Republic of Guinea v Democratic Republic of the Congo), 2007, paragraph 39).

Therefore, we will apply customary international law in the matter of diplomatic protection, as reflected in the ILC's Draft Articles on Diplomatic Protection.

In addition, we will also apply the ICCPR and the CAT, to which both States are parties.

[1] Report of the Commission to the General Assembly on the work of its fiftieth session, *Yearbook of the International Law Commission*, Vol II (1998) 49, para 108.

2. Violation of an international rule with regards to a foreigner

In order for Saoseo to be able to exercise diplomatic protection, it has first to be shown that there was a violation of a rule which was directly owed to a foreigner.

In our case, Oscar Lai was arrested at random at a peaceful demonstration, he was held in custody without knowing what charges he faced and without the possibility of contacting anyone, and he was beaten by policemen during interrogation, which caused him several broken ribs. The last act could potentially qualify as torture, or at least as inhuman treatment, under Article 1 CAT: Oscar was beaten and his ribs broken, which causes severe physical pain. Furthermore, these beatings were done intentionally and only after Oscar was not able to give the expected answer. So we could say that these police officers (who are—like all members of the police forces—public officials) started to beat him to get information or a confession from him.

In addition, we can say that Alzasca did not only violate the CAT, but also the ICCPR, namely Article 7 (torture), Article 9 (no arbitrary arrest or detention; prompt information about the charges) and eventually also Article 10 (person deprived of their liberty has to be treated with humanity and respect). It is important to stress here that what has to be shown at this stage is that there is a *claim* concerning such a violation of a right of a foreigner. It is not necessary that it is already now established beyond all reasonable doubt that the acts in question amount to these violations. This is a matter to be determined by the courts later on.

It is furthermore clear that the injured individual, ie Oscar Lai, is a foreigner, since he is a national from Saoseo and not from Alzasca. Thus the condition *ratione personae* is satisfied. The condition *ratione materiae* is equally fulfilled, since human rights which are violated here are owed directly to any individual (regardless of their nationality) within the jurisdiction of the State, thus of Alzasca (see eg Article 2 ICCPR).

Thus, we have established that there is indeed a violation of an international norm with regards to a foreigner.

3. Link of nationality

The second element necessary for a State to exercise diplomatic protection is the link of nationality between the injured individual and the State in question. Thereby, three separate elements have to be tested.

(a) Validity

It has to be ascertained whether the nationality has been validly granted. This is usually not contested, since it falls within the competence of each State to decide how and to whom it grants its nationality. This has been recognised by the Permanent Court of International Justice in the *Nationality Decrees in Tunis and Morocco* advisory opinion (PCIJ, Advisory Opinion, *Nationality Decrees Issued in Tunis and Morocco*, 1923, 22–24), but is now also reflected in Article 4 of the Draft Articles when it mentions that the nationality of the person is 'acquired in accordance with the law of that State'.

Thus, in our case Oscar Lai is a national of Saoseo and there is nothing that indicates that this nationality was not validly acquired.

(b) Continuity

In order to exercise diplomatic protection, the nationality of the State wishing to exercise this protection has to exist both at the time of the commission of the violation and at the time of the presentation of the claim. This customary rule is reflected in Article 5 of the Draft Articles.

This does not pose any problems here either, since Oscar Lai was a national of Saoseo both at the time when his human rights were violated by Alzasca and now, at the time when Saoseo wants to bring the claim for diplomatic protection. Hence, the second element is also fulfilled.

(c) Opposability

Since Oscar Lai only has one nationality, no difficult issues concerning the potential parallel exercise of diplomatic protection arises. Only Saoseo as the national State of Oscar is entitled to exercise diplomatic protection. Even though the ICJ in the *Nottebohm* case (ICJ, Judgment, *Nottebohm* (Liechtenstein v Guatemala), 1955, 21–23) raised some doubts whether or not the 'genuine link' requirement had to be examined also in case of single nationals, it is today accepted that single nationalities are ipso facto opposable to other States. This solution is also reflected in Article 4 of the Draft Articles. Were it otherwise, millions of people with one nationality but not living in their State of nationality (so potentially with no genuine link to their State of nationality) would be rendered 'stateless' for the purpose of diplomatic protection: the State of nationality could never protect them due to the lack of a genuine link, but neither could any other State, including the State of habitual residence, exercise diplomatic protection, due to the lack of a link of nationality.

Therefore, the nationality from Saoseo of Oscar is automatically opposable to Alzasca and we can conclude that a link of nationality between Oscar and Saoseo exists.

4. Exhaustion of local remedies

The last element to be assessed is whether local remedies have been exhausted. A State can only exercise diplomatic protection on behalf of one of its nationals after all the local remedies have been exhausted. The underlying reason is to give the 'wrongdoing' State a chance to 'make the wrong right'. This customary rule is also reflected in Article 14 of the Draft Articles and has for example been set out by the ICJ in the *Interhandel* case (ICJ, Judgment on Preliminary Objections, *Interhandel* (Switzerland v United States of America), 1959, 27).

In our case, Oscar Lai brought his case to the courts of Alzasca and he even went as far as the High Court, the highest instance. But all the courts rejected his claims, for reasons which are not totally clear. In any event, local remedies have been exhausted. Therefore, the last element is also fulfilled.

5. Conclusion

Seeing that all three elements—violation, link of nationality and exhaustion of local remedies—are fulfilled, we can conclude that Saoseo is entitled to exercise diplomatic protection on behalf of its national Oscar Lai against Alzasca.

It is important to recall here that the exercise of diplomatic protection is a discretionary right of the State and not a right of the individual. Thus, even if all the elements are established as in the present case, there is no obligation in international law that Saoseao *has* to exercise diplomatic protection, but the conclusion is rather that it *can* do so if it wishes.

Suggested Solution—Case 2.2

Abbreviations used

ECHR = European Convention on Human Rights
ICCPR = International Covenant on Civil and Political Rights
ICJ = International Court of Justice
ILC = International Law Commission
PCIJ = Permanent Court of International Justice

1. Applicable law

We will apply the International Law Commission's (ILC) Draft Articles on Diplomatic Protection adopted in 2006 (hereinafter the Draft Articles). It is important to note that this is not a treaty and thus not legally binding as such. But it is widely acknowledged that most of the Draft Articles reflect customary law. The International Court of Justice (ICJ) has recognised this, for example in the *Diallo* case (ICJ, Judgment on Preliminary Objections, *Ahamdou Sadio Diallo* (Republic of Guinea v Democratic Republic of the Congo), 2007, paragraph 39).

Furthermore, we will also apply the International Covenant on Civil and Political Rights (ICCPR), and the European Convention on Human Rights (ECHR), to which Thoris, Mantiko and Behem are all parties and therefore bound by their obligations.

In order for a State to be able to exercise diplomatic protection on behalf of one of its nationals, three main elements need to be fulfilled: violation of an international obligation owed to a foreigner, link of nationality and exhaustion of local remedies.

2. Violation of an international rule with regards to a foreigner

There needs to be a violation of a rule of international law; that rule must be owed directly to an individual and in addition that individual needs to be a foreigner.

Lily Fenix is arrested in 2006 and questioned about the criminal activities of her husband. Although the police has to accept that she does not know anything and is not involved in criminal activities, she is not released but kept in prison for roughly four more years (she is released in 2010). During all that time she has never been charged with anything. She has basically been held as a hostage by the government of Thoris in the hope of luring her husband back, but without success.

Article 9 ICCPR provides that everyone has the right to liberty and security of person and that no one shall be subjected to arbitrary arrest or detention (paragraph 1). Furthermore, everyone shall promptly be informed about the charges against him/her (paragraph 2) and everyone arrested on criminal charges shall be brought promptly before a judge and is entitled to a trial within a reasonable delay (paragraph 3).

No charges are ever brought against Lily Fenix, but nevertheless she has been kept in custody for four years. However, holding someone in custody for such a long time without any charges, and consequently also no trial, clearly violates Article 9 ICCPR. While maybe her arrest was not arbitrary since she was suspected of being the accomplice of her husband, the prolonged detention after the police realised that she was innocent was purely arbitrary and violated her right to liberty enshrined in Article 9 ICCPR.

Article 5 ECHR contains a similar right to liberty and security, which is consequently also violated by Thoris.

The victim of these violations in Thoris is Lily Fenix, a national of Behem and Mantiko. Thoris has rejected her request for nationalisation in Thoris. She is therefore clearly a foreigner in Thoris, and hence fulfils the condition *ratione personae* concerning the violation of the international norm.

In addition, to fulfil the condition *ratione materiae*, it is necessary that this international rule be directly owed to that foreigner. Human rights such as those in the ICCPR and the ECHR are directly owed to individuals as human beings. Therefore, this condition is also fulfilled.

We can consequently conclude that Thoris has indeed violated an international norm with regard to a foreigner by imprisoning Lily Fenix for four years without charges. The first argument made by Thoris—that there is no violation—hence cannot be accepted.

3. Link of nationality

In order to be able to exercise diplomatic protection, it is crucial to establish the necessary link of nationality. There are three points that need to be ascertained.

(a) Validity

It is widely accepted that the conditions under which a State wants to grant its nationality to a person forms part of each State's reserved domain. This has, for example, been recognised by the Permanent Court of International Justice in the *Nationality Decrees in Tunis and Morocco* case (PCIJ, Advisory Opinion, *Nationality Decrees Issued in Tunis and Morocco*, 1923, 22–24). Therefore, if there is no evidence to the contrary, it is usually assumed that the nationality has been granted validly. This has also been incorporated in Article 4 of the Draft Articles.

Lily Fenix is a national of both Behem and Mantiko.

The national law of Behem provides that every person born in its territory will automatically acquire the nationality of Behem. Since Lily Fenix is born in Behem, this nationality has been validly acquired. Mantiko, on the other hand, grants its nationality according to the *jus sanguinis* rule, that is when the parents are nationals from Mantiko, their children will also be nationals of Mantiko, regardless of their place of birth. Lily Fenix's parents are both nationals from Mantiko, consequently Lily's Mantikoan nationality has also been validly acquired.

(b) Continuity

For the purposes of diplomatic protection, it is important that the nationality of the State wanting to exercise this protection existed at the time when the violation occurred and at the time when the claim of diplomatic protection is presented. This rule has been codified in Article 5 of the Draft Articles.

This condition is not problematic in our case, since Lily Fenix was a national of Behem and especially Mantiko both at the time of the human rights violations (from 2006 to 2010) and now, at the time when Mantiko wants to exercise diplomatic protection on her behalf.

(c) Opposability

We are confronted here with a case of double nationality, where the claim of diplomatic protection is exercised against a third State.

It is true that in the past situations of double nationals have been more problematic than those of single nationals for the purpose of diplomatic protection. However, an Arbitral Tribunal in the *Salem* case (Arbitral Tribunal, Award, *Salem Case* (Egypt v USA), 1932, 1188) established as long ago as 1932 that if diplomatic protection is to be exercised on behalf of a double national against a third State (ie not a State of nationality), there is no need to establish an effective link. This makes sense, since exercising diplomatic protection against a third State is not violating in any way the sovereignty of that third State, since it has no special right over this person which is not its national. This solution has also been codified in Article 6 of the Draft Articles, clearly stating that '*any* State of which a dual or multiple national is a national may exercise diplomatic protection in respect of that national against a State of which that person is not a national'.

Therefore, it is not necessary to establish an effective link as shown in the ICJ's *Nottebohm* case (ICJ, Judgment, *Nottebohm* (Liechtenstein v Guatemala), 1955, 22) between Lily and Mantiko. The fact that Lily has never lived in Mantiko is therefore irrelevant in this case against Thoris. Thus, Thoris's second argument has to be rejected as well. In addition, Thoris's third argument, that the only real links are to Thoris and hence no other State can exercise diplomatic protection, is also not valid either. Diplomatic protection can be exercised only by States of nationality. Since Thoris is not a State of nationality of Lily, it can consequently not exercise diplomatic protection on her behalf and also cannot bar other States such as Mantiko from doing so.

Concluding, we can say that the link of nationality between Lily Fenix and Mantiko is existent and that there is no need to establish an effective link since Thoris is a third State and not a State of nationality.

4. Exhaustion of local remedies

The last element to be assessed is whether local remedies have been exhausted. A State can only exercise diplomatic protection on behalf of one of its nationals after all the local remedies have been exhausted. The underlying reason is to give the State that has violated an international obligation a chance to 'make the wrong right'. This condition is in fact a customary rule and is also reflected in Article 14 of the Draft Articles. It has also, for example, been set out by the ICJ in the *Interhandel* case (ICJ, Judgment on Preliminary Objections, *Interhandel* (Switzerland v United States of America), 1959, 27).

In our case, Lily Fenix has indeed brought her case to justice in Thoris up to the Supreme Court. Yet, the courts have all rejected her claim by stating that the fight against criminal activities is more important than human rights. Since Lily has not had any success in getting redress in the national system, the local remedies can indeed be said to be exhausted.

Consequently, the third necessary element is also fulfilled.

5. Conclusion

In conclusion, we can say that since the necessary three elements are fulfilled, Mantiko as one of the States of nationality of Lily Fenix is entitled (but not obliged) to exercise diplomatic protection on her behalf against the State of Thoris.

Suggested Solution—Case 2.3

Abbreviations used

ICCPR = International Covenant on Civil and Political Rights
ICJ = International Court of Justice
ILC = International Law Commission
PCIJ = Permanent Court of International Justice

1. Applicable law

We will apply the International Law Commission's (ILC) Draft Articles on Diplomatic Protection adopted in 2006 (hereinafter the Draft Articles). It is important to note that this is not a treaty and thus not legally binding as such. But it is widely acknowledged that most of the Draft Articles reflect customary law. The International Court of Justice has recognised, for example in the *Diallo* case (ICJ, Judgment on Preliminary Objections, *Ahamdou Sadio Diallo* (Republic of Guinea v Democratic Republic of the Congo), 2007, paragraph 39), that some of the rules are customary law. Furthermore, the ILC working group on Diplomatic Protection stated that they based themselves on customary law when elaborating the Draft Articles.[2]

[2] Report of the Commission to the General Assembly on the work of its fiftieth session, *Yearbook of the International Law Commission*, Vol II (1998) 49, para 108.

In addition, we will also apply the International Covenant on Civil and Political Rights (ICCPR), to which Toissa is a party.

Three elements need to be fulfilled in order for a State to be able to exercise diplomatic protection on behalf of one of its nationals: violation of an international obligation owed to a foreigner, link of nationality and exhaustion of local remedies.

2. Violation of an international rule with regards to a foreigner

There needs to be a violation of a rule of international law, that rule must be owed directly to an individual and in addition that individual needs to be a foreigner.

In our case, Mischa Dom is arrested without charges and is kept in jail for three days without being informed of the reasons for his detention. This can amount to a violation of Article 9 ICCPR, which States that no one shall be subjected to arbitrary arrest or detention and, if detained, everyone should promptly be informed about the reasons for the arrest. Nevertheless, Mischa Dom is never informed about the reasons for his detention.

Furthermore, Article 19 ICCPR could also be seen as violated. Article 19 provides for the freedom of expression. The newspaper of Mischa Dom and his articles were censured by the government authorities. And, when he is released from prison, Mischa Dom is threatened with 'serious consequences' if he does not stop writing his (critical) articles. This is a violation of the freedom of expression, since what is sought to be achieved is that Mischa Dom can no longer express his opinion. The exceptions found in paragraph 3 of Article 19 do not seem to be applicable since by exposing the truth about corruption and nepotism, it can hardly be said that national security is endangered and no *right* of someone else is affected.

It is important to point out that it is not necessary to provide full evidence that these violations have actually happened and fulfil all the necessary elements under a specific Article. We only have to show that there is a *claim* that these violations happened, which thus just needs some factual elements but no proof 'beyond all reasonable doubt'.

The victim of the violations noted above is Mischa Dom. He is both a foreigner (national of Etzel) and a national of Toissa. However, at this stage we are not concerned in establishing the 'primacy' of any of his two nationalities. It is enough to note here that Mischa Dom, being also a national of Etzel, can indeed satisfy the personal conditions, namely that the victim of the violation must be a foreigner. In addition, the rights that are allegedly violated must be directly owed to the individual in question. Like all human rights, the rights contained in the ICCPR are indeed directly owed to the individual, as can be seen in Article 2 ICCPR. Therefore, the condition *ratione materiae* is also satisfied.

Thus, the first condition, existence of a violation with regards to a foreigner, is satisfied.

3. Link of nationality

Under this criterion, three points have to be assessed.

(a) Validity

It is widely accepted that it is up to each State to determine the conditions under which it wants to grant its nationality to a person. This has, for example, been recognised by the Permanent Court of International Justice in the *Nationality Decrees in Tunis and Morocco* case (PCIJ, Advisory Opinion, *Nationality Decrees Issued in Tunis and Morocco*, 1923, 22–24). Therefore, if there is no evidence to the contrary, it is usually assumed that the nationality has been granted validly. This has also been incorporated in Article 4 of the Draft Articles.

Mischa Dom has had the nationality of Etzel since he was born and nothing suggests that this is not a valid nationality. As for his Toissan nationality, Mischa Dom acquired it through marriage to a national of Toissa, in conformity with the national law of this State. Therefore, this nationality too seems to be valid.

(b) Continuity

Continuity means that the nationality of the State that wants to exercise diplomatic protection existed continuously from the time of the violation to the time of the presentation of the claim. This requirement has also been codified in Article 5 of the Draft Articles.

This does not seem to be a problem here either, since both nationalities of Mischa Dom existed at the time of the violation as well as at the time when the claim is made (or considered to be made).

(c) Opposability

Our case is a case of multiple nationalities, where the claim is brought against one of the States of nationality. This is the most complex situation concerning opposability. Previously it was considered that under these circumstances no diplomatic protection was possible at all. The reason was that the opposed States were both States of nationality of the individual in question and so they had the same 'claim' to the individual and no one could be 'prime' over the other. However, over the years another approach has emerged, namely to allow the State with which the individual had the 'more genuine link' to exercise diplomatic protection against the other State of nationality. Article 7 of the Draft Articles has also incorporated this solution, by speaking of a 'predominant nationality'. The origin of the genuine link or predominance test can be found in the ICJ judgment in the *Nottebohm* case (ICJ, Judgment, *Nottebohm* (Liechtenstein v Guatemala), 1955, 22). There, the ICJ also gives some indications concerning what to look at when assessing the genuine link of an individual. It mentioned habitual place of residence, family ties, work, 'centre of life' and so on.

Mischa Dom has first lived in Etzel but after his studies moved to Toissa, where he has lived and worked ever since. He is married to a citizen of Toissa and has a house there. Furthermore, it is stated that the couple went to Etzel only for holidays and that after his parents have passed away in 2004 until early 2011 (when all the court proceedings have ended) they went back to Etzel only twice. It seems, therefore, that Mischa Dom's most important ties (family, work, habitual place of residence) are all in Toissa. Therefore, we have to consider that there is a genuine link with Toissa, but not with Etzel.

As a consequence, Etzel cannot exercise diplomatic protection on behalf of Mischa Dom against his other State of nationality, Toissa.

4. Conclusion

Since we have established above that the opposability of the nationality of Etzel is lacking and that therefore Etzel cannot exercise diplomatic protection, we do not have to assess whether all local remedies have been exhausted. The lack in the criterion of the link of nationality has as a consequence that Etzel in any event cannot exercise diplomatic protection on behalf of Mischa Dom against Toissa, regardless of whether or not local remedies have been exhausted.

Suggested Solution—Case 2.4

Abbreviations used

BI = Beverages Inc (company)
ECHR = European Convention on Human Rights
ICJ = International Court of Justice
ILC = International Law Commission

1. Applicable law

There is no legally binding convention on the rules of diplomatic protection. However, the International Law Commission (ILC) has adopted in 2006 Draft Articles on Diplomatic Protection (hereinafter the Draft Articles). It is widely recognised that these Draft Articles reflect international customary law in the matter of diplomatic protection. This has also been pointed out for some Articles in the *Diallo* case (ICJ, Judgment on Preliminary Objections, *Ahamdou Sadio Diallo* (Republic of Guinea v Democratic Republic of the Congo), 2007, paragraph 39). Therefore, we will apply customary law concerning diplomatic protection, as reflected in the ILC's Draft Articles.

Furthermore, we will also apply the European Convention on Human Rights (ECHR) and all its protocols, to which both States in question are parties.

2. Violation of an international obligation with regards to a foreigner

According to Article 1 of Protocol 1 to the ECHR 'Every natural or legal person is entitled to the peaceful enjoyment of his possessions. No one shall be deprived of his possessions except in the public interest and subject to the conditions provided for by law and by the general principles of international law.' Thus, by expropriating BI and not paying any compensation at all, Sico can be said to have violated this provision.

[*Depending on how you argue, it might be possible—although a little far fetched—to claim that the expropriation of BI was done for reasons of public interest, namely the protection of health of the population and would thus be justified. Yet, under international law it is undisputed that* some *form of compensation is due to the expropriated company. Thus, Article 1 of Protocol 1 would most likely have been violated nevertheless, due to the lack of compensation. However, it should be noted that there are differing views on the appropriate level of compensation, ranging from 'full' to 'just' and 'appropriate' compensation.*[3] *While each of these terms is subject to differing interpretations, it seems that in most instances a sort of balancing will have to be done to determine the appropriate level of compensation*].

The victim of this violation is a foreign legal person, namely BI, which is registered in Kala and only has subsidiaries in Sico. Thus, the condition *ratione personae* is also fulfilled. Moreover, the obligation not to be deprived of one's property is directly owed to natural and legal persons, so the condition *ratione materiae* is also fulfilled.

In conclusion we can therefore say that the authorities of Sico have indeed committed a violation of an international obligation with regards to a foreigner.

3. Link of nationality

There needs to exist a link of nationality between the 'victim' and the State wishing to exercise diplomatic protection on his behalf. This link needs to be established based on three elements.

(a) Validity

In our case, the victim is not a natural but a legal person, a company. For companies, it has been held that normally the State of incorporation will be seen as the State of nationality. This approach has also been incorporated in Article 9 of the Draft Articles. In our case, it is clearly stated that BI is incorporated in Kala. We do not know anything about incorporation in Sico and can therefore assume that this was not a necessary condition to do business there. Thus, Kala as the State of incorporation can be considered as the State of nationality of BI and thus this 'nationality' is validly granted.

(b) Continuity

As with natural persons, it is necessary that the same nationality existed continuously from the date of the violation to the date of the presentation of the claim. Concerning companies this has been set out in Article 10 of the Draft Articles. Here, BI was incorporated and thus a national of Kala both at the time of the commission of the expropriation and at the time of the presentation of the claim and thus this requirement is also fulfilled.

(c) Opposability

This does not constitute a problem in our case, since there is no other State which could

[3] See eg the *Chorzów Factory* case (PCIJ, Judgment, *Case Concerning the Factory at Chorzów (Claim for Indemnity, Merits)*, 1928, 47 (as the first case on the issue); see also decisions by the Iran–US Claims Tribunal or relevant decisions by courts and tribunals such as the International Center for the Settlement of Investment Disputes (ICSID), as well as the European Court of Human Rights and the Inter-American Court of Human Rights. For an overview see eg www.wfu.edu/~palmitar/Law&Valuation/Papers/2001/Smith.htm.

also be considered to be a State of nationality of BI. Thus, the nationality of Kala is opposable to Sico.

We have therefore established that there indeed exists a link of nationality between BI and Kala.

5. Exhaustion of local remedies

The last element to be tested before we can conclude on the exercise of diplomatic protection by Kala is whether local remedies have been exhausted by BI in Sico. The requirement that local remedies must be exhausted first has been codified in Article 14 of the Draft Articles and was for example explicitly mentioned by the ICJ in the *Interhandel* case (ICJ, Judgment on Preliminary Objections, *Interhandel* (Switzerland v United States of America), 1959, 27). The underlying reason is that the State which has violated an international obligation should get a chance to redress the situation on its own, ie through its national courts.

It should be noted here that in our case local remedies do not seem to have been exhausted. The manager of BI only went to the first court and not all the way up to the highest instance. However, the fact that he was told (at the court but also by other sources) that BI could never bring a claim to a national court of Sico since it was a foreign company is very relevant. Customary law reflected in Article 15 of the Draft Articles foresees some exceptional circumstances when local remedies have not to be exhausted. One possible exception is thereby letter (d), stating that local remedies have not to be exhausted if 'the injured person is manifestly precluded from pursuing local remedies'. This seems to be applicable here, since even though there are local remedies, it appears that BI as a foreign company cannot bring a claim there. It would be unreasonable to expect in these circumstances that an injured person has to exhaust local remedies, since this is simply not possible and consequently these persons could never be protected by their State of nationality under diplomatic protection.

Thus, it is clear that in our case there is an exception to the requirement of exhausting local remedies and therefore these remedies do not need to be exhausted.

5. Conclusion

Since all three elements explained above (violation, link of nationality, exhaustion of local remedies) are fulfilled, we can concluded that Kala is entitled (but not obliged) to exercise diplomatic protection on behalf of the company BI against Sico.

Suggested Solution—Case 2.5

Abbreviations used

CPE	= Council for the Protection of the Environment
ICJ	= International Court of Justice
PCIJ	= Permanent Court of International Justice
The Convention	= Convention on the Privileges and Immunities of the United Nations of 13 February 1946
UN	= United Nations

1. Applicable law

In order to solve this question we will apply the Convention on the Privileges and Immunities of the United Nations of 13 February 1946 (hereinafter the Convention). Brutland, the State which has arrested and imprisoned Mr Fleurrose and which denies him immunity, is a party to this Convention, which is thus applicable to it.

In addition we will also apply customary international law in the matter of diplomatic protection. These rules are reflected in the ILC Draft Articles on Diplomatic Protection from 2006 (hereinafter the Draft Articles). The ICJ has confirmed the customary nature of most of these draft rules, for example in the *Diallo* case (ICJ, Judgment on Preliminary Objections, *Ahamdou Sadio Diallo* (Republic of Guinea v Democratic Republic of the Congo), 2007, paragraph 39).

2. Question asked by the General Assembly: is the Convention on the Privileges and Immunities of the United Nations of 13 February 1946 applicable to experts of the CPE?

First of all, it should be noted that the CPE is created by the UN General Assembly as one of its subsidiary organs. It is therefore part of the United Nations. According to the Convention's preamble it is applicable to the organisation of the United Nations, which consequently would include the CPE as part of this organisation.

Furthermore, the Convention divides the staff members of the UN into three different categories for the purposes of immunities and thus also for functional protection:

1. The Secretary-General and Assistant Secretary-Generals have immunities *ratione personae* (Article V paragraph 19).
2. All other officials of the organisation enjoy immunities *ratione materiae* (Article V paragraph 18(a)).
3. Experts on mission also have immunities *ratione materiae* as well as some limited personal inviolability (immunity *ratione personae*) in light to their need to travel freely in the performance of their mission (Article VI paragraph 22).

In our case, Mr Fleurrose is an official of the UN (ie of a UN organ, namely the CPE). He is sent on a mission to Brutland by the CPE and should therefore rather be considered to be an expert on mission and consequently benefit from this protection.

Particularly relevant to our case is Article VI paragraph 22(b), which provides that experts on mission shall benefit from 'immunity from legal process of every kind' for 'words spoken or written and acts done by them in the course of the performance of their mission'.

Since, as seen above, experts on mission mainly enjoy immunities *ratione materiae* it is relevant to determine what exactly constitutes an 'official act', ie an act 'done in the course of the performance of their mission'. In particular, it is important to clarify who determines what an official act is or is not, since often—as is also the case here—there seems to be disagreement between the UN who declares something to be an official act, and the State who holds it is not an official act and thus the expert does not benefit from his immunity. The ICJ was confronted with a similar question in the so-called *Cumaraswamy* case (ICJ, Advisory Opinion, *Difference Relating to Immunity from Legal Process of a Special Rapporteur of the Commission on Human Rights*, 1999, paragraphs 60, 61). There, the ICJ held that when a national court has to deal with a case involving the immunity of a UN agent, the national court should be informed about any finding by the UN Secretary General concerning this immunity. The finding of immunity then creates a presumption which can only be set aside by the national court 'for the most compelling reasons'. Thus, in the end it is the national court which has to make the final determination whether or not an act constitutes an official act. However, if the UN itself declares this to be an official act and thus benefiting from immunity, the national court can only go against this finding if it has very good and pressing reasons.

In our case, the UN legal advisor asked the permanent representative of Brutland to inform the relevant national court that Mr Fluerrose enjoyed immunity from jurisdiction for the acts done during his mission and that he could thus not be judged. There is thus a strong presumption that Mr Fleurrose indeed has immunity and the national court needs to show 'the most compelling reasons' if it does not want to respect this immunity. Simply stating that giving interviews and defaming State companies were not part of the official functions of an expert would not satisfy the requirement of 'most compelling reasons'. In addition, as mentioned above, Article VI paragraph 22(b) clearly States that experts on mission benefit from immunity from jurisdiction also for 'words spoken' during their mission. Mr Fleurrose gave the interview in his *official* capacity as an expert of the CPE. Thus, the interview was clearly connected to the exercise of his mission, namely to ascertain the behavior of the two oil companies in Brutland. Therefore, Article VI paragraph 22(b) is applicable and further strengthens the presumption that Mr Fleurrose indeed benefits from immunity from jurisdiction (in that sense, see the *Cumaraswamy* case (ICJ, Advisory Opinion, *Difference Relating to Immunity from Legal Process of a Special Rapporteur of the Commission on Human Rights*, 1999, paragraphs 50–52).

Hence, we can conclude that the Convention is indeed applicable to Mr Fleurrose, an expert on mission from the CPE, and that he benefits from immunity from jurisdiction also for the interviews he has given.

Since the Convention is applicable, this also means that the UN is entitled to exercise functional protection for the benefit of Mr Fleurrose.

3. Can Tulipland exercise diplomatic protection on behalf of Mr Fleurrose, excluding the protection granted under the Convention on the Privileges and Immunities of the United Nations of 13 February 1946?

In this question we are not only asked to clarify whether Tulipland can exercise diplomatic protection on behalf of Mr Fleurrose, but also whether in the exercise of diplomatic protection Tulipland can bar the UN from exercising its functional protection established above.

The main difference to be noted between diplomatic and functional protection is the link which is required between the individual and the entity wanting to exercise protection. While in diplomatic protection, this link is based on the nationality of the individual, in functional protection the link is based on the individual's status as an agent of the organisation.

To give an answer to this question, we have first to ascertain whether or not Tulipland can exercise diplomatic protection at all.

Violation of an international rule with regards to a foreigner

There needs to be a violation of a rule of international law, that rule must be owed directly to an individual and in addition that individual needs to be a foreigner.

Mr Fleurrose is a national from Tulipland, so he clearly is a foreigner in Brutland. In addition, he has been the victim of torture while he was imprisoned in Brutland. The prohibition of torture is a well-established rule of customary international law; it is therefore not necessary to know whether Brutland is bound by any of the human rights instruments prohibiting torture. Furthermore, such human rights obligations are directly owed to the individual, since it is the individual as human being who is directly protected (and benefiting) from them.

Therefore, we can conclude that there has indeed been a violation of an international rule with regards to a foreigner.

Link of nationality

Under this element three points need to be assessed.

(a) Validity

A nationality has to be validly granted. It is, however, well accepted that it is up to each State to determine under which conditions it wants to grant its nationalities. This has been confirmed by the PCIJ in the *Nationality Decrees in Tunis and Morocco* case (PCIJ, Advisory Opinion, *Nationality Decrees Issued in Tunis and Morocco*, 1923, 22–24). Hence, if there is no evidence to the contrary, it is usually assumed that the nationality has been validly granted. This approach has also been adopted by the ILC in Article 4 of the Draft Articles.

There is nothing that would suggest that the nationality from Tulipland of Mr Fleurrose would not be valid. Consequently, we can assume that it has been validly granted.

(b) Continuity

Secondly, it is necessary that the nationality existed both at the time of the violation and at the time when the State brings the claim under diplomatic protection (see the customary rule in Article 5 of the Draft Articles).

In our case, Mr Fleurrose has not changed his nationality and thus was a national of Tulipland both at the time when he was tortured and now when his State of nationality plans to exercise diplomatic protection on his behalf.

(c) Opposability

Mr Fleurrose is apparently a single national. The exercise of diplomatic protection does not therefore pose any particular problem in this regard. In case of single nationals it is not necessary to show any 'genuine link', a requirement hinted at by the ICJ in the *Nottebohm* case (ICJ, Judgment, *Nottebohm* (Liechtenstein v Guatemala), 1955, 21–23) even for single nationals. Nevertheless, today it is widely accepted that single nationalities are ipso facto opposable to other States, since they do not create any problem in the exercise of State sovereignty of national States and since otherwise millions of people not living in their State of nationality would be rendered stateless for the purpose of diplomatic protection. This solution has also been endorsed by the ILC in Article 4 of the Draft Articles.

It seems, therefore, that the second element—the link of nationality—is also fulfilled.

Exhaustion of local remedies

It is essential to ascertain if local remedies have been exhausted. A State can only bring a claim in diplomatic protection if those remedies have been exhausted (or if it can be concluded that no such reasonable remedies are available). The reason is that a 'wrongdoing' State should get the chance to remedy the wrong before it is lifted up to an international dispute between two States. The ICJ has confirmed this customary rule in the *Interhandel* case (ICJ, Judgment on Preliminary Objections, *Interhandel* (Switzerland v United States of America), 1959, 27) and the ILC has incorporated it in Article 14 of the Draft Articles.

Nevertheless, in our case it seems that local remedies have not been exhausted, since there is no mention of any court proceedings. Therefore, Tulipland would not (yet) be competent to bring a claim under diplomatic protection for the benefit of Mr Fleurrose. [*In light of missing information of such importance it would have to be very well justified if you would assume the contrary, namely that local remedies have been exhausted. Of course, if local remedies were exhausted, Tulipland could exercise diplomatic protection on behalf of Mr Fleurrose, since all three criteria would be satisfied.*]

4. Functional vs diplomatic protection

Nevertheless, the question asked as to whether Tulipland can exercise its diplomatic protection while excluding functional protection by the UN is an important one. [*Despite the question's importance, it would be justifiable not to deal with this issue in your answer since it is partly premised on the situation where Tulipland actually could exercise diplomatic protection, which is not (yet) the case as we have seen above. However, the situation of functional vs diplomatic protection has been added here for completeness.*]

As stated above, it also has to be kept in mind that these two forms of protection are based on different links of the individuals and are thus slightly different. It is, however, conceivable, as is the case here, that a violation of the rights of a specific individual might lead to an actual 'competition' between the individual's national State and the organisation for which the individual has been an agent. Nevertheless, the ICJ has clearly established in the *Reparation for Injuries* Advisory Opinion (ICJ, Advisory Opinion, *Reparation for Injuries Suffered in the Service of the United Nations,* 1949, 185, 186) that there are no rules in international law establishing a hierarchy between functional and diplomatic protection. The only issue which is clear according to the ICJ is that the defendant State cannot be forced to pay the necessary compensation twice. It seems, therefore, that the State of nationality and the organisation involved need to come to a conclusion through negotiation or through a general agreement.

Arguments as to the priority of one or the other can both be made and seem equally valid [*in an exam you can indicate that both solutions are possible, but in the end you should decide which position to take and give arguments supporting your choice*]. One could, for example, argue that since Mr Fleurrose's rights were violated in the course of the exercise of his official mission for the CPE, the UN should have priority to exercise functional protection since it was also its right (according to the ICJ in the Advisory Opinion on the *Reparation for Injuries Suffered in the Service of the United Nation,* 184, this is the UN's 'right to secure respect for undertakings entered into towards the organisation') which was violated. On the other hand, it was obviously also the right of Tulipland (ie Tulipland's right to see the international rights of its nationals respected) which can be said to be violated when Mr Fleurrose was arrested and tortured. Therefore, a prioritisation proves to be difficult and in the absence of an agreement between the UN and Tulipland any proposed solution can only largely be based on the personal convictions and preferences of the legal advisor.

5. Conclusion

As seen above, there is no hierarchy between the functional protection exercised by the UN on behalf of Mr Fleurrose and the diplomatic protection exercised by Tulipland as the national State of Mr Fleurrose on his behalf.

Functional protection seems to be possible in our case since the Convention is applicable to experts of the CPE such as Mr Fleurrose and he is protected by immunities *ratione materiae* for all his official acts during his missions, including for interviews given in connection with his mission. On the other hand, diplomatic protection by Tulipland is not (yet) possible since local remedies have not (yet) been exhausted.

Therefore, for the time being only functional protection by the UN on behalf of Mr Fleurrose is possible and the difficult question of the competing relationship between functional and diplomatic protection thus does not have to be solved.

Chapter 3

SUGGESTED SOLUTIONS
Treaty Law

SUGGESTED SOLUTIONS
Applicability of the Vienna Convention on the Law of Treaties (VCLT)

Suggested Solution—Case 3.1

Abbreviations used

FEE = Treaty on Friendship and Economic Exchange
TEOS = Treaty on the Exchange of Oil against Sugar
VCLT = Vienna Convention on the Law of Treaties

(a) A: A ratified the VCLT on 25 May 1978, so before the entry into force of the VCLT itself. Thus the entry into force for A is according to Article 84 paragraph 1 VCLT: this Article provides that the VCLT enters into force on the 30th day after the deposit of the 35th instrument of ratification or accession. Therefore this means the VCLT enters into force for A on the general date of entry into force of the VCLT, on 27 January 1980.

B: B acceded to the VCLT after its entry into force, on 13 October 1985. As a consequence, the VCLT enters into force for B according to Article 84 paragraph 2 VCLT, ie on the 30th day after the deposit of its instrument of accession. Therefore, the VCLT enters into force for B on the 13 November 1985.

FEE: The FEE has been concluded by A and B on 5 June 1988. The non-retroactivity principle in Article 4 VCLT provides that the VCLT is only applicable to treaties which have been concluded after its (the VCLT's) entry into force for the respective State parties to the treaty in question. In our case, at the date of conclusion of the FEE, the VCLT is in force for both A and B. Therefore, Article 4 VCLT is fulfilled and the VCLT is applicable to the FEE. The date of entry into force of the FEE, on the other hand, is completely irrelevant for the question of the applicability of the VCLT, since it is the date of conclusion that matters.

(b) O: O has ratified the VCLT on 3 February 1973, so before the entry into force of the VCLT as such. Article 84 paragraph 1 VCLT provides that the VCLT enters into force 30 days after the deposit of the 35th instrument of ratification. Since O's instrument of ratification is part of the necessary 35 instruments, the VCLT enters into force for O on 27 January 1980.

X: This State has already ratified the VCLT on 19 April 1970. As for O, the VCLT therefore enters into force for X according to Article 84 paragraph 1 VCLT on 27 January 1980.

Treaty: The treaty has been concluded on 8 August 1977. (The date of entry into force is irrelevant for the determination of the applicability of the VCLT.) Article 4 VCLT, the non-retroactivity principle, provides that the VCLT is only applicable to treaties which have been concluded after the entry into force of the VCLT for the State parties to the treaty. In our case, the VCLT is not yet in force for X and O when they conclude the treaty in question, even though they have both ratified the VCLT before concluding this treaty. However, as seen above, the VCLT only enters into force for those States on 27 January 1980. As a consequence, the VCLT is not applicable as such, ie it is not applicable as a convention. However, we can apply the customary reflection contained in the VCLT. The International Court of Justice confirmed, for example in the *Gabčíkovo-Nagymaros* case (ICJ, Judgment, *Gabčíkovo-Nagymaros Project* (Hungary/Slovakia), 1997, paragraph 46), that the VCLT reflects customary treaty law.

(c) L: L has ratified the VCLT on 14 April 1983, ie after the general entry into force of the VCLT. According to Article 84 paragraph 2 VCLT, the VCLT therefore enters into force for this State 30 days after the deposit of its instrument of ratification. Hence, the VCLT enters into force for L on 14 May 1983.

C: C has never ratified the VCLT and is thus not a party to it.

TEOS: The TEOS has been concluded between C and L on 31 May 2010. Article 4 VCLT, the non-retroactivity principle, provides that the VCLT is only applicable to treaties which have been concluded after its entry into force for the State parties to the treaty ('such States'). While the VCLT is in force for L since it is a party to it, C is not a party and is thus also not bound by the VCLT. Therefore, the condition set in Article 4 is not fulfilled, since only one of the two State parties to the TEOS is also a party to the VCLT. However, even though the VCLT as a convention is not applicable we can apply the customary reflection contained in this instrument. The International Court of Justice confirmed, for example in the *Gabčíkovo-Nagymaros* case (ICJ, Judgment, *Gabčíkovo-Nagymaros Project* (Hungary/Slovakia), 1997, paragraph 46), the reflection of customary treaty law in the VCLT.

(d) F: It is said that F is a party to the VCLT since 3 September 1995. 'Being a party' means that at that date the VCLT must have entered into force for F, since before then they cannot be considered a fully fledged party, but would rather be only a signatory.

M: M has ratified the VCLT on 10 March 2009. Therefore, according to Article 84 paragraph 2 VCLT the VCLT will enter into force for M 30 days later, ie on 10 April 2009.

Water treaty: The Water treaty is concluded between M and F on 15 March 2009. According to the non-retroactivity principle contained in Article 4 VCLT, the VCLT is only applicable to treaties which have been concluded at a time when the VCLT was in force for all State parties to the treaty in question. In our case, however, the VCLT is not in force for M at the time of conclusion of the Water treaty. The treaty is concluded on 15 March 2009, while the VCLT will come into force for M only on 10 April 2009. The non-retroactivity principle is thus not fulfilled and as a consequence the VCLT is not applicable as such. However, we can still apply the customary reflection in the matter of treaty law contained in the VCLT. That the VCLT indeed reflects such customary law has been affirmed by the International Court of Justice, for example in the *Gabčíkovo-Nagymaros* case (ICJ, Judgment, *Gabčíkovo-Nagymaros Project* (Hungary/Slovakia), 1997, paragraph 46).

(e) T: T has ratified the VCLT on 5 May 1972, ie before the entry into force of the VCLT as such. According to Article 84 paragraph 1 VCLT, the convention enters into force for T 30 days after the deposit of the 35th instrument of ratification. Thus, the VCLT enters into force for T on 27 January 1980.

E: E has ratified the VCLT on 29 November 1979. As for T, the VCLT enters into force for E according to Article 84 paragraph 1 VCLT on 27 January 1980.

S: S has ratified the VCLT on 16 September 1998. According to Article 84 paragraph 2 VCLT, the Convention enters into force 30 days after the deposit of its instrument of ratification, ie on 16 October 1998.

K: K has ratified the VCLT on 7 December 1990. Therefore, as for S, the VCLT enters into force for K according to Article 84 paragraph 2, ie on 7 January 1991.

N: N has never ratified the VCLT and is thus not a party to it.

Disarmament treaty: The treaty has been concluded on 25 July 2007. The problem, however, is that one of the State parties, N, is not a party to the VCLT. According to the non-retroactivity principle contained in Article 4 VCLT, the VCLT must be in force for all State parties at the time of conclusion of the treaty in order to be applicable to that treaty. Since N is not a party to the VCLT, the VCLT as such will thus not be applicable, but its customary reflection will be applicable. In the *Gabčíkovo-Nagymaros* case the International Court of Justice has, for example, confirmed that the VCLT is a reflection of customary law in the matter of treaty law (ICJ, Judgment, *Gabčíkovo-Nagymaros Project* (Hungary/Slovakia), 1997, paragraph 46).

[*However, if we imagine that there might arise a problem only between States K and S, for example, the VCLT as such could be applied to the dispute/problem at hand because both States in question are parties to the VCLT.*]

SUGGESTED SOLUTIONS
Reservations

Suggested Solution—Case 3.2

Abbreviations used

ECtHR	=	European Court of Human Rights
ICJ	=	International Court of Justice
TOCAS	=	Treaty on the Co-operation Against Smugglers
VCLT	=	Vienna Convention on the Law of Treaties

1. Applicable law

First, we have to determine the applicable law. All four States are parties to the Vienna Convention on the Law of Treaties (VCLT) since its entry into force, ie since 27 January 1980. The treaty in question, the TOCAS, was concluded on 5 August 2008, ie after the entry into force of the VCLT for the four State parties. Article 4 VCLT, the non-retroactivity principle, States that the VCLT is only applicable to treaties concluded by States after the entry into force of the VCLT for these States. Hence, in our case this principle is satisfied, since the TOCAS was concluded after all the State parties to it were also parties to the VCLT. Therefore, the VCLT is applicable.

2. Clarification of terms

Tuor makes a reservation, while Bibiton claims to make an 'interpretative declaration'. It has therefore to be assessed whether they are indeed a reservation and an interpretative declaration, respectively. (The reason is that the law of treaties contains a series of rules regulating reservations, while interpretative declarations are not regulated there, mainly because they do not intend to change the treaty and do not have any legal value as such. Hence, the legal effects of reservations and interpretative declarations are different. In that sense see also the case *Belilos v Switzerland* from the European Court of Human Rights (ECtHR, *Belilos v Switzerland*, Judgment, Application No 10328/83, 29 April 1988, especially paragraphs 38–60).)

A reservation is defined in Article 2 paragraph 1(d) VCLT. It is a unilateral statement made at the time of ratifying, acceding, signing or otherwise expressing the State's consent to be bound by the treaty and it 'purports to exclude or to modify the legal effect of certain provisions of the treaty'. The most important factor is thus the exclusion or modification of the legal effects.

Tuor in its reservation intends to replace the patrols by airplanes with patrols by ships. Hence, this is indeed a reservation, since Tuor wants to *modify* the provision on common patrols and hence its legal effects.

If we look at Bibiton's interpretative declaration, we see that Bibiton actually intends to eliminate the obligation concerning the monthly meetings contained in Article 45 TOCAS. Hence, this is not an interpretative declaration simply stating how a term will be interpreted, but it actually wants to *exclude* Article 45 TOCAS. As a consequence, it has to be considered as a reservation as well and thus has to be assessed under the relevant provisions of the VCLT.

3. Procedure and admissibility of Tuor's reservation (the modifying reservation)

Article 19 VCLT States that a reservation has to be made at the time of ratification, signature, acceptance, approval or accession, while Article 23 VLCT adds that the reservation has to be made in writing and has to be communicated to the other States. This seems to be satisfied in the case at hand, since Tuor deposits the reservation together with its instrument of ratification. It thereby fulfils the timing in Article 19 VCLT as well as the conditions posed in Article 23 VCLT, since a deposition together with the instrument of ratification suggests a written form of the reservation (otherwise it cannot be deposited), as well as information for the other States which are normally informed of further ratification of treaties to which they are parties.

Article 19 VCLT further indicates the conditions under which the admissibility of a reservation has to be assessed. Since the TOCAS is silent on the matter of reservations, we only have to consider letter (c) of Article 19 VCLT, namely whether the reservation is against the object and purpose of the treaty. The object of the treaty as stated in the preamble is co-operation to combat smuggling and drug trafficking. Tuor does not contest this main purpose and is also not against common patrols as a means of co-operation. It only wants to effectuate the patrols by boat and not by airplane. This does not seem to put the overarching goal into jeopardy and the reservation made by Tuor can be deemed to be compatible with the object and purpose of the TOCAS. The reservation is thus admissible.

4. Opposability and consequences of Tuor's reservation

Concerning Tuor's reservation, both Apro and Bibition have remained silent. According to Article 20 paragraph 5 VCLT, silence is deemed to be an acceptance of the reservation after a period of 12 months. Therefore, since it is nowhere in the facts stated that Apro or Bibiton object later on, we can consider these two States as accepting States after a period of 12 months. Fenis, on the other hand, objects to the reservation made by Tuor, but at the same time does not preclude the entry into force of the treaty. This is hence a 'simple objection' (as opposed to a 'radical objection'), which is regulated under Article 20 paragraph 4(b) VCLT: the objection of a State to the reservation of another does not preclude the entry into force of the treaty between the two parties unless the objecting State has expressly stated that it wishes the treaty concerned not to enter into force between the two of them.

[*It is interesting to consider briefly the question as to when a reserving State can be considered to be a party to the treaty. As is well known, the approach changed with the Advisory Opinion of the ICJ concerning the* Reservations to the Genocide Convention *(ICJ, Advisory Opinion*, Reservations to the Convention on the Prevention and Punishment of the Crime of Genocide*, 1951, 21–26). Before this advisory opinion, in order for a reserving State to become a party to the treaty, it was necessary that the reservation was accepted by all other State parties to the treaty. The ICJ changed this* *in its advisory opinion, saying that it is not necessary that all other States accept the reservation. Even though the ICJ had limited its answers to the Genocide Convention, the advisory opinion combined with subsequent developments led the International Law Commission to the adoption of Article 20 paragraph 4(c) VCLT, stating that one acceptance by at least one other contracting State is enough to make of the reserving State a party to the treaty. In our case, both Apro and Bibiton express tacit acceptance and hence Tuor can be considered as a party to the TOCAS, at least after the 12-month period of silence required for tacit acceptance.]*

The legal effects of the reservation are regulated in Article 21 VCLT. The relationship between Tuor and each of the two accepting States (Apro and Bibiton) is regulated by Article 21 paragraph 1(a) and (b). According to this Article, the treaty is modified to the extent of the reservation for both the reserving and the accepting State in their mutual relation. In our case, the reservation was a modifying reservation (ships instead of airplanes), which means in practice that the common patrols between Tuor and Apro and Tuor and Bibiton will be carried out by ship and not airplane. Article 21 paragraph 3 regulates the case of the simple objector: in that case, the provision to which the reservation is made does not apply between the reserving and the objecting State 'to the extent of the reservation'. Here, this means that Article 57 TOCAS on the common patrols does not apply between Tuor and Fenis (the simple objector) at all, since there is no ground of agreement: Tuor wants patrols by ships and Fenis does not want patrols by ships (but supposedly by airplanes as is stated in the original Article 57 TOCAS). They will therefore have to negotiate and find a solution on how to effectuate these common patrols, but the TOCAS no longer regulates this question between the two of them. Between all the other States except the reserving State Tuor, however, the TOCAS applies unmodified according to Article 21 paragraph 2 VCLT. That is between Apro, Bibiton and Fenis *inter se*, Article 57 TOCAS applies with common patrols by airplanes.

5. Procedure and admissibility of Bibiton's reservation

As pointed out above for Tuor's reservation, the procedural conditions for reservations are found in Article 19 VCLT (time of making a reservation) and Article 23 VCLT (written form and communication to other States). Similar to Tuor's case we can argue that the conditions are fulfilled here. It is expressly stated that Bibiton informs the other States that it attaches to its instrument of ratification an 'interpretative declaration', thereby showing that it is in a written form, since otherwise it cannot be attached to an instrument of ratification which is usually in written form.

It has already been established above that Bibiton's 'interpretative declaration' is in fact an (excluding) reservation. Thus, we have to analyse its admissibility, opposability and effects under the VCLT. Admissibility is to be assessed under Article 19 VCLT. Since the TOCAS is silent on the matter of reservations, we only have to check whether the reservation is compatible with the object and purpose of the treaty (Article 19(c) VCLT). Bibiton wants to exclude the monthly meetings provided in Article 45 TOCAS 'due to high costs of travel'. This Article was inserted to 'establish good personal relations' among the heads of the police forces. Article 45 TOCAS as such, unlike Article 44 TOCAS, does not talk about any co-operative goals but has been established to create good personal relations. It is true that regular meetings might also be beneficial for the mutual co-operation, but Bibiton does not seem to want to exclude this co-operation as such, since it has not made any other reservation on a clear co-operation clause. Thus, it seems to go too far to conclude that this reservation would be incompatible with the object and purpose of the treaty, and, as a consequence, Bibiton's reservation is admissible.

[*The opposite conclusion is nevertheless also possible, if it is argued that good personal relations are indispensable for co-operation and thus that Article 45 is an essential part of the goal of the TOCAS to establish co-operation. Then the reservation made by Bibiton would not be admissible. As a consequence a discussion of whether the instrument of ratification, which contains this invalid reservation, remains valid as such would be necessary in order to conclude whether or not Bibiton can be seen as having ratified the treaty and thus being a party to the TOCAS (see eg Belilos case before the ECtHR). In this regard it should be pointed out that there are generally two opposing positions. The first one says that an instrument of ratification containing an invalid reservation is per se invalid as well, since the State making the reservation only wants to ratify the treaty in question under the condition of this reservation. If thus this reservation is not accepted, the instrument of ratificaiton falls as well. The other position rather undertakes a sort of balancing. Proponents hold that the invalid reservation can be severed from the instrument of ratification which would thus remain valid. The rationale is to say that after all the State had an interest in joining this treaty, expressed in its submission of the instrument of ratification, and thus it should still be considered as having validly ratified the treaty in question. Both types of arguments are valid and have their merits. If you are confronted with such an issue you should—after having set out the two theoretical positions—decide which line of argument seems more convincing to you (also eventually taking into account present circumstances such as statements made by the State in question) and argue the case accordingly.*]

6. Opposability and consequences of Bibiton's reservation

Tuor expressly accepts the reservation made by Bibiton and thus according to Article 20 paragraph 4(a) VCLT Bibiton becomes a party to the TOCAS with regard to Tuor. We can also point out that as a consequence Article 20 paragraph 4(c) VCLT is fulfilled, which requires, as we have seen above in more detail, that a reserving State only becomes a party to a treaty if at least one other State has accepted the reservation. This is the case here and thus Bibiton is a party to the TOCAS. Apro has again remained silent. Under Article 20 paragraph 5 VCLT Apro will be considered to be an accepting State after 12 months of silence. Fenis, on the other hand, has also protested against this reservation. However, it is again a simple objection according to Article 20 paragraph 4(b) VCLT, since Fenis does not preclude the entry into force of the TOCAS between Bibiton and itself.

As a consequence, the TOCAS will apply as follows: between Bibiton and each of the two accepting States (Tuor and after 12 months Apro), the treaty applies according to Article 21 paragraph 1(a) and (b). That means that the TOCAS between Bibiton and Apro, and Bibiton and Tuor applies without Article 45 TOCAS, so there is no longer an applicable provision providing for monthly meetings. This is due to the reservation itself which has been accepted by both parties. However, for the relation between Bibiton and Fenis we have to apply Article 21 paragraph 3 VCLT. The result, though, is the same: the TOCAS applies without Article 45. But this is not due to the reservation (which has not been accepted by Fenis), but rather to treaty law as such (the application of Article 21 paragraph 3 VCLT), since there is no agreement between the parties and thus the disputed provision cannot apply between them. As for the relation between the non-reserving States, in this case Apro, Tuor and Fenis, we apply Article 21 paragraph 2 VCLT. Consequently, the TOCAS applies unmodified, ie with Article 45 TOCAS (and thus the monthly meetings).

7. Conclusion

As we have seen above, the reservations of both Bibiton and Tuor are admissible and thus modify the application of the TOCAS between all the parties.

The reservation made by Bibiton modifies the treaty by excluding the application of Article 45 TOCAS between Bibition and each of the three other parties. In relation to Tuor and Apro this is due to their acceptance, while in relation to Fenis this is due to the application of Article 21 paragraph 3 VCLT. The reservation does not change the relation between Tuor, Apro and Fenis *inter se*.

The reservation made by Tuor, on the other hand, modifies the application of Article 57 TOCAS between Tuor and Apro, and Tuor and Bibiton, while this Article is not applicable in Tuor's relation with Fenis due to Fenis's simple objection. Again, the reservation does not change the relation between the non-reserving States inter se, here Apro, Bibiton and Fenis.

Suggested Solution—Case 3.3

Abbreviations used

CJT = Convention on Joint Telecommunication
ECtHR = European Court of Human Rights
VCLT = Vienna Convention on the Law of Treaties

1. Applicable law

All State parties to the Convention on Joint Telecommunication (CJT) are parties to the Vienna Convention on the Law Treaties (VCLT) since its entry into force. Following Article 84 paragraph 1 VCLT, this Convention entered into force for these States on the 30th day after the deposit of the 35th instrument of ratification, ie on 27 January 1980. The CJT has been concluded on 3 March 2009, hence at a time when the VCLT was already in force for all State parties to the CJT. This is a condition of the applicability of the VCLT to a specific treaty, stated in Article 4 VCLT (the non-retroactivity principle). This principle is thus fulfilled and the VCLT is applicable to the CJT as such.

2. Clarification of terms

None of the State parties contests that the two reservations made by Vignar and Oskam are indeed reservations. A short analysis of the definition of a reservation confirms that they are indeed reservations. According to Article 2 paragraph 1(d) VCLT, a reservation is a unilateral statement by a State made at the time of expressing its consent to be bound by the treaty and which seeks to exclude or modify the legal effects of a treaty for that State. As is easy to see, both statements made by Vignar and Oskam want to exclude something from the treaty (Vignar wants to exclude part of the dispute-settlement provision, while Oskam wants to exclude a specific frequency). Hence, they have indeed entered reservations to the CJT.

3. Procedure and admissibility of the reservations

According to Article 19 VCLT, a reservation has to be made at the time when the State in question is signing, ratifying, accepting, approving or acceding to the treaty in question. This is fulfilled for both reservations made by Vignar and Oskam, since they attach their reservations to their respective instruments of ratification. In addition, Article 23 paragraph 1 VCLT stipulates that reservations have to be made in writing and have to be communicated to the other State parties. This seems to be fulfilled as well, since it is stated that the reservation was written (for Vignar) and was attached to the instrument of ratification (for Oskam), which suggests that the reservation is also made in a written form. In addition, the other States seem to be informed about these reservations, since normally States are informed about further ratification of treaties to which they are parties and thus also of the reservations. Indeed some of the States react to the reservations, showing that they have been informed.

Concerning the admissibility of the reservations we have to consider Article 19 VCLT. In letter (a) of this Article it is provided that reservations are not admissible when the treaty prohibits them. The CJT indeed provides in its Article 18 that reservations to a number of provisions are prohibited. Under these provisions figures also Article 15 CJT, the dispute-settlement clause. As a consequence, the reservation made by Vignar to Article 15 CJT is not admissible, ie it cannot be made. It has thus to be analysed whether Vignar, which attached this reservation to its instrument of ratification of the CJT, will still be a party to this treaty. The question is not regulated in the law of treaties and there are two possible positions which can be taken: one is to say that Vignar is still a party because its ratification can be separated from the reservation, since it wanted to become a party to the CJT and thus this would be more important for it than having the reservation. Consequently, Vignar would still be a party to the CJT, but without the reservation. It is, however, also possible to argue that Vignar only chose to become a party to the CJT because it had the possibility of entering such a reservation. Without the reservation it would thus no longer want to become bound by the treaty. [*Both positions can be validly taken. To answer the question, you should decide and consequently provide arguments on which one you find more convincing and thus applicable here.*] In our opinion, we should privilege the first approach in this case, which has also been used by the European Court of Human Rights in the *Belilos v Switzerland* case (ECtHR, *Belilos v Switzerland*, Judgment, Application No 10328/83,

29 April 1988, especially paragraphs 38–60)). Furthermore, in our case Vignar could have known from the beginning that its reservation would not be admissible, since this was clearly indicated in the CJT itself (Article 18 clearly lists the articles to which reservations are not allowed). The fact that it still made the reservation, knowing that it would be inadmissible under Article 19 VCLT, could be seen as indicating that it was indeed more important for Vignar to become a party to the CJT than really having this reservation applicable.

This leaves us to assess Oskam's reservation. Oskam's reservation is made to Article 7 paragraph 5 CJT. According to Article 18 CJT, it is not prohibited to make a reservation to Article 7. Thus, Article 19(a) VCLT is not applicable, nor is Article 19(b), since the CJT does not say anything on specific reservations that can be made. But we have to assess whether Article 19(c) VCLT, the compatibility of the reservation with the object and purpose of a treaty, is fulfilled. The object and purpose of the CJT is to establish a joint communication system, to which Oskam does not seem to be opposed at all. Article 7 CJT lists over 20 frequencies which will be used for telecommunication purposes and Oskam only wants to exclude one of them in its country, because that frequency is used for other purposes. While it is true that it can be seen as careless that Oskam did not previously object to the use of this particular frequency, it seems to go a bit far to hold that by doing this Oskam would actually go against the object and purpose of the treaty. The object and purpose of a treaty usually are the big goals that the treaty wants to achieve. In the light of so many frequencies, it is hard to imagine that the exclusion of one would actually defeat the whole object and purpose of the CJT, even though Rayte's argument seems to point in this direction. Nevertheless, also in light of the fact that the other parties remain silent, it is our opinion that the reservation made by Oskam is admissible.

[*If you are of the opinion that the reservation is not admissible since you argue that this frequency is equally important to the object and purpose of the treaty than any other frequency and that it defeats the goal of the treaty to exclude one, the reservation made by Oskam would have to be declared inadmissible under Article 19(c) VCLT. In this case, the next step would be to argue for or against the continued validity of Oskam's instrument of ratification containing the invalid reservation, as seen above with Vignar. A further point which has not been completely clarified in international law that could be discussed in this regard is what happens if States accept an invalid reservation and thus make the reserving State a party to the treaty (as is the case here within 12 months in virtue of Article 20 paragraph 5 VCLT, since all States except Rayte have remained silent). One possibility would be to say that the VCLT provides that invalid reservations are not admissible and thus they can never be accepted (with the consequences on the instrument of ratification to be discussed, as seen above). Another position could be to say that States are free to enter into treaty relations, thus they are also free to accept invalid reservations (at least if they are not expressly prohibited by the treaty). Thus, since the majority of States here seems to accept the reservation, it could be considered as valid in relation to those accepting States (and consequently the instrument of ratification would also be valid). It has, however, to be recognised that this later position would somewhat weaken Article 19 VCLT.*]

4. Opposability and consequences of the reservation

Concerning the reservation made by Vignar it has to be recalled that it has been declared inadmissible and is thus non-existent. The CJT is therefore not affected and applies normally between all the parties.

Concerning the reservation made by Oskam, it should be clarified whether Article 20 paragraph 2 VCLT is applicable. That paragraph states that if it is clear from the restricted number of State parties and the object and purpose of the treaty that its application in its entirety (ie the same for every party) is an essential condition of the consent of all the parties, then the reservation has to be accepted by all parties. However, in our case nothing suggests that the application of the treaty in its entirety was an essential condition for the State's consent. On the contrary, most States remain silent, thereby working towards acceptance as we will see. In addition, as stated above, it is not clear from the object and purpose of the treaty that it requires the application in its entirety. Therefore, it seems advisable not to invoke Article 20 paragraph 2 VCLT here.

There is according to the facts only one State, Rayte, which reacts to the reservation made by Oskam. All the others seem to remain silent. According to Article 20 paragraph 5 VCLT, silence for 12 months after the States in question were notified of the reservation or expressed their consent to be bound by the treaty, whichever date is later, is deemed acceptance. In our case, notification of the reservation is later, since Oskam deposited its reservation at the beginning of June, while the other States had already ratified the CJT in May. Hence, we can say that one year later (in May 2010), the reservation of Oskam has clearly been accepted by Aleta, Carmon, Tamra and Vignar since we do not know of any objection made by one of these States. Thus, Article 20 paragraph 4(c), which provides that in order for the reserving State to be considered a party to the treaty in question there needs to be at least one State accepting its reservation, is also clearly fulfilled in May 2010. (It can be assumed that the treaty can be already applied beforehand if none of these States objects, but in case of dispute over the application of the treaty the States would have to negotiate since until May 2010 Oskam was not formally a party to the CJT.)

Article 21 paragraph 1(a) and (b) VCLT establishes the consequences of an accepted reservation (an 'established reservation') between the accepting and the reserving States. Thereby, the reservation modifies the provisions of the treaty to which the reservation relates to the extent of the reservation. In our case, we are dealing with an excluding reservation since Oskam wants to exclude a certain frequency from the treaty. Therefore, Article 7 paragraph 5 CJT containing this frequency will not be applicable between Oskam and Aleta, Oskam and Carmon, Oskam and Tamra, and Oskam and Vignar, and this specific frequency will not be used.

The case is different concerning Rayte. Rayte has made a radical objection to Oskam's reservation. That means, in accordance with Article 20 paragraph 4(b) VCLT *in fine* that Rayte has not only objected to the reservation but has also objected to becoming a party to the treaty with regards to Oskam.

The consequence of this can be found in Article 21 VCLT *a contrario*. Nowhere in Article 21 VCLT can be found anything on the situation of a radical objector. Thus, and also due to logic since the States do not agree at all with each other, we can conclude that there is no treaty relation whatsoever between Rayte and Oskam regarding the CJT.

In the relations between all the other States *inter se* including Rayte (ie between

Aleta, Camron, Tamra, Vignar and Rayte) the CJT remains, however, unmodified according to Article 21 paragraph 2 VCLT. This means that Article 7 paragraph 5 CJT is in force between all those parties and the frequency excluded by Oskam can be used among these five States.

5. Conclusion

As demonstrated above, Vignar's reservation is not admissible, but Vignar will continue to be a member of the CJT. On the other hand, Oskam's reservation is admissible. It will modify the treaty between Oskam and all the other States accepting the reservation accordingly, ie it will exclude the frequency mentioned in Article 7 paragraph 5 CJT between Oskam and all other accepting States, while there will be no treaty relation at all between Oskam and Rayte. For all the other States except Oskam *inter se*, the CJT will not be modified.

[*Depending on your arguments above the conclusion will obviously change. If you concluded that the instrument of ratification of Vignar is no longer valid due to the inadmissible reservation, then Vignar is not a party to the CJT—unless of course it submits a new instrument of ratification. The same goes for Oskam if you declared its reservation as inadmissible and consequently its instrument of ratification as invalid. If you decide that the instrument of ratification retains its validity without the reservation, then Oskam would be a party to the CJT, which would, however, be unmodified since the reservation would no longer exist. It is to be assumed in this scenario that the radical objector Rayte would no longer object to a treaty relation with Oskam, since the reason for its radical objection—the reservation—is no longer present.*]

SUGGESTED SOLUTIONS
Competence to conclude treaties

Suggested Solution—Case 3.4

Abbreviations used

ICJ = International Court of Justice
OPNE = Organisation for the Protection of the Natural Environment
TEMT = Treaty on the Exchange of Military Technology
TPIF = Treaty on the Increased Protection of Marine Animal and Plant Species against Industrial Fishing
VCLT = Vienna Convention on the Law of Treaties

Situation (a)

1. Applicable law

We do not have any information whether or not Peaceland and Warland are parties to the Vienna Convention on the Law of Treaties (VCLT). However, in any event the ICJ has confirmed in several cases, for example in the *Gabčíkovo-Nagymaros* case (ICJ,

Judgment, *Gabčíkovo-Nagymaros Project* (Hungary/Slovakia), 1997, paragraph 46), that the VCLT articles are a reflection of customary international law in the matter of treaty law and can thus be applied as such.

2. Full powers

Article 7 VCLT deals with 'full powers' in relation to the conclusion of treaties. This Article provides in paragraph 2(a) that in virtue of their function, heads of States or governments do not have to produce full powers when performing 'all acts relating to the conclusion of a treaty'. Presidents, as here in our case, are undoubtedly heads of States or governments (depending on the national system).

Thus, the presidents of Peaceland and Warland were entitled to negotiate the treaty but also to conclude and sign it.

3. Consent to be bound expressed by signature

As to the simple signature that is enough to conclude the TEMT and to make it binding on the parties, this is not problematic since it seems that the two States agreed during the negotiations that the signature would have such an effect. According to Article 12 paragraph 1(c) VCLT (second part of the provision), the consent to be bound expressed by signature is valid when the parties have agreed during the negotiation that the signature would have this effect. Here, the two parties indeed agreed 'during the negotiations' that a simple signature by the presidents would be enough to express the State's consent to be bound by the treaty.

[*You could also envisage justifying the simple signature as being enough to express the States' consent to be bound under Article 12 paragraph 1(b) VCLT. This would not be substantially wrong. However, since it is clearly provided that the parties agreed to this mode during negotiations and since this is one possibility which is clearly provided for in the disjunctive wording of Article 12 paragraph 1(c) VCLT (the agreement appears from the full powers of the representative OR was expressed during negotiations), it seems that invoking Article 12 paragraph 1(c) VCLT is more convincing in the case at hand.*]

4. Conclusion

For all the above reasons we can conclude that the TEMT has been validly concluded.

Situation (b)

1. Applicable law

We do not have any information available indicating whether or not the relevant State parties are also parties to the VCLT. However, being a reflection of customary international law, the VCLT can in any event be applied to the case at hand. The customary nature of the VCLT has been confirmed by the ICJ in the *Gabčíkovo-Nagymaros* case (ICJ, Judgment, *Gabčíkovo-Nagymaros Project* (Hungary/Slovakia), 1997, paragraph 46).

2. Full powers

In this case we have to examine two different situations: the case of the permanent representative of Souchiland to OPNE and the case of the leader of the Green Party of Cyanoland.

The main issue is whether they have full powers to conclude such treaties. According to the facts, none of the two officially presented full powers.

Concerning the permanent representative of Souchiland

Article 7 paragraph 2 VCLT explains which groups of persons can represent their State without presenting full powers. Letter (c) foresees that representatives to international organisations are deemed to represent their State for the purpose of adopting the text of a treaty in this organisation.

The person in question is indeed a permanent representative to an international organisation—the OPNE—under which auspices the international conference adopting the TPIF has been held. It has to be kept in mind, however, that this permanent representative only has the power to *adopt* the text. He does not have the power to express his State's consent to be bound by the TPIF. We do not know whether signature of the TPIF equals giving its consent to be bound (ie this would be possible under Article 12 VCLT, but there is no information on this). If this is not the case, then an additional step by Souchiland would be necessary to express its consent to be bound by the TPIF. If signature equals expression of consent to be bound, then the TPIF is not validly concluded, since the permanent representative's powers are limited to the adoption of the text. Unless he has always been engaging his State's consent to be bound in the same manner before, or unless he produces full powers, we cannot say that the permanent representative validly concluded the TPIF in the sense that he could not express his State's consent to be bound by this treaty.

Concerning the leader of the Green Party of Cyanoland

The leader of a national political party does not fall under the persons mentioned in Article 7 paragraph 2 VCLT. He has never been granted an accreditation by his State to an international conference, even though Cyanoland has apparently repeatedly been sending him to conferences. Consequently he cannot fall under Article 7 paragraph 2(c) VCLT. Thus, in general such a person needs full powers to act. Yet, Article 7 paragraph 1(b) VCLT provides that when it has been the practice of the State concerned that this particular person has full powers in such negotiations, then this person will be deemed to have full powers even without producing them.

In our case, Cyanoland has been sending the leader of the Green Party to such conferences and negotiations for years. Thus, there is a clear State practice in this regard, which in addition also seems to be accepted by the other States, which appreciate the presence of the leader of the Green Party.

Thus, the leader of the Green Party can express Cyanoland's consent to be bound if it is agreed by the parties that a simple signature will have this effect.

3. Conclusion

Without producing full powers, the leader of the Green Party can express Cyanoland's consent to be bound based on State practice (Article 7 paragraph 1(b) VCLT), while the permanent representative of Souchiland is only entitled to adopt the text of a treaty but not to engage his State (Article 7 paragraph 2(c) VCLT).

SUGGESTED SOLUTIONS
'Pathologies' of treaties: invalidity, termination and suspension

Suggested Solution—Case 3.5

Abbreviations used

ICJ = International Court of Justice
MFA = Minister of Foreign Affairs
MLT = Military Liquidation Treaty
PCIJ = Permanent Court of International Justice
VCLT = Vienna Convention on the Law of Treaties

1. Applicable law

In order for the VCLT to be applicable there are two important dates: the date of the entry into force of the VCLT for the States parties to the treaty and the date of conclusion of the treaty. According to Article 4 VCLT, the non-retroactivity principle, the VCLT is only applicable to treaties where the former date is before the latter, thus the VCLT has to have entered into force for all the States parties at the time when the treaty in question is concluded.

In our case, Fedeland and Nationland are parties to the VCLT since its entry into force, which occurred in accordance with Article 84 paragraph 1 VCLT on 27 January 1980. Oportunor is a canton of Fedeland and not an independent State. In international law it is the States which are bound by international law, which, however, then also binds their constituting entities such as the cantons in a federal State. This well-accepted principle can, for example, also be seen in Article 28 VCLT, where it is explicitly said that, unless otherwise stated or agreed, a treaty is 'binding upon each party in respect of its entire territory'. Quite logically, cantons are part of the territory of a State and therefore, Oportunor is also bound by the VCLT 'via' Fedeland.

The VCLT is thus applicable to the MLT.

2. Can Oportunor conclude international treaties?

Nothing in the VCLT expressly regulates this question. It is only provided that every *State* possesses the capacity to conclude treaties (Article 6 VCLT). However, in an earlier version of the VCLT this Article had a second paragraph, stating that 'States members of a federal union may possess a capacity to conclude treaties if such capacity is admitted by the federal constitution and within the limits there laid down' (former Article 5 paragraph 2 VCLT). One of the reasons why this paragraph was deleted might reside in the fact that States felt uneasy to regulate such a matter, rather falling within the domestic law of States. However, the fact that it is no longer mentioned in the VCLT cannot lead us to the conclusion that it is prohibited that federal entities conclude international treaties. Applying the *Lotus* principle (see PCIJ, Judgment, *Lotus*, 1927, 18), we can therefore say that until such a prohibition is proven, the conduct in question is allowed. Indeed, it is rather for the federal State itself to decide whether or not it allows its federal constituents to conclude international treaty and if yes within which limits.

In our case, the constitution of Fedeland in its Article 47 clearly authorises the cantons to conclude international treaties with other sovereign States. Therefore, in principle Oportunor had the capacity to conclude a treaty with Natioland. Yet, this capacity was limited by the constitution itself, which has to be analysed now.

3. Has the MLT been validly concluded?

Generally, the MFA of Natioland is right when he says that a State cannot invoke its internal law in order not to respect its international commitments. This is very clearly stated in Article 27 VCLT, and the primacy of international law over national law has been confirmed also by the ICJ in instances such as the *Applicability of the Obligation to Arbitrate* advisory opinion (ICJ, Advisory Opinion, *Applicability of the Obligation to Arbitrate under Section 21 of the United Nations Headquarters Agreement of 26 June 1947*, 1988, paragraph 57) or the *LaGrand* case (ICJ, Judgment, *LaGrand* (Germany v United States of America), 2001, paragraphs 90, 91) and the *Avena* case (ICJ, Judgment, *Avena and other Mexican Nationals* (Mexico v United States of America), 2004, paragraphs 111–113). However, it is well accepted that this rule contains an exception, which is contained in Article 46 VCLT.

Article 46 VCLT provides that under certain circumstances a State can invoke a provision of its internal law which was violated to invalidate a treaty. (Here it is important to note that under this rule only invalidity of a treaty is possible and not termination as claimed by the MFA of Fedeland. The distinction is relevant due to the different consequences: according to Article 69 VCLT an invalid treaty is void ab intio and deemed to have never produced any legal effect. All the acts taken under such a treaty are invalid. If a treaty is terminated, the effects are according to Article 70 VCLT *ex nunc* (from 'now' on) and all the previous acts retain their validity.)

In order to satisfy Article 46 VCLT, two cumulative conditions have to be fulfilled: first of all, the rule violated must be a rule of fundamental importance concerning the capacity to conclude treaties; and secondly, the violation must have been manifest.

In our case, Article 47 of the Constitution of Fedeland gives the cantons the right to conclude treaties. However, this right is limited to matters which do not fall within the competence of the federal government. Article 46 of the Constitution provides that treaties dealing with military or economic questions in a wider sense fall within the competence of the federal government. The MLT concluded by Oportunor involves the sale of military equipment to Natioland. Yet, military equipment clearly falls within 'military questions' for which only the federal government is competent to conclude treaties in accordance with the two provisions of the Constitution explained above. Therefore, the conclusion of the MLT has violated Article 47 of the Constitution of Fedeland.

The constitution of a State is recognised to be the most fundamental law of a State, since it is the highest – or as the MFA puts it, the supreme – law of the State. Consequently, there is indeed a rule of fundamental importance in relation to the competence to conclude treaties which is violated and thus the first element is fulfilled.

Generally it is true, as the MFA of Nationland States, that States are not required to know the internal law of all other States. This has, for example, been acknowledged by the ICJ in the case *Cameroon v Nigeria* (ICJ, Judgment, *Land and Maritime Boundary between Cameroon and Nigeria* (Cameroon v Nigeria), 2002, paragraph 266).

Therefore, the violation of this fundamental internal law also has to be *manifest*.

Article 46 paragraph 2 VCLT explains that a violation is manifest 'if it would be objectively evident to any State conducting itself in the matter in accordance with normal practice and in good faith'.

In our case, Natioland and Fedeland have concluded already numerous treaties on different issues, among other things even treaties on the supply of military equipment. Therefore, one could assume that Natioland was aware that such treaties can only be concluded by the federal government. In addition, the two States, and especially also the two MFAs, had very close and good relations. It can therefore be assumed that they knew more about each other's internal law as compared to a distant State with whom a treaty is concluded for the first time. (Furthermore, it has to be admitted that normally international treaties—be they bilateral or multilateral—are concluded by States properly speaking and not by their federal entities. Thus, in the rather exceptional circumstance where federal entities are negotiating and concluding an international treaty, it can be expected that the other party will take extra care to ascertain that this conclusion is valid.)

Therefore we can conclude that the violation of the Constitution of Fedeland was manifest.

Consequently, Fedeland is entitled to invoke Article 46 VCLT in order to invalidate (and not terminate) the MLT.

4. Acquiescence

Nevertheless, before making this finding final, we have to assess whether Fedeland acquiesced in the validity of the MLT either explicitly (Article 45(a) VCLT) or implicitly by its conduct (Article 45(b) VCLT). Article 46 VCLT is a cause of relative invalidity (voidability) and thus acquiescence is theoretically possible. However, as soon as the federal government of Fedeland becomes aware of the MLT it protests. Thus there is clearly no acquiescence.

5. Separability

In addition, we have to check whether the treaty could be 'saved' under Article 44 VCLT. In the case of Article 46 VCLT, separation is mandatory if the conditions listed in paragraph 3 of this Article are cumulatively satisfied. However, since the whole treaty deals with 'military questions', the whole treaty is concerned with the violation of Article 46 VCLT and none of the clauses can be separated.

6. Consequence and conclusion

As a conclusion we can therefore say that Fedeland has the right to invoke Article 46 VCLT to invalidate the MLT. Invalidity according to Article 69 VCLT has effects ab initio. This means that the MLT is deemed to have never existed. Furthermore, under paragraph 2 the parties can ask each other to re-establish the situation that would have existed if the treaty would never have been concluded (except for acts in good faith which retain their validity). Since it cannot be said that Natioland (and Oportunor) acted in good faith, knowing that the MLT violated the Constitution of Fedeland, the sale of the military equipment is invalid and Fedeland can—as the MFA does—ask for the restitution of all the equipment. Yet, at the same time, Oportunor will also have to restitute any money already paid by Natioland to Natioland.

Suggested Solution—Case 3.6

Abbreviations used
ACUA = Agreement on the Cetaca, its Use and Apportionment
ICJ = International Court of Justice
VCLT = Vienna Convention on the Law of Treaties

1. Applicable law

All four States are parties to the Vienna Convention on the Law of Treaties (VCLT) since its entry into force. According to Article 84 paragraph 1 VCLT, the VCLT thus entered into force for those four States on 27 January 1980. However, the ACUA has been concluded on 30 July 1979, ie *before* the entry into force of the VCLT itself. The fact that the VCLT entered into force before the entry into force of the ACUA (six months after its conclusion, hence roughly at the end of January 1980) is irrelevant for this question. The determining date for the applicability of the VCLT is the date of *conclusion* of the treaty in question and not the date of its entry into force. As a consequence, Article 4 VCLT, the non-retroactivity principle, is not fulfilled since the VCLT 'applies only to treaties which are concluded by States after the entry into force of the present Convention with regard to such States' and the ACUA has been concluded before the entry into force of the VCLT for the four States in question. Therefore, the VCLT as such cannot be applied. However, it has repeatedly been confirmed by the International Court of Justice (ICJ) that the VCLT reflects customary law in the matter of international treaty law (see eg ICJ, Judgment, *Case concerning the Gabčíkovo-*

Nagymaros Project (Hungary/Slovakia), 1997, paragraph 46). Therefore, we will apply the customary reflection contained in the VCLT in this case.

2. Clarification of terms

We are confronted with the question of deciding whether the ACUA can continue to be applied. It seems, however, that Patello is making a slight confusion when it talks about considering the ACUA, which is based on incorrect maps, to be *terminated*. If Patello wants to invoke an error, as it seems to do by talking about 'wrong maps', then this is not a ground for terminating a treaty but on the contrary invalidates the treaty. The distinction between these two terms is crucial since the consequences are very different. Termination, according to Article 70 VCLT used as customary reflection, means that the treaty concerned ends 'from now on', but all the acts performed before remain valid. By invoking invalidity on the other hand, following the customary reflection contained in Article 69 VCLT, the treaty will be void ab initio. It will be considered that the treaty should never have produced legal effects and as a consequence all the legal acts performed before become void (with the exception of acts performed in good faith). It is therefore necessary to see what Patello can invoke.

3. Termination? (Adding this section would make a very complete answer but is not absolutely necessary for your answer to be a good answer)

Considering the grounds for terminating a treaty exhaustively enumerated in the VCLT (and used as a customary reflection), we can see that one Article, namely Article 56 VCLT used as a customary reflection, should be analysed in more detail. As we know, the ACUA does not contain any denunciation clause. Article 56 VCLT deals with this situation and sets out that when it can be established that the parties intended that the silent treaty can nevertheless be terminated or when the nature of the treaty seems to allow this, then a treaty silent on the subject of termination can nevertheless be terminated. Article 56 VCLT should be interpreted restrictively. Since the ACUA has been concluded for an undetermined time it seems difficult to argue that the parties actually wanted to allow the possibility of terminating the treaty. Rather, the contrary seems to be the case. Furthermore, the ACUA at least in part fixes boundaries. Boundary treaties, however, are not treaties whose 'nature' implies that they can be terminated. Allowing this possibility would put many negotiated boundaries in danger since parties could simply claim that the 'nature' of the treaty allows them to terminate. On the contrary, boundary treaties are probably among the most 'fixed' treaties, as opposed to political or alliance treaties where it can indeed often be implied that their 'nature' allows termination (since the political context frequently changes). For the foregoing reasons it seems to be reasonable to conclude that Article 56 could not be used, even if that had been the intention of Patello.

Thus, we can conclude that Patello has no possibility of invoking Articles regulating termination. We thus have to turn to what Patello seems to be really invoking, namely 'wrong maps'.

4. Invalidity

Invoking 'wrong maps', Patello is actually having recourse to 'error', regulated in Article 48 VCLT, used as a customary reflection. This is a ground of relative invalidity of a treaty (also called voidability). In order to be able to invoke error, two elements have to be shown: first that the error related to a fact or situation which was deemed to exist at the time of conclusion of the treaty; and second that this fact or situation constituted an essential basis of consent for the party in question. It can thus be said that an error is a wrong or inexact representation of reality, which was, however, the basis of consent. The ICJ was confronted to a similar case in the *Temple of Preah Vihear* case (ICJ, Judgment, *Temple of Preah Vihear* (Cambodia v Thailand), 1962, 26), where it confirmed the customary nature of the rule on error as contained in Article 48 VCLT.

The first element, that the error is related to a fact or situation, seems to be fulfilled. There was indeed an error in the map, since the source of the Cetaca was shown to be on the right side of a mountain ridge, while in reality it was on the left side. Thus there is indeed a wrong representation of reality. The ACUA was also set up to fix the boundaries between the States. Patello has based itself on the wrong maps when negotiating and consenting to the treaty. And according to the facts, the 'accurate' maps played a crucial part in convincing Patello to accept and sign the ACUA. Thus, since these maps showed wrong boundaries we can indeed argue that they were an essential basis of consent. The factual situation which was represented wrong and which constituted an essential basis of consent consequently cannot only be limited to the wrong location of the source of the Cetaca but has to be seen in relation to the other boundaries established on the basis of these wrong maps. Thus, the second element of error (essential basis of consent) is also satisfied.

Before finally concluding whether or not Patello can invoke error we have to consider the exception contained in Article 48 paragraph 2. If a State contributed to the error itself, it cannot invoke the error in order to invalidate the treaty. However, Patello did not contribute to the error since it did not have the means to draw the maps itself and was at the time of drawing the maps very occupied in fighting rebels, a conflict that used up most of its resources. In addition, the source of the Cetaca is located in a very remote and hardly accessible area, where it is not possible just to pass by to check whether the maps are correct. Thus, the exception is not applicable and Patello could invoke error to invalidate the ACUA.

However, as the secret documents revealed show, the error was actually *deliberately* introduced into the maps by Glossida. Therefore, it is in any event no longer a simple error, but can be classified as fraud. Fraud shares with error the fact that there is a wrong or inexact representation of reality, but in addition needs a fraudulent conduct which has led the other State to consent to the treaty. In that sense in our case (but not necessarily always) error is 'incorporated' into fraud. [*We will thus rather invoke fraud than error as a ground for invalidity, since fraud contains this extra element of fraudulent conduct. Invoking error would in that sense not be wrong, but would not capture the entire situation. It is also envisageable to invoke both error and fraud at the same time. While this might make sense in less clear-cut cases where fraud is not easily shown, it seems to be slightly exaggerated here, since one clause of invalidity is generally enough to invalidate a treaty. Yet, it would certainly not be wrong to use both Articles on error and fraud.*] Fraud is regulated in the VCLT in Article 49 (used as a customary reflection here). According to this Article, a State can invoke the fraudulent conduct of another negotiating State in order to invalidate its consent to be bound by the treaty if that fraudulent conduct induced the State in question to conclude the treaty. As we know, Glossida deliberately let the maps to be drawn incorrectly, because this offered advantages to it, namely the construction of a dam, which was only possible at the source of the Cetaca. Glossida deliberately persuaded Arapam to fake the maps to its advantage. Thus Arapam, which was also a negotiating State of the ACUA, has engaged in fraudulent conduct, but so has Glossida. Patello, on the other hand, was so impressed by the maps that this was the main argument which convinced them to sign the ACUA. It can therefore be said that it was really the maps that 'induced' Patello to sign. Hence, all the elements for fraud seem to be fulfilled and Patello can invoke fraud to invalidate its consent to be bound by the ACUA.

Fraud is a case of relative invalidity that means first of all that only the State which is a victim of the fraud (as well as of the error dealt with above) can invoke it. Thus Larida can neither invoke error nor fraud. The fact that it would be affected by the reduction of the water flowing in the Cetaca by the dam is not relevant for either error or fraud, since the project was announced after the conclusion of the ACUA (and is not regulated by it). Thus, this cannot have been an essential basis of consent of Larida. In addition, nothing indicated that the wrong maps were an essential basis of consent of Larida either, which would, however, be necessary for error or fraud.

Relative invalidity, however, also means that acquiescence and separability are possible (unlike with absolute causes of invalidity) and thus have to be analysed.

5. Acquiescence

Article 45 VCLT is explicitly applicable to cases of fraud (and error). Under Article 45 VCLT used as a customary reflection a State can no longer invoke a ground for invalidating its consent if it either expressly (letter a) or implicitly (letter b) has acquiesced that the treaty shall continue to be applied despite its 'flaw'.

However, in our case Patello immediately protests after having learnt first of the wrongly indicated location of the source, but also after the secret documents have been published. This clearly indicates that Patello is not willing to acquiesce.

6. Separability

Generally, for error (Article 48 VCLT) separability is mandatory if the three cumulative conditions in paragraph 3 are fulfilled. However, we know from the above reasoning that Patello can actually not only invoke error but rather is invoking fraud. In cases falling under Article 49 VCLT (fraud), Article 44 paragraph 4 provides that the party which is entitled to invoke the fraud can chose to invoke the fraud either with respect to the whole treaty or only with respect to the particular clause affected by the fraud (in case all three cumulative conditions under paragraph 3 are fulfilled). Patello States that it considers the whole ACUA to be dead, and it seems thus to be clear that it chooses to invoke invalidity based on fraud concerning the whole treaty. We therefore do not necessarily have to consider whether separability under paragraph 3 would be possible, but we can conclude that the ACUA is not separated.

[*In any event, it can also be argued that even if Patello chose to invoke invalidity not in relation to the whole treaty, the second element of Article 44 paragraph 3 VCLT ((b) essential basis of consent) would not be satisfied: although the clauses establishing the boundaries could be separated under (a), these clauses constituted very likely an essential basis of consent of the parties. This seems to be true especially for Patello, which was induced by the wrong maps and the boundaries fixed therein to sign the ACUA. Yet, the conditions under Article 33 paragraph 3 VCLT are cumulative, meaning that all of them need to be fulfilled in order for the clauses to be separable from the rest. In addition to letter (b) also the fulfilment of letter (c) (the continued performance of the treaty would not be unjust) could be questioned, especially in light of the fact that Glossida wants—based on the deliberately faked maps—to construct a dam (not regulated in the treaty) which heavily impacts all the other States. Consequently, leaving the treaty as it is might indeed be seen as unjust. Thus, the ACUA cannot be separated in any event.*]

7. Consequences and conclusion

As stated in the beginning, the consequences of invalidity are set out in Article 69 VCLT. An invalid treaty is void ab initio and deemed to have never produced legal effects (paragraph 1). It has to be pointed out that since this is a multilateral treaty, the invalidity of the ACUA can be invoked by Patello in its relations with the other States, but will not invalidate the ACUA among the three other States *inter se* (Arapam, Glossida and Larida). This follows from the customary reflection contained in Article 69 paragraph 4 VCLT.

Under paragraph 2(a) of this Article, every party can ask the other one to re-establish as far as possible the situation which would have existed if the treaty had never been concluded. That is, Patello can ask Glossida among other things to eliminate the few preparatory measures for the dam, since they were not done in good faith. In addition, paragraph 3 specifies that the party that is responsible for the fraud cannot benefit from paragraph 2. Thus, Glossida (but also Arapam) could under no circumstances ask Patello to re-establish the previous situation. However, it is also important to note that acts conducted in good faith (which mainly concerns Larida and Patello which did not know about the fraud) will not become unlawful (Article 69 paragraph 2(b)).

Concluding we can say that Patello can invalidate the ACUA based especially on fraud (Article 49), which is in that sense incorporating error (and having the additional element of fraudulent conduct). Patello can ask Glossida to re-establish the situation that existed before it started to build the dam. Patello is under no circumstances bound by the ACUA, which is deemed to have never produced legal effects.

Suggested Solution—Case 3.7

Abbreviations used
AEPOR = Agreement on the Exploitation and Production of Oil Resources
MFA = Ministers of Foreign Affairs
VCLT = Vienna Convention on the Law of Treaties

1. Applicable law: Applicability of the VCLT to the AEPOR

According to its Article 4, incorporating the non-retroactivity principle, the 1969 Vienna Convention on the Law of Treaties (VCLT) 'applies only to treaties which are concluded by States after the entry into force of the present Convention with regard to such States'. Thus there are two important dates to be considered when assessing the applicability of the VCLT to a particular treaty: the date of the conclusion of the treaty to which we would like to apply the VCLT, and the date of entry into force of the VCLT in relation to the States concluding the treaty. The latter date is determined in conformity with Article 84 VCLT. The date of the conclusion of the treaty has to be after the entry into force of the VCLT for the States in question.

According to the facts of the case the two States Suhmiland and Tyraland are parties to the VCLT since its entry into force. In conformity with Article 84 paragraph 1 VCLT the latter thus entered into force for Suhmiland and Tyraland on 27 January 1980.

The AEPOR is a bilateral treaty which has been concluded in simplified form. This means that a simple signature is enough to conclude the treaty. The date of conclusion of the AEPOR is not indicated in the case. However, we can assume that it has been concluded during June 2008 or the latest at the beginning of July 2008. They negotiated for five days and the treaty was signed during this period. Consequently, the AEPOR was concluded with the signature of the Ministers of Foreign Affairs (MFAs) of Suhmiland and Tyraland. Therefore, we can argue that this treaty has been concluded during June 2008 or at the latest at the beginning July 2008.

In any event, the conclusion of the AEPOR is after the entry into force of the VCLT for Suhmiland and Tyraland. Thus, the VCLT is applicable to the AEPOR.

2. Invalidity

First of all, we can note that Article 7 paragraph 2(a) VCLT specifies that the MFA is considered to represent his/her State for the purpose of performing all acts related to the conclusion of a treaty without having to produce full powers. Since both Mr Walter and Mr Blackgold are the MFAs of their respective States, this aspect is not problematic in our case.

As stated in Article 42 paragraph 1 VCLT, the causes of invalidity of a treaty are enumerated exhaustively in the VCLT.

Article 51 VCLT, dealing with coercion of a State representative, provides that 'the expression of a State's consent to be bound by a treaty which has been procured by the coercion of its representative through acts or threats directed against him shall be without any legal effect'. This Article spells out an absolute cause of invalidity (voidness) of a treaty.

First of all, there needs to be coercion through acts or threats. According to the Report of the International Law Commission on its draft articles on treaty law, Article 51 VCLT refers to all kind of forms of threats or coercion against a representative of a State. The Report specifies that the coercion needs to be exercised against the person as an individual and not as a representative of the State. While obviously every physical act or threat against a person is coercion, the threat to ruin his career by making public certain information on his private life or to threaten to injure a member of the representative's family can also be seen to constitute coercion in the sense of Article 51 VCLT.[1]

In addition, according to Article 51 VCLT, this coercion has to be directed against the representative of a State who has the capacity to express the consent of the State to be bound by the treaty. In other words, there has to be a causal link between the coercion and the expressed consent to be bound by the treaty.

In our case, by pressing his Magnum 357 against the temple of Mr Walter, Mr Hics has clearly threatened a person (Mr Walter), thereby fulfilling the first criterion of Article 51 VCLT. This coercion was directed against Mr Walter, who in his capacity as MFA of Suhmiland is a representative capable of concluding treaties on behalf of Suhmiland (see Article 7 paragraph 2(a) VCLT). When Mr Walter signed the AEPOR, he has hence expressed his State's consent to be bound by this international treaty. Finally, as to the necessary casual link, we can note that without the threat by Mr Hics and his gun, Mr Walter would never have signed the treaty. In fact, Mr Walter did not want to accord more than 35% of the extracted crude oil to Tyraland. However, the final treaty foresees that Tyraland receives 90% of the crude oil, a percentage which is clearly higher than what Mr Walter was ready to grant Tyraland in the first place. Thus, there was indeed coercion in the sense of Article 51 VCLT exercised on Mr Walter, the representative of Suhmiland, in order to obtain his signature expressing Suhmiland's consent to be bound by the AEPOR.

3. Acquiescence

In the case of absolute invalidity, acquiescence is impossible. This can be inferred from an *a contrario* reading of Article 45 VCLT.

Article 51 VCLT contains such a cause of absolute invalidity (voidness). Hence, the question of a potential acquiescence by Suhmiland does not arise.

4. Separability

According to Article 44 paragraph 2 VCLT, invalidity can only be invoked with respect to the whole treaty, except in the situations regulated in paragraphs 3 and 4, where separability is, respectively, mandatory or voluntary.

However, Article 51 does not fall under those two paragraphs. According to Article 44 paragraph 5 VCLT, 'in cases falling under Articles 51, 52 and 53, no separation of

[1] Report of the International Law Commission on the work of its 18th session, 4 May–19 July 1966, Geneva, in *Yearbook of the International Law Commission* (1966) Vol II, 246, para 2.

the provisions of the treaty is permitted'. Yet, we have concluded that the AEPOR is invalid on the basis of Article 51 VCLT. Consequently, the AEPOR cannot be separated and the cause of invalidity has to be invoked with respect to the whole treaty.

5. Consequences

The consequences of the invalidity of a treaty can be found in Article 69 VCLT, as long as the treaty does not conflict with a norm of *jus cogens*. According to paragraph 1 of Article 69 VCLT, an invalid treaty is void, meaning that it has no legal force. Invalidity has effects ab initio.

In our case, the invalidity of the AEPOR has been established under Article 51 VCLT. Thus, this treaty is void and deemed to never have produced legal effects.

It must be pointed out that if Tyraland has undertaken some acts between the conclusion of the AEPOR and the invocation of its invalidity by Suhmiland, these acts could not benefit from Article 69 paragraph 2, since Tyraland is responsible for the coercion exercised on Mr Walter through its agent Mr Hics (see Article 69 paragraph 3 VCLT).

6. Conclusion

In conclusion, we can say that the AEPOR has not been validly concluded. It is void and deemed to never have produced legal effects. Suhmiland is thus under no circumstances bound by the AEPOR.

Suggested Solution—Case 3.8

Abbreviations used
AT = Art Treaty
VCLT = Vienna Convention on the Law of Treaties

1. Applicable law

Litemonte is party to the Vienna Convention on the Law of Treaties (VCLT) since its entry into force, which occurred in accordance with Article 84 paragraph 1 VCLT, 30 days after the deposit of the 35th instrument of ratification, on 27 January 1980. Fappa, on the other hand, has ratified the VCLT on 5 January 1999, ie after the general entry into force of the VCLT itself. According to Article 84 paragraph 2 VCLT, the VCLT enters into force for States depositing their instrument of ratification after the general entry into force of the VCLT itself 30 days after they have deposited the said instrument of ratification. Therefore, the VCLT enters into force for Fappa on 5 February 1999.

The Art Treaty (AT) has been concluded on 14 September 2006. Therefore, Article 4 VCLT, the non-retroactivity principle, is satisfied: at the time of the conclusion of the treaty (the AT), both State parties are also parties to the VCLT. As a consequence, the VCLT is applicable.

2. Termination

The AT is limited to five years since after this time the paintings of Trebol were supposed to go back from Litemonte to Fappa. It does not mean, however, that the AT contains a clause of termination related to any prior termination. Article 56 VCLT deals with the situation of treaties having no clause regulating termination. These treaties can nevertheless be terminated if it can be inferred that granting such a right was the will of the parties or if the 'nature' of the treaty implies this right. However, in our case nothing indicates that the two parties intended to establish a right to terminate the treaty earlier than these five years. Furthermore, treaties whose 'nature' allows termination are usually political or alliance treaties since international political realities indeed change quickly. However, to read the 'nature' of any other treaty as allowing earlier termination would be dangerous and would open the door to abuse. An art treaty seems not specifically predestined to be of a nature which would allow its termination. Therefore, we have to conclude that the application of Article 56 VCLT is not appropriate.

More appropriate seems to be the application of Article 61 VCLT—supervening impossibility of performance. Article 61 provides in paragraph 1 that the impossibility of performance of a treaty can be invoked by a party if this impossibility results from the 'permanent disappearance or destruction of an object indispensable for the execution of the treaty'. In our case it is clear that the paintings of Trebol were 'an object indispensable for the execution of the treaty'. Without these paintings there would be no treaty at all and without the paintings the treaty cannot be executed since it would be essentially one-sided (only Litemonte having an obligation, namely to pay, and Fappa having no obligation since it can no longer lend the paintings). However, the paintings of Trebol have been burnt by the fire beyond repair and thus are permanently destroyed. Therefore, the elements required in paragraph 1 seem to be satisfied and termination of the AT is possible. Paragraph 1 of Article 61 VLCT further points out that if the impossibility is only temporary, then only suspension can be invoked. However, the destruction of these paintings is not only temporary; they are lost forever. Furthermore, since all the works of Trebol which were in the possession of the National Museum of Fappa have been burnt, it is not possible to argue that they could replace the 30 promised works with other ones. Before we can undoubtedly conclude that Article 61 VCLT can be invoked we also have to have a look at its paragraph 2. This paragraph excludes the applicability of Article 61 VCLT if the impossibility of performance of a treaty is due to a breach of an obligation under that treaty or any other international obligation by the party wanting to invoke Article 61 VCLT. In our case it seems to be Litemonte that wants to get out of the treaty. However, Litemonte did not breach any obligation at all which might have led to the destruction of the paintings. This sad event was only due to the occurrence of natural causes, namely an earthquake and fire, and thus Litemonte but also Fappa did in no way contribute to their destruction.

We can therefore conclude that Article 61 VCLT can indeed be invoked by Litemonte.

[*Of course one might think that we could also (or in addition) try to argue that this was a fundamental change of circumstances (Article 62 VCLT). It is true that on the face of it, it was indeed a fundamental change of circumstances. However, a careful analysis of the Article (backed by the commentaries of the International Law Commission) shows that there is an important difference between Articles 61 and 62 VCLT.*

Under Article 61 it is virtually impossible to execute the treaty at all. Under Article 62 it is, however, not absolutely impossible to go on to execute the treaty, but its execution is made very burdensome for the party, in fact so burdensome that it cannot be reasonably expected from the party to go on executing this treaty. This can be inferred from Article 62 paragraph 1(b), talking about the condition that the change must have radically *transformed the* 'extent of obligations still to be performed under the treaty*'.*

In our case it is, however, clear that due to the destruction of the paintings it is not just more difficult but truly impossible to execute the treaty. Therefore, Article 62 VCLT is not appropriate in our case.

Furthermore, also Article 60 VCLT seems not very appropriate. Article 60 paragraph 1 VCLT provides that a material breach of a bilateral treaty by one of the parties entitles the other party to terminate or suspend the treaty in whole or in part. A material breach, as defined in paragraph 3 of the same Article, includes the violation of a provision essential to the accomplishment of the object and purpose of the treaty. In our case, it could be argued that there is indeed a material breach by Fappa by not delivering the paintings. However, this has to be seen in the context that it is no longer possible for Fappa to execute this obligation. It is therefore very questionable whether Litemonte could invoke this provision to terminate the AT. Furthermore, it could also be said that Litemonte has committed a material breach by not paying, under which circumstances it would, however, not be possible for Litemonte to invoke Article 60 VCLT, since it is itself the violating party and can therefore not take advantage of termination. For all these reasons it appears that Article 60 VCLT is rather problematic in our case and could not be invoked.]

3. Acquiescence

A reading *a contrario* of Article 45 VCLT shows that acquiescence in the case of Article 61 is not possible. Article 61 is not mentioned, while all the other articles to which Article 45 can be applied are expressly mentioned. Therefore, it is apparent that acquiescence is not possible in our case. This is a logical solution, because if the object indispensable for the execution of the treaty has disappeared, it does not make any sense to acquiesce in the further application of this treaty.

4. Separability

Article 44 VCLT does not specifically mention Article 61. Therefore, the general provision, ie paragraph 3 of Article 44 VCLT, has to be applied. All three conditions contained in paragraph 3 need to be cumulatively fulfilled in order for the treaty to be separable. If we look at these conditions it becomes quickly clear that letter (c) will certainly not be fulfilled: taking the clauses about the paintings, which have burnt, out would render the continued performance of the treaty unjust since it would be only one-sided. However, letter (b) too cannot be considered to be fulfilled since the inclusion of the provisions on the lending of the paintings was of course an essential basis of consent for Litemonte and indeed the main purposes of the AT. Therefore, separability is not possible in our case.

5. Conclusion

As a consequence we can conclude that Litemonte is indeed entitled to invoke supervening impossibility of performance (Article 61 VCLT) in order to terminate the treaty. The procedures to be followed by Litemonte are set out in Articles 65 and 67 VCLT.

[Procedure: *It is true that according to Article 65 paragraph 1 VCLT the party wishing to terminate the treaty has to notify the other party. We do not have any knowledge that Litemonte acutally sent a written notification to Fappa in this regard. (The requirement that the notification be written is to be found in Article 67 paragraph 1 VCLT.) Yet, Article 65 paragraph 5 VCLT clearly provides that the fact that a State has not yet made such a notification shall not be prevented to do so 'in answer to another party claiming performance of the treaty'. It is reasonable to assume that Litemonte did not consider it necessary to write such a notification of termination, since the AT without the paintings of Trebol is so one-sided that no one could be expected to continue its execution. Thus, when Fappa insits on the fulfilment of the AT, Litemonte has all the right in accordance with Article 65 paragraph 5 VCLT still to make this notification. However, it should be stressed that an oral notification is not sufficient but that Litemonte needs to add to this a written one.*]

The consequence of termination is spelled out in Article 70 VCLT. Termination means that the treaty ends *ex nunc*, that is from 'now' on. According to Article 70 paragraph 1, the parties are freed from the obligation to perform the treaty further, but at the same time, any acts or situations created during the prior execution of the treaty remain valid.

Suggested Solution—Case 3.9

Abbreviations used

MFA = Minister of Foreign Affairs
TCB = Treaty on the Construction of the Bigpower Dam
VCLT = Vienna Convention on the Law of Treaties

1. Applicable law

There are two important dates to take into account when assessing whether the Vienna Convention on the Law of Treaties (VCLT) is applicable to a particular treaty. The first date is the entry into force of the VCLT for the States parties to that treaty, and the second date is the date of conclusion of the treaty. Thereby, Article 4 VCLT (the non-retroactivity principle) provides that the date of the entry into force of the VCLT for the States parties to the treaty in question has to be before the date of the conclusion of the treaty itself. Otherwise, the VCLT will not be applicable as such.

In our case, Candleland and Nucland have been parties to the VCLT since its entry into force. According to Article 84 paragraph 1, the VCLT entered into force 30 days after the deposit of the 35th instrument of ratification. Consequently, the VCLT entered into force (also for our two States) on 27 January 1980.

The TCB, on the other hand, has been concluded on 13 May 2009, ie after the entry into force of the VCLT for the two State parties. Therefore, Article 4 VCLT is fulfilled and the VCLT is applicable to the TCB.

2. Termination of the TCB

According to Article 42 paragraph 2 VCLT, a treaty can only be terminated in accordance with the rules found in the VCLT. Thus, all the grounds for termination are exhaustively enumerated in the VCLT and no further grounds can be sought outside the convention.

There are two Articles in the VCLT that have to be looked at more closely.

The first one is Article 61—supervening impossibility of performance. The condition in order to invoke this provision is the 'permanent disappearance or destruction of an object indispensable for the execution of the treaty', thus hinting at an absolute impossibility of further execution of the treaty. Yet, the earthquake and subsequent tsunami have not destroyed any 'object' related to the construction of the dam. On the contrary, the dam was not touched by the natural catastrophe at all. Therefore, no 'object indispensable for the execution of the treaty' has been destroyed. Of course, one could argue that there is no more money from the side of Nucland for the construction of the dam. Yet, money as such is not an object which can be 'destroyed or disappeared' in the sense of Article 61 VCLT. This Article needs a physical object to be destroyed.

Therefore, we have to turn to Article 62 VCLT—fundamental change of circumstances. The negative formulation of this Article ('may *not* be invoked') indicates that this provision can only be applicable in exceptional circumstances. First of all, according to paragraph 1 of Article 62 VCLT, two cumulative conditions need to be satisfied.

First, the existence of those circumstances that fundamentally changed must have constituted an essential basis of consent of the parties to be bound by the treaty. Secondly, the effect of this fundamental change is to transform radically the extent of obligations which have still to be performed under the treaty.

In our case, the earthquake followed by the tsunami largely destroyed Nucland, which therefore has to allocate its budget differently and has no money left for the dam project. The circumstances that radically changed can therefore said to be the existence of the necessary money for the dam project or, to put it differently, the economic circumstances.

Yet, the existence of this money was an essential basis of consent for both parties. It was agreed that they would split costs 50–50 and it is also clear from the facts that Candleland cannot finance the dam alone. Therefore, we can indeed assume that this was an essential basis of consent for both States. Furthermore, two additional but connected arguments have to be considered. It has to be kept in mind that if Nucland would go on financing the dam, it would—according to the experts—go bankrupt. It is, however, not reasonable to expect that a State would willingly risk its own bankruptcy and the very serious consequences thereof. Moreover, the decision of the government of Nucland was also motivated by the concern for the security and the well-being of its own population. Therefore, the shortage of money in Nucland is not the only reason to be considered in isolation, but the consequences of further spending (and thus honouring the TCB) have also to be taken into account to see that there is indeed a fundamental change in circumstances due to the earthquake and tsunami.

In addition, the fact that there is now no money available from Nucland has indeed the effect of radically transforming the obligations still to be performed under the treaty. If Candleland would go on building the dam, it would have to finance the construction on its own, which it is not able to. Therefore, the obligations relating to the construction of the dam, as well as its administration, are radically transformed.

Consequently, it appears that Article 62 paragraph 1 is satisfied.

Before concluding we have, however, also to look at the other paragraphs. According to paragraph 2 of this Article, a fundamental change of circumstance cannot be invoked if the treaty establishes a boundary or if the change is actually due to a violation of the State invoking it. However, the TCB does not establish a boundary and in addition the change in circumstances is not due to any violation of an international obligation by the parties. On the contrary, the change in circumstances—ie the difficult ecnomic and monetary situation—is due to a natural catastrophe which cannot be influenced by States or humans.

Consequently, we can conclude that Nucland is indeed entitled to invoke a fundamental change of circumstances based on Article 62 VCLT as a ground for terminating the TCB.

According to Article 62 paragraph 3, a State able to invoke this Article to terminate a treaty can also invoke the same provision to suspend the operation of the treaty. However, from the statements made by Nucland we can deduce that it indeed wishes to terminate and not only to suspend the treaty.

3. Acquiescence

Article 45 VCLT provides that a State that has, after becoming aware of the facts, either explicitly (letter (a)) or implicitly through its conduct (letter (b)) acquiesced in the validity of the treaty loses its right to invoke the ground for termination.

The catastrophe hit Nucland on 17 November 2010 and the MFA informs Candleland on 25 November 2010 that it wishes to terminate the treaty. These few days are too short to talk about acquiescence by conduct, especially also in light of the difficult situation in which Nucland found itself. Since there is also no explicit acquiescence, Nucland can still invoke the termination of the TCB.

4. Separability

If the conditions under Article 44 paragraph 3 are cumulatively fulfilled, the treaty has to be mandatorily separated. Yet, the whole treaty rather than only some clauses are concerned about the fundamental change of circumstances. The clauses on financing cannot be separated since without them the goal of the treaty—the construction and administration of the hydroelectric dam—cannot be realised anymore.

Therefore, separability is not possible.

5. Consequences and conclusion

Nucland can invoke the termination of the TCB.

Articles 65 and 67 VCLT set out the procedure to be followed. According to these Articles, the other State parties need to be informed about the intention to terminate a treaty. The notification needs to explain the reasons for the termination and the treaty can only be terminated after a period of three months after the notification has been made (except in situations of urgency) (Article 65 VCLT). In addition, Article 67 provides that this notification needs to be in writing and needs to be signed by the MFA or the head of State or government.

These procedural conditions seem largely to be fulfilled in our case. It is the MFA of Nucland that sends a letter (notification in writing, by 'diplomatic post') to his counterpart in Candleland. The notification gives the reasons for the termination and we can assume that the MFA also signed his letter. Yet, it also indicates that the termination is to be effective from 1 February onwards. Since the notification was made on 25 November 2010, this leaves a little more than two months for the termination to become effective. However, as pointed out above, in situations of urgency this delay can be shorter. In light of the serious situation of Nucland it would appear that a bit more than two months notice would be sufficient to satisfy the procedural condition.

After this time, the TCB can be terminated in accordance with Article 70 VCLT. The effects of termination are *ex nunc*, that is from 'now' on and not retroactively as is the case with invalidity. Furthermore, all the acts performed under the treaty so far remain valid. The parties are simply released from the further performance of the treaty.

[*Even though following Article 62 VCLT Nucland seems to have every right to terminate the treaty, as its advisor it might be a good idea to suggest that they only suspend the treaty, which is also possible under this Article (paragraph 3). A suspension allows parties to resume the excution of the treaty later on, while releasing them from the obligation to execute the treaty from 'now' on (*ex nunc*, see Article 72 VCLT). First of all Nucland might still be interested in changing its energy supply later on and thus continue the construction of the dam once it has rebuilt itself. Secondly, the solution of only suspending the treaty would also seem the more prudent one in the interest of good neighbourly relations. The parties can freely agree on the time of suspension, which can be a long period, thus giving Nucland enough time to rebuild.*]

Suggested Solution—Case 3.10

Abbreviations used

ICJ = International Court of Justice
PoD = Pact on Disarmament
VCLT = Vienna Convention on the Law of Treaties

1. Applicable law

First of all we have to determine whether the Vienna Convention on the Law of Treaties (VCLT) is applicable to the Pact on Disarmament (PoD). Ignis has been a party to the VCLT since its entry into force, ie in application of Article 84 paragraph 1 VCLT (the

VCLT enters into force 30 days after the deposit of the 35th instrument of ratification), since 27 January 1980. Aura, on the other hand, has ratified the VCLT on 29 May 1985, thus after the general entry into force of the VCLT. According to Article 84 paragraph 2 VCLT, for States depositing their instrument of ratification after the deposit of the 35th instrument of ratification, the VCLT enters into force on the 30th day after they have deposited their instrument of ratification. As a consequence, the VCLT enters into force for Aura on 29 June 1985.

As to Tellus and Unda, they have only signed the VCLT. However, as is stated in Article 82 VCLT, this convention is subject to ratification. Hence, simply signing is not enough to become a party to the VCLT and therefore both Tellus and Unda are not (yet) parties to the VCLT.

The non-retroactivity principle in Article 4 VCLT States that the VCLT is only applicable to treaties which have been concluded after the entry into force of the VCLT for all State parties to the treaty. In our case, not all State parties were parties to the VCLT at the time of the conclusion of the PoD (4 March 2004), as seen above. As a consequence, the VCLT is not applicable as such to the PoD. However, it has been confirmed by the International Court of Justice (ICJ), for example in the *Gabčíkovo-Nagymaros* case (ICJ, Judgment, *Gabčíkovo-Nagymaros Project* (Hungary/Slovakia), 1997, paragraph 46), that most of the VCLT actually reflects customary international law. Therefore, we can apply the customary reflection contained in the VCLT.

2. Invalidity/Termination/Suspension

[*The question concerns only what Aura can do under 'international treaty law'. It would therefore go too far to address issues such as peaceful settlement of disputes or State responsibility.*]

It has to be recalled that according to Article 42 VCLT, applied here as customary reflection, a treaty can only be invalidated, terminated or suspended in accordance with the provisions of the VCLT. Thus, the grounds for invalidity, termination or suspension are enumerated exhaustively in the VCLT and no other grounds can be found outside the VCLT.

After having looked at the different causes of invalidity, termination and suspension, the most likely Article to be applied seems to be Article 60 of the VCLT (ie the customary reflection of this Article, which has been confirmed by the ICJ in its *Namibia* Advisory Opinion (ICJ, Advisory Opinion, *Legal Consequences for States of the Continued Presence of South Africa in Namibia (South West Africa) notwithstanding Security Council Resolution 276 (1970)*, 1971, paragraph 94). Article 60 VCLT provides that in case of a material breach it is possible to terminate, or depending on the circumstances, to suspend, the treaty. Paragraph 3 of this Article clarifies what has to be understood under 'material breach': it is either a repudiation of the whole treaty not in conformity with the VCLT, or it is a violation of a provision essential to the accomplishment of the object and purpose of the treaty. The latter provision has for example been applied in the *Rainbow Warrior* case (Arbitral Tribunal, Award, *Case concerning the difference between New Zealand and France concerning the interpretation or application of two agreements, concluded on 9 July 1986 between the two States and which related to the problems arising from the Rainbow Warrior Affair*, 1990, paragraph 100).

In our case, Unda seems indeed to be responsible even for a number of material breaches. The object—or main aim—of the PoD was disarmament. Several PoD Articles, eg Articles 5–7, lay down obligations for the parties to reduce their different weapon arsenals within two years by half of what they had at the time of the conclusion of the treaty. However, there is evidence that Unda has actually not been disarming but has increased the number of biological and chemical weapons. This is against Articles 6 and 7 PoD, which not only establish a disarmament obligation (and thus arming is logically already a violation), but explicitly State that increasing the weapons arsenal is not permitted under any circumstance. Breaching these Articles amounts to a material breach in the sense of Article 60 paragraph 3(b), namely a 'violation of a provision essential to the accomplishment of the object of the treaty'. Violating disarmament obligations clearly violates a disarmament treaty.

Furthermore, Article 11 PoD establishes that State parties have to allow the inspectors to enter their territory at any time in order to control but also ensure the fulfilment of the obligations (namely disarmament) of the treaty. Unda, however, refuses to let the inspectors in. This too could be seen as a material breach of the PoD: the whole point of Article 11 was to make sure through the control by these independent inspectors that disarmament (which is the aim of the PoD) was actually carried out. Without these controls, disarmament would be less likely since no one could control or verify whether States are actually complying with their disarmament obligations. Hence, the requirements of a material breach in Article 60 paragraph 3(b) VCLT used as a customary reflection seems again to be satisfied.

In addition, we could also consider that Article 3 PoD is breached by Unda, since in order to achieve disarmament, Article 3 provided that the numbers of weapons shall be disclosed as well as be controlled by independent international inspectors. However, by not voluntarily presenting the number of its weapons (but stating that evidence about its increase in weapons are only rumours), as well as its refusal to co-operate with the inspectors, Unda has indeed also violated this provision, which can said to be 'essential to the accomplishment of the object of the treaty', namely disarmament.

Since the treaty under consideration is a multilateral treaty, we have to analyse the necessary consequences under paragraph 2 of Article 60 VCLT, dealing with this kind of treaties. Letter (a) cannot be invoked, since visibly there is no unanimous agreement among the parties to the treaty as to either suspension or termination of the PoD due to its material breach. Tellus and Ignis only 'call upon Unda' and want to give it more time and hence are clearly not ready to take any concrete measures. Letter (b) of the same paragraph does not seem to be wholly appropriate either. It is difficult to see why Aura should be considered a 'specially affected' party. In fact, Aura, Tellus and Ignis are all affected in the same way by the material breach by Unda and none of them can be singled out. This leaves letter (c). According to this provision, any party (except the defaulting State) can invoke the material breach for suspending the treaty between itself and the defaulting State, if it can be shown that the treaty in question is of such a nature that a material breach radically changes the position of every party concerning the further performance of the treaty. Disarmament treaties normally heavily depend on mutual performance (and also mutual trust). If one party decides to increase its number of weapons instead of decreasing it, it is difficult to see why the other States party to the treaty should not also increase their weapons for their own security. In that sense, a breach of a disarmament treaty indeed radically changes the position of every other

State party because it will not have any incentive at all itself to conform to the treaty and to go on to honour the obligations contained therein. Therefore, we can conclude that the customary reflection of Article 60 paragraph 2(c) is applicable in our case. Aura can invoke it to suspend the PoD between itself and all the other States (but the PoD will remain in force between between Tellus, Ignis and Unda *inter se*). It is important to note that Aura can only suspend the treaty and not terminate it.

3. Acquiesence

According to the customary reflection of Article 45 VCLT acquiesence is possible for Article 60 VCLT. However, seeing the protest and the fact that Aura wants actively to take steps, it is clear that this is not an option for this State. Thus, there is neither explicit nor implicit acquiesence.

4. Separability

Article 44 VCLT in its paragraph 2 (used as a reflection of customary law) mentions that Article 60 VCLT contains itself rules on the separability of treaties. Indeed, the provisions in paragraph 2 of Article 60 VCLT each allows the States to terminate or suspend the treaty 'in whole or in part'. The PoD is a disarmament treaty, thus its breach can be seen as undermining the whole regime rather than a few clauses only. Furthermore, from the facts of the case, and in light of the numerous material breaches, it does not seem that Aura is willing to suspend some specific clauses only, but rather that it wants to suspend the whole PoD. Under Article 60 paragraph 2(c) it is its right to suspend the whole treaty if it wishes so. Consequently, there is no separability in this case.

5. Consequences of suspension and conclusion

The consequences of suspension can be found in Article 72 VCLT, used as a customary reflection. According to it, suspension means that the parties between which the treaty is suspended do not momentarily have any obligation to perform the treaty (Article 72 paragraph 1(a) VCLT). However, the treaty as such, as well as all acts executed under it, remain perfectly valid (unlike invalidity, where in general all acts performed since the beginning of the treaty become void, and also unlike termination where the treaty ends). Therefore, the PoD can be resumed later on between Aura and the other States if the parties so agree. States have, however to be reminded of paragraph 2 of Article 72 VCLT, which States that in the period of suspension, States should refrain from taking any measures which would block the resumption of the treaty later on.

Chapter 4

SUGGESTED SOLUTIONS
Responsibility of States for Internationally Wrongful Acts

SUGGESTED SOLUTIONS
Attribution and violation of an international obligation

Suggested Solution—Case 4.1

Abbreviations used

ICJ = International Court of Justice
ILC = International Law Commission
PCIJ = Permanent Court of International Justice
SRA = ILC Articles on Responsibility of States for Internationally Wrongful Acts from 2001 (State Responsibility Articles)
UN = United Nations

1. Applicable law

The law applicable to this case is first and foremost contained in the ILC Articles on Responsibility of States for Internationally Wrongful Acts from 2001 (State Responsibility Articles; SRA). These Articles are not a treaty, even though they have been accepted by the UN General Assembly. However, it is generally recognised that the rules formulated by the ILC in these Articles reflect customary law. This has, for example, been confirmed by the International Court of Justice in the *Genocide* case (ICJ, Judgment, *Application of the Convention on the Prevention and Punishment of the Crime of Genocide* (Bosnia and Herzegovina v Serbia and Montenegro), 2007, paragraph 401) or the *Gabčíkovo-Nagymaros* case (ICJ, Judgment, *Gabčíkovo-Nagymaros Project* (Hungary/Slovakia), 1997, paragraph 47).

Apart from the SRA, the applicable law also includes the UN Charter to which both States are parties.

It is clear from Article 1 SRA that a State is responsible for its own international wrongful acts. In order to hold a State responsible for a particular act or omission, Article 2 SRA sets out two necessary conditions. First, the act or omission in question must be attributable to the State in question; and second, this act or omission must constitute a violation of an international obligation of the State. We have to analyse these two elements in turn. It should also be mentioned that according to Article 3 SRA it is international law—and not a State's internal law—which determines whether or not an act is internationally wrongful.

2. Attribution

Articles 4–11 SRA deal with the question of attribution.

Article 4 SRA holds that the State is responsible for the acts of all its organs, regardless of its function (executive, judicial, legislative or any other function), the position or characterisation of that organ. Furthermore, paragraph 2 clarifies that under this Article all organs which have the status as State organs under internal law will be included.

In our case, the act (the accidental firing of five missiles) is performed by the military of Styrom. Normally the military is considered to be an organ of the State, since it is usually the State itself which has the prerogative of public power in States. Therefore, the actions of the military can be attributed to the State of Styrom under Article 4 SRA.

3. Violation

Before analysing the potential violation we have to establish some fundamental points concerning the violation. According to Article 12 SRA there is a breach of an international obligation when a State does not act in conformity with what is expected from it under its international obligations. Thereby, the character or the international norm violated does not matter. This means that the international obligation can be of conventional but also of customary nature. In addition, Article 13 SRA makes clear that an act or omission can only be considered as a breach of an international obligation if at the time of the commission of the act or omission this international obligation was in force for the State in question.

Under Article 2 paragraph 4 of the UN Charter, States have the obligation to refrain from the use or threat of use of force against the territorial integrity or political independence of other States.

It is clear that firing missiles onto the territory of another State is an undisputable use of force against the territorial integrity of the other State, even though this act of course does not amount to an aggression by Styrom against the Kingdom of Kachan.

The fact that the launch of the missiles was an accident can be considered as being immaterial to the question of State responsibility. It is generally accepted (even though not completely undisputed) that it is not necessary that an act has been committed in bad faith or with any intention in order to be internationally wrongful. The SRA are in this sense completely neutral to the question of eventual intent or negligence with which an act has or has not been committed. Thus, whenever there has been a breach of an international obligation of a State and when that breach is attributable to the State, that State will be responsible (this is also called strict liability).

Therefore, we can conclude that even though the launch of the missiles onto the territory of the Kingdom of Kachan was an accident and not intended by Styrom, Styrom breached an international obligation (Article 2 paragraph 4 of the UN Charter) which was in force for Styrom at the time of the breach (since it is a UN member). Furthermore, the act is attributable to Styrom, as seen above, because it was its own military that fired the missiles.

4. Circumstance precluding wrongfulness

You are not asked to deal with this here.

5. Consequences

There is an obligation to make reparations for the injuries caused, contained in Article 31 SRA. This obligation is customary law, as has been recognised already by the Permanent Court of International Justice in the *Chorzów Factory* case (PCIJ, Judgment, *Case concerning the Factory at Chorzów (Claim for Indemnity)*, 1927, 21). Article 31 paragraph 2 SRA defines injuries as material or moral damage.

Restitution (Article 35 SRA) is in our case not possible: it is 'materially impossible' (letter (a)) to 're-establish the situation which existed before', since there is nothing that can be physically 'given back'. The village is partly destroyed and two villagers are dead.

Therefore, reparation will have to take the form of compensation (Article 36 SRA), eg by paying damages or reconstructing the houses, and/or the form of satisfaction (Article 37 SRA), eg by a public apology by Styrom. What the exact form of reparation will be is up to either the States to determine in negotiations, or for an international court seized of the matter to decide.

6. Conclusion

Styrom can be held responsible for having accidently launched five missiles onto the territory of the Kingdom of Kachan.

Suggested Solution—Case 4.2

Abbreviations used

ICJ = International Court of Justice
ICTY = International Criminal Tribunal for the Former-Yugoslavia
ICL = International Law Commission
PCIJ = Permanent Court of International Justice
SAFE = Safety As First End (Private Security Company)
SRA = ILC Articles on Responsibility of States for Internationally Wrongful Acts 2001 (State Responsibility Articles)
VCDR = Vienna Convention on Diplomatic Relations

1. Applicable law

To solve this issue we will have to apply the ILC's State Responsibility Articles from 2001 (SRA). It is important to note that these Articles are not a convention. However, they are nevertheless legally binding, since it is generally recognised that they reflect customary international law on the matter of State responsibility. This has, for example, been confirmed by the International Court of Justice in the *Genocide* case between Bosnia and Herzegovina and Serbia and Montenegro in 2007 (ICJ, Judgment, *Application of the Convention on the Prevention and Punishment of the Crime of Genocide* (Bosnia and Herzegovina v Serbia and Montenegro), 2007, paragraph 401).

In addition, since this is a case involving diplomats, we will also apply the Vienna Convention on Diplomatic Relations (VCDR) from 1961, to which both States are parties.

Article 1 SRA confirms that every internationally wrongful act of a State makes that State internationally responsible.

To arrive at the conclusion whether or not a State is responsible, we have first and foremost to analyse two elements of an internationally wrongful act, which are to be found in Article 2 SRA. First, the act or omission in question has to be attributable to the State; and second, the act or omission must constitute a breach of an international obligation incumbent on this State. It does not matter which one of the elements is considered first.

2. Attribution: the soccer fans

Attribution has to be found under Articles 4–11 SRA. Acts of private individuals can only be attributable to the State under specific circumstances.

In our case, the group of soccer fans beating the diplomats from Pomal seem indeed to have been private individuals. Therefore, they cannot be considered a de jure organ and neither a de facto organ of Allenda. Due to lack of 'complete dependency' as established by the ICJ in the *Nicaragua* case (ICJ, Judgment on the Merits, *Military and Paramilitary Activities in and against Nicaragua* (Nicaragua v United States of America), 1986, paragraphs 109–112) and the *Genocide* case (ICJ, Judgment, *Application of the Convention on the Prevention and Punishment of the Crime of Genocide* (Bosnia and Herzegovina v Serbia and Montenegro), 2007, paragraphs 390–395)), attribution under Article 4 SRA is not possible. In addition, Article 5 SRA does not seem to be possible, since the group of soccer fans is not 'mandated by a law or decree' of the State to 'exercise governmental authority'.

Article 8 SRA attributes to the State acts of a group of private individuals if that group acts upon instruction or under direction or control of the State. The ICJ has established in its *Nicaragua* case (ICJ, Judgment on the Merits, *Military and Paramilitary Activities in and against Nicaragua* (Nicaragua v United States of America), 1986, paragraphs 105–116) and later on also in the *Genocide* case (ICJ, Judgment, *Application of the Convention on the Prevention and Punishment of the Crime of Genocide* (Bosnia and Herzegovina v Serbia and Montenegro), 2007, paragraphs 396–407) that for Article 8 SRA to be applicable effective control over that group was needed. The ICJ in the *Genocide* case rejected the overall control test established by the ICTY in the *Tadić* case (ICTY, Appeals Chamber, Judgment, *Tadić*, 1999 (Case No. IT-94-1-A), paragraphs 99–145). This means that virtually every act has to be controlled and ordered by the State. Simply supporting the group with, for example, weapons or training would not be enough for effective control. However, in our case there is no indication whatsoever that the State of Allenda ordered the soccer fans to beat up the diplomats from Pomal. Therefore, attribution under Article 8 SRA is not possible either.

Finally, Article 11 SRA deals with the situation when a State accepts an act of a group of private persons as its own act after the commission of this act. This has, for example, been the situation in Iran, when the government adopted the occupation of the US Embassy by students as its own act and supported the students. However, in order for this Article to be satisfied, the government needs to have very clearly and directly expressed that it acknowledges this act as its own. Simply not condemning an act would hence not be enough. Therefore, statements made by Allenda after the incident, eg denying responsibility or talking about 'rightfully disappointed fans of Allenda's national soccer team', would not be enough. Consequently, there is also no attribution under Article 11 SRA.

Therefore, it seems that the act of beating up the diplomats from Pomal as such cannot be attributed to Allenda, since the only ones beating the diplomats were the private soccer fans.

However, we should consider what international obligations Allenda had with respect to those diplomats to determine whether this State can be held responsible for some other act or omission than the beating up itself. Thus, it is now most convenient to study the question of violation.

[*As stated above, there is no obligation to follow this order. You can also first continue with attribution and then analyse any potential violation.*]

3. Violation

For convenience in this case we will first look at possible violations.

According to Article 12 SRA, there is a breach of an international obligation as soon as an act or omission of the State is not in conformity with what this obligation requires. Hence, the character of the obligation breached does not matter: it can be of conventional but also of customary nature.

Article 13 SRA then adds the condition that in order to constitute a violation, the obligation breached must have been in force for the State in question at the time of the commission of the act.

If we look at the VCDR, we find that Article 29 of this Convention provides that the person of the diplomat is inviolable and that the receiving State has a duty to 'take all appropriate steps to prevent any attack on his person, freedom and dignity'.

In our case, the duty to make sure that diplomats will not be attacked was a binding treaty obligation on Allenda (Article 12 SRA), since it was a party to the VCDR at the time of the commission of the beating (Article 13 SRA). Beating up diplomats clearly violates Article 29 VCDR, but what is even more important in our case is that *not preventing* private individuals from beating up diplomats is also a violation of this Article. The State has after all an obligation to 'take all appropriate steps' to prevent such attacks. However, the members of the private security firm SAFE were just standing there and watching in silence as the diplomats were beaten. It would have been their duty (and hence they would have taken all appropriate steps) to intervene to protect the diplomats whom they clearly recognised. Hence, there is a clear omission in our case, namely an omission concerning the duty to protect diplomats of a foreign State under Article 29 VCDR.

Since there is an omission established, we have to consider attribution of that omission to Allenda, since both elements are necessary to determine State responsibility.

4. Attribution: the private security firm

The private security firm SAFE has been authorised by the State of Allenda by a governmental decree 'to maintain law and public order' in the capital of Allenda, Yema. In short, it is mandated to exercise police functions since the police force of Allenda has been almost totally eliminated.

It is clear that SAFE is not a de jure organ of Allenda in the sense of Article 4, nor is it a de facto organ under that article, since again the necessary 'complete dependency' (as established by the ICJ in the *Nicaragua* case and the *Genocide* case mentioned above) is lacking.

Article 5 SRA provides that a conduct is attributable to the State when the person or entity exercising the act or omission is—even though not an organ in the sense of Article 4 SRA—empowered by the law of that State to exercise elements of governmental authority. In addition, Article 5 clarifies that the conduct in question is only attributable to the State if the person or entity acted in the capacity of exercising governmental authority granted to them. This Article seems to match our situation. SAFE is a private security firm, not an organ of Allenda. However, SAFE is authorised by a governmental decree having the force of law (so an internal law of the State of Allenda) to 'maintain law and public order'. Maintaining law and order is, however, usually seen as a governmental function since the State has the monopoly of power in its territory. In addition, the members of SAFE that did not protect the diplomats were actually on patrol, ie on duty, and therefore were 'acting in that capacity [of exercising governmental authority] in the particular instance'. All elements necessary for Article 5 seem therefore to be fulfilled.

Hence we can conclude that the omission—the non-protection of the diplomats as was the State's duty under Article 29 VCDR—is indeed attributable to Allenda under

Article 5 SRA. Therefore, Allenda is responsible under international law for this omission of not protecting the diplomats of Pomal from harm, but not for the act of beating the diplomats, which was committed by purely private individuals and thus cannot be attributed to the State.

5. Circumstances precluding wrongfulness

You are not asked to deal with the circumstances precluding wrongfulness.

6. Consequences and conclusion

As stated in the *Chorzów Factory* case of the Permanent Court of International Justice (PCIJ, Judgment, *Case concerning the Factory at Chorzów (Claim for Indemnity)*, 1927, 21), it is a rule of customary international law that a State that is responsible for an internationally wrongful act has a duty to make reparations for the injury caused. This customary obligation can be found in the SRA in Article 31.

Allenda has thus an obligation to make reparations.

There are different forms of reparation, but not all are possible in this case. Restitution (Article 35 SRA) is not possible in our case, since it is simply impossible to 're-establish the situation which existed before'. A beating cannot be undone and also nothing has been taken away that could be given back.

This leaves as a possible option compensation (Article 36 SRA), eg financial payments to Pomal and eventually also to the diplomats for the harm done. Another, or even additional, possibility is satisfaction (Article 37 SRA), eg an apology by Allenda to Pomal, or also the arrest and conviction of the private individuals responsible for the beating and/or of the SAFE members who did not intervene. Which form the reparation will take in the end is for the States to settle through negotiations, or for a court seized of the matter to determine.

Suggested Solution—Case 4.3

Abbreviations used

ICJ = International Court of Justice
ILC = International Law Commission
PCIJ = Permanent Court of International Justice
SRA = ILC Articles on Responsibility of States for Internationally Wrongful Acts 2001 (State Responsibility Articles)
SPP = Service for the Protection of Personalitites
VCDR = Vienna Convention on Diplomatic Relations

1. Applicable law

To answer this question we will apply the ILC Articles on Responsibility of States for Internationally Wrongful Acts (2001), also called the State Responsibility Articles (SRA).

The SRA are not a treaty, but it is well accepted that they reflect international customary law in the matter of State responsibility. This has been confirmed by the ICJ in cases such as the *Iran Hostages* case (ICJ, Judgment, *United States Diplomatic and Consular Staff in Teheran* (United States of America v Iran), 1980, paragraphs 56–92), the *Gabčíkovo-Nagymaros* case (ICJ, Judgment, *Gabčíkovo-Nagymaros Project* (Hungary/Slovakia), 1997, paragraph 47) and most recently the *Genocide* case (ICJ, Judgment, *Application of the Convention on the Prevention and Punishment of the Crime of Genocide* (Bosnia and Herzegovina v Serbia and Montenegro), 2007, paragraph 401).

In addition we will also apply the Vienna Convention on Diplomatic Relations (VCDR) to which both States are parties.

Article 1 SRA provides that a State is internationally responsible for every one of its internationally wrongful acts. Article 2 then sets out the two necessary elements to find an internationally wrongful act. First of all, the act or omission needs to be attributable to the State in question; and secondly, the act or omission must constitute a violation of an international obligation of the State in question.

2. Attribution

The act in question is the abduction of Madam Diamgold, the wife of the ambassador of Petroland. This act has been perpetrated by Gideon and Tristan, two agents of the Service for the Protection of Personalities (SPP) of the State of Monailand.

Since it is stated that the SPP is a service of the *State* of Monailand we can assume that the SPP therefore can be seen as an organ of that State. This assumption is confirmed by the fact that later on Monailand speaks of 'its agents' when talking about the attribution of Gideon and Tristan's act. Article 4 SRA provides that the conduct of every organ of the State is attributable to the State. Therefore, it does not matter what function or characteristic this organ had, but it needs to have its statute as an organ of the State according to the internal law of the State.

Assuming that the SPP has such a statute under the internal law of Monailand (there is nothing to make us doubt that they do not have such a statute), we can therefore conclude that the acts of all agents of the SPP are attributable to Monailand.

Monailand argues that the conduct could not be attributable to it because it was done with a purely private goal. Yet, unlike under Article 5 SRA, in the case of State organs under Article 4 SRA *all* acts of these organs are attributable to the State. The private or public goal of the act is therefore completely irrelevant and acts of organs under Article 4 SRA can be attributable even if the person belonging to the organ in question did not act in that capacity at the time of the commission of the act (this results from a comparative reading with Article 5 SRA). Consequently, Monailand's first argument needs to be rejected.

Monailand further argues that a State can never be responsible for acts of its agents when they have clearly exceeded their authority.

However, Article 7 SRA provides that the conduct of an organ of the State is attributable to the State even if the organs/agents in question exceed their authority or contravene instructions. Under this Article it is, however, necessary that the organ/agent has acted in its capacity as organ/agent at the moment of the facts, and in that sense lead outside persons to believe that it was an organ of the State acting in its official capacity when committing the act. As stated by the Arbitral Tribunal in the *Youmans* case (Arbitral Tribunal, Award, *Thomas H Youmans (USA) v United Mexican States*, 1926, paragraphs 12–14), for example, police officers acting in their uniform can be said to act in their capacity as State organs charged with keeping peace and order in the State. Thus any of their acts committed in uniform, even if they exceed their authorities or contravene instructions, are attributable to the State in question under Article 7 SRA.

In our case, by abducting Madam Diamgold and finally accidentally killing her Gideon and Tristan clearly contravened instructions (which were to bring Madam Diamgold to the airport) and also exceeded their authority (which did not include abduction and killings). When they abducted the wife of the ambassador they were both wearing their uniforms and carrying their weapons. Furthermore, they had picked her up following a normal order and in their function as SPP agents charged with the protection of foreign ambassadors. They therefore acted clearly 'in their capacity' as SPP agents, who are—as seen above—State organs.

Therefore, Article 7 SRA applies and the second argument of Monailand has to be rejected as well.

Consequently, the abduction of the wife of the ambassador by Gideon and Tristan is clearly attributable to Monailand under Articles 4 and 7 SRA in combination.

3. Violation

Article 12 SRA provides that there is a violation of an international obligation if a State does not act in conformity with what is expected from it in accordance with international law. Therefore it does not matter whether the obligation arises from a treaty or from customary law.

Article 13 SRA, however, adds that the obligation must be in force for the State at the moment of the alleged violation, otherwise this cannot constitute a violation of an international obligation.

According to Article 37 paragraph 1 VCDR, members of the family of a diplomatic agent forming part of his household benefit from the same privileges and immunities as the diplomats under Articles 29–36 VCDR. Among these, Article 29 VCDR provides that the person of a diplomatic agent is inviolable. Consequently, in applying Article 37 paragraph 1 the person of, for example, the wife of the diplomat is also inviolable.

Madam Diamgold is the wife of the ambassador of Petroland, and thus under Article 37 paragraph 1 VCDR entitled to the same protection as the ambassador himself. Abducting and killing Madam Diamgold has very clearly violated her inviolability, granted under Article 29 VCDR. The obligations under the VCDR are in force for Monailand on 14 May 2010 when the acts occur, since Monailand is a member of the VCDR since its entry into force (which was on 24 April 1964).

Consequently, there is a violation of an international obligation incumbent on Monailand, namely of Article 29 VCDR combined with Article 37 VCDR. As seen above, this violation is attributable to Monailand.

4. Circumstances precluding wrongfulness

You are not required to deal with this issue here.

5. Consequences and conclusion

First of all, according to Article 30 SRA, Monailand has to give appropriate guarantees to Petroland that a similar incident will not occur again. Furthermore, it is well accepted under international law that a State responsible for an internationally wrongful act has the duty to make reparations. This has been confirmed as a customary rule by the Permanent Court of International Justice in the *Chorzów Factory* case (PCIJ, Judgment, *Case concerning the Factory at Chorzów (Claim for Indemnity)*, 1927, 21) and is also contained in Article 31 SRA.

There are different forms of reparation (Article 34 SRA). Unfortunately, restitution (Article 35 SRA) is materially impossible since there is nothing to 'give back'. The wife of the ambassador is dead and a life cannot be 'given back'.

An appropriate form of reparation would be compensation (Article 36 SRA) by making financial payments to remedy the damages. Damages—as defined by Article 31 paragraph 2 SRA—include both material and moral injuries. As the commentary of the ILC reveals, compensation has been used frequently also in cases of loss of life. In addition, satisfaction (Article 37 SRA) also seems to be appropriate, eg in the form of public apologies of Monailand to Petroland, or/and by prosecuting the two agents responsible, Gideon and Tristan. The exact form of reparation will have to be decided by the States in negotiations or by a competent court or tribunal.

Suggested Solution—Case 4.4

Abbreviations used

EC	= Equalisation Committee
ICJ	= International Court of Justice
ICTY	= International Criminal Tribunal for the Former-Yugoslavia
ILC	= International Law Commission
PCIJ	= Permanent Court of International Justice
SRA	= ILC Articles on Responsibility of States for Internationally Wrongful Acts 2001 (State Responsibility Articles)
UN	= United Nations

1. Applicable law

The law we will be applying in this case is first and foremost the State Responsibility Articles (SRA) from the International Law Commission from 2001. It is important to note that these Articles are not a treaty. Nevertheless, they are binding as customary international law which has, among other things, been confirmed by the International Court of Justice in the *Genocide* case in 2007 (ICJ, Judgment, *Application of the Convention on the Prevention and Punishment of the Crime of Genocide* (Bosnia and

Herzegovina v Serbia and Montenegro), 2007, paragraph 401). Therefore, we can apply the Articles as customary law, which is binding on all States.

In addition, we will also apply the Charter of the United Nations, to which both States in question are parties and which is hence also binding on them.

Article 1 SRA clarifies that a State is responsible for every of its internationally wrongful acts. In order to have an internationally wrongful act, there need to be two elements present (as set out in Article 2 SRA): first, the act or omission in question has to be attributable to the State; and second, this act or omission has to amount to a breach of an international obligation incumbent on that State. We have to analyse these two elements in turn.

2. Attribution

The question of attribution is regulated by Articles 4–11 SRA.

In our case, it is clear that the Equalisation Committee (EC) is not a State organ, as is envisaged under Article 4 SRA: it is not given this status under an internal law of the State, since it is mentioned that it does not have any official status and is not mentioned in any official document or law either.

In addition, attribution under Article 5 SRA can be excluded since there is no law empowering the group to exercise governmental functions.

Looking at the remaining Articles dealing with attribution, Article 8 SRA seems to be the most appropriate one. According to Article 8 SRA, the act of a group or person is attributable to the State if it can be shown that this group or person actually acted on the instruction of, *or* under the direction *or* control of the State when it was committing its acts (or omissions). From the Article as such it is, however, not clear what kind or level of control is necessary in order to satisfy this Article.

The International Court of Justice (ICJ) in the *Nicaragua* case (ICJ, Judgment on the Merits, *Military and Paramilitary Activities in and against Nicaragua* (Nicaragua v United States of America), 1986, paragraphs 105–116) has established the test of 'effective control'. This means that not only is the State financing, training or equipping the group in question, but it also controls all their actions in the sense that it is the State that orders the group to engage in a specific conduct. In this scenario, the group of private individuals or rebels is effectively the 'puppet' of the State.

Later, the International Criminal Tribunal for the Former Yugoslavia (ICTY) established another test, with a lower threshold. The 'overall control' test set out in the *Tadić* case (ICTY, Appeals Chamber, Judgment, *Tadić*, 1999 (Case No. IT-94-1-A) paragraphs 99–145) essentially provides that it is enough that the State finances, equips or trains a particular group to make all the acts of that group attributable to the State in question. It is thus not necessary to show that the State was exercising any control over the actions as such.

The ICJ in the *Genocide* case (ICJ, Judgment, *Application of the Convention on the Prevention and Punishment of the Crime of Genocide* (Bosnia and Herzegovina v Serbia and Montenegro), 2007, paragraphs 396–407) however reaffirmed the 'effective control' test for the purpose of State responsibility, arguing on the one hand that the ICTY was concerned with a different issue (namely the classification of conflicts and not State responsibility), and on the other hand saying that it would be dangerous to broaden the applicability of State responsibility too much. In any event, even if the situation might not be totally clear as of today, it is advisable to employ so far the higher standard of the 'effective control' test established by the ICJ, reaffirmed by the International Law Commission and many scholars.

[*It would not be necessarily wrong to argue based on the 'overall control' test (lower threshold, thus easier to find attribution of acts of groups or persons to the State under Article 8 SRA). However, any such departure from generally accepted standards in international law needs to be very well argued.*]

We have now to consider the application of these theoretical considerations to our case.

The EC is a group of persons that has been trained and equipped by military officers of Corle. More importantly, the secret documents show that the EC has been created by order of the current president of Corle, Mr Leon. Moreover, President Leon has explicitly ordered the attack on the factory of Mata and thereby necessarily also the attack on Mata (since the forces had to cross the border before getting to the factory, which they did in a violent fashion). In addition, he stated that the EC should get the construction plans 'at any cost'. Thus, we can argue that even though he might not have directly ordered the killings of who ever stands in their way he must at least have accepted the possibility that there would be casualties. It seems that the 'effective control' test is satisfied since the EC acted on the instructions of President Leon, who is representing the State. Therefore, the acts of the EC—attacking the State of Mata, breaking into the factory to steal the plans and killing several persons in the process—are clearly attributable to the State of Corle under Article 8 SRA.

However, there is no evidence at all that the State of Corle or its President also ordered the attack on the ship in the territorial waters of Mata. Rather, it seems that this act was carried out by the EC alone. Therefore, although this would arguably satisfy the 'overall control' test, since the EC was nevertheless still equipped and trained by Corle, it does not fulfil the 'effective control' test (there was no order by the State to attack and rob the ship in the territorial waters of Mata). Hence, this second act of the EC cannot be attributed to Corle under Article 8 SRA.

In conclusion, we can say that the first acts of the EC—attacking Mata, breaking into the factory and killing several persons—is attributable to Corle under Article 8 while the second act of the EC is not attributable.

3. Violation

Before we analyse the potential violation it is relevant to point out that according to Article 12 SRA there is an international breach if the State in question does not comply with what is required from it under its international obligations. Hence the character of the obligation breached does not matter, ie it can be an obligation of conventional or customary origin. In addition, Article 13 SRA importantly points out that a breach of an international obligation can only be considered to be a breach if at the time of the commission of the breach the State in question was bound by that obligation.

Both States are bound by the UN Charter. Article 2 paragraph 4 of the UN Charter establishes the non-use of force principle: it is prohibited to use or threat to use force against the 'territorial integrity or political independence' of another State, 'or in any other manner inconsistent with the purposes of the United Nations'. Furthermore, the UN General Assembly resolution 2625, also called the Friendly Relations resolution, provides that States should refrain from 'organizing or encouraging the organisation of irregular forces or armed bands, including mercenaries, for incursion into the territory of another State'. It is true that UN General Assembly resolutions are not legally binding as such. However, in this case it can be argued that this resolution only explains and spells out what is already contained in the UN Charter, eg under Article 2 paragraph 4 of the UN Charter. Thus, the resolution does not set out new obligations but helps to clarify how Article 2 paragraph 4 of the UN Charter should be understood.

The EC attacks Mata in order to cross Mata's border. This constitutes a clear violation of the prohibition to use force against the territorial integrity of another State contained in Article 2 paragraph 4 of the UN Charter, as explained in resolution 2625 (since the EC constitute 'irregular forces' which were organised by Corle itself). In addition, the purposes of the United Nations include, among others, maintaining international peace and security. By attacking Mata, breaking into the factory and killing several people it can also be argued that this is to be seen as an attack 'inconsistent with the purposes of the United Nations'. At the time of the commission of this attack, Corle was a party to the UN Charter (it has been a party since its independence in 1973) and thus these obligations were in force for it.

[*Potentially, we could also argue that the EC, and thus Corle, violated the right to life (the right not to be arbitrarily deprived of one's life) of the people that were killed in the attack. We do not know from the facts whether Corle is a party to instruments such as the International Convention on Civil and Political Rights (ICCPR) containing the right to life. However, the right to life is usually accepted to be of customary nature. Since according to Article 12 SRA the origin of the international obligation does not matter, we could argue that Corle is also responsible for a violation of the right to life of the persons killed. Yet, the problem here is that this obligation is not directly owed to the State of Mata as such, but to the dead individuals. Thus, before Mata can invoke this violation for the purpose of State responsibility, it has—according to Article 44(b) SRA—to be ascertained that local remedies were all exhausted in Corle in order to get redress for this violation. Since we do not know from the facts of the case whether local remedies have been exhausted, we will not consider the issue of the violation of the right to life any further.*]

We can consequently conclude that in any event there was a violation of an international obligation of the State of Corle, namely a violation of Article 2 paragraph 4 of the UN Charter.

4. Circumstances precluding wrongfulness

You do not need to deal with these here.

5. Consequences and conclusion

It is a well-established principle of customary law recognised, for example, in the *Chorzów Factory* case (PCIJ, Judgment, *Case concerning the Factory at Chorzów*

(Claim for Indemnity), 1927, 21) that a State that is responsible for an act or omission under international law has an obligation to make reparations for the injury caused. This obligation has also been incorporated in Article 31 SRA.

There are different forms of reparation. First, we could consider restitution (Article 35 SRA). There can be no restitution for the attack as such and the killings. These are facts that cannot be undone and thus it is 'materially impossible' to restitute. However, since the EC managed to steal construction plans for high-precision instruments, Corle is obliged to give these plans back to Mata.

In addition, compensation under Article 36 SRA is a possibility, eg by financial payments made by Corle to Mata for the damage (material and moral) that is financially assessable (ie excluding, for example, payments for the affront made to the State, but only related to material or moral damage to property and persons—see Article 36 paragraph 2 SRA). Furthermore, under Article 37 SRA (satisfaction) Corle could be obliged to make, for example, public apologies.

In addition to these possible forms of reparation (to be determined by a court or by the States through negotiations), we can also consider that under Article 30(b) SRA the State of Corle also has a duty to give guarantees that it will not use the EC to attack Mata again (or attack Mata at all, for that matter). This might be necessary to re-establish a certain level of trust between the two States.

Suggested Solution—Case 4.5

Abbreviations used

ICJ = International Court of Justice
ILC = International Law Commission
PCIJ = Permanent Court of International Justice
SRA = ILC Articles on Responsibility of States for Internationally Wrongful Acts 2001 (State Responsibility Articles)
VCCR = Vienna Convention on Consular Relations

1. Applicable law

We will apply the ILC Articles on Responsibility of States for Internationally Wrongful Acts (2001), also called the State Responsibility Articles (SRA).

The SRA are not a treaty, but it is well accepted that they reflect international customary law in the matter of State responsibility. This has been confirmed by the ICJ in cases such as the *Iran Hostages* case (ICJ, Judgment, *United States Diplomatic and Consular Staff in Teheran* (United States of America v Iran), 1980, paragraphs 56–92), the *Gabčíkovo-Nagymaros* case (ICJ, Judgment, *Gabčíkovo-Nagymaros Project* (Hungary/Slovakia), 1997, paragraph 47) and most recently the *Genocide* case ICJ, Judgment, *Application of the Convention on the Prevention and Punishment of the Crime of Genocide* (Bosnia and Herzegovina v Serbia and Montenegro), 2007, paragraph 401).

Since we do not have any information as to whether the States in question are parties to the Vienna Convention on Consular Relations (VCCR, 1963), we will apply customary international law. It is widely agreed that the VCCR reflects customary international law in the matter. This can also be inferred from the preamble of the VCCR itself, which in one paragraph affirms 'that the rules of customary international law *continue* to govern matters not expressly regulated by the provisions of the present Convention' (emphasis added).

Article 1 SRA provides that a State is internationally responsible for every of its internationally wrongful acts. Article 2 then sets out the two necessary elements to find an internationally wrongful act. First of all, the act or omission needs to be attributable to the State in question; and secondly, the act or omission must constitute a violation of an international obligation of the State in question.

2. Attribution

The act in question is the seizing of the consulate of Waïkiland by a group of inhabitants from Nicetown in order to detain looters.

Generally, Unluckland is right to say that acts of private persons are not attributable to States. Yet, analyzing the Articles on attribution in the SRA (Articles 4–11 SRA), we can see that there are nevertheless some circumstances were such acts can be attributed to the State.

The most appropriate Article in our case seems to be Article 9 SRA. This Article provides that acts of persons or groups of persons are to be considered acts of the State if these persons or groups have in fact been 'exercising elements of governmental authority' in the absence of the official authorities. In addition, circumstances have to be such as 'to call for the exercise of those elements of authority'. It is clear from the reference to 'persons or groups of persons' that in this Article, unlike in Articles 4–6, we are not talking about persons constituting an organ of the State. On the contrary, these are private individuals, who in a situation of need and in the absence of the official authorities of the State take over functions of governmental authority.

Generally, maintaining law and public order, and thereby providing security and arresting looters, is a prerogative of the State, ie a 'function of governmental authority'. The situation in Nicetown was very serious. It was cut off from the rest of the country and there were also many victims among the police force and rescue teams. Therefore, there were not enough police officers to maintain peace and security in the town. However, it was also not possible to get help from the 'outside', since the lava had built a wall which made it in the beginning impossible to reach the town by land or sea, and the ashes spitting into the sky made any approach by helicopter or airplane impossible as well. Therefore, there was indeed an absence (or at least a very serious shortage) of official authorities and a situation of need in which it was required that some persons take over some of the functions normally discharged by the police and other security forces, such as arresting looters. The group of Nicetownians in question indeed was exercising only this governmental function when arresting looters. Since the consulate of Waïkiland seems to have been one of the few relatively undamaged buildings, the group expelled the inhabitants to use the basement as a detention centre for looters. Even if the way this has been done might be questionable, detaining people responsible for looting can still be seen as a State function.

It seems that based on the above arguments attribution under Article 9 SRA is possible. This means, therefore, that all acts surrounding this exercise of governmental authority—including the seizing of the consulate—are attributable to Unluckland under Article 9 SRA.

3. Violation

Article 12 SRA provides that there is a violation of an international obligation if a State does not act in conformity with what is expected from it in accordance with international law; it does not matter whether this obligation arises from a treaty or from customary law.

Article 13 SRA, however, adds that the obligation must be in force for the State at the moment of the alleged violation, otherwise this cannot constitute a violation of an international obligation.

As stated above, we will apply customary international law in the matter of consular relations, which are at least partially reflected in the VCCR. Since we are dealing with customary international law (the origin of the obligation does not matter—Article 12 SRA), these obligations are binding on all States (Article 13 SRA), regardless of whether or not they are parties to the VCCR.

Article 31 VCCR, reflecting customary law, States that the premises of consulates are inviolable and can only be entered by the authorities of the host State with the permission of the consul. In our case, the 'authorities' of the host State were made up by this group of Nicetownians, since they were at that time exercising functions of governmental authority. Very obviously they did not ask the consul to enter the consulate or to use it as a detention centre, since otherwise, had the consul agreed, it would not have been necessary to expel the consul and his staff. Therefore, there is a clear violation of the customary rule of inviolability of consular premises contained in Article 31 VCCR.

Since we have found attribution and a violation of an international obligation, we can conclude that prima facie Unluckland is responsible for an internationally wrongful act.

4. Circumstances precluding wrongfulness

You are not required to deal with this issue here.

5. Consequences and conclusion

First of all, according to Article 30 SRA, Unluckland has to assure Waïkiland that such a seizure of one of its consulate will not reproduce itself. In addition, it is well accepted under international law that a State responsible for an internationally wrongful act has the duty to make reparations. This customary rule has been confirmed, for example, by the Permanent Court of International Justice in the *Chorzów Factory* case (PCIJ, Judgment, *Case concerning the Factory at Chorzów (Claim for Indemnity)*, 1927, 21) and is also contained in Article 31 SRA.

There are different forms of reparation (Article 34 SRA).

The most appropriate form seems here to be first of all restitution (Article 35 SRA), by handing back the consulate to Waïkiland. In addition, Unluckland could also have recourse to compensation (Article 36 SRA) by making financial payments to Waïkiland for the damages caused. In addition, satisfaction (Article 37 SRA) also seems to be appropriate, eg in the form of public apologies of Unluckland to Waïkiland. The exact form of reparation will have to be decided by the States in negotiations or by a competent court or tribunal.

Suggested Solution—Case 4.6

Abbreviations used
ICJ = International Court of Justice
ILC = International Law Commission
PCIJ = Permanent Court of International Justice
SRA = ILC Articles on Responsibility of States for Internationally Wrongful Acts, 2001 (State Responsibility Articles)
UN = United Nations
VCDR = Vienna Convention on Diplomatic Relations

1. Applicable law

We will apply the International Law Commission's Articles on State Responsibility from 2001 (SRA) in this case. It is important to note that these Articles are not a treaty. However, they are still legally binding, namely as customary law. It has been confirmed by the International Court of Justice (ICJ), for example in the *Iran Hostages* case (ICJ, Judgment, *United States Diplomatic and Consular Staff in Teheran* (United States of America v Iran), 1980, paragraphs 56–92) or in the *Genocide* case (ICJ, Judgment, *Application of the Convention on the Prevention and Punishment of the Crime of Genocide* (Bosnia and Herzegovina v Serbia and Montenegro), 2007, paragraph 401), that the State Responsibility Articles indeed reflect customary law and are thus binding on all States.

Furthermore, we will be using the 1961 Vienna Convention on Diplomatic Relations (VCDR) to which both States are parties.

Article 1 SRA specifies that every internationally wrongful act of a State will entail the international responsibility of that State. Article 2 SRA sets out the two necessary elements for an internationally wrongful act. First, the act or the omission in question needs to be attributable to the State; and second, the act or omission must amount to a violation of an international obligation of that State. Thus, we have to look at both elements in turn.

2. Attribution

Tiranoc is generally right when it says that acts of private persons are usually not attributable to a State. To be attributable an act or omission needs some sort of link to the State. All possibilities of attribution are set out in Articles 4–11 SRA. Very clearly, the students cannot be considered organs of the State, but they remain private individuals. They are not State organs according to Tiranoc's internal law; they are not de facto State organs since there is no 'complete dependence' (*Nicaragua* case; ICJ, Judgment on the Merits, *Military and Paramilitary Activities in and against Nicaragua (Nicaragua v United States of America)*, 1986, paragraphs 109–112); and there is no internal law mandating them with the exercise of a governmental function. Thus there can be no attribution under Articles such as Articles 4 and 5 SRA. In addition, there seems to be no evidence that it was actually Tiranoc itself that ordered the students to storm the embassy. Rather, it seems that this was a spontaneous act. Therefore, attribution under Article 8 SRA is also not possible.

The most likely Article for attribution is Article 11 SRA, which is inspired by the events leading to the *Iran Hostages* case decided by the ICJ in 1980 (ICJ, Judgment, *United States Diplomatic and Consular Staff in Teheran* (United States of America v Iran), 1980, especially paragraphs 56–92). According to this Article, a conduct that is not attributable to the State under any of the foregoing Articles can nevertheless be attributed to the State if that State 'acknowledges and adopts the conduct in question as its own'. In our case there is, as we have seen, clearly no attribution possible under any of the Articles preceeding Article 11 SRA. Furthermore, the President of Tiranoc in his public statements congratulates the students and openly supports them, even with providing them with food and water to go on in what they are doing. All these actions show that Tiranoc acknowledged and also clearly supported the acts of the students. However, in order to satisfy Article 11 SRA the State must also adopt the conduct as its own. Tiranoc's President added that the acts of the students have to be seen as part of the official policy of Tiranoc. By making the actions of the students part of their official policy, it can be argued that Tiranoc has recognised these acts as their own acts (therefore also part of their own policy). Thus, we can indeed find attribution under Article 11 SRA.

Here it is, however, important to note that under Article 11 only acts which the State has 'acknowledged and adopted as their own' will be attributable to the State and not just any act of this group. Tiranoc clearly adopted the storming and occupation of the embassy as 'their own act', as shown above. However, the President also strongly condemned the searching and destruction of the archives of the embassy. Thus, it cannot be said that Tiranoc adopted the destruction of the archives as its own act. Therefore, only the storming of the embassy and not the destruction of the archives is attributable to Tiranoc under Article 11 (without prejudice to the analysis of the violation). As we can see, Tiranoc is hence not totally correct when it States that the acts of the students can under no circumstances be attributed to it.

It has to be kept in mind that not only acts but also omissions are attributable to the States and can lead to State responsibility. In our case, there is no evidence that the police or military forces of Tiranoc actually protected the embassy of Saphery or tried to stop the students from storming the embassy. Without prejudice to the analysis of the violation, we can say that such an omission would indeed be attributable to Tiranoc under Article 4 SRA. The police or military are normally considered to be organs of the State, since it is the State that has the prerogatives of public power. Therefore, we can find attribution to Tiranoc for an omission of its security apparatus under Article 4 SRA.

3. Violation

Before we start the analysis of any potential violation, we should note two issues concerning the violation. First, according to Article 12 SRA there is a breach if a State does not behave according to what is expected from it under its international obligations: the nature of the violation does not matter. That is, the obligation breached can be of conventional but also of customary nature. Second, Article 13 SRA makes clear that there can only be a breach of an international obligation if that obligation at the time of the commission was actually in force for the State in question.

In our case, both States are parties to the VCDR, which is in force for them at the moment of the facts. According to Article 22 of this Convention, the premises of the embassy in a foreign State are inviolable (paragraph 1) and the receiving State has a duty to take all appropriate steps to protect these premises against any intrusion or damage and to prevent any disturbance of the peace of the embassy (paragraph 2). In our case, the students violated the premises of the embassy by forcibly entering into them. This constitutes a violation of Article 22 paragraph 1 VCDR. Furthermore, it seems that the State did also not take any steps actually to protect the embassy. As mentioned above, this is an omission by Tiranoc, which also constitutes a violation of an international obligation, namely of Article 22 paragraph 2 VCDR. According to Article 24 VCDR, archives of embassies are also inviolable and thus we have an additional breach of an international obligation here, since the students destroyed the archives. But, as noted above, this act by private persons is not attributable to Tiranoc because it condemned rather than adopted this conduct as its own.

In conclusion we can say that the violation of Article 24 VCDR is not attributable to Tiranoc, the violation of Article 22 paragraph 1 VCDR is attributable to Tiranoc under Article 11 SRA and the violation by omission of paragraph 2 of the same Article of the VCDR has to be seen as being attributable to Tiranoc under Article 4 SRA. Consequently, Tiranoc can be held responsible for all acts for which attribution was found as exposed above.

4. Circumstances precluding wrongfulness

You do not need to deal with these.

5. Consequences and conclusion

There is a duty in customary international law that a State which is internationally responsible has a duty to make reparations (see *Chorzów Factory* case; PCIJ, Judgment, *Case concerning the Factory at Chorzów (Claim for Indemnity)*, 1927, 21). This rule has been incorporated by the ILC in Article 31 SRA.

There are different forms of reparation. Restitution (Article 35 SRA) might be relevant here, in the sense that Tiranoc gives the embassy building back to Saphery. Also compensation (Article 36 SRA, eg financial payments for the material damage caused to the embassy) and/or satisfaction (Article 37 SRA) are options. Seeing that the damages for which Tiranoc can be held responsible are rather limited (remember that the destruction of the archives cannot be attributed to Tiranoc and thus it does not have to make reparation for it), it seems that in addition to restituting the embassy building, satisfaction (eg in the form of an apology or by holding the students responsible) would be the most appropriate form. However, this does not exclude any form of compensation. It is up to the two States through negotiations, or to a competent international court, to determine how reparation should be made in this case.

SUGGESTED SOLUTIONS
Circumstances precluding wrongfulness

Suggested Solution—Case 4.7

Abbreviations used

ICJ = International Court of Justice
ILC = International Law Commission
MPT = Military Passage Treaty
SRA = ILC Articles on Responsibility of States for Internationally Wrongful Acts 2001 (State Responsibility Articles)
UN = United Nations
VCLT = Vienna Convention on the Law of Treaties

1. Applicable law

The law applicable in our case is first and foremost the Articles on State Responsibility (SRA) adopted by the International Law Commission in 2001. These Articles are not a treaty. Nevertheless, they are recognised to reflect customary international law in the matter of State responsibility and are thus binding on all States. The customary nature of the SRA has been confirmed, for example, by the International Court of Justice in the *Genocide* case in 2007 (ICJ, Judgment, *Application of the Convention on the Prevention and Punishment of the Crime of Genocide* (Bosnia and Herzegovina v Serbia and Montenegro), 2007, paragraph 401).

Furthermore, we will also apply the United Nations Charter to which both States in question are parties.

Moreover, we will also apply the Vienna Convention on the Law of Treaties (VCLT). Both States are parties to the VCLT since its entry into force, which occurred in accordance with Article 84 paragraph 1 VCLT on 27 January 1980. The non-retroactivity principle enshrined in Article 4 VCLT provides that the VCLT is only applicable to treaties which have been concluded after the entry into force of the VCLT for the States party to that treaty. In our case, the MPT is concluded in 2010, while both Jemm and Alindor have been parties to the VCLT since 27 January 1980. Therefore, the non-retroactivity principle is clearly fulfilled and the VCLT is applicable.

What we are dealing with here is the responsibility of States for a breach of an international obligation. Article 1 SRA clearly says that a State is internationally responsible for every one of its internationally wrongful acts. To show the existence of an international wrongful act we have to analyse two issues specified in Article 2 SRA: first, can the act or omission in question be attributed to the State; and second, does the act constitute a violation of an international obligation?

2. Attribution

The act that is at issue here is the passage of three warships of Alindor through the territorial waters of Jemm. It has thus to be analysed whether actions of a navy can be attributed to a State.

Under Article 4 SRA any action of an organ of a State is attributable to the State. Hence it does not matter what position or characteristic this organ has (ie it can be a legislative, executive, judicial or any other organ). What counts is that the organ is considered to be such an organ in the internal law of the State in question. Normally, the military is undoubtedly seen as an organ of the State since it is the State that has the prerogative of public power and has thus also the monopoly when it comes to the organisation of an army. Thus, the navy of Alindor is an organ of that State and all its actions can be attributed to Alindor.

3. Violation

Before analysing the violation in question it is important to stress a few points. First of all, according to Article 12 SRA there is a breach of an international obligation if the State in question does not act in conformity with what is to be expected from it under its international obligations. Hence it does not matter whether the obligation violated has a conventional or a customary character. Thus, a State cannot claim that there is no violation because the rule violated was not a treaty but a customary rule. However, the obligation breached has to be in force for the State allegedly responsible for the breach at the time the wrongful conduct was committed (Article 13 SRA).

Article 2 paragraph 1 of the UN Charter establishes the principle of sovereign equality of States, ie no State shall violate the (territorial) sovereignty of another State. On the face of it, Alindor has indeed violated the sovereignty of Jemm by sending warships through its territorial waters. [*The fact that Article 2 paragraph 1 UN Charter speaks about the respect of the sovereign equality of 'all its Members' does not matter. First of all, both States are parties to the UN Charter and thus members of the organisation. Furthermore, it is well established that sovereign equality is part of customary international law (eg held by the ICJ in the* Nicaragua *case; ICJ, Judgment on the Merits,* Military and Paramilitary Activities in and against Nicaragua *(Nicaragua v United States of America), 1986, paragraphs 202–209), and therefore applicable to all States, members and non-members of the UN alike.*]

In addition, Article 2 paragraph 4 of the UN Charter establishes the rule that no force or threat of use of force should be used against the territorial integrity of a State. Thus, any attack but also military intervention of the territory of another State is seen as a violation of this 'non-use of force' rule. We cannot deny that the three warships of Alindor have entered territorial waters of Jemm. In addition, because it was a military operation (warships), it could be argued to be a use of force. The intention of the State sending the warships is not relevant since the assessment of the responsibility of a

State is an 'objective' exercise. In other words, according to the majority opinion it is not necessary that the State had any bad intention, but it will be objectively asserted whether it used any type of force against the territorial integrity of another State. We can in our case unfortunately not deny that normally the entry of foreign warships into the territorial waters of a State would satisfy the situation described in Article 2 paragraph 4 of the UN Charter and thus amounts to a violation of an international obligation.

Both Article 2 paragraph 1 and Article 2 paragraph 4 of the UN Charter are in force for Alindor, since it is an original member of the United Nations.

However, we cannot stop our analysis here: it is crucial to consider whether there are any circumstances precluding wrongfulness which might justify the conduct of Alindor and exempt it from responsibility.

4. Circumstances precluding wrongfulness

Looking at the circumstances precluding wrongfulness enumerated in Chapter V SRA, Article 20 on consent seems to be the most appropriate one. This Article provides that the valid consent by a State to the commission of an act precludes the wrongfulness of that act in relation to the State which commits the act. The Article adds a caveat, however, namely that the wrongfulness of the act will only be precluded as long as the act in question remains within the limits of the consent given.

In our case, there is in fact a treaty between Jemm and Alindor whereby Jemm *consents* that warships of Alindor can pass its territorial waters in the strait to reach the open sea. A treaty is a very clear form of consent. Article 20 SRA stresses, however, that the consent must also be valid. The validity of the consent to a treaty is not an issue which is regulated under the SRA but we have to look briefly at the Vienna Convention on the Law of Treaties. Nothing in the paragraph dealing with the invalidity of treaties seems to be applicable. There has been no coercion, no violation of internal law (both parliaments ratified the treaty in accordance with the State's respective constitutions) and none of the other Articles seems to be applicable. Furthermore, also no Articles dealing with the termination or suspension of a treaty can be applied (eg *the election of the new president does not satisfy the elements of 'fundamental change of circumstances' in Article 62 VCLT, first because a change in the political system of a State can never be seen as satisfying this Article (see eg the* Tinoco Arbiration*; Arbitral Tribunal, Award,* Aguilar-Amory and Royal Bank of Canada claim*s (Tinoco case) (Great Britain v Costa Rica), 1923, 377, 378, setting out the principle of the continuity of the State), and second because also the previous situation, ie the presence of the old President, was not an essential basis of consent as required under Article 62 VCLT*). Thus, the consent has indeed been validly given by Jemm. Furthermore, the new President does not mention the treaty at all. Thus, he is not invoking any problem in relation to the treaty as such. Rather it seems as if he would not be aware of the existence of this treaty.

Next to the fact that the consent needs to be valid we have to assess whether the second element, namely that the act remained within the limits of the consent, has also been respected. The treaty permits the navy of Alindor to pass through the territorial waters (the strait) of Jemm after having informed the Ministry of Defence of Jemm at least 12 hours in advance and for the purpose of exercises in the open sea. In our case Alindor notified the Ministry of Defence of Jemm one day (24 hours) before the warships passed the strait. Furthermore, the ships were indeed on their way to a military exercise of the regional defence organisation. Thus, all the conditions set in the treaty seem to be fulfilled and hence we can confirm that the conduct remained within the limits of the consent given.

In conclusion, the new President of Jemm is mistaken to accuse Alindor of violating international law and asking for reparation. Indeed, if looked at the conduct of the warships in isolation it could be argued that this is a violation of Article 2 paragraph 1 or even Article 2 paragraph 4 of the UN Charter as explained above. However, the consent given by Jemm concerning the passage of the warships in its territorial waters precludes the wrongfulness of the conduct and thus Alindor is not responsible under international law.

5. Consequences and conclusion

It is logical that a State has no obligation to make reparations if it has been found not to be responsible for an internationally wrongful act. This can also be inferred from an *a contrario* reading of Article 31 SRA. However, Article 27 SRA makes clear that even when circumstances precluding wrongfulness can be invoked, this does not relieve the State from complying with the obligation in question (a), and in addition does not relieve it from paying for material damages caused (b). This means in our case that Alindor cannot chose not to comply with Article 2 paragraph 1 and Article 2 paragraph 4 of the UN Charter in general or in relation to Jemm outside the strictly construed consent given by Jemm in the MPT. But since there are no material damages that arose from the passage of the warships, Alindor has no obligation whatsoever to make financial payments.

Suggested Solution—Case 4.8

Abbreviations used

ICJ = International Court of Justice
ILC = International Law Commission
PCIJ = Permanent Court of International Justice
SRA = ILC Articles on Responsibility of States for Internationally Wrongful Acts 2001 (State Responsibility Articles)
TOFT = Treaty on the Over Flight of Territories

1. Applicable law

We will apply the ILC Articles on Responsibility of States for Internationally Wrongful Acts (2001), also called the State Responsibility Articles (SRA).

The SRA are not a treaty, but it is well accepted that they reflect international customary law in the matter of State responsibility. This has been confirmed by the ICJ in cases such as the *Iran Hostages* case (ICJ, Judgment, *United States Diplomatic and*

Consular Staff in Teheran (United States of America v Iran), 1980, paragraphs 56–92), the *Gabčíkovo-Nagymaros* case (ICJ, Judgment, *Gabčíkovo-Nagymaros Project* (Hungary/Slovakia), 1997, paragraph 47) and most recently the *Genocide* case (ICJ, Judgment, *Application of the Convention on the Prevention and Punishment of the Crime of Genocide* (Bosnia and Herzegovina v Serbia and Montenegro), 2007, paragraph 401).

In addition we will also apply the TOFT, the treaty regulating the free flight of commercial flights over the territory of the two States in question.

Article 1 SRA provides that a State is internationally responsible for every of its internationally wrongful acts. Article 2 then sets out the two necessary elements to find an internationally wrongful act. First of all, the act or omission needs to be attributable to the State in question; and secondly, the act or omission must constitute a violation of an international obligation of the State in question.

2. Attribution

We are asked here to deal with the potential State responsibility of Spaceland and not of Airstate. This has to be borne in mind in the following analysis.

The act we are analysing is the prohibition by Spaceland to fly over its territory which is directed towards all flights from Airstate, including commercial flights.

Article 4 SRA provides that all acts of organs of the State are attributable to the State. The characteristic or exact function of this organ does not therefore matter.

In our case, it is apparently the government which has decided to enact and maintain this prohibition. Furthermore, judging from the threat made by Spaceland, we can assume that it is the military of Spaceland that is charged with taking care that the prohibition is enforced should an Airstatian airplane venture into the airspace of Spaceland despite the prohibition. Both the government and the military are undoubtedly organs of the State in the sense of Article 4 SRA.

Therefore, the act in question is attributable to Spaceland. We now have to judge whether the act is a violation of an international obligation.

3. Violation

Article 12 SRA provides that there is a violation of an international obligation if a State does not act in conformity with what is expected from it in accordance with international law. Hence it does not matter whether the obligation arises from a treaty or from customary law.

Article 13 SRA, however, adds that the obligation must be in force for the State at the moment of the alleged violation, otherwise this cannot constitute a violation of an international obligation.

The TOFT is a bilateral treaty between Spaceland and Airstate (Article 12 SRA). It has been concluded in 1974 and judging from its execution it has also entered into force. The provisions in this treaty are thus in force and binding on both State parties (Article 13 SRA).

Article 4 TOFT clearly provides that commercial flights transporting passengers are allowed to fly freely over the territory of Spaceland. While the blocking of military flights over its territory might not be a violation of the TOFT, the prohibition to commercial flights to fly over its territory clearly is a violation of Article 4 TOFT. Thus, by blocking all flights including commercial flights, Spaceland was not acting in conformity with what could have been expected from it under the TOFT.

Therefore, since there is attribution and a violation of an international obligation we can conclude that prima facie Spaceland is responsible for an international wrongful act.

4. Circumstances precluding wrongfulness

However, no analysis of State responsibility is complete without taking into account the circumstances precluding wrongfulness. These circumstances are set out in Chapter V SRA.

Consent (Article 20 SRA), force majeure (Article 23 SRA), distress (Article 24 SRA) and necessity (Article 25 SRA) all seem not to be applicable. In addition, self-defence (Article 21 SRA) is difficult to argue, since to take self-defence in conformity with the UN Charter there needs to be an armed attack. [*While it is not absolutely impossible to argue that the military flights over the territory constitute an armed attack, this nevertheless seems to stretch the argument a bit too far.*]

Therefore, the only possibility left is Article 22 SRA, countermeasures. The wrongfulness of an internationally wrongful act is precluded if that act was taken as a countermeasure. The conditions to be fulfilled in order to constitute a lawful countermeasure are found in Chapter II of Part Three of the SRA.

According to Article 49 paragraph 1 SRA, an injured State can only take countermeasures in order to induce the wrongdoing State to comply with its international obligations.

Therefore, we first have to determine whether Airstate is also responsible for an international wrongful act, since otherwise countermeasures are by definition excluded.

Attribution

The act we are assessing here is the flight of military transports over the territory of Spaceland, which according to Airstate is justified under the TOFT.

Similar to the situation of Spaceland, the organ acting here is the military and the government of Airstate (giving the order to fly over Spaceland). As seen above, acts by the military and the government are attributable to the State under Article 4 SRA.

Violation

First of all, the TOFT clearly limited the free overflight to commercial flights (Article 2 TOFT). Spaceland is right to say that two previous military overflights are not enough to constitute a relevant precedent to change the interpretation of the TOFT. In addition, as argued by Spaceland, the different purpose of the military flights (humanitarian assistance versus armed conflict) has to be taken into account. Therefore, there is no relevant precedent to be interpreted into the TOFT to justify the overflight of military transporters to bring troops to an armed conflict.

Furthermore, Article 2 paragraph 1 of the UN Charter provides that the sovereignty of States should not be violated. By penetrating into the airspace of Spaceland with military flights and without the authorisation of Spaceland, Airstate has violated—as argued by Spaceland—the territorial sovereignty of this State. The rule contained in Article 2 paragraph 1 UN Charter is well accepted to be also part of customary international law (see eg the ICJ in the *Nicaragua* case; ICJ, Judgment on the Merits, *Military and Paramilitary Activities in and against Nicaragua (Nicaragua v United States of America)*, 1986, paragraphs 202–209) and is thus binding on Airstate in any event.

In conclusion, we can say that Airstate is responsible for two internationally wrongful acts, namely the violation of Article 2 paragraph 1 UN Charter and the violation of Article 2 TOFT (and thus indirectly also Article 4 TOFT).

Unlike in the case of Spaceland, there seem to be no circumstances precluding wrongfulness applicable here.

To satisfy Article 49 paragraph 1 SRA, we have established above that there was indeed an internationally wrongful act by Airstate and that the injured State is Spaceland. The measures taken by Spaceland are furthermore taken with the aim of stopping Airstate from violating the TOFT. Hence the requirement that countermeasures need to be taken to 'induce that State to comply with its obligations' is also satisfied.

Article 49 paragraph 2 SRA provides that countermeasures are limited to the non-performance of international obligations. Indeed, Spaceland has just decided not to perform its obligations under the TOFT, namely to allow free overflight for commercial flights (military flights having never been permitted anyway). Thus, paragraph 2 is also satisfied. And the countermeasures taken are clearly of a nature as to resume the obligation suspended later on, as is required by Article 49 paragraph 3 SRA. It will not be difficult to lift the overflight ban on aircraft from Airstate and consequently Spaceland would be in compliance with the TOFT again.

Article 50 paragraph 1(a) SRA clearly provides that force cannot be used as a countermeasure. However, even though Spaceland mentioned that it would use its military to divert flights coming from Airstate, this cannot be necessarily seen as a use of force in the sense of the UN Charter. It does not mean that they will shoot at the airplanes, but rather that they will make them land. Furthermore, it will not actually use force against another State, but the military will only become active to ensure the pronounced prohibition of overflight once the airplane concerned crosses into the territory of Spaceland. Furthermore, we do not have any indication of the facts that the military actually became active (or used force for that matter).

The proportionality requirement under Article 51 SRA also seems to be satisfied. Confronting the violation of territorial sovereignty and of a bilateral treaty by Airstate with the non-performance for the time being of a part of the bilateral treaty by Spaceland appears to be a balanced response.

It seems, therefore, that Spaceland's acts can be seen as lawful countermeasures which thus preclude the wrongfulness of its acts.

However, one last Article has to be analysed, namely Article 52 SRA. Paragraph 1 seems to be fulfilled: Spaceland called upon Airstate to stop the violation as is requested in letter (a), and also informed it about the measures it would take if the violations continued (letter (b)). However, under paragraph 3 of the same Article countermeasures cannot be taken, or if taken have to be suspended, if (a) the wrongful act has ceased and (b) the dispute is pending before a competent international court.

[*Despite the 'and' in the text, it would be unreasonable to read this as two cumulative conditions. Otherwise, for example, if the wrongful act has ceased (so there are no longer any reasons for countermeasures), a State could continue exercising countermeasures by arguing that the dispute was not (yet) pending before an international court. Taking into account the reason and justification of countermeasures—to induce a State to stop the violation of an obligation and to comply with it—this solution would thus make no sense. Consequently, only either (a) or (b) have to be fulfilled in order for Article 52 paragraph 3 SRA to be applicable.*]

The dispute is undoubtedly pending before a competent international court, since the ICJ has declared itself competent to hear the case. Consequently, Spaceland should immediately lift its prohibition of overflight concerning commercial flights in order to be back in conformity with the TOFT. Otherwise, the countermeasure, which has lawfully been taken, risks becoming unlawful.

5. Consequences and conclusion

A State whose act has been 'excused' under the circumstances precluding wrongfulness does not have an obligation as such to make reparation, since there is no internationally wrongful act anymore. However, Article 27 SRA provides that States benefiting from a circumstance precluding wrongfulness nevertheless have the obligation to pay for material damages. In our case we are not aware of any material damages to Airstate. [*It would be possible, however, to say that the loss of income of the commercial airlines of Airstate was a material damage, since the loss of earnings can be seen as material damage. Yet, according to the ILC Commentary on the SRA, the material loss is suffered 'by any* State *directly affected' (86, emphasis added). Thus, it would first have to be argued that the economic damages are actually damages to the State of Airstate (ie because the Airline is State owned) or Airstate—in case the companies are private—at least would need to take up their case and invoke their loss under diplomatic protection. Following this line of argument, the conclusion would be that even though Spaceland is not responsible for an international wrongful act since it benefits from a circumstance precluding wrongfulness, this does not preclude that it might have to pay any eventual material damages suffered by Airstate. The exact amount and extent of damages will have to be determined in negotiations or by a competent international court or tribunal.*]

Both States in question are responsible for an internationally wrongful act. However, unlike Airstate, Spaceland is excused by a circumstance precluding wrongfulness, namely countermeasures taken against the wrongful act of Airstate. Nevertheless, if Spaceland does not immediately stop its countermeasures (ie lifts the prohibition on commercial over flights), the risk is that its countermeasures are no longer seen as lawful.

Suggested Solution—Case 4.9

Abbreviations used
ICJ = International Court of Justice
ILC = International Law Commission
PCIJ = Permanent Court of International Justice
SRA = ILC Articles on Responsibility of States for Internationally Wrongful Acts 2001 (State Responsibility Articles)
UN = United Nations

1. Applicable law

The applicable law includes first of all the ILC's Articles on State Responsibility (SRA) from 2001. It is important to note that these Articles are not a treaty. However, it is generally recognised that they reflect customary law and are thus binding on all States as customary law. The customary nature of the SRA have, for example, been confirmed by the ICJ in the *Genocide* case from 2007 (ICJ, Judgment, *Application of the Convention on the Prevention and Punishment of the Crime of Genocide* (Bosnia and Herzegovina v Serbia and Montenegro), 2007, paragraph 401).

In addition, we will also apply the United Nations Charter to our case. Both States are members of the UN and therefore party to the UN Charter.

According to Article 1 SRA, a State is internationally responsible for its wrongful acts. Article 2 SRA then identifies the two necessary elements to recognise an internationally wrongful act. First of all, the act or omission has to be attributable to the State in question; and secondly, the act of omission must constitute a breach of an international obligation of that State. To clarify the situation at hand, we have to examine both elements.

2. Attribution

The question of attribution is regulated in the SRA in Articles 4–11.

Article 4 SRA provides that an act carried out by any of the organs of the State, irrespective of its character or position, is attributable to that State.

In our case, the act for which Apteno invokes the responsibility of Eudyp is the bombing of a military ship belonging to and registered in Apteno. Three military airplanes of Eudyp have carried out the bombing.

In general, it is uncontested that the military is an organ of the State, since also the prerogative of public power is incumbent on the State. Therefore, it seems to be clear here that the act—the bombing of the ship—by the military of Eudyp in indeed attributable to Eudyp under Article 4 SRA.

3. Violation

Having to analyse the possible violation, it is useful to first clarify a few points regarding the breach of an international obligation. First of all, as stated in Article 12 SRA, there exists a breach of an international obligation if the State in question did not act in a way that was expected from it under its international obligations. Concerning the breached obligation, it does not matter what character it had. This means that the obligation can be contained in a treaty but also in customary law. However, Article 13 SRA adds that there can only be a breach of an international obligation if this obligation was in force for the State accused of its breach at the time of the commission of the conduct.

In the UN Charter, Article 2 paragraph 4 makes it clear that the use of force or the threat to use force against the territorial integrity or political independence of another State is prohibited. That is, any attack (or also threat to attack) on another State is prohibited. Previously, ships in general were considered to be an extension of the territory of the State (a sort of 'floating territory'). Today, this extension is usually no longer made, with the possible exception of warships due to their close connection to territorial sovereignty. Here, the bombed ship was indeed a warship. Thus, the bombing of the ship registered in Apteno can indeed be said to be an attack on the 'territory' of Apteno and thus a violation of Article 2 paragraph 4 of the UN Charter. Since Eudyp is a member of the UN, the UN Charter is in force for it and thus Article 2 paragraph 4 is binding at the time of the commission of the bombing. That the bombing was carried out with good intentions (to stop the oil spill) is irrelevant for the question of whether there was a violation or not. This is an objective determination.

Thus, it seems that Apteno is right in invoking Eudyp's international responsibility. However, no analysis of international responsibility is complete without the assessment of the circumstances precluding wrongfulness and thus we should not draw premature conclusions.

4. Circumstances precluding wrongfulness

Looking at the different circumstances precluding wrongfulness in Chapter V SRA, it seems that the most appropriate Article is Article 25 SRA, necessity. As the negative formulation of this Article shows, it is in general not possible to invoke necessity, *unless* the two cumulative conditions contained in paragraph 1 are met. Under the first condition it has to be shown that there was a 'grave and imminent peril' endangering an essential interest of the State, and that the act (or omission) was the only means to safeguard that essential interest. Furthermore, under the second condition it has to be proven that the act was proportionate, ie that it did not impair an essential interest of another State or the international community as a whole.

Indeed, in our case there was a grave and imminent peril endangering an essential interest of the State. The oil spill flowing in the direction of the coast of Eudyp and the island off its coast constituted a very grave danger both to the rare penguin population and the lobster production in the area. It could be argued that an oil spill is a grave danger to the ecosystem of the region as a whole. In addition, the protection of the environment, in our case the protection of the rare species of penguins which live almost exclusively on this island, can without a doubt be seen as an essential interest of a State. Indeed, in several previous cases the protection of the natural environment has been invoked as an essential interest of a State (see eg the *Gabčíkovo-Nagymaros Project* case (ICJ, Judgment, *Gabčíkovo-Nagymaros Project* (Hungary/Slovakia), 1997) or the *Fur Seal* Arbitration (Arbitral Tribunal, Award, *Award between the United States and the United Kingdom relating to the rights of jurisdiction of United States in the Bering's sea and the preservation of fur seals*, 1893)).

Moreover, there is also a danger to the fishing industry of Eudyp, of which the lobster production seems to make up a big part. Protecting its industry can also be seen as an essential interest of a State (regardless of the size of the industry). As is well known, the consequences of oil spills can be disastrous for ecosystems, and—in our case—there is even the danger of extinction of the penguins. Therefore, the danger was undoubtedly grave. Additionally, it was also imminent, since the oil was already on its way and more and more oil was flowing out of the ship by the hour. Urgent measures were needed to stop the outflow. As has been established by the expert body, the only way to stop the outflow of oil immediately was to cause explosions in and on the ship. This was achieved by the bombing, which thus constitutes the 'only means' for Eudyp to protect the environment as well as its economy. Thus the first element in paragraph 1 of Article 25 SRA seems to be satisfied.

Next, we need to look at the question of proportionality (Article 25 paragraph 1(b) SRA). Did the bombing impair an essential interest of another State? The destruction of the ship did certainly affect an interest of Apteno, but whether this is an essential interest is questionable. According to the information we have the ship was already on the point of breaking apart, so it is questionable whether it could have been used afterwards again. Therefore, the destruction of the ship as such might indeed not affect an *essential* interest of Apteno. Furthermore, even though a military ship can be equated with the territory of a State, it is clear that it was not the intention of Eudyp actually to attack Apteno as a State and thus no *essential* interest was affected. Any proportionality requirement such as the one in letter (b) always needs balancing between the interests involved. It would be very difficult to weigh up the destruction of one ship against the destruction of an ecosystem, the quasi-extinction of a whole species and widespread economic damage. Thus, the approach by Eudyp can be judged to be proportionate and thus the second condition is fulfilled.

Before making a final determination on the applicability of necessity as a circumstance precluding wrongfulness, we have to take into account the second paragraph of Article 25 SRA. A State cannot invoke necessity if the international obligation in question excludes the possibility to invoke necessity or if the State itself contributed to the situation of necessity.

For sure, Eudyp has not contributed to the situation of necessity. They had nothing to do with the ship and its running aground on the rocks in the high sea. Furthermore, there is nothing in the UN Charter which would suggest that necessity cannot be invoked for Article 2 paragraph 4.

[*It might be appropriate here to make clear why, for example, force majeure (Article 23 SRA) and distress (Article 24 SRA) are not applicable in our case. Force majeure involves involuntary or coerced behaviour, so there is no choice in action. However, in our case there was actually no involuntary behaviour, but the bombing of the ship was a voluntary act and there were other possibilities (even though admittedly the alternative of letting the oil pollute the region is not very appealing as an alternative, it is nevertheless a possibility). Therefore, force majeure could not be invoked. Distress, on the other hand, is the situation when the danger is to the life of persons in the care of the author of the wrongful act and there is no other reasonable way to save that person's life. In our case, the life of persons is not (directly) endangered, thus it is impossible to apply distress.*]

Before concluding, we have to analyse Article 26 SRA. This Article provides that the non-compliance with a norm of *jus cogens* can never be justified under the circumstances precluding wrongfulness. It is true that generally the prohibition of aggression is said to be a norm of *jus cogens*. However, the bombing of a ship to stop the outflow of oil in order to protect the environment cannot be said to amount to an act of aggression. Eudyp had no intention to harm or directly attack Apteno, but was only concerned with the protection of its essential interests.

In conclusion, we can say that necessity seems to be applicable as a circumstance precluding wrongfulness and thus Eudyp cannot be held responsible under international law.

5. Consequences and conclusion

Since Eudyp is not responsible under international law, it also does not have any obligation to make reparations as indicated by an *a contrario* reading of Article 31 SRA. This Article States that the *responsible* State is under the obligation to make full reparations, but since Eudyp is not responsible, it cannot be under such an obligation.

Nevertheless we have to look at Article 27 SRA. It provides that even if a State can invoke circumstances precluding wrongfulness, this is without prejudice to the question of compensation for material loss caused by the action. Therefore, Eudyp should pay financial compensation for the destruction of the ship to Apteno. However, whether or not financial compensation will be made and the exact amount is subject to negotiation between the States (or up to a determination by a competent court). In any event, such assessments would have to take into account the fact that the ship was already in very bad shape after it had hit the rocks and that the destruction of the ship by the bombs of Eudyp did not cause all the material damage to the ship.

Suggested Solution—Case 4.10

Abbreviations used

ICJ = International Court of Justice
ILC = International Law Commission
PCIJ = Permanent Court of International Justice
SRA = ILC Articles on Responsibility of States for Internationally Wrongful Acts 2001 (State Responsibility Articles)

1. Applicable law

The law applicable in our case is first and foremost the Articles on State Responsibility (SRA) adopted by the International Law Commission in 2001. These Articles are not a treaty. However, they are recognised to reflect customary international law in the matter of State responsibility and are thus binding (and are even binding on all States). The customary nature of the SRA has been confirmed for example by the International Court of Justice in the *Iran Hostages* case (ICJ, Judgment, *United States Diplomatic and Consular Staff in Teheran* (United States of America v Iran), 1980, paragraphs 56–92), the *Gabčíkovo-Nagymaros* case (ICJ, Judgment, *Gabčíkovo-Nagymaros Project* (Hungary/Slovakia), 1997, paragraph 47) and the *Genocide* case (ICJ, Judgment, *Application of the Convention on the Prevention and Punishment of the Crime of Genocide* (Bosnia and Herzegovina v Serbia and Montenegro), 2007, paragraph 401).

Furthermore, we will also apply customary international law in matters of use of force and respect of international sovereignty. These rules are reflected, for example, in Article 2 paragraphs 1 and 4 of the UN Charter. The ICJ has confirmed in the *Nicaragua* case (ICJ, Judgment on the Merits, *Military and Paramilitary Activities in and against Nicaragua* (Nicaragua v United States of America), 1986, paragraphs 187–192, 202–209) that these rules reflect the relevant customary law.

We are dealing here with the responsibility of States for an alleged breach of an international obligation. Article 1 SRA clearly says that a State is internationally responsible for every of its internationally wrongful acts. To show the existence of an international wrongful act we have to analyse two issues specified in Article 2 SRA: first, can the act or omission in question be attributed to the State; and second, does the act constitute a violation of an international obligation.

2. Attribution

The act we are analysing is the penetration without authorisation of a military submarine from Mecanoland into the territorial waters of Paradiland.

Under Article 4 SRA any action of an organ of a State is attributable to the State. It does not matter what position or characteristic this organ has (ie it can be a legislative, executive, judicial or any other organ). What counts is that the organ is considered to be such an organ in the internal law of the State in question.

In our case, the submarine, Commander Luck and his crew were all parts of the military of Mecanoland. Normally, the military is undoubtedly seen as an organ of the State since it is the State which has the prerogative of public power and has thus also the monopoly when it comes to the organisation of armed forces. Thus, the navy of Mecanoland is an organ of that State and all its actions can be attributed to Mecanoland in conformity with Article 4 SRA.

3. Violation

Before analyzing the violation in question it is important to stress a few points. First of all, according to Article 12 SRA there is a breach of an international obligation if the State in question does not act in conformity with what is to be expected from it under its international obligations. It does not matter whether the obligation violated has a conventional or a customary character. Thus, a State cannot claim that there is no violation because the rule violated was a customary but not a treaty rule. However, the obligation breached has to be in force for the State allegedly responsible for the breach at the time the wrongful conduct was committed (Article 13 SRA).

Article 2 paragraph 1 of the UN Charter establishes the principle of sovereign equality of States, ie no State shall violate the (territorial) sovereignty of another State. On the face of it, Mecanoland can be said to have violated the sovereignty of Paradisland when its military submarine penetrated the latter's territorial waters without authorisation. It has to be kept in mind that territorial waters constitute an integral part of the territory of a State, and thus their violation is to be analysed in the same vein as any violation of a State's territory.

It is well established that sovereign equality is part of customary international law (eg held by the ICJ in the *Nicaragua* case; ICJ, Judgment on the Merits, *Military and Paramilitary Activities in and against Nicaragua* (Nicaragua v United States of America), 1986, paragraphs 202–209), and therefore applicable to all States, members and non-members of the UN alike. There is a clear violation of Article 2 paragraph 1 of the UN Charter which is binding on Mecanoland due to its customary nature. It is thus not necessary to know whether Mecanoland is a member of the UN or not.

In addition, Article 2 paragraph 4 of the UN Charter establishes the rule that no force or threat of use of force should be used against the territorial integrity of a State. Thus, any attack but also military intervention on the territory of another State is seen as a violation of this 'non-use of force' rule. In our case, a military submarine has entered the territorial waters of Paradisland. Therefore, it could be argued to be a use of force. The intention of the State sending the warships is not relevant since the assessment of the responsibility of a State is an 'objective' exercise. In other words, it is not necessary that the State had any bad intention, but it will be objectively asserted whether it used any type of force against the territorial integrity of another State. Nevertheless, normally the entry of foreign warships or submarines into the territorial waters of a State can be said to satisfy the situation described in Article 2 paragraph 4 UN Charter and would thus amount to a violation of an international obligation.

As stated above, Article 2 paragraph 4 UN Charter has also been confirmed by the ICJ to be of customary nature (ICJ, Judgment on the Merits, *Military and Paramilitary Activities in and against Nicaragua* (Nicaragua v United States of America), 1986, paragraphs 187–192) and is thus binding on Mecanoland.

In conclusion we can say that there has certainly been violation of Article 2 paragraph 1 of the UN Charter and possibly (*depending on how you argue*) also of Article 2 paragraph 4 UN Charter. Since both violations are attributable to Mecanoland as seen above, this State is prima facie responsible for an internationally wrongful act.

However, we cannot stop our analysis here: it is crucial to consider whether there are any circumstances precluding wrongfulness which might justify the conduct and exempt Mecanoland from responsibility.

4. Circumstances precluding wrongfulness

Looking at the circumstances precluding wrongfulness enumerated in Chapter V SRA, Article 24 (distress) seems to be the most appropriate possibility.

Under distress, the wrongful act resulted from the fact that the author of the wrongful act did not have any other reasonable choice to save his life and/or the lives of persons under his care. There are thus two cumulative conditions to be satisfied: there must not have been any other *reasonable* choice, and the author of the act must have sought to save his life and/or the lives of persons under his care.

In our case, due to the leakage of the nuclear reactor there was the danger that the whole submarine would be contaminated and in addition the danger that the nuclear engine would explode. Both situations are undoubtedly situations where the lives of the people on board of the submarine were in serious danger. Thus, by calling at the port of Orchycity, Commander Luck just wanted to save his life and the lives of the 125 crew members under his command (under his 'care'). In addition, there was no reasonable other way of saving them all. Of course, Commander Luck could have respected international law by not penetrating into the territorial waters of Paradisland, with the likely result of the engine exploding and killing them all. Therefore, there was a 'choice' there: penetrating the territorial waters of Paradisland in order to reach the port of Orchycity to repair the engine; or accept the contamination and explosion of the reactor, resulting in their death. Yet, it cannot convincingly be argued that the latter is a *reasonable* way to act in order to save 'the author's life or the lives entrusted to the author's care'. Therefore, distress seems to be applicable in our case.

Article 24 paragraph 2 SRA provides, however, for situations when paragraph 1 cannot be invoked. This also needs to be analysed. Distress cannot be invoked if the situation of distress is due in some way to the conduct of the State invoking it (a) or if the act in question is likely to create a comparable or greater peril (b) (proportionality).

Concerning letter (a) it is clear that Mecanoland cannot be said to have contributed to the situation of distress. The nuclear engine in the submarine had been working well for over five months. The fact that errors and accidents such as the leak in the engine are always a possibility cannot lead to the conclusion that Mecanoland actually *contributed* to this serious situation.

As for letter (b), it was obviously a great risk the crew took when calling at the port of Orchycity. The island is classified as a UNESCO World Heritage site, and damage to its fauna and flora resulting from a nuclear explosion could have been devastating. Furthermore, the majority of the people of the island live in the capital city. A nuclear explosion would also have endangered them all.

It is possible to argue that by calling at this port Commander Luck was indeed creating a greater peril than the one which he sought to avoid. It could be said that with the likelihood of the nuclear engine exploding (which was after all one of the reasons why they needed to get to a port quickly so as to repair the engine) it was too dangerous to approach Orchycity in the first place. By nevertheless approaching it, Commander Luck took his chance and it was only pure luck that everything went well. This was, however, far from clear when the decision to reach Orchycity was made. The danger posed to a large population and a unique ecosystem could thus not be balanced against the life of 125 crew members on the nuclear submarine. Following this argumentation it should be concluded that there are no circumstances precluding wrongfulness that can be invoked, since Article 24 paragraph 2(b) SRA is satisfied, thus excluding the possibility of applying the whole Article.

[*However, it is also possible to argue that the explosion of the engine was only a possibility which was said to happen if the engine could not be repaired quickly. Yet, this repair seemed to have been possible at any port. Furthermore, Commander Luck had extensive experience and he also judged that the repair was possible. Therefore, the risk they took in case the repair was not possible seems to be completely proportionate with the danger they would have faced had they not sought safety in Paradisland. The fact that radioactivity was not increased on the island and that the ecosystem remained unharmed by the incident confirm this. Nevertheless, it should be pointed out that these facts cannot of course be taken as a full argument, since the risk and proportionality referred to in paragraph 2(b) have to be judged ex ante and not after the act has taken place. Under this reasoning it could be justified to say that Mecanoland can invoke distress as a circumstance precluding wrongfulness.*]

In our case, force majeure (Article 23 SRA) would not be applicable since under force majeure it is impossible to carry out the obligation (eg the obligation not to penetrate into the territorial waters of Pardisland). Thus, there is absolutely no element of free choice at all, meaning that the performance of the obligation must be *impossible*, not just more difficult. Yet, as explained above, in the case of distress the person is not acting involuntarily. There is still a choice, even though the choice is actually nullified by the perilous situation ('no other reasonable way'). This suggests that there are still other ways, even though unreasonable ones. As seen above, there was a choice in our case (which was, however, an unreasonable one). There was no 'irresistible force' which is necessary to show for force majeure.

Hence, there seems to be no circumstance precluding wrongfulness which can be invoked.

[*Or, if you argued that distress was applicable: Hence, distress seems to be applicable as the only circumstance precluding wrongfulness. Cases where distress was accepted as a circumstance precluding wrongfulness include the* Rainbow Warrior *case, where the arbitral tribunal held that the evacuation of the two French agents was excused under distress, due to extreme urgency involving medical and other 'humanitarian' considerations.*]

5. Consequences and conclusion

Since Mecanoland cannot benefit from a circumstance precluding wrongfulness, it is responsible for an internationally wrongful act as explained above. Under Article 31 SRA a State responsible for such an act has the obligation to make reparations—an obligation also recognised to be customary law by the PCIJ in the *Chorzów Factory* case (PCIJ, Judgment, *Case concerning the Factory at Chorzów (Claim for Indemnity)*, 1927, 2).

There are different forms of reparation (Article 34 SRA). Restitution (Article 35 SRA) does not seem to be appropriate here, since there was no physical object which has been taken away which could now be 'given back' (restituted). Compensation under Article 36 SRA does not seem to be suitable either. Compensation is made for 'financially assessable' damage (Article 36 paragraph 2 SRA), ie both moral and material damages to physical objects and persons. It does not, however, include 'moral damages' to a State in the sense of an affront or 'injury caused by a violation of rights not associated with actual damage to property or persons' (ILC Commentary on State Responsibility Articles, 99). We are here not aware of any material or moral damage caused by the submarine to property or persons. This leaves thus satisfaction (Article 37 SRA) as the most likely form of reparation, eg in the form of apologies.

[*If you concluded that distress can be invoked, the conclusion would run as follows: It is logical that a State has no obligation to make reparations if it has been found not to be responsible for an internationally wrongful act. This can be inferred from an* a contrario *reading of Article 31 SRA.*

However, Article 27 SRA makes clear that even when circumstances precluding wrongfulness can be invoked, this does not relieve the State from complying with the obligation in question (a), and in addition it does not relieve it from paying for material damages caused (b). This means in our case that Mecanoland in future has to comply with Article 2 paragraphs 1 and 4 of the UN Charter (and their customary reflection) and cannot see this as a precedent not to respect these obligations anymore. In addition, Mecanoland has to pay for any material damages created if there were any.]

Chapter 5

SUGGESTED SOLUTIONS
International Dispute Settlement: The International Court of Justice

SUGGESTED SOLUTIONS
Issues of personal jurisdiction

Suggested Solution—Case 5.1

Abbreviations used
ICJ = International Court of Justice
PCIJ = Permanent Court of International Justice
UN = United Nations

1. Applicable law

To answer this question we will apply the ICJ Statute to which both States are parties. In addition we will also apply the UN Charter where necessary. It should be kept in mind that according to Article 92 UN Charter, the ICJ Statute is an integral part of the UN Charter.

In order for the ICJ to have jurisdiction, three elements need to be fulfilled: there needs to be personal jurisdiction, subject matter jurisdiction and finally consent to the compulsory jurisdiction of the Court.

2. Personal jurisdiction (jurisdiction *ratione personae*)

In every case the ICJ checks on its own (ex officio) whether it has personal jurisdiction or not.

In order to have personal jurisdiction two elements need to be fulfilled.

According to Article 34 paragraph 1 ICJ Statute, only States can be parties to a dispute in front of the ICJ. However, there is no doubt and no indication to the contrary that both Farstate and Westland are indeed States. Therefore, this point is fulfilled.

Article 35 paragraph 1 ICJ Statute further provides that the ICJ is only open to States which are parties to its Statute.

Farstate is a member of the UN. Article 93 paragraph 1 of the UN Charter provides that all UN members are ipso facto, ie automatically, parties to the ICJ Statute.

Westland, on the other hand, is not a member of the UN. However, it is according to the facts provided nevertheless a party to the ICJ Statute. This is made possible under Article 93 paragraph 2 of the UN Charter which provides that States not members of the UN can also become parties to the ICJ Statute under conditions to be determined by the General Assembly upon recommendation of the Security Council.

Therefore, since both States are parties to the ICJ Statute, Article 35 paragraph 1 is fulfilled. Consequently, we can conclude that the ICJ has personal jurisdiction to hear the case.

3. Subject matter jurisdiction (jurisdiction *ratione materiae*)

The ICJ examines this part of jurisdiction ex officio as well. The ICJ is only competent to hear cases relating to legal disputes under international law (see eg Article 38 of its Statute).

The most commonly accepted definition of a dispute can be found in the *Mavrommatis* case of the Permanent Court of International Justice (PCIJ, Judgment on the Objection to the Jurisdiction of the Court, *The Mavrommatis Palestine Concessions*, 1924, 11). There, the Court held that a dispute is a disagreement on a point of law or fact between two persons.

Apparently here Westland and Farstate do not agree on the alleged violation of a commercial treaty by Farstate. Therefore, there is clearly a disagreement on a point of law and thus a legal dispute. Since the dispute concerns a commercial treaty between two States which is furthermore governed by international law in the matter of treaty law, the legal dispute is also a dispute under international law.

Consequently, the ICJ also has subject matter jurisdiction in that case.

4. Consensual jurisdiction (jurisdiction *ratione consensus*)

Consent to the Court's jurisdiction is an essential principle, as the ICJ has confirmed itself, for example in the *East Timor* case (ICJ, Judgment, *Case concerning East Timor* (Portugal v Australia), 1995, paragraph 26). Nevertheless, this element is normally not examined ex officio by the ICJ, but is only dealt with if the parties contest the Court's consensual jurisdiction in preliminary objections. In our case none of the parties contested the jurisdiction of the Court, and therefore we can assume that the ICJ is competent.

Furthermore this assumption is confirmed by the fact that both States have made optional clause declarations under Article 36 paragraph 2 of the Statute. With this reciprocal system States agree to the compulsory jurisdiction of the ICJ for all disputes in relation to States which have accepted the same obligation. Since there are two optional clause declarations the system can fully work and the ICJ has consensual jurisdiction based on the two optional clause declarations made by the two parties to the dispute.

5. Conclusion

As shown above, the ICJ has personal, subject matter as well as consensual jurisdiction in this case. Consequently, the ICJ is competent to deal with the case between Farstate and Westland.

Suggested Solution—Case 5.2

Abbreviations used
ICJ = International Court of Justice
UN = United Nations

1. Applicable law

The law which we will apply to determine whether or not the ICJ has jurisdiction is first and foremost its own Statute. The Statute of the ICJ forms an integral part of the Charter of the United Nations (Article 92 of the UN Charter). The States in question are both parties to the UN Charter, which can thus be applied.

2. Personal jurisdiction

The first point to be clarified in any assessment of the jurisdiction of the ICJ is jurisdiction *ratione personae*. This means whether the ICJ has any competence over cases brought by the specific parties.

According to Article 34 paragraph 1, only States can be parties in contentious cases before the ICJ. This is very clear and no exception whatsoever is provided.

In our case, however, the party bringing the claim is not a State but a company (Cany), which cannot be a party to any dispute before the ICJ.

Thus, we have to conclude that the ICJ does not have personal jurisdiction to hear this case.

3. Conclusion

The ICJ is not competent to deal with the case since this Court is only open to disputes between States.

SUGGESTED SOLUTIONS
Forms of consent – reservations to optional clause declarations

Suggested Solution—Case 5.3

Abbreviations used
ICJ = International Court of Justice
PCIJ = Permanent Court of International Justice
TOE = Treaty on Oil Exports
UN = United Nations

1. Applicable law

The law that will be applied are the United Nations Charter and the Statute of the International Court of Justice (ICJ), which is an integral part of the UN Charter (Article 92 UN Charter). Both States involved in the dispute are members of the UN and thus the UN Charter and the ICJ Statute can be applied.

To determine whether or not the ICJ has jurisdiction to deal with the present case between Skir and Reggo we will make a full analysis of the three jurisdictional aspects necessary, namely personal, subject matter and consensual jurisdiction. The two first aspects are usually raised ex officio by the Court, while the last aspect is only dealt with if one of the parties contests the jurisdiction of the ICJ on this ground.

2. Personal jurisdiction (jurisdiction *ratione personae*)

According to Article 34 paragraph 1 of the ICJ Statute, only States can be parties in contentious cases before the Court. In our case, there is no doubt that Skir and Reggo are States. This is supported by the fact that both States are members of the UN, which only permits States to be members (Article 4 paragraph 1 UN Charter).

Furthermore, Article 35 paragraph 1 ICJ Statute provides that the Court is only open to States which are parties to the Statute of the Court. Article 93 paragraph 1 of the UN Charter declares that every UN member is, ipso facto, a party to the ICJ Statute. Thus, since Skir and Reggo are both UN members, they are automatically also parties to the ICJ Statute.

As a consequence, personal jurisdiction for the ICJ exists.

3. Subject matter jurisdiction (jurisdiction *ratione materiae*)

It is generally accepted that the ICJ as the 'principle judicial organ of the UN' (Article 1 ICJ Statute) is only competent to deal with legal disputes under international law. This can, for example, be inferred from Article 38 of the ICJ Statute, where it is said that the function of the ICJ is to 'decide in accordance with international law such disputes as are submitted to it'.

The most frequently used definition of a dispute can be found in the *Mavrommatis Palestine Concessions* case by the Permanent Court of International Justice (PCIJ, Judgment on the Objection to the Jurisdiction of the Court, *The Mavrommatis Palestine Concessions*, 1924, 11). There, the Court said that a dispute is a disagreement on a point of law or fact between two persons. It is also important to point out that it is irrelevant whether the two parties say or think that such a dispute does or does not exist. It is alone for the Court to determine objectively whether such a dispute is present (see eg the ICJ's judgment on the preliminary objections in the *Lockerbie* case (ICJ, Judgment on Preliminary Objections, *Questions of Interpretation and Application of the 1971 Montreal Convention arising from the Aerial Incident at Lockerbie* (Libyan Arab Jamahiriya v United States of America), 1998, paragraph 21) or the Advisory Opinion on the *Interpretation of Peace Treaties* (ICJ, Advisory Opinion, First Phase, *Interpretation of Peace Treaties with Bulgaria, Hungary and Romania*, 1950, 74)).

Between our two States, there clearly is a disagreement on a point of law, namely whether or not the TOE provides that all payments need to be made in the local currency of Reggo. This disagreement on a question of treaty interpretation is consequently a *legal* dispute and since it is an international treaty the dispute is also subject to international rather than national law.

Thus, the ICJ also has subject matter jurisdiction in the present case.

4. Consensual jurisdiction (jurisdiction *ratione consensus*)

It is well known that the two jurisdictional aspects alone are not enough to declare the ICJ competent to hear a case. There exists no compulsory jurisdiction without consent. Thus, the jurisdiction of the ICJ essentially depends on the consent given by the parties, as can be inferred from Article 36 of the ICJ Statute. The importance of consent in order to establish the ICJ's jurisdiction has, for example, also been affirmed in the *East Timor* case (ICJ, Judgment, *Case concerning East Timor* (Portugal v Australia), 1995, paragraph 26).

In our case there are two optional clause declarations. Optional clause declarations constitute one of the four modes of consenting to the ICJ's jurisdiction and are made under Article 36 paragraph 2 of the ICJ Statute. The optional clause declaration made by Reggo is made without reservation, while Skir has attached a reservation to its declaration.

This first raises the question of whether it is permitted to make reservations to optional clause declarations. Article 36 paragraph 3 of the ICJ Statute, which provides that optional clause declarations can be made unconditionally or subject to some conditions, has usually been read as indicating that reservations to optional clause declarations are allowed. Of course this should be seen within the limits imposed by Article 19 of the Vienna Convention on the Law of Treaties, namely that in the case of silence of a treaty concerning reservations, reservations are only allowed if they do not violate the object and purpose of the treaty. In its practice, the ICJ has usually accepted reservations. Furthermore, reservations excluding from the jurisdiction of the Court issues relating to oil in a rather broad sense can hardly be said to violate the object and purpose of the ICJ Statute. In addition, this reservation by Skir is not an automatic reservation and thus does not prevent the ICJ from making its own determination concerning its jurisdiction, in accordance with Article 36 paragraph 6 of its Statute. Thus, the reservation made by Skir is in conformity with the object and the purpose of the ICJ Statute and hence admissible.

Reservations only become limiting on the ICJ's jurisdiction if they are invoked by the parties, since this is not an issue the ICJ raises ex officio. Thus, the next question to be clarified is whether Reggo, not having a reservation, can actually invoke the reservation made by Skir. The ICJ in the *Norwegian Loans* case (ICJ, Judgment, *Certain Norwegian Loans* (France v Norway), 1957, 22–27) recognised that Norway (the non-reserving State) could invoke France's reservation.

The underlying reason is that optional clauses are dependent on reciprocity. Article 36 paragraph 2 of the ICJ Statute declares that States making an optional clause declaration recognise the compulsory jurisdiction of the ICJ *in respect of any other State accepting the same obligation*. Thus, optional clauses only give the ICJ jurisdiction on the 'lowest common denominator' (on this see, for example, the *Anlgo-Iranian Oil* case (ICJ, Judgment, *Anglo-Iranian Oil Co* (United Kingdom v Iran), 1952, 103)). This means that both declarations have to give the ICJ jurisdiction for the dispute under consideration. If one of the parties excludes this jurisdiction by way of a reservation, the non-reserving State is entitled to invoke this reservation to preserve reciprocity. Therefore, it is acceptable for Reggo to invoke Skir's reservation. This reservation excludes all cases relating to 'oil, oil extraction, oil exports or oil products'. It can be said that the present case is related to oil exports (namely the payment of such exports). Due to the overarching importance of consent to the jurisdiction of the Court, reservations cannot be read restrictively. Thus, it would probably go against the original will of Skir to read its reservation as not excluding oil payment issues, since payment and money transactions constitute an integral part of exports. Thus, on basis of the doctrine of the 'lowest common denominator', there is no consent between the parties to the dispute as to the jurisdiction of the ICJ in the case. There is no consensus given to the ICJ's jurisdiction.

5. Conclusion

Consequently we have to declare that the ICJ does not have jurisdiction and hence is not competent to hear the case in question based on the two optional clause declarations.

In addition, there is no indication that the TOE contains a compromissory clause which could serve as a basis of jurisdiction for the ICJ.

Therefore, we have to conclude that at the present moment the ICJ is not competent to hear the case under dispute here.

Suggested Solution—Case 5.4

Abbreviations used

FISH = Formulation of International Safeguards for Herrings
ICJ = International Court of Justice
PCIJ = Permanent Court of International Justice
UN = United Nations
VCLT = Vienna Convention on the Law of Treaties

1. Applicable law

To determine the jurisdiction of the International Court of Justice (ICJ) in the present case, the applicable law will be the Statute of the ICJ and the Charter of the United Nations. According to Article 92 of the UN Charter, the ICJ Statute is an integral part of the UN Charter. Since both States are original members of the UN, the UN Charter, and consequently also the ICJ Statute, are applicable to them.

In order for the ICJ to have jurisdiction to deal with the case, it has to be established that it has personal jurisdiction, subject matter jurisdiction and consensual jurisdiction.

2. Personal jurisdiction (jurisdiction *ratione personae*)

Personal jurisdiction is always assessed by the ICJ ex officio.

Article 34 paragraph 1 of the ICJ Statute makes clear that only States can be parties in disputes before the ICJ. It is not in dispute in our case that both Clupe and Scombria are States. They are even original members of the United Nations, an organisation that only allows States as members, as can be seen from Article 4 paragraph 1 of the UN Charter. Thus, Article 34 is fulfilled.

In addition, Article 35 paragraph 1 of the ICJ Statute provides that the ICJ is only open to States that are parties to the ICJ Statute. Article 93 paragraph 1 of the UN Charter, however, provides that every member of the UN is, ipso facto, also party to the ICJ Statute. Since, as we have seen above, the two States in question are UN members, they are consequently also parties to the ICJ Statute.

Therefore, we can conclude that personal jurisdiction is established.

3. Subject matter jurisdiction (jurisdiction *ratione materiae*)

The ICJ raises also this part of jurisdiction ex officio. The ICJ is only competent to hear cases relating to legal disputes under international law (see for example Article 38 of its Statute).

The most commonly accepted definition of a dispute can be found in the *Mavrommatis Palestine Concessions* case of the PCIJ (PCIJ, Judgment on the Objection to the Jurisdiction of the Court, *The Mavrommatis Palestine Concessions*, 1924, 11). There, the Court held that a dispute is a disagreement on a point of law or fact between two persons.

Here, we clearly have at least two disputes. Clupe and Scombria do not agree with each other, first, as to whether or not Scombria has, by exceeding its fishing quota, violated the FISH; and second, whether Clupe has, by intercepting and forcibly boarding the *Raptor* by its ship *Poseidon*, violated international law. It is also clear that the disputes are legal disputes, related to treaties (the FISH and potentially the United Nations Convention on the Law of the Sea) and issues of State responsibility. These legal disputes are also disputes under international law, since international treaties as well as State responsibility are part of and governed by international law.

Thus, subject matter jurisdiction is also fulfilled.

4. Consensual jurisdiction (jurisdiction *ratione consensus*)

In addition to the two jurisdictional aspects examined above, it is also indispensable that States have consented to the jurisdiction of the Court. This has been confirmed by the ICJ, eg in the *East Timor* case (ICJ, Judgment, *Case concerning East Timor* (Portugal v Australia), 1995, paragraph 26).

Both States in question have made optional clause declarations under Article 36 paragraph 2 of the Statute and both have attached a reservation. As we can see from Article 36 paragraph 3 ICJ Statute, reservations to optional clause declarations are allowed. They have, however, to satisfy Article 19(c) VCLT, ie not to be incompatible with the object and purpose of the treaty, namely the ICJ Statute. The ICJ has in practice accepted reservations on a very wide basis. Such reservations as those from Clupe and Scombria would be considered as being compatible with the object and purpose of the ICJ Statute. They do not frustrate the ICJ Statute as such and since they are not automatic reservations leave enough leeway for the ICJ to decide on its own competence in accordance with Article 36 paragraph 6 ICJ Statute should the question arise.

Scombria's reservation, dealing with textile production and exports, does not seem to be relevant in our case and hence does not need to be considered further. However, Clupe made a reservation to its optional clause declaration excluding the jurisdiction of the ICJ for all matters falling within fisheries. At least one part of the disputes does fall under the issue of fisheries, namely the question whether Scombria has violated the FISH, a treaty for the protection of herrings. It can also be argued that the other dispute, the boarding of the *Raptor* by the crew of the *Poseidon* on the high seas, is related to fisheries issues, since the aim was to control whether the *Raptor* had caught too many herrings. Do we therefore have to conclude that the ICJ is not competent to deal with the disputes in question? No, this is not the case.

Unlike the two previous jurisdictional aspects, issues related to jurisdiction *ratione consensus* are not raised ex officio by the ICJ. This means that the ICJ will not deal with the question of consent given to its jurisdiction unless one of the States raises this issue and contests the jurisdiction of the Court in preliminary objections.

In our case, there seem, however, to be no such objections to the Court's jurisdiction. The reserving State, Clupe, is the one that has brought the case, so it is highly unlikely (although of course not totally excluded) that it will invoke its own reservation in order to prevent the ICJ from having jurisdiction. But Scombria too does not seem to want to contest the ICJ's jurisdiction or to invoke Clupe's reservation (the optional clause system is based on reciprocity and therefore the non-reserving State is allowed to invoke also the reservations of the reserving States if it wishes to do so—see eg the

Norwegian Loans case (ICJ, Judgment, *Certain Norwegian Loans* (France v Norway), 1957, 22–27)). On the contrary, Scombria welcomes that Clupe has brought the case to the ICJ and according to its statements it will also appear and participate in the proceedings. Nothing therefore indicates that the reservation of Clupe, which potentially could indeed have the consequence of preventing the ICJ from having jurisdiction, is invoked by one of the two States. Thus, the ICJ will not consider this issue. Consequently, since there are no objections to its consensual jurisdiction, the last aspect of the ICJ's jurisdiction is also fulfilled.

[*The question asked by the President is expressly limited to jurisdiction established on the basis of the two optional clause declarations. Thus, any considerations on other ways of consenting to the ICJ's jurisdiction, such as* forum prorogatum *do not have to be made since they fall outside the question asked.*]

5. Conclusion

Since all three elements of jurisdiction are satisfied, the ICJ has jurisdiction and will thus be able to deal with the disputes pending between Clupe and Scombria.

Suggested Solution—Case 5.5

Abbreviations used

ECtHR = European Court of Human Rights
ICJ = International Court of Justice
PCIJ = Permanent Court of International Justice
UN = United Nations
VCLT = Vienna Convention on the Law of Treaties

1. Applicable law

To determine whether the International Court of Justice (ICJ) has jurisdiction in this case we will apply the United Nations Charter and the ICJ Statute, which is an integral part of the UN Charter (Article 92 UN Charter). The UN Charter and the ICJ Statute are both applicable since both States in question are members of the UN.

2. Personal jurisdiction (jurisdiction *ratione personae*)

According to Article 34 paragraph 1 of the Statute, only States can be parties to disputes before the ICJ. It is not disputed in our case that both Melusina and Karabo are States. In addition, the fact that both are UN members is sufficient proof that they are States for our purposes, since according to Article 4 paragraph 1 of the UN Charter only States can become members of the UN.

Article 35 paragraph 1 adds a further requirement for the establishment of personal jurisdiction, namely that the ICJ is only open to States which are parties to the ICJ Statute. Article 93 paragraph 1 of the UN Charter indicates that all UN members are automatically also parties to the Statute of the ICJ. Since, as we have seen above, Melusina and Karabo are both UN members, they are also parties to the ICJ Statute. Consequently, the requirements for personal jurisdiction are fulfilled.

3. Subject matter jurisdiction (jurisdiction *ratione materiae*)

The ICJ is only competent to deal with legal disputes under international law. The most widely accepted definition of a 'dispute' can be found in the *Mavrommatis Palestine Concessions* case (PCIJ, Judgment on the Objection to the Jurisdiction of the Court, *The Mavrommatis Palestine Concessions*, 1924, 11). There, the PCIJ held that a dispute is a disagreement on a point of law or fact between two persons.

It is also important to point out that it is irrelevant whether the two parties say or think that such a dispute does or does not exist. This is to be determined objectively (see ICJ, Advisory Opinion, First Phase, *Interpretation of Peace Treaties with Bulgaria, Hungary and Romania*, 1950, 74) and it is alone for the Court to make this determination objectively on the existence of a dispute. This has, for example, been held in the *Lockerbie* case (ICJ, Judgment on Preliminary Objections, *Questions of Interpretation and Application of the 1971 Montreal Convention arising from the Aerial Incident at Lockerbie* (Libyan Arab Jamahiriya v United States of America), 1998, paragraph 21).

In our case, there clearly is a disagreement on a point of law, namely whether Karabo can impose visa requirements on nationals from Melusina despite the fact that a commercial treaty between the two of them has abolished such requirements. This dispute is a legal dispute (since it is related to treaty law and treaty interpretation) and it is a dispute under international law, since a treaty between two States by definition is part of but also regulated by international law. In this regard we can add that when international treaties are concluded by States on certain issues, these issues are no longer exclusively within the reserved domain or domestic jurisdiction. Therefore, the arguments made by Karabo by saying that immigration issues are protected under equal sovereignty and against foreign interference are not founded.

Thus, the second jurisdictional element is also fulfilled.

4. Consensual jurisdiction (jurisdiction *ratione consensus*)

This third jurisdictional element is the most difficult one in our case. Nevertheless, consensus is indispensable to establish the jurisdiction of the Court (see *East Timor* case, ICJ, Judgment, *Case concerning East Timor* (Portugal v Australia), 1995, paragraph 26). Since Karabo has raised preliminary objections, the ICJ will have to consider the issue of jurisdiction *ratione consensus*. This issue, unlike the first two, is not raised ex officio by the ICJ, but has to be brought up by the parties.

As there is no information on an eventual compromissory clause in the treaty between Karabo and Melusina, we cannot base ourselves on this treaty as a basis of consent.

Nevertheless, in the case at hand there are two optional clause declarations made under Article 36 paragraph 2 of the ICJ Statute. The optional clause system is a reciprocal system, in which jurisdiction is established on the 'least common denominator' between the two parties as has been said by the ICJ in the *Anglo Iranian Oil* case (ICJ, Judgment, *Anglo-Iranian Oil Co* (United Kingdom v Iran), 1952, 103).

One of the optional clauses at hand has a reservation attached to it. This first of all raises the question whether it is allowed to make reservations to optional clause declarations. Reading paragraph 3 of Article 36 seems to indicate that reservations are generally allowed, since it States that these declarations can either be made unconditionally or on condition of some requirements. Even though the listed requirements are quite narrow, it has generally been accepted that reservations can in principle be attached to optional clause declarations. However, the next question which has to be answered is whether the reservation is a valid one, ie whether it is compatible with Article 19(c) VCLT. We are confronted here with a very special kind of reservation, a so-called 'automatic' or 'self-judging' reservation, since it is the State that reserves the right to determine whether a particular issue will fall under its 'domestic jurisdiction', which has as a consequence that the ICJ will not be competent to hear the case (since it is only competent for issues under international, but not national law).

Are such reservations admissible? The ICJ has so far never had to pronounce itself on the validity of such an automatic reservation, therefore any answer will not necessarily be final.

However, several judges in the *Interhandel* case (ICJ, Judgment on Preliminary Objections, *Interhandel* (Switzerland v United States of America), 1959; Separate Opinion of Judge Spender, 56, 57; Dissenting Opinion of President Klaestad, 76, 77; Dissenting Opinion of Judge Lauterpacht, 115, 116; Dissenting Opinion of Judge Armand-Ugon, 91–94) declared that such automatic reservations would not be admissible mainly for two reasons: first, States making such reservations do not in fact assume any legal obligations under their optional clause declarations since they can always decide themselves whether or not an issue falls within their domestic jurisdiction. Secondly, it was also argued that this type of reservation conflicted with Article 36 paragraph 6 of the ICJ Statute, the provision establishing that the ICJ is competent to decide on its own competence (*Kompetenz-Kompetenz* principle): it would not be the ICJ that decides whether it is competent to hear the case, but the reserving State.

These two arguments seem to be convincing, so that we can conclude that automatic reservations are not compatible with the object and purpose of the ICJ Statute and thus are not admissible. Consequently, Karabo's reservation is invalid.

However, this leads to the question of what happens to the optional clause declaration to which this invalid reservation was attached. There are mainly two positions that can be taken (again, the ICJ itself has so far never pronounced on this). In his Dissenting Opinion, Judge Lauterpacht in the *Interhandel* case (ICJ, Judgment on Preliminary Objections, *Interhandel* (Switzerland v United States of America), 1959, Dissenting Opinion of Judge Lauterpacht, 116–119) essentially argued that the declaration could not stand without the reservation, since the State in question only had made this optional clause declaration because it had the possibility to attach a reservation. Thus, since the reservation was invalid, the whole optional clause declaration would have to be considered invalid, and due to the lack of consent the ICJ would consequently not be competent to deal with the case.

Judge Klaestad in his Dissenting Opinion in the same case (ICJ, Judgment on Preliminary Objections, *Interhandel* (Switzerland v United States of America), 1959, Dissenting Opinion of Judge Klaestad, 76–78) was, however, of the opinion that the invalid reservation was actually severable from the optional clause declaration, since the State in question truly had had the intention of making such a declaration accepting the ICJ's jurisdiction. Thus, this intention should be considered as more important, and the reservation could be separated from the optional clause declaration, which consequently would remain valid and on which the ICJ could base its jurisdiction.

[*You should now argue for either one of the solutions theoretically explained above.*]

In our opinion, the position of Judge Klaestad seems to be more convincing, especially also in the light of the decision of the European Court of Human Rights in the *Belilos v Switzerland* case (ECtHR, *Belilos v Switzerland*, Judgment, Application No 10328/83, 29 April 1988, paragraphs 38–60), where it held that the invalid reservation of Switzerland could be separated from the valid consent of Switzerland. This solution is also preferable in light of international justice, since it prevents the creation of gaps in jurisdiction. Therefore, we can conclude that the automatic reservation made by Karabo is invalid, but is severable from its optional clause declaration, which thus remains in force.

[*If you found the position of Judge Lauterpacht more convincing—which is an equally valid position in this unsettled question—you could argue, for example, that there is no obligation on States actually to make such optional clause declarations at all. There are in fact enough other possibilities to give consent to the ICJ's jurisdiction should the need arise. Furthermore, an optional clause declaration is potentially giving the ICJ jurisdiction in a multitude of cases, since once this declaration is made, every other State having such a declaration could bring a case against this State, for which the ICJ would be competent based on these optional clause declarations. The motivation thus to limit the ICJ's jurisdiction is wholly understandable. Consequently, a State having made such an optional clause declaration does not make any rash decisions but carefully prepares this voluntary statement. Hence, it can truly be assumed that this State only made this optional clause declaration because it had the possibility of attaching a reservation to it. If now this reservation for whatever reason would be declared invalid, the whole optional clause declaration logically needs to fall, since the now unprotected State no longer has any interest in the existence of this optional clause declaration. Therefore, we can conclude that since the automatic reservation made by Karabo has been declared invalid, this State's optional clause declaration also becomes invalid.*]

5. Conclusion

Thus, there exist now two optional clause declarations (one from Karabo and one from Melusina) with no relevant reservations, satisfying the reciprocal nature of the optional clause system. Therefore, also the third aspect of jurisdiction, jurisdiction *ratione consensus*, exists and the ICJ is competent to hear the case between Karabo and Melusina.

[*If you argued that the optional clause declaration of Karabo is no longer valid, your conclusion could read as follows: Consequently, only one optional clause declaration—the one from Melusina—exists. However, the optional clause system is a reciprocal system and only works if the two parties have both made such declarations. This is clearly provided in Article 36 paragraph 2 ICJ Statute where it says that a State making an optional clause declaration recognises the Court's competence 'in relation to any other State accepting the* same *obligation' (emphasis added). Thus, it is clear that two optional clause declarations are necessary to establish consent on this basis (see eg the* Certain Norwegian Loans *case (ICJ, Judgment,* Certain Norwegian Loans *(France v Norway), 1957, 23, 24). Since we cannot rely on any of the other modes of giving consent to the Court either (such as special provision in the treaty, a special agreement or* forum prorogatum*, we have to conclude that the ICJ does not have jurisdiction and is thus not competent to deal with the case.*]

SUGGESTED SOLUTIONS
Other forms of consent

Suggested Solution—Case 5.6

Abbreviations used
ICJ = International Court of Justice
TUW = Treaty on the Use of the Waterflo
PCIJ = Permanent Court of International Justice
UN = United Nations

1. Applicable law

We will apply the ICJ Statute and the UN Charter. According to Article 92 UN Charter, the ICJ Statute is an integral part of the UN Charter. Since both parties involved in the dispute are parties to the UN Charter since its entry into force (and thus are necessarily also members of the UN), the UN Charter and consequently also the ICJ Statute is applicable.

In order for the ICJ to be competent to hear the case, three different types of jurisdiction need to be established: personal jurisdiction, subject matter jurisdiction and consensual jurisdiction.

2. Personal jurisdiction (jurisdiction *ratione personae*)

Article 34 paragraph 1 ICJ Statute provides that only States can be parties to disputes in front of the ICJ. There is nothing in the facts that lets us suspect that Attaland and Defland are not States. Their statehood is also confirmed by the fact that they are members of the UN, since the UN is only open to States (Article 4 paragraph 1 UN Charter). Therefore, the first requirement in order to satisfy this element is fulfilled.

In addition, Article 35 paragraph 1 ICJ Statute further provides that the ICJ is only open to States that are parties to its Statute. However, Article 93 paragraph 1 UN Charter declares that all members of the UN are, ipso facto, parties to the ICJ Statute. Consequently, since both Attaland and Defland are parties to the UN Charter and thus members of the UN, they are automatically also parties to the ICJ Statute and the second requirement for personal jurisdiction is fulfilled.

We can therefore conclude that the ICJ has personal jurisdiction to hear the case.

3. Subject matter jurisdiction (jurisdiction *ratione materiae*)

The ICJ is only competent to deal with legal disputes under international law, which can for example be inferred from Article 38 ICJ Statute.

The most often used definition of a legal dispute can be found in the *Mavrommatis Palestine Concessions* case by the PCIJ (PCIJ, Judgment on the Objection to the Jurisdiction of the Court, *The Mavrommatis Palestine Concessions*, 1924, 11). There, the PCIJ said that a dispute was a disagreement on a point of law or fact between two persons.

Indeed, in our case there seems to be a dispute between Attaland and Defland, since Attaland considers that the construction of a dam was a clear violation of the TUW, while it can be assumed that Defland is of a different opinion. This can be assumed first of all because Defland constructs this dam. If we do not suppose that Defland manifestly would act in bad faith and would deliberately violate an international treaty, then the conclusion is that Defland assumes that constructing a dam is permitted under the TUW. Secondly, if there were not a disagreement on facts but rather both parties were in agreement, it would not be necessary to bring the dispute to the ICJ. In this regard it might be important to point out that it is irrelevant whether the two parties say or think that such a dispute does or does not exist. It is for the Court alone to determine objectively whether such a dispute is present (see eg the ICJ's judgment on the preliminary objections in the *Lockerbie* case (ICJ, Judgment on Preliminary Objections, *Questions of Interpretation and Application of the 1971 Montreal Convention arising from the Aerial Incident at Lockerbie* (Libyan Arab Jamahiriya v United States of America), 1998, paragraph 21)). Thus, even if Defland—the defendant—were to argue that there is no such dispute, an objective determination by the ICJ will clarify the matter and will have to conclude that there is indeed a legal dispute on the interpretation of a bilateral treaty.

In addition, the dispute falls under international law, since it concerns an international (bilateral) treaty. Furthermore, international treaties are also governed by international treaty law and therefore the dispute is indeed a legal dispute under international law.

Consequently, the ICJ also has subject matter jurisdiction to hear the case.

4. Consensual jurisdiction (jurisdiction *ratione consensus*)

Even if the foregoing elements are all fulfilled, it is crucial that there is consent by the State parties to the jurisdiction of the Court. There is no compulsory jurisdiction of the ICJ as such without the agreement of the parties concerned. The ICJ itself has confirmed this, for example in the *East Timor* case (ICJ, Judgment, *Case concerning East Timor* (Portugal v Australia), 1995, paragraph 26) or in the *Monetary Gold* case (ICJ, Judgment, *Monetary Gold Removed from Rome in 1943* (Italy v France, United Kingdom of Great Britain and Northern Ireland and United States of America), 1954, 32).

Normally, the matter of consensus is—unlike the two previous elements—not dealt with ex officio by the ICJ. However, since we do not know whether or not Defland contests the ICJ's jurisdiction, it is more appropriate also to analyse this element.

Only one of the four possibilities to consent to the ICJ's jurisdiction *ratione consensus* seems to be relevant here.

The TUW contains in its Article 48 a so-called compromissory clause. In such a clause, parties to the treaty have agreed how and under which conditions they will settle their disputes in relation to the treaty. Compromissory clauses give the ICJ jurisdiction *ratione consensus* under Article 36 paragraph 1 ICJ Statute.

In our case Article 48 TUW does not contain any condition for the competence of the ICJ such as previous failure of negotiations. In addition, it seems that one party alone can bring the case to the ICJ. This is logical because the TUW is a bilateral treaty and were it otherwise such a condition would have to be clearly stated in the compromissory clause. Therefore, the ICJ's consensual jurisdiction based on the compromissory clause in Article 48 TUW is established.

5. Conclusion

As seen above, all necessary elements for the ICJ's jurisdiction are fulfilled. Therefore, the ICJ is competent to deal with the dispute between Attaland and Defland.

Suggested Solution—Case 5.7

Abbreviations used

ICJ = International Court of Justice
PCIJ = Permanent Court of International Justice
TEST = Treaty on the Exchange of Sugar against Tin
UN = United Nations
VCLT = Vienna Convention on the Law of Treaties

1. Applicable Law

We will apply the UN Charter and the Statute of the ICJ. The latter is, according to Article 92 of the UN Charter, an integral part of the UN Charter.

Both States in question are original members of the UN and therefore bound by this instrument.

In order to find that the ICJ is competent to hear the case in question, three conditions need to be fulfilled: personal jurisdiction, subject matter jurisdiction and consensual jurisdiction.

2. Personal jurisdiction (jurisdiction *ratione personae*)

Whether or not the ICJ has personal jurisdiction is a matter which is ascertained ex officio by the ICJ itself.

Article 34 paragraph 1 of the ICJ Statute provides that only States can be parties in disputes before the ICJ. This means that other entities such as companies but also international organisations are excluded from the contentious function of the ICJ.

In our case, there is no doubt that both Hanchez and Bonnat are States. This is also shown by the fact that they are both members of the UN, to which according to Article 4 paragraph 1 of the UN Charter only States can become parties.

In addition, Article 35 paragraph 1 of the ICJ Statute provides that the ICJ is only open to States which are parties to the ICJ Statute.

According to Article 93 paragraph 1 of the UN Charter all UN members are, however, ipso facto parties to the Statute of the ICJ. Since both States in question are members of the UN, they are automatically also parties to the ICJ Statute.

Hence we can conclude that the necessary conditions for the establishment of personal jurisdiction are fulfilled and the ICJ has personal jurisdiction in that case.

3. Subject matter jurisdiction (jurisdiction *ratione materiae*)

The existence of subject matter jurisdiction is also examined ex officio by the ICJ. The ICJ is only competent to deal with legal disputes under international law. This can be inferred, for example, from Article 38 paragraph 1 of the ICJ Statute. Therefore, the ICJ would not be competent to deal with purely political disputes. However, political aspects or implications of a legal question do not prevent the ICJ from finding jurisdiction *ratione materiae*.

The most widely used definition of a dispute can be found in the *Mavrommatis Palestine Concessions* case (PCIJ, Judgment on the Objection to the Jurisdiction of the Court, *The Mavrommatis Palestine Concessions*, 1924, 11). There, the PCIJ held that a dispute is a disagreement on a point of law or fact between two persons. It is also important to point out that it is irrelevant whether the two parties say or think that such a dispute does or does not exist. Whether there exists such dispute is to be determined objectively (ICJ, Advisory Opinion, First Phase, *Interpretation of Peace Treaties with Bulgaria, Hungary and Romania*, 1950, 74). It is up to the Court to make this determination (see eg the *Lockerbie* case, (ICJ, Judgment on Preliminary Objections, *Questions of Interpretation and Application of the 1971 Montreal Convention arising from the Aerial Incident at Lockerbie* (Libyan Arab Jamahiriya v United States of America), 1998, paragraph 21)).

In our case, there seems indeed to be a legal dispute between Hanchez and Bonnat. The two States do not agree on the (correct) application of the TEST and its eventual termination under Article 60 VCLT. This is therefore a disagreement on a point of law. In addition the dispute is a legal one since the issue is treaty law and the application of a treaty. It has furthermore to be kept in mind that the ICJ is only competent to deal with cases that arise under international law. Also this condition seems to be fulfilled since there is an international treaty (the TEST) between two States. Thus, the issue clearly falls under international law.

Consequently, we can conclude that subject matter jurisdiction also exists in our case at hand.

4. Consensual jurisdiction (jurisdiction *ratione consensus*)

For ICJ jurisdiction it is not enough to have established personal and subject matter jurisdiction. Consent by the parties to the jurisdiction is essential, a factor that has been stressed by the ICJ, for example in the *Monetary Gold* case (ICJ, Judgment, *Monetary Gold Removed from Rome in 1943* (Italy v France, United Kingdom of Great Britain and Northern Ireland and United States of America), 1954, 32) and the *East Timor* case (ICJ, Judgment, *Case concerning East Timor* (Portugal v Australia), 1995, paragraph 26).

This third aspect of jurisdiction is normally not raised ex officio by the ICJ. It is up to the parties to raise issues of consent in preliminary objections. Nevertheless, since the question with which we are confronted asks whether we would consider the ICJ to be competent to hear the case, an assessment of jurisdiction *ratione consensus* is indispensable.

There are different possibilities for States to express their consent to be bound by the compulsory jurisdiction of the ICJ.

One possibility is a so-called compromissory clause in a treaty (Article 36 paragraph 1 ICJ Statute). These are clauses in a treaty which stipulate under which conditions State parties to the treaty can have recourse to the ICJ in order to settle a dispute relating to the treaty in question. However, in our case there is nothing in the facts indicating that the TEST contains such a compromissory clause. We have therefore to assume that it does not contain such a clause and thus cannot serve as a basis of jurisdiction for the ICJ here.

Another possibility are optional clause declarations, made under Article 36 paragraph 2 of the ICJ Statute. These are unilateral declarations by States, declaring that they 'recognise the compulsory jurisdiction of the ICJ ipso facto and without special agreement in relation to any other State accepting the same obligation'. As indicated in the second part of this sentence, optional clause declarations only work on a reciprocal basis, meaning that there need to be two optional clause declarations to establish the basis of jurisdiction of the ICJ (see eg the *Certain Norwegian Loans* case (ICJ, Judgment, *Certain Norwegian Loans* (France v Norway), 1957, 23, 24)). Since in our case only Hanchez has made an optional clause declaration, this form cannot serve as basis of jurisdiction for the ICJ.

Next to written forms of consenting to the ICJ's jurisdiction, there is one non-written form. It is called *forum prorogatum*. This is the situation when a defending State does not contest the jurisdiction of the ICJ in the case in question, but immediately starts to argue on the merits of the case. It is important to stress that *forum prorogatum* can only exist when the arguments are made on the *merits* of the case. Any argument on the competence of the ICJ is to be seen as a preliminary objection and hence cannot be said to be *forum prorogatum*. (On *forum prorogatum*, see eg the *Corfu Channel* case (ICJ, Judgment on Preliminary Objections, *Corfu Channel* (United Kingdom of Great Britain and Northern Ireland v Albania), 1948, 27, 28) or the case on *Questions of Mutual Assistance in Criminal Matters* (ICJ, Judgment, *Certain Questions of Mutual Assistance in Criminal Matters* (Djibouti v France), 2008, paragraphs 60–95).)

In our case, Hanchez brings the dispute to the ICJ. As soon as Bonnat—the defendant State—is informed it starts to argue on the merits by outlining its arguments why in its opinion the TEST is properly applied and could not be terminated under Article 60

VCLT. Bonnat does not contest the jurisdiction of the ICJ in the case at hand and even says that it believes in the importance of international justice as deployed by the ICJ.

Therefore, this is a situation of *forum prorogatum*, a tacit consent by the States to the ICJ's jurisdiction. Consequently, the third element necessary for ICJ jurisdiction has been established.

5. Conclusion

Since all three elements—personal, subject matter and consensual jurisdiction—are fulfilled, the ICJ has jurisdiction to deal with the dispute between Hanchez and Bonat.

Suggested Solution—Case 5.8

Abbreviations used

ICJ = International Court of Justice
PCIJ = Permanent Court of International Justice
UN = United Nations

Applicable law

The law applicable to our case is the UN Charter and the Statute of the ICJ, which is according to Article 92 UN Charter an integral part of the UN Charter. Both States party to the dispute are members of the UN, making the UN Charter applicable.

In addition we will also apply the agreement concluded between Nemesis and Titania on 31 May 2010.

2. Personal jurisdiction (jurisdiction *ratione personae*)

According to Article 34 paragraph 1 of the ICJ Statute, only States can be parties to disputes before the Court. Other entities such as international organisations as well as individuals or private companies are excluded.

However, there is no doubt that Nemesis and Titania are both States. This can also be inferred from the fact that they are both members of the UN. According to Article 4 paragraph 1 UN Charter, membership in this organisation is only open to States.

Article 35 paragraph 1 of the ICJ Statute adds a further condition, namely that States which wish to be parties to a dispute in front of the ICJ need to be parties to the ICJ Statute. However, Article 93 paragraph 1 of the UN Charter specifies that every UN member is ipso facto, ie automatically, a party to the ICJ Statute. Since, as seen above, both Titania and Nemesis are members of the UN, they are hence also parties to the ICJ Statute.

Consequently, personal jurisdiction of the ICJ in the present case over Nemesis and Titania is established.

3. Subject matter jurisdiction (jurisdiction *ratione materiae*)

The ICJ is only competent to deal with legal disputes under international law. It is thus not competent to deal, for example, with purely political questions (although a political implication of a legal question or dispute will not prevent the ICJ from having jurisdiction *ratione materiae*). As for personal jurisdiction, the ICJ has to ascertain ex officio whether subject matter jurisdiction exists.

The most widely used definition of a dispute can be found in the *Mavrommatis Palestine Concessions* case (PCIJ, Judgment on the Objection to the Jurisdiction of the Court, *The Mavrommatis Palestine Concessions*, 1924, 11). There, the PCIJ held that a dispute is a disagreement on a point of law or fact between two persons. It is also important to point out that it is irrelevant whether the two parties say or think that such a dispute does or does not exist. It is alone for the Court to determine objectively whether such a dispute is present (see eg the *Lockerbie* case, (ICJ, Judgment on Preliminary Objections, *Questions of Interpretation and Application of the 1971 Montreal Convention arising from the Aerial Incident at Lockerbie* (Libyan Arab Jamahiriya v United States of America), 1998, paragraph 21), see also ICJ, Advisory Opinion, First Phase, *Interpretation of Peace Treaties with Bulgaria, Hungary and Romania*, 1950, 74).

In our case, there is indeed a dispute between the two parties since they do not agree on the course of their common border, especially in the region where diamonds were found. The dispute is also an internationally legal one as the determination of State boundaries is a question under international law, which determines the territory of a State and thus also the extension of its sovereignty.

Thus, we can conclude that there is indeed an internationally legal dispute present between Nemesis and Titania and thus subject matter jurisdiction of the ICJ is established.

4. Consensual jurisdiction (jurisdiction *ratione consensus*)

Despite having established the presence of personal and subject matter jurisdiction, the ICJ can never have jurisdiction to hear a case without the consent of the parties involved, ie there is no compulsory jurisdiction without consent (see eg the ICJ in the *East Timor* case (ICJ, Judgment, *Case concerning East Timor* (Portugal v Australia), 1995, paragraph 26) or in the *Monetary Gold* case (ICJ, Judgment, *Monetary Gold Removed from Rome in 1943* (Italy v France, United Kingdom of Great Britain and Northern Ireland and United States of America), 1954, 32)).

This third aspect of jurisdiction is normally not raised ex officio by the ICJ. It is up to the parties to raise issues of consent in preliminary objections. Nevertheless, since the question with which we are confronted asks whether we would consider the ICJ to be competent to hear the case, an assessment of jurisdiction *ratione consensus* should be made.

Nemesis has made an optional clause declaration under Article 36 paragraph 2 of the ICJ Statute. However, Titania has not made such a declaration. The optional clause system is a reciprocal system, establishing a web of relations between States. Therefore, this system can only serve as basis of consent to the ICJ's jurisdiction if there are two optional clause declarations covering the same subject matter. This basis of jurisdiction can therefore be excluded here.

When Nemesis brought the case to the ICJ it also transmitted an agreement between itself and Titania. This is a so-called 'special agreement', whereby two States consent to bring a particular case to the ICJ after the dispute has arisen. The special agreement between Nemesis and Titania is validly concluded and has entered into force at the day of signature, ie on 31 May 2010. It can therefore be applied and serves as basis for jurisdiction in accordance with Article 36 paragraph 1 of the ICJ Statute. It foresees that the ICJ shall draw the border between the two States in the region where the diamonds were found and that in addition it should also specify which law is applicable to this determination of the borders. It is relevant to note that the question that the ICJ is asked to answer is limited: only the border in the region of the diamond mine shall be determined by the ICJ. Any other parts of the common border which might still be undefined are not included and the ICJ is not authorised under this special agreement to pronounce itself on them.

Nevertheless, the special agreement establishes the parties' consent to the ICJ's jurisdiction to deal with the specific dispute between Nemesis and Titania.

5. Conclusion

Personal, subject matter and consensual jurisdiction have been established, as argued above. Thus, we can conclude that the ICJ is competent to deal with the case on the delimitation of the border between Nemesis and Titania in the region of the diamond mine, as foreseen in the special agreement concluded by the two parties in May 2010.

SUGGESTED SOLUTIONS
Issues of admissibility

Suggested Solution—Case 5.9

Abbreviations used

BT = Boundary Treaty
ICJ = International Court of Justice
PCIJ = Permanent Court of International Justice
UN = United Nations

1. Applicable law

In this case, we will apply the Statute of the ICJ, which is, according to Article 92 of the UN Charter, an integral part of the UN Charter. Both States involved in the proceedings, Boja and Lesta, as well as the third State, Nyfor, are original members of the UN. Thus, the UN Charter is applicable in its entirety.

In addition, the applicable law comprises also the Boundary Treaty, concluded on 26 February 1984 between Boja, Lesta and Nyfor.

Boja generally contests the jurisdiction of the ICJ. Therefore, we have first to analyse the three main elements of jurisdiction of the ICJ: personal, material and consensual jurisdiction.

2. Personal jurisdiction (jurisdiction *ratione personae*)

According to Article 34 paragraph 1 ICJ Statute, only States can be parties in contentious cases before the Court. This requirement does not pose any problem here, since both parties involved in the dispute brought before the Court, namely Boja and Lesta, are States. No one contests this and furthermore they are members of the UN, an organisation that only permits States to become members (Article 4 paragraph 1 UN Charter).

In addition, Article 35 paragraph 1 of the ICJ Statute provides that the Court is only open to States which are also parties to the Statute of the Court. Article 93 paragraph 1 of the UN Charter States that all the members of the UN are ipso facto, ie automatically, parties to the ICJ Statute. Since, as seen above, both Boja and Lesta are members of the UN, they are also parties to the ICJ Statute and thus Article 35 paragraph 1 is fulfilled.

We can therefore conclude that the ICJ has personal jurisdiction to hear the case.

3. Subject matter jurisdiction (jurisdiction *ratione materiae*)

The ICJ is only competent to deal with legal disputes under international law. This can be seen in Article 38 of the ICJ Statute which says that the Court's function is to 'decide in accordance with international law such disputes as are submitted to it'.

It has been the Permanent Court of International Justice which gave the most used definition of a dispute in its *Mavrommatis Palestine Concessions* case in 1924 (PCIJ, Judgment on the Objection to the Jurisdiction of the Court, *The Mavrommatis Palestine Concessions*, 1924, 11). There the PCIJ said that a dispute is a 'disagreement on a point of law or fact, a conflict of legal views or interests between two persons'.

Here we clearly have a dispute, namely whether or not Boja violated the maritime boundaries between itself and Lesta. Furthermore, the dispute is also a legal one, since issues of territorial sovereignty but also issues concerning the BT (which after all has established those maritime boundaries) are raised. These are clearly issues which have legal aspects. In addition, as a third element, the ICJ can only deal with disputes under international law. This is also fulfilled here, since it involves an international treaty—the BT—which is governed by the international law on treaties, and in addition the subject of boundaries falls under international and not national law.

Thus, the ICJ also has subject matter jurisdiction, since it is indeed confronted with a legal dispute under international law.

4. Consensual jurisdiction (jurisdiction *ratione consensus*)

Unlike with the two previous elements, the consensual jurisdiction is normally not analysed ex officio by the ICJ. However, since Boja contests the jurisdiction of the ICJ in general, we have to analyse the jurisdiction *ratione consensus*.

As is well known the ICJ can only deal with a case if the parties to the dispute have given their consent to the jurisdiction of the Court. This important point has been confirmed by the ICJ for example in the *East Timor* case (ICJ, Judgment, *Case concerning East Timor* (Portugal v Australia), 1995, paragraph 26).

In our case the consent to the jurisdiction of the ICJ can be found in a so-called compromissory clause in the BT. Those compromissory clauses are recognised as a means of consenting to the ICJ under Article 36 paragraph 1 of the ICJ Statute. The compromissory clause in Article 77 BT foresees that every party to this treaty can bring a dispute about the interpretation or application of the treaty to the ICJ. There is, however, a condition: prior negotiations must have failed.

We know from the facts that Lesta has offered several times to negotiate with Boja, but Boja has either refused or ignored this. Therefore, it can be said that negotiations have failed. It would be unreasonable to expect that negotiations have actually to have taken place and failed in order to fulfil this condition. This would create a means for the State not willing to negotiate to permanently block any solution of the dispute by preventing the case from being referred to the ICJ.

Furthermore, we can note that the BT authorises that States bring the dispute unilaterally, since it speaks of 'any party to this dispute'.

Hence, both States did consent to the jurisdiction of the ICJ in the compromissory clause contained in the BT.

In conclusion, we can say that the ICJ has jurisdiction to hear the case at hand and Boja was wrong to contest this.

However, Boja also raises issues falling under the admissibility of cases.

5. Admissibility

Boja claims that since the dispute concerns a treaty to which a State not involved in the dispute—Nyfor—is a party, the ICJ would not be competent to hear the case.

Boja is thereby referring to what is known as the 'legal interest of third States'. This argument against admissibility has been raised in a number of cases, such as the *Monetary Gold* case (ICJ, Judgment, *Monetary Gold Removed from Rome in 1943* (Italy v France, United Kingdom of Great Britain and Northern Ireland and United States of America), 1954, 32), the *Nicaragua* case (ICJ, Judgment on the Jurisdiction of the Court and the Admissibility of the Application, *Military and Paramilitary Activities in and against Nicaragua* (Nicaragua v United States of America), 1984, paragraph 88) or the *East Timor* case (ICJ, Judgment, *Case concerning East Timor* (Portugal v Australia), 1995, paragraphs 28–29).

According to the *Monetary Gold* case referred to above, it has to be assessed whether the legal interest of the third State not involved in the dispute actually constitutes the 'very subject-matter' of the dispute. Or, as the ICJ specified later on in the *Nicaragua* case cited above, whether these legal interests were only 'affected' by the decision of the ICJ (which, it should be remembered, is according to Article 59 only binding on the parties to the dispute in question and therefore not on any third States).

It is true that any decision involving the BT would potentially have an effect on

Nyfor. However, the 'very subject-matter' of the dispute is the alleged non-respect of the boundaries determined by the BT by Boja in relation to Lesta. Nyfor is not involved there. It thus cannot be said that the legal interests of Nyfor in the treaty would be the 'very subject-matter' of the dispute, but its interests would at most be 'affected'. Thus, the case has to be declared admissible.

In addition, under Article 62 of the ICJ Statute Nyfor—as a State whose legal interest might be affected by the decision in the case—can submit a request to the ICJ to be permitted to intervene in the case. Therefore, Nyfor's potential legal interest could be safeguarded in any event.

6. Conclusion

The case between Lesta and Boja is admissible and the ICJ also has jurisdiction to deal with the case. Thus, the ICJ is competent to deal with the dispute in the merits phase.

SUGGESTED SOLUTIONS
Advisory opinions

Suggested Solution—Case 5.10

Abbreviations used
ICJ = International Court of Justice
TWOOS = Treaty on the World Organisation for Outer Space
UN = United Nations
WOOS = World Organisation for Outer Space

1. Applicable law

In order to reply to this question of the registrar, we will have recourse to the ICJ Statute and the UN Charter. It should be noted that, according to Article 92 of the UN Charter, the ICJ Statute is an integral part of this Charter. Thus they should be applied together.

In addition, we will also have to take a look at the founding treaty of the WOOS, the TWOOS and the Outer Space Treaty.

2. 'Personal jurisdiction' (jurisdiction *ratione personae*)

Article 65 paragraph 1 of the ICJ Statute provides that the Court can give advisory opinions on any legal question at the request of whatever body which is authorised in accordance with the UN Charter to ask such questions. Therefore, we need to look at the UN Charter in order to see who is allowed to ask such questions.

In Article 96 paragraph 1 UN Charter it is stated that the UN General Assembly and the UN Security Council can ask advisory opinions on 'any legal question'. Yet, the question in our case does not come from the UN General Assembly, but from the General Assembly of the WOOS, a specialised agency within the UN system.

Therefore, we have to look at Article 96 paragraph 2 UN Charter which provides that UN organs other than the two mentioned in paragraph 1 and organs of specialised agencies which are authorised by the UN General Assembly can ask advisory opinions on 'legal questions arising within the scope of their activities'.

In our case, the WOOS has been authorised by the UN General Assembly in resolution 95/504 adopted on 7 June 2011 to ask advisory opinions to the ICJ.

Therefore, in accordance with Article 96 paragraph 2 UN Charter, the General Assembly of the WOOS is entitled to request an advisory opinion of the ICJ.

3. Subject matter jurisdiction (jurisdiction *ratione materiae*)

As already seen above, Article 96 UN Charter distinguishes questions that can be asked between paragraphs 1 and 2. While under paragraph 1 the UN General Assembly and the Security Council are entitled to ask 'all legal questions', organs entitled to request advisory opinions under paragraph 2 can only do so on 'legal questions arising within the scope of their activities'. The same restriction has also been incorporated into General Assembly resolution 95/504, which, however, also added that the WOOS cannot ask questions in relation to the reciprocal relations between the WOOS and the UN or other specialised organisations. However, it is clear that the question asked by the WOOS does not fall within the second limit posed by the UN General Assembly Resolution.

First of all, we have to make sure that the question asked is indeed a legal question, since otherwise the Court as a judicial organ will not be competent to answer it. The question deals with liabilities and, among other things, with the interpretation and application of Article VII of the Outer Space Treaty. Thus, the question is indeed in relation to legal issues such as liabilities and treaty interpretation.

In addition, we have to ascertain whether the question asked falls within the scope of activities of the WOOS.

The question asked deals with the liability for damages resulting from the launch of space shuttles by the WOOS, without the direct participation of a State. It is apparently not clear whether the WOOS will be liable in such cases or whether the State making its territory available for this launch will be liable for potential damages (in accordance with Article VII of the Outer Space Treaty). If we look at the goals and competences of the WOOS, it soon becomes clear that the WOOS is entitled to launch space shuttle missions for scientific purposes on its own, ie without the participation of any State. Therefore, the question of liability for such launches of the WOOS is a pertinent one which clearly falls within the scope of the WOOS's activities.

Therefore, the ICJ should declare itself competent to answer the question asked by the General Assembly of the WOOS.

In addition, we might note the conditions posed in Article 65 paragraph 2 ICJ Statute concerning the question asked. The question has to be submitted in writing and needs to contain an exact statement of the question upon which the advisory opinion is sought.

In our case, the question is a very precise question transmitted in writing in the resolution adopted by the General Assembly of the WOOS to the Court.

We can also assume that the necessary documents will be delivered to the Court to help it clarify the question.

4. Conclusion

For all the reasons above, we can conclude that the ICJ would be competent to deal with the advisory opinion requested by the General Assembly of the WOOS. Nevertheless, we have to note that there is no obligation on the ICJ to give advisory opinions even if all the necessary conditions are fulfilled (see Article 65 paragraph 1 'the Court *may* give advisory opinions') and thus it is up to the Court to decide whether or not to take up this question. This discretionary right of the Court has been confirmed by the ICJ itself in numerous advisory opinions, such as the *Wall* case (ICJ, Advisory Opinion, *Legal Consequences of the Construction of a Wall in the Occupied Palestinian Territory*, 2004, paragraph 44), the Advisory Opinion on the *Legality of the Use of Nuclear Weapons* (ICJ, Advisory Opinion, *Legality of the Use by a State of Nuclear Weapons in Armed Conflict*, 1996, paragraph 14) and the Advisory Opinion on the *Reservations to the Genocide Convention* (ICJ, Advisory Opinion, *Reservations to the Convention on the Prevention and Punishment of the Crime of Genocide*, 1951, 19).

However, at the same time it has to be recognised that the ICJ has equally often stressed that as principal judicial organ of the UN it should in principle not refuse to give an advisory opinion, unless it has 'compelling reasons' for such a refusal (see eg the *Certain Expenses* Advisory Opinion (ICJ, Advisory Opinion, *Certain Expenses of the United Nations (Article 17, paragraph 2, of the Charter)*, 1962, 155)).

Thus, since the ICJ is competent to answer the advisory opinion requested by the WOOS, it can be expected that it will indeed give such an answer.

Chapter 6

SUGGESTED SOLUTIONS
Use of Force

SUGGESTED SOLUTIONS
Article 2 paragraph 4 of the UN Charter

Suggested Solution—Case 6.1

Abbreviations used

GA = General Assembly
ICJ = International Court of Justice
SRA = State Responsibility Articles
UN = United Nations

1. Applicable law

We will apply the UN Charter to which both States are parties. In addition, we will also apply relevant resolutions from the General Assembly (GA), such as resolution 2625, also called the Declaration on Principles of International Law concerning Friendly Relations and Co-operation among States in Accordance with the Charter of the United Nations, adopted in 1970.

This raises a preliminary question concerning the legal value of GA resolutions. It is well known that the GA only has the power to make *recommendations* (see Articles 10–14 of the UN Charter, dealing with the functions and powers of the GA). Thus, GA resolutions are not legally binding as such and therefore cannot be the source of legal obligations of States. However, talking here specifically about GA resolution 2625 we could first consider that most of the principles it enumerates are actually principles of international customary law and therefore binding on all States. Second, GA resolution 2625 has actually been adopted to clarify the different principles of friendly relations, such as peaceful settlement of disputes or non-use of force, contained in the UN Charter. In that sense, these principles do not add any new obligations on States but only interpret and clarify already existing obligations under the UN Charter (or also customary law).

In any event, it can be considered that GA resolution 2625 can be applied here and clarifies obligations of States under the UN Charter.

In addition, we will also use the ILC's Articles on Responsibility of States for Internationally Wrongful Acts (SRA), which are not a treaty but are binding as customary law, as has been confirmed by the ICJ, for example in the *Genocide* case in 2007 (ICJ, Judgment, *Application of the Convention on the Prevention and Punishment of the Crime of Genocide* (Bosnia and Herzegovina v Serbia and Montenegro), 2007, paragraph 401).

2. Article 2 paragraph 4 UN Charter: threat or use of force

Generally the use of force is prohibited under the UN Charter (Article 2 paragraph 4), with the exception of self-defence and the authorisation of use of force by the Security Council.

It is clear from the facts that Lyreco has not (yet) used force against Assuria but has only threatened to use it.

There are several reasons why in addition to the use of force the threat to use force was also prohibited by the drafters of the UN Charter. It is logical to prohibit the threats if the use itself is afterwards prohibited. Threats are often already sufficient to poison international relations and disturb relations between States. This is even more so if the threatening State is a powerful one, for whom threats might be enough to coerce smaller States in doing what it wants. Lastly, in order not to lose their credibility, many States tend actually to use force in one way or another once they have threatened to do so. Therefore, the threat needs to be prohibited at the outset to avoid that States feel 'obliged' to realise their threats in order to 'keep face'.

We have to consider whether the different acts can constitute threats to use force.

The first acts to be considered are the statements made by the President of Lyreco, Mr Prid, and his ministers.

In GA resolution 2625, under the principle that States shall refrain from the use or threat of use of force against the territorial integrity of a State, we can find the indication that this principle also incorporates the duty of States to refrain from propaganda for wars of aggression.

It is true that the government of Lyreco never openly speaks of a war of aggression. However, when Mr Prid says that Assuria 'should be prepared for the day when the glorious Lyreco takes over their miserable country', this could be said to amount to a threat to use force against Assuria, since it is not conceivable how one country can take over another against the latter's will without using force. 'Propaganda' means in general that something—an idea or action—is 'advertised' and made popular. Statements by governmental officials can indeed amount to propaganda. Thus, with their statements the government of Lyreco can indeed be said to have made (or at least attempted to make) propaganda for a future war of aggression against Assuria. This can consequently be said to be a first potential violation of Article 2 paragraph 4, clarified in GA resolution 2625.

The next act to consider is the mobilisation of Lyreco's army and its deployment at the border of Assuria. The army does not cross the border but remains close to it for several days. It is probably difficult to find a more obvious example of the threat of use of force against the territorial integrity of a State than the deployment of an army at the border of a neighbouring State. Thus, Article 2 paragraph 4 is again violated. In addition, it can be said that the threat is continuing, since even though Lyreco's army has retreated, a large battalion remains close to the border. Thus, the threat to use force against the territorial integrity of Assuria remains.

Thirdly, the group called the Xerox is an armed organisation whose plan is to attack Assuria in order to get back the territory which Lyreco in general thinks is rightfully its. Since the Xerox is a non-State actor, we have shortly to consider whether the acts of the Xerox are attributable to Lyreco, since otherwise they cannot be said to violate Article 2 paragraph 4 of the UN Charter also on this account.

As we know, a State is responsible for every internationally wrongful act it commits (Article 1 SRA). For this responsibility we need to find attribution and a breach of an international obligation owed to that State (Article 2 SRA).

Looking at Articles 4–11 SRA on attribution, the most relevant Article appears to be Article 11 SRA. The Xerox is certainly not a State organ, nor is the State controlling it 'effectively' as is required for Article 8 SRA. Nevertheless, since Lyreco States that it agrees and supports the measures taken by the Xerox, this could be seen as endorsing the Xerox's actions as part of Lyreco's campaign against Assuria and could be seen as being enough to find attribution under Article 11 SRA.

[*You could, however, also argue that the President's statement is too weak to consider this as a conclusive 'endorsement' under the rather high threshold of Article 11 SRA. You could, for example, argue that this was only a statement made in the heat of circumstances and was not calculated to express the government's support of the Xerox's actions. Following this argument, then, you would conclude that no attribution under the SRA is possible. However, if no attribution is found under Article 11 SRA, it would, for example, still be possible to argue that Lyreco is responsible for having encouraged and/or tolerated on its territory acts involving the use or threat of use of force against another State. This would be equally inconsistent with the principles of GA resolution 2625 analysed here. Yet, since this would be Lyreco's own violation (ie the violation of the government of Lyreco), it would not be necessary to find attribution of the acts of the Xerox under the SRA.*]

So far, according to the facts, the action of the Xerox is limited to making threatening statements, similar to the ones made by the government of Lyreco. Thus, we can conclude that this could be seen as propaganda for a war of aggression as well. Since the actions of the Xerox are attributable to Lyreco under Article 11 SRA, Lyreco will also be responsible for this violation of Article 2 paragraph 4 UN Charter, as clarified by GA resolution 2625. [*Or, alternatively or even in addition—depending on how you argue—Lyreco will be responsible for its own violation, as argued above.*]

Since there are from the facts clearly no circumstances precluding wrongfulness, this violation of Article 2 paragraph 4 UN Charter can be attributed to Lyreco.

In addition to the specific violation made by the Xerox—and regardless of whether their actions have been found to be attributable to Lyreco or not—we can note a few further potential violations by Lyreco of Article 2 paragraph 4 UN Charter as set out in GA resolution 2625. The resolution specifies that this Article is also violated when a State encourages 'the organisation of irregular forces for incursion into the territory of another State'. In addition, States also have to refrain from 'acquiescing in organised activities within its territory' when these activities (acts of civil strife or terrorist acts) are directed against another State and involve the threat or use of force.

Lyreco neither condemns the plans of the Xerox, nor does it seem to take any measures against them, but rather publicly supports the Xerox and its plans. This is obviously encouraging for the Xerox. However, this explanation speaks of encouragement in connection with the *formation* of such groups and not with their encouragement once they exist. We do not know from the facts whether Lyreco actually encouraged the formation of the Xerox. There is nothing that would indicate this. Therefore, we cannot conclude that this would apply here.

Nevertheless, by saying that they support the activities of the Xerox, Lyreco clearly acquiesces in these acts. The threatened acts involve attacks on Assuria, including the planting of bombs. These can be seen as threatened 'terrorist acts', even though it has to be kept in mind that no universally accepted definition of terrorism exists. [*It should, however, be kept in mind that no acts have happened so far, so all remains on the level of threats, which makes a difference for finding a violation by the Xerox which might or might not be attributable to the State.*]

All the violations of Lyreco mentioned above—with the exception of acts by Xerox attributable (*or not*) to Lyreco—have been carried out by the government (ie the President and/or Ministers). Under Article 4 SRA, these are clearly organs of the State of Lyreco. Thus, since attribution is found in addition to violations, Lyreco is internationally responsible.

3. Conclusion

As a general conclusion we can say that Lyreco has repeatedly used threats to use force against Assuria. As clarified by GA resolution 2625, Article 2 paragraph 4 is broader than just the threat of physical force by one State against the other. Thus, Lyreco has violated Article 2 paragraph 4 not only by deploying its army to the border with Assuria (and keeping a battalion there), but potentially also by making propaganda for an aggressive war and by acquiescing in the threats and potential violent acts of the Xerox.

Suggested Solution—Case 6.2

Abbreviations used

GA = General Assembly
ICJ = International Court of Justice
MTL = Movement against Tyranny and for Liberty
SRA = State Responsibility Articles
UN = United Nations

1. Applicable law

We will apply the UN Charter to which both States are parties. In addition, we will also apply relevant resolutions from the GA, such as resolution 2625, also called the Declaration on Principles of International Law concerning Friendly Relations and Cooperation among States in Accordance with the Charter of the United Nations, adopted in 1970.

However, the application of this GA resolution 2625 raises questions concerning the legal value of such GA resolutions.

According to the UN Charter, the GA only has the power to make recommendations (Articles 10–14 of the UN Charter, dealing with the functions and powers of the GA). Thus, GA resolutions are not legally binding as such and therefore cannot be the source of legal obligations of States. However, concerning GA resolution 2625 we can argue that most of the principles it enumerates are principles of international customary law and therefore binding on all States. Second, GA resolution 2625 has been adopted to clarify the different principles of friendly relations, such as peaceful settlement of disputes or non-use of force, contained in the UN Charter. In that sense, these principles do not add any new obligations on States but only interpret and clarify already existing obligations under the UN Charter (or also customary law).

In any event, it can be considered that GA resolution 2625 can be applied here and clarifies obligations of States under the UN Charter.

In addition, we will also use the ILC's Articles on Responsibility of States for Internationally Wrongful Acts (SRA), which are not a treaty but which are binding as customary law, as has been confirmed by the ICJ for example in the *Genocide* case (ICJ, Judgment, *Application of the Convention on the Prevention and Punishment of the Crime of Genocide* (Bosnia and Herzegovina v Serbia and Montenegro), 2007, paragraph 401).

2. Article 2 paragraph 4 UN Charter: threat or use of force

Violation

The prohibition to use force is one of the most fundamental provisions in the UN Charter but also under customary international law (the ICJ confirmed the customary nature of this prohibition in the *Nicaragua* case (ICJ, Judgment on the Merits, *Military and Paramilitary Activities in and against Nicaragua* (Nicaragua v United States of America), 1986, paragraphs 187–192)). The use of force is prohibited under the UN Charter in Article 2 paragraph 4 UN Charter, with the exception of self-defence and the authorisation of use of force by the Security Council.

It is clear in our case that the MTL has used force when it attacked four different targets in Missland in September 2009. However, the question is not whether the MTL has used force but whether it can be said that Armeland has used force.

It is clear that Armeland has not used force directly, since neither its army, police nor any other organs were involved in the attacks. We have therefore to consider what has to be understood under the use of force as prohibited under Article 2 paragraph 4 UN Charter. Since the Article itself does not give any additional indications, we have to have recourse to GA resolution 2625, which—as explained above—clarifies what is to be understood under the different principles contained in the Charter. The first principle in this resolution is the principle of non-use of force. Under this principle the following is among other things provided:

> Every State has the duty to refrain from organizing, instigating, assisting or participating in acts of civil strife or *terrorist acts in another State or acquiescing in organised activities within its territory directed towards the commission of such acts*, when the acts referred to in the present paragraph involve a threat or use of force. (emphasis added)

Armeland was apparently aware of the presence of the MTL and supposedly also of its activities (even though this is not entirely sure). Yet, it did not take any measures against the MTL. Therefore, it can be said that by not taking action to hinder the MTL present in its territory from carrying out terrorist acts in another State (Missland), Armeland has acquiesced in these organised activities within its territory. Furthermore, the acts perpetrated by the MTL clearly involved the use of force, as argued above. Therefore, we can conclude that there has been indeed a violation of the principle of non-use of force by Armeland.

According to the SRA, there is a violation of an international obligation if a State does not act in conformity with what is required from it by an international customary or conventional obligation (Article 12 SRA) which is in force for the State in question at the time of the commission of the act (Article 13 SRA).

Armeland as a member of the UN is bound by Article 2 paragraph 4 of the UN Charter and was also bound by this obligation at the time when it ignored the presence of the MTL on its territory. As explained by UN GA resolution 2625, the prohibition not to use force has to be understood in a broad fashion, also including acquiescence. Therefore, we have to conclude there is a violation of an international obligation incumbent on Armeland.

Attribution

However, before concluding on Armeland's responsibility, we have also to deal with the necessary attribution. Article 2 SRA clearly provides that in order for a State to incur international responsibility the act in question must be attributable to the State and must constitute a violation of an international obligation.

It has to be kept in mind that we have to ascertain attribution not for the attack of the MTL, but for Armeland's *own* violation established above, namely the acquiescence in organised activities on its territory leading to terrorist attacks in another State. Armeland is in that sense right to argue that the acts of the MTL cannot be attributed to it since MTL members are private individuals. It seems also that Armeland does not have any control over the MTL, nor is it financing or training the organisation. In addition, Armeland does not adopt the conduct of the MTL as its own either, but simply tolerates its actions. Therefore, attribution of the acts of the MTL is clearly not possible in any event.

Nevertheless, Armeland's own violation explained above seems to be attributable to it. It would be the task of the police or the military to hinder organisations such as the MTL in training and planning their attacks on the territory of Armeland. In addition, it would have probably been for the government of Armeland to decide on measures against the MTL and if lacking to create the necessary legal basis for action. All these organs mentioned above are, however, clearly organs of the State in the sense of Article 4 SRA. Therefore, the acquiescence described above is attributable to Armeland.

Circumstances precluding wrongfulness

Looking at the different circumstances precluding wrongfulness available under the SRA, it becomes quickly clear that none of them is applicable in our case.

Therefore, we have to conclude that Armeland is indeed responsible for a violation of the prohibition to use force, since this prohibition is, according to UN GA resolution 2625, also violated in case that States acquiesce in the organised activities of groups directing terrorist attacks or other acts using force against another State. It has, however, to be stressed again that Armeland is responsible for its *own* violation—namely the acquiescence—and not directly for the attacks by the MTL. This has also an influence on the reparation to be made by Armeland.

Consequences

First of all, Armeland has to stop acquiescing to the presence of the MTL on its territory and to give guarantees to Missland that it will not do the same in the future again (Article 30 SRA). In addition, since Armeland is internationally responsible, it has also to make reparation. This is a well-established principle in international customary law (see PCIJ in the *Chórzow Factory* case (PCIJ, Judgment, *Case concerning the Factory at Chorzów (Claim for Indemnity)*, 1927, 21) and Article 31 SRA).

The most appropriate form of reparation seems to be satisfaction (Article 37 SRA), eg by prosecuting or extraditing MTL members or by making public apologies. It is also possible to argue that Armeland has to make financial reparations in the form of compensation (Article 36 SRA), but again it has to be stressed that Armeland can only be held responsible for its own violation and not the attacks of the MTL as such. This will necessarily considerably diminish the amount of money to be paid.

3. Conclusion

As seen above, Armeland is responsible for a violation of the prohibition on the use of force since according to UN GA resolution 2625 also acquiescing in such activities amounts to a violation of Article 2 paragraph 4 of the UN Charter.

SUGGESTED SOLUTIONS
Article 51 of the United Nations Charter

Suggested Solution—Case 6.3

Abbreviations used
ICJ = International Court of Justice
UN = United Nations

1. Applicable law

In order to solve this question we will have recourse to the UN Charter to which both Endo and Preg are parties.

In addition, we will, if necessary, use customary international law in the matter of use of force and self-defence.

2. The general rule and the two exceptions

It is true that the non-use of force provision found in Article 2 paragraph 4 of the UN Charter is one of the most fundamental provisions. It prohibits any State from using or threatening to use force against the territorial integrity or political independence of any other country. Furthermore, it is widely accepted that the non-use of force rule is a norm of *jus cogens*, and that it is therefore an absolute rule (see eg the pronouncement of the International Court of Justice in the *Nicaragua* case in this regard; ICJ, Judgment on the Merits, *Military and Paramilitary Activities in and against Nicaragua* (Nicaragua v United States of America), 1986, paragraph 190).

However, it is equally well accepted that there are two exceptions in the UN Charter itself in relation to the prohibition to use force. One exception is the power of the UN Security Council to authorise the use of force under Article 42 of the UN Charter, and the other exception is the 'inherent right of self-defence' found in Article 51 of the UN Charter. Since the force used was not authorised by the Security Council, the only other possibly exception is self-defence.

3. The conditions of self-defence

Article 51 of the UN Charter authorises self-defence of individual States or groups of States if there was an *armed attack* against this State. Self-defence is only authorised as long as the Security Council has not taken 'measures necessary to maintain international peace and security'. Furthermore, the State (or States) resorting to self-defence have to inform the Security Council immediately of the steps taken. These are all important conditions; however, what the 'inherent right of self-defence' really is, is not defined in the UN Charter. We have therefore to have recourse in addition to customary international law. There, we can find that there are two important conditions for the exercise of self-defence. Both conditions arose out of the *Caroline* incident, between the UK and the USA.

(a) The first condition is 'necessity'. This means that the use of force taken in self-defence was necessary and there was no other peaceful way (eg negotiations) to stop the attack of the other State. There is therefore a certain element of 'imminence' inherent in that first condition.
(b) The second condition is 'proportionality'. This refers to the requirement that measures taken in response to the attack cannot be disproportionate. It is, however, not completely clear to what the response has to be proportionate: has it to be proportionate to the means used in the attack, or to the threat posed by the attack or to the possibility of further attacks? Usually, it is used to refer to the proportionality concerning the means employed by the two parties. For example, the use of a nuclear bomb in response to the simple bombing and sinking of a warship would clearly not be proportionate. [*Due to the doctrinal uncertainty it is possible to take a different stance on this issue, keeping in mind, however, that the proportionality of means is the majority opinion. Thus, any contrary position needs to be well argued.*]

Let us now look at whether all the conditions named above, from Article 51 of the UN Charter as well as the customary clarifications, are fulfilled in our case.

To start with, Article 51 is only applicable in the case of an armed attack of one State against another. This is clearly fulfilled here, since it is Preg—a State—which attacks with its army as well as by launching missiles another State, namely Endo (see UN GA resolution 3314, Article 3(a) and (b)).

Was the use of force by Endo necessary? The armed attack occurred in the night of 6/7 May. The attack was hence already 'in full swing' and there was no other peaceful possibility available at that moment to stop the attack. In addition, it is highly unlikely that negotiations would have been successful, since Preg has turned down negotiation requests before. Therefore, the threat was not only imminent but actually already very real and the use of force by Endo necessary. Thus, the first customary element of self-defence seems to be fulfilled.

Also the element of proportionality does not seem to pose particular problems. Preg was using ground forces and missiles; Endo was using ground forces and air power to fight back. This does not seem to be out of proportion.

In addition, Article 51 imposes on the State resorting to self-defence the obligation to inform the Security Council immediately of the steps taken. The President of Endo has also fulfilled this condition, since immediately after ordering the attack on the forces of Preg he called the representative of Teny, the State which at that moment had the presidency of the Security Council, and informed him about the measures taken. Moreover, it is stated that the Security Council was kept up to date in the following days. Therefore, this condition for the exercise of self-defence in conformity with international law is also fulfilled.

Article 51 specifies that self-defence can only be exercised as long as the Security Council has not adopted the necessary measures to restore peace and security. This does not seem to be applicable in our case, since we do not know about any measures taken or even discussed by the Security Council.

Thus, we can say that the intellectuals criticising the President of Endo for his alleged violation of the rule of non-use of force are wrong. Indeed, all the conditions necessary for the exercise of self-defence—legal both under the UN Charter (Article 51) and customary international law—are fulfilled and hence the President did not violate international law. The only possible reproach that could be directed at the President is that he did not call upon the Security Council (or the General Assembly) to take measures earlier. However, once the attack started, the only viable option was indeed self-defence. If the war had taken longer than a few days, however, the Security Council should have pronounced itself on the issue.

4. Preventive or pre-emptive self-defence?

Another critique addressed to the President is that he had waited too long and not done anything before. This raises the difficult question of preventive or pre-emptive self-defence. Preventive self-defence usually means that an attack on the 'enemy' is launched with no imminent or known threat present. Pre-emptive self-defence, on the other hand, is normally understood to take place in a situation where there is an immediate threat, although nothing (no armed aggression) has happened yet.

It is widely debated whether a right for preventive self-defence exists. Normally, such a pure right in the case of mere suspicions or allegations is denied, since it would open the door to abuses of the right of self-defence in cases where there are only suspicions concerning the activities of States. In these situations the use of force would potentially become more frequent since States could claim the right to self-defence to justify all their (dubious) actions.

Pre-emptive self-defence (in a rather strict form) seems, however, to be overall better accepted, although there is no unanimity on this topic either. In particular, there are discussions on how 'imminent' the threat has to be in order to justify an action in self-defence. Nevertheless, it is, for example, well accepted that a State seeing the missiles coming does not have to wait until they hit its territory before it can take counter-measures and use force against the State that launched the missiles in the first place.

However, although the situation was tense between Endo and Preg, we cannot assimilate it to the situation of pre-emptive self-defence described above since for a long time nothing was happening. Suspicions, even justified ones, are not necessarily enough to resort to self-defence, which in this case would have been preventive self-defence due to the lack of a clear imminent attack. There is a very fine line between self-defence used in a preventive manner and aggression. Therefore, it was probably wise of the President not to take action against Preg before the attack.

[*While it seems clear that preventive self-defence cannot be justified, it might be possible to argue for the applicability of pre-emptive self-defence. You would have to show that the threats posed by Preg were indeed 'imminent' and clear, so that a pre-emptive action could have been justified. This needs to be well argued since it somewhat softens the prohibition on the use of force. Under this scenario the President of Endo would indeed have had the (legal) possibility to justify earlier action. However, it should be noted that this is a right of the State, not an obligation. Thus, it cannot be said that by not taking action earlier the President of Endo violated any existing obligation.*]

5. Conclusion

As seen above, all the criteria for the exercise of self-defence are fulfilled. Therefore, the President of Endo has acted in conformity with international law when he ordered the attack on the forces of Preg. Furthermore, the President did not have any other legal means to take prior actions, since preventive self-defence is not well accepted and heavily disputed, while pre-emptive self-defence is only admissible under strict circumstances that seem not to be present here. Furthermore, Preg had refused invitations to negotiate, barring the road to a peaceful solution.

Suggested Solution—Case 6.4

Abbreviations used
ICJ = International Court of Justice
UN = United Nations

1. Applicable law

In order to reply to the question asked by the Minister of Foreign Affairs of Bouland, we will apply the UN Charter as well as customary international law in the matter of use of force and self-defence. In fact, the rules on the use of force and self-defence contained in the UN Charter do not necessarily constitute customary international law in the matter of self-defence as will be seen later. Therefore, customary international law, which is by definition binding on all States, seems to be more important in our case.

The question to be solved asks whether the reaction of Tareland, and especially its attack on the region of Areagold, can be seen as legitimate self-defence.

2. Self-defence—an exception to the prohibition to use force

It is true that the non-use of force provision found in Article 2 paragraph 4 of the UN Charter is one of the most fundamental provisions. It prohibits any State from using or threatening to use force against the territorial integrity or political independence of any other country. This prohibition to use force undoubtedly is also customary law, as has been confirmed by the ICJ, for example in the *Nicaragua* case (ICJ, Judgment on the Merits, *Military and Paramilitary Activities in and against Nicaragua* (Nicaragua v United States of America), 1986, paragraphs 187–192).

However, it is equally well accepted that there are exceptions to this prohibition to use force. The UN Charter itself contains two such exceptions: one exception is the power of the UN Security Council to authorise the use of force under Article 42 of the UN Charter, and the other exception is the 'inherent right of self-defence' found in Article 51 of the UN Charter. Customary international law, on the other hand, only knows the inherent right of self-defence as an exception to the prohibition to use force.

3. The conditions of self-defence

Article 51 of the UN Charter authorises self-defence of individual States or also groups of States if there was an *armed attack* against this State. Self-defence is only authorised as long as the Security Council has not taken 'measures necessary to maintain international peace and security' and the State (or the States) resorting to self-defence have to inform the Security Council immediately of the steps taken.

However, in our case it has to be kept in mind that Tareland is not a member of the UN and is thus not bound by the conditions set in the UN Charter. For example, a non-UN member could not be obliged to inform the Security Council of the UN about the measures taken in self-defence. Therefore, the more important conditions, to clarify what the 'right of self-defence' really entails, are to be found in international customary law.

In fact, there are two important conditions for the exercise of self-defence found in customary international law. Both conditions arose out of the *Caroline* incident, between the UK and the USA.

(a) The first condition is 'necessity'. This means that the use of force taken in self-defence was necessary and there was no other peaceful way (eg negotiations) to stop the attack of the other State. There is therefore a certain element of 'imminence' inherent in that first condition.
(b) The second condition is 'proportionality'. This refers to the requirement that measures taken in response to the attack cannot be disproportionate. Usually proportionality is seen as referring to the proportionality of the means employed by the two parties, even though this is not completely clear and is sometimes debated.

Another important element, inherent in the expression 'self-defence' and connected to the condition of proportionality, has to be mentioned here. Self-defence can only be used to push an aggressor back, or in other words, to defend one's territory. Going beyond this and using the opportunity to invade and especially occupy in turn the other country would go beyond self-defence but instead turn from a defence to an attack. Thus, it can be said that such a reaction would no longer be proportionate.

Let us consider whether the conditions explained above are applicable to the reaction of Tareland.

It is clear that under customary law, as is the case under Article 51 UN Charter, self-defence is only allowed in case of an armed attack. Yet, Warnland has indeed first attacked Tareland, which was thus prima facie entitled to resort to the use of force in self-defence.

Nevertheless, this use of force has to satisfy the conditions of necessity and proportionality.

Necessity

When Tareland reacted, the attack by Warnland had already taken place. There is therefore certainly an element of 'imminence' present, which required Tareland to take immediate action. It was therefore not necessary that Tareland first tried to solve the problem with peaceful solutions such as negotiations, since this would have meant standing by and watching as Warnland realised its goal of taking the capital and overthrowing the government in power in Tareland. Thus, it seems that there was indeed an element of necessity present at the beginning. Nevertheless, it is questionable whether it was actually 'necessary' to invade the region of Areagold in the exercise of self-defence. Nothing indicates that this was in any way essential or needed for Tareland.

Proportionality

The element of proportionality also seems to be partly problematic. At first, Tareland was bombarding the backlines of the advancing army of Warnland in order to cut off supplies. This can still be seen as being a proportionate means to the attack by Warnland.

However, when the troops of Tareland were winning, this State decided to mount a blitz operation after which it controlled the region of Areagold, which it had wanted to control for a long time. It is true that Warnland had wanted to take the capital of Tareland and overthrow its government and is therefore clearly responsible for an aggression. Yet, as explained above, invading and controlling whole regions normally goes beyond self-defence. Thus, since only self-defence and nothing more is allowed, even when facing such an aggression as posed by Warnland, it is not possible to go significantly beyond ones own borders and especially not to control whole regions in the other State. In addition, it is not clear that the control of the region Areagold gives Tareland any military advantage, for example in preventing any further attacks by Warnland. Thus, while proportionality was satisfied in the beginning, Tareland's invasion into the region of Areagold clearly went beyond what is permitted under customary law and the condition of proportionality.

In our case, it is not necessary to assess the other conditions contained in Article 51 of the UN Charter, such as notification to the Security Council, since Tareland is not a member of the UN. Thus, it has also no obligation to inform the Security Council about any measures taken.

4. Conclusion

As seen above, at the beginning, the actions of Tareland in reaction to the attack of Warnland satisfied the important requirements for the exercise of self-defence such as necessity and proportionality. Thus, self-defence was legally justified. However, by taking and finally controlling the region of Areagold in Warnland, Tareland has gone beyond what is allowed under self-defence, especially under the principles of proportionality and necessity. This action therefore constitutes an attack upon another State, which is clearly prohibited by international law and is illegal.

Suggested Solution—Case 6.5

Abbreviations used

GA = General Assembly
MFS = Movement for a Free Spartland
UN = United Nations
SRA = ILC Articles on Responsibility of States for Internationally Wrongful Acts 2001 (State Responsibility Articles)

1. Applicable law

We will use the UN Charter, to which both States are parties, as well as customary international law in the matter of use of force and self-defence.

2. Use of force and self-defence

The question we are asked to clarify is whether Spartland is allowed to bombard and launch missiles against the territory of Vikiland (ie in short to use force against this State). This question has to be answered in light of the attack of the MFS and the preparation of the army of Vikiland at the border.

In general, it is true that the non-use of force provision found in Article 2 paragraph 4 of the UN Charter is one of the most fundamental provisions. According to the ICJ in the *Nicaragua* case, this prohibition is an absolute rule (ICJ, Judgment on the Merits, *Military and Paramilitary Activities in and against Nicaragua* (Nicaragua v United States of America), 1986, paragraph 190).

At the same time, the UN Charter itself recognises two important exceptions to this prohibition. One is the power of the UN Security Council to authorise the use of force under Article 42 of the UN Charter, and the other is the 'inherent right of self-defence' found in Article 51 of the UN Charter.

3. The conditions of self-defence

Article 51 of the UN Charter authorises self-defence of individual States or also groups of States if there was an *armed attack* against this State. Self-defence is only authorised as long as the Security Council has not taken 'measures necessary to maintain international peace and security'. In addition, the State (or States) resorting to self-defence has to inform the Security Council immediately of the steps taken.

In order to judge what the 'inherent right of self-defence' really is, it is necessary to have recourse to international customary law in the matter, since this is not specified in the UN Charter. There, we can find that there are two important conditions for the exercise of self-defence. Both conditions arose out of the *Caroline* incident, between the UK and the USA.

(a) The first condition is 'necessity'. This means that the use of force taken in self-defence was necessary and there was no other peaceful way (eg negotiations) to stop the attack of the other State. There is therefore a certain element of 'imminence' inherent in that first condition.

(b) The second condition is 'proportionality'. This refers to the requirement that measures taken in response to the attack cannot be disproportionate. Usually, proportionality is taken to refer to proportionality of the means employed by the parties (eg the use of a nuclear bomb in response to the simple bombing and sinking of a warship would clearly not be proportionate), even though there are sometimes also arguments saying that means have to be proportionate to the threat or the possibility of further attacks.

Let us now look whether all the conditions named above, from Article 51 of the UN Charter as well as the customary clarifications, are fulfilled in our case.

Armed attack

According to Article 51 UN Charter, by which both States are bound, self-defence can only be used against an armed attack.

There has clearly been an armed attack by the MFS on the military installations of Spartland in the region of Diamsberg. However, even though the armed attack of rebels as such of course allows the attacked State to fight the rebels, it does not give it the right to directly attack another State. Such an attack could only be justified when the attack came in one way or another from this State. In other words, it has to be ascertained whether the attack by the rebels can in one way or another be attributed to Vikiland in order to justify an armed reaction against the territory of Vikiland.

It is in this case helpful to look at the UN GA resolution 3314. It is true that in general UN GA resolutions are not legally binding since the GA only has the power to make recommendations (Articles 10–14 UN Charter). However, it is recognised that resolution 3314 reflects customary international law and is therefore legally binding.

Article 3(g) of this resolution 3314 indicates that the 'sending by or on behalf of a State of armed bands, groups, irregular or mercenaries, which carry out acts of armed force against another State' which amount to attacks or invasions of the territory of this State, shall be seen as acts of aggression. In our case, Vikiland did not want to attack the military installations of Spartland in Diamsberg on its own, but instead made a deal with the rebels of the MFS. The MFS was to attack these installations in exchange for financing and arming by Vikiland. The MFS was also instructed and specifically trained for this task. It seems therefore clear that Vikiland actually sent the MFS to perpetrate these attacks. Without this request (and the support) of Vikiland, the MFS would probably not have attacked specifically these military installations in Diamsberg. The MFS was thus sent by Vikiland to perpetrate the attack (acts of armed force) against Spartland. This consequently amounts to an act of aggression.

It is clear that this act of aggression is a violation of international law (customary law and Article 2 paragraph 4 UN Charter) in force for Vikiland (Articles 12 and 13 SRA). In order, however, to determine the responsibility of Vikiland in accordance with the customary SRA, we have in addition to the violation also to find attribution (Article 2 SRA).

Looking at the Articles dealing with attribution, the only possibility seems to be Article 8 SRA. For this Article to be applicable it is, however, necessary to show that Vikiland had effective control over the MFS (effective control test established by the ICJ in the *Nicaragua* case (ICJ, Judgment on the Merits, *Military and Paramilitary Activities in and against Nicaragua* (Nicaragua v United States of America), 1986, paragraphs 105–116) and confirmed in the *Genocide* case (ICJ, Judgment, *Application of the Convention on the Prevention and Punishment of the Crime of Genocide* (Bosnia and Herzegovina v Serbia and Montenegro), 2007, paragraphs 396–407)) and not just overall control (overall control test established by the ICTY in the *Tadić* case (ICTY, Appeals Chamber, Judgment, *Tadić*, 1999, (Case No IT-94-1-A), paragraphs 99–145))).

Under the effective control test it is necessary that the State in question not only financed or trained the rebels (which would be enough to satisfy the overall control test), but the State actually needs to control the actions of the rebels.

In our case, Vikiland finances, arms and trains the MFS. In addition, concerning the attack on the military installations in Diamsberg Vikiland gives the MFS detailed instructions and training in order to ensure that the operation goes smoothly. It can therefore be said that Vikiland directs and controls the MFS and consequently the actions of the MFS in the attack on Spartland are attributable to Vikiland.

It is therefore clear that the element of an armed attack is satisfied. Seeing that this armed attack comes from Vikiland, it would also be justified to use self-defence against this State.

Necessity

In addition, it is important that there is a certain element of 'imminence' which justifies the use of force in self-defence. Very clearly, the attacks by the MFS satisfy this element, since they are already occurring. In addition, however, seeing that Vikiland is pulling together its troops at the border, we can also argue that the element of necessity is satisfied there.

It is true that there is a quite sensitive discussion concerning the right of preventive or preemptive self-defence. It is equally true that this right has to be strictly construed so as not to give States the chance to resort to so-called 'self-defence' on the mere suspicion of armed activities of another State. But on the other hand where there is a clear threat it does not make sense for a State to wait in the exercise of self-defence until the enemy has launched its troops. In our case, Vikiland is known to have aspirations to control Diamsberg. It is equally known that it is Vikiland that is the responsible actor behind the attack of the MFS on the military installations in that region. Now this State is concentrating its troops at the border of Spartland, which makes the assumption of a planned attack reasonable. Therefore, the use of force in self-defence against Vikiland would not violate the element of necessity needed for self-defence, since in addition to the attacks of the MFS, the threat posed by the army of Vikiland can equally be seen as imminent.

Proportionality

According to the majority opinion, the means employed in self-defence need to be proportionate to the means used by the enemy. The MFS attacked Spartland and the army of Vikiland stands at its border. Launching missiles and bombing the area of the High Peaks (where the base of the MSF is located) seems to be quite proportionate. Care has, however, to be taken to avoid any civilian or excessive damage in the heavy bombings announced.

Inform the UN Security Council

An additional condition found in Article 51 of the UN Charter is that the UN Security Council is immediately informed of the steps taken. Thus before starting the bombings it would be necessary for Spartland to inform the Security Council. Without this notification, the exercise of self-defence will not be in accordance with the UN Charter (by which Spartland as a member is bound). Also, it has to be kept in mind that the exercise of self-defence by Spartland is only lawful as long as the Security Council has not taken measures to maintain international peace and security.

4. Conclusion

As seen above, it seems that Spartland is entitled to exercise self-defence against

Vikiland, which is also responsible for the attack of the MFS. Yet, in order to fulfil completely all the necessary conditions of self-defence under customary international law and the UN Charter, the UN Security Council must be regularly informed about the steps taken by Spartland.

SUGGESTED SOLUTIONS
Chapter VII of the United Nations Charter

Suggested Solution—Case 6.6

Abbreviation used
UN = United Nations

1. Applicable law

In order to determine whether the measures taken by Ayent are lawful under international law, we will mainly have recourse to the UN Charter, to which both States are parties. Therefore, the UN Charter is binding on both of them.

2. The application of Article 41 by the Security Council

The Security Council resolution on which Ayent bases its measures is adopted under Chapter VII of the UN Charter, and specifically indicates measures to be taken under Article 41 of the UN Charter.

In order for the Security Council to be able to apply either Article 41 (coercive measure falling short of the use of force) or Article 42 (coercive measures involving the use of force) of the UN Charter, it has first to pass the 'entry point' of Chapter VII, namely Article 39.

To 'activate' Chapter VII, the Security Council has—in accordance with Article 39—to 'determine the existence of any threat to the peace, breach of the peace, or act of aggression'. Only once the situation is qualified as falling under one of these categories can the Security Council decide what measures under Articles 41 or 42 should be taken.

In our case, the Security Council has stated that the situation is a threat to the peace, thereby indicating that henceforth it can be considered under Chapter VII. Thus, the adoption of the Security Council resolution indicating measures to be taken under Article 41 was done in full accordance with the necessary procedure established by the UN Charter.

Concerning Article 41, it is important to note that there is no obligation on the Security Council to adopt such measures once it has found a situation to qualify for Article 39 and has made decisions/recommendations on it. The Article clearly indicates this by saying that the Security Council *may* decide. Furthermore, the list of measures provided in the second part of the Article is only indicative and not exhaustive. This is clear from the wording ('may include'), but also from the drafting history of this provision. Thus, the Security Council is free to adopt under Article 41 any other measure not involving the use of force as long as it remains within the limits of Chapter VII.

Concerning the measures taken in the concrete case, there does not seem to be any problem. They do not involve the use of force and do not go beyond Chapter VII as might be the case if measures for the peaceful settlement of disputes would be decided.

3. The measures taken by Ayent under the Security Council resolution

It is clear that the measures decided by the Security Council have to be implemented by the States.

Decisions taken by the Security Council under Chapter VII are binding on the UN Member States and they are hence obliged to implement them and to carry them out. This is made clear by Article 25 of the UN Charter, stating that members of the United Nations 'agree to accept and carry out the decisions of the Security Council'. Thus, Ayent is in fact under an obligation to adopt measures to implement the Security Council resolution.

Furthermore, it is very important to stress that according to Article 103 of the UN Charter, obligations under the UN Charter take primacy over obligations States might have under other international instruments. That means that in case of conflict between a treaty and an obligation under the UN Charter (including resolutions by the Security Council), the latter will prevail over the former.

According to the Security Council resolution in our case there are three measures to be taken: (a) to stop exports of certain goods listed in Annex I to interrupt economic relations; (b) to interrupt postal relations; (c) to impose a travel ban on certain persons.

We will now look at the measures taken by Ayent to fulfil the Security Council resolution.

(a) Stop the export of certain goods

Ayent has stopped its exports of replacement parts for oil pumps which are apparently used in Haida. According to Annex I, goods for the extraction of oil fall under the economic embargo imposed by the Security Council. Since oil pumps are used for oil extraction, replacement parts of these oil pumps are also covered by the embargo (since they are an important condition for keeping the pumps running).

(b) Interruption of postal relations

In the time of internet and smart phones this measure does not seem to make a lot of sense, even though it has been used in the past (eg in the embargo imposed on Southern Rhodesia). However, we do not have to question the sensibility of measures adopted by the Security Council here, but we are merely concerned with the question whether Ayent has validly acted under international law.

Similar to the argument above, the Security Council resolution obliges Ayent to take necessary measure to interrupt postal relations. By no longer delivering stamps, Ayent, the main stamp provider for Haida, is taking measures to implement this interruption. Thus, the second measure taken by Ayent is also in conformity with the Security Council resolution and thus international law.

(c) Travel ban

The last measure decided by the Security Council is a travel ban for certain persons. There is a bilateral treaty between Ayent and Haida on the free movement of persons which has abolished all controls of persons at the common border of Haida and Ayent. However, now Ayent has reintroduced these controls and wants to check all persons coming from Haida. This effectively violates the bilateral treaty concluded in 1980. Yet, as explained above, obligations under the UN Charter prevail over any other obligation States might have under international law. Thus, obligations coming from a Security Council resolution (which is adopted in conformity with the UN Charter) will always take primacy over treaty provisions between States. Consequently, the actions of Ayent in this regard are still in conformity with international law even though it goes against the bilateral treaty.

4. Conclusion

As argued above, all the measures taken by Ayent are in full conformity with the Security Council resolution and the United Nations Charter.

Suggested Solution—Case 6.7

Abbreviations used
ICJ = International Court of Justice
UN = United Nations

1. Applicable law

The applicable law in order to decide on the legality of the actions taken by Anxieuland is the UN Charter. The UN Charter is applicable since both States involved are original members of the UN and thus bound by its Charter.

2. The prohibition to use force and two exceptions

The prohibition to use force contained in Article 2 paragraph 4 of the UN Charter is one of the most fundamental provisions in the UN Charter. The ICJ has recognised the absolute character of this prohibition, for example in the *Nicaragua* case (ICJ, Judgment on the Merits, *Military and Paramilitary Activities in and against Nicaragua* (Nicaragua v United States of America), 1986, paragraph 190).

Nevertheless, at the same time it is well accepted that the UN Charter itself contains two exceptions to the non-use of force. One is the inherent right of self-defence (Article 51 UN Charter) and the other one is the authorisation of the Security Council to use all necessary means (including the use of force) to maintain or restore international peace and security under Article 42 of the UN Charter.

In our case, self-defence is difficult to argue for Anxieuland, since it is not attacked and there seems, according to the facts, also to be no imminent threat of an attack against Anxieuland. Since preventive self-defence in case of speculation rather than a clear threat is not allowed, self-defence is not an option. Furthermore, in the absence of an evident imminent threat, pre-emptive self-defence too cannot be argued.

Therefore, we have to consider whether Anxieuland's actions can be justified under a UN Security Council resolution based on Article 42 UN Charter. It is necessary that this resolution refers to Article 42 UN Charter since the use of force is only allowed under this Article. Article 41 UN Charter, for example, clearly provides that in its application the Security Council can only decide on measures falling short of the use of armed force.

3. The application of Article 42 by the Security Council and the use of force by Anxieuland

In order for the Security Council to be able to apply Article 42 (measures involving the use of force) of the UN Charter, it has first to pass the 'entry point' of Chapter VII, namely Article 39.

To 'activate' Chapter VII, the Security Council has—in accordance with Article 39—to 'determine the existence of any threat to the peace, breach of the peace, or act of aggression'. Only once the situation is qualified as falling under one of these categories can the Security Council decide what measures under Article 42 (or Article 41 for that matter) should be taken.

In our case, the Security Council has determined in its resolution 1945 that the situation is a danger to international peace and security. However, it is important to note that this resolution 1945 does not mention Article 42 UN Charter in any way, nor does it authorise States to 'use all necessary means'.

At the time when Anxieuland intervenes militarily in Tyraland, there was thus no Security Council resolution authorising the use of force by States against Tyraland. The start of this military operation was thus illegal.

However, one day after the military intervention by Anxieuland the UN Security Council adopts resolution 1946 in which it authorises the States to adopt all necessary means to stop the cruelties occurring in Tyraland. Thus, from this day on forward it cannot be denied that Anxieuland was acting in conformity and with the 'blessing' of the UN Charter.

4. Conclusion

As argued above, the start of the military intervention by Anxieuland was illegal since at that time the UN Security Council had not yet authorised the use of force against Tyraland. However, after the adoption of UN Security Council Resolution 1946 authorizing States to use all necessary means, which includes the use of force, the action of Anxieuland has to be considered as being in conformity with international law.

Chapter 7

SUGGESTED SOLUTIONS
Interconnected Cases

Suggested Solution—Case 7.1

Abbreviations used

ECtHR = European Court of Human Rights
ELF = Enemy Listeners and Fighters
ICJ = International Court of Justice
ICTY = International Criminal Tribunal for the Former Yugoslavia
ILC = International Law Commission
PAC = Protocol Against Criminals
PCIJ = Permanent Court of International Justice
SRA = ILC Articles on Responsibility of States for Internationally Wrongful Acts 2001 (State Responsibility Articles)
UN = United Nations
VCLT = Vienna Convention on the Law of Treaties

Question 1: How does the PAC apply between the parties (in particular before 2009) and is Arda right to argue for its invalidity?

1. Applicable law

Arda and Valinor are parties to the Vienna Convention on the Law of Treaties (VCLT) since its entry into force. In accordance with Article 84 paragraph 1 VCLT, the VCLT as such entered into force on the 30th day after the deposit of the 35th instrument of ratification, ie on 27 January 1980. Therefore, the VCLT entered into force for both Arda and Valinor also on this date.

Sindar has ratified the VCLT on 30 April 1987. According to Article 84 paragraph 2 VCLT, for every State ratifying or acceding to the VCLT after the deposit of the first 35 ratifications, the VCLT will enter into force 30 days after the deposit of the State's instrument of ratification. This means that the VCLT enters into force for Sindar on 30 May 1987.

Naggaroth has ratified the VCLT on 6 June 2004. Following Article 84 paragraph 2 VCLT as explained above, the VCLT enters into force for that State on 6 July 2004.

The PAC has been concluded on 4 June 2002. Article 4 VCLT provides that the VCLT is only applicable to treaties which are concluded by States after the entry into force of the VCLT for these State parties. However, the PAC has been concluded in 2002, at a time when not all four State parties were parties to the VCLT, since Naggaroth only became a party to the VCLT in 2004. Thus, the VCLT is not applicable to the PAC as such.

However, it is well established that the VCLT reflects customary international law in matters of treaty law. This has, for example, been confirmed by the ICJ in the *Gabčíkovo-Nagymaros* case (ICJ, Judgment, *Gabčíkovo-Nagymaros Project* (Hungary/Slovakia), 1997, paragraph 46). Consequently, we will apply the customary reflection contained in the VCLT. Any reference to the VCLT should henceforth be read as a reference to its customary reflection.

2. Is the PAC a treaty?

Sindar contends that the PAC is not a treaty but 'only a Protocol' and that therefore the VCLT would not be applicable to it, nor would then its customary reflection.

Article 2 paragraph 1(a) VCLT contains a definition of what 'treaty' means for the purposes of the VCLT.

As noted above, however, the VCLT is not applicable as such in our case and the definition provided above only applies 'for the purposes of the VCLT'. Therefore, we have to apply the customary law definition of a treaty. It is similar to the VCLT definition, but broader, since in the customary definition a 'treaty' is not limited to treaties between States but can also include treaties between other entities. In addition, under customary international law, treaties are not limited to written treaties, but can also include oral treaties. In essence, a treaty under customary international law is defined as an expression of concurring wills between two or more subjects of international law, which has been concluded with the intention to produce legal effects and which is governed by international law. Its denomination does not matter (see also ICJ, Judgment on Preliminary Objections, *South West Africa* (Liberia v South Africa and Ethiopia v South Africa), 1962, 331).

In our case, the PAC is concluded between four States (which clearly are subjects of international law) in a written form. It was concluded with the idea of fighting criminals also beyond borders and through various means of collaboration and thus to produce legal effects. In addition, nothing indicates that it is governed by national law, but—as is normally the case for multilateral treaties—it is governed by international law. Consequently, the PAC falls easily within the larger customary law definition. Hence, the fact that it is called 'protocol' instead of 'treaty' does not change its nature as a legally binding treaty to which the customary international law in the matters of treaties is applicable.

3. Interpretative declarations or reservations?

Clarification of terms

At the moment of signing the PAC (which is at the same time also ratification, since the treaty is concluded in simplified form, see Article 12 paragraph 1(a) VCLT) Sindar presents two 'interpretative declarations'. One has always to be careful concerning interpretative declarations, since they are often hidden reservations to treaties.

Article 2 paragraph 1(d) VCLT used as a customary reflection defines a reservation: this is a unilateral statement made at the time when a State expresses its consent to be bound by the treaty (signature, ratification, accession, etc), whereby this State purports to exclude or modify the legal effects of a certain provision of the treaty in its application to that State.

When reading the two interpretative declarations made by Sindar it is clear that this State indeed wants to 'modify or exclude the legal effect' of some provisions. It does not simply want to give an interpretation of a specific term or expression. Therefore, these two statements need to be considered as reservations and consequently analysed as such in order to determine how the treaty applies between the parties (especially also before 2009 when the issue of validity of the PAC arose).

Validity (Article 19 VCLT)

A State can only make reservations according to Article 19 VCLT used as a customary reflection when the treaty does not prohibit this reservation or the reservation is not incompatible with the object and purpose of the treaty.

The PAC in its Article 67 prohibits reservations to Article 56 PAC, to which Sindar has, however, made a reservation. According to Article 19(a), reservations that are prohibited by the treaty cannot be made. Consequently, this first reservation by Sindar is invalid.

It is not entirely clear what happens to the consent to be bound accompanied by a reservation which is declared to be invalid. One position is to say that the State only consented to be bound because it had the possibility to attach a reservation. If the reservation is declared invalid, the consent to be bound needs therefore to be seen as no longer existing. However, others argue that the consent to be bound was more important for the State than the reservation as such since otherwise it would not have consented in the first place, and thus this consent remains valid also without reservation. The latter is the approach taken by the European Court of Human Rights in the *Belilos v Switzerland* case (ECtHR, *Belilos v Switzerland*, Judgment, Application No 10328/83, 29 April 1988, paragraphs 38–60). [*After setting out the two theoretical possibilities, you should now argue your position for or against one of them to go on with the case. Both positions are equally valid and it depends on your own convictions and the arguments you make which one you privilege.*]

In the interest of sound treaty relations, and keeping in mind that in our case it can be argued that Sindar knew—or should have known—from the beginning that reservations to Article 56 PAC were prohibited, it seems justified to privilege the second position. In nevertheless signing the treaty with such a reservation, Sindar indicated that signature was indeed more important than the reservation, since it should have expected from the beginning that this particular reservation might be declared invalid. Consequently, Sindar's consent to be bound remains valid.

[*If you privileged the first option, then Sindar's consent to be bound becomes invalid at the time its reservation is declared invalid. Thus, this means that Sindar is not a party to the PAC, since there is no consent to be bound. This would relieve you from considering the effects of the second reservation to Article 31 PAC since in any event in relation to the PAC there are no longer any treaty relations between Sindar and any of the other States.*]

Sindar's other reservation to Article 31 PAC is not prohibited by the PAC itself and thus does not fall under Article 19(a) (nor under Article 19(b), since the PAC does not specifically authorise any reservation). It has, however, to be assessed whether the reservation to Article 31 is compatible with the object and purpose of the PAC, as required in Article 19(c). The object and purpose of the PAC is to fight criminals. However, the reservation only excludes the meetings between the heads of the police forces of the four countries every three months. It does not exclude the passing on of information or any other collaboration. It would go too far to declare that rejecting some meetings would go against the purpose of fighting criminals. Therefore, we can declare that the reservation made by Sindar is admissible.

Opposability (Article 20 VCLT)

Since the reservation to Article 56 PAC has been declared invalid, we only need to assess the opposability and consequences of the reservation made to Article 31 PAC.

Arda and Naggaroth remain silent concerning the reservation made by Sindar. According to Article 20 paragraph 5 VCLT, silence of a State concerning a reservation is to be considered as acceptance if this State has not objected to the reservation by the end of a period of 12 months after the notification of the reservation. It is true that deadlines and time spans are not necessarily customary law but what is required is rather a 'reasonable delay'. However, a time period of around 12 months seems to give the silent State enough time to object if it wishes to and on the other hand it does not seem to be an excessively long period of uncertainty. It is therefore suggested to accept the time period of 12 months as applicable also in our case. Thus, since Arda and Naggaroth do not seem to object, we can consider that they have accepted the reservation made by Sindar 12 months after the notification has been made, ie on 4 June 2003.

Valinor has, on the other hand, objected to Sindar's reservation. Article 20 paragraph 4(b) VCLT provides that an objection to a reservation does not preclude the entry into force of the treaty between the reserving and the objecting State, unless the objecting State has expressly stated its intention of not becoming a party to the treaty in relation to the reserving State. In our case, Valinor has objected to the reservation since it considers the meetings as an important element of the treaty, but it has nowhere expressed that it did not want to enter into a treaty relation with Sindar, the reserving State. Therefore, Valinor is a so-called simple objector and there will be a treaty relation between Valinor and Sindar, as we will see.

It is necessary to take a short look also at Article 20 paragraph 4(c) VCLT, which provides that a reserving State is considered to be a party to the treaty in question (its consent to be bound by the treaty is effective) as soon as at least one other State has accepted its reservation. This solution—one acceptance by another State is enough to make the reserving State a party to the treaty—has been adopted by the ICJ in its Advisory Opinion on the *Reservations to the Genocide Convention* (ICJ, Advisory Opinion, *Reservations to the Convention on the Prevention and Punishment of the Crime of Genocide*, 1951, 21–26). This means in our case that Sindar can be seen as a party to the PAC due to the tacit acceptance by Arda and Naggaroth, which is, however, only clear beyond all doubt after the period of 12 months has passed.

Consequences (Article 21 VCLT)

The consequences of reservations are regulated in Article 21 VCLT, used here as customary reflection.

Between Sindar and the two accepting States, Arda and Naggaroth, the relationship will be regulated by Article 21 paragraph 1(a) and (b) VCLT. The Article provides that the treaty is modified to the extent of the reservation between the reserving and the accepting States. In our concrete case this means that the meetings foreseen in Article 31 PAC will not be held between Sindar and Arda, and Sindar and Naggaroth.

The relation between Sindar and the objecting State Valinor is regulated by Article 21 paragraph 3 VCLT. It provides that between the reserving State and the simple objector, the treaty applies without the provision on which the reservation was made. This is logical, since obviously there is no agreement between the two States on this specific point. Therefore, the PAC applies between Sindar and Valinor without Article 31.

Between the non-reserving States *inter se* (Arda, Naggaroth and Valinor), the PAC applies according to Article 21 paragraph 2 VCLT unchanged, ie with Article 31 PAC.

4. Invalidity of the PAC

Arda claims that the PAC is invalid as soon as it becomes known that the ambassador of Arda signed the PAC after having received a fake fax.

First of all, it is relevant to point out that a treaty can only be found to be invalid in accordance with the VCLT (or its customary reflection) or with its own provisions. All the grounds for invalidity, as well as for termination and suspension, are listed in the VCLT in an exhaustive manner, as is provided in Article 42 VCLT.

After having looked at all the grounds of invalidity, the most likely ground in our case seems to be fraud, according to Article 49 VCLT (used as a customary reflection). Fraud as a ground for invalidity of a treaty is the situation when a State has been induced to conclude a treaty by the fraudulent conduct of another negotiating State. This is a case of voidability of a treaty (relative invalidity), meaning that only the 'victim' State can invoke this ground for invalidating the treaty.

In our case, the ambassador of Arda only signed the treaty because he received a fax, which seemed to come from the bureau of the President of Arda, that told him that it was OK to sign now. According to the facts, the fax presented the necessary official signs, though these were reduced in clarity due to the bad quality of the print-out. Nevertheless, there was no reason to doubt their authenticity. However, as the facts further show the fax did not come from Arda but from Sindar instead, which through this act induced Arda to sign the PAC. Sindar's behaviour by sending a fake fax to Arda in order to make them sign can clearly be qualified as fraud.

In addition, Arda clearly is the 'victim', since without this fax they might not have signed the PAC at that moment.

Therefore, based on Article 49 VCLT, Arda can indeed invoke fraud to invalidate the treaty.

However, before concluding on its invalidity, we need to check whether the PAC can nevertheless be 'saved'.

Article 45 VCLT (acquiescence) provides that a State loses its right to invoke a ground of invalidity of a treaty if it has either expressly or by its conduct agreed to continue to apply the treaty as it is. The time span which has to be considered to judge a State's behaviour in this regard starts at the moment when the facts leading to invalidity become known, and not at the time when the action leading to invalidity (ie the fraud) was committed.

In our case, as soon as Arda becomes aware of the fraud by Sindar it protests and wants to invalidate the treaty. Hence, it clearly did not acquiesce.

Article 44 VCLT sets out under which circumstances a treaty can be separated, ie the clause on which the invalidity relies can be taken out and the rest of the treaty remains valid. Article 44 paragraph 4 VCLT provides that in the case of fraud, the victim State can chose whether it wants to invalidate the whole treaty or—if the conditions under paragraph 3 are fulfilled—to separate the affected clause.

In our case, Arda clearly wants to invalidate the whole treaty, which is their right under paragraph 4. However, even if it would be otherwise, the cumulative conditions in Article 44 paragraph 3 VCLT would not be fulfilled, since the fraud concerns the whole treaty and not just simply a specific clause which can then be separated.

Thus, Arda can indeed invoke the invalidity of the PAC based on fraud by Sindar. Seeing nothing contrary in the facts, we can assume that the procedural aspects do not pose any problem in this case. (Besides, the procedural provisions are the only parts of the VCLT which are not customary.)

The consequences of invalidity of a treaty can be found in Article 69 VCLT. The treaty is to be considered void ab initio, ie it is deemed to have never produced any legal effects. According to paragraph 2, acts which have already been performed under the treaty in good faith remain, however, valid (b), but if possible, any State can ask the other parties to re-establish the situation that would have existed if the treaty had never been concluded (a). Yet, paragraph 3 clarifies that the party responsible for fraud—in our case Sindar—cannot benefit from paragraph 2, meaning it is not entitled to a re-establishment of the previous situation and its previous acts are no longer valid (they are by necessity not in good faith since it knew that the treaty had been concluded under fraud).

Article 69 paragraph 4 then specifies the situation for multilateral treaties, meaning that the PAC will be invalid between Arda and all the other States, but not between the other three States *inter se*.

5. Conclusion

Sindar made two reservations of which one was declared to be inadmissible. The second reservation, however, changes the treaty relations between the reserving and the accepting States and the reserving and simple objecting State accordingly, as shown above.

In addition, we have established that Arda is correct in invoking fraud as a ground for invalidating the PAC and after the necessary analysis we can conclude that the PAC is invalid between Arda and Sindar.

Question 2: Has Sindar engaged its international responsibility by kidnapping Mr Malekith?

1. Applicable law

We will mainly apply the ILC Articles on Responsibility of States for Internationally Wrongful Acts from 2001 (SRA). These Articles are not a treaty, but it is widely accepted that they reflect customary international law in matters of State responsibility. This has also been confirmed by the ICJ in several cases, for example the *Gabčíkovo-Nagymaros* case (ICJ, Judgment, *Gabčíkovo-Nagymaros Project* (Hungary/Slovakia), 1997, paragraph 47), the *Iran Hostages* case (ICJ, Judgment, *United States Diplomatic and Consular Staff in Teheran* (United States of America v Iran), 1980, paragraphs 56–92) and most recently in the *Genocide* case from 2007 (ICJ, Judgment, *Application of the Convention on the Prevention and Punishment of the Crime of Genocide* (Bosnia and Herzegovina v Serbia and Montenegro), 2007, paragraph 401).

In addition, we will also apply the UN Charter, to which both States involved are parties.

Article 1 SRA provides that every internationally wrongful act of a State leads to the international responsibility of the State. Article 2 SRA then sets out the two necessary elements in order to find an internationally wrongful act: first, the act needs to be attributable to the State in question; and second, the act needs to constitute a breach of an international obligation of that State.

2. Attribution

Attribution is regulated in Articles 4–11 SRA.

The act in question is the kidnapping of Mr Malekith from Arda by the ELF.

The ELF, even though its members are spies, is clearly not part of the official secret service of Sindar. Nor is there truly 'complete dependence' as established by the ICJ in the *Nicaragua* case (ICJ, Judgment on the Merits, *Military and Paramilitary Activities in and against Nicaragua* (Nicaragua v United States of America), 1986, paragraphs 109–112) and the *Genocide* case (ICJ, Judgment, *Application of the Convention on the Prevention and Punishment of the Crime of Genocide* (Bosnia and Herzegovina v Serbia and Montenegro), 2007, paragraphs 390–395) to find that the ELF qualifies as organs of Sindar.

However, Article 8 SRA seems to be appropriate. Article 8 SRA provides that the conduct of a person or a group shall be attributable to the State if this person or group in carrying out that conduct acts on the instructions of or under the direction or control of that State.

To clarify the extent of direction or control, the ICJ established in its *Nicaragua* case (ICJ, Judgment on the Merits, *Military and Paramilitary Activities in and against Nicaragua* (Nicaragua v United States of America), 1986, paragraphs 105–116) the so-called 'effective control' test. This test sets out that it is not enough to finance or train certain persons or groups, but that the State needs to control and order their actions. A few years later, the ICTY in the *Tadić* case (ICTY, Appeals Chamber, Judgment, *Tadić*, 1999 (Case No IT-94-1-A), paragraphs 99–145) declared that the appropriate test would be the 'overall control' test, whereby training and financing would be sufficient to find attribution to the State. In the *Genocide* case (ICJ, Judgment, *Application of the Convention on the Prevention and Punishment of the Crime of Genocide* (Bosnia and Herzegovina v Serbia and Montenegro), 2007, paragraphs 396–407), the ICJ rejected the 'overall control' test and held that for the purpose of State responsibility the appropriate test was the 'effective control' test.

In our case, Sindar has created the ELF itself. The ELF is trained and also equipped by the secret service of Sindar. This would not be enough to satisfy the 'effective control' test, but it is in fact the President of Sindar himself who gives the order to the ELF to kidnap Mr Malekith 'no matter' what. Therefore, the ELF in this case only acts on the instruction of the President of Sindar, thereby fulfilling the 'effective control' test.

Consequently, the act of kidnapping Mr Malekith—as well as the accidental wounding of the border guards in the execution of the order—is attributable to Sindar.

3. Violation

Article 12 SRA provides that a breach of an international obligation exists when a State does not act in conformity with what is required from it by that obligation. Thereby, it does not matter whether the origin of the obligation is a treaty or customary international law.

Article 13 SRA then establishes that the obligation in question needs to be in force for the State in order to constitute a breach.

In our case, the ELF penetrated from Sindar into Arda, kidnapped Mr Malekith and wounded some border guards on its way back. It is well established that a State has exclusive jurisdiction on its territory. Therefore, States are not allowed to penetrate into other States' territories and to kidnap people. This constitutes a violation of the sovereignty of a State, which is guaranteed in Article 2 paragraph 1 of the UN Charter (see also the case of the abduction of Eichmann from Argentina by members of the Israeli secret service).

We can hence conclude that there is indeed a violation of an international obligation incumbent on Sindar, namely of Article 2 paragraph 1 UN Charter. This obligation is in force for Sindar since—in addition to being a customary rule—Sindar is a UN member and thus bound by the UN Charter.

4. Circumstances precluding wrongfulness

After having studied all the circumstances precluding wrongfulness contained in the SRA we have to conclude that none of them is applicable.

Consequently, Sindar is indeed responsible for an internationally wrongful act.

5. Consequences

First of all, Sindar should—in accordance with Article 30(b) SRA—give appropriate assurances to Arda that such violations will not be repeated and that the territorial sovereignty of Arda will henceforth be respected.

In addition, there is in customary international law a well-established duty to make reparations. This duty has been confirmed by the Permanent Court of International Justice in the *Chorzów Factory* case (PCIJ, Judgment, *Case concerning the Factory at Chorzów (Claim for Indemnity)*, 1927, 21) and has been incorporated in Article 31 SRA.

There are several forms of making reparations (Article 34 SRA). In our case, the most appropriate one seems first to be restitution (Article 35), meaning simply 'giving back' (restituting) Mr Malekith to Arda. In addition, compensation (Article 36) could also be relevant, for example for the injuries inflicted upon the border guards. Lastly, also satisfaction (Article 37) could be envisaged, notably by official apologies from Sindar.

However, what the exact form of reparation will be has to be negotiated by the two States in question or decided by a competent tribunal.

6. Conclusion

Sindar has indeed engaged its international responsibility by kidnapping Mr Malekith. The act is attributable to Sindar and constitutes a violation of its international obligations, as shown above.

As a consequence, Sindar has to make reparations, ideally in the form of restitution, but also compensation and satisfaction might be appropriate additional means of reparation.

Question 3: Is the International Court of Justice competent to deal with the dispute(s); and if yes, on which basis?

1. Applicable law

We will mostly apply the ICJ Statute and the UN Charter. According to Article 92 UN Charter, the ICJ Statute is an integral part of the UN Charter.

The UN Charter is applicable since all States in question are members of the UN and thus parties to its Charter.

In order to ascertain whether or not the ICJ has jurisdiction to hear the present case, three elements need to be fulfilled, namely personal jurisdiction, subject matter jurisdiction and consensual jurisdiction.

2. Personal jurisdiction (jurisdiction *ratione personae*)

The ICJ verifies ex officio whether parties to the disputes fulfil the criteria of personal jurisdiction.

According to Article 34 paragraph 1 of the ICJ Statute, only States can be parties to disputes in front of the ICJ. This is not a problem here since both Arda and Sindar are undoubtedly States. This can also be seen from the fact that they are members of the UN, which is only open to States (Article 4 paragraph 1 UN Charter).

In addition, Article 35 paragraph 1 ICJ Statute declares that the ICJ is only open to States which are parties to its Statute. Yet, Article 93 paragraph 1 of the UN Charter provides that all UN members are, ipso facto, parties to the ICJ Statute. Thus, since in our case both Arda and Sindar are members of the UN they are automatically also parties to the ICJ Statute and fulfil the requirement in Article 35 paragraph 1.

In conclusion, we can say that the ICJ has personal jurisdiction in this case.

3. Subject matter jurisdiction (jurisdiction *ratione materiae*)

This too is an issue which the ICJ checks ex officio.

The ICJ is only competent to hear legal disputes under international law, as can for example be inferred from Article 38 ICJ Statute.

The most famous definition of a 'dispute' has been provided by the Permanent Court of International Justice (PCIJ) in the *Mavrommatis Palestine Concessions* case (PCIJ, Judgment on the Objection to the Jurisdiction of the Court, *The Mavrommatis Palestine Concessions*, 1924, 11). There, the PCIJ said that a dispute was a disagreement on a point of law or fact between two persons. In addition, it is relevant to point out that the existence of a dispute is an objective determination made by the Court. It does not matter what the parties say in this regards. This has been explained by the ICJ, for example in the *Lockerbie* case (ICJ, Judgment on Preliminary Objections, *Questions of Interpretation and Application of the 1971 Montreal Convention arising from the Aerial Incident at Lockerbie* (Libyan Arab Jamahiriya v United States of America), 1998, paragraph 21) and the Advisory Opinion on the *Interpretation of Peace Treaties* (ICJ, Advisory Opinion, First Phase, *Interpretation of Peace Treaties with Bulgaria, Hungary and Romania*, 1950, 74).

In our case, Sindar and Arda indeed disagree on several points of law, namely on the invalidity or not of the PAC and on whether Sindar is internationally responsible for the kidnapping of Mr Malekith. Treaty law issues and State responsibility issues are legal by nature. In addition, they are also legal disputes under international law, since they are regulated by international rather than by national law.

Thus, there exists a legal dispute under international law between Arda and Sindar and consequently the ICJ also has jurisdiction *ratione materiae*.

4. Consensual jurisdiction (jurisdiction *ratione consensus*)

Having established the two previous points is not enough, however, to make the ICJ competent to deal with a case: consensus to the ICJ's jurisdiction is a crucial element, which has also been confirmed by the ICJ itself, for example in the *East Timor* case (ICJ, Judgment, *Case concerning East Timor* (Portugal v Australia), 1995, paragraph 26).

Consensus is, however, not ascertained ex officio by the ICJ, but the issue has to be raised by the parties. Since Sindar contests the jurisdiction of the Court, it is necessary that the ICJ examines also this point.

There are four different ways of consenting to the ICJ's jurisdiction. Only two of them are relevant here.

Optional clause declaration

Optional clause declarations are unilateral statements based on Article 36 paragraph 2 ICJ Statute, with which a State consents to the ICJ's compulsory jurisdiction ipso facto and without special agreement in relation to any other State that has made the same declaration. Thus, the optional clause system is based on reciprocity and thus needs the same basis from two States.

In our case, Arda has made an optional clause declaration without any reservation. Sindar has also made an optional clause declaration to which it attached, however, a reservation. Generally, reservations to optional clause declarations are allowed under Article 36 paragraph 3 ICJ Statute. Nevertheless, we have to test whether the reservation is compatible with the object and purpose of the ICJ Statute (Article 19(c) VCLT). Sindar's reservation excludes from the ICJ's jurisdiction cases of multilateral treaties when not all parties are present before the Court. While this is certainly a serious limitation on the ICJ's jurisdiction, it is not clear whether it is really incompatible with the object and purpose of the ICJ. It does not necessarily hinder the ICJ to pronounce itself on a case, especially because it can still decide on its own competence (Article 36 paragraph 6 ICJ Statute). In addition, keeping in mind that the ICJ has in the past been rather generous when assessing a reservation's compatibility with its Statute and that the USA had a similar reservation, we should conclude that the reservation is indeed compatible with the object and purpose of the ICJ Statute.

Yet, since the reservation is valid, it limits the jurisdiction of the ICJ. This jurisdiction is always based on the 'least common denominator' of the two optional clause declarations, as has been held by the ICJ in the *Anglo Iranian Oil* case (ICJ, Judgment, *Anglo-Iranian Oil Co.* (United Kingdom v Iran), 1952, 103). Since the PAC is a multilateral treaty but only two out of its four Member States are parties to the dispute before the ICJ, the ICJ is consequently not competent to hear the dispute on the PAC based on the optional clause declarations.

However, based on the two optional clause declarations the ICJ is competent to hear the part on the State responsibility of Sindar. The SRA are not a multilateral treaty but customary law. It is true that the UN Charter, which is involved because of the alleged violation of its Article 2 paragraph 1 by Sindar, is a multilateral treaty. Yet, it has been held by the ICJ in the *Nicaragua* case (ICJ, Judgment on the Merits, *Military and Paramilitary Activities in and against Nicaragua* (Nicaragua v United States of America), 1986, paragraphs 172–179 for the UN Charter in general, paragraphs 202–209 for Article 2 paragraph 1 UN Charter specifically) that most of the UN Charter and especially also Article 2 of the Charter are customary international law and that both the Charter and the customary rules coexist and do not mutually exclude each other. Therefore, the ICJ can apply Article 2 paragraph 1 as customary law and is thus not limited by Sindar's reservation.

Compromissory clause in the PAC

The PAC contains in its Article 56 a compromissory clause, which can serve as a basis of jurisdiction for the ICJ under Article 36 paragraph 1 ICJ Statute. It is true that the PAC is invalid; however, it is widely accepted that the compromissory clause remains valid in such cases. This is logical, since the dispute is exactly on the question whether or not the PAC is invalid. Were the compromissory clause automatically to be invalid as soon as a State claims the treaty in question is invalid, then the ICJ would never be competent to hear a case about an allegedly invalid treaty. The continuing validity of compromissory clauses has been confirmed by the ICJ in the *Fisheries Jurisdiction* case (ICJ, Judgment on the Jurisdiction of the Court, *Fisheries Jurisdiction* (United Kingdom of Great Britain and Northern Ireland v Iceland), 1973, paragraphs 43–45).

Yet, the compromissory clause cannot serve as a basis of jurisdiction in our case since it provides that the ICJ is competent when two State parties bring a case *jointly* to the Court. However, the case in question has only been brought by Arda alone. Therefore, the ICJ is not competent to hear the dispute on the basis of the compromissory clause in the PAC.

5. Conclusion

In conclusion, we can say that the ICJ is not competent to hear the case involving the invalidity of the PAC due to a lack of consent. However, the ICJ is competent to hear the case on the State responsibility issue based on the optional clause declarations made by both Sindar and Arda.

Suggested Solution—Case 7.2

Abbreviations used

EEZ	= Exclusive Economic Zone
GA	= General Assembly (of the United Nations)
ICJ	= International Court of Justice
ICTY	= International Criminal Tribunal for the Former Yugoslavia
ILC	= International Law Commission
MFS	= Movement for Freedom in Silla
NCS	= National Cartography Service of Silla
PCIJ	= Permanent Court of International Justice
SRA	= ILC Articles on Responsibility of States for Internationally Wrongful Acts 2001 (State Responsibility Articles)
TEMR	= Treaty on the Exploitation of Maritime Resources
UN	= United Nations
VCLT	= Vienna Convention on the Law of Treaties

Question 1: Is the TEMR (still) in force between the parties, and especially also between Silla and Munkus? Address all the legal arguments made by the parties.

1. Applicable law

All three States are parties to the VCLT since its entry into force. Concerning the entry into force of the VCLT, Article 84 paragraph 1 VCLT provides that the VCLT enters into force 30 days after the deposit of the 35th instrument of ratification of the convention. Following this Article the VCLT entered into force on 27 January 1980, including for Munkus, Silla and Aspara.

The relevant date concerning the TEMR for the purpose of the applicability of the VCLT is its date of conclusion (and not its date of entry into force). The TEMR was concluded on 25 June 1973.

Article 4 VCLT provides that the VCLT is only applicable to treaties which have been concluded by States after the VCLT has entered into force for these State parties. However, at the time of the conclusion of the TEMR in June 1973, none of the contracting States was a party to the VCLT because the VCLT had not yet entered into force.

Consequently, the VCLT is not applicable to the TEMR. Yet, as has been established by the ICJ in cases such as the *Gabčíkovo-Nagymaros* case (ICJ, Judgment, *Gabčíkovo-Nagymaros Project* (Hungary/Slovakia), 1997, paragraph 46), most articles of the VCLT reflect customary international law in the matter of treaty law. Thus, we will apply the customary reflection contained in the VCLT. Hence, any reference to the VCLT should be read as referring to its customary reflection rather than to the convention itself.

2. Reservation made by Munkus

When depositing its instrument of ratification, Munkus circulates a so-called 'declaration'. However, we have to check whether this declaration is in fact not a hidden reservation.

Reservations are defined in Article 2 paragraph 1(d) VCLT used as customary reflection. A reservation is a unilateral statement made by a State at the time of giving its consent to be bound by the treaty in question, with which the State seeks to exclude or modify the legal effects of a certain provision of the treaty. In fact, Munkus's 'declaration' does not simply State how it will interpret a certain expression or term. On the contrary, with the inclusion of the shearwaters on the endangered list Munkus seeks to modify the legal effect of Article 37 TEMR by extending the legally agreed protection accorded to species on the protected list also to this seabird. Therefore, this declaration has to be seen as a reservation and to be treated accordingly.

Validity

First of all we have to ascertain whether the reservation made by Munkus is valid.

Article 19 VCLT used as a customary reflection sets out the conditions under which a reservation is to be considered as valid. The reservation must be made at the time of ratifying, signing, acceding to, accepting or approving a treaty. This is fulfilled since Munkus communicates its reservation when it is submitting its instrument of ratification of the TEMR.

In addition, Article 19(a) provides that a reservation is only valid if the treaty itself does not prohibit it. The TEMR in its Article 68 indeed lists a series of Articles to which no reservations can be made. Article 37 is not on this list, suggesting that reservations to this Article are allowed. Article 19(b) VCLT is not relevant in this case, because the TEMR does not expressly allow any reservations. However, we have to see whether Article 19(c) VCLT is also fulfilled. Article 19(c) provides that any reservation in order to be valid has to be compatible with the object and purpose of the treaty in question. In our case, the object and purpose of the TEMR is on the one hand to establish the borders of each State's EEZ and on the other hand to regulate the use of natural resources and to provide for the protection of maritime species. Yet, with its reservation Munkus only seeks to protect also the shearwaters, not to influence or change any of the objects of the TEMR. Consequently, adding an additional bird to the list of protected species is not defeating the object and purpose of the TEMR in any way. The reservation made by Munkus is thus valid.

Opposability

Aspara does not react to the announcement of the reservation and remains silent. Thus, according to Article 20 paragraph 5 VCLT used as a customary reflection, Aspara can be considered to have accepted the reservation made by Munkus at the end of a period of 12 months of silence. (We have to note that deadlines and time spans are not usually seen as customary law but what is required is rather a 'reasonable delay'. However, a time period of around 12 months seems to give the silent State enough time to object if it wishes to and on the other hand it does not seem to be an excessively long period of uncertainty. It is therefore suggested to accept the time period of 12 months as applicable also in our case.)

Therefore, Aspara can be seen as an accepting State for the purpose of the reservation, for sure and undoubtedly at the end of the 12 months period after it has been informed about the reservation.

Silla, on the other hand, States that it does not agree with this reservation. Article 20 paragraph 4(b) VCLT used as a customary reflection provides that an objection to a reservation does not preclude the entry into force of the treaty between the reserving and the objecting State as long as the latter has not clearly expressed its intention not to enter into any treaty relation with the reserving State. In our case, Silla has objected to the reservation but it has not said that it did not wish the TEMR to apply between itself and Munkus. Therefore, Silla is a simple objector (in opposition to a radical objector), and the TEMR will enter into force between Silla and Munkus despite Silla's objection.

We should also shortly consider Article 20 paragraph 4(c) VCLT used as a customary reflection. This Article provides that a reserving State is to be seen as a party to the treaty in question only from the moment when there is at least one other contracting State that has accepted the reservation. That only one acceptance is necessary to constitute the reserving State as a party to the treaty has also been the solution adopted by the ICJ in the Advisory Opinion on *Reservations to the Genocide Convention* (ICJ, Advisory Opinion, *Reservations to the Convention on the Prevention and Punishment of the Crime of Genocide*, 1951, 21–26).

In our case Munkus can be considered to be a party to the TEMR since Aspara has silently accepted its reservation. This is, however, only undoubtedly clear after the 12-month period.

Consequences

It is nevertheless important to clarify the consequences of the application of the reservation.

The relation between Aspara—the accepting State—and Munkus—the reserving

State—will be regulated by Article 2 paragraph 1(a) and (b) VCLT (customary reflection). This Article provides that the reservation will modify the provisions of the treaty to which the reservation relates to the extent of the reservation between the reserving and the accepting State. This means that in our case Article 37 TEMR will be changed by the reservation and thus the shearwaters will be included on the list of protected species in the relation between Apsara and Munkus.

Article 21 paragraph 3 VCLT regulates the relation between Munkuas and Silla—the simple objector. According to this Article the provision to which the reservation relates does not apply between the reserving and the objecting State to the extent of the reservation. In our case this means that Article 37 TEMR does not apply between Munkus and Silla 'to the extent of the reservation', meaning that the shearwaters will not be included on the list of the protected species between these two States, since this is the part where the two States do not agree.

As for the relation between Aspara and Silla, it is regulated by Article 21 paragraph 2 VCLT. The reservation made by Munkus does not change anything in the treaty relation between those two States *inter se*, ie Article 37 TEMR applies in an unchanged way (without the shearwaters on the list).

As is apparent from our analysis above, there are treaty relations between all three States. Munkus is therefore wrong to claim that there is no treaty at all between the parties due to Silla's simple objection.

3. Invalidity of the TEMR

Clarification of terms

Munkus further argues that the TEMR is terminated since it is based on incorrect maps. Yet, incorrect maps can only be a ground for invalidating a treaty under error, and not a ground for terminating a treaty. In fact, Article 42 VCLT used as a customary reflection provides that a treaty can only be invalidated or terminated in accordance with the grounds found in the VCLT, thus the grounds for invalidity or termination are exhaustively enumerated in this instrument (and consequently in its customary reflection). Therefore, based on the facts and the statements made by Munkus it seems indeed to invoke error and thus a ground for invalidating and not terminating the treaty.

The distinction between invalidity and termination is important due to their different consequences. An invalid treaty is void ab initio, is deemed to have never produced any legal effect and acts performed under it are no longer valid (Article 69 VCLT used as customary reflection). Termination, on the other hand, has effects *ex nunc*, that is from 'now' on. It has no retroactive effects on acts previously performed under that treaty (Article 70 VLCT used as customary reflection).

Error as a ground for invalidating a treaty is contained in Article 48 VCLT used as a customary reflection. In order for a State to invoke an error to invalidate a treaty, it is necessary that this error relates to a fact or situation which was assumed by that State to exist at the moment when the treaty was concluded and which in addition formed an essential basis of consent of the State to be bound by the treaty.

At the time of negotiating the TEMR Munkus—and indeed the two other States as well—assumed that the island in question was located at the place indicated on the maps. The map was drawn incorrectly, yet this was not done with bad intentions as is shown by the internal investigation conducted after this mistake is discovered. (Consequently, the situation cannot be qualified as fraud.) The determination of boundaries is in general very important. In fact, the three States considered it as very important to define the limits of each State's territorial sea and adjacent EEZ, especially also for the exploitation of natural sources. Therefore, we can argue that the presented boundaries on the wrong map were indeed an essential basis of consent for Munkus.

Before concluding that Munkus can indeed invoke error to invalidate the TEMR, we need to have a look also at paragraph 2 of Article 48 VCLT. An error cannot be invoked if the State invoking the error contributed by its own conduct to the error or the circumstances were such as to put this State on notice of the error. However, in our case Munkus did not contribute to the error. The maps were drawn by the NCS since both Munkus and Aspara did not have the necessary cartographic capabilities. There was also nothing that should have put Munkus or any of the other States on alert as to an error. The NCS seems to be in general a reliable organisation, which can be seen in the fact that it publicly apologises and conducts an internal investigation as soon as the error is discovered. Thus, there was no reason why Munkus should not have trusted the NCS.

Consequently, Munkus is entitled to invoke an error based on Article 48 VCLT as invalidating the TEMR.

Nevertheless, before concluding definitely on the fate of the TEMR we have to take a look at Article 45 VCLT (acquiescence). This Article provides that a State loses its right to invoke a ground to invalidate a treaty if, after it has become aware of the relevant facts, it consented expressly or implicitly by its conduct to the validity of the treaty. The error becomes public in 1976 and is subsequently also reported in several newspapers in all three States. Yet, none of the States, including Munkus, reacts, but they continue to apply the TEMR as it is. Only 21 years later, in 1997 when the oil field is discovered, does Munkus start to argue that the TEMR is invalid. A continuous application of the TEMR for 21 years is too long to claim that Munkus did not consent to its validity by its conduct (Article 45(b) VCLT). Thus, Munkus has acquiesced to the validity of the TEMR and has consequently lost its right to invoke error as a ground for invalidating the treaty.

Since we have established acquiescence, there is no need to look at separability of the TEMR under Article 44 VCLT.

4. Conclusion

As seen above, the reservation made by Munkus is applicable and changes the treaty relations between the reserving and the other States (one acceptance and one simple objection) accordingly. However, the simple objection does not lead to 'no treaty relation at all', as claimed by Munkus.

Furthermore, even though the TEMR is affected by an error, Munkus has lost its right to invoke this ground of invalidity to invalidate the TEMR since it has acquiesced in its continued application for 21 years. Consequently, we can conclude that the TEMR is still valid and in force between all three States.

Question 2: Can Munkus be held responsible for an internationally wrongful act? If yes, what are the consequences?

1. Applicable law

First of all we will apply the ILC Articles on Responsibility of States for Internationally Wrongful Acts 2001 (SRA). It is important to note that these Articles are despite their acceptance by the UN General Assembly not a legally binding treaty. Nevertheless, they are legally binding as customary international law. Their customary character has been recognised by the ICJ, for example in the *Iran Hostages* case (ICJ, Judgment, *United States Diplomatic and Consular Staff in Teheran* (United States of America v Iran), 1980, paragraphs 56–92), the *Gabčíkovo-Nagymaros* case (ICJ, Judgment, *Gabčíkovo-Nagymaros Project* (Hungary/Slovakia), 1997, paragraph 47) and most recently in the *Genocide* case (ICJ, Judgment, *Application of the Convention on the Prevention and Punishment of the Crime of Genocide* (Bosnia and Herzegovina v Serbia and Montenegro), 2007, paragraph 401).

In addition, we will also apply the UN Charter, which is applicable since both States involved in the issue are members of the UN.

Article 1 SRA holds that every internationally wrongful act of a State entails the international responsibility of this State. Article 2 then establishes the two necessary criteria to find an internationally wrongful act: first, the act or omission must be attributable to the State in question; and second, the act or omission must constitute a breach of an international obligation of that State.

2. Attribution 1

First, we need to check whether the acts committed by the MFS (attacks on undefended villages, killing villagers, attacks on and destruction of oil extraction facilities) are attributable to Munkus.

Undoubtedly the MFS cannot be qualified as an organ of the State of Munkus. This is a rebel group from neighbouring Silla and is not involved in the government of Munkus, nor does it exercise any sort of governmental authority in Munkus.

Another possibility would be to find attribution under Article 8 SRA. Under this Article acts of persons or groups can be attributed to the State if the person or group acts on the instructions or the direction or control of the State. According to the ICJ in the *Nicaragua* case (ICJ, Judgment on the Merits, *Military and Paramilitary Activities in and against Nicaragua* (Nicaragua v United States of America), 1986, paragraphs 105–116), the relevant test for this Article is whether Munkus exercises 'effective control' over the MFS. Effective control means that Munkus would not only be training and financing the MFS, but would also give it concrete instructions concerning its actions. The ICTY in its *Tadić* case (ICTY, Appeals Chamber, Judgment, *Tadić*, 1999 (Case No IT-94-1-A), paragraphs 99–145) held that it was not necessary to show 'effective control', but 'overall control' would be sufficient to find attribution. Under this 'overall control' test financing and/or training of rebels would be enough to attribute their acts to the State. The ICJ in its *Genocide* case (ICJ, Judgment, *Application of the Convention on the Prevention and Punishment of the Crime of Genocide* (Bosnia and Herzegovina v Serbia and Montenegro), 2007, paragraphs 396–407) vehemently rejected the ICTY's arguments and re-established the 'effective control' test as the appropriate test for the purpose of State responsibility. However, Munkus did not finance or train the MFS, nor did it give it any instructions or orders to attack the villages or the oil extraction facilities. In fact, Munkus just did nothing at all; it does not even communicate with the MFS. Therefore, it is impossible to find attribution under Article 8 SRA.

In addition, Article 11 SRA is not suitable. Following this Article it is possible to find attribution if a State acknowledges and adopts a certain conduct by a group or person as the State's own conduct. But in order to satisfy this Article an express acknowledgement by the State is necessary. The fact that Munkus does not condemn the acts of the MFS cannot be seen as meaning that it adopts them as its own acts.

Thus, it is impossible to find direct attribution concerning the acts committed by the MFS.

It might be helpful to analyse what other potential violations exist that could be attributed to the State of Munkus in a second analysis of attribution.

3. Violations

Article 12 SRA provides that there is a breach of an international obligation of the State if that State does not act in conformity with what is required by it under an international obligation. Whether that obligation is thereby of customary or conventional nature does not matter. Article 13 SRA adds to this that in order to constitute a breach the obligation in question needs to be in force for the State at the time of the alleged violation.

Munkus did not directly attack Silla itself. Therefore, a more refined analysis is necessary.

Several possibilities can be found in the GA resolution 2625 (also called the Friendly Relations Resolution).

For example, under the first principle of this resolution—the non-use of force principle—it is provided that 'every State has the duty to refrain from … *acquiescing* in organised activities within its territory directed towards the commission of such acts [ie acts of civil strife or terrorist acts], when the acts referred to in the present paragraph involve a threat or user of force' (emphasis added).

In our case, despite the lack of a general definition of terrorism, the attacks on the oil extraction facilities by the MFS could be qualified as terrorist acts, while the attacks on the villages would rather fit under acts of civil strife. In any event, the attacks of the MFS clearly involve the use of force against Silla. Munkus, by remaining silent and not doing anything to prevent the attacks or at least inform Silla, has clearly tacitly acquiesced in these acts. By their passivity Munkus therefore violated its obligation under this part of the GA resolution 2625.

In addition, a further violation can be found under principle three of GA resolution 2625—the duty not to intervene in matters within the domestic jurisdiction of another State. There it is stated that 'no State shall organise, assist, foment, finance, incite or *tolerate* subversive, terrorist or armed activities directed towards the violent overthrow of the regime of another State' (emphasis added). Munkus obviously tolerated the armed and terrorist activities by the MFS, since it had first-hand information about all the acts and nevertheless did not take any action at all. Furthermore, Munkus must have known as well that the MFS was fighting against the government of Silla and recently switched from peaceful means to armed struggle. The acts of the MFS were directed towards the overthrow of the government of Silla, and Munkus tolerated these acts.

Thirdly, GA resolution 2625 contains in its principle four—the duty to co-operate—in letter (a) the obligation that 'States shall co-operate with other States in the maintenance of international peace and security'. By not even informing Silla about the imminent threat to its security, Munkus evidently violated its duty to co-operate.

Thus, it seems that Munkus could be responsible for two acts (acquiescing in organised activities within its territory directed towards another State and tolerating armed and terrorist activities against another State) as well as for one omission (not co-operating).

Yet an important point has to be addressed, namely the legal value of such GA resolutions as 2625. Normally, GA resolutions are not legally binding since the GA's power is limited to making recommendations (see Articles 10–15 UN Charter). However, it can be argued that GA resolution 2625 actually only explains and specifies what is provided in Articles 1 and 2 of the UN Charter in a short form. Thus, GA resolution 2625 does not impose any new obligations but just clarifies what has to be understood, for example under Article 2 paragraph 4—the non-use of force provision. Consequently, these explanations are binding 'via' the UN Charter. In addition, the clarifications set out in GA resolution 2625 have arguably become international customary law today.

Thus, there exist international legal obligations for Munkus as a member of the UN, in the form of the UN Charter and its clarifications in GA resolution 2625. Some of these obligations have been violated by Munkus, as seen above.

4. Attribution 2

After having found violations, it is necessary to determine under which provision of the SRA attribution can be found.

The army and the secret service observe and infiltrate the MFS. The government is informed and it is the government of Munkus that decides not to take any action. Thus, it can be said that it is mainly the government which violated the duty to co-operate, and tolerated and acquiesced in the presence of the MFS even though it was very clearly informed about the latter's goals. Article 4 SRA provides that the conduct of any State organ is attributable to the State, regardless of its function, position or character. The government clearly is an organ of the State in the sense of Article 4 SRA.

Thus, the violations found above are attributable to Munkus and this State is prima facie responsible for a violation of international law.

5. Circumstances precluding wrongfulness

No analysis of State responsibility is complete without analysing the circumstances precluding wrongfulness. However, in our case clearly none of these Articles is applicable.

6. Consequences

First of all, Munkus should, according to Article 30(b), offer appropriate guarantees and assurances of non-repetition. Under Article 30(a) one could also consider that Munkus has an obligation to co-operate with Silla to end the threat posed by the MSF still present in Munkus's territory, since one can consider that as long as Munkus is still tolerating the MFS on its territory the violation of its obligations (toleration, non co-operation) continues.

It is a well-established principle of international customary law that the responsible State has an obligation to make reparations. This obligation has been confirmed by the Permanent Court of International Justice in the *Chorzów Factory* case (PCIJ, Judgment, *Case concerning the Factory at Chorzów (Claim for Indemnity)*, 1927, 21) and has been incorporated in Article 31 SRA.

There are different forms of reparation (Article 34). When assessing which form of reparation is appropriate, it should be kept in mind that Munkus is responsible for its *own* acts (and ommissions) and *not* the acts by the MSF. Therefore, restitution (Article 35 SRA) does not seem to be appropriate since it was not Munkus that destroyed the oil-extraction facilities and villages. (Furthermore, restitution would in any event not be appropriate: there is nothing that can be 'given back', since the oil-extraction facilities and villages are destroyed and many villagers dead.) Moreover, compensation (Article 36 SRA) seems not necessarily to be appropriate since Munkus itself did not inflict and is not directly responsible for the damages. However, satisfaction (Article 37 SRA), eg in the form of public apologies by Munkus, does seem to be suitable. The exact form of reparation has, however, to be negotiated between the two States or decided by a competent court or tribunal.

[*It might be possible to argue that because Munkus acquiesced in the conduct of the MSF and tolerated it being on its territory, the acts of this group became possible in the first place. Therefore, although Munkus is legally not necessarily directly responsible for the acts of the MSF, it can be argued that the destruction that was caused should nevertheless play a role when assessing the appropriate form and amount of Munkus' reparation.*]

7. Conclusion

As shown above, Munkus is indeed responsible for several breaches of international law, through acts but also omissions. It is important to stress that Munkus is only responsible for its *own* acts and omissions and not the acts of the MFS, since they cannot be attributed to Munkus. There are in addition no circumstances precluding wrongfulness which would preclude the responsibility of Munkus.

Therefore, Munkus has the obligation to make reparations to Silla, most likely in the form of satisfaction.

Question 3: Is the ICJ competent to deal with the disputes submitted to it? Analyse all the possible jurisdictional bases.

1. Applicable law

We will first and foremost apply the Statute of the ICJ, which is according to Article 92 UN Charter an integral part of the UN Charter. Since both States in question are members of the UN and thus parties to the UN Charter, the ICJ Statute is also applicable.

In order for the ICJ to be competent to hear a case, three elements need to be established: personal jurisdiction, subject matter jurisdiction and consent.

2. Personal jurisdiction (jurisdiction *ratione personae*)

According to Article 34 paragraph 1 ICJ Statute, only States can be parties to disputes before the Court. Both Munkus and Silla are States. This is undisputed and is further proven by the fact that they are members of the UN, an organisation which is only open to States as members (Article 4 paragraph 1 UN Charter). Therefore, this first requirement is fulfilled.

In addition, Article 35 paragraph 1 holds that the ICJ is only open to States which are parties to the ICJ Statute. According to Article 93 paragraph 1 of the UN Charter all the UN members are ipso facto parties to the ICJ Statute. Since Munkus and Silla are both UN members they are also parties to the ICJ Statute.

Consequently, personal jurisdiction is established.

3. Subject matter jurisdiction (jurisdiction *ratione materiae*)

The ICJ is only competent to hear legal disputes under international law, as can be inferred, for example, from Article 38 ICJ Statute.

In the *Mavrommatis Palestine Concessions* case (PCIJ, Judgment on the Objection to the Jurisdiction of the Court, *The Mavrommatis Palestine Concessions*, 1924, 11), the Permanent Court of International Justice (PCIJ) has most famously provided a definition of a dispute. There, the PCIJ said that a dispute was a disagreement on a point of law or fact between two persons. Thereby, a simple statement that there is a dispute is not enough, but positive opposition has to be shown (see ICJ, Judgment on Preliminary Objections, *South West Africa* (Liberia v South Africa and Ethiopia v South Africa), 1962, 328). This is thus an objective determination, as the ICJ held in the *Lockerbie* case (ICJ, Judgment on Preliminary Objections, *Questions of Interpretation and Application of the 1971 Montreal Convention arising from the Aerial Incident at Lockerbie* (Libyan Arab Jamahiriya v United States of America), 1998, paragraph 21).

In our case, Munkus and Silla indeed positively disagree on several points of law, namely on the reservations to and invalidity of the TEMR, as well as on the potential State responsibility of Munkus. Treaty law issues and State responsibility issues are legal by nature. In addition they are also legal disputes under international law, since they are regulated by international rather than by national law.

Thus, there exists a legal dispute under international law between Munkus and Silla and consequently the ICJ also has jurisdiction *ratione materiae*.

4. Consensus (jurisdiction *ratione consensus*)

Consensus to the compulsory jurisdiction of the ICJ is crucial for the establishment of the ICJ's jurisdiction. The ICJ itself has confirmed this for example in the *East Timor* case (ICJ, Judgment, *Case concerning East Timor* (Portugal v Australia), 1995, paragraph 26).

There are four possible ways for States to give consent. But only two are relevant in our case.

Optional clause declarations (Article 36 paragraph 2 ICJ Statute)

Silla has not made an optional clause declaration based on Article 36 paragraph 2 of the ICJ Statute. However, it has made such an optional clause declaration under the Statute of the PCIJ and has never revoked it. Article 36 paragraph 5 ICJ Statute foresees that declarations made under the Statute of the PCIJ and which are still in force shall be seen as acceptance of the compulsory jurisdiction of the ICJ. Thus, Silla's optional clause declaration is applicable under the ICJ and can serve as a basis of jurisdiction in our case.

However, the optional clause system is based on reciprocity, meaning that there need to be optional clause declarations by both parties to the dispute in order to serve as a basis of jurisdiction.

Munkus has also made an optional clause declaration, which is accompanied by a reservation. However, since none of the parties invokes the reservation, and since this is an issue which is not dealt with ex officio by the Court, it is not necessary to analyse this reservation.

[*Indeed, the issue of the reservation to bar the Court's jurisdiction has to be raised by parties in preliminary objections. If the parties do not do so, as is the case here, the ICJ would not go into the matter of analysing the reservation and its applicability. Yet, in case students analysed the reservation nonetheless, we would like to provide a suggested reasoning below, so that students can check their answer on this point.*

Generally, reservations to optional clause declarations are allowed according to Article 36 paragraph 3 ICJ Statute. Nevertheless, it has to be checked whether the reservation is compatible with the object and purpose of the ICJ Statute (Article 19(c) VCLT). It is crucial to point out that Munkus' reservation is not a so-called 'automatic' reservation. The essential part for being an automatic reservation is lacking: a true automatic reservation would read 'Munkus excludes from the jurisdiction of the International Court of Justice matters which essentially fall within the domestic jurisdiction and domestic law of Munkus, as determined by Munkus.*' The most relevant part of an automatic reservation is the emphasised part. It is also this part that makes automatic reservations so problematic since it deprives the ICJ of its competence to decide on its own competence (Article 36 paragraph 6 ICJ Statute). However, since this part is lacking, Munkus' reservation is a normal, albeit a rather useless reservation. It is useless because the ICJ is in any event not competent to deal with issue falling 'exclusively within the domestic jurisdiction' of a State, since the ICJ can only deal with disputes under international law, as shown above. Therefore, the reservation is not incompatible with the object and purpose of the ICJ Statute. On the other hand it is in our case also no limitation of the ICJ's jurisdiction.*]

The optional clause declarations by Munkus and Silla give the ICJ the necessary consensual jurisdiction in order to deal both with the State responsibility and the treaty law aspects of the dispute.

5. Forum prorogatum

Forum prorogatum is the situation when a case is brought to the ICJ and the defendant State does not contest the jurisdiction of the ICJ but immediately starts to argue on the merits of the case. This form of consent has been recognised by the ICJ, for example in the *Corfu Channel* case (ICJ, Judgment on Preliminary Objections, *Corfu Channel* (United Kingdom of Great Britain and Northern Ireland v Albania), 1948, 27, 28). It is important to stress that the arguments by the defendant have to be on the merits in order to find *forum prorogatum*. If the State presents arguments in order to contest the ICJ's jurisdiction, this cannot be seen as *forum prorogatum*.

Munkus, as soon as it is informed that a case has been brought against it, presents arguments why in its opinion it was not responsible for anything in relation to the MFS and why the TEMR was invalid. Therefore, this is a situation of *forum prorogatum*. On this basis, the ICJ is also competent to deal with the disputes between Silla and Munkus.

6. Conclusion

After our analysis above, we can conclude that the ICJ is competent to hear the disputes between Silla and Munkus both based on the optional clause declarations and *forum prorogatum*.

Suggested Solution—Case 7.3

Abbreviations used

ICJ	= International Court of Justice
ICTY	= International Criminal Tribunal for the Former Yugoslavia
ILC	= International Law Commission
MOILEX	= Memorandum on Oil Extraction
PCIJ	= Permanent Court of International Justice
SRA	= ILC Articles on Responsibility of States for Internationally Wrongful Acts 2001 (State Responsibility Articles)
UN	= United Nations
VCLT	= Vienna Convention on the Law of Treaties

Question 1: Is the MOILEX a treaty and if yes can it be terminated on the grounds presented by Coru?

1. Applicable law

There are two important dates to resolve the question of the applicability of the Vienna Convention on the Law of Treaties (VCLT) to a particular treaty. One is the date of entry into force of the VCLT itself for the State parties to the treaty in question; the other date is the date of conclusion of this treaty. Thereby, according to the non-retroactivity principle in Article 4 VCLT, the date of conclusion of the treaty has to be after the date of the entry into force of the VCLT for the State parties to the treaty.

In our case, we know that both Coru and Ottis are parties to the VCLT 'since its entry into force'. Thus, the VCLT enters into force for both Coru and Ottis on 27 January 1980, according to Article 84 paragraph 1 VCLT.

The MOILEX, however, has been concluded in 1976, ie before the entry into force of the VCLT in general (and thus also before the entry into force for Coru and Ottis). Consequently, the non-retroactivity principle in Article 4 VCLT is not fulfilled.

However, it is well accepted that most of the VCLT reflects customary international law. This has, for example, been confirmed by the International Court of Justice (ICJ) in the *Gabčíkovo-Nagymaros Project* case (ICJ, Judgment, *Gabčíkovo-Nagymaros Project* (Hungary/Slovakia), 1997, paragraph 46). Therefore, we will apply the customary reflection contained in the VCLT.

2. Determination of the instrument: is the MOILEX a treaty?

The next question that has to be clarified is whether or not the MOILEX is a treaty.

Article 2 paragraph 1(a) VCLT defines the term 'treaty': an 'international agreement concluded between States in written form and governed by international law'; the designation of the instrument is irrelevant. However, it has to be kept in mind that this definition is the definition of a treaty for the purpose of the VCLT and is thus limited. Since the VCLT is not applicable in our case here, we have to apply the customary international law definition of a treaty, which is broader than the VCLT definition in several respects. Generally, a treaty under international customary law is defined as an expression of concurring wills between at least two subjects of international law, concluded with the intention to produce legal effects and governed by international law. Thus, this definition is broader since it is not limited to treaties between States only, and because it includes also treaties concluded in a non-written form. It is, however, equally true that under customary international law the denomination of a treaty does not matter (see ICJ, Judgment on Preliminary Objections, *South West Africa* (Liberia v South Africa and Ethiopia v South Africa), 1962, 331). See, for example, the *Aegean Sea* case (ICJ, Judgment on the Jurisdiction of the Court, *Aegean Sea Continental Shelf* (Greece v Turkey), 1978, paragraph 96), where the ICJ held that even a joint communiqué could be a treaty, or the *Case concerning Maritime Delimitation and Territorial Questions between Qatar and Bahrain* (ICJ, Judgment on Jurisdiction and Admissibility, *Maritime Delimitation and Territorial Questions between Qatar and Bahrain* (Qatar v Bahrain), 1994, paragraphs 23–25) where the ICJ found that minutes and exchanges of letters can also constitute a treaty. What matters is the intention of the parties.

The President of Coru questions whether the MOILEX is a treaty mainly because it is called 'memorandum' and not 'treaty'. Since, as we have seen above, the name given to a particular instrument is not important, this argument cannot be accepted. Nevertheless, we have to analyse whether the main elements contained in the customary treaty definition set out above are fulfilled.

(a) Expression of concurring wills: when concluding the MOILEX the two parties did agree in this instrument that Ottis could extract oil in the territorial waters of Coru and how much oil it could keep. Thus there was indeed a concurring will. That this will apparently no longer exists is irrelevant for the existence of the treaty.
(b) Concluded between at least two subjects of international law: there is no doubt that Ottis and Coru are States and thus subjects of international law.
(c) Intention to produce legal effects: the idea of the MOILEX was to regulate the oil extraction by Ottis in the territorial waters of Coru and to distribute that oil afterwards. Thus, the MOILEX is indeed intended to produce legal effects.
(d) Governed by international law: since the MOILEX is concluded between two States and since there is nothing that indicates that the parties determined that the treaty should be governed by one of their national laws, we can safely assume that this memorandum is governed by international law, as is usually the case for international treaties.

Seeing that all four main elements in order to qualify as a treaty for the purposes of international customary law are fulfilled, we can conclude that the MOILEX is, despite its name, a treaty.

As a next step we now have to consider President Nardin's argument that the treaty is terminated.

3. Termination

It has to be pointed out at the outset that the clauses for termination are enumerated exhaustively in the VCLT (see Article 42 paragraph 2 VCLT, used as a customary reflection). There thus cannot be any other grounds for termination.

Coru makes several arguments why it considers the MOILEX to be terminated.

(a) The treaty was concluded by a non-legitimate government

It is true that the Eberhard government was a dictatorship which was not recognised by all States in the international community. We do not know whether or not Ottis has recognised this government. Yet, in any event this is not relevant, since the Eberhard regime was the de facto regime for 44 years, without any internal or external challenges to its power. Consequently, this government could act as the sovereign government of Ottis and could also conclude treaties. The new government remains bound by the treaties concluded by its predecessor, since it is actually the *State* which is bound by international treaties, and not the government. This solution has also been adopted in the *Tinoco Arbitration* (Arbitral Tribunal, Award, *Aguilar-Amory and Royal Bank of Canada claims* (*Tinoco case*) (Great Britain v Costa Rica), 1923, 377, 378). Changes in government will generally not affect the international obligations of States, since States usually 'live' for a much longer time than governments. This idea has also been termed the 'principle of the continuity of the State'. Besides, it would be fatal for the stability of the international treaty regime if it would be allowed that treaties are terminated at will after every change of government.

(b) The MOILEX is an unfair/unequal treaty

As pointed out above, the grounds for terminating, invalidating or suspending a treaty are exhaustively enumerated in the VCLT (Article 42 VCLT). This is also true for international customary law. However, unequal treaties are not a ground for terminating a treaty and thus cannot be invoked.

(c) Fundamental change of circumstances

Coru also invokes a fundamental change of circumstances from a dictatorial to a democratic regime to argue for the termination of the MOILEX. It is true that a fundamental change of circumstances is, according to Article 62 VCLT, a ground for terminating a treaty. The customary nature of this Article has been confirmed by the ICJ, for example in the *Fisheries Jurisdiction* case (UK v Iceland) (ICJ, Judgment on the Jurisdiction of the Court, *Fisheries Jurisdiction* (United Kingdom of Great Britain and Northern Ireland v Iceland), 1973, paragraph 36).

International relations are changing constantly. Therefore, the threshold of Article 62 VCLT is very high in order to reduce the danger posed to international treaties by the possibility of invoking some changes as being 'fundamental' in order to end treaties. The restrictive nature of this Article can be seen in its negative formulation, which provides that a fundamental change of circumstances 'may *not* be invoked as a ground for terminating or withdrawing from a treaty *unless*'. In practice, this ground for termination has only very rarely been accepted.

Under paragraph 1 of Article 62 VCLT used as a customary reflection, two cumulative conditions have to be satisfied in order to invoke a fundamental change of circumstances. First, these circumstances were an essential basis of consent of the parties to be bound by the treaty; and second, the change in circumstances has as effect that the extent of obligations which is still to be performed under the treaty is radically transformed. In addition, the ICJ held in the *Gabčíkovo-Nagymaros* case (ICJ, Judgment, *Gabčíkovo-Nagymaros Project* (Hungary/Slovakia), 1997, paragraph 104) that 'a fundamental change of circumstances must have been unforeseen'.

In our case, the circumstance that is said to have radically changed is the change of government, from a dictatorship to a democratic government. Thus, these are political circumstances that have changed. It cannot convincingly be argued that the existence of the dictatorship was an 'essential basis of consent of the parties to be bound by the treaty'. It is true that this political system might have facilitated the conclusion of such a treaty as the MOILEX, but then it has at most affected this conclusion and was still not an essential basis of consent for both parties.

Furthermore, the nature of the regime does not seem to be relevant at all for the obligations under the MOILEX as such. Thus, the fact that the government has changed now does not transform in any way the obligations under this treaty. That the new democratic government is unhappy with the unfair distribution of the oil or concerned about the environmental impact of the oil extraction does not affect the obligations of the parties under the treaty (but might be reasons to propose a renegotiation of the MOILEX).

Thus, we can say that both of the conditions which have cumulatively to be satisfied under the customary reflection of Article 62 VCLT to invoke a fundamental change of circumstances are not fulfilled.

Consequently, the MOILEX cannot be terminated on this ground.

Looking at other clauses for termination it seems that none is applicable. In addition, the treaty has been concluded for an undetermined time and without any denunciation clause, thereby indicating that the parties did not intend to allow for such an option.

4. Conclusion

As seen above, both arguments made by the President of Coru have to be rejected. First of all, the MOILEX is a treaty, regardless of its name. Second, the MOILEX cannot be terminated based on Article 62 VCLT or any other of the provisions on termination in the customary reflection of the VCLT. Therefore, the MOILEX is still in force between Coru and Ottis.

Question 2: Is President Neil right to say that Ottis is responsible for all acts of the 'Carlists'; and if yes, what are the consequences?

1. Applicable law

The applicable law are mainly the ILC Articles on Responsibility of States for Internationally Wrongful Acts 2001 (SRA). These Articles are not a treaty, but they reflect customary international law, as has been confirmed by the ICJ in cases such as the *Iran Hostages* case (ICJ, Judgment, *United States Diplomatic and Consular Staff in Teheran* (United States of America v Iran), 1980, paragraphs 56–92), the *Gabčíkovo-Nagymaros* case (ICJ, Judgment, *Gabčíkovo-Nagymaros Project* (Hungary/Slovakia),

1997, paragraph 104) and most recently the *Genocide* case (ICJ, Judgment, *Application of the Convention on the Prevention and Punishment of the Crime of Genocide* (Bosnia and Herzegovina v Serbia and Montenegro), 2007, paragraph 401).

Furthermore, we will also apply the UN Charter, which is applicable since both States are UN members.

Article 1 SRA holds that States are responsible for all their internationally wrongful acts. The definition of an internationally wrongful act can be found in Article 2 SRA. Two cumulative elements are necessary: first, the action or omission must be attributable to the State in question; and second, the act or omission must constitute a breach of an international obligation of that State.

2. Attribution

Attribution is regulated in Articles 4–11 SRA.

The Carlists are certainly not de jure organs of Ottis under Article 4, since they do not have any position according to internal law of Ottis. Neither can they be seen as de facto organs under Article 4, following the 'complete dependence' test established by the ICJ in the *Nicaragua* case (ICJ, Judgment on the Merits, *Military and Paramilitary Activities in and against Nicaragua* (Nicaragua v United States of America), 1986, paragraphs 109–112) and the *Genocide* case (ICJ, Judgment, *Application of the Convention on the Prevention and Punishment of the Crime of Genocide* (Bosnia and Herzegovina v Serbia and Montenegro), 2007, paragraphs 390–395). Complete dependency means that the group is a mere instrument, a puppet of the government and has no autonomy at all. If the person or group still has a slight degree of autonomy for their acts, then the complete dependency test would not be satisfied. In our case, Ottis does not create the Carlists and they also act independently, as can be seen in their attack on the power station. Thus, the Carlists are not organs of the State of Ottis.

The only other possibility to find attribution for acts or omissions committed by persons or other entities which seems applicable here is Article 8 SRA. Under this Article, there is attribution of an act or omission exercised by a group or person to the State if that group or person acts under the 'instruction of, or under the direction or control of, that State in carrying out the conduct'. The question is, however, what has to be understood under 'instruction of, or direction or control'.

The ICJ in the *Nicaragua* case (ICJ, Judgment on the Merits, *Military and Paramilitary Activities in and against Nicaragua* (Nicaragua v United States of America), 1986, paragraphs 105–116) established as the necessary degree of control the so-called 'effective control' test. According to this criterion, it is not enough only to finance, train or give logistical support to the group; the State needs effectively to control what they are doing, for example by ordering them to do something. In particular, the State needs to have effective control over the conduct during which the alleged violation occurred. However, the ICTY in the *Tadić* case (ICTY, Appeals Chamber, Judgment, *Tadić*, 1999 (Case No IT-94-1-A), paragraphs 99–145) said that the appropriate test of control was the 'overall control' test. This test has a lower threshold, whereby financing or training a certain group can be enough to find attribution. The ICJ in the *Genocide* case (ICJ, Judgment, *Application of the Convention on the Prevention and Punishment of the Crime of Genocide* (Bosnia and Herzegovina v Serbia and Montenegro), 2007, paragraphs 396–407), however, firmly rejected the ICTY's approach and re-established the 'effective control' test as the correct test for the purposes of State responsibility.

In our case, the Carlists are financed and for some time also trained by Ottis. This would as such not be enough to find attribution under the 'effective control' test. However, Ottis directly instructed the Carlists to mine the port in Coru. This would be enough to satisfy the 'effective control' test and attribution can be found. It is, however, important that attribution can only be found for this conduct alone. The other attack by the Carlist on the power station was not ordered by Ottis and is consequently not attributable to it (Ottis had no control over this act).

3. Violation

Article 12 SRA specifies that there is a breach of an international obligation if a State does not act in accordance with what is required from it under its international obligation. Whether these obligations are of a customary or conventional nature does not matter. Article 13 SRA adds that in order to find a breach, the obligation in question must have been in force for the State in question at the time of the violation.

The mining of a port can be seen as a breach of the territorial sovereignty of a State (violation of Article 2 paragraph 1 of the UN Charter), as well as a prohibited use of force against a State's integrity (violation of Article 2 paragraph 4 UN Charter). The UN Charter is in force for Ottis, since it is an original member of the UN.

Therefore, Ottis is responsible for this violation of the UN Charter towards Coru.

In addition, Ottis's support of the Carlists can also be seen as a violation of the principle of non-interference in the domestic jurisdiction of a State. In this respect, General Assembly resolution 2625 provides that 'no State shall organise, assist, foment, finance, incite or tolerate subversive, terrorist or armed activities directed towards the violent overthrow of the regime of another State'. It is true that General Assembly resolutions as such are not legally binding since the General Assembly only has recommendatory powers (Articles 10–15 UN Charter). However, General Assembly resolution 2625, apart from being seen as customary by many, is basically only clarifying the provisions found in the UN Charter (in our case, for example, Article 2 paragraph 1 of the UN Charter). It is not creating new obligations and the violation as such is a violation of the Charter, not of the General Assembly resolution.

Of course, for this last violation attribution is to be found under Article 4 SRA, since it is the government and secret service of Ottis—both clearly organs of the State under Article 4 SRA—which finance, support and train the Carlists.

Therefore, we can say that Ottis is prima facie responsible for violations of the UN Charter, Article 2 paragraph 4 and 'twice' Article 2 paragraph 1, once through the acts of the Carlists attributable to it under Article 8 SRA and once for its own violation of this Article.

4. Circumstances precluding wrongfulness

No analysis of State responsibility is complete without an analysis of potential circumstances precluding wrongfulness. However, in our case there seem to be none of those circumstances applicable and Ottis is consequently responsible.

5. Consequences

First of all, Ottis has a duty to cease its violations and to give appropriate guarantees of non-repetition (Article 30 SRA). Cessation of the violation would, for example, mean that Ottis immediately stops any financial or other support (in our case weapons) to the Carlists.

In addition, making reparation for a breach of international law is an obligation under customary international law, as has been confirmed by the PCIJ in the *Chorzów Factory* case (PCIJ, Judgment, *Case concerning the Factory at Chorzów (Claim for Indemnity)*, 1927, 21). Article 31 SRA also sets out this obligation.

There are different forms of reparation according to Article 34 SRA. Restitution (Article 35 SRA), ie giving something back, is not appropriate here since there is nothing material to give back. However, Ottis should pay compensation (Article 36 SRA) for the materially assessable damage to the port. In addition, it would also be appropriate to use satisfaction (Article 37 SRA) as a means of reparation, eg in the form of a public apology.

6. Conclusion

President Neil is only partly correct when he is saying that Ottis is responsible for all acts of the Carlists. As shown above, only the act of mining the port can be attributed to Ottis under Article 8 SRA. The attack on the power station, however, cannot be attributed to Ottis, which is thus not responsible for this act. It is, though, also responsible for its own violation of international law, namely supporting and financing the Carlists, which can be seen—through the General Assembly resolution 2625—as a violation of Article 2 paragraph 1 UN Charter.

The appropriate consequences in this case, next to cessation and guarantees of non-repetition, are compensation and satisfaction.

Question 3: Is the ICJ competent to deal with the dispute(s) in issue?

1. Applicable law

First of all, we will apply the ICJ Statute and the UN Charter. According to Article 92 UN Charter, the ICJ Statute is an integral part of the UN Charter. The UN Charter is applicable since both States in question are members of the UN and thus parties to its Charter.

In addition, we will also apply the regional dispute settlement treaty concluded in 1949, to which both Ottis and Coru are parties.

In order to ascertain whether or not the ICJ has jurisdiction to hear the present case, three elements need to be fulfilled, namely personal jurisdiction, subject matter jurisdiction and consensual jurisdiction.

2. Personal jurisdiction (jurisdiction *ratione personae*)

According to Article 34 paragraph 1 of the ICJ Statute, only States can be parties to disputes in front of the ICJ. Both Ottis and Coru are States. This is not disputed and can also be seen from the fact that they are members of the UN, which is only open to States (Article 4 paragraph 1 UN Charter).

In addition, Article 35 paragraph 1 ICJ Statute declares that the ICJ is only open to States which are parties to its Statute; Article 93 paragraph 1 of the UN Charter provides that all UN members are, ipso facto, parties to the ICJ Statute. In our case both States are members of the UN, thus they are automatically also parties to the ICJ Statute and fulfil the requirement in Article 35 paragraph 1.

Seeing that both necessary elements are fulfilled, we can say that the ICJ has personal jurisdiction in this case.

3. Subject matter jurisdiction (jurisdiction *ratione materiae*)

The ICJ is only competent to hear legal disputes under international law, as can be inferred, for example, from Article 38 ICJ Statute.

Disputes have most famously been defined by the PCIJ in the *Mavrommatis Palestine Concessions* case (PCIJ, Judgment on the Objection to the Jurisdiction of the Court, *The Mavrommatis Palestine Concessions*, 1924, 11). There, the PCIJ said that a dispute was a disagreement on a point of law or fact between two persons.

In our case, Ottis and Coru indeed disagree on several points of law. There seem in fact to be two disputes: one related to the termination of the MOILEX and the other one to the question of whether or not Ottis is responsible for the acts of the Carlists. Treaty law issues and State responsibility issues are legal by nature. In addition, they are also legal disputes under international law, since they are regulated by international rather than by national law.

Thus, there exists legal disputes under international law between Ottis and Coru and consequently the ICJ also has jurisdiction *ratione materiae*.

4. Consensual jurisdiction (jurisdiction *ratione consensus*)

The consent of the parties to the jurisdiction of the ICJ is crucial, since there is no direct compulsory jurisdiction of the ICJ. The ICJ stressed the importance of consent to its jurisdiction for example in the *East Timor* case (ICJ, Judgment, *Case concerning East Timor* (Portugal v Australia), 1995, paragraph 26).

There are four different ways for a State to give its consent. In our case, only one possibility seems to be relevant, since none of the parties seems to have made optional clause declarations and since the MOILEX does apparently not contain a compromissory clause.

The basis of jurisdiction invoked by Coru is a regional dispute settlement treaty concluded in 1949. Dispute settlement treaties are a well-established basis of jurisdiction under Article 36 paragraph 1 of the ICJ Statute. The argument by Ottis that this treaty cannot be invoked because it is older than the dispute cannot be accepted. Indeed, the idea of such general dispute settlement treaties is to secure adjudication to peacefully solve *future* disputes. In addition, the dispute settlement treaty is not limited in substance. Consequently, this dispute settlement treaty can serve as a basis of jurisdiction for both disputes.

Article 6 of the dispute settlement treaty provides two possibilities for the settlement of disputes. One possibility (paragraph 1) is arbitration, which is, however, not a precondition for seizing the ICJ.

The other possibility (paragraph 2) is to bring the case unilaterally to the ICJ, on the precondition that previous negotiations have failed. The practice of the ICJ shows that the State seizing the court, in our case Coru, needs to present sufficient evidence that it attempted such negotiations.

It is true that Coru attempted to negotiate with Ottis regarding the alleged State responsibility of the latter State. These negotiations were, however, rejected by Ottis. This could therefore be seen as a failed attempt to negotiate.

On the other hand, regarding the termination issue surrounding the MOILEX, it is Ottis that offered negotiations which were rejected by Coru. However, by engaging the Carlists to mine the port to 'change their approach', it is questionable whether Ottis's offer to negotiate can be seen as a good faith offer. In addition, Ottis later on categorically rejects all negotiations 'regardless of the subject or the problem'. This indicates that Ottis would now no longer be willing to negotiate on the application of the MOILEX either. It has also to be noted, however, that it seems that Coru never in fact offered to negotiate concerning the MOILEX, even though this is not completely clear from the facts.

5. Conclusion

We can say that there have been clearly failed negotiations between Coru and Ottis regarding the State responsibility issue, where Ottis rejected to negotiate. Thus, the precondition in Article 6 paragraph 2 of the dispute settlement treaty is fulfilled and this treaty can serve as a basis of jurisdiction of the ICJ.

As for the dispute on the MOILEX, prima facie the precondition of failed negotiations is not fulfilled because Coru has never offered such negotiations and rejected such an offer coming from Ottis. Thus, the ICJ is not competent to deal with this dispute on the basis of the dispute settlement treaty (which is the only basis of jurisdiction here). Had Coru offered negotiations and had Ottis rejected them (as is likely—yet not completely certain—since they refuse any sort of negotiations), then Article 6 paragraph 2 would be fulfilled and the ICJ would be competent to hear also that dispute.

[*It is possible to argue that it seems clear from the categorical rejection of negotiations by Ottis and its attempt to deal with problems 'its own way' that negotiations between Coru and Ottis are not likely. This is also owing to the disrupted level of trust between the two parties. Therefore, it could be said that requiring that Coru offer negotiations only to be turned down (which seems likely) is an unnecessary procedural step. It would mean that Coru would have to make the offer, be turned down and introduce the same case on the MOILEX again a few days later, which seems to be an unnecessary waste of resources and time. Under these circumstances it could be said that the condition to negotiate found in Article 6 paragraph 2 of the dispute settlement treaty can be seen as fulfilled as well for the dispute surrounding the MOILEX. Consequently, the ICJ is competent to hear also this dispute in addition to the one on State responsibility issues.*]

Suggested Solution—Case 7.4

Abbreviations used

AMR	= Agreement on Movement and Residence
GA	= General Assembly (of the United Nations)
ICJ	= International Court of Justice
ICTY	= International Criminal Tribunal for the Former Yugoslavia
ILC	= International Law Commission
PCIJ	= Permanent Court of International Justice
SRA	= ILC Articles on Responsibility of States for Internationally Wrongful Acts 2001 (State Responsibility Articles)
UN	= United Nations
VCLT	= Vienna Convention on the Law of Treaties

Question 1: Is the AMR still in force between the four State parties?

1. Applicable law

Concerning the applicability of the Vienna Convention on the Law of Treaties (VCLT), there are two sets of important dates that have to be assessed: the entry into force of the VCLT for all the respective State parties, and the date of conclusion (and not the date of entry into force) of the treaty in question. Article 4 VCLT—the non-retroactivity principle—provides that the VCLT is only applicable to treaties which have been concluded after the entry into force of the VCLT for the respective State parties.

Jada and Chardun are parties to the VCLT since its entry into force. This means that according to Article 84 paragraph 1 VCLT, which provides that the VCLT entered into force 30 days after the deposit of the 35th instrument of ratification, the VCLT entered into force also for these two States on 27 January 1980.

Barat has ratified the VCLT on 9 September 1985. Article 84 paragraph 2 VCLT provides that after its entry into force following Article 84 paragraph 1, the VCLT enters into force for States 30 days after they deposited their instrument of ratification or accession. Therefore, the VCLT entered into force for Barat on 9 October 1985.

Ruvi has ratified the VCLT on 7 July 1993. As explained above, following Article 84 paragraph 2, the VCLT entered into force for Ruvi on 7 August 1993.

The AMR has been concluded on 4 March 1995. At this date, all the State parties to the AMR were also State parties to the VCLT. Therefore, Article 4, as explained above, is fulfilled and the VCLT is applicable to the AMR.

2. Invalidity of the AMR

Ruvi, via its High Court, argues that the AMR is invalid since it has been concluded in violation of the internal law of Ruvi, since it has not been ratified by the Parliament.

First of all, it should be pointed out that the grounds for invalidating, terminating and suspending a treaty are enumerated exhaustively in the VCLT, as is provided by Article 42 VCLT. Therefore, no other grounds outside the VCLT can be found and invoked.

In general, a State cannot invoke provisions of its internal law to justify a violation of a treaty (Article 27 VCLT). However, there is an explicit exception, which is contained in Article 46 VCLT. This Article provides that invalidity of a treaty on grounds of a violation of the State's internal law concerning the competence to conclude treaties can be invoked if two cumulative conditions are satisfied: (a) the violation must have been manifest; and (b) it must have concerned a rule of fundamental importance. Paragraph 2 explains that a violation is manifest when it would be objectively clear to any State conducting itself in accordance with normal practice and good faith that this is a violation.

It is true that the constitution of a State is said usually to contain rules of fundamental importance, since it is the highest law of a State. In our case, Article 42 of the Ruvian constitution indeed provides that all treaties (except treaties dealing only with commodity exchange) have to be ratified by the Parliament. There is therefore a rule of fundamental importance concerning the conclusion of treaties in Ruvi.

It is debatable, however, whether the violation of the rule was manifest. States are not required to be familiar with the internal law of other States. While most treaties seem to need to be ratified by the Parliament in Ruvi, this is not the case for all treaties. Moreover, whether or not a treaty needs to be ratified by Parliament apparently depends on an internal classification, which is not necessarily clear to all States and where, as in our case, internal mistakes can also happen (which are even less apparent and obviously also not a concern for other States). On the other hand, we have to acknowledge that Jada—the depositor—noticed that ratification by the Parliament of Ruvi was lacking, which can be seen as indicating that the rule was indeed known to other States and that the violation was thus manifest. Following this argument, we could argue that Article 46 VCLT is fulfilled and that Ruvi can indeed invoke this Article to invalidate the AMR. Article 46 VCLT is a relative ground of invalidity (voidability) and only the 'victim' State, ie Ruvi, can invoke it.

However, before making any final conclusion, we have to look at acquiescence (Article 45 VCLT). Article 45 VCLT provides that a State loses its right to invoke a ground for invalidity or termination if it has acquiesced to the validity of the treaty, either (a) in an express statement or (b) through its conduct. When Jada contacts Ruvi concerning the lack of parliamentary ratification the government of Ruvi holds consultations with the Parliament. Afterwards, the Foreign Minister of Ruvi informs Jada that 'even though the ratification of the Parliament was missing, Ruvi could be considered to be fully bound by the AMR'. This means that Ruiv has expressly confirmed the validity of the AMR despite the lacking parliamentary ratification and thus fulfils Article 45(a) VCLT. In addition, the AMR is applied for more than 10 years without any contestation, either from Ruvi or from any other State party. Therefore, we can say that Ruvi has also acquiesced to the validity of the AMR through its conduct, as is laid down in Article 45(b) VCLT.

In any event, irrespective of the arguments made above concerning the applicability of Article 46 VCLT, it is clear that Ruvi has acquiesced to the validity of the AMR in conformity with Article 45 VCLT and thus can no longer invoke the invalidity of the AMR.

As to the statement made by the High Court that it is Ruvi's right to pass laws in its territory and that it was clear from the new law that it were no longer considered itself bound by the AMR, we can respond as follows. It is true that States are sovereign in their territories, meaning that they can also pass their own laws. However, as pointed out above, it is a general rule in international law that the internal law of a State does not justify the violation or non-performance of an international agreement (Article 27 VCLT). It is thus the State's obligation to ensure that its internal law is in conformity with, or at least not hindering, the execution of international obligations. Consequently, this statement by the High Court needs to be rejected and can under no circumstances justify a non-performance of the AMR.

3. Conclusion

The AMR is still in force between all the parties, since Ruvi cannot invoke Article 46 VCLT as a ground for invalidating this treaty, due to the fact that it acquiesced in this treaty's validity. Furthermore, the passing of a new law in violation of the AMR (an international treaty) cannot justify the violation of the provisions of this treaty, since international obligations take primacy over national ones. Therefore, the arguments made by the High Court regarding the validity of the AMR need to be rejected.

Question 2: Can Ruvi be held responsible for violation(s) of international law? If yes, how and what are the consequences? Analyse all the potential possibilities.

1. Applicable law

In order to resolve the question on State responsibility we will apply the ILC Articles on Responsibility of States for Internationally Wrongful Acts from 2001 (SRA). These Articles are not a legally binding treaty, but they reflect customary international law and are thus applicable as such. The ICJ has confirmed the customary character of the SRA in numerous cases, such as the *Iran Hostages* case (ICJ, Judgment, *United States Diplomatic and Consular Staff in Teheran* (United States of America v Iran), 1980, paragraphs 56–92), the *Gabčíkovo-Nagymaros* case (ICJ, Judgment, *Gabčíkovo-Nagymaros Project* (Hungary/Slovakia), 1997, paragraph 47) and most recently the *Genocide* case (ICJ, Judgment, *Application of the Convention on the Prevention and Punishment of the Crime of Genocide* (Bosnia and Herzegovina v Serbia and Montenegro), 2007, paragraph 401).

In addition, we will also apply the AMR which is binding on all four States in this case.

Article 1 SRA provides that a State is internationally responsible for every one of its internationally wrongful acts. Article 2 SRA sets out the two necessary elements for an internationally wrongful act. First, the act or omission must be attributable to the State in question; and second, the act or omission must constitute a breach of an international obligation of that State.

2. Attribution

It seems that there are two potential violations that should be analysed. There is on one hand the passing of the law prohibiting foreigners to buy houses, and on the other hand there is the judgment of the High Court in that matter. Both presumably violate the AMR.

Concerning the adoption of the new law, it is stated that it was the government that adopted it. The government is clearly an organ in the sense of Article 4 SRA. Article 4 SRA provides that the conduct of any State organ is to be seen as an act of the State, regardless of the function or character the organ exercises. Indeed, executive functions are expressly mentioned in the Article, leaving no doubt that acts of the government, such as passing laws, can be attributable to the State of Ruvi.

In addition, courts or other judicial organs are also to be considered organs of the State under Article 4 SRA. Article 4 SRA also expressly mentions that acts or omissions of organs exercising judicial functions shall be considered as acts of the State. Therefore, the judgment of the High Court is attributable to Ruvi as well.

Thus, Ruvi's argument that national courts can never be held responsible under international law, and consequently neither the State, is not totally correct. It is true that national courts as such are not directly responsible themselves on the international level. But national courts are organs of the State as any other organ. Since the *State* is responsible for acts and omissions of all its organs, this naturally also includes acts and omissions of national courts.

3. Violation

Article 12 SRA explains that there is a violation of an international obligation when a State does not act in conformity with what is expected from it under its international obligations. Whether this obligation is of customary or conventional nature does not therefore matter.

In addition, Article 13 SRA specifies that there is only a breach of an international obligation if at the time of the alleged breach the obligation in question was in force for the State.

The AMR provides in its Article 15 that foreigners can take up residence wherever they want in the territory of the contracting parties. Article 16 AMR holds that foreigners have the same rights as nationals of the contracting parties when it comes to purchasing or selling houses, apartments and so on.

Nevertheless, the government of Ruvi has passed a law prohibiting all foreigners to buy houses. This is a clear violation of international law, namely Article 16 AMR to which Ruvi is a party and by which it is consequently bound. Nevertheless, it is debatable whether the mere adoption of a law contrary to international law is to be seen as a violation. One could imagine a situation where a law contrary to international law is adopted but never applied. Thus, there would actually be no violation concerning the international obligation with which the internal law is in conflict. In our opinion, it is therefore more convincing to argue that the adoption of a law violating an international obligation of the State per se is not a violation in the sense of the SRA. Only when this law is applied can there be a violation (which is, however, then the act of *applying* the law and not the act of *passing* the law).

The judgment of the High Court is applying the newly passed law to the detriment of a foreign national. This is therefore a clear violation of Article 16 AMR. In addition, the High Court seems to suggest that foreigners could not just live where they want, thereby restricting their freedom of movement and directly violating Article 15 AMR, which provides for the liberty of living wherever the foreigners want in the territory of the contracting States.

In addition, as has been shown above, Article 27 VCLT provides that an internal law can never be invoked to justify a State's failure to respect a treaty. Furthermore, Article 3 SRA States that the characterisation of an act as unlawful is done under international law. The fact that the same act (thus prohibiting foreigners to buy houses) is lawful under national law is irrelevant for the purposes of State responsibility. Here, the AMR sets out clear obligations in the matter at hand, allowing foreigners to buy houses and to reside where they like. Even though the High Court 'only' follows the new law passed by the government, this qualification as lawful by an internal law does not preclude the violation of international law (ie the AMR).

Consequently, there is a violation of international law in force for Ruvi (a violation of the AMR), which is attributable to Ruvi, since it is its State organ (the High Court) that renders this judgment.

In addition the argument made by the President of the High Court Tonin Dalia that it is the State that signs international treaties and not the judges needs to be rejected. While it is true that judges do normally not sign international treaties, it has to be kept in mind that it is always the *State* which is bound by international treaties (see eg the *Tinoco Arbitration* (Arbitral Tribunal, Award, *Aguilar-Amory and Royal Bank of Canada claims* (*Tinoco case*) (Great Britain v Costa Rica), 1923, at 377, 378)).

However, a State is obviously an abstract entity, which acts only through its organs. These organs are therefore automatically bound by all international obligations of the State, as can very clearly be seen from Article 4 SRA. Since, as pointed out above, courts are organs of the State, they are also bound by international law, regardless of whether the judges like it or not. They have thus the obligation to interpret their internal law in conformity with the international obligations of the State.

[*There is no information on whether expropriations have already been conducted and if yes what (and if) compensation has been paid. Therefore, it is not possible to analyse this potential violation here.*]

Consequently, Ruvi is prima facie responsible for a breach of an international obligation.

4. Circumstances precluding wrongfulness

No analysis of State responsibility is complete without analysing the circumstances precluding wrongfulness. However, in our case, none of these circumstances is applicable.

Therefore, we can conclude that Ruvi is indeed responsible for an internationally wrongful act, namely the violation of the AMR through the judgment of the High Court, especially its Article 15 and 16.

5. Consequences and conclusion

A very important first consequence is contained in Article 30 SRA, namely cessation of the act (a) and non-repetition (b). This means that the High Court of Ruvi should reverse its judgment (cessation of the violation, since as long as this judgment remains, the AMR is violated) and that Ruvi should make assurances that the law will be changed in order to avoid further violations (non-repetition).

In addition, it is well established in customary international law that every State responsible for an internationally wrongful act has an obligation to make reparations. This was already established by the PCIJ in the *Chorzów Factory* case (PCIJ, Judgment, *Case concerning the Factory at Chorzów (Claim for Indemnity)*, 1927, 21) and has been codified also in Article 31 SRA.

There are different forms of reparation (Article 34 SRA). Restitution (Article 35 SRA) means that 'something is given back' to the victim State. If this is not possible, or also just in addition, compensation (Article 36 SRA) is a possibility. This means financial compensation for damages. Finally, satisfaction under Article 37 SRA is also an option, which can, for example, take the form of a public apology by Ruvi.

In this case, the most appropriate form seems to be satisfaction (Article 37 SRA). As far as we know, there have been no financially assessable damages to another State and no possibility for restitution. Any damage to an individual national of a State (eg for a potential expropriation) would need to be addressed under diplomatic protection since it is only indirectly the State's right that is violated. The exact forms have to be negotiated by the States or decided by a competent court or tribunal.

Ruvi is internationally responsible for the violation of the AMR and has thus to make reparation.

Question 3: Is the ICJ competent to deal with the dispute?

1. Applicable law

We will apply the ICJ Statute and the UN Charter. According to Article 92 UN Charter, the ICJ Statute is an integral part of the UN Charter. Since both parties involved in the dispute, Ruvi and Jada, are original members of the United Nations, the UN Charter and consequently also the ICJ Statute is applicable.

In order for the ICJ to have jurisdiction to hear the case, three elements need to be established: personal jurisdiction, subject matter jurisdiction and consensual jurisdiction.

2. Personal jurisdiction (jurisdiction *ratione personae*)

Article 34 paragraph 1 ICJ Statute provides that only States can be parties to disputes in front of the ICJ. Both Ruvi and Jada are undoubtedly States. This is also confirmed by the fact that they are original members of the UN, since the UN is only open to States (Article 4 UN Charter). Therefore, the first requirement in order to satisfy this element is fulfilled.

Article 35 paragraph 1 ICJ Statute further provides that the ICJ is only open to States that are parties to its Statute. Yet, Article 93 paragraph 1 UN Charter declares that all members of the UN are, ipso facto, parties to the ICJ Statute. Consequently, since both Jada and Ruvi are members of the UN they are automatically also parties to the ICJ Statute and the second requirement for personal jurisdiction is fulfilled.

We can therefore conclude that the ICJ has personal jurisdiction to hear the case.

3. Subject matter jurisdiction (jurisdiction *ratione materiae*)

The ICJ is only competent to deal with legal disputes under international law.

The most often used definition of a dispute can be found in the *Mavrommatis Palestine Concessions* case (PCIJ, Judgment on the Objection to the Jurisdiction of the Court, *The Mavrommatis Palestine Concessions*, 1924, 11). There, the PCIJ said that a dispute was a disagreement on a point of law or fact between two persons.

Indeed, in our case two 'persons', namely Ruvi and Jada, do not agree on points of law, namely whether the AMR is still valid and whether Ruvi is internationally responsible. Thus, since these are disagreements on points of law, they are clearly legal disputes.

In addition, the disputes fall under international law, since they concern an international treaty, international treaty law and the international rules on State responsibility.

Consequently, the ICJ also has subject matter jurisdiction to hear the case.

4. Consensual jurisdiction (jurisdiction *ratione consensus*)

Even if the foregoing elements are all fulfilled, it is crucial that there is consent by the State parties to the compulsory jurisdiction of the Court. This has been confirmed by the ICJ itself, for example in the *Monetary Gold* case (ICJ, Judgment, *Monetary Gold Removed from Rome in 1943* (Italy v France, United Kingdom of Great Britain and Northern Ireland and United States of America), 1954, 32) as well as in the *East Timor* case (ICJ, Judgment, *Case concerning East Timor* (Portugal v Australia), 1995, paragraph 26). Normally, the matter of consensus is—unlike the two previous elements—not dealt with ex officio by the ICJ. But if one party contests the ICJ's jurisdiction (as is the case here), then the ICJ needs to assess whether there is the necessary consent to its jurisdiction.

Generally there are four ways of giving the ICJ jurisdiction: optional clause declarations, compromissory clauses, special agreements and *forum prorogatum*.

Optional clause declarations made under Article 36 paragraph 2 ICJ Statute only operate on the basis of reciprocity. This means that there need to be at least two States accepting the jurisdiction of the ICJ on this basis. Since here only Jada has made an optional clause declaration, this cannot serve as a basis of jurisdiction.

The AMR, on the other hand, contains in Article 85 a so-called compromissory clause, which can serve as basis of jurisdiction according to Article 36 paragraph 1 ICJ Statute. In Article 85 AMR, the parties agreed that 'All disputes on the interpretation or application of the present treaty can be brought to the International Court of Justice by unilateral application.' We have established before that the AMR is still in force. However, even if we had reached the opposite conclusion and had declared the AMR as invalid, its compromissory clause would still remain operational and could serve as a basis of jurisdiction. Otherwise, it would never be possible to have recourse to the ICJ to solve disputes on the validity or termination of a treaty where one party alleges its invalidity/termination and the other party contests this. The ICJ confirmed the continued applicability of the compromissory clauses, for example in the *Fisheries Jurisdiction* case (ICJ, Judgment on the Jurisdiction of the Court, *Fisheries Jurisdiction* (United Kingdom of Great Britain and Northern Ireland v Iceland), 1973, paragraphs 43–45).

In our case, Jada brought the disputes with Ruvi to the ICJ, thus by unilateral application. Therefore, consent to the jurisdiction of the ICJ can be based on Article 85 AMR, the compromissory clause. In fact, this compromissory clause can serve as a basis of jurisdiction for both disputes in question, ie the dispute on the validity of the AMR and the dispute on the violation of the AMR by Ruvi entailing its State responsibility. Both disputes are related to the 'application or interpretation' of the AMR and thus fall under its compromissory clause. The argument made by Ruvi contesting the jurisdiction of the ICJ on this basis has thus to be rejected.

Consequently, the ICJ has jurisdiction to deal with the case.

5. Admissibility

Ruvi makes an additional argument not related to the jurisdiction of the ICJ, but to the admissibility of the case. The difference between jurisdiction and admissibility is the following. Very broadly speaking it can be said that if there is no jurisdiction, then the ICJ can never hear the case. On the contrary, if the case is not admissible, the ICJ is just not competent to hear the case *now*, but might have been competent in the past or might be competent in the future.

In our case, Ruvi makes an argument related to the legal interests of third States. It says that since the dispute surrounds the AMR, to which also Barat and Chardun are parties, these two States also need to be parties to the dispute, since their interests will be affected by the interpretations of the ICJ. As seen above, consent to the jurisdiction of the ICJ is crucial. Yet, such a third party has not given its consent to the jurisdiction of the ICJ and thus the ICJ should declare the case inadmissible.

There are indeed a few cases where the ICJ declared a case inadmissible because of the legal interests of a third State. However, there is a crucial difference to be made.

The case is only inadmissible if the legal interests of this third State are the *very subject matter* of the dispute, when they are indispensable to solving the dispute. On the other hand, if the legal interests of a third State are only *affected*, this will not be a bar to admissibility. Indeed, in international law very often the legal interest of a third

State might be affected, be it because a multilateral treaty needs to be interpreted or also because the ICJ pronounces itself on some customary law rules. It is inconceivable that all these cases could be declared inadmissible. On the other hand, if the legal interests of the third State are the heart of the matter, this third State needs to have given its consent to the ICJ's jurisdiction and needs to have a chance to defend itself, which it can only do if it is a party to the dispute. Thus, in these cases the ICJ would declare a case as inadmissible.

For example, in the *Monetary Gold* case (ICJ, Judgment, *Monetary Gold Removed from Rome in 1943* (Italy v France, United Kingdom of Great Britain and Northern Ireland and United States of America), 1954, 32), the ICJ held that the legal interests of Albania, not a party to the dispute, were the very subject matter of the dispute and thus the ICJ could not continue with the proceedings. Similarly, in the *East Timor* case (ICJ, Judgment, *Case concerning East Timor* (Portugal v Australia), 1995, paragraphs 28–29), the ICJ declared that the case between Portugal and Australia could not be assessed without first addressing the question of why Indonesia could not have legally concluded the 1989 treaty. Thus, the legal interests of a third State (Indonesia) were the very subject matter of the dispute and the case had thus to be declared inadmissible. On the other hand, in the *Nicaragua* case (ICJ, Judgment on the Jurisdiction of the Court and the Admissibility of the Application, *Military and Paramilitary Activities in and against Nicaragua* (Nicaragua v United States of America), 1984, paragraph 88), the ICJ decided that the legal interests of third States (Costa Rica and El Salvador) were at most only 'affected' and that none of these States was 'truly indispensable' for the proceedings. Thus, the case was admissible.

In our case, Jada brings a case against Ruvi, among other things concerning the validity of the AMR. It is certainly true that the legal interests of Barat and Chardun will be affected, since any decision of the AMR will also affect them. Yet, there is nothing which would make these States indispensable for the proceedings and their legal interests are not the very subject matter of the disputes. Thus, their legal interests will at most be affected, which is not enough to bar the jurisdiction of the Court. In addition, if Barat and Chardun really consider that their legal interests will be affected in the case at hand, they can chose to request the ICJ to allow them to intervene in this case in accordance with Article 62 paragraph 1 ICJ Statute. Since the treaty under dispute is a multilateral treaty, parties in fact have the right to intervene in the proceedings if they want to (Article 63 ICJ Statute). However, if they decide to do so, the judgment becomes binding on the intervening State as well (Article 63 paragraph 2 ICJ Statute).

6. Conclusion

We can conclude that the ICJ is competent to deal with the disputes between Ruvi and Jada based on the compromissory clause contained in Article 85 AMR. The case is in addition admissible, since the legal interests of third States are at most only affected and are not the very subject matter of the dispute.

Suggested Solution—Case 7.5

Abbreviations used

APT = Agricultural Products Treaty
GA = General Assembly (of the United Nations)
ICJ = International Court of Justice
ICTY = International Criminal Tribunal for the Former Yugoslavia
ILC = International Law Commission
PCIJ = Permanent Court of International Justice
SRA = ILC Articles on Responsibility of States for Internationally Wrongful Acts 2001 (State Responsibility Articles)
UN = United Nations
VCLT = Vienna Convention on the Law of Treaties

Question 1: How does the APT apply between all the respective parties and is it still in force between them?

1. Applicable law

Concerning the applicability of the Vienna Convention on the Law of Treaties (VCLT), we have to consider two sets of important dates, namely the date of the entry into force of the VCLT for all the respective State parties to the treaty, and the date of conclusion (and not the date of entry into force) of the treaty in question. Article 4 VCLT—the non-retroactivity principle—provides that the VCLT is only applicable to treaties that have been concluded after the entry into force of the VCLT for the respective State parties.

In our case Sambu has ratified the VCLT on 27 November 1997. This is after the general entry into force of the VCLT on 27 January 1980. Therefore, according to Article 84 paragraph 2 VCLT, the VCLT enters into force for Sambu 30 days after the deposit of its instrument of ratification. Consequently, the VCLT enters into force for Sambu on 27 December 1997.

Conyza, on the other hand, has ratified the VCLT on 19 July 2001. In accordance with Article 84 paragraph 2 VCLT, the VCLT entered thus on 19 August 2001 in force for Conyza.

Pulica has signed the VCLT on 8 October 1999. Yet, it is clearly stated in Article 82 VCLT that this convention is subject to ratification. Therefore, only signing but apparently not ratifying the VCLT does not make Pulica a party to the VCLT, which is therefore not in force for Pulica.

The ATP has been concluded in 2003. However, at that time not all three State parties of the ATP were parties to the VCLT, since Pulica only signed but did not ratify the VCLT. Hence, Article 4 VCLT, the non-retroactivity principle as explained above, is not fulfilled and the VCLT as such is not applicable.

Yet, it is well established that most of the VCLT reflects customary international law in the matter of treaty law. The ICJ has confirmed this, for example in the *Gabčíkovo-Nagymaros* case (ICJ, Judgment, *Gabčíkovo-Nagymaros Project* (Hungary/Slovakia), 1997, paragraph 46). We will therefore apply the customary reflection contained in the VCLT. Any further reference to the VCLT should be read as referring to its customary reflection.

2. Reservation made by Pulica

Pulica attached a reservation to Article 9 APT to its instrument of ratification. Reservations are usually said to be unilateral statements made by States with which they seek to modify or exclude the application of a specific provision (see also Article 2 paragraph 1(d) VCLT). Since Pulica seeks to exclude the application of Article 9 APT, this clearly is a reservation. Any reservation changes the application of the treaty among the parties and has therefore to be considered carefully.

Admissibility

First of all, we have to ascertain whether or not the reservation is valid. The ICJ has declared in the *Case concerning Border and Transborder Armed Action* (ICJ, Judgment on the Jurisdiction of the Court and Admissibility of the Application, *Border and Transborder Armed Actions* (Nicaragua v Honduras), 1988, paragraph 35) that the regime of reservations contained in the VCLT is indeed a reflection of customary international law. Article 19 VCLT used as customary reflection indicates that reservations can only be made at the time when the State signs, ratifies, accepts, approves or accedes to the treaty in question. Furthermore, the reservation must not be prohibited by the treaty itself and it must be compatible with the object and purpose of the treaty.

In our case, Pulica indeed makes the reservation at the time when ratifying the ATP, thereby fulfilling the temporal element. Since the ATP itself is silent on the matters of reservations, letters (a) and (b) of Article 19 VCLT are not relevant. However, the reservation still has to be compatible with the object and purpose of the treaty (Article 19(c) VCLT)). The ATP is a treaty on the sale of wheat and sugar by Pulica to Sambu and Conyza. A reservation to its dispute settlement provision can hardly be said to be incompatible with an economic treaty. In any event, Article 9 ATP is not the only dispute settlement provision in the ATP. The ATP still allows for a dispute settlement in cases of disputes under Article 10 ATP. Therefore, since Pulica's reservation cannot be said to be incompatible with the object and purpose of the ATP, the reservation is admissible.

Opposability

Once the reservation has been declared admissible, it is then necessary to determine the opposability of the reservation—or in other words to determine the type of relationship between the reserving and the other States.

Article 20 paragraph 4(a) VCLT used as a customary reflection provides that the acceptance of the reservation by another State makes the reserving State a party to the treaty in relation to that accepting State. Without any acceptance (tacit or implicit under Article 20 paragraph 5 VCLT) a reserving State cannot be considered to be a party to the treaty in question, as is clearly provided in Article 20 paragraph 4(c) ('an act expressing a State's consent to be bound by the treaty and containing a reservation is ***effective*** *as soon as at least one other contracting State has* ***accepted*** *the reservation*', emphasis added). This is the new practice in relation to reservations adopted in the *Reservations to the Genocide Convention A*dvisory Opinion by the ICJ (ICJ, Advisory Opinion, *Reservations to the Convention on the Prevention and Punishment of the*

Crime of Genocide, 1951, 21–26). Prior to this, multilateral treaties required unanimous acceptance of reservations in order for the reserving State to become a party to the treaty in question.

Upon being informed about Pulica's reservation, Conyza declares that it accepts this reservation. Therefore, in accordance with the customary reflection in Article 20 paragraph 4(a) and (c) VCLT, Pulica is first of all a party to the ATP as such and is especially also a party in relation to Conyza.

Sambu, on the other hand, does not accept the reservation, but objects to it. According to Article 20 paragraph 4(b), an objection to a reservation does not preclude the entry into force of the treaty between the reserving State and the State making a so-called simple objection. A simple objection—as opposed to a radical or qualified objection—is the situation in which a State protests against a reservation but nevertheless does not indicate that there should be no treaty relation between the two States. This is the situation of Sambu: it protests against the reservation, but by stating at the same time that it is 'looking forward to the execution of the ATP' it clearly indicates its wish to enter into a treaty relation with Pulica. Consequently, Sambu is a simple objector in accordance with the customary reflection contained in Article 20 paragraph 4(b) VCLT.

Consequences

As stated above, reservations have consequences on the application of the treaty between the parties. These consequences are regulated in the customary reflection contained in Article 21 VCLT.

The customary law reflected in Article 21 paragraph 1(a) and (b) VCLT sets out the situation between the reserving and the accepting State: the consequence is that the treaty is modified to the extent of the reservation in its application between these two States. This means in our case that the ATP between Conyza (the accepting State) and Pulica (the reserving State) applies without Article 9 of this treaty, since Pulica's reservation accepted by Conyza has excluded the application of this Article.

Customary law contained in Article 21 paragraph 3 clarifies the situation between the simple objector and the reserving State. According to this, the provision to which the reservation relates does not apply between the two States to the extent of the reservation. This is a logical consequence, since by definition the objecting and the reserving State do not agree on the application of a certain provision. When there is no common ground of understanding there can also be no treaty rule applicable. Therefore, Article 9 ATP does not apply between Sambu and Pulica.

It is true that the final result in the application of the reservation for Sambu and Conyza is the same, yet the underlying reasons are entirely different. While for Conyza the non-application of Article 9 ATP results from Article 21 paragraph 1 VCLT, for Sambu this is based on Article 21 paragraph 3 VCLT and the non-existence of a common ground of understanding.

Between Sambu and Conyza, on the other hand, the consequences are regulated by the customary law reflected in Article 21 paragraph 2 VCLT: the treaty is not changed between all non-reserving States *inter se*. Therefore, between Sambu and Conyza Article 9 ATP is applicable.

3. Termination of the ATP

As a result of the destruction of its wheat and sugar production by the volcanic eruption, Pulica argues that the ATP could be terminated.

It has to be kept in mind that Article 42 paragraph 2 VCLT clearly provides that the grounds for termination of a treaty are enumerated exhaustively in the VCLT. The same applies for customary law, where no additional ground for terminating a treaty not contained in the VCLT can be found.

Having a look at the different provisions regulating the termination of treaties, two Articles might be possible.

The first one is Article 61, supervening impossibility of performance. It is the theory of force majeure which is contained in this Article. It can be invoked as a ground for terminating a treaty when there was a 'permanent disappearance or destruction of an object indispensable for the execution of the treaty'. However, when the destruction or disappearance is only temporary, the treaty can only be suspended. It is true that most of the wheat and sugar production of Pulica has been destroyed. Since the ATP was about selling wheat and sugar to the two other States, it could indeed be argued that they were 'objects indispensable for the execution of the treaty', since without them the ATP cannot work. The destruction by the volcano was an unforeseen event and there was nothing that could have stopped the destruction by these natural forces, thereby also fulfilling the necessary elements of force majeure. However, in any event the destruction of the wheat and sugar production is only temporary, since in a couple of years Pulica will be able to produce these two goods again. Consequently, under Article 61 VCLT used as customary reflection, it would in only be possible to suspend the ATP and not to terminate it.

However, it is also questionable whether it is really appropriate to apply Article 61 VCLT or whether it would not be more appropriate to apply Article 62 VCLT—fundamental change of circumstance. It is clear that almost by definition situations of supervening impossibilities of performances are situations where there have been fundamental changes of circumstances. What is, however, important is to ascertain the impossibility of the performance as such. In order for Article 61 VCLT to apply, the performance of the treaty must (for the time being) truly be impossible. The example most frequently given is the submerging of an island or the drying up of a river. Yet, when the execution of the treaty is not truly impossible but has only become very difficult and burdensome, this would not be enough to satisfy Article 61 VCLT but would rather fall under Article 62 VCLT. In our case, it is true that almost the entire wheat and sugar production has been destroyed, leaving hardly enough for Pulica's own needs. While this is a difficult situation, we can argue that it is still not completely impossible to execute the ATP. There are at least two possibilities, which are extremely burdensome and rather unreasonable, but which make the execution of the ATP possible. The first possibility would be to honour the ATP as well as possible and to export parts of the wheat and sugar needed for Pulica's own population. The second possibility would be for Pulica to buy wheat and sugar on the world market to deliver it to Conyza and Sambu. Admitteldy, Pulcia would lose financially in this exercise, since apparently the world market prices are above the agreed maximum prices in the ATP (and it can be assumed that with the shortage created by the volcanic eruption the prices will increase further) but Conyza and Sambu still would only pay the maximum prices agreed to in the ATP. These two scenarios illustrate that the execution of the ATP is not completely impossible, thereby not fulfilling the requirements under Article 61.

We have therefore to turn to a closer examination of Article 62 VCLT. The customary nature of this Article has been confirmed by the ICJ in the *Fisheries Jurisdiction* case (UK v Iceland) (ICJ, Judgment on the Jurisdiction of the Court, *Fisheries Jurisdiction* (United Kingdom of Great Britain and Northern Ireland v Iceland), 1973, paragraph 36). It has to be kept in mind that this Article has been very strictly construed (see eg the ICJ in the *Gabčíkovo-Nagymaros* case (ICJ, Judgment, *Gabčíkovo-Nagymaros Project* (Hungary/Slovakia), 1997, paragraph 104)). The strict application of Article 62 VCLT is also visible in its negative formulation ('may not be invoked … unless').

Under paragraph 1 of Article 62 VCLT used as a customary reflection, two cumulative conditions have to be satisfied in order to invoke a fundamental change of circumstances. First, the circumstances in question need to have been an essential basis of consent of the parties to be bound by the treaty. Second, the change in circumstances has as effect that the extent of obligations which is still to be performed under the treaty is radically transformed. (From this latter condition it is therefore clearly visible that unlike Article 61—supervening impossibility of performance—it is not impossible to execute the treaty under Article 62, but this execution can only be done under very difficult circumstances). In addition, the ICJ held that 'a fundamental change of circumstances must have been unforeseen' (*Gabčíkovo-Nagymaros* case quoted above) and that it made the obligations to be executed under the treaty more burdensome in such a way as to change radically the obligations to be executed under the treaty from what was previously agreed to (*Fisheries Jurisdiction* case quoted above).

In our case, first of all the change of circumstances relates to the non-existence of wheat and sugar, destroyed by a natural catastrophe. The existence of this wheat and sugar was obviously an essential basis of consent, since without their existence the ATP would never have been concluded at all. In addition, without the necessary wheat and sugar the extent of the obligations to be performed under the ATP is radically transformed. As argued above, while it might not be impossible to execute the ATP, it is very burdensome for Pulica, going well beyond what is required from this State in the ATP (namely either having to spend a fortune on the world market or having to starve its own population). Furthermore, the eruption of the volcano, which had been inactive for over a century, was indeed an unforeseen event as required by the ICJ. Therefore, all the conditions set out in paragraph 1 of Article 62 used as a customary reflection seem to be satisfied.

Yet, we also have to assess that the conditions in paragraph 2 are fulfilled. The ATP is not a boundary treaty, therefore Article 62 paragraph 2(a) used as customary reflection is not an obstacle to the termination of the ATP. Furthermore, letter (b) of the same paragraph provides that the Article cannot be invoked if the fundamental change of circumstances is a result of a breach of an international obligation by the party invoking the breach. However, the eruption of the volcano was a natural event not influenced in any way by the State of Pulica. Therefore, Article 62 VCLT seems to be applicable and Pulica can indeed invoke the termination of the ATP based on a fundamental change of circumstance.

Acquiescence

The customary rule contained in Article 45 VCLT provides that a State can no longer invoke a ground for terminating a treaty if it has either explicitly (letter (a)) or implicitly (letter (b)) acquiesced in the validity of the treaty. However, as soon as the natural catastrophe has destroyed the wheat and sugar production, Pulica argues for termination. Therefore, there is neither explicit nor implicit acquiescence.

Separability

If the conditions under Article 44 paragraph 3 VCLT, used as a customary reflection, are cumulatively fulfilled, then the treaty has to be separated. Yet, no specific clause is concerned but the whole treaty is affected by the fundamental change of circumstances. Therefore, the conditions under paragraph 3 cannot be fulfilled and the ATP is not separable.

Consequence

Consequently, Pulica can invoke the termination of the ATP. The consequence of termination is specified in the customary law reflected in Article 70 VCLT. Consequences of the termination of a treaty are *ex nunc*, meaning that the consequences take effect from now on and have no retroactive application. Termination means that the terminated treaty no longer needs to be performed and ends.

4. Conclusion

As seen above, the reservation made by Pulica is applicable and changes the relation between the three contracting States accordingly.

Furthermore, due to the destruction of its wheat and sugar production by the eruption of the volcano Gali, it seems possible for Pulica to invoke the termination of the ATP based on the customary reflection of Article 62 VCLT (fundamental change of circumstances).

Question 2: Is someone, and if yes who, internationally responsible for the attack on Sambu? Explain all the potential responsibilities of all parties involved. In case responsibility is found, what are the consequences?

1. Applicable law

In order to resolve the question on State responsibility we will apply the ILC Articles on Responsibility of States for Internationally Wrongful Acts from 2001 (SRA). These Articles are not a legally binding treaty, but they reflect customary international law and are thus applicable as such. The ICJ has confirmed the customary character of the SRA in numerous cases, such as the *Iran Hostages* case (ICJ, Judgment, *United States Diplomatic and Consular Staff in Teheran* (United States of America v Iran),

1980, paragraphs 56–92), the *Gabčíkovo-Nagymaros* case (ICJ, Judgment, *Gabčíkovo-Nagymaros Project* (Hungary/Slovakia), 1997, paragraph 47) and most recently the *Genocide* case (ICJ, Judgment, *Application of the Convention on the Prevention and Punishment of the Crime of Genocide* (Bosnia and Herzegovina v Serbia and Montenegro), 2007, paragraph 401).

In addition, we will also apply the UN Charter, to which all three States are parties since they are members of the UN.

Article 1 SRA provides that a State is internationally responsible for every of its internationally wrongful acts. Article 2 SRA sets out the two necessary elements for an internationally wrongful act. First, the act or omission must be attributable to the State in question; and second, the act or omission must constitute a breach of an international obligation of that State.

We have to deal with the potential responsibility of two States, namely Conyza and Pulica, for the attack on Sambu.

We will start with Conyza, since this case is rather clear cut.

2. Attribution

Article 4 SRA provides that the acts or omissions of any State organ—regardless of its function or character—is attributable to the State.

The army of a State is undoubtedly an organ of the State, since it is also the State that has the prerogatives of public powers. Consequently, all the actions of the army of Conyza are attributable to that State. Since the attack on Sambu was perpetrated by the army of Conyza, this act is clearly attributable to Conyza.

3. Violation

Before looking at the specific violation it has to be recalled that Article 12 SRA provides that there is a breach of an international obligation when a State does not act in conformity with what could have been expected from it under its international obligations. It does not matter whether this obligation is of customary or conventional origin.

In addition, Article 13 SRA provides that in order to amount to a violation, this obligation must have been in force for the State in question at the moment of the commission of the act.

Article 2 paragraph 4 UN Charter clearly prohibits the use of force against the territorial integrity of any State. Furthermore, Article 3(a) of UN GA resolution 3314 provides that 'any invasion or attack by armed forces of a State of the territory of another State' is an act of aggression and therefore prohibited under international law. By attacking Sambu with its army, Conyza has thereby clearly violated its international obligations under the UN Charter (but also under general international law since aggression amounts to a violation of a *jus cogens* rule).

Since Conyza was a UN member at the time of the attack, the obligation not to use force against any other State was clearly in force for this State.

Thus, there is in addition to attribution also a violation.

4. Circumstances precluding wrongfulness

No analysis of State responsibility is complete without having a look at the circumstances precluding wrongfulness. Nevertheless, it becomes quickly clear that such an aggression cannot be justified by any of the applicable Articles. Dependency on another State is not a circumstance precluding wrongfulness. In addition, since the prohibition of aggression is a peremptory norm of international law, this violation can in accordance with Article 26 SRA never be justified by a circumstance precluding wrongfulness.

5. The situation of Pulica

Before dealing with the consequences, let us have a look at the situation of Pulica.

It is true, as Pulica argues, that it was not its own army that attacked Sambu. Therefore, an attribution under Article 4 SRA is not possible. In addition, an analysis of the other Articles of attribution show that none really seems to match this situation. [*Article 8 SRA, for example, does not match the situation since Pulica, even though it practically orders Conyza to carry out the attack, does not have 'effective' control over the army of Conyza. Even though some consider the government of Conyza as a mere puppet of Pulica, there is no evidence in the facts that it is Pulica that trains, finances and controls this army. Thus, Article 8 SRA is not applicable.*]

Yet, Article 17 SRA provides that a State which directs and controls another State in the commission of an internationally wrongful act is also responsible for that act if the former State knew about the circumstances of the internationally wrongful act and if the act would also have been an internationally wrongful act if that former State had executed it alone.

It is known that Conyza is very much influenced by Pulica. Indeed, Conyza is seen by some as only a puppet of the latter. In addition, the secret service's reliable investigations have shown that Pulica has in effect ordered Conyza to attack Sambu in exchange for economic favours. While we do not have enough information to conclude that Conyza was coerced into attacking Sambu (Article 18 SRA), it seems to be clear that Pulica directed (or ordered) Conyza to attack its neighbour. In addition, calling it a puppet indicates that Pulica is indeed controlling Conyza to a certain extent.

Pulica knew very well what it was ordering Conzya to do and intentionally did so in order to distract attention from the termination of the ATP. In addition, such an attack on Sambu would also have been an internationally wrongful act if directly perpetrated by Pulica. Therefore, all necessary conditions of Article 17 SRA are fulfilled and Pulica is equally responsible for the breach of the international obligation contained in Article 2 paragraph 4 UN Charter (and also binding on it since Pulica is a UN member as well). None of the circumstances precluding wrongfulness are applicable either.

6. Consequences

A very important first consequence is contained in Article 30 SRA, namely cessation of the act (a) and non-repetition (b). This means that both Conyza and Pulica have to make appropriate guarantees of not repeating such attacks.

In addition, it is well established in customary international law that every State responsible for an internationally wrongful act has an obligation to make reparations. This was already established by the PCIJ in the *Chorzów Factory* case (PCIJ, Judgment, *Case concerning the Factory at Chorzów (Claim for Indemnity)*, 1927, 21) and has been codified also in Article 31 SRA.

There are different forms of reparation (Article 34 SRA). Restitution (Article 35 SRA) means that 'something is given back' to the victim State. If this is not possible or also just in addition, compensation (Article 36 SRA) is a possibility. This means financial compensation for damages. Finally, satisfaction under Article 37 SRA is also an option.

In this case, restitution does not seem to be possible since there is nothing to be given back. However, both compensation for the materially assessable damage and satisfaction (eg in the form of public apologies of both attacking States) seem to be possible forms of reparation. The exact forms have to be negotiated by the States or decided by a competent court or tribunal.

7. Conclusion

As argued above, we have concluded that both Conyza and Pulica are responsible for an internationally wrongful act, namely of attacking Sambu, thereby violating Article 2 paragraph 4 of the UN Charter.

Question 3: Is the ICJ competent to hear the case, and if yes, what is the basis of jurisdiction? Provide all the potential possibilities.

1. Applicable law

We will apply the ICJ Statute and the UN Charter. According to Article 92 UN Charter, the ICJ Statute is an integral part of the UN Charter. Since all three States involved in the disputes are original members of the UN, the UN Charter and consequently also the ICJ Statute is applicable.

In order for the ICJ to have jurisdiction to hear cases, three elements need to be established: personal jurisdiction, subject matter jurisdiction and consensual jurisdiction.

2. Personal jurisdiction (jurisdiction *ratione personae*)

Article 34 paragraph 1 ICJ Statute provides that only States can be parties to disputes in front of the ICJ. There is no doubt that Pulica, Sambu and Conyza are States. This is also confirmed by the fact that they are original members of the UN, since the UN is only open to States (Article 4 UN Charter). Therefore, the first requirement in order to satisfy this element is fulfilled.

Article 35 paragraph 1 ICJ Statute further provides that the ICJ is only open to States that are parties to its Statute. Yet, Article 93 paragraph 1 UN Charter declares that all members of the UN are, ipso facto, parties to the ICJ Statute. Consequently, since as stated above the three States are members of the UN, they are also parties to the ICJ Statute.

Thus, we can conclude that the ICJ has personal jurisdiction to deal with the cases in question.

3. Subject matter jurisdiction (jurisdiction *ratione materiae*)

The ICJ is only competent to deal with legal disputes under international law.

The most often used definition of a dispute can be found in the *Mavrommatis Palestine Concessions* case (PCIJ, Judgment on the Objection to the Jurisdiction of the Court, *The Mavrommatis Palestine Concessions*, 1924, 11). There, the PCIJ said that a dispute was a disagreement on a point of law or fact between two persons. What has to be shown is a positive opposition between two parties and not just an assertion that there is a dispute, as stated by the ICJ in the *South West Africa* case (ICJ, Judgment on Preliminary Objections, *South West Africa* (Liberia v South Africa and Ethiopia v South Africa), 1962, 328).

In our case, Sambu brought two disputes: one against Conyza and one against Pulica. They seem to deal with State responsibility issues as well as the applicability of the ATP. Certainly, there is a disagreement on the responsibility of Pulica concerning the attack on Sambu, as well as a disagreement with this State on the termination or not of the ATP. Both disputes turn on legal questions under international law.

As for the disputes with Conyza, this is more difficult, since Conyza usually does not say anything. This does not necessarily mean, however, that there is no dispute between Conyza and Sambu existing. The qualification by the parties of the existence or non-existence of a dispute does not matter. The determination of the existence of a dispute is an objective exercise made by the ICJ ex officio. This has been explained by the ICJ, for example in its Advisory Opinion on the *Interpretation of Peace Treaties* (ICJ, Advisory Opinion, First Phase, *Interpretation of Peace Treaties with Bulgaria, Hungary and Romania*, 1950, 74). Since at least the State responsibility issue seems to be a rather unresolved issue we can assume that the ICJ would indeed also find a legal dispute under international law here.

Consequently, we can conclude that the ICJ also has subject matter jurisdiction.

4. Consensual jurisdiction (jurisdiction *ratione consensus*)

Even if the foregoing elements are all fulfilled, it is crucial that there is consent by the State parties to the compulsory jurisdiction of the Court. This has been confirmed by the ICJ itself, for example in the *East Timor* case (ICJ, Judgment, *Case concerning East Timor* (Portugal v Australia), 1995, paragraph 26). Normally, the matter of consensus is—unlike the two previous elements—not dealt with ex officio by the ICJ.

But if one party contests the ICJ's jurisdiction—as is the case here—then the ICJ needs to assess whether there is the necessary consent to its jurisdiction.

Generally there are four ways of giving the ICJ jurisdiction: optional clause declarations, compromissory clauses, special agreements and *forum prorogatum*.

Here, a compromissory clause and optional clause declarations seem to be relevant.

Compromissory clause

A compromissory clause is a clause in a treaty providing for the jurisdiction of the Court in case of disputes surrounding the treaty. This is a basis of jurisdiction under Article 36 paragraph 1 ICJ Statute.

In our case, the ATP contains such a compromissory clause in its Article 9. It is true that we have concluded before that the ATP can be terminated. However, it is well accepted that the compromissory clause remains valid. This is logical, since the dispute is exactly on the question whether or not the ATP is terminated. Were the compromissory clause to be automatically terminated as soon as a State claims the treaty in question ends, then the ICJ would never be competent to hear a case about an allegedly terminated treaty. The continuing validity of compromissory clauses has in fact been confirmed by the ICJ in the *Fisheries Jurisdiction* case (ICJ, Judgment on the Jurisdiction of the Court, *Fisheries Jurisdiction* (United Kingdom of Great Britain and Northern Ireland v Iceland), 1973, paragraphs 43–45).

On the other hand, we have also concluded above that Pulica's reservation is valid and thus applies. Consequently, as seen above, the compromissory clause in Article 9 ATP does not apply between Sambu and Pulica. Therefore, the compromissory clause cannot serve as a basis of jurisdiction for the dispute between Sambu and Pulica, since Article 9 ATP is not applicable between them.

Yet, Article 9 ATP is applicable between Sambu and Conyza, since Pulica's reservation has not changed their relation *inter se*. However, it has to be kept in mind that this compromissory clause can only serve as a basis of jurisdiction for disputes relating to the application or interpretation of the ATP. Thus, this cannot serve as a basis of jurisdiction for the State responsibility issue between Sambu and Conyza. (And there seems to be no dispute between Conyza and Sambu in relation to the ATP.)

Optional clause declarations

Optional clause declarations are unilateral declarations made by States under Article 36 paragraph 2 ICJ Statute. According to these declarations, States consent to the ICJ's jurisdiction in relation to all disputes involving States having also such an optional clause declaration. Thus, the optional clause system is very much based on reciprocity.

Pulica argues that Sambu cannot base itself on its optional clause since the latter made this declaration only three days before bringing the case and Pulica had not yet been informed that Sambu had made such an optional clause declaration. However, this argument appears to be unfounded. First of all, the conditions contained in Article 36 paragraph 4 in relation to such optional clause declarations are clear: these declarations have to be deposited with the Secretary General of the UN and they will be valid from the moment of the deposit onwards. This is indeed the only clear moment in the process. Were it necessary to have first notified all other States concerning this declaration, then it would never be quite clear when this new declaration would be valid. Some States can be informed quicker, some States have a slower diplomatic and administrative machinery, so that it would be unclear from when on all States would be notified. Thus, it is only necessary to deposit the declaration with the UN Secretary General, as was done by Sambu.

In addition, any State such as Pulica having made an optional clause declaration accepts that the ICJ will be competent to deal with disputes in relation to States having also made such an optional clause declaration. The rights of Pulica were thus in no way violated, but it should have known that the system is based on reciprocity. Thus, as soon as one other State fulfils this condition, it can bring a case against Pulica.

In fact, the ICJ itself has accepted that it is not necessary that the defendant State is informed beforehand concerning the new optional clause declaration made by the State bringing a case against it (*Right of Passage* case (ICJ, Judgment on Preliminary Objections, *Right of Passage over Indian Territory* (Portugal v India), 1957, 146, 147)).

Thus, the argument made by Pulica against the application of the optional clause declaration by Sambu cannot be accepted.

In addition, the reservation made by Pulica to its optional clause declaration is not applicable in our case, since the disputes concern, on one hand, the termination of an international treaty and, on the other, the potential responsibility of Pulica for an internationally wrongful act. None has to do with international fisheries.

Since all three States have made optional clause declarations, they can serve as basis of jurisdiction for both sets of disputes: between Sambu and Pulica and between Samub and Conyza. In addition, none of the optional clauses limits the jurisdiction of the ICJ in any way. Therefore, they can serve as basis of jurisdiction for both the disputes on the termination of the ATP as well as the dispute in relation to the State responsibility issue.

5. Conclusion

The ICJ is competent to deal with the cases between Sambu and Pulica and Sambu and Conyza based on the respective optional clause declarations made by the three States. On the other hand, the compromissory clause in the ATP is not applicable due to Pulica's reservation and can thus not serve as a basis of jurisdiction between Sambu and Pulica.

Suggested Solution—Case 7.6

Abbreviations used

ICJ = International Court of Justice
ILC = International Law Commission
MET = Military Exercise Treaty
PCIJ = Permanent Court of International Justice
SRA = ILC Articles on Responsibility of States for Internationally Wrongful Acts 2001 (State Responsibility Articles)
UN = United Nations
VCLT = Vienna Convention on the Law of Treaties

Question 1: Is the MET in force between the two States? Address all the arguments made by the parties.

1. Applicable law

Article 4 VCLT—the non-retroactivity principle—provides that the VCLT is only applicable to treaties which have been concluded after the entry into force of the VCLT for all the respective State parties. Therefore, we have to analyse whether the VCLT entered into force for the two States in question before they concluded the treaty under discussion.

Mollugo is a party to the VCLT since its entry into force. Article 84 paragraph 1 VCLT provides that the VCLT enters into force 30 days after the deposit of the 35th instrument of ratification. Following these conditions the VCLT entered into force for these 35 States (including Mollugo) on 27 January 1980.

Farfa, on the other hand, has ratified the VCLT later, namely on 8 July 1999. According to Article 84 paragraph 2 VCLT, the VCLT enters into force for States ratifying it after its general entry into force 30 days after the deposit of their instrument of ratification. Consequently, the VCLT entered into force for Farfa on 8 August 1999.

The MET was concluded on 16 September 2010, ie well after the entry into force of the VCLT for the two State parties. Therefore, the non-retroactivity principle contained in Article 4 VCLT is fulfilled and the VCLT is applicable to the MET.

2. Invalidity due to restricted full powers

Mollugo argues that it is not bound by the MET since the full powers of its Foreign Minister Mr Lucidum had been restricted by a governmental decree.

Article 7 VCLT regulates the question of full powers for the purpose of acts in relation to the conclusion of treaties. Article 7 paragraph 2(a) specifies that Ministers of Foreign Affairs, due to their official function, do not have to present full powers in order to be entitled to perform 'all acts relating to the conclusion of a treaty'. Mr Lucidum was the Foreign Minister of Mollugo, sent on official mission to Farfa to negotiate the MET. It was therefore not necessary for him to present any full powers in order to negotiate, conclude but also ratify by signature the treaty in question.

Yet, at the same time nothing prohibits a State from limiting the full powers of its negotiators, including the Minister of Foreign Affairs. Therefore, Article 47 VCLT has also to be considered. This Article provides that the authority of a representative of the State to express the consent of the State to be bound by the treaty (ie to ratify) can be restricted. If this representative failed to respect this restriction, this *cannot* be invoked in order to invalidate the consent to be bound *unless* the restriction was communicated to the other negotiating party prior to the expression of consent.

In our case, there was indeed a decree by the government of Mollugo, restricting the authority of Mr Lucidum. While he could perform acts such as negotiating or signing treaties, he could not, according to this restriction, ratify treaties and thereby express the consent of Mollugo to be bound. However, this governmental decree was never communicated to Farfa. The Ministry of Foreign Affairs did not forward the decree and Mr Lucidum did not inform Farfa about it beforehand either, since he considered this limitation of his powers as a disgrace. Under these circumstances and considering that Mr Lucidum was a serving Minister of Foreign Affairs normally having all necessary full powers under Article 7 VCLT, it cannot be expected that Farfa asked for the production of full powers or inquired about any potential limitation. This is also clearly reflected in Article 47 VCLT, which provides that the non-respect of the restriction by the representative of the State cannot serve to invalidate the consent to a treaty, *unless* this limitation was communicated beforehand. Since, as seen above, this restriction was not communicated to Farfa beforehand, Mollugo cannot invoke it to invalidate its consent to be bound by the MET.

3. Invalidity due to the corruption of the representative of the State

One month after the signature of the MET Mr Lucidum finally confesses to the Vice-Foreign Minister that he was offered large sums of money and a villa at a fashionable seaside resort if he finally signed the MET.

Article 42 VCLT clearly specifies that a treaty can only be invalidated, terminated or suspended in accordance with the relevant articles contained in the VCLT. The grounds for invalidity, termination and suspension are thus exhaustively enumerated in the convention and there can be no further grounds found outside the convention. Looking at the different possibilities to terminate or invalidate a treaty, we can see that one possibility is Article 50 VCLT, corruption of a representative of a State.

Article 50 VCLT provides that if the consent of the representative of a State has been procured through corruption of this representative by another negotiating State, the consent to be bound by this treaty can be invalidated. During the negotiations, the representative of Farfa offered Mr Lucidum a lot of money and also a villa. These material gifts finally led Mr Lucidum to sign the MET. Offering someone money or other goods in order to procure his or her consent or goodwill clearly amounts to corruption and thus Farfa clearly has corrupted the Foreign Minister of Mollugo.

Consequently, Mollugo is entitled to invoke Article 50 VCLT—corruption of a representative of a State—to invalidate the MET.

In this respect it is important to clarify a slight confusion of terms. The President of Mollugo, when invoking the corruption of Mr Lucidum, talks about the 'termination' of the treaty. However, the corruption of a representative of a State is not a ground for termination but a ground of invalidity of a treaty. The distinction between termination and invalidity is important due to the different consequences. While under termination (Article 70 VCLT) the treaty ends *ex nunc* (from now on), invalidity (Article 69 VCLT) of a treaty has more severe consequences since it invalidates the treaty ab initio, ie from the beginning. The treaty is thus deemed never to have existed and acts performed under it become invalid, while acts previously performed under a terminated treaty retain their full validity.

By invoking corruption, the only possibility is thus invalidity and not termination of the MET.

Acquiescence

However, we first also have to determine whether Mollugo has lost its right to invoke the invalidity of the MET by either explicitly or implicitly consenting to its validity, as foreseen in Article 45 VCLT.

When considering whether or not there is tacit acquiescence by conduct (Article 45(b) VCLT), the time starts at the moment of the discovery of the facts leading to the invalidity or termination. It does not thus start at the moment when these facts were actually committed. Mollugo has half-heartedly executed the treaty for about a month. But as soon as the corruption of Mr Lucidum becomes known (which was not known before), Mollugo protests and declares the treaty to be terminated (which is supposed to mean invalidity here as explained above).

Therefore, there was no acquiescence in our case.

Separability

In addition, it has to be ascertained whether the affected treaty provisions cannot be separated in order to save the rest of the treaty. Separability is done in accordance with Article 44 VCLT.

Article 44 paragraph 4 VCLT provides that in the case of fraud (Article 49 VCLT) and corruption (Article 50), the 'victim' State entitled to invoke it can choose whether it wants to invoke the invalidity for the whole treaty or—if the conditions for separability under paragraph 3 are fulfilled—only for particular clauses. In our case, it seems clear that Mollugo wants to invalidate the whole treaty since it does not mention any specific clauses which should be separated.

Therefore, separability is not an option and Mollugo can declare the MET as invalid.

Consequence

As briefly mentioned above, the consequences of invalidity are regulated in Article 69 VCLT. Invalidity means that a treaty is void ab initio and it is deemed to have never produced any legal effects. Consequently, all the acts previously performed under the treaty become invalid, except if they have been performed in good faith (Article 69 paragraph 2(b) VCLT). Yet, Farfa had to be aware of the corruption of Mr Lucidum since it was its own act. Therefore, it cannot be argued that the acts previously performed under the MET (namely the first exercises) were done in good faith. Thus, all the acts performed under the MET, ie all the military exercises involving penetration into the territory of Mollugo, become invalid.

4. Conclusion

Mollugo can invalidate the MET based on Article 50 VCLT (corruption of a representative of a State), but it cannot invoke the governmental decree limiting the authority of its own Foreign Minister as a ground for invalidating the MET. It follows from the reasoning above that the MET is not in force between Farfa and Mollugo, and since it is invalid is deemed to have never existed.

Question 2: Can Farfa be held responsible for a violation of international law due to its military exercises, and if yes, what are the consequences?

1. Applicable law

In order to resolve the question on State responsibility we will apply the ILC Articles on Responsibility of States for Internationally Wrongful Acts from 2001 (SRA). These Articles are not a legally binding treaty, but they reflect customary international law and are thus applicable as such. The ICJ has confirmed the customary character of the State Responsibility Articles in numerous cases, such as the *Gabčíkovo-Nagymaros* case (ICJ, Judgment, *Gabčíkovo-Nagymaros Project* (Hungary/Slovakia), 1997, paragraph 47) and most recently the *Genocide* case (ICJ, Judgment, *Application of the Convention on the Prevention and Punishment of the Crime of Genocide* (Bosnia and Herzegovina v Serbia and Montenegro), 2007, paragraph 401).

In addition, we will also apply the UN Charter and customary law contained therein.

Article 1 SRA provides that a State is internationally responsible for every of its internationally wrongful acts. Article 2 SRA sets out that in order for an internationally wrongful act to exist, the act or omission must be attributable to the State in question and the act or omission must constitute a breach of an international obligation of that State.

2. Attribution

The acts we are analysing here are the military exercises of Farfa, partially held in the territory of Mollugo.

Article 4 SRA provides that all acts and omissions of organs of the State are attributable to the State: it does not matter what function or character or position this organ had, it only needs to have this status as an organ of the State according to the internal law of the State.

Normally, the military is undoubtedly considered to be an organ of the State, also because it is the State which has the prerogatives of public power. In our case nothing indicates that the military of Farfa would not be an organ of that State. Therefore, all acts of the military of Farfa, including the navy, the airforce and the ground troops, are attributable to Farfa.

3. Violation

Article 12 SRA explains that there is a violation of an international obligation when a State does not act in conformity with what is expected from it under its international obligations. Whether this obligation is of customary or conventional nature does not therefore matter.

In addition, Article 13 SRA specifies that there is only a breach of an international obligation if at the time of the alleged breach the obligation in question was in force for the State.

Article 2 paragraph 4 of the UN Charter clearly provides that the use of force against the territorial integrity of another State is prohibited. In addition, UN GA resolution 3314—which is to be seen as customary law and as a clarification of the UN Charter itself—declares in its Article 3(a) that any invasion or attack by one State against another one is to be seen as an aggression.

It is true that Farfa is not a member of the UN and is therefore not bound by the UN Charter. Yet, it is widely accepted that the prohibition to use force contained in Article 2 paragraph 4 of the UN Charter as well as the principle of sovereign equality contained in Article 2 paragraph 1 UN Charter are rules of customary international law and thus binding on all States. The ICJ has confirmed this customary nature, for example in the *Nicaragua* case (ICJ, Judgment on the Merits, *Military and Paramilitary Activities in and against Nicaragua* (Nicaragua v United States of America), 1986, paragraphs 187–192 and 202–209). In addition, as mentioned above, UN General Assembly resolution 3314 is also seen as part of customary international law and since it only clarifies other customary rules it can also be seen as binding via these rules.

In our case we can argue that by penetrating into the territory (including the airspace and territorial waters) of Mollugo with its military forces, Farfa has used force against Mollugo. This would thus constitute a violation of the customary rule contained in Article 2 paragraph 4 of the UN Charter, which is binding on Farfa since customary law is binding on all States.

However, it would in our opinion go a bit too far to declare that this was actually an aggression perpetrated against Mollugo. It is true that generally the theory of strict liability is accepted for the purposes of State responsibility. This means that, for example, the fact that a specific act violating international law was an accident does not exonerate the State to which that acts is attributable from responsibility. It is thus not necessary that the act was committed in bad faith to give rise to State responsibility. Yet, aggression is a very particular and grave act and care should be taken not to label everything immediately as aggression. It can be argued that for aggression it is not enough to simply violate the territorial integrity of a State, but that something more is needed such as an attack with the goal of destroying or invading the other State or parts of the other State. Were it otherwise, every small (and even accidental) border incident would have to be called 'aggression', which clearly seems to go too far.

In our case, Farfa had no intention of invading or destroying Mollugo. We are not even aware of any material damages caused by the military of Farfa. Thus, while penetrating with its military into the territory of another State without the latter's permission can be termed a use of force in violation of the prohibition to use force (and potential also a violation of the sovereign equality of States), it would go too far to call it an aggression.

In conclusion, we can say that there is indeed a violation the customary rule of prohibiting the use of force and potentially also of the principle of sovereign equality. Both violations are attributable to Farfa.

4. Circumstances precluding wrongfulness

However, no analysis of State responsibility is complete without the analysis of the circumstances precluding wrongfulness.

Looking at the exhaustively enumerated circumstances precluding wrongfulness in Chapter V SRA, it becomes quickly clear that the only potential possibility is Article 20 SRA, consent.

According to this Article, the valid consent of a State to the commission of a given act precludes the wrongfulness of that act if it stays within the limits of the consent.

It is true that under the MET it seemed that Mollugo actually consented to the military exercises of Farfa held in the former's territory. It also seems that Farfa did not exceed the consent given in these exercises. However, it is crucial to note that the consent has to be valid in order to preclude the wrongfulness. As we have seen above, the consent given in the MET was, however, invalid due to the corruption of Mr Lucidum. Therefore, no valid consent exists in our case and thus there is also no circumstance precluding wrongfulness applicable.

Indeed, as pointed out above, since under an invalid treaty all previously performed acts lose their validity, it cannot even be argued that the military exercises performed before the corruption became known and Mollugo invoked the invalidity of the MET are precluded from wrongfulness. On the contrary, all military exercises have to be considered as violations.

5. Consequence

Since there are no circumstances precluding wrongfulness applicable, Farfa is consequently responsible for an internationally wrongful act.

The first consequence is to be found in Article 30 SRA. This Article specifies that the responsible State has the obligation to cease the wrongful act (letter (a)) and to make appropriate guarantees of non-repetition (letter (b)). This means that Farfa has to stop immediately all military exercises in the territory of Mollugo. In addition, it has to give guarantees to Mollugo that without the latter's consent it will respect Mollugo's territorial integrity in the future, including when undertaking military exercises.

Furthermore it is well established in international customary law that a State being responsible for an internationally wrongful act has an obligation to make reparations. This customary rule was confirmed by the PCIJ in the *Chórzow Factory* case (PCIJ, Judgment, *Case concerning the Factory at Chorzów (Claim for Indemnity)*, 1927, 21) and is now enshrined in Article 31 SRA.

There are different forms of reparation (Article 34 SRA). Restitution, ie 'giving back' something that has been taken away (Article 35 SRA), does not seem to be appropriate here, since Farfa did not take anything away from Mollugo. Compensation (Article 36 SRA) might be a possibility, if there are any financially assessable damages.

Since we are not aware of any such damages, we cannot come to a final conclusion. In any event satisfaction (Article 37), eg in the form of public apologies, seems to be an appropriate form of reparation.

However, the specific form of reparation has to be determined by the two States through negotiations or has to be fixed by a competent court or tribunal.

6. Conclusion

As seen above, through its military exercises Farfa has indeed become responsible for an internationally wrongful act. There is no circumstance precluding wrongfulness applicable, since the consent given in the MET was invalid. Therefore, Farfa should at least make excuses as a form of reparation.

Question 3: Is the ICJ competent to hear the case, and if yes, what is (are) the basis of jurisdiction?

1. Applicable law

We will apply the ICJ Statute and the UN Charter. According to Article 92 UN Charter the ICJ Statute is an integral part of the UN Charter. Mollugo is a UN member and is thus bound by both the UN Charter and the ICJ Statute. Farfa is not a UN member. It is, however, a party to the ICJ Statute, in accordance with Article 93 paragraph 2 of the UN Charter. Thus, while the ICJ Statute is applicable between the two parties, the UN Charter is not. We will consequently apply the relevant customary international law reflected in the UN Charter.

Furthermore, where necessary we will also apply the MET.

In order for the ICJ to have jurisdiction to hear the case, three elements need to be established: personal jurisdiction, subject matter jurisdiction and consensual jurisdiction.

2. Personal jurisdiction (jurisdiction *ratione personae*)

Article 34 paragraph 1 ICJ Statute provides that only States can be parties to disputes in front of the ICJ. There is nothing in the facts that lets us suspect that Mollugo and Farfa are not States. Therefore, the first requirement in order to satisfy this element is fulfilled.

In addition, Article 35 paragraph 1 ICJ Statute further provides that the ICJ is only open to States that are parties to its Statute.

This is not a problem for Mollugo, since this State is an original member of the UN. Article 93 paragraph 1 UN Charter declares that all members of the UN are, ipso facto, parties to the ICJ Statute. Consequently, Mollugo is automatically also a party to the ICJ Statute and the requirement for personal jurisdiction contained in Article 35 paragraph 1 is fulfilled.

Farfa, on the other hand, is not a member of the UN and is thus not automatically a party to the ICJ Statute. However, according to Article 93 paragraph 2 UN Charter it is possible that non-UN members can become parties to the ICJ Statute. Farfa has made such a request in 1950, which has been accepted by the Security Council. In addition, Farfa also fulfils the necessary financial conditions posed. Therefore, Farfa is also a party to the ICJ Statute and therefore also fulfils Article 35 paragraph 1 of the ICJ Statute. [*And not Article 35 paragraph 2 ICJ Statute, since Farfa is, according to Article 93 paragraph 2, also a party to the ICJ Statute and thus not* another *State to which Article 35 paragraph 2 ICJ Statute refers.*]

Consequently, Farfa's argument that the ICJ is not competent to hear the case simply because it is not a UN member cannot be accepted.

On the contrary, we can conclude that the ICJ has personal jurisdiction to hear the case.

3. Subject matter jurisdiction (jurisdiction *ratione materiae*)

The ICJ is only competent to deal with legal disputes under international law, which can for example be inferred from Article 38 ICJ Statute.

The most often used definition of a dispute can be found in the *Mavrommatis Palestine Concessions* case (PCIJ, Judgment on the Objection to the Jurisdiction of the Court, *The Mavrommatis Palestine Concessions*, 1924, 11). There, the PCIJ said that a dispute was a disagreement on a point of law or fact between two persons. It is not enough just to claim that there exists a dispute, but a positive opposition needs to be shown in an objective determination done by the Court (see eg ICJ, Advisory Opinion, First Phase, *Interpretation of Peace Treaties with Bulgaria, Hungary and Romania*, 1950, 74).

Indeed, in our case there is a dispute between Mollugo and Farfa, since they do not agree on points of law, namely whether or not the MET is invalid, and there is also a dispute surrounding the potential responsibility of Farfa due to its military exercises performed in the territory of Mollugo. These disagreements turn on points of law (treaty law and the rules on State responsibility) and are thus legal disputes.

In addition, the disputes fall under international law, since they concern an international treaty, international treaty law and the international rules on State responsibility.

Consequently, the ICJ also has subject matter jurisdiction to hear the case.

4. Consensual jurisdiction (jurisdiction *ratione consensus*)

Even if the foregoing elements are all fulfilled, it is crucial that there is consent by the State parties to the jurisdiction of the Court. There is no compulsory jurisdiction of the ICJ as such without the agreement of the parties concerned. This has been confirmed by the ICJ itself, for example in the *East Timor* case (ICJ, Judgment, *Case concerning East Timor* (Portugal v Australia), 1995, paragraph 26) or in the *Monetary Gold* case (ICJ, Judgment, *Monetary Gold Removed from Rome in 1943* (Italy v France, United Kingdom of Great Britain and Northern Ireland and United States of America), 1954, 32).

Normally, the matter of consensus is—unlike the two previous elements—not dealt with ex officio by the ICJ. However, if one party contests the ICJ's jurisdiction—as is the case here—then the ICJ needs to assess whether there is the necessary consent to its jurisdiction.

There are four possibilities to consent to the ICJ's jurisdiction *ratione consensus*: compromissory clauses in a treaty, optional clause declarations in accordance with Article 36 paragraph 2 ICJ Statute, a special agreement or *forum prorogatum*. Only one possibility, namely the compromissory clause contained in Article 44 of the MET, seems to be relevant here.

It is true that we have declared above that the MET is invalid, which has also prevented its application as a circumstance precluding wrongfulness. Yet, it is well accepted that compromissory clauses in treaties that have been declared invalid (or terminated) remain valid. This is logical conclusion, since the dispute is exactly on the question whether or not the treaty in question—here the MET—is invalid. Were the compromissory clause automatically invalid as soon as a State claims the invalidity of a treaty, then the ICJ would never be competent to hear a case about an allegedly invalid treaty. In addition, the continuing validity of compromissory clauses has been confirmed by the ICJ in the *Fisheries Jurisdiction* case (UK v Iceland) (ICJ, Judgment on the Jurisdiction of the Court, *Fisheries Jurisdiction* (United Kingdom of Great Britain and Northern Ireland v Iceland), 1973, paragraphs 43–45). It has also to be kept in mind that only a minority of States has made optional clause declarations to consent to the jurisdiction of the ICJ and that for most of them the consent is based on treaties (special agreements or compromissory clauses in treaties). To exclude the applicability of compromissory clauses in the case where one party claims the invalidity or termination of a treaty would dangerously weaken the international dispute settlement system.

Nevertheless, it has to be clarified for which disputes this compromissory clause in the MET can serve as basis of jurisdiction. There are two disputes in our case: the dispute on the validity of the MET itself, and the dispute surrounding the State responsibility of Farfa due to its military exercises. Article 44 MET gives the ICJ jurisdiction for the 'disputes concerning the application or interpretation of the present treaty'. It is clear that on this basis the ICJ is competent to deal with the dispute on the validity of the MET, since this goes to the heart of the application of the treaty. In addition it can, however, also be argued that this compromissory clause also gives the ICJ jurisdiction for the State responsibility issue, since it is tightly connected to the application of the MET as well. Without the MET, Farfa would never have performed such military exercises and it is again the question of the MET's invalidity that essentially determines whether or not Farfa is responsible or can benefit from a circumstance precluding wrongfulness (consent). Thus, it can be held that Article 44 MET can serve as consent for both disputes.

In addition, Article 44 MET specifies that the dispute can be brought to the ICJ by 'any of the parties'. There are thus no further conditions such as prior negotiations. Mollugo, a pary to the MET, brought the case. Therefore, the compromissory clause in Article 44 MET can serve as basis of consent for the ICJ and we can thus conclude that the third requirement in order for the ICJ to have jurisdiction is also fulfilled.

5. Conclusion

The ICJ is competent to hear the dispute on the validity of the MET and the State responsibility issue based on the compromissory clause in Article 44 MET.

Suggested Solution—Case 7.7

Abbreviations used

CAT	=	Convention Against Torture and Other Cruel, Inhuman or Degrading Treatment or Punishment
Draft Articles	=	ILC Draft Articles on Diplomatic Protection, 2006
ICCPR	=	International Covenant on Civil and Political Rights
ICJ	=	International Court of Justice
ICTY	=	International Criminal Tribunal for the Former Yugoslavia
ILC	=	International Law Commission
PCIJ	=	Permanent Court of International Justice
SRA	=	ILC Articles on Responsibility of States for Internationally Wrongful Acts 2001 (State Responsibility Articles)
UN	=	United Nations
VCLT	=	Vienna Convention on the Law of Treaties

Question 1: Can Acero exercise diplomatic protection on behalf of Mr Alfred Mill and Ms Elisa Montana-Mill?

1. Applicable law

To solve questions of diplomatic protection we will apply the ILC Draft Articles on Diplomatic Protection from 2006 (hereinafter the Draft Articles). It is important to note that these Draft Articles are not a treaty and thus not legally binding as such. However, the ICJ has confirmed, for example in the *Ahmadou Sadio Diallo* case (ICJ, Judgment on Preliminary Objections, *Ahamdou Sadio Diallo* (Republic of Guinea v Democratic Republic of the Congo), 2007, paragraph 39), that most of the rules contained in the Draft Articles are customary and thus nevertheless binding on all States.

In addition to the Draft Articles we will also apply the CAT and the ICCPR in our answer. They are applicable since Carpinus is a party to both of these instruments.

2. Diplomatic protection—introduction

It is widely recognised that State sovereignty not only entails rights but also duties, such as the duty to protect foreign nationals from any violations of international obligations or rights. This was, for example, held in the Arbitral Award on the *Islands of Palmas* case by the single arbitrator Max Huber (Arbitral Tribunal, Award, *Island of Palmas case* (Netherlands, USA), 1928, 839).

In exercising diplomatic protection, the State of nationality of the injured individual takes up the case on behalf of the individual. Using a legal fiction, famously stated in the *Mavrommatis Palestine Concessions* case (PCIJ, Judgment on the Objection to the Jurisdiction of the Court, *The Mavrommatis Palestine Concessions*, 1924, 12), it is often said that in diplomatic protection, the State is actually protecting its *own* right, namely to see the rights of its nationals respected by foreign States. Yet, Article 1 of the Draft Articles no longer contains this legal fiction.

In any event, it has to be kept in mind, however, that exercising diplomatic protection is the discretionary right of the State and not a right of the individual concerned (see eg the ICJ in the *Barcelona Traction* case (ICJ, Judgment Second Phase, *Barcelona Traction, Light and Power Company Limited* (Belgium v Spain), 1970, paragraphs 78, 79) and a UK court in the *Abbasi* case (*Abbasi and Anor, R v Secretary of State for Foreign and Commonwealth Affairs & Secretary of State for the Home Department*, 6 November 2002, [2002] EWCA Civ 1598, paragraph 99)).

In order for a State to exercise diplomatic protection once it has decided to do so—as in our case Acero—three main elements need to be fulfilled: there must be a violation of an international rule with regards to foreigners, there must be a link of nationality and local remedies need to be exhausted.

3. Violation of an international rule with regards to foreigners

In order to satisfy this element, there needs to be a violation of a rule of international law, that rule must be owed directly to an individual (condition *ratione materiae*) and in addition that individual needs to be a foreigner (condition *ratione personae*).

Condition ratione personae

The injured natural or legal person must be a foreigner.

In our case, we are concerned with two persons, namely Alfred Mill and Elisa Montana-Mill.

Elisa is certainly a foreigner in Carpinus, since she is not a national of that State. Alfred, on the other hand, is a national of Acero and Carpinus. We will have to analyse these two nationalities in more detail below, yet seeing that Alfred is not exclusively a national from Carpinus we can prima facie assume that he could also be a foreigner.

Thus, we can consider the condition *ratione personae* as fulfilled.

Condition ratione materiae

There must be violations of international rules by the State and these rules must be directly owed to the injured natural or legal person.

In the *Diallo* case (ICJ, Judgment on Preliminary Objections, *Ahamdou Sadio Diallo* (Republic of Guinea v Democratic Republic of the Congo), 2007, paragraph 39), the ICJ held that these violations include also violations of fundamental human rights and are no longer limited only to the so-called international minimum standard of treatment. Human rights are indeed directly owed to the individuals, since they are directly protected under them.

In our case, there are several potential violations. In this regard, it is also important to note that for the purpose of an action of diplomatic protection it is enough to have a claim that these violations occurred. It is thus not necessary to prove that these violations occurred 'beyond all reasonable doubt'. This will be the task of the court or tribunal seized of the case.

Concerning Alfred, we can argue that there is clearly a violation of the CAT. The CAT, to which Carpinus is a party, prohibits torture by State officials or other persons acting in official capacity with the acquiescence or consent of the State. Alfred has been repeatedly tortured by police forces, which clearly are State officials. In addition, we can also find a violation of Article 7 ICCPR (torture) and Article 9 ICCPR (arbitrary arrest and detention). Alfred has been held in custody for months, apparently without formal charges against him, and his wife was not informed of his whereabouts. This prolonged incommunicado detention is contrary to Article 9 ICCPR.

As for Elisa, she too has been tortured in prison. Therefore, we can also find a violation of the CAT and of Article 7 ICCPR in her case. In addition, the fact that she has not been informed about the whereabouts of her husband for months could be seen as an additional form of (mental) torture. Furthermore, she was arrested without charges and has never been informed of the reasons for her arrest. Thus, this is also a violation of Article 9 ICCPR, prohibiting arbitrary arrest and detention.

In conclusion, we can say that Elisa and Alfred can both be considered as foreigners, who have suffered violations at the hand of Carpinus of rights which, as human rights, were directly owed to them. Therefore, the first element in order to exercise diplomatic protection—the violation of an international rule with regards to foreigners—is fulfilled.

4. Link of nationality

To establish this element, three points need to be checked: validity, continuity and opposability.

Validity

The nationality must be validly granted. It has to be kept in mind that the conditions under which a State grants its nationality to a person forms part of the reserved domain of the State. Thus, as recognised by the PCIJ in the *Nationality Decrees in Tunis and Morocco* case (PCIJ, Advisory Opinion, *Nationality Decrees Issued in Tunis and Morocco*, 1923, 22–24), the validity of a nationality is determined by national law. This condition is also codified in Article 4 of the Draft Articles.

In our case, Alfred is a national of Acero by birth. As nothing seems to suggest the contrary, this nationality is valid. This is particularly relevant, since it is Acero that wishes to exercise diplomatic protection.

Nevertheless, Alfred is also a national of Carpinus. According to the national law of that State, foreigners can acquire the nationality of Carpinus after having lived for three years in the same city in Carpinus and after successfully passing a test. Alfred has lived in Carpinus for more than three years and also has passed the test. Therefore, his nationality of Carpinus is also valid.

Elisa is a national by Betula by birth and this nationality is hence valid. Furthermore, she is also a national of Acero through marriage. The national law of Acero provides that its nationality can be transmitted by marriage. Since Elisa has married Alfred—a national of Acero—she has validly acquired Aceron nationality. Both nationalities are equally valid. The argument of Carpinus that the only real nationality of Elisa was her first one from Betula is therefore not acceptable.

Thus, the nationalities of both Alfred and Elisa are valid.

Continuity

Customary law reflected in Article 5 of the Draft Articles provides that the nationality of the State wishing to exercise diplomatic protection needs to exist both at the time of the commission of the alleged violation and at the time of presenting the claim of diplomatic protection.

In our case, Alfred and Elisa are nationals of Acero (which is particularly relevant since it has decided to exercise diplomatic protection on their behalf) well before the violations occurred and they are still its nationals now, at the time of the presentation of the claim.

The nationality of Betula (for Elisa) and of Carpinus (for Alfred) existed both at the time of the violation and at the time of the presentation of the claim. This is, however, less relevant since it is Acero seeking to exercise diplomatic protection.

Opposability

Finally, opposability has to be tested. This is particularly tricky in our case, since we have two different situations of double nationals.

In the case of Alfred, one State of his nationality (Acero) wishes to exercise diplomatic protection against another State of his nationality (Carpinus). Traditionally, it has been impossible for one State of nationality to exercise diplomatic protection against another State of nationality (see *Reparations for Injuries* Advisory Opinion (ICJ, Advisory Opinion, *Reparations for Injuries Suffered in the Service of the United Nations*, 1949, 186)). The reason was that both States claim sovereignty over their national and it is impossible to say that the sovereignty of one State has primacy over the other. Yet, recognizing that such nationals would virtually be without any protection on the international level and under the influence of the development of human rights, the practice has changed. It has been held in cases such as the *Mergé* case (Italian–United States Conciliation Commission, Decision No 55, *Mergé Case*, 1955, 247) and the *Esphahanian* case (Iran–United States Claims Tribunal, Award No 31-157-2, *Nasser Esphahanian (Claimant) v Bank Tejarat (Respondent)* (Case No 157), 1983, reproduced in *Iran–United States Claims Tribunal Reports,* Vol 2, 1983 (I), Grotius Publications Limited, Cambridge, 157, at 161–164) that diplomatic protection of one State of nationality against another State of nationality is possible if there is an 'effective' or 'predominant' link with the State wishing to exercise diplomatic protection. This solution has finally also been adopted in Article 7 of the Draft Articles. It is therefore not correct to say, as Caprinus does, that it is still impossible for a State of nationality to exercise diplomatic protection against another State of nationality.

The criteria to establish the existence of an 'effective link' have been set out by the ICJ in the *Nottebohm* case (ICJ, Judgment, *Nottebohm* (Liechtenstein v Guatemala), 1955, 22). Following this case we can look at elements such as habitual residence, family ties, usual centre of the life, but also time spent in one country.

Alfred has lived and worked all his live in Acero, except for the last three and a half years. He frequently travels back to Acero where his children live. His family ties, except to his wife, are still all in Acero. Together with his wife, Elisa, he plans to move back to Acero once her contract is terminated in a few years. Therefore, they have also kept their house there. It seems that the ties to Acero are stronger in the case of Alfred, since he lived there for such a long time and plans to move back in a few years. Carpinus is only a short 'stop' for business purposes. In addition, he has only acquired Carpinusian nationality because this was beneficial for him since he was working in one of its State companies. For all these reasons, it seems to be convincing to argue that the nationality of Acero is more effective in Alfred's case.

Therefore, we can say that Acero is entitled to exercise diplomatic protection on behalf of Alfred.

[*You can argue the contrary. You could say that even though Alfred has lived for a long time in Acero, what matters is his current habitual residence. This residence, as well as his work, is at present to be found in Carpinus. Furthermore, his family life too seems to be more established in Carpinus, since his wife also lives there, while their children living in Acero are already grown up and thus no longer share a common home. Current residency and work are very important elements for determining the effectiveness of a nationality. The 'frequent' visits to Acero can thus not deny that Alfred is clearly living and working in Carpinus. After all, he is coming back to Carpinus after every visit. All these elements lead us to conclude that the predominant nationality of Alfred is that of Carpinus. Consequently, it is not possible for Acero to exercise diplomatic protection on behalf of Alfred (see Article 7 Draft Articles.*]

The case of Elisa is easier, since she is not a national of Carpinus. There, one State of nationality (Acero) wants to exercises diplomatic protection against a third State (Carpinus). Even though in the past it was also necessary to establish an effective link in this case, this approach has been changed, as can be seen, for example, in the *Salem* case (Arbitral Tribunal, Award, *Salem Case*, (Egypt v USA), 1932, 1188). Consequently, no effective link requirement is incorporated in Article 6 of the Draft Articles. This is logical, since in this situation it is not two States of nationality having equal sovereignty over an individual that confront each other, but only one State of nationality against a third State. The fact that the injured individual is a double national does not change this, but it simply means that the two States of nationality could each exercise diplomatic protection (or even do it jointly).

Therefore, Acero is entitled to exercise diplomatic protection on behalf of Elisa.

5. Exhaustion of local remedies

The requirement of having exhausted local remedies codified in Article 14 of the Draft Articles is a well-established customary rule, which has, for example, been confirmed by the ICJ in the *Elettronica Sicula* case (ICJ, Judgment, *Elettronica Sicula SpA (ELSI)* (United States of America v Italy), 1989, paragraph 50) or the *Internandel* case (ICJ, Judgment on Preliminary Objections, *Interhandel* (Switzerland v United States of America), 1959, 27). The reason behind this rule is that a 'wrong-doing' State has to have the possibility to make a wrong right.

Alfred and Elisa bring their case to court in Carpinus, but all the courts seem to reject their case, including the Supreme Court. From the fact that their case is 'rejected' it seems that their case is not even treated by the courts, thus one could say that local remedies are not truly exhausted. However, there are five customary exceptions to the rule of exhaustion of local remedies, which are codified in Article 15 of the Draft Articles. Letter (a) provides that local remedies need not be exhausted when there are no reasonably available remedies. In this case, the courts reject their case on flimsy grounds before they even really consider it. Therefore, it can be said that there are in fact no local remedies reasonably available to Alfred and Elisa. Consequently, local remedies do not need to be exhausted and the last element can be seen as fulfilled as well.

6. Conclusion

Based on the foregoing reasoning, we can conclude that contrary to what Carpinus contends, Acero can exercise diplomatic protection on behalf of both Alfred and Elisa, since the three necessary elements are all fulfilled.

[*Or, if you concluded above that Acero cannot exercise diplomatic protection on behalf of Alfred: Based on the foregoing arguments, we can conclude that while Acero can exercise diplomatic protection against Carpinus on behalf of Elisa, it cannot do so on behalf of Alfred, since the latter's predominant nationality is from Carpinus.*]

Question 2: Is Carpinus responsible for an international wrongful act as alleged by Betula and is the action of suspending a commercial treaty taken by Betula in conformity with international law?

1. Applicable law

In this question, we will apply the ILC Articles on Responsibility of States for Internationally Wrongful Acts 2001 (SRA). These Articles are not a treaty but are binding as customary international law, as has been confirmed by the ICJ in cases such as the *Iran Hostages* case (ICJ, Judgment, *United States Diplomatic and Consular Staff in Teheran* (United States of America v Iran), 1980, paragraphs 56–92), the *Gabčíkovo-Nagymaros* case (ICJ, Judgment, *Gabčíkovo-Nagymaros Project* (Hungary/Slovakia), 1997, paragraph 47) and the *Genocide* case (ICJ, Judgment, *Application of the Convention on the Prevention and Punishment of the Crime of Genocide* (Bosnia and Herzegovina v Serbia and Montenegro), 2007, paragraph 401).

In addition we will also apply the CAT and the ICCPR to which the two States concerned, ie Betual and Carpinus, both are parties.

Article 1 SRA holds that a State is responsible for every of its internationally wrongful acts.

Article 2 SRA then defines internationally wrongful acts. For such an act, two cumulative elements are necessary: the act must be attributable to the State in question, and it must constitute a violation of an international obligation of the State.

2. Attribution

The acts in question here, mainly torture but also a violation of the right to security and against arbitrary detention, needs to be attributable to Carpinus.

Attribution is regulated under Articles 4–11 SRA.

Article 4 provides that every act of an organ of the State is attributable to the State. Thereby it does not matter which function or character this organ has: it simply must have this status according to the internal law of the State.

In our case, Elisa and Alfred were tortured by the police of Carpinus while in custody in that country. It is also the police or security apparatus that held them there without formal charges, and without giving any information about his whereabouts in the case of Alfred. It is the State that has the prerogatives of public power within its territory. Therefore, a police force is usually clearly considered to be an organ of the State in the sense of Article 4 SRA.

Consequently, we can find that the acts are attributable to Carpinus.

3. Violation

According to Article 12 SRA, there is a breach of an international norm if the State in question does not act in conformity with what is expected of it under international law: it does not matter whether the violated rule is a treaty or a customary law rule.

Article 13 SRA adds that in order to be a breach, the obligation must be in force for the State in question at the time of the commission of the offence.

Carpinus is a party to both the CAT and the ICCPR without any reservation, and these conventions prohibit the use of torture; Article 9 ICCPR provides also for the liberty and security of the person. In addition, the CAT provides for the criminalisation of acts of torture, which is clearly not happening in Carpinus, seeing that the claims presented by Elisa and Alfred are all rejected. Therefore, we can say that in conformity with Article 12 SRA, Carpinus did not act as had to be expected by a State party to the CAT and the ICCPR (ie ban and prevent torture, prosecute torturers, prevent violations of the right of liberty, etc). In addition, at the moment when the violations occurred, the CAT and the ICCPR were both in force for Carpinus, which has been a party to those treaties since 1990.

For the above reasons we can conclude that there is indeed a violation of an international norm and this violation is attributable, as seen above.

Consequently, Carpinus is prima facie responsible for an internationally wrongful act.

4. Circumstances precluding wrongfulness

No analysis of State responsibility is complete without looking at the circumstances precluding wrongfulness. However, none of these circumstances—set out in Articles 20–25 SRA—seems to be applicable in our case. In addition, Article 26 SRA is very important. This Article provides that nothing can preclude the wrongfulness of an act which is violating a peremptory norm of international law. Yet, it is well established that the prohibition of torture forms part of *jus cogens*. Thus, the wrongfulness of these violations in our case can under no circumstances be precluded.

As a result, we can conclude that Carpinus is definitely responsible for an internationally wrongful act.

5. Consequences

First of all, under Article 30 SRA Carpinus has the obligation to stop the violation (ie stop torturing) and to offer adequate guarantees of non-repetition.

Second, it is well established in customary international law that there is an obligation to make reparations (see the PCIJ in the *Chorzów Factory* case (PCIJ, Judgment, *Case concerning the Factory at Chorzów (Claim for Indemnity)*, 1927, 21) and Article 31 SRA). There are different forms of reparation (Article 34 SRA) of which financial compensation in particular (Article 36 SRA) and even more satisfaction (Article 37 SRA), eg in the form of a public apology, seem to be appropriate.

6. Measures by Betula

In order to determine whether the measures taken by Betula when suspending the commercial treaty are lawful countermeasures, we first have to assess whether Betula can actually invoke the responsibility of Carpinus.

Article 42 SRA determines when a State is an injured State and can consequently invoke the other State's responsibility. It is clear that the obligations violated under CAT and the ICCPR are not individually owed to Betula, and therefore Betula cannot be considered as an injured State under Article 42(a) SRA.

Letter (b) of the same Article provides that when the obligation was owed to a group of States or the international community as a whole, the breach must either (i) specifically affect the State invoking State responsibility, or (ii) the breach must radically change the position of all other States with regard to the further performance of the obligation.

It cannot be convincingly argued that (ii) is applicable, since the fact that one State party violates the CAT or the ICCPR does not change the position of the other State parties in such a way that they can decide to change their application or respect of the provisions of these treaties. Yet, it can be argued that Betula is specifically affected by the violation of the CAT and the ICCPR, since one of its nationals, Elisa, has been tortured. As explained above in the part on diplomatic protection, every State has the right that the rights of its nationals are respected abroad. Thus, we could conclude that Betula can indeed invoke Carpinus's responsibility as a specially affected State.

[*Alternatively, we can argue that none of the States is specially affected, so that the only possibility is Article 48 SRA, under which any State other than the injured State can invoke the responsibility of the violating State if the obligation breaches is (a) either owed to a group of States including that State and is established for the protection of a collective interest, or (b) the obligation breached is owed to the international community as a whole. Since as a norm of* jus cogens *the prohibition of torture is also a norm* erga omnes *and thus owed to the international community as a whole, Betula is entitled to invoke the responsibility of Carpinus under this Article.*]

In any event, it is necessary to check Article 44 SRA which provides that the responsibility of a State cannot be invoked if (a) the claim is not brought in accordance with the rules relating to the nationality of claims (if applicable), and (b) if the claim is subject to a rule of exhaustion of local remedies and such remedies have not been exhausted (if applicable).

However, Elisa is a national of Betula. As we have seen above, this nationality is valid and since Carpinus is not a State of nationality of Elisa any measure taken by Betula on behalf of its national is not problematic. Besides, the fact that Acero is already exercising diplomatic protection on behalf of Elisa is not necessarily barring Betula from taking action in a field other than diplomatic protection. Furthermore, the Draft Articles on Diplomatic Protection expressly allow States also to act jointly against a third State (Article 6), indicating that an action by one State does not prevent the other from taking action. Furthermore, concerning letter (b), we have established above that local remedies do not have to be exhausted since there are no reasonably available remedies in Carpinus. Therefore, we can consider Article 44 SRA as fulfilled and Betula can invoke the responsibility of Carpinus.

According to Article 49 SRA, countermeasures can only be taken to induce a State to comply with its international obligations (paragraph 1). Furthermore, paragraph 2 explains that countermeasures are limited to the temporal non-performance of an international obligation of the State taking those measures towards the violating State. In addition, all measures taken should be taken in such a way as to resume their performance of the obligation non-performed in the future (paragraph 3).

Indeed, the commercial treaty between Betula and Carpinus is an obligation of Betula towards Carpinus and its suspension thus fulfils the requirements of Article 49 paragraph 2 SRA. Furthermore, Betula has clearly stated that it suspends the treaty in order to bring Carpinus to respect the prohibition on torture, thereby satisfying Article 49 paragraph 1 SRA. Then, Betula only suspended the commercial treaty, which allows in accordance with Article 72 VCLT that the execution of the treaty can be resumed in future, thereby also satisfying Article 49 paragraph 3 SRA.

Article 50 SRA outlines obligations which can under no circumstance be affected by countermeasures. For example, it is not allowed to use force as a countermeasure or to violate any norms of *jus cogens* nature. Yet, the suspension of a commercial treaty does not fall under any of the prohibited categories of countermeasures and is thus lawful.

Article 51 SRA sets out that the countermeasures taken must be proportionate to the injury suffered, taking into account the gravity of the internationally wrongful act. In our case, the wrongful act—violating the CAT and the ICCPR by torturing—is graver than the suspension of a commercial treaty. It thus cannot be held to be a disproportionate measure and is consequently lawful.

Article 52 SRA deals with the procedure to be taken when resorting to countermeasures. In accordance with paragraph 1(a) the responsible State must first be called upon to respect its obligations and paragraph 1(b) sets out that the responsible State has to be notified of any decision to take countermeasures against it and negotiations have to be offered. Betula has indeed first called on Carpinus to stop torturing and honour its obligations under the CAT and the ICCPR. Carpinus, however, does not react. In addition, Betula informs Carpinus that it will suspend the commercial treaty. Therefore, Article

51 paragraph 1 is satisfied. However, it has to be noted that under Article 52 paragraph 3(b), countermeasures cannot be taken if the dispute is pending before a competent court or tribunal which can take binding decisions. Thus, if we can conclude under question 3 that the ICJ is competent to hear the dispute relating to Carpinus's State responsibility, then following Article 52 paragraph 3(b) Betula is not entitled to take countermeasures (ie has to resume the execution of the commercial treaty). However, until this question has been clarified and the ICJ has declared itself competent, Betula is lawfully entitled to suspend the commercial treaty as a countermeasure.

[*Following the alternative conclusion above that Betula is not a specially affected State but could invoke Carpinus's responsibility only under Article 48 SRA, we can hold that Betula is in accordance with Article 54 SRA nevertheless entitled to take countermeasures. The same reasoning on the lawfulness of the measures taken would then have to follow. Furthermore, it should be noted that under Article 54 SRA countermeasures can only be taken to achieve cessation of the breach and reparation in the interest of the beneficiaries of the obligation breached.*]

7. Conclusion

We can conclude first of all that Carpinus is indeed responsible for an internationally wrongful act as shown above. Secondly, our analysis has shown that (regardless of whether Betula is found to be a specially affected State or not) Betula is entitled to suspend a commercial treaty with Carpinus as a countermeasure.

Question 3: Is the ICJ competent to hear the disputes between Carpinus and Acero and Carpinus and Betula? Explain all the possible bases for jurisdiction.

1. Applicable law

We will apply the ICJ Statute, which is according to Article 92 of the UN Charter an integral part of the UN Charter. All three States are members of the UN, thus the Charter and hence also the ICJ Statute are applicable.

In addition, we will also apply the CAT, which is applicable between Betula and Carpinus, but not in relation to Acero, since the latter is not a party to this treaty.

In order for the ICJ to have jurisdiction, we need to establish personal jurisdiction, subject matter jurisdiction and consensual jurisdiction for both sets of disputes, ie between Carpinus and Acero and between Carpinus and Betula.

2. Personal jurisdiction (jurisdiction *ratione personae*)

Article 34 paragraph 1 of the ICJ Statute holds that only States can be parties to disputes before the ICJ. It is not in doubt that Acero, Betula and Carpinus are States. This can also be proven by the fact that all three are members of the UN, which according to Article 4 UN Charter is only open to States as members.

Article 35 paragraph 1 of the ICJ Statue further provides that the ICJ is only open to States parties to its Statute. Article 93 paragraph 1 of the UN Charter holds that members of the UN are, ipso facto, parties to the ICJ Statute. Since all three States in question are members of the UN, they are automatically also parties to the ICJ Statute.

Therefore, the two necessary elements to find personal jurisdiction have been fulfilled and the ICJ has personal jurisdiction in both sets of disputes.

3. Subject matter jurisdiction (jurisdiction *ratione materiae*)

The ICJ is only competent to deal with legal disputes under international law, as can be seen, for example, in Article 38 of its Statute. It would thus not be competent to hear a purely political dispute.

The most famous definition of a dispute has been made by the PCIJ in the *Mavrommatis Palestine Concessions* case (PCIJ, Judgment on the Objection to the Jurisdiction of the Court, *The Mavrommatis Palestine Concessions*, 1924, 11). There, the PCIJ held that a dispute is a disagreement on a point of law or fact between two persons. In addition, the ICJ held, however, that it is not enough to have a simple assertion that a dispute exists, but that a positive opposition has to be shown (ICJ, Judgment on Preliminary Objections, *South West Africa* (Liberia v South Africa and Ethiopia v South Africa), 1962, 328). This is an objective determination which is to be made by the Court, and not by the parties (see eg ICJ, Advisory Opinion, First Phase, *Interpretation of Peace Treaties with Bulgaria, Hungary and Romania*, 1950, 74).

In our case, the three States indeed do not agree on points of law, namely on Acero's possibility to exercise diplomatic protection on behalf of Alfred and Elisa, on Carpinus's potential State responsibility and on the lawfulness of Betula's action in suspending a commercial treaty. These are all clearly legal disputes. In addition these disputes are also taking place under international rather than national law. It is international law such as the customary law on diplomatic protection, the CAT and ICCPR (international treaties) and the customary law in the matter of State responsibility that govern these disputes.

Consequently, we can conclude that the ICJ also has subject matter jurisdiction in the disputes between Acero and Carpinus and Betula and Carpinus.

4. Consensual jurisdiction (jurisdiction *ratione consensus*)

If none of the States contests the jurisdiction of the ICJ at this point, the ICJ does not deal with this matter ex officio (unlike with the two other points above, which are always ascertained by the ICJ). However, since the journalist asked us about the competence of the ICJ on all possible bases of jurisdiction, we have to assess this last point as well.

Indeed, the ICJ has itself held, for example in the *East Timor* case (ICJ, Judgment, *Case concerning East Timor* (Portugal v Australia), 1995, paragraph 26) and in the *Monetary Gold* case (ICJ, Judgment, *Monetary Gold Removed from Rome in 1943* (Italy v France, United Kingdom of Great Britain and Northern Ireland and United States of America), 1954, 32), that consent to its jurisdiction is absolutely crucial in order for the Court to be competent to deal with the case in question.

There seem to be three possibilities in our case.

Optional clause declaration

The first possibility are the optional clause declarations under Article 36 paragraph 2 ICJ Statute. The optional clause system is a reciprocal system, meaning that both States need to have made such a declaration in order for the ICJ to be competent. Since Betula has never made an optional clause declaration, this cannot serve as a basis of jurisdiction between this State and Carpinus. But Carpinus and Acero have both made an optional clause declaration, which could thus potentially serve as basis of jurisdiction.

Acero has made this declaration in accordance with Article 36 paragraph 2 ICJ Statute without any reservation. Carpinus, however, has attached to its optional clause declaration a reservation to exclude from the jurisdiction of the Court disputes in which Carpinus's police, military or other security organs are involved. According to Article 36 paragraph 3 ICJ Statute, reservations to optional clause declarations can generally be seen as being admissible. Yet, following Article 19(c) VCLT a reservation always has to be compatible with the object and purpose of the treaty to which the reservation is made. It is obvious that any reservation limiting the jurisdiction of the ICJ is somewhat problematic since the object and purpose of the ICJ Statute is, among others, to allow the peaceful settlement of disputes by the ICJ. However, it has to be kept in mind that in practice the ICJ has been rather generous in accepting reservations to optional clause declarations (which are all per se limiting its jurisdiction). Therefore, Carpinus's reservation cannot be seen as necessarily more problematic than a reservation excluding, for example, fisheries issues. In addition, the reservation in our case is not a so-called 'automatic' reservation. Therefore, it is in accordance with Article 36 paragraph 6 ICJ Statute up to the ICJ to decide on its own competence and if necessary to declare the reservation as invalid. This step would, however, necessarily need an analysis of the continued validity or not of the optional clause declaration itself.

In light of the generous practice of the ICJ it seems to be most appropriate to accept Carpinus's reservation as valid. The ICJ is only competent to deal with disputes falling under the least common denominator between two optional clause declarations, as stated by the ICJ in the *Anglo-Iranian Oil* case (ICJ, Judgment, *Anglo-Iranian Oil Co* (United Kingdom v Iran), 1952, 103). Thus, in our case disputes 'in which Carpinus's police, military or other security organ are involved' are excluded from the ICJ's jurisdiction. The dispute between Acero and Carpinus relates to the possibility of the former exercising diplomatic protection on behalf of Alfred and Elisa. Since in order to be able to exercise diplomatic protection it is crucial to analyse the alleged violation, and since in our case the alleged violations such as torture have been inflicted by the police of Carpinus, it can be argued that the ICJ would be barred from dealing with the issue due to the reservation.

Following this line of argument we can conclude that the ICJ is not competent to deal with the dispute between Acero and Carpinus on this basis. There are, however, still other possibilities.

Compromissory clause

There is a compromissory clause in the CAT (Article 30 paragraph 1 CAT). Since

Acero is not a party to the CAT, this compromissory clause can only serve as a basis of jurisdiction between Betula and Carpinus. The State responsibility issue pending between these two States is directly linked to the application or interpretation of the CAT, which can thus potentially serve as a basis of jurisdiction.

According to this Article, an attempt should be made first to settle the disputes by negotiation, before submitting it to arbitration. In our case, Betula indeed tries to negotiate with Carpinus but they are unable to find a solution. Therefore, Betula suggests recourse to arbitration, which is also accepted by Carpinus.

Article 30 paragraph 1 CAT further provides that if within six months after the requests for arbitration has been made the parties are unable to agree on the modalities, any of the parties involved in the dispute can bring the dispute to the ICJ. In our case, eight months after the decision to have recourse to arbitration the States involved were still unable to set up the arbitral tribunal, mainly because Carpinus wants to included among the judges a person who is absolutely unacceptable to Betula. Carpinus is therefore entitled to bring the dispute to the ICJ, which is competent on the basis of Article 30 paragraph 1 CAT to hear the dispute between Carpinus and Betula.

Forum prorogatum

As a last (and maybe the best) possibility in this case we need to have a look at *forum prorogatum*. *Forum prorogatum* designates the situation when a defendant State upon being informed of the case brought against it immediately starts to argue on the merits of the case and does not contest the jurisdiction of the Court. The ICJ has recognised this as a valid basis of jurisdiction in numerous cases, for example in the *Corfu Channel* case (ICJ, Judgment on Preliminary Objections, *Corfu Channel* (United Kingdom of Great Britain and Northern Ireland v Albania), 1948, 27, 28) and the *Case concerning Certain Questions of Mutual Assistance in Criminal Matters* (ICJ, Judgment, *Certain Questions of Mutual Assistance in Criminal Matters* (Djibouti v France), 2008, paragraphs 60–95).

In our case, as soon as they are informed about the cases brought against them, both Betula and Acero start to present their arguments why in their opinion Caprinus has violated international law and do not contest the jurisdiction of the ICJ. This is thus a classical case of *forum prorogatum*.

5. Conclusion

The ICJ is competent to hear the disputes between Carpinus and Acero and Carpinus and Betula based on *forum prorogatum*. In addition, in the dispute between Carpinus and Betula Article 30 paragraph 1 CAT—the compromissory clause—can also serve as a valid basis of consent. Consequently, following the reasoning presented above, the ICJ is competent to hear the disputes.

Suggested Solution—Case 7.8

Abbreviations used

APMF	= Agreement on the Protection of Migratory Fish
FF	= Friends of the Fishes
ICJ	= International Court of Justice
ILC	= International Law Commission
PCIJ	= Permanent Court of International Justice
SRA	= ILC Articles on Responsibility of States for Internationally Wrongful Acts 2001 (State Responsibility Articles)
TF	= Tiny fish or *Piscarius pusillus*
UN	= United Nations
VCLT	= Vienna Convention on the Law of Treaties
VCDR	= Vienna Convention on Diplomatic Relations

Question 1: Is the APMF still in force between the parties or not?

1. Applicable law

First of all we have to determine whether the Vienna Convention on the Law of Treaties (VCLT) is applicable to the APMF. There are two relevant sets of dates that have to be analysed: first, the entry into force of the VCLT for all the State parties, and second, the date of conclusion of the treaty. The latter date must be after the former, in order to satisfy the non-retroactivity principle in Article 4 VCLT. This Article holds that the VCLT is only applicable to treaties which are concluded by States after the VCLT has entered into force for all these States.

Perca and Tinca are parties to the VCLT since its entry into force. The general entry into force of the VCLT occurred in accordance with Article 84 paragraph 1 VCLT 30 days after the deposit of the 35th instrument of ratification. Thus the VCLT entered into force (also for Percan and Tinca) on 27 January 1980.

The three other States have deposited their instruments of ratification later. Article 84 paragraph 2 VCLT provides that for States depositing their instrument of ratification after the entry into force of the VCLT as such, the VCLT enters into force 30 days after the deposit of their instrument of ratification.

Lampetra deposited its instrument of ratification on 6 August 1985. In accordance with Article 84 paragraph 2 VCLT, the VCLT thus enters into force for that State on 6 September 1985.

Salmo has ratified and deposited its instrument on 15 March 2000. Therefore, the VCLT enters into force for Salmo on 15 April 2000 in accordance with Article 84 paragraph 2 VCLT.

Finally, Esox has deposited its instrument of ratification on 30 January 2002. Following Article 84 paragraph 2 VCLT, the VCLT thus enters into force for Esox on 1 March 2002.

As stated above, the relevant date for the APMF is its date of conclusion and not its date of entry into force. Thus, the APMF is concluded on 6 February 2002. This is before the VCLT has entered into force for all State parties, since the VCLT enters into force for Esox only on 1 March 2002.

Consequently the VCLT is not applicable as such. However, it is well established that the VCLT reflects customary international law in the matter of treaty law. This has been confirmed by the ICJ, for example in the *Gabčíkovo-Nagymaros* case (ICJ, Judgment, *Gabčíkovo-Nagymaros Project* (Hungary/Slovakia), 1997, paragraph 46). Thus, we will apply the customary reflection of the VCLT and any references to the VCLT should be read as a reference to its customary reflection.

2. Termination of the APMF

Article 42 paragraph 2 VCLT, used as a customary reflection, holds that the grounds for terminating a treaty are listed exhaustively in the VCLT (and are thus also limited under international customary law).

Salmo, speaking on behalf of all State parties to the APMF except Esox, declares that the APMF should be seen as terminated, which Esox contests. Therefore, termination cannot take place in accordance with the customary reflection of Article 54 VCLT, since for this Article to be applicable it is necessary that all parties agree. This is clearly not the case here, since Esox does not agree.

In addition, we also know that the APMF has been concluded for an undetermined time and does not contain a clause of denunciation or withdrawal. Consequently, it cannot be argued that the parties intended to admit the possibility of denunciation, in accordance with Article 56 paragraph 1(a). Furthermore, the 'nature' of the APMF as an environmental protection treaty seems not simply to allow termination either (Article 56 paragraph 1(b). On the contrary, since the environment must be carefully protected, which takes a long time or is even an endless task, it would undermine the force of these treaties if it would be concluded that their 'nature' allows their termination. Thus, termination under Article 56 is not possible either.

Since we are dealing here with the situation where four States agree to terminate the treaty in consequence of a breach of the treaty by another State, the most appropriate customary rule applicable seems to be the one codified in Article 60 VCLT: termination due to a material breach of the treaty.

Article 60 paragraph 3 VCLT defines a material breach. It is either (a) a repudiation of the whole treaty not in conformity with the VCLT or (b) the violation of a provision which is essential for the accomplishment of the object and purpose of the treaty.

The object and purpose of the APMF is the protection of migratory fish, but especially the protection of the so-called 'tiny fish' (TF) in order to safeguard the aquatic ecosystems in the region (since the TF are vital for these aquatic ecosystems). Therefore, it is of the utmost importance that the threatened species of the TF are not fished in order to regain their normal population. Esox has started to fish the TF again, even though the fishing of the TF is prohibited by Article 5 APMF. Exceptions to this Article are only possible if the specifically established scientific committee declares that the TF can be fished again and allocates quotas to the participating States (Article 7 APMF). However, the scientific committee has never allowed the catch of the TF in the past years and has even stated that it would need an additional five to ten years to re-establish a balanced stock of TF and to allow fishing. Therefore, Esox by fishing the TF, has violated Article 5 APMF, which is essential for the whole purpose of protecting the TF, but also other migratory fish species and the aquatic ecosystem in general. Consequently, there has indeed been a material breach in this case (Article 60 paragraph 3(b) VCLT).

Article 60 paragraph 2(a) VCLT sets out that States other than the defaulting State can by unanimous agreement declare the treaty terminated either between themselves and the defaulting State (i) or between all the parties (ii). It seems that there is indeed unanimous agreement between the four States that have respected the APMF. From the statements made by Salmo it can be inferred that the agreement is to terminate the APMF between all the parties in accordance with the customary reflection contained in Article 60 paragraph 2(a)(ii) VCLT.

Since the APMF does not contain any provision in relation to termination as stated above, Article 60 paragraph 4 VCLT does not pose any problem to the invocation of the termination either.

Acquiescence

However, before drawing conclusions we have to check whether acquiescence can 'save' the treaty. In accordance with the customary reflection of Article 45 VCLT a State loses its right to invoke the termination of a treaty if it has expressly (a) or by its conduct (b) acquiesced to the continued valid application of the treaty. Yet, as soon as it becomes clear that Esox is continuously violating the APMF, the four other State parties meet and decide on the termination of this treaty. Therefore, there is no acquiescence present in our case, neither expressly, nor by conduct.

Separability

We also have to check whether a separation of the treaty in accordance with the customary law reflected in Article 44 could be a solution. From Article 44 paragraph 2 it is clear that in the case of Article 60 there is no mandatory separation but the issue of termination is regulated by Article 60 itself, which has already been assessed above. The parties to the APMF other than the defaulting State decided to terminate the whole treaty. There is thus no separability applicable here.

Procedure

Following the necessary procedure, termination can indeed be invoked—though the procedural aspects of the VCLT are commonly said not to reflect customary law. However, looking at the relevant Articles in the VCLT (Articles 65 and 67 VCLT), it is clear that some sort of notification of the termination must be made to the defaulting State in writing and that there must be a reasonable time accorded before the termination actually takes effect. We do not know whether in addition to the public announcement made a written notification is also sent to Esox, indicating moreover a date from which the AMPF will be terminated. However, due to the lack of information on this point, as well as the lack of protest from Esox in this regard, we can conclude that this is not an issue in the case. In fact, Esox only protests against the termination of the treaty in general, but not on procedural grounds.

3. Consequences

The consequences of termination of a treaty can be found in the customary reflection of Article 70 VCLT. The effects of termination are *ex nunc*, ie from 'now' on. This means that (after a specified date) the treaty no longer exists and the parties consequently no longer have any obligations under this treaty. However, unlike with invalidity, all the acts performed in conformity with the treaty before the termination of the treaty remain valid (Article 70 paragraph 1(b)).

4. Conclusion

We can conclude that Salmo, Perca, Tinca and Lampetra are indeed entitled to invoke the termination of the APMF based on a material breach of this treaty by Esox. A material breach is a ground for terminating a treaty under the customary reflection of Article 60 VCLT. The AMPF is thus no longer in force between the five States and Esox's argument that a treaty cannot be terminated because not all the parties to the treaty were involved has thus to be rejected.

Question 2: Is Salmo responsible for an internationally wrongful act as is claimed by Esox, and if yes, what are the consequences?

1. Applicable law

We will apply the ILC Articles on Responsibility of States for Internationally Wrongful Acts from 2001 (SRA). These Articles are not a treaty, but it is widely accepted that they reflect customary international law in matters of State responsibility. This has also been confirmed by the ICJ in several cases, for example the *Gabčíkovo-Nagymaros* case (ICJ, Judgment, *Gabčíkovo-Nagymaros Project* (Hungary/Slovakia), 1997, paragraph 47), the *Iran Hostages* case (ICJ, Judgment, *United States Diplomatic and Consular Staff in Teheran* (United States of America v Iran), 1980, paragraphs 56–92) and most recently in the *Genocide* case from 2007 (ICJ, Judgment, *Application of the Convention on the Prevention and Punishment of the Crime of Genocide* (Bosnia and Herzegovina v Serbia and Montenegro), 2007, paragraph 401).

In addition, we will also apply the Vienna Convention on Diplomatic Relations, to which all five States are parties.

Article 1 SRA provides that every internationally wrongful act of a State leads to the international responsibility of that State. Article 2 SRA then sets out the two necessary elements in order to find an internationally wrongful act: first, the act needs to be attributable to the State in question, and second, the act needs to constitute a breach of an international obligation of that State.

2. Attribution

The act for which State responsibility is alleged is the beating and shooting of the ambassador of Esox in Salmo.

It is clear that the FF is not an official organ of the State of Salmo in accordance with Article 4 SRA.

Article 5 SRA provides that the conduct of a person or organ which is not an organ under Article 4 SRA can nevertheless be attributed to the State if that organ is empowered by the law of that State to exercise 'elements of governmental authority'. Yet, in order for the act to be attributable under this Article, the person or organ must have acted in its capacity of 'exercising elements of governmental authority' at the time of the commission of the act. The FF is mandated under the law on fisheries of Salmo to monitor the different internal waters of Salmo and to punish anyone fishing there (since fishing is now prohibited in Salmo). With this, the FF takes over a task which has previously been exercised by the police. Thus, the FF is mandated under the internal law of Salmo to exercise particular functions of governmental authority (namely what the police previously did: controlling and punishing fishermen). In addition, at the moment when the ambassador of Esox was beaten and shot, the two members of the FF were acting in their official capacity (they were on patrol).

The acts of the FF are therefore attributable to Salmo and Salmo's argument that the acts were not attributable to it because the FF is a private organisation needs to be rejected.

Yet, under the domestic law of Salmo, the members of the FF are not allowed to use any physical force, least of all to carry a gun with them, but are under an obligation to call the police should they encounter any problems needing a physical enforcement action. By not calling the police, beating the ambassador of Esox (physical force) and carrying a gun with which the Ambassador is shot at, the two members of the FF have thus violated the internal law of Salmo and have acted ultra vires. This is also an argument made by Salmo. However, Article 7 SRA clearly provides that the conduct of an organ of the State (be this an organ under Article 4, 5 or 6 SRA) is to be considered an act of the State when the organ acts in its official capacity even if it exceeds its authority or contravenes instructions. The customary nature of this rule has been confirmed by an Arbitral tribunal in the *Youmans* case between the USA and Mexico (Arbitral Tribunal, Award, *Thomas H Youmans (USA) v United Mexican States*, 1926, paragraphs 12–14).

The limitation to this rule is that the organ in question must have acted in its capacity as an organ of the State at the moment of the fact.

In our case, both members of the FF clearly acted in their official capacity when they encounter the ambassador of Esox. Their acts are clearly ultra vires as explained above, exceeding their authority but also contravening instructions (not to carry guns, for example). Nevertheless, as established by Article 7 SRA the acts of the FF remain attributable to Salmo.

3. Violation

Article 12 SRA specifies that there is a breach of an international obligation if a State does not act in accordance to what is required from it under its international obligations. Whether these obligations are of customary or conventional nature does not matter. Article 13 SRA adds that in order to find a breach, the obligation in question must have been in force for the State in question at the time of the violation.

According to Article 29 VCDR, the person of the diplomat is inviolable and thus cannot simply be attacked. Thus, by beating and shooting the ambassador, the members of the FF have violated this provision. Since these acts are attributable to Salmo, it is thus responsible for this violation of the VCDR. Salmo and Esox are both parties to the VCDR. Therefore, there clearly is a violation of an international conventional obligation, which is in force for Salmo at the time the act occurs.

Thus, prima facie Salmo is responsible for an internationally wrongful act.

4. Circumstances precluding wrongfulness

Before making a final determination, it has to be assessed whether any of the circumstances precluding wrongfulness are applicable. However, a short look at these provisions in Articles 20–25 SRA shows that none of these Articles is applicable.

Consequently, Salmo is responsible for an internationally wrongful act.

5. Consequences

One of the first consequences is to be found in Article 30(b) SRA: Salmo should offer appropriate assurances to Esox that a similar violation will not occur again.

In addition, it is well established in customary international law that if a State is responsible for an internationally wrongful act, there is an obligation to make reparations. This has already been stated by the PCIJ in the *Chorzów Factory* case (PCIJ, Judgment, *Case concerning the Factory at Chorzów (Claim for Indemnity)*, 1927, 21) and is also reflected in Article 31 SRA.

There are different means to make reparation (Article 34 SRA).

Restitution (Article 35 SRA) is not appropriate here, since there is nothing that can materially be 'given back' to Esox. Financial compensation in accordance with Article 36 SRA might be an option, as well as satisfaction (Article 37). Satisfaction could, for example, include that the two members of the FF who attacked the Ambassador be punished and that Salmo publicly apologises. The exact form of reparation has to be determined either through negotiations between the concerned States, ie Esox and Salmo, or by a competent court or tribunal.

6. Conclusion

Salmo is indeed responsible for an internationally wrongful act and has to make reparations, eg in the form of compensation and/or satisfaction.

Question 3: Is the ICJ competent to hear the disputes between Salmo and Esox?

1. Applicable law

We will apply the ICJ Statute, which is according to Article 92 of the UN Charter an integral part of the UN Charter. Both Esox and Salmo are members of the UN, thus the Charter and hence also the Statute are applicable.

In order for the ICJ to have jurisdiction, three elements need to be established: personal jurisdiction, subject matter jurisdiction and consensual jurisdiction.

2. Personal jurisdiction (jurisdiction *ratione personae*)

Article 34 paragraph 1 of the ICJ Statute holds that only States can be parties to disputes before the ICJ. It is not in doubt that Salmo and Esox are States. This can also be proven by the fact that they both are members of the UN, which according to Article 4 UN Charter only accepts States as members.

Article 35 paragraph 1 of the ICJ Statute further provides that the ICJ is only open to State parties to its Statute. Article 93 paragraph 1 of the UN Charter holds that members of the UN are, ipso facto, parties to the ICJ Statute. Since both States in question are members of the UN, they are automatically also parties to the ICJ Statute.

Therefore, the two necessary elements to find personal jurisdiction have been fulfilled and the ICJ has personal jurisdiction in this case.

3. Subject matter jurisdiction (jurisdiction *ratione materiae*)

The ICJ is only competent to deal with legal disputes under international law, as can be seen, for example, in Article 38 of its Statute. It would thus not be competent to hear a purely political dispute, but at the same time political aspects of a legal dispute do not bar the ICJ from having jurisdiction *ratione materiae*.

The most famous definition of a dispute has been provided by the PCIJ in the *Mavrommatis Palestine Concessions* case (PCIJ, Judgment on the Objection to the Jurisdiction of the Court, *The Mavrommatis Palestine Concessions*, 1924, 11). There, the PCIJ held that a dispute is a disagreement on a point of law or fact between two persons. Furthermore, according to the ICJ in the *South West Africa* case, (ICJ, Judgment on Preliminary Objections, *South West Africa* (Liberia v South Africa and Ethiopia v South Africa), 1962, 328) it has to be shown that there is a positive opposition and not just a mere assertion of the existence of a dispute. Finally, it is the ICJ and not the parties which has to objectively determine the existence of a dispute (ICJ, Advisory Opinion, First Phase, *Interpretation of Peace Treaties with Bulgaria, Hungary and Romania*, 1950, 74 and ICJ, Judgment on Preliminary Objections, *Questions of Interpretation and Application of the 1971 Montreal Convention arising from the Aerial Incident at Lockerbie* (Libyan Arab Jamahiriya v United States of America), 1998, paragraph 21).

In our case, Esox and Salmo indeed do not agree on points of law, namely on Salmo's potential State responsibility and on the possibility to terminate the APMF lawfully. These are all clearly legal disputes. In addition, these disputes are also taking place under international rather than national law, since they are taking place between two States and are governed by customary international law in the matters of treaty law and of State responsibility.

Consequently, we can conclude that the ICJ also has subject matter jurisdiction in the disputes between Salmo and Esox.

4. Consensual jurisdiction (jurisdiction *ratione consensus*)

Unlike the two previous points, consensus is not checked by the ICJ ex officio. However, since in our case Esox contests the jurisdiction of the ICJ in making preliminary objections, the ICJ is obliged to make sure jurisdiction *ratione consensus* exists. Indeed, it has been held by the ICJ itself, for example in the *East Timor* case (ICJ, Judgment, *Case concerning East Timor* (Portugal v Australia), 1995, paragraph 26), that consent to its jurisdiction was absolutely crucial.

There are four different possibilities to give its consent to the jurisdiction of the ICJ: through optional clause declarations (Article 36 paragraph 2 ICJ Statute), special agreements (Article 36 paragraph 1 ICJ Statute), compromissory clauses in a treaty (Article 36 paragraph 1 ICJ Statute) and finally *forum prorogatum*, which is not expressly contained in the ICJ Statute but which is established in customary law and accepted by the ICJ (see eg ICJ, Judgment, *Certain Questions of Mutual Assistance in Criminal Matters* (Djibouti v France), 2008, paragraphs 60–95).

The only possible basis of jurisdiction in our case seems to be the optional clause declarations made by the parties in accordance with Article 36 paragraph 2 of the ICJ Statute. The optional clause system is a reciprocal system, meaning that both parties to a dispute must have made such an optional clause declaration in order to serve as basis of consent for the compulsory jurisdiction of the ICJ. Esox has made such an optional clause declaration. Moreover Salmo has made an optional clause declaration in conformity with Article 36 paragraph 2 ICJ Statute, but it has attached a reservation to its declaration, excluding from the jurisdiction of the Court 'disputes involving the matters of fisheries'.

From Article 36 paragraph 3 ICJ Statute it can be inferred that, in general, reservations to optional clause declarations are allowed. Since the ICJ Statute and the UN Charter both do not contain any rules specific to reservations, Article 19(c) VCLT applies (as customary reflection). That is, it has to be ascertained whether the reservation is compatible with the object and purpose of the treaty to which the reservation is made.

It is true that any limitation of the jurisdiction of the ICJ to solve disputes can be seen as problematic. On the other hand, saying that a reservation excluding one particular type of disputes only would go against the object and purpose of the much broader ICJ Statute might be going a bit far. In addition, under such a reservation as the one from Salmo, the ICJ is not precluded to decide whether or not it is competent to hear the case (Kompetenz–Kompetenz, in accordance with Article 36 paragraph 6 ICJ Statute), and thus could always reject the application of such a reservation. However, in the light of the fact that most reservations to optional clause declarations have been accepted in the past and were not seen to be particularly problematic, we can conclude that the reservation made by Salmo is valid.

It is important to note that it was Salmo that brought the case to the ICJ. Salmo did not invoke its own reservation, though this is now invoked by Esox, the defendant. Salmo argues that this is not possible. As stated above, however, the acceptance of the ICJ's jurisdiction under Article 36 paragraph 2—the optional clause system—is based on the principle of reciprocity. The ICJ held in the case of *Certain Norwegian Loans* (ICJ, Judgment, *Certain Norwegian Loans* (France v Norway), 1957, 22–27) that in order to have true reciprocity, one State is also allowed to invoke the reservation made by the other State to its optional clause declaration. Therefore, in the spirit of reciprocity, Esox is indeed entitled to invoke Salmo's reservation.

As stated above, a reservation necessarily limits the jurisdiction of the ICJ, since the Court's jurisdiction is always based on the least common denominator to be found between two optional clause declarations (on this see eg the ICJ's *Anlgo-Iranian Oil* case (ICJ, Judgment, *Anglo-Iranian Oil Co.* (United Kingdom v Iran), 1952, 103)). Therefore, in accordance with Salmo's reservation invoked by Esox, the ICJ will not be competent to deal with disputes involving the matters of fisheries due to lack of consent.

There are two disputes between Salmo and Esox. The first one relates to Salmo's alleged State responsibility due to the beating and shooting of the ambassador of Esox by members of the FF. The second dispute concerns the termination of the APMF.

Unfortunately, the APMF is a treaty dealing with fisheries, namely the protection of fish species, especially the TF, and it also contains rules on the catching of fish such as the TF. Since the ICJ does not have jurisdiction on disputes involving matters of fisheries due to Salmo's own reservation, the ICJ will have to declare that it is not competent to hear the case on the termination of the APMF.

On the other hand, the State responsibility issue is not directly concerned with 'matters of fisheries', but rather with a violation of the VCDR by Salmo. The fact that the 'triggering factor' for the violation of the VCDR has been an issue related to fisheries is irrelevant, since the dispute as such in this case does not relate to fisheries.

Therefore, the ICJ is competent to deal with the case of the alleged State responsibility of Salmo.

5. Conclusion

The ICJ is not competent to hear the dispute between Salmo and Esox on the termination of the APMF. The reason is that there is no consent to the compulsory jurisdiction of the ICJ in that case, due to a reservation made by Salmo, limiting the consent given under the optional clause declarations.

However, the ICJ is competent to deal with the dispute involving the State responsibility issue based on the two optional clause declarations made by Esox and Salmo.

Suggested Solution—Case 7.9

Abbreviations used

ECtHR = European Court of Human Rights
ERCT = Emission Reduction and Compensation Treaty
ICJ = International Court of Justice
ILC = International Law Commission
PCIJ = Permanent Court of International Justice
SRA = ILC Articles on Responsibility of States for Internationally Wrongful Acts 2001 (State Responsibility Articles)
UN = United Nations
VCLT = Vienna Convention on the Law of Treaties
VCDR = Vienna Convention on Diplomatic Relations

Question 1: How does the ERCT apply between all the parties after the reservations made by Tellur and is the ERCT still in force between the parties?

1. Applicable law

We have to ascertain whether the VCLT is applicable to the ERCT. First we have to check the dates of entry into force of the VCLT for the State parties to the treaty in question. Second, the date of the conclusion of the treaty, here of the ERCT has to be taken into account. Hence, the first dates (the entry into force of the VCLT for the States) need to be before the date of conclusion of the treaty in order to satisfy the non-retroactivity principle in Article 4 VCLT. Only if this Article is fulfilled is the VCLT applicable to the treaty under discussion.

Niob, Tellur and Osmium are parties to the VCLT since its entry into force. Article 84 paragraph 1 VCLT provides that the VCLT enters into force 30 days after the deposit of the 35th instrument of ratification of the VCLT. In accordance with this Article, the VCLT entered into force—also for Niob, Tellur and Osmium—on 27 January 1980.

Astat has ratified the VCLT on 7 January 1999, ie after its general entry into force. According to Article 84 paragraph 2, the VCLT enters into force for such States 30 days after they deposited their instrument of ratification. Therefore, the VCLT enters into force for Astat on 7 February 1999.

The ERCT was concluded on 28 October 2009, ie more than ten years after the VCLT has entered into force for Astat. Consequently, at the time of the conclusion of the ERCT, the VCLT had entered into force for all State parties to the ERCT, thereby fulfilling Article 4 VCLT. The VCLT is thus applicable in our case.

2. Reservations

Tellur has made two reservations to the ERCT.

A reservation is defined in Article 2 paragraph 1(d) VCLT. It is a unilateral statement made by a State 'at the time when signing, ratifying, accepting, approving or acceding to a treaty, whereby it purports to exclude or to modify the legal effect of certain provisions of the treaty in their application to that State'. Looking at the reservations made by Tellur, we can indeed say that these unilateral statements made at the time of ratification aim to exclude certain provisions of the ERCT, namely Articles 5 and 62. They are thus indeed reservations and need to be analysed as such.

Validity

First of all, we have to test whether or not the reservations are valid. For this, we will have recourse to Article 19 VCLT.

The ERCT is silent on the matter of reservations. Therefore, we only have to look at Article 19(c) VCLT—are the reservations compatible with the object and purpose of the treaty?

Article 5 ERCT specifies the precise function of the compensation scheme established by the ERCT and the method of calculation used. As stated in the preamble of the ERCT, the main aim is to reduce CO_2 and other greenhouse gases. Thus, as further stated in the preamble, the reduction and compensation scheme is to be seen as the 'heart' of the treaty. By excluding Article 5 ERCT, it is virtually impossible for the compensation and reduction scheme to work, since it is this Article that clarifies the functions of this scheme as well as the calculation method on which it is based. However, this scheme has been declared to be the main object of the treaty in order to reduce CO_2 and other greenhouse gases. Therefore, we have to declare that the reservation made by Tellur on Article 5 ERCT cannot be seen as compatible with the object and purpose of the ERCT and is thus invalid.

The other reservation on Article 62 ERCT (the dispute settlement clause) does not concern a matter which is at the heart of the treaty. Therefore, this reservation is compatible with the object and purpose of the ERCT and thus admissible.

The question, however, is what happens to the validity of the instrument of ratification when a reservation has been declared as inadmissible. This is not entirely clear in the legal literature. Some argue that the State only ratified the treaty because it had the possibility to make such a reservation. If the reservation is declared invalid, then the consent to be bound also falls, since without the reservation the State would not agree to be bound by that treaty. This is, for example, the position of Judge Lauterpacht (ICJ, Judgment on Preliminary Objections, *Interhandel* (Switzerland v United States of America, 1959, Dissenting Opinion of Judge Lauterpacht, 116–119). Others argue that the State wanted to be bound by the treaty; otherwise it would not have ratified it in the first place. Thus, the consent to be bound by the treaty is to be seen as more important than the reservation, and the consent could be separated from the invalid reservation and remain valid on its own. This would be supported for example by the Dissenting Opinion of Judge Klaestad also in the *Interhandel* case (ICJ, Judgment on Preliminary Objections, *Interhandel* (Switzerland v United States of America), 1959, Dissenting Opinion of Judge Klaestad, 76–78). The latter approach has also been taken by the European Court of Human Rights in the *Bellilos v Switzerland* case (ECtHR, *Belilos v Switzerland*, Judgment, Application No 10328/83, 29 April 1988, paragraphs 38–60), where the ECtHR held that despite the fact that a reservation by Switzerland was declared inadmissible, Switzerland remained bound by the European Convention on Human Rights.

[*There are thus two possible ways to argue: either Tellur's instrument of ratification is invalid due to the invalid reservation, or the instrument of ratification and the invalid reservation can be separated and the former remains in force. You should after a short theoretical explanation of the two legal possibilities take a position and provide your arguments why this solution is, in this case, more convincing.*]

In our case, it seems that Tellur actually wanted to become a party to the ERCT since it was concerned about global warming like the other States. In addition, only one of the two reservations made by Tellur is declared inadmissible. Furthermore, in the interest of protecting treaty relations it is more beneficial to accept that Tellur's consent to be bound remains valid. For all those reasons, we can consider that Tellur remains bound by the ERCT. We can thus proceed to the opposability of the remaining valid reservation against Article 62 ERCT.

[*Or you can argue: In our case, we do not know whether one of the reservations made by Tellur was especially important to this State, and therefore the fact that only one has been declared invalid is not necessarily relevant. Furthermore, it is clear that Tellur's consent to be bound by the ERCT has to be read together with the two reservations, since this State made these reservations deliberately and was apparently only ready to ratify the ERCT when issuing such reservations. By declaring one reservation as invalid, Tellur's consent to be bound is no longer its original consent and has thus to be declared as no longer existing.*

If this is your conclusion, then you can skip the remaining analysis of the reservations, since Tellur would not be a party to the ERCT at all and thus both of its reservations would no longer be relevant.]

Opposability

The issue of opposability is dealt with in Article 20 VCLT. The three States other than the reserving State each react in a different manner.

Article 20 paragraph 4(a) VCLT provides that the acceptance of a reservation by a State makes the reserving State a party to that treaty in relation to the accepting State. This Article thus applies to Osmium, which has accepted all the reservations made by Tellur. Yet, because the reservation to Article 5 ERCT is inadmissible, we should no longer consider it. Article 20 paragraph 4(c) VCLT specifies that a reserving State can only be considered to be a State party to the treaty if at least one other State has accepted its reservation. Thus, the acceptance of Osmium has the effect of making Tellur's consent to be bound by the ERCT effective.

[*The following point could optionally be discussed in relation to Osmium's acceptance. It is still unclear in international law whether States can actually accept invalid reservations—as Osmium does—and thus make the reserving State a party to the treaty. One possibility would be to say that the VCLT provides that invalid reservations are not admissible and thus they can never be accepted. Another position could be to say that States are free to enter into treaty relations, thus they are also free to accept invalid reservations (at least if they are not expressly prohibited by the treaty). It has, however, to be recognised that this later position would somewhat weaken Article 19 VCLT. Here only one reservation is invalid, but Osmium accepts both (and thus makes Tellur a party to the ERCT). The big question is thus whether this would in any way 'invalidate' Osmium's acceptance, since one of the reservations has been declared not admissible. There is no clear answer and you should provide your own arguments on this based on the two positions above.*]

Astat, on the other hand, has objected to the reservation made by Tellur. It has not, however, expressed its intention not to be bound by the ERCT in relation to Tellur. Astat has consequently made a simple objection and there will still be a treaty relation between it and Tellur. The situation of the simple objector is governed by Article 20 paragraph 4(b) VCLT.

Yet, Article 20 paragraph 4(b) *in fine* provides for the radical or qualified objector. This is a State that not only objects to the reservations, but in addition expresses its will not to enter into a treaty relation with the reserving State in this case. Niob has made such a radical objection by saying that it preferred not to have anything to do with Tellur in relation to the ERCT.

Consequences

Between Tellur and Osmium (the accepting State), the situation is regulated by Article 21 paragraph 1(a) and (b) VCLT. This means that the ERCT is changed for both the reserving and the accepting State, ie Article 62 ERCT does not apply between these two States. This result is due to the application of the reservation: Tellur did not want Article 62 to be applicable and Osmium agreed to this in its relation with Tellur.

Between Tellur and Astat (the simple objector), it is Article 21 paragraph 3 VCLT which is applicable. Under this rule, the provision to which the reservation relates does not apply between the reserving and the simple objecting State. This means that the ERCT applies without Article 62 between Tellur and Astat. It is true that this is the same result as above between Tellur and Osmium, but, unlike above, this form of application results from the application of Article 21 paragraph 3 VCLT and not from the application of the reservation.

Between Tellur and Niob (the radical objector), however, there is no treaty relation at all. This is clear from Article 20 paragraph 4(b) *in fine*, but also from the fact that no situation between the reserving State and the radical objector is contained in Article 21 VCLT (Article 21 VCLT *a contrario*).

The relationship between the non-reserving States, ie Osmium, Astat and Niob *inter se*, is governed by Article 21 paragraph 2 VCLT. The ERCT is not changed between these States, and thus Article 62 ERCT applies between these States.

3. Invalidity

Niob alleges that the ERCT is invalid. To justify its argument it invokes a paper published in *Science* which has discovered a scientific error in the method of calculation normally used for compensation and reduction of greenhouse gases which has also been used in Article 5 of the ERCT.

Under Article 48 VCLT, an error can indeed be a ground for invalidating a treaty.

In order to be able to invoke Article 48 VCLT, it has to be shown that the error relates to a fact or situation which was assumed by the State to exist at the time of the conclusion of the treaty. In addition, it is necessary that this fact or situation was for that State an essential basis of consent to be bound by the treaty.

A scientific error, as in our case, indeed relates to a fact that was assumed to exist at the time the ERCT was concluded. The calculation method was widely accepted and generally used and so far no one had noticed that it contained a scientific error but all assumed that this method would be correct. In addition, Niob was for a long time sceptical concerning the ERCT and was only ready to sign it when it saw the detailed calculation method contained in Article 5. Thus, this method, which is now based on a scientific error, was indeed an essential basis for Niob's consent.

Paragraph 2 of Article 48 VCLT indicates that States which contributed to the error, or which should have been aware of such a possible error, cannot invoke error in order to invalidate the treaty. However, the calculation method was well established and widely used. There was thus no particular reason why Niob or any other State should have suspected that it contained an error. Furthermore, Niob did obviously not contribute to the error, since the calculation method was not established by this State but was a generally available and widely used scientific formula.

Therefore, it seems that Niob can indeed invoke Article 48 VCLT in order to invalidate the ERCT.

Acquiescence

Under Article 45 VCLT it is possible to 'save' the treaty when the State invoking the invalidity has either explicitly or through its conduct acquiesced to the continued valid application of the treaty in question. However, as soon as Niob is aware of the paper in *Science*, it invokes the invalidity. Therefore, it cannot be argued that it acquiesced.

Separability

In addition, separability under Article 44 VCLT does not seem to be possible either. Under Article 44 paragraph 3 separability is mandatory if all three elements are fulfilled. Yet, it is impossible to separate Article 5 out of the ERCT, since the further application of the treaty without the regulation of the compensation scheme would not make any sense (Article 44 paragraph 3(a) and also (c)). We do not know whether Article 5 ERCT was also an essential basis of consent for the other parties (Article 44 paragraph 3(b)), but since all three conditions in paragraph 3 must be cumulatively fulfilled, separability is not possible.

Consequently, Niob is entitled to invoke the invalidity of the ERCT based on Article 48 ERCT.

Consequences

The consequences of invalidity are specified in Article 69 VCLT. The treaty is void ab initio and is deemed never to have produced any legal effects. All the acts already performed will become invalid, except those acts performed in good faith (Article 69 paragraph 2(b)). This will probably apply to all acts in our case: none of the acts were performed in bad faith, since none of the State parties knew there was an error.

In accordance with Article 69 paragraph 4, Niob can thus invalidate the ERCT between itself and the three other parties to the ERCT. However, it cannot invalidate the ERCT between those States *inter se*, which seem—judging from their reaction to Niob's announcement—rather inclined to keep the treaty.

4. Conclusion

Only the reservation to Article 62 ERCT is admissible and changes the treaty relations between the reserving State Tellur and the other States accordingly as described above. It does not, however, change the treaty relation between the three non-reserving States *inter se*.

In addition, Niob is entitled to invoke the invalidity of the ERCT based on Article 48—error. However, it can only invalidate the ERCT between itself and the other three States and not between the other three States *inter se*.

Question 2: Did Tellur and/or Niob breach international law and engage their international responsibility by the actions of their armies? If yes, what are the consequences?

1. Applicable law

We will apply the ILC Articles on Responsibility of States for Internationally Wrongful Acts from 2001 (SRA). These Articles are not a treaty, but it is widely accepted that they reflect customary international law in matters of State responsibility. This has been confirmed by the ICJ in several cases, for example the *Gabčíkovo-Nagymaros* case (ICJ, Judgment, *Gabčíkovo-Nagymaros Project* (Hungary/Slovakia), 1997, paragraph 47), the *Iran Hostages* case (ICJ, Judgment, *United States Diplomatic and Consular Staff in Teheran* (United States of America v Iran), 1980, paragraphs 56–92) and most recently in the *Genocide* case from 2007 (ICJ, Judgment, *Application of the Convention on the Prevention and Punishment of the Crime of Genocide* (Bosnia and Herzegovina v Serbia and Montenegro), 2007, paragraph 401).

In addition, we will also apply the UN Charter, to which both Tellur and Niob are parties.

Article 1 SRA provides that every internationally wrongful act of a State leads to the international responsibility of the State. Article 2 SRA sets out the two necessary elements in order to find an internationally wrongful act: first, the act needs to be attributable to the State in question, and second, the act needs to constitute a breach of an international obligation of that State.

2. Attribution

The acts we are talking about here refer to the acts of the armies of Tellur and Niob in the events in August 2010, but also the border crossing of the protesters from Niob, which leads to Tellur's reaction.

The acts of the two armies: under Article 4 SRA, all acts of all State organs are considered to be acts of the State. It does not matter what function this organ exercised or what characteristics it had, but it needs to be an organ of the State according to the internal law of that State. We do not have any information about the internal law of the two States. However, it is generally well accepted that the military is to be considered as an organ of the State. This is also due to the fact that it is the State that exercises the prerogatives of public power and thus delegates the exercise of this power to its organs. Consequently, it is undisputed that the military is an organ of the State.

Thus, the actions of the armies of Tellur and Niob are attributable to their respective States.

The acts of the private protesters, however, do not seem to be attributable to Niob. They act as private parties, whose acts normally are not attributable to the State. There is no evidence to indicate that Niob has in one way or another controlled or sent the protesters (ie Article 8 SRA) and the government does not endorse the protesters' actions as its own either (ie Article 11 SRA). None of the other articles of attribution seem to be applicable. Consequently, the border crossing of the protesters is not attributable to Niob. Since the two conditions in Article 2 SRA are cumulative, we do not need to analyse further the protesters' action in relation to a potential violation of international law.

3. Violation

Article 12 SRA provides that a breach of an international obligation exists when a State does not act in conformity with what is required from it by that obligation. Thus, it does not matter whether the origin of the obligation is a treaty or customary international law.

Article 13 SRA then establishes that the obligation in question needs to be in force for the State in order to constitute a breach.

In our case, the army of Tellur pushes the protesters from Niob back over the border to Niob. However, they do not stop there, but invade Niob, attacking and plundering villages.

Article 2 paragraph 4 of the UN Charter prohibits the use of force.

While Tellur had the right to push the unarmed protesters back to Niob, it is a clear violation of Article 2 paragraph 4 to continue into Niob and to invade it. Tellur thereby clearly used force against the territorial integrity of Niob, in violation of Article 2 paragraph 4 of the UN Charter which is in force for Tellur at the time of the commission of the act. (In addition to the violation of the UN Charter on grounds of Article 2 paragraph 4 UN Charter, Tellur also violated numerous rules of international humanitarian law by plundering and attacking undefended villages.)

However, Niob also uses force when its own army attacks the army of Tellur, driving it back over the border with Tellur. The use of force per se is a violation of Article 2 paragraph 4 of the UN Charter. Therefore, there is prima facie a violation of international law attributable to both Telllur and Niob.

4. Circumstances precluding wrongfulness

Before making the final conclusion it is necessary to check whether any circumstance precluding wrongfulness can be invoked that would—as its name suggests—preclude the wrongfulness of an act and thus the responsibility of the State.

Looking at those circumstances, the only possibility is Article 21 SRA—self-defence. It has to be kept in mind that under the UN Charter there are two exceptions to the general prohibition to use force contained in Article 2 paragraph 4. The first exception is the use of self-defence in accordance with Article 51 UN Charter and the second exception concerns actions mandated by the Security Council under Chapter VII of the UN Charter. Article 21 SRA accordingly acknowledges that the lawful exercise of self-defence by a State, even though involving the use of force, can be excused. Article 21 SRA, however, also stipulates that self-defence has to be taken in accordance with the UN Charter in order to be lawful.

Article 51 of the UN Charter provides that a State has the right to take measures of self-defence against an armed attack, but only until the UN Security Council has taken the necessary measures. In addition, the State taking measures in self-defence has to inform the Security Council immediately about the measures taken. Two further conditions of legitimate self-defence not contained in Article 51 UN Charter but well established in customary international law (see the *Caroline* case) are necessity and proportionality. Necessity refers to the fact that the use of force taken in self-defence was necessary and there was no other peaceful way to stop the attack of the other State (element of imminence). As for proportionality, it is clear that the response has to be proportionate, but it is not so clear to what the response has to be proportionate (to the threat posed; the means used in the attack; the possibility of future attacks; etc?). However, most often it is understood as meaning that the means taken in self-defence need to be proportionate to the means employed in the attack.

Tellur cannot convincingly argue for the application of self-defence in its case. The protesters that provoked the action of the army in the first place were unarmed. Thus, their march into Tellur could hardly qualify as an 'armed attack' on Tellur (in accordance with Article 51 UN Charter). As acknowledged above, taking measures against the protesters was lawful, but the continuance into the territory of Niob was a violation, which cannot be justified by a reference to self-defence.

The case is different for Niob. Niob was attacked by Tellur, which was plundering and destroying villages in Niob, an action that clearly constitutes an armed attack by one State against another. This thus triggers Niob's right to take measures in self-defence. In addition, Niob has informed the Security Council that it would take measures in self-defence against Tellur. Since the direct confrontation ended after a few days, we are not aware of any measures taken by the Security Council. Concerning the element of necessity, there is indeed an element of imminence present: the army of Tellur has already crossed the border and is plundering and attacking the villages. There seems to be no other way to stop Tellur, since Tellur does not react to the calls of Niob to stop and continues to plunder for several days until the army of Niob drives them back. Thus, there is indeed necessity as required under customary international law. Concerning the proportionality requirement, it seems to be fulfilled as well, since Niob uses its army against the army of Tellur. We do not have any information that Niob would use weapons against Tellur which would be clearly disproportionate, such as an atomic bomb.

In conclusion, we can say that in the case of Niob, the circumstance precluding wrongfulness of self-defence (Article 21 SRA) applies. The same is not true for Tellur, which is thus responsible for an internationally wrongful act.

5. Consequences

Since Niob's actions are excused, there are no further consequences, except for Article 27 SRA: this Article provides that Niob might have to pay compensation for material damage.

As for Tellur, the first consequence is Article 30 SRA, whereby Tellur has to make appropriate assurances to Niob that the same violation will not occur again (letter (b)).

In addition, it is well established that there is an obligation under international law to make reparations. This has been confirmed by the PCIJ in the *Chorzów Factory* case (PCIJ, Judgment, *Case concerning the Factory at Chorzów (Claim for Indemnity)*, 1927, 21) and has been codified in Article 31 SRA.

There are different ways of making reparation (Article 34 SRA). All three ways—restitution, compensation and satisfaction—seem to be appropriate. Under restitution (Article 35 SRA), Tellur would have to give back all the goods taken away during its plundering, where this is still materially possible (ie where these goods have not been destroyed). Further, for all the destruction and loss of life, Tellur will have to pay compensation in accordance with Article 36 SRA. Lastly, satisfaction (Article 37 SRA) is also appropriate, eg in the form of a public apology. The exact form and combination of reparation will have to be negotiated by the States or decided by a competent international court or tribunal.

6. Conclusion

As seen above, Niob is exempted from responsibility because in its case self-defence as a circumstance precluding wrongfulness was applicable. This was not the case for Tellur, which is consequently responsible for its international wrongful act and has thus to make reparation.

Question 3: Is the ICJ competent to hear the disputes between Niob and Tellur and Niob and Astat respectively? Provide all possible bases of jurisdiction.

1. Applicable law

In order to solve this question we will apply the ICJ Statute and the UN Charter. According to Article 92 UN Charter, the ICJ Statute is an integral part of the UN Charter.

The UN Charter is applicable since all three States in question are members of the UN and thus parties to its Charter.

In order to ascertain whether or not the ICJ has jurisdiction to hear the present cases, three elements need to be fulfilled, namely personal jurisdiction, subject matter jurisdiction and consensual jurisdiction.

2. Personal jurisdiction (jurisdiction *ratione personae*)

The ICJ verifies ex officio whether parties to the disputes fulfil the criteria of personal jurisdiction.

According to Article 34 paragraph 1 of the ICJ Statute, only States can be parties to disputes in front of the ICJ. This is not a problem here since Tellur, Niob and Astat are undoubtedly States. This can also be seen from the fact that they are members of the UN, which is only open to States (Article 4 paragraph 1 UN Charter).

In addition, Article 35 paragraph 1 ICJ Statute declares that the ICJ is only open to States which are parties to its Statute. Yet, Article 93 paragraph 1 of the UN Charter provides that all UN members are, ipso facto, parties to the ICJ Statute. Thus, since in our case all three States are members of the UN they are automatically also parties to the ICJ Statute and fulfil the requirement in Article 35 paragraph 1.

Hence we can conclude that the ICJ has personal jurisdiction in this case.

3. Subject matter jurisdiction (jurisdiction *ratione materiae*)

This too is an issue which the ICJ checks ex officio.

The ICJ is only competent to hear legal disputes under international law, as can be inferred, for example, from Article 38 ICJ Statute.

The most widely used definition of a dispute has been given by the Permanent Court of International Justice (PCIJ) in the *Mavrommatis Palestine Concessions* case (PCIJ, Judgment on the Objection to the Jurisdiction of the Court, *The Mavrommatis Palestine Concessions*, 1924, 11). There, the PCIJ said that a dispute was a disagreement on a point of law or fact between two persons. At the same time, it is not enough simply to claim that a dispute exists, but a positive opposition needs to be shown, as the ICJ has confirmed in the *South West Africa* case (ICJ, Judgment on Preliminary Objections, *South West Africa* (Liberia v South Africa and Ethiopia v South Africa), 1962, 328).

In our case, Niob and Tellur indeed disagree on several points of law, namely on the invalidity or not of the ERCT and on their respective alleged State responsibility in relation to the actions of their armies. Treaty law issues and State responsibility issues are legal by nature. In addition they are also legal disputes under international law, since they are disputes between two States and are regulated by international rather than by national law.

In addition, there exists also a legal dispute under international law between Astat and Niob, namely on the alleged invalidity of the ERCT.

Thus, there exist legal dispute under international law between Niob and Tellur and between Astat and Niob. Consequently, the ICJ also has jurisdiction *ratione materiae*.

4. Consensual jurisdiction (jurisdiction *ratione consensus*)

Having established the two previous points is not enough, however, to make the ICJ competent to deal with a case. Consensus with the ICJ's jurisdiction is a crucial element, which has also been confirmed by the ICJ, for example in the *East Timor* case (ICJ, Judgment, *Case concerning East Timor* (Portugal v Australia), 1995, paragraph 26).

Consensus is not ascertained ex officio by the ICJ, but the issue has to be raised by the parties. Here, Tellur contests the jurisdiction of the ICJ in its dispute with Niob, while Niob contests the jurisdiction of the Court in its dispute with Astat. Therefore, the ICJ has also to deal with that issue.

There are four different ways of consenting to the ICJ's jurisdiction, namely compromissory clauses (Article 36 paragraph 1 ICJ Statute), special agreements (Article 36 paragraph 1 ICJ Statute), optional clause declarations (Article 36 paragraph 2 ICJ Statute) and *forum prorogatum* (not contained in the Charter but well established in customary law—see eg ICJ, Judgment on Preliminary Objections, *Corfu Channel* (United Kingdom of Great Britain and Northern Ireland v Albania), 1948, 27, 28).

In our case, however, the only possibility seems to be a compromissory clause as basis of jurisdiction, namely Article 62 ERCT (basis of jurisdiction in accordance with Article 36 paragraph 1 ICJ Statute). None of the three States present before the ICJ has made an optional clause declaration in accordance with Article 36 paragraph 2 ICJ Statute, nor is there a special agreement existing between them. In addition, since on the one hand Tellur and on the other Niob contest the jurisdiction of the ICJ, there is certainly also no *forum prorogatum*.

Niob bases both its disputes with Tellur on the compromissory clause in Article 62 ERCT.

First of all, the compromissory clause cannot serve as a basis of jurisdiction for the State responsibility issue, since Article 62 ERCT is limited to disputes on the interpretation and application of the ERCT. The State responsibility issue, however, has nothing to do with the ERCT. Since there is no other basis of jurisdiction existing in this case, the ICJ is not competent to hear the dispute between Niob and Tellur on their respective State responsibility.

Secondly, an additional serious problem is that the ERCT is not applicable at all between Tellur and Niob due to Niob's radical objection to Tellur's reservation, as seen in the answer to the first question. Logically, a treaty not existing between two parties cannot serve as basis of jurisdiction between the same two parties. In addition, it has to be kept in mind that Tellur has made a reservation to Article 62 ERCT, thereby excluding its application in its—Tellur's—regard. We have previously declared this reservation as being admissible, thus the compromissory clause in Article 62 ERCT could never serve as a basis for jurisdiction for the ICJ for a dispute between Tellur and any of the other three State parties.

Consequently, for the above reasons we have to conclude that the ICJ is not competent to hear both disputes between Niob and Tellur.

However, the ERCT is normally applicable between Astat and Niob. As seen in the answer to the first question, the reservation by Tellur does not in any way change the treaty relation between the non-reserving States *inter se*. Thus, Article 62 ERCT is applicable between Astat and Niob. This Article provides that any dispute on the application or interpretation of the ERCT can be brought to the ICJ by any party. It is true that we have previously declared that Niob can invalidate the ERCT in its relation with the other States. Yet, this is exactly what the dispute is about: can the ERCT be invalidated or not. It would therefore be illogical if compromissory clauses would become invalid when one State alleges that the treaty containing them is invalid. This would mean that the ICJ could never use a compromissory clause as a basis to solve disputes about the invalidity or also termination and suspension of a treaty. Such a solution would dangerously weaken the system of peaceful settlement of disputes in international law. The ICJ has in the *Fisheries Jurisdiction* case (UK v Iceland) (ICJ, Judgment on the Jurisdiction of the Court, *Fisheries Jurisdiction* (United Kingdom of Great Britain and Northern Ireland v Iceland), 1973, paragraphs 43–45) indeed also concluded that compromissory clauses retain their validity in the case of an allegedly invalid treaty in order to allow adjudication of the dispute.

Consequently, the compromissory clause in Article 62 ERCT is applicable and serves as a basis of jurisdiction for the ICJ for the dispute between Astat and Niob.

5. Conclusion

The ICJ is not competent to deal with the disputes between Niob and Tellur, because there is no consent to its jurisdiction.

However, the ICJ is competent to hear the dispute on the validity of the ERCT between Astate and Niob, based on the compromissory clause contained in Article 62 ERCT.

Suggested Solution—Case 7.10

Abbreviations used

CREP = Convention on Rare Earth Production
ICJ = International Court of Justice
ICTY = International Criminal Tribunal for the Former Yugoslavia
ILC = International Law Commission
PCIJ = Permanent Court of International Justice
SRA = ILC Articles on Responsibility of States for Internationally Wrongful Acts 2001 (State Responsibility Articles)
UN = United Nations
VCLT = Vienna Convention on the Law of Treaties

Question 1: Is the CREP still in force between the two parties?

1. Applicable law

Concerning the applicability of the Vienna Convention on the Law of Treaties (VCLT), there are two sets of important dates that have to be assessed: first of all the entry into force of the VCLT for all the respective State parties, and second, the date of conclusion (and not the date of entry into force) of the treaty in question. Article 4 VCLT—the non-retroactivity principle—provides that the VCLT is only applicable to treaties that have been concluded after the entry into force of the VCLT for all the respective State parties.

According to Article 84 paragraph 1 VCLT, the VCLT entered into force on 27 January 1980. Zelos has ratified the VCLT on 5 November 1980, ie after the general entry into force of the VCLT. Article 84 paragraph 2 VCLT provides that after its entry into force following Article 84 paragraph 1, the VCLT enters into force for States 30 days after they deposited their instrument of ratification or accession. Therefore, the VCLT entered into force for Zelos on 5 December 1980.

Erebos however, has apparently only signed the VCLT but has never ratified it. Yet, in order to enter into force, the VCLT needs to be ratified, which can clearly be seen from Article 84 VCLT. Therefore, due to lack of ratification Erebos is not a party to the VCLT.

The CREP was concluded in 1985, but Erebos was at that time not a party to the VCLT. Consequently, Article 4 VCLT, as explained above, is not fulfilled and the VCLT is not applicable to the CREP as such.

However, it is well accepted that the VCLT reflects customary international law in the matter of treaty law. The ICJ has confirmed this, for example in the *Gabčíkovo-Nagymaros* case (ICJ, Judgment, *Gabčíkovo-Nagymaros Project* (Hungary/Slovakia), 1997, paragraph 46). As a consequence, we will apply the customary reflection contained in the VCLT. Any further reference to the VCLT should be read as meaning a reference to the customary reflection of the VCLT.

2. Argument by Zelos: invalidity due to violation of internal law

First of all, it has to be recalled that in general a State cannot invoke its internal law to justify the non-performance of a treaty (customary reflection in Article 27 VCLT). However, this rule has an exception contained in Article 46 VCLT. The Arbitral Tribunal in the *Maritime Frontier* case between Guinea-Bissau and Senegal (Arbitral Tribunal, Award, *Case concerning the delimitation of maritime boundary between Guinea-Bissau and Senegal*, 1989, paragraphs 54, 55) confirmed that Article 46 indeed reflects customary law.

In order for the customary rule to be satisfied, two cumulative conditions need to be fulfilled. First of all, the violation must concern a rule of the State's internal law which is of fundamental importance and which relates to the competence to conclude treaties, and second, the violation must have been manifest.

Zelos's constitution indeed contains a rule concerning the conclusion of treaties in its Article 189. It is generally agreed that rules found in the constitution of a country are to be considered rules of fundamental importance since the constitution is the highest law in a country. In our case, however, the rule in Article 189 foresees that only peace treaties and treaties or agreements concerning the cessation or annexation of territory have to be ratified or approved by the Parliament. This rule thus applies only to some treaties, but not to all. The CREP, however, is not a peace treaty, nor does it deal with the annexation or cessation of territory, but it is about the production of rare earths and the distribution of the corresponding profits. Therefore, as it does not fall into the category of treaties covered by Article 189, there is no rule of fundamental importance applicable here.

Since the conditions in Article 46 VCLT have to be cumulatively satisfied, it is actually not necessary to analyse whether the violation had been a 'manifest' violation in the sense of paragraph 2 of this Article. [*It is, however, in any event debatable whether the violation had been manifest, since no State is obliged to know the internal law of another State and it might therefore not be 'objectively evident to any State conducting itself in the matter in accordance with normal practice and good faith' that a rule such as Article 189 existed.*]

In conclusion, we can say that since there is no rule of fundamental importance applicable in our case, the customary rule reflected in Article 46 is not fulfilled and Zelos cannot invoke its internal law to invalidate the CREP.

3. Argument by Erebos: invalidity due to fraud

After having looked at the VCLT Articles on invalidity and termination, it seems that Article 49 VCLT (fraud) is most appropriate in the case of Mr Ate's action.

Article 49 provides that a State can invoke fraud to invalidate its consent to be bound by a treaty, if its consent to be bound by that treaty had been induced by the fraudulent conduct of another negotiating State.

In our case, apparently the most difficult point during the negotiations had been the attribution of the profits. While Erebos was only ready to give 45%, Zelos wanted at least 50%. The Minister of Foreign Affairs of Zelos in his autobiography confesses that he had hacked the computer of the President of Erebos, in order to send the Minister of Foreign Affairs of Erebos an e-mail, indicating that he should sign the CREP, giving 50% of the profits to Zelos. The Minister of Foreign Affairs from Erebos had followed this alleged order of his President, known for changing his mind quickly. (Foreign Ministers are entitled to conclude treaties according to the customary reflection contained in Article 7 VCLT, so this is not a problem).

Fraud means to deceive someone else intentionally, in order to gain an advantage. Pretending to be another person (in our case the President of Erebos) by sending a e-mail from his normal account which was hacked, in order to induce the Foreign Minister of Erebos to sign the CREP in a more advantageous manner for Zelos (50% of the profit instead of 45%) clearly can be seen as fraud. Fraud is an instance of voidability (relative invalidity), which can only be invoked by the victim State, ie Erebos.

Yet, even though the customary reflection of Article 49 is satisfied, we cannot yet finally conclude that Erebos can indeed invoke Article 49 to invalidate the treaty.

Acquiescence

Article 45 VCLT provides that a State can no longer invoke a ground for invalidating a treaty when, after becoming aware of the facts, it has either expressly (letter (a)) or implicitly through its conduct (letter (b)) acquiesced in the validity of the treaty.

The facts relating to the fraud became publicly known in January 1996, when the former Foreign Minster of Zelos Mr Ate publishes his autobiography. However, Ereobs does not react at that point, but claims invalidity of the CREP based on fraud only two years later after March 1998. Two years is too long to claim that Erebos needed time to think about such a serious issue and to take measures. Therefore, by its silence Erebos has acquiesced in the validity of the CREP as it stands, ie with the 50% profit instead of 45% profit.

Since Erebos has acquiesced, it is also not necessary to check whether the CREP could be separated under Article 44 VCLT.

So, even though we have been able to establish that there has been fraud, Erebos has lost its right to invoke this ground of invalidity since it has acquiesced in the validity of the CREP. Consequently, the CREP is still valid between the two parties.

4. Argument by Erebos: non-existence of the CREP due to its non-registration

Erebos later on argues that the CREP was non-existent because it had never been registered with the UN Secretary General. Article 80 VCLT provides that after their entry into force treaties shall be transmitted to the UN Secretary General in order to be registered. It is not certain whether Article 80 VCLT is a reflection of customary law since procedural provisions are most often not considered to be customary. However, Article 102 paragraph 1 of the UN Charter—to which both States are parties—contains the same obligation. Yet, neither Article 80 VCLT nor Article 102 UN Charter provides that non-registered treaties are invalid (non-existent). The only consequence of non-registration is, according to Article 102 paragraph 2 UN Charter, that such non-registered treaties cannot be invoked in front of any UN organ. This has no influence, however, on the validity of these treaties as such.

In addition, it should not be forgotten that Article 42 VCLT, which is also a reflection of customary law, recalls that the grounds for invalidating or terminating a treaty are exhaustively listed in the VCLT. Yet, none of these grounds includes the non-registration of a treaty as a reason to invalidate or terminate it.

Erebos's argument in this regard must therefore be rejected.

5. Conclusion

The CREP cannot be invalidated based on the alleged violation of internal law of Zelos, nor based on fraud or its non-registration with the UN Secretary General. The CREP is consequently still in force and fully applicable between Zelos and Erebos.

Question 2: Is the international responsibility of Zelos engaged by the incident of 4 March 1998, and if yes, what are the consequences?

1. Applicable law

In order to resolve the question on State responsibility we will apply the ILC Articles on Responsibility of States for Internationally Wrongful Acts from 2001 (SRA). These Articles are not a legally binding treaty, but they reflect customary international law and are thus applicable as such. The ICJ has confirmed the customary character of the SRA in numerous cases, such as the *Iran Hostages* case (ICJ, Judgment, *United States Diplomatic and Consular Staff in Teheran* (United States of America v Iran), 1980, paragraphs 56–92), the *Gabčíkovo-Nagymaros* case (ICJ, Judgment, *Gabčíkovo-Nagymaros Project* (Hungary/Slovakia), 1997, paragraph 47) and most recently the *Genocide* case (ICJ, Judgment, *Application of the Convention on the Prevention and Punishment of the Crime of Genocide* (Bosnia and Herzegovina v Serbia and Montenegro), 2007, paragraph 401).

In addition, we will also apply the UN Charter, to which both States are parties.

Article 1 SRA provides that a State is internationally responsible for every one of its internationally wrongful acts. Article 2 SRA sets out the two necessary elements for an internationally wrongful act. First, the act or omission must be attributable to the State in question, and second, the act or omission must constitute a breach of an international obligation of that State.

2. Attribution

The act we are talking about here is the penetration of a warship of Zelos into the territorial waters of Erebos without the authorisation of the latter.

According to Article 4 SRA, all acts of de jure organs of the State are attributable to the State.

The military is generally seen as a clear de jure organ of the State, among others also because it is the State that has the prerogatives of public power. Therefore, all the acts of the military of Zelos—and thus also of the warship in question—are attributable to Zelos.

3. Violation

Article 12 SRA explains that there is a violation of an international obligation when a State does not act in conformity with what is expected of it under its international obligations. Whether this obligation is of customary or conventional nature does not therefore matter.

In addition, Article 13 SRA specifies that there is only a breach of an international obligation if at the time of the alleged breach the obligation in question was in force for the State.

The warship of Zelos penetrated into the territorial waters of Erebos without the latter's authorisation. On the contrary, the authorities of Erebos had prohibited the entry and had ordered the ship to proceed.

Article 2 paragraph 1 of the UN Charter sets out the sovereign equality of all UN members and is usually read as prohibiting the violation of territorial sovereignty. Territorial waters undoubtedly form an integral part of a State's territory. Therefore, an unauthorised penetration into territorial waters constitutes a violation of the territorial sovereignty of that particular State. Thus, through the acts of its warship, Zelos has clearly violated Article 2 paragraph 1 of the UN Charter.

In addition, Article 2 paragraph 4 of the UN Charter prohibits the use of force against the threat or use of force against the territorial integrity and political independence of a State. As seen above, territorial waters are part of the territory of a State. Therefore, the crossing into territorial waters with a military ship and without authorisation can be equated to an invasion (or an attack) upon the territorial integrity of this State (see eg also UN General Assembly resolution 3314). Consequently, we can argue that through the acts of its military ship, Zelos has violated Article 2 paragraph 4 of the UN Charter since it did not act in conformity with this provision, which was, however, in force for Zelos since it is a member of the UN. Besides, the non-use of force provision is also well-accepted customary law and thus binding on all States anyway (see eg the ICJ's *Nicaragua* case (ICJ, Judgment on the Merits, *Military and Paramilitary Activities in and against Nicaragua* (Nicaragua v United States of America), 1986, paragraphs 187–192)).

Thus, Zelos is prima facie responsible for an internationally wrongful act.

4. Circumstances precluding wrongfulness

No determination of State responsibility is complete without having looked at the circumstances precluding wrongfulness.

The provision which seems to be applicable here is Article 24 SRA—distress. Under distress, the wrongful act results from the fact that the author of the wrongful act did not have any other reasonable choice to save his life and/or the lives of persons under his care. There are thus two cumulative conditions to be satisfied: no other reasonable choice, and saving the life or lives of persons under the author's care.

In our case, the captain of the warship of Zelos indeed wanted to save his life and the lives of the 120 persons on the boat under his command. In addition, there was no other reasonable way of saving them all. Due to the storm and the fact that the ship had already hit rocks, it was unable to regain its own territorial waters. The nearest port where they could reach safety was a port of Erebos. Of course, the captain could have respected the order by Erebos and not have entered its territorial waters, very likely exposing them all to death. Therefore, there was a choice, another way than violating the territorial waters of Erebos, yet it cannot be argued that exposing hundreds of people to death would be a reasonable way to act in order to save 'the author's life or the lives entrusted to the author's care'.

In our case, force majeure (Article 23 SRA) would not be applicable since under force majeure it is *impossible* to carry out the obligation (eg not penetrating into the territorial waters of Erebos, respecting Article 2 paragraph 4 UN Charter). Thus, there is absolutely no element of free choice at all, meaning that the performance of the obligation must be impossible, not just more difficult. Yet, as explained above, in case of distress the person is *not* acting involuntarily. There is still a choice, even though the choice is actually nullified by the perilous situation ('no other *reasonable* way'). This suggests that there are still other ways, even though unreasonable ones.

In addition, we could not argue that this is a situation of necessity (Article 25 SRA) either. Necessity is a situation in which the only way a State can safeguard an essential interest threatened by a grave and imminent peril is not to perform a certain obligation. Unlike force majeure, necessity does not involve involuntary or coerced behavior (so there are other possibilities). And unlike distress, necessity consists not in danger to the lives of individuals in the charge of a State official but in a grave danger either to the essential interests of the State or of the international community as a whole. Thus, in necessity there is an element of choice between respecting the international obligations and safeguarding the legitimate interest of a State. Here, no essential interest of Erebos was in question.

Hence, distress seems to be applicable as the only circumstance precluding wrongfulness. Cases where distress was accepted as a circumstance precluding wrongfulness include the *Rainbow Warrior* case (Arbitral Tribunal, Award, *Case concerning the dif-*

ference between New Zealand and France concerning the interpretation or application of two agreements, concluded on 9 July 1986 between the two States and which related to the problems arising from the Rainbow Warrior Affair, 1990, especially paragraphs 78–101), where the arbitral tribunal held that the evacuation of the two French agents was excused under distress, due to extreme urgency involving medical and other 'humanitarian' considerations.

5. Consequence and conclusion

As shown above, the wrongfulness attributable to Zelos due to the penetration of its warship into the territorial waters of Erebos is precluded by distress (Article 24 SRA).

Therefore, Zelos has no obligation to make reparation as such, with the exception of Article 27 SRA. This Article provides that the invocation of circumstances precluding wrongfulness does not exempt the State from paying for any *material* loss (and not moral damage) caused in the question. From the facts, we are not aware of any material damage or loss caused to Erebos. Therefore, on the basis of what we know, we have to reject the claim by Erebos for financial compensation.

Question 3: What are the *legal* possibilities to settle the various disputes between the two States?

1. Applicable law

We will apply the ICJ Statute and the UN Charter. According to Article 92 UN Charter, the ICJ Statute is an integral part of the UN Charter. Since both parties involved in the dispute are founding members of the UN, the UN Charter and, consequently also the ICJ Statute, is applicable.

The first legal possibility to settle the disputes between Zelos and Erebos is to have recourse to the ICJ

In order for the ICJ to have jurisdiction to hear the case, three elements need to be established: personal jurisdiction, subject matter jurisdiction and consensual jurisdiction.

2. Personal jurisdiction (jurisdiction *ratione personae*)

Article 34 paragraph 1 ICJ Statute provides that only States can be parties to disputes in front of the ICJ. Both Zelos and Erebos are undoubtedly States. This is also confirmed by the fact that they are members of the UN, since the UN is only open to States (Article 4 UN Charter). Therefore, the first requirement in order to satisfy this element is fulfilled.

In addition, Article 35 paragraph 1 ICJ Statute further provides that the ICJ is only open to States that are parties to its Statute. Yet, Article 93 paragraph 1 UN Charter declares that all members of the UN are, ipso facto, parties to the ICJ Statute. Consequently, since both Erebos and Zelos are members of the UN, they are automatically also parties to the ICJ Statute and the second requirement for personal jurisdiction is fulfilled.

We can therefore conclude that the ICJ has personal jurisdiction to hear the case.

3. Subject matter jurisdiction (jurisdiction *ratione materiae*)

The ICJ is only competent to deal with legal disputes under international law, which can for example be inferred from Article 38 ICJ Statute.

The most frequently used definition of a legal dispute can be found in the *Mavrommatis Palestine Concessions* case (PCIJ, Judgment on the Objection to the Jurisdiction of the Court, *The Mavrommatis Palestine Concessions*, 1924, 11). There, the PCIJ said that a dispute was a disagreement on a point of law or fact between two persons. The existence of this dispute has, however, not only to be asserted, but there has to be shown a positive opposition, as the ICJ held in the *South West Africa* case (ICJ, Judgment on Preliminary Objections, *South West Africa* (Liberia v South Africa and Ethiopia v South Africa), 1962, 328). The existence of a dispute is thus an objective determination to be made by the Court (see ICJ, Advisory Opinion, First Phase, *Interpretation of Peace Treaties with Bulgaria, Hungary and Romania*, 1950, 74 and ICJ, Judgment on Preliminary Objections, *Questions of Interpretation and Application of the 1971 Montreal Convention arising from the Aerial Incident at Lockerbie* (Libyan Arab Jamahiriya v United States of America), 1998, paragraph 21).

Indeed, in our case there is a positive dispute between Erebos and Zelos, since they do not agree on points of law, namely whether the CREP is still applicable between them and on the legality of the events taking place on 4 March 1998. Thus, these disputes are legal disputes.

In addition, the disputes fall under international law, since they concern an international treaty, international treaty law and the international rules on State responsibility.

Consequently, the ICJ also has subject matter jurisdiction to hear the case.

4. Consensual jurisdiction (jurisdiction *ratione consensus*)

Even if the foregoing elements are all fulfilled, it is crucial that there is consent by the State parties to the jurisdiction of the Court. There is no compulsory jurisdiction of the ICJ as such without the agreement of the parties concerned. The ICJ has confirmed this, for example in the *East Timor* case (ICJ, Judgment, *Case concerning East Timor* (Portugal v Australia), 1995, paragraph 26) or in the *Monetary Gold* case (ICJ, Judgment, *Monetary Gold Removed from Rome in 1943* (Italy v France, United Kingdom of Great Britain and Northern Ireland and United States of America), 1954, 32).

Normally, the matter of consensus is—unlike the two previous elements—not dealt with ex officio by the ICJ. However, if one party contests the ICJ's jurisdiction—as is the case here—then the ICJ needs to assess whether there is the necessary consent to its jurisdiction.

Out of the four possibilities to consent to the ICJ's jurisdiction *ratione consensus* only two need to be dealt with here.

Optional clause declarations

Under Article 36 paragraph 2 ICJ Statute a State can unilaterally make so-called optional clause declarations in which it consents to the jurisdiction of the ICJ in all cases where another State has accepted the same obligations. Thus, the optional clause system is necessarily based on reciprocity and can only work if two States have made such declarations. In our case, however, only Zelos has made an optional clause declaration but not Erebos. Therefore, the optional clause system cannot work and thus cannot serve as basis of jurisdiction of the ICJ.

Compromissory clause

Another possibility would be a compromissory clause in a treaty. Article 22 CREP seems at first sight to be such a clause. However, this clause cannot serve as a basis of jurisdiction for two reasons.

First of all, the CREP has never been registered with the UN Secretary General. As mentioned above in the answer to the first question, the consequence of non-registration is, according to Article 102 paragraph 2 UN Charter, that such a treaty can never be invoked before any organ of the UN. The ICJ is, however, an organ of the UN, as is clearly provided in Article 7 paragraph 1 of the UN Charter. Thus, Article 22 CREP cannot be invoked before the ICJ since the whole non-registered CREP cannot be invoked in front of the ICJ.

In addition, it can be noted that Article 22 rather just regulates the relation between recourse to arbitration and the ICJ. It seems that under Article 22 the competence of the ICJ needs to be established on another basis, meaning a basis outside the CREP. If this jurisdiction is established, then the ICJ will have precedence over recourse to arbitration. However, this clause does not directly give the ICJ jurisdiction. Since there is no other basis of jurisdiction applicable here, Article 22 CREP cannot give precedence to the ICJ. Thus, Article 22 is in any event not a real compromissory clause.

Thus, the ICJ is not competent to deal with the case.

5. Arbitration

The second legal possibility to settle the dispute between Erebos and Zelos is indeed to have recourse to arbitration. This can be based on Article 22 CREP, which provides for arbitration unless the competence of the ICJ can be established on a different basis.

The fact that the States argue that the CREP is invalid (for different reasons) is thereby not relevant. It is well established that clauses providing for the settlement of disputes in a treaty retain their validity even though it is argued that the treaty containing them is invalid. This has been confirmed by the ICJ in the *Fisheries Jurisdiction* case (UK v Iceland) (ICJ, Judgment on the Jurisdiction of the Court, *Fisheries Jurisdiction* (United Kingdom of Great Britain and Northern Ireland v Iceland), 1973, paragraphs 43–45)). Otherwise, it would never be possible peacefully to resolve disputes between States concerning the alleged invalidity or termination of a treaty.

Yet, it has to be kept in mind that Article 22 CREP is only a basis of jurisdiction for an arbitral tribunal concerning the validity of the CREP itself. Since the legality of the acts on 4 March 1998 are in no way connected with the CREP, Article 22 CREP cannot serve as a basis of jurisdiction for the State responsibility issue.

6. Conclusion

The ICJ is not competent to hear the disputes between Zelos and Erebos because the necessary consensus to the ICJ's jurisdiction is lacking.

Nevertheless, an arbitral tribunal can solve the dispute on the validity of the CREP in accordance with Article 22 CREP. However, since this Article cannot serve as basis for jurisdiction for the State responsibility issue, the arbitral tribunal established under Article 22 CREP could not be competent to deal with this issue on the basis of Article 22 CREP.

In order to solve the State responsibility issue legally, the two States would need to conclude, for example, a special agreement giving either the ICJ or an arbitral tribunal the competence to hear the case. Otherwise, only the recourse to non-legal means such as negotiation, mediation and conciliation remains.

Suggested Solution—Case 7.11

Abbreviations used

ICJ = International Court of Justice
ILC = International Law Commission
MST = Military Stationing Treaty
PCIJ = Permanent Court of International Justice
SRA = ILC Articles on Responsibility of States for Internationally Wrongful Acts 2001 (State Responsibility Articles)
UN = United Nations
VCLT = Vienna Convention on the Law of Treaties

Question 1: Is Carboxy according to international law an independent State or not? Address all the arguments made by the parties.

1. Applicable law

First of all it is important to acknowledge that there is no legally binding definition of a State. The most widely used definition can be found in the Montevideo Convention on the Rights and Duties of States from 1933 (hereinafter the Montevideo Convention). However, since this Convention has been concluded only among some Latin American States, it is not universally binding, nor is it generally accepted that this definition reflects customary international law and would thus be binding as such. Nevertheless, the definition of a State contained in Article 1 of the Montevideo Convention is usually used to define and determine a State.

According to Article 1 of the Montevideo Convention there are four elements that have to be satisfied in order to recognise that a particular entity is a State:

(a) a permanent population;
(b) a defined territory;
(c) a government;
(d) capacity to enter into relations with other States.

Thus, in order to answer the first question we have to look at all four elements in turn.

(a) A permanent population

This criterion means that there needs to be a population that always ('permanently') lives on the territory or under the sovereignty of the entity in question.

It is important to stress that the size of the population does not matter. Contrary to what Amino claims, there is no minimum requirement or minimum number necessary. It would be very difficult to establish such a minimum number. Moreover, such a minimum could also mean that very small States (population-wise) existing today, such as Nauru, Monaco or Lichtenstein,[1] could no longer be regarded as States. Thus, Amino's argument needs to be rejected. A population of 150,000 people is sufficient to satisfy this first criterion. In addition, nothing indicates that this population is not permanent. Thus, it seems that Carboxy indeed has a permanent population.

(b) Defined territory

Carboxy clearly occupies a physical territory. Furthermore, from the facts it seems that the borders of the region of Carboxy which declared itself to be a State are rather clear. At least there is no dispute on this ground. In addition, it is important to note that the size of the territory or the fact that some of its borders might still be disputed is not relevant for this criterion. Thus, we can conclude that there is also a defined territory in the case of Carboxy.

(c) A government

First of all, this clearly means that the entity has some governing organs such as a government (executive) and a parliament. However, this is usually not seen as being enough, but it is necessary that this entity has internal sovereignty and control over its whole territory to the exclusion of other States.

After the declaration of independence in 1997, the former regional government declares itself as the government of the newly created State. Furthermore, it created a parliament and a high court. Thus, there are clearly legislative, executive and even judicial organs present in Carboxy; in particular, the existence of a government and a parliament satisfy this third requirement.

Yet, in addition internal sovereignty and control over its territory is also necessary. According to the facts, Carboxy created its own police force, which was very efficient in securing law and order in the region. It was indeed so efficient that Amino withdrew its own police force in 1999, leaving all law enforcement to the police force of

[1] Nauru: 9,378 inhabitants; Monaco: 30,510 inhabitants; Lichtenstein: 36,713 inhabitants. All numbers are estimates of July 2012, from the CIA World Factbook, available at www.cia.gov/library/publications/the-world-factbook/rankorder/2119rank.html (accessed 22 August 2012).

Carboxy. Thus, we can say that at least from 1999 onwards, Carboxy controls its own territory to the exclusion of any other State, in this case Amino. Furthermore, it seems that Carboxy has extended its competences considerably and is now handling many matters a sovereign State normally deals with. The fact that it handles all administrative matters on its own, but is also competent in tax, security and many other matters, clearly shows that Carboxy has internal sovereignty. It seems to be able to decide on its own how to organise its State. In addition, it seems also to be able to exploit the gold and coal found in its territory, and use the profits from its exports as it chooses (which gives them a certain financial independence).

Thus, for all the above reasons we can declare that Carboxy also fulfils the third criterion, at least from 1999 onwards. This is the time when Amino's police left the region and it can clearly be said that Carboxy exercised full control over its territory. Thus, Carboxy's claim that it has been independent since 1997 has to be nuanced, since their internal sovereignty is only likely to have existed since 1999.

(d) Capacity to enter into legal relations with other States

This criterion is often called 'external sovereignty', in opposition to the internal sovereignty seen above. Arguably, this is the most political of all the criteria. Recognition is crucial to fulfil this criterion, but recognition by other States is largely a political process. If no State recognises a State as an equal in order to enter into treaty relations with each other, it cannot be considered to be a State (since it is not capable of entering into legal relations with other States). It is difficult to say how many States need to have recognised a new State. There is no absolute number, but it can be argued that today with over 190 States it has to be a certain number of them.

We know that Carobxy has concluded a series of economic and commercial treaties with other States (and even a military treaty with Leucin), which makes it clear that other States recognise Carboxy as an equal partner. Thus, Carboxy is able to enter into legal relations with other States. Curiously, Amino does not seem to protest when these treaties are concluded (it only protests later when the MST is concluded), despite the fact that its constitution prohibits the conclusion of international treaties by its composite regions.

As far as recognition is concerned, Carboxy has not yet applied for membership of the UN. The granting of such membership would be a very clear indication of the considered statehood of an entity (recognition), since only States can become members of the UN (Article 4 UN Charter).

Instead, we know that in December 2009 about 65 States have recognised Carboxy as an independent State. This is about a third of today's international community of over 190 States. It is not clear whether this number would suffice as such. However, since Carboxy is clearly able to conclude treaties and not even Amino protests about most of these, we could convincingly argue that Carboxy indeed also possesses external sovereignty.

It seems therefore that Carboxy is indeed an independent State, at least from 1999 onwards.

[*The fulfilment of the three first criteria does not seem to pose problems in general. Yet, it is of course possible to argue on the fourth criterion that today, with such a large number of States in the world, recognition by only 65 of them would not suffice.*]

2. Is the declaration of independence lawful?

The fact that Amino argues that Carboxy could not declare itself independent could be seen as suggesting that Amino considers this declaration of independence to be unlawful. However, the ICJ has held in its *Kosovo* Advisory Opinion (ICJ, Advisory Opinion, *Accordance with international law of the unilateral declaration of independence in respect of Kosovo*, 2010, paragraphs 79–81) that declarations of independence have been and are generally not seen as contrary to international law. This is so regardless of whether the entity or people declaring its independence could do so under the premise of the 'self-determination of peoples' or not. Therefore, we do not have to analyse the question of whether the population of Carboxy as a linguistic minority had the right of 'self-determination'.

Since it is generally not unlawful to declare one's independence this will have no influence whatsoever on the above finding of statehood of Carboxy.

3. Conclusion

In light of the above analysis we can conclude that there are enough reasons to consider Carboxy as an independent State at least from 1999 onwards when Amino's police left the region. This will obviously influence the answers to the other questions as well.

[*If you decided that any of the four elements is missing—most likely the fourth or eventually the third one—then your conclusion would be that Carboxy cannot be considered a State.*]

Question 2: Did Leucin violate international law by establishing a military basis in Carboxy, and if yes, what are the consequences? Argue on the basis of the ILC SRA and address all the relevant arguments made by the parties.

1. Applicable law

We have to solve this issue raised by Amino based on the ILC SRA. The question generally asked is whether Leucin has violated international law, independently from the fact that Carboxy itself has never argued that the establishment of Leucin's military base in its territory constitutes a violation. However, the determination of a violation is an objective exercise.

The SRA are not a legally binding treaty, but they reflect customary international law and are thus applicable as such to all States. The ICJ has confirmed the customary character of the SRA in numerous cases, such as the *Iran Hostages* case (ICJ, Judgment, *United States Diplomatic and Consular Staff in Teheran* (United States of America v Iran), 1980, paragraphs 56–92), the *Gabčíkovo-Nagymaros* case (ICJ, Judgment, *Gabčíkovo-Nagymaros Project* (Hungary/Slovakia), 1997, paragraph 47) and most recently the *Genocide* case (ICJ, Judgment, *Application of the Convention on the Prevention and Punishment of the Crime of Genocide* (Bosnia and Herzegovina v Serbia and Montenegro), 2007, paragraph 401).

In addition, we will also apply the MST, which is binding on Leucin and Carboxy.

Article 1 SRA provides that a State is internationally responsible for every of its internationally wrongful acts. Article 2 SRA sets out the two necessary elements for an internationally wrongful act. First, the act or omission must be attributable to the State in question and second, the act or omission must constitute a breach of an international obligation of that State.

2. Attribution

The act that has to be analysed is the presence and the establishment of a military base of the army of Leucin in the territory of Carboxy.

The military of Leucin is present in Carboxy. Furthermore, Leucin builds a military base on Carboxy's territory. Thus, it is the military and the government of Leucin acting.

According to Article 4 SRA the conduct of any State organ is to be seen as an act of the State, regardless of the function or character the organ exercises. It just needs to have the status of an organ of the State according to the internal law of the State.

The government clearly is an organ of the State and is even expressly mentioned by Article 4 SRA ('executive function'). Furthermore, the army is normally considered to be an organ of the State as well since it is the State which has the prerogatives of public power. Thus, any act of its military and its government is attributable to Leucin under Article 4 SRA.

3. Violation

Article 12 SRA explains that there is a violation of an international obligation when a State does not act in conformity with what is expected from it under its international obligations. Whether this obligation is of customary or conventional nature does not therefore matter.

In addition, Article 13 SRA specifies that there is only a breach of an international obligation if at the time of the alleged breach the obligation in question was in force for the State.

Article 2 paragraph 4 of the UN Charter provides that States should refrain from the use of force against other States. In addition, Article 2 paragraph 1 UN Charter contains the sovereign equality principle.

By penetrating with its army into the territory of another State, Leucin can indeed be said to have at least violated the sovereign equality principle contained in Article 2 paragraph 1 UN Charter. It perhaps goes a bit far to argue that Leucin has also used force in violation of Article 2 paragraph 4 UN Charter. However, such an argument can be made when considering that the use of an army as such, regardless of any deaths or damages, is always to be seen as a use of force. Thus, a violation of Article 2 paragraph 4 UN Charter could also be found. Yet, this violation certainly does not amount to an aggression.

Since Leucin is an original member of the UN, the UN Charter was in force for it in 2010 when the acts happened. Thus, there are indeed violations of international law which are furthermore attributable to Leucin.

4. Circumstances precluding wrongfulness

We cannot conclude any analysis on State responsibility if we have not analysed the circumstances precluding wrongfulness.

It seems that therefore the only possibility is Article 20 SRA. Article 20 SRA provides that the wrongfulness of an act against a State is precluded if there was a valid consent of this State to the commission of that act. In our case, there is indeed the MST, a treaty concluded between Carboxy and Leucin, in which Leucin is allowed to set up some military basis in the territory of Carboxy. Yet, the consent given must be 'valid'. Since, as established above, Carboxy is an independent State, it is correct to argue that it can conclude treaties on whatever subject and with whomever it wants. There is furthermore nothing in the facts suggesting that the MST is affected by invalidity, termination or suspension. Thus, we can hold that from what we know the MST has been validly concluded between two sovereign States and is consequently a valid basis of consent.

Therefore, Article 20 precludes the wrongfulness of Leucin's acts and Leucin is not internationally responsible.

As a consequence, Leucin has no obligation to make reparations (see Article 31 SRA *a contrario*). Yet, Article 27 SRA stresses that even if the State is not responsible this does not mean that it should not pay for material loss caused by the action. However, we are not aware of any material loss caused by the establishment of the military basis and thus cannot apply Article 27 SRA to the case.

[*If you concluded above that Carboxy is not a State, the last part of your argument is of course entirely different. While attribution under Article 4 SRA and the violation (Article 2 paragraph 1 UN Charter and maybe—depending on the arguments—Article 2 paragraph 4 UN Charter) largely stay the same in relation to Amino (of which Caraboxy only is a region), the assessment of circumstances precluding wrongfulness changes. It is clearly provided in Article 20 SRA that the consent must be valid in order to amount to a circumstance precluding wrongfulness. Yet, if Carboxy is not an independent State but still a part of Amino's territory, it has no right to conclude international treaties. This is clearly provided in Amino's constitution, where it says that the regions of the State of Amino can 'under no circumstances' conclude international treaties. Thus, Carboxy did not have the competence to conclude such a treaty, which is thus not valid. This could be based on Article 46 VCLT (or its customary reflection, since we do not know whether the States in question are parties to the VCLT). A treaty is invalid if it violated an internal law of fundamental importance in relation to the conclusion of treaties, and when this violation was manifest. Certainly, the consitution of Amino has been violated by Carboxy's action, since it prohibits the regions from concluding international treaties. The constitution of a State is usually the most important law of a country and thus of fundamental importance. A violation is according to Article 46 paragraph 2 manifest when it would be 'objectively evident to any State conducting itself in the matter in accordance with normal practice and good faith'. This condition might be more difficult to fulfil. It is clear that no State has the obligation to know the internal laws of another State. However, it could be argued that in case of doubt whether Carboxy was or was not a State, Leucin should have acted especially carefully and should have ascertained that the treaty could be validly concluded. On the other hand, it has to be kept in mind that Carboxy has been recongised by a number of States, including Leucin, which would thus in good faith assume that Carboxy was a State. Thus, the answer as to whether the MST can be invalidated under Article 46 VCLT is difficult and depends on your own convictions. In any event, it could be added that under the customary law definition of a treaty it is usually provided that it is the expression of a concurring will between two* subjects of international law. *Yet, regions of States are normally not subjects of international law and thus usually cannot simply conclude international treaties. Therefore, should Carboxy not be a State, the MST has to be considered as not validly concluded, regardless of the application of Article 46 VCLT. This means, however, that there is no consent to the presence of Leucin's military in Carboxy (the territory of Amino) and consequently there is no circumstance precluding wrongfulness applicable. Thus, Leucin would be responsible for an internationally wrongful act, and would have the obligation to make reparations (Article 31 SRA), eg in the form of restitution (of the land) under Article 35 SRA, compensation for the financially assessable damages caused (Article 36 SRA) and eventually satisfaction, ie apologies (Article 37 SRA).*]

5. Conclusion

Leucin is not responsible for an internationally wrongful act, since there is a valid consent of Carboxy as to the establishment of Leucin's military basis in its territory. Thus, the wrongfulness is precluded according to Article 20 SRA.

[*Or alternatively: Since there is no circumstance precluding wrongfulness applicable in the case, Leucin is responsible for an internationally wrongful act and has thus to make reparations (Article 31 SRA).*]

Question 3: Is the ICJ competent to hear the case between Amino and Leucin?

1. Applicable law

We will apply the ICJ Statute, which is according to Article 92 of the UN Charter an integral part of the UN Charter. It has to be kept in mind that the dispute brought to the ICJ is between Amino and Leucin. Both are members of the UN and thus the Charter, and consequently also the ICJ Statute, are applicable.

In order for the ICJ to have jurisdiction, three elements need to be established: personal jurisdiction, subject matter jurisdiction and consensual jurisdiction.

2. Personal jurisdiction (jurisdiction *ratione personae*)

Article 34 paragraph 1 of the ICJ Statute provides that only States can be parties to disputes before the ICJ. It is not contested that Leucin and Amino are States. This can also be proven by the fact that both are members of the UN, which according to Article 4 UN Charter is only open to States, as seen above.

Article 35 paragraph 1 of the ICJ Statue further provides that the ICJ is only open to State parties to its Statute. Article 93 paragraph 1 of the UN Charter holds that members of the UN are, ipso facto, parties to the ICJ Statute. Since both States in question are members of the UN, they are automatically also parties to the ICJ Statute.

Therefore, the two necessary elements to find personal jurisdiction have been fulfilled and the ICJ has personal jurisdiction in this case.

3. Subject matter jurisdiction (jurisdiction *ratione materiae*)

The ICJ is only competent to deal with legal disputes under international law, as can be seen for example in Article 38 of its Statute. It would thus not be competent to hear a purely political dispute, but at the same time political aspects of a legal dispute do not bar the ICJ from having jurisdiction *ratione materiae*.

The most famous definition of a legal dispute has been made by the PCIJ in the *Mavrommatis Palestine Concessions* case (PCIJ, Judgment on the Objection to the Jurisdiction of the Court, *The Mavrommatis Palestine Concessions*, 1924, 11). There, the PCIJ held that a dispute is a disagreement on a point of law or fact between two persons. In addition, it is necessary to show that there was a positive opposition between the parties to the dispute and not a mere assertion of the existence of such a dispute, as stated by the ICJ in the *South West Africa* case (ICJ, Judgment on Preliminary Objections, *South West Africa* (Liberia v South Africa and Ethiopia v South Africa), 1962, 328). It is the ICJ that has to make an objective determination of the existence of a dispute, regardless of the relevant claims made by the parties (see ICJ, Judgment on Preliminary Objections, *Questions of Interpretation and Application of the 1971 Montreal Convention arising from the Aerial Incident at Lockerbie* (Libyan Arab Jamahiriya v United States of America), 1998, paragraph 21 and ICJ, Advisory Opinion, First Phase, *Interpretation of Peace Treaties with Bulgaria, Hungary and Romania*, 1950, 74).

In our case, Amino claims that Leucin has violated international law by establishing a military basis in the territory of Carboxy, considered by Amino to be an integral part of its own territory. Leucin contests that it has violated international law by saying that Carboxy is an independent State with which Leucin concluded an international treaty allowing the establishment of such a military base. A dispute referring to the violation of international law can per se be seen as a legal dispute under international law. Furthermore, it is clearly also a positive opposition of views.

Consequently, we can conclude that the ICJ also has subject matter jurisdiction in the dispute between Amino and Leucin.

4. Consensual jurisdiction (jurisdiction *ratione consensus*)

Since Leucin contests the jurisdiction of the Court, the ICJ has to deal with the question of consensual jurisdiction. Unlike the two previous points, however, consenst is not checked by the ICJ ex officio. Nevertheless, consent to its jurisdiction is absolutely crucial, which the ICJ has confirmed itself, for example in the *East Timor* case (ICJ, Judgment, *Case concerning East Timor* (Portugal v Australia), 1995, paragraph 26).

From the four possibilities to consent to the ICJ's jurisdiction, only one seems to be relevant: optional clause declarations made in accordance with Article 36 paragraph 2

ICJ Statute. The optional clause system is based on reciprocity. This means first of all that both parties to a dispute must have made such an optional clause declaration in order to serve as basis of consent to the compulsory jurisdiction of the ICJ. Both Leucin and Amino have made such an optional clause declaration. While Leucin has not made any reservation, Amino has with a reservation excluded the competence of the Court for 'disputes involving the interpretation or application of multilateral treaties where not all State parties to this treaty are parties to the dispute before the Court'.

From Article 36 paragraph 3 ICJ Statute it can be inferred that, in general, reservations to optional clause declarations are allowed. Since the ICJ Statute and the UN Charter both do not contain any rules specific to reservations, Article 19(c) VCLT applies (as reflection of customary law since we do not know whether the two States are parties to the VCLT). That is, it has to be ascertained whether the reservation is compatible with the object and purpose of the treaty to which the reservation is made.

It is true that any limitation of the jurisdiction of the ICJ to solve disputes can be seen as problematic. On the other hand, saying that a reservation excluding one particular type of disputes would go against the object and purpose of the much broader ICJ Statute might go a bit far. In addition, under such 'normal' reservations the ICJ is not precluded from deciding whether or not it is competent to hear the case (Kompetenz–Kompetenz, in accordance with Article 36 paragraph 6 ICJ Statute), and thus it could always reject the application of such a reservation. Furthermore, in the light of the fact that most reservations to optional clause declarations have been accepted in the past and were not seen to be particularly problematic, we can conclude that the reservation made by Amino is valid.

Obviously, Amino did not invoke its own reservation when it brought the case to the ICJ. However, Leucin argues that it can invoke Amino's reservation, a fact that is contested by Amino. However, as stated above, the optional clause system under Article 36 paragraph 2 is based on the principle of reciprocity. The ICJ held in the case of *Certain Norwegian Loans* (ICJ, Judgment, *Certain Norwegian Loans* (France v Norway), 1957, 22–27) that in order to have true reciprocity, one State is also allowed to invoke the reservation made by the other State to its optional clause declaration. Therefore, in the spirit of reciprocity, Leucin is indeed entitled to invoke Amino's reservation. Amino's argument that only the State making the reservation can also invoke it has thus to be rejected.

A reservation limits the jurisdiction of the ICJ, since the Court's jurisdiction is always based on the least common denominator to be found between two optional clause declarations (on this see eg the ICJ's *Anlgo-Iranian Oil* case (ICJ, Judgment, *Anglo-Iranian Oil Co.* (United Kingdom v Iran), 1952, 103)). Leucin argues that the ICJ is barred from hearing the case because it involves the application of the UN Charter, a multilateral treaty, without all UN members being parties to the dispute at hand. Thus, Amino's reservation invoked by Leucin precludes in Leucin's opinion the ICJ from hearing the case.

It is true that the dispute involves the UN Charter on issues such as use of force and violation of sovereignty. However, as the ICJ has held in the *Nicaragua* case (ICJ, Judgment on the Merits, *Military and Paramilitary Activities in and against Nicaragua* (Nicaragua v United States of America), 1986, paragraphs 172–79), these rules contained in the UN Charter—and indeed most of the UN Charter—are also customary law. Thus, in order to solve the dispute it is not necessary for the ICJ to apply the UN

Charter, it can just apply its customary reflection. Therefore, the reservation made by Amino and invoked by Leucin does not bar the jurisdiction of the Court.

On the contrary, we can concluded that based on the two optional clause declarations the ICJ indeed also has consensual jurisdiction.

5. Consequence

Since all three elements necessary for the ICJ's jurisdiction are established, as argued above, we can declare that the ICJ would be competent to hear the case.

6. Admissibility

Yet, Leucin makes an additional argument not related to the jurisdiction of the ICJ, but to the admissibility of the case. It makes the so-called 'legal interest of a third State' argument, by invoking that 'the legal interests of Carboxy were directly affected'.

There are indeed a few cases where the ICJ declared a case inadmissible because of the legal interests of a third State. There is, however, an important difference to be made.

The legal interests of a third State are only a bar to the admissibility if those legal interests are the *very subject matter* of the dispute, ie when they are indispensable to solve the dispute. If, on the other hand, those legal interests are only *affected*, then they do not cause the inadmissibility of the case. It is a fact that there are many situations in international law where the legal interests of third States are affected, eg when the ICJ interprets a multilateral treaty or pronounces itself on customary rules. However, it would undermine the international legal system if all these cases could be declared inadmissible. Consequently, *affected* legal interests of a third State do not bar the admissibility of the case. On the other hand, if the legal interests of a third State are indeed the heart of the dispute, this State needs to have a say in the course of the dispute in order to be able to defend itself. It thus needs to consent to the ICJ's jurisdiction as well and needs to get the chance be a party to the dispute in question. Only then could the ICJ declare such a case as admissible.

For example, in the *Monetary Gold* case (ICJ, Judgment, *Monetary Gold Removed from Rome in 1943* (Italy v France, United Kingdom of Great Britain and Northern Ireland and United States of America), 1954, 32), the ICJ held that the legal interests of Albania, not a party to the dispute, were the very subject matter of the dispute and thus the ICJ could not continue with the proceedings. Similarly, in the *East Timor* case (ICJ, Judgment, *Case concerning East Timor* (Portugal v Australia), 1995, paragraphs 28–29), the ICJ declared that the case between Portugal and Australia could not be assessed without first addressing the question of why Indonesia could not have legally concluded the 1989 treaty. Thus, the legal interests of a third State (Indonesia) were the very subject matter of the dispute and the case had thus to be declared inadmissible. On the other hand, in the *Nicaragua* case (ICJ, Judgment on the Jurisdiction of the Court and the Admissibility of the Application, *Military and Paramilitary Activities in and against Nicaragua* (Nicaragua v United States of America), 1984, paragraph 88), the ICJ decided that the legal interests of third States (Costa Rica and El Salvador) were at most only 'affected' and that none of these States was 'truly indispensable' for the proceedings. Thus, the case was admissible.

In our case, the question of whether Carboxy is or is not a State is absolutely crucial for the solution of the dispute. If the conclusion is that it is a State, then the MST has been validly concluded and Leucin is not internationally responsible for a violation of an international obligation. However, if Carboxy is said not to be a State, the MST has not been validly concluded and Leucin has indeed violated the territorial integrity of Amino, which has not consented to the establishment of a military base on its territory. Thus, the question of the statehood of Carboxy is the heart of the dispute.

The question is, however, a very difficult one: admissibility is barred when legal interests of a third *State* are the very subject matter of the dispute. We have already concluded that Carboxy is a State, but could the ICJ make the same conclusion for a dispute where this question is in fact the whole underlying issue? By admitting that the legal interests of a third State are an obstacle to admissibility in this case, the ICJ would implicitly recognise that Carboxy is a State, without however properly having considered the question (since this is the preliminary objections and not the merits phase). However, if the ICJ goes on to consider the question of the statehood of Carboxy, parting from the premise that it is not clear whether it is a State and that thus its legal interest could not influence the admissibility of the case, the problem arises that as soon as the ICJ declares Carboxy a State, its legal interests are naturally involved. However, potentially this second solution is to be preferred for the following reason: when the ICJ declares that Carboxy is not a State, then there are no legal interests of a third *State* which could be affected anyway and thus could bar the ICJ's admissibility. On the other hand, when the ICJ declares that Carboxy is a State, it is true that this State's legal interests are affected, but at least not to its detriment since it has officially been recognised as a State. The problem is, however, that in either case Carboxy as a most affected entity would not get the right to appear before the Court to defend its case since only States can appear before the ICJ or ask for the permission to intervene in the case (Article 62 paragraph 1 ICJ Statute) and that it is exactly this question of statehood which is the problem and the heart of the dispute.

In our opinion, it is not possible for the ICJ to solve this dilemma satisfactorily; it is after all also a political issue. An option would be for Leucin to try to bring the UN General Assembly to ask an advisory opinion on the question or to convince Carboxy to apply for UN membership. Based on the result of this application it would be clear whether or not Carboxy is indeed considered as a State by the international community as we have argued above.

7. Conclusion

As argued above, the ICJ has jurisdiction to deal with the case.

However, it is unclear whether it can be argued that the case is admissible or not. Since the ICJ is unable to solve the rather political dilemma, it should declare the case inadmissible, which means that the ICJ cannot hear the case *now*, but might be able to do so in the future.

Chapter 8

SUGGESTED SOLUTIONS
Specialised Branches of International Law

SUGGESTED SOLUTIONS
International Human Rights Law

Suggested Solution—Case 8.1

Abbreviations used
ECHR = European Convention on Human Rights
ECtHR = European Court of Human Rights

1. Applicable law

We are asked to give an objective legal opinion on the territorial jurisdiction (jurisdiction *ratione loci*) of the European Court of Human Rights (ECtHR).

The claimants allege that the State Kata, which is a party to the European Convention on Human Rights (ECHR), has violated this convention through acts that took place on the territory of another State, Tredor, which is not a party to the ECHR. In order to determine the competence of the ECtHR, it is necessary first to determine whether the ECHR is applicable to the situations at hand. The problem submitted to our attention requires an analysis on the extra-territorial application of the ECHR. For this analysis we will mainly look at Article 1 ECHR.

Extra-territorial application of the ECHR

Article 1 ECHR provides that the ECHR applies to everyone within the jurisdiction of a High Contracting Party. The central element is therefore the expression 'jurisdiction'. This term has been clarified in the jurisprudence of the Court, of which a brief review is necessary in order to answer the question asked.

In 1975 and 1978, the European Commission on Human Rights held that 'jurisdiction' in Article 1 ECHR did not mean that the application of the ECHR was limited to the national territory of High Contracting Parties. In arguing this point, the Commission stated in one of the *Cyprus v Turkey* cases that 'it is clear from the language, in particular of the French text, and the object of this Article, and from the purpose of the Convention as a whole, that the High Contracting Parties are bound to secure the said rights and freedoms to all persons under their actual authority and responsibility, whether that authority is exercised within their own territory or abroad' (see European Commission on Human Rights, *Cyprus v Turkey*, Applications No 6780/74 and No 6950/75, 26 May 1975, paragraph 8). The Commission confirmed this interpretation three years later in another case involving Cyprus and Turkey (see European Commission on Human Rights, *Cyprus v Turkey*, Application No 8007/77, 10 July 1978, paragraph 19).

The ECtHR followed these considerations and considered 'jurisdiction' as not being limited to the national territory of a State. In the *Loizidou* case, the ECtHR further added that a Contracting Party is also bound by the ECHR—thus that persons are 'within the jurisdiction' of a State party—in situations where this State exercises effective control over the territory of another State, for example after a military action (see ECtHR, *Case of Loizidou v Turkey*, Preliminary Objections, Application No 15318/89, 23 March 1995, paragraph 62). In the same case in the decision on the merits, the Court somewhat softened this criterion. It stated that detailed control over the actions and policies of the local authorities on the foreign territories was not necessary. Rather, in order for persons affected by actions and policies of local authorities or agents to fall within the 'jurisdiction' of a State party, it is enough that the State party exercises global control over these local authorities (see ECtHR, *Case of Loizidou v Turkey*, Judgment, Application No 15318/89, 18 December 1996, paragraph 56).

In the *Banković* case—a case involving bombardments carried out by NATO troops in Kosovo—the ECtHR considered that the term 'jurisdiction' should be understood in the same sense as that of a State exercising competences in public international law. The Court in this respect recalled that the jurisdiction of a State is essentially territorial. Only exceptionally can this jurisdiction be exercised extra-territorially, eg in the case of a military occupation or upon the invitation or consent of the State on the territory of which the jurisdiction will be exercised (see ECtHR, *Banković and others v Belgium and others*, Decision on Admissibility, Application No 52207/99, paragraphs 59, 60). Summarising its own position, the ECtHR argued that

> its recognition of the exercise of extra-territorial jurisdiction by a Contracting State is exceptional: it has done so when the respondent State, through the effective control of the relevant territory and its inhabitants abroad as a consequence of military occupation or through the consent, invitation or acquiescence of the Government of that territory, exercises all or some of the public powers normally to be exercised by that Government. (ECtHR, *Banković and others v Belgium and others*, Decision on Admissibility, Application No 52207/99, paragraph 71)

Finally, in the *Assanidze v Georgia* case, Judge Loucaides explained in his concurring opinion, that the notion of 'jurisdiction' is to be understood as meaning 'actual authority', that is the capacity to impose the will of a State on every individual, regardless of whether this imposition takes place in or outside the territory of that State (see ECtHR, *Assanidze v Georgia*, Judgment, Application No 71503/01, Concurring Opinion of Judge Loucaides, 8 April 2004).

2. Application of the law to the facts

We now need to apply our theoretical considerations above to the facts of the case at hand. In order to do this, we will consider the two periods under discussion separately.

(a) Period from 17 May to 17 June 2012

During this first period, the air force of Kata bombarded the territory of Mirscha, but did not send its ground troops to Tredor. Kata limited itself to carrying out aerial operations in Mirscha, with the goal of preparing for a future invasion by ground troops.

In light of the relevant case law analysed above we can conclude that Kata did not exercise any control on the territory of Tredor. In particular, Kata did not exercise global or effective control, which would allow it to impose its own authority on the inhabitants of the region Mirscha. Consequently, these individuals fell neither under the authority nor the responsibility of Kata.

Consequently, in the time period under consideration the applicants did not find themselves within the jurisdiction of Kata in the sense of Article 1 ECHR.

(b) Period from 28 June to 15 November 2012

In the second phase under consideration, Kata's ground troops invaded the region of Mirscha and took control. The level of control exercised by the army of Kata was sufficient to allow agents from Kata to expel, imprison and execute members of the Tredorian population. Through their presence on this territory, the agents of Kata have thus exercised actual authority over the inhabitants of the region of Mirscha, allowing Kata to impose its will to regain full sovereignty over this area. This authority arguably amounts to enough control of the territory of Mirscha to engage Kata's responsibility.

Consequently, the acts committed during this time period fall within the jurisdiction of Kata in the sense of Article 1 ECHR.

3. Conclusion

As we have seen above, the acts committed during the time period 17 May–17 June 2012 do not fall within the jurisdiction of Kata in the sense of Article 1 ECHR. Consequently, the ECtHR is not competent *ratione loci* to deal with these acts.

However, the acts committed during the time of 28 June to 15 November 2012 do fall within the jurisdiction of Kata. Kata does exercise sufficient control over the region of Mirscha in this period to satisfy the 'jurisdiction' requirement in Article 1 ECHR, as developed by the ECtHR's jurisprudence. Therefore, the ECtHR's territorial jurisdiction obligation is satisfied and the ECtHR is competent to deal with the acts during that period.

Suggested Solution—Case 8.2

Abbreviations used

ATL 2012	= Anti-Terrorist Law 2012
ECHR	= European Convention on Human Rights
ECtHR	= European Court of Human Rights
ICTY	= International Criminal Tribunal for the former Yugoslavia

1. Applicable law

Scissorland is a party to the European Convention on Human Rights (ECHR). We will thus apply this legal instrument to the case at hand. In order to assess the allegations made by Mr Alfred Pasnette, we first have to analyse the derogation mechanism contained in the ECHR.

Derogations under the ECHR

Article 15 ECHR sets out the derogation system of this convention. In accordance with this provision, a State party can in exceptional circumstances suspend some of the rights contained in the convention. However, as is clearly stated in Article 15 paragraph 2 ECHR, there exist some non-derogable rights, which can never be suspended by a State party under any circumstance.

The exceptional circumstances under which derogation might be permissible include, for example, war or a public emergency that is threatening the life of the nation (Article 15 paragraph 1 ECHR ab initio). The meaning of 'public emergency threatening the life of the nation' has been clarified by the jurisprudence of the European Court of Human Rights (ECtHR). According to the Court in the *Lawless* case, a 'public emergency threatening the life of a nation' exists when there is an exceptional situation of emergency or crisis, affecting the whole population and constituting a threat to the organised life of the community (ECtHR, *Case of Lawless v Ireland (No 3)*, Judgment, Application No 332/57, 1 July 1961, paragraph 28). This public danger cannot be just hypothetical or in the future. It needs to be of certain imminence. Nevertheless, in the determination of whether such a public emergency exists, the State enjoys a wide margin of appreciation (see ECtHR, *Case of Ireland v The United Kingdom*, Judgment, Application No 5310/71, 18 January 1978, paragraph 207).

It should be noted that the derogation mechanism set out in Article 15 ECHR can only be invoked where the situation strictly requires it (Article 15 paragraph 1 ECHR). In fact, it can only be used when the ordinary legislation has proven to be unable to deal with the danger, as the ECtHR explained in the *Lawless* case (ECtHR, *Case of Lawless v Ireland (No 3)*, Judgment, Application No 332/57, 1 July 1961, paragraph 36). However, the State in question benefits also here from a wide margin of appreciation.

As the ECtHR said in the case of *Brannigan and McBride*, in order to determine the lawfulness of the derogatory measures taken by the State, it is necessary to take into account factors such as the nature of the rights affected or suspended under the derogation, as well as the situation leading to and the duration of the emergency situation (ECtHR, *Case of Brannigan and McBride v The United Kingdom*, Judgment,

Applications No 4553/89 and No 14554/89, 25 May 1993, paragraph 43). Concerning the case of administrative detention, we also have to take into account the duration of the detention and the availability of judicial guarantees (ECtHR, *Case of Lawless v Ireland (No 3)*, Judgment, Application No 332/57, 1 July 1961, paragraph 37).

In addition, Article 15 paragraph 1 ECHR also provides that derogations are only allowed if they are not inconsistent with the State's other obligations under international law.

When invoking its right of derogation, the State in question has to respect the procedural requirement contained in Article 15 paragraph 3 ECHR. This provision holds that the State has to inform the Secretary General of the Council of Europe about the measures taken as well as the reasons for taking them. The Court clarified in the *Lawless* case that the Secretary General has to be notified without delay (see ECtHR, *Case of Lawless v Ireland (No 3)*, Judgment, Application No 332/57, 1 July 1961, paragraphs 42ff).

Mr Alfred Pasnette alleged that Scissorland violated both Article 3 ECHR and Article 5 ECHR. To analyse his allegations, we will consider these two Articles separately under the derogation mechanism of Article 15 ECHR.

2. Violation of Article 3 ECHR

We can point out at the outset that the prohibition of torture contained in Article 3 ECHR is part of the non-derogable rights listed in Article 15 paragraph 2 ECHR. Consequently, the Anti-Terrorist Law 2012 (ATL 2012) enacted by Scissorland under Article 15 ECHR cannot derogate from the prohibition of torture. This means that Scissorland cannot base itself on the ATL 2012 to justify any violation of Article 3 ECHR.

To respond to Mr Pasnette's allegations, we need to assess whether he has been subject to acts of torture. The prohibition of torture is an absolute right, to which no derogation or exception can apply. It is considered as one of the fundamental values of a democratic society and clearly is part of the so-called *jus cogens* norms, as has been confirmed by several international courts (see eg ECtHR, *Case of Soering v The United Kingdom*, Judgment, Application No 14038/88, paragraph 88; and ICTY, Trial Chamber, Judgment, *Prosecutor v Furundžija*, 1998 (Case No IT-95-17/1-T) paragraph 153). Torture in the sense of Article 3 ECHR means severe pain or suffering, which can be both mental as well as physical. In order to amount to acts of torture, this pain or suffering has to be of certain intensity and needs to be inflicted intentionally. In the *Ireland v United Kingdom* case from 1978, the ECtHR clarified that torture means 'deliberate inhuman treatment causing very serious and cruel suffering' (ECtHR, *Case of Ireland v The United Kingdom*, Judgment, Application No 5310/71, 18 January 1978, paragraph 167).

The assessment of the necessary level of intensity in order to find an act of torture is a relative assessment, containing two parts. The first part is the internal part. Therefore, as was held by the ECtHR, the pain and suffering needs to be examined on a case-by-case basis, taking into account particularities of the person concerned, such as his/her age, gender and general health condition (ECtHR, *Case of Ireland v The United Kingdom*, Judgment, Application No 5310/71, 18 January 1978, paragraph 162). In the *Selmouni* case the ECtHR specified that in addition the duration of the act as well as its physical or mental effects are points to be considered here (ECtHR, *Case of Selmouni v France*, Judgment, Application No 25803/94, 28 July 1999, paragraph 100).

The second part of the analysis is external and is subject to an evolutionary interpretation. The necessary level of intensity is subject to change over time, as a function of how the conception of law develops in the jurisdictions and societies concerned (see ECtHR, *Case of Selmouni v France*, Judgment, Application No 25803/94, 28 July 1999, paragraph 102). In particular, directly relevant for the case under consideration here, the ECtHR has confirmed in the *Askoy* case that the technique of 'Palestinian hanging' is a form of torture (ECtHR, *Case of Askoy v Turkey*, Judgment, Application No 21987/93, 18 December 1996, paragraph 64).

In the case under consideration here, Mr Alfred Pasnette was subject to 'Palestinian hanging', as well as waterboarding and sleep deprivation. It is clear, as seen above, that the Court sees 'Palestinian hanging' as an act of torture. Waterboarding leads the victim to experience the feeling of drowning, and is capable of causing extreme pain and physical damage due to oxygen deprivation. It is thus clear that this treatment only has severe adverse effects on an individual, both physically and mentally. Finally, it is well established that prolonged sleep deprivation can have devastating mental effects. All these acts were inflicted on Mr Alfred Pasnette during his 38 days in detention. We also know from the facts that he is marked for life by this detention, and is unable ever to live a normal life again. It is therefore obvious that this treatment had severe consequences on the health and life of Mr Alfred Pasnette.

Judging from the duration as well as the nature of the acts inflicted on Mr Alfred Pasnette, it seems clear that they reach the necessary level of intensity in order to amount to torture, as defined by the jurisprudence reviewed above. The elements at our disposal are sufficient to make this determination, despite the fact that we do not dispose of any information as to the particular personal characteristics of Mr Pasnette. Finally, we can also note that Mr Pasnette was subjected to this treatment deliberately, in order to obtain from him information on the separatist group MalikaLibre.

In conclusion, we can hold that the treatment experienced by Mr Alfred Pasnette during 38 days in detention amounts to acts of torture in the sense of Article 3 ECHR. Since a State can never derogate from the prohibition of torture, not even in situations of emergency as provided in Article 15 paragraph 2 ECHR, Scissorland has through its police agents violated Article 3 ECHR.

3. Violation of Article 5 ECHR

Unlike Article 3 ECHR, the right to liberty, or more precisely the right not to be subject to arbitrary detention, contained in Article 5 ECHR is not an absolute right and can thus be subject to derogation (Article 15 paragraph 2 ECHR *a contrario*) and limitations (Article 5 paragraph 1 ECHR, second phrase).

By adopting the ATL 2012 on 14 August 2012, Scissorland invoked its right to derogate from Article 5 ECHR on the basis of the derogation mechanism contained in Article 15 ECHR. We have theoretically analysed this derogation mechanism above. Here, we now have to assess the compliance of the ATL 2012 with Article 15 ECHR.

We know from the facts that Scissorland is fighting a terrorist group, which has the capacity to perpetrate attacks anytime, anywhere and against any person. The group in question—the MalikaLibre—has already perpetrated numerous attacks, leading to more than 300 deaths in a few months. This situation has created a climate of fear among the entire civilian population of Scissorland.

We can resolve that there exists indeed an exceptional danger. In addition, this danger is concrete, since attacks have already been perpetrated. Thus, the element of imminence of the danger is also satisfied. The entire population is affected by the resulting climate of terror. Finally, since the MalikaLibre can strike at any time, any place and against any person, we can say that there exists indeed a danger for the organised life of the community composing Scissorland.

Consequently, there exists a public emergency threatening the life of the nation on the territory of Scissorland. Based on this determination, the derogation mechanism in Article 15 ECHR can be used by Scissorland. In fact, the situation of public emergency has officially been proclaimed when the Parliament of Scissorland decreed a State of emergency.

It is necessary that the ATL 2012 conforms to the conditions that are strictly necessary for the situation at hand. We can note in this regard that the ATL 2012 does not mention which rights are suspended. Therefore, we can assume that it suspends all rights, which are subject to derogation. We can further note that the ATL 2012 does not contain a time limit and thus provides for an emergency regime to apply for an unlimited period. The emergency regime was enacted in response to the terrorist attacks perpetrated by the MalikaLibre. According to the facts, the legislation of Scissorland did not prove to be effective in this situation. That is why the authorities decided to have recourse to the derogation mechanism of Article 15 ECHR. Finally, the ATL 2012 provides for administrative detention for a maximum of 40 days (Article 4 ATL 2012) without any judicial guarantees, especially without the possibility to have recourse to a counsel and to have the legality of the detention reviewed by a judge.

Seeing all these elements, it is difficult to conclude that the ATL 2012 conforms to the conditions that are strictly necessary for the current situation.

It is true that the circumstances at the origin of the measures adopted in ATL 2012, ie widespread terrorist attacks, can justify the application of the derogation mechanism of Article 15 ECHR. In addition, in conformity with Article 15 paragraph 3 ECHR, the Secretary General of the Council of Europe has been notified concerning the adoption of this law. (There are no specific dates provided, but in the absence of contrary information we can assume that the notification was done without delay.)

But it seems that overall the ATL 2012 goes too far and goes beyond what is allowed under the derogation mechanism. Under the ATL 2012, all the derogable human rights contained in the ECHR are suspended, and not just those that are strictly necessary to deal with the situation of terrorist attacks. Furthermore, the ATL 2012 does not contain any time limit and is thus susceptible to be applied in perpetuity. And lastly, allowing administrative detention for 40 days without any judicial guarantee attached seems largely to exceed the margin of appreciation accorded to States when adopting their specific derogation measures.

Since we do not dispose of any information regarding other obligations of Scissorland under international law, we cannot conclusively analyse the last condition laid down in Article 15 paragraph 1 ECHR.

In conclusion, we can hold that Scissorland has exceeded its margin of appreciation by establishing such a derogation regime in ATL 2012. This law goes beyond what is strictly necessary to deal with the situation. Consequently, Mr Alfred Pasnette could not have been lawfully detained for 38 days without any judicial guarantee. Under these conditions, Scissorland cannot invoke the ATL 2012 to justify the detention of Mr Pasnette.

Scissorland has thus not validly applied the derogation mechanism contained in Article 15 ECHR and therefore has to respect Article 5 ECHR.

However, both the duration of the detention as well as the absence of judicial guarantees is in violation of Article 5 ECHR, in particular paragraph 4 of this provision. Consequently, Scissorland has arbitrarily detained Mr Alfred Pasnette, in violation of Article 5 ECHR.

4. Conclusion

As we have established above, Scissorland has violated its obligations both under Article 3 and Article 5 ECHR. Furthermore, the derogation to the latter provision by adopting the ATL 2012 was not valid. Mr Alfred Pasnette's allegations have therefore proven to be correct.

Suggested Solution—Case 8.3

Abbreviations used

ECHR = European Convention on Human Rights
EComHR = European Commission on Human Rights
ECtHR = European Court of Human Rights

1. Applicable law

As the legal counsel of Guy Badkopf's parents, we are tasked to show that Nowdstate has violated its obligations, thus leading to the death of Guy Badkopf. For this purpose, and seeing that we are acting before the European Court of Human Rights (ECtHR), we will apply the European Convention on Human Rights (ECHR). Nowdstate is a party to this Convention since its entry into force and there thus exists no obstacle to its application.

2. *[Jurisdiction of the European Court of Human Rights*

If students, acting as a legal counsel in this case, have assessed whether or not the ECtHR possesses jurisdiction to hear the case, this would certainly not be wrong. The necessary elements of this analysis are set out below, in order to give students addressing this question an opportunity to check their answers. However, seeing that the question is actually limited to determine the existence of a violation of the right to life, it would not be expected from students to analyse the jurisdictional question as well.

For the Court to be competent to hear a case, the ECHR needs to be applicable, since the Court's jurisdiction is limited to the application and interpretation of the ECHR, as provided in Article 32 paragraph 1 ECHR. This does not pose a problem here since, as seen above, Nowdstate is a party to the ECHR since its entry into force.

Only individuals, non-governmental organisations and groups of individuals can bring cases to the ECtHR (Article 34 ECHR) and only if they are claiming to be the victim of a violation of a right contained in the Convention. 'Victim' in that sense is not necessarily limited to one person alone. In our case, the claim made concerns the violation of the right to life by the death of Guy Badkopf. His parents are to be seen as victims of this tragedy as well (especially since Guy is dead) and they are individuals. Therefore, they can bring a case before the ECtHR.

In addition, an important requirement is that local remedies need to be exhausted before the ECtHR is competent to hear a case (Article 35 paragraph 1 ECHR). In the facts at our disposal it is stated that after the closure of the case following a more than sketchy investigation, the parents of Guy Badkopf complained to the superior authorities about the lack of diligence and impartiality of the police. Yet, all their requests remain without consequence. One could of course argue that local remedies have not been exhausted, since the parents did not go all the way up to the Supreme Court. Article 35 paragraph 1 states that this exhaustion has to be done in accordance with 'generally recognized rules of international law'. However, it is widely accepted that local remedies need not be exhausted if this requirement would be unreasonable or if there is undue delay (see eg a clear statement in this regard in Article 41 paragraph 1(c) of the International Covenant on Civil and Political Rights and Article 15 of the Draft Articles on Diplomatic Protection).

Here, it seems that the authorities of Nowdstate will not undertake any steps, regardless of all the attempts made by Guy Badkopf's parents. Therefore, it can reasonably be said that local remedies are unavailable (or at least not reasonably available) and that thus the requirement to exhaust local remedies should not be seen as barring the ECtHR from accepting the case.]

3. Right to life

Article 2 paragraph 1 ECHR guarantees everyone the right to life. The right to life is one of the supreme rights of human beings. It constitutes the precondition to have access to all other human rights and represents a fundamental value of democratic societies, as the ECtHR held in the *McCann* case (ECtHR, *Case of McCann and others v The United Kingdom*, Judgment, Application No 18984/91, 27 September 1995, paragraph 147). Yet, even though it is considered as a non-derogable right according to Article 15 paragraph 2 ECHR, it can be subject to restrictions and limitations. For this purpose, Article 2 paragraph 2 sets out the situations in which it is lawful to use lethal force against a person. The list in this provision is exhaustive and the situations mentioned have to be strictly construed.

According to Article 2 paragraph 2 ECHR, lethal force can lawfully be used against a person in defending another person from unlawful violence (a), in order to arrest someone or to prevent a lawfully arrested person from escaping (b), and in actions that are lawfully taken for the purpose of quelling a riot or insurrection (c). For our case, only the first and the last situation are relevant.

The Convention does not provide a definition of the first circumstance, the situation of self-defence. According to case law, a situation of self-defence in the sense of Article 2 paragraph 2(a) exists when there is a threat to life or physical integrity of another person. In addition, this threat has to be imminent and the use of force has to be proportionate to the threat.

Concerning the situation mentioned in letter (c) of Article 2 paragraph 2 ECHR, riots have not been defined either in the ECHR. Both the European Commission on Human Rights (EComHR) and the ECtHR adopt an empirical approach. This means that the existence of a riot has to be assessed on a case-by-case basis in light of all the relevant circumstances. Case law has given some useful hints in order to determine whether a riot exists. Elements that can be considered include, for example, the presence of a hostile crowd of more than 150 persons, throwing of stones and bottles against military or police forces, the risk of injuries and the context in which these troubles take place. (See on this eg EComHR, *Stewart v United Kingdom*, Decision on Admissibility, Application No 10044/82, 10 July 1984, paragraph 25; ECtHR, *Case of Güleç v Turkey*, Judgment, Application No 54/1997/838/1044, 27 July 1998, paragraph 71.)

Finally, the specific use of force has to be absolutely necessary, as is clearly provided in Article 2 paragraph 2, for all three situations listed therein. The Convention contains in this regard a proportionality element, which needs to be interpreted strictly, as the ECtHR and the EComHR have held in various cases (EComHR, *Stewart v United Kingdom*, Decision on Admissibility, Application No 10044/82, 10 July 1984, paragraph 18; ECtHR, *Case of McCann and others v The United Kingdom*, Judgment, Application No 18984/91, 27 September 1995, paragraph 149; ECtHR, *Case of Güleç v Turkey*, Judgment, Application No 54/1997/838/1044, 27 July 1998, paragraph 71; ECtHR, *Case of Isayeva v Russia*, Judgment, Application No 57950/00, 24 February 2005, paragraph 173). Factors to be taken into account in this proportionality assessment include the nature of the goal sought by using force, the danger for human lives and physical integrity inherent in the situation, and the extent to which the use of force is a risk for other persons.

In addition, prior to the proportionality principle, the precautionary principle needs to be included in the analysis. As the ECtHR argued in the *Ergi* case, the precautionary principle requires that all measures be taken to minimise the risks associated with the use of lethal force for the population (ECtHR, *Case of Ergi v Turkey*, Judgment, Application No 66/1997/850/1057, 28 July 1998, paragraph 79). In this regard, all necessary precautions need to be taken, both in the planning stage and the phase of actual use of force (see ECtHR, *Case of McCann and others v The United Kingdom*, Judgment, Application No 18984/91, 27 September 1995, paragraph 194). There thus exists an obligation to anticipate and to prevent risk (ECtHR, *Case of Isayeva v Russia*, Judgment, Application No 57950/00, 24 February 2005, paragraph 175). The more foreseeable a situation was and the more the use of force was prepared in advance, the more precautionary measures need to be taken.

Finally, Article 2 ECHR does not only protect people against the arbitrary deprivation of life. Implicitly, this provision also contains positive obligations falling upon the State party, such as the obligation to make investigations, to prosecute and to make reparations. In particular, the obligation to make investigations applies as soon as the authorities are informed about the death of a person. The latter should not have to be the subject of a complaint. The investigation has to be independent, impartial and prompt and has to involve as far as possible the relatives of the deceased person. In addition, the investigation has to contain a certain form of public scrutiny (see ECtHR, *Case of McCann and others v The United Kingdom*, Judgment, Application No 18984/91, 27 September 1995, paragraphs 161, 162; ECtHR, *Case of Güleç v Turkey*, Judgment, Application No 54/1997/838/1044, 27 July 1998, paragraph 78).

4. Application of the law to the facts

In our case, a large demonstration took place on 14 January 2012. The demonstration quickly got violent and protestors were pelting the police with glass bottles and stones. We do not know the exact number of participants in this demonstration, but the facts indicate that it was 'very large'. We can therefore assume that more than 150 persons participated.

Throwing bottles and stones can be very dangerous to the physical integrity and even life of a person. Glass bottles are susceptible to break into pieces, thereby seriously cutting the affected persons. As for stones, they are, depending on their size and weight, very dangerous blunt objects or even weapons. They present, therefore, a significant risk of injury as well.

The demonstration took place in a difficult economic climate, in which the government had adopted new austerity measures to fight the State's debts. As we can deduce from the facts, this situation has existed for a while, since Nowdstate had astronomic debts and was moreover used to this kind of protest.

Taking all these elements together, we can thus conclude that there was indeed a riot on 14 January 2012, in the sense of Article 2 paragraph 2(c) ECHR and as developed by case law. Thus, prima facie, the police had the right to use lethal force in order to master and end this situation. Since Guy Badkopf clearly took part in the riot, the police sergeant Ted Shooter had the right to shoot at him.

However, using live ammunition in the middle of a supposedly dense crowd presents a very high risk of collateral damage. Even though glass bottles and stones pose a danger to the physical integrity and life of persons, it does not seem to be proportionate to use live ammunition against the protesters. It seems that the goal of the action was only to disperse the crowd. Yet, this could have been achieved with other means than live ammunition.

It is true that the police first used water canons. This measure was planned and prepared before the operation and thus constitutes a good precautionary measure. Unfortunately, the water canons were not effective at dispersing the crowd. However, the precautionary principle would require the police also to prepare other measures presenting less risk than the use of live ammunition in case the water canons should prove not to be sufficient. We know from the facts that Nowdstate was used to this kind of protest action. Moreover, it was also well known that violent thugs frequently participated in these demonstrations. Nevertheless, even though violent, nothing in the facts suggests that these thugs were actually armed, other than with glass bottles and stones. All these facts, known by the police, should have led the police to prepare less harmful measures, such as the use of rubber bullets or tear gas. However, this was not done. By authorising the use of live ammunition, as a backup should the water canons fail, Nowdstate did not take all the precautions that the situation at hand demanded. This lack of precaution finally led to the death of the teenager Guy Badkopf.

In particular, it was police sergeant Ted Shooter who shot Guy Badkopf. From the facts of the case we know that Ted Shooter is a very experienced police officer and a former army sharpshooter. His excellent shooting capabilities are confirmed by the fact that in a generally chaotic situation he was able to aim at the head of the teenager. The principle of proportionality as well as his experience as police sergeant required that if he was able intentionally to fire such a shot, he should have targeted a less vital part of the body of Guy. It should be recalled in this context that the goal of shooting at Guy was only to neutralise him, since Ted Shooter (wrongly) thought that the teenager was about to throw a glass bottle at him. Thus, this use of lethal force was not at all necessary to end the riot and particularly to neutralise Guy Badkopf, especially when we also take into account Ted Shooter's capabilities and experience as police officer and sharpshooter.

For the same reasons this use of lethal force could not be justified under Article 2 paragraph 2(a) ECHR either. As pointed out above, throwing glass bottles and stones can indeed present a danger to the life and physical integrity of persons. However, objectively speaking, Guy was not about to throw anything at the police forces, but was simply throwing an empty soda can to the ground. It is true that in the chaotic and hostile situation, which Ted Shooter had to face, it might be understandable why he felt himself threatened by Guy. Nevertheless, his capacities as an experienced police sergeant and former army sharpshooter and the intentional character of the shot are elements that have to be taken into account when assessing the proportionality of his action. As argued above, his experience should have allowed him to aim at another less vital part of Guy's body than his head. Thus, this shot does not appear to be absolutely necessary in light of Article 2 paragraph 2(a) ECHR either.

It appears from our analysis that the police force of Nowdstate did not respect the precautionary principle and the principle of proportionality contained in Article 2 paragraph 2 ECHR. In addition, by shooting at the head of Guy Badkopf, Ted Shooter has exceeded the limits of the strict proportionality to be applied in all instances of use of lethal force. Consequently, Nowdstate violated the obligation contained in Article 2 paragraph 1 ECHR towards Guy Badkopf.

Furthermore, by classifying the case after only sketchy investigation on the events of 14 January 2012 and by not taking any steps to deal with the complaints of Guy Badkopf's parents, the authorities of Nowdstate also violated their obligation to investigate, implicitly contained in Article 2 paragraph 1 ECHR.

5. Conclusion

In conclusion, the applicants respectfully ask the Court to adjudge and declare that Nowdstate has violated Article 2 paragraph 1 ECHR: (1) by not taking all precautionary measures when preparing the operation to quell the riot on 14 January 2012, resulting in the death of Guy Badkopf; (2) by using lethal force in violation of the principle of proportionality, especially in relation to the shot to the head of Guy Badkopf by Ted Shooter; and finally, (3) by not respecting its obligation to conduct an investigation following the death of the teenager Guy Badkopf.

SUGGESTED SOLUTIONS
International Refugee Law

Suggested Solution—Case 8.4

Abbreviations used

Cartagena Declaration	=	1984 Cartagena Declaration on Refugees
YSL	=	Young Socialist League
1951 Convention	=	1951 Convention Relating to the Status of Refugees
1967 Protocol	=	1967 Protocol to the 1951 Convention Relating to the Status of Refugees

1. Applicable law

In order to determine whether Pascal, Tom and Ben are refugees, we will first of all apply the 1951 Convention Relating to the Statues of Refugees (1951 Convention) and where necessary the 1967 Protocol to this Convention. Luren is a party to the 1951 Convention, which is thus applicable to this State. Since Desor is not a party to the 1951 Convention, this Convention as such is not directly applicable to it. In the case of Desor, we will apply its own national law definition of refugees, which essentially repeats the definition found in the 1984 Cartagena Declaration on Refugees (Cartagena Declaration). The Cartagena Declaration is not formally binding and the proposed refugee definition is only recommended. However, like Desor, several States (mainly from Latin America) have incorporated the Cartagena Declaration's principles and its refugee definition into their own national laws. Thus, through this incorporation the definition contained in the Cartagena Declaration becomes binding on Desor as national law.

2. Elements in order to be recognised as a refugee

In order to be recognised as a refugee under the 1951 Convention, there are at least three elements that need to be considered. These are the so-called inclusion clauses or criteria: (1) the person in question must be outside his/her country of nationality; (2) she or he must be suffering from a well-founded fear of persecution based on one of the five convention grounds; and (3) she or he must be unable or unwilling to get protection from his/her State of nationality.

[*If you prefer, you can also say that the analysis of the refugee statues is a five-step approach, by splitting the second criterion: (1) the person in question must be outside his/her country of nationality; (2) she/he must have a well-founded fear; (3) this fear must relate to persecution; (4) this persecution must occur on the basis of one of the five grounds enumerated in the 1951 Convention; and finally (5) the person seeking asylum must be unwilling or unable to get protection from his/her country of nationality. The number of steps taken does not really matter. It is, however, important that all elements are carefully assessed. Furthermore, it does for the solution not matter whether all the criteria are assessed simultaneously for all three applicants, or whether one applicant is dealt with after another.*

It should also be noted that in refugee law it is very important how certain actions or circumstances are viewed by the person making the assessment. Different assessments of the same case are therefore possible.]

3. Preliminary clarifications regarding the applicability of the 1951 Convention refugee definition

As specified above, Desor is not a party to the 1951 Convention. However, it has incorporated into its own national law the definition found in the Cartagena Declaration. Article III paragraph 3 of the Cartagena Declaration containing this definition specifies that a person will be recognised as a refugee when she/he fulfils the 1951 Convention criteria (see above) or is fleeing from additional situations not connected to the 1951 Convention grounds, such as fleeing massive human rights violations or foreign domination. The reference to the general refugee definition contained in the 1951 Convention is made without specification or limitation. This indicates that this general definition will be applicable to whomever chooses to adopt the Cartagena Declaration definition (ie in national law). Thus, the 1951 Convention is not applicable to Tom claiming asylum in Desor as such and consequently if recognised as a refugee he cannot benefit from the rights contained in this Convention. Yet, the criteria contained in the 1951 Convention are nevertheless used to determine whether he is a refugee, since the Cartagena Declaration incorporated into national law provides for this. Legally speaking—and for the applicable rights and obligations of the refugee—it makes a difference, however, which legal instrument is applied—national law based on the Cartagena Declaration or an international treaty such as the 1951 Convention.

4. Outside the country of nationality

In order to be a refugee, the person in question has to have crossed an international border and to be consequently outside his/her country of nationality.

Pascal—a national of Apoka—is in Luren indeed outside his country of nationality. Tom, also a national of Apoka, is outside his country of nationality as well since he fled to Desor.

Ben—a national of Apoka and Conda—is also outside his countries of nationalities since he is in Luren. However, Article 1A paragraph 2 of the 1951 Convention clearly provides that in the case of multiple nationalities the expression 'country of his nationality' means each of his countries of nationality. It further adds that a person is not seen as lacking protection of his State of nationality if there is no well-founded fear in that other country as well and he has not sought the protection of this other country of nationality. Indeed, Ben is also a national of Conda. We have no indication about any well-founded fear he might have in this State. Thus, concluding based on the information provided, we can say that Ben is not fulfilling these first requirements in order to be a refugee, since he has another State of nationality to go to and to seek protection from. We will thus not investigate his case further.

5. Well-founded fear of persecution based on a convention ground

This criterion of well-founded fear is composed of a subjective element (fear) referring to a State of mind and an objective element (well-founded). The subjective element is necessarily difficult to assess, and thus it matters whether the applicants appear to be credible. Having applied for refugee status is thereby in practice often taken as indicating fear. The 'well-foundedness' of the fear needs to be assessed in the context prevailing in the applicant's country of nationality, as well as the applicant's personal situation in connection to that. The credibility of the applicant and his/her fear have to be evaluated against the objective information available on his/her country of origin and the conditions found there. Thereby, it is not necessary that it is absolutely certain that the applicant would suffer harm in his/her country of nationality. It has only to be shown that there is a 'reasonable possibility' that the person concerned would face harm if returned to the country of origin. (For example the US Supreme Court in *INS v Cardoza-Fonseca* held that it has to be shown that 'it is more likely than not that the alien would be subject to persecution' if he had to go back (*Immigration and Naturalization Service v Cardoza-Fonseca,* US Supreme Court, 1987, 480 US 421)).

Furthermore, the well-founded fear has to be related to persecution on one of the five convention grounds. Thus, persons fleeing from other situations than persecution—eg famine—would not satisfy the 1951 Convention definition. Persecution is not clearly defined in international law, but it is generally understood as the systematic mistreatment of an individual or group by another group, by using threats to life or physical freedom as well as other serious violations of basic human rights. Persecution often has a systematic element. As stated above, the 1951 Convention only recognises persons as refugees who flee from persecution for reasons of race, religion, nationality, membership of a particular social group or political opinion.

Applying these theoretical considerations to our case at hand, we can argue the following. Both brothers have applied for refugee status, indicating already that they are afraid. They were both active in the political party YSL. The government of Apoka is arresting political activists, including both current and former members of the YSL. The arrested activists are systematically tortured and sometimes also killed. If Pascal and Tom were to return to Apoka it is very likely that they would suffer the same treatment. An indication in Tom's case could also be the fact that his apartment has already been searched by the police, who apparently also sought to arrest him (but he was not there). Thus, in light of this context and their personal situation the fear of the two brothers seems to be well-founded.

In addition, this well-founded fear needs to relate to persecution. The government systematically commits several violent acts against political opponents. Arbitrary arrest, detention, torture and extrajudicial killings are all serious violations of internationally recognised human rights guarantees, which mostly are also customary in nature (it violates, for example, the UN Convention Against Torture, but also numerous provisions of the International Covenant on Civil and Political Rights such as Article 6 ICCPR (right to life), Article 7 ICCPR (freedom from torture), Article 9 ICCPR (liberty and no arbitrary arrest/detention)). Thus, there is indeed persecution present.

Furthermore, it is clear that the reason why the brothers are persecuted is their political opinion, a convention ground.

Consequently, both Pascal and Tom have a well-founded fear of being persecuted due to their political opinion.

6. Unable or unwilling to avail him/herself of the protection of the State of nationality

In order to be recognised as a refugee, the applicant must also be unable or unwilling to seek the protection of his/her State of nationality.

It seems quite obvious that Pascal and Tom are both unable and unwilling to seek protection from Apoka. Since the government of their State of nationality is in fact persecuting political opponents like them, it is highly unlikely that it would protect them. From the facts it also seems that since it is the government of Apoka that is responsible for the persecution, this persecution extends to the whole territory and the brothers could not find protection in another part of the country (as would, for example, be the case if it was a local government responsible for the persecution). In addition, under the present circumstances it cannot be expected that Pascal and Tom would actually ask Apoka for protection.

7. Exclusion from refugee status

The general exclusion clauses, namely Article 1F of the 1951 Convention, do not seem to be applicable. Normally, these clauses are not applied systematically but only if there are 'serious reasons for considering' that the person in question has committed any of the acts enumerated in this Article. There are no such 'serious reasons' here.

However, we need to consider Article 1E with respect to Pascal. This Article provides that a person shall not be recognised as a refugee if she/he has in her/his country of residence basically the same rights and obligations as a national of that State. Pascal has indeed been living for two years in Luren, and thus it can be said that he 'has taken residence' there. We know for sure that he does not have Lurenian nationality. However, we have no information at all on his rights and obligations there and whether or not they would be the same as a national of that State. In light of what is at stake and the uncertainty on this crucial point, this gap should not be treated lightly. It should therefore not be assumed that Pascal would benefit from the same rights and obligations as Luren's nationals and could thus be excluded from refugee status.

8. Conclusion

Both Pascal and Tom fulfil the requirements in order to be recognised as refugees—Pascal under the 1951 Convention and Tom under the national law incorporating the Cartagena Declaration.

It could be added that Pascal is a so-called refugee *sur place* since when he left Apoka two years ago he was not yet a refugee (there was no reason for him to have a well-founded fear then). Becoming a refugee outside one's country is, however, not prohibited.

Suggested Solution—Case 8.5

Abbreviations used

CAT	=	UN Convention against Torture and other Cruel, Inhuman or Degrading Treatment or Punishment
ExCom	=	Executive Committee (of UNHCR)
ICCPR	=	International Covenant on Civil and Political Rights
ICJ	=	International Court of Justice
PCIJ	=	Permanent Court of International Justice
UNHCR	=	Office of the United Nations High Commissioner for Refugees
1951 Convention	=	1951 Convention Relating to the Status of Refugees

1. Applicable law

Naret is a party to the UN Convention against Torture and other Cruel, Inhuman or Degrading Treatment or Punishment (CAT) and the International Covenant on Civil and Political Rights (ICCPR). Therefore, we will be able to apply these two conventions.

The question posed asks us to consider the legality of the expulsion of the Shasta from Naret. To put it into other words, we are asked to test whether there is a violation of the *non-refoulement* rule. Such a prohibition expressly aimed at refugees is also contained in Article 33 of the 1951 Convention Relating to the Status of Refugees (1951 Convention). However, Naret is not a party to this instrument. Therefore, since the question asks us to consider both treaty and customary law, we will ascertain as a first step whether it can be said that the *non-refoulement* rule contained in Article 33 of the 1951 Convention is customary law.

2. Is the *non-refoulement* rule contained in Article 33 customary law?

As we have said above, the government of Naret is not a party to the 1951 Convention, and hence the Convention as such cannot be applied to protect the Shasta from *refoulement*. Therefore, we have to consider whether *non-refoulement* is customary law. Customary law applies to all States, regardless of whether or not they are party to a particular treaty containing this rule. Furthermore, it is well established that customary and treaty rules can independently exist side by side, even if they relate to the exact same matter. The ICJ has confirmed this independent existence of treaty and customary rules, for example in the *Nicaragua* case (ICJ, Judgment on the Merits, *Military and Paramilitary Activities in and against Nicaragua* (Nicaragua v United Sates of America), 1986, paragraphs 172–182). While the rules exist independently, the relationship between treaty and customary rules is nevertheless rather close. Treaties can in fact codify existing customary rules (declaratory effect), they can crystallise an emerging customary rule (crystallising effect) or the treaty rule can develop later into a customary rule (generating effect). The ICJ has pronounced itself several times on the relationship between treaty and custom, most famously in the *North Sea Continental Shelf* case (ICJ, Judgment, *North Sea Continental Shelf case*, (Germany v Netherlands/Denmark), 1969, paragraphs 60–83).

Thus, the fact that the 1951 Convention contains in its Article 33 a *non-refoulement* rule as a treaty rule does not prevent it from existing in customary international law.

At the same time, its existence as a treaty rule does not confirm the existence of such a customary rule either.

In order to conclude that a rule of customary law exists, it is according to the 'two-element theory' necessary to establish two elements, namely State practice and *opinio juris*. These two elements have been clearly established by the ICJ as being necessary to find a customary rule (see ICJ, Judgment, *North Sea Continental Shelf case*, (Germany v Netherlands/Denmark), 1969, paragraphs 70–79). Admittedly, it is in practice not always easy or sometimes not even possible to distinguish them.

[*There are numerous possibilities and elements to be used when assessing the practice and* opinio juris *of States regarding* non-refoulement. *It should therefore be noted that the elements provided below constitute only a selection and should in no way be regarded as exhaustive. Other elements can—and should—be provided. Furthermore, as pointed out above, the difference between practice and* opinio juris *is not always clear cut and there can be different assessments of specific elements. It is therefore possible that students decide rather to include some specific element contained here in State practice in* opinio juris.]

(a) State practice

State practice means that States (or other relevant entities such as international organisations) are actually respecting and following the rule in question. Positive acts are very important, but as the PCIJ held in the *Lotus* case, abstentions can also count (PCIJ, Judgment, *Lotus*, 1927, 28). It is often held that also statements of States or General Assembly resolutions are an expression of State practice. [*Although statements are often used as evidence of State practice, it should be noted that this is controversial. Not all legal scholars agree that statements can be part of custom, but for them only positive acts or abstentions should be taken into account. The student should here decide on his/her own position whether or not to accept such statements as part of State practice*].

It should be noted that it is not necessary that there is absolute uniform practice by all States all the time in order to fulfil this element. Rather, as the ICJ noted in the *Nicaragua* case, the practice should be consistent 'in general' (ICJ, Judgment on the Merits, *Military and Paramilitary Activities in and against Nicaragua* (Nicaragua v United States of America), 1986, paragraph 186). Yet, when looking at the practice of States, the ICJ held that we should look mostly at the practice of 'States whose interests [are] specially affected', since these are the States that can significantly contribute to the development of law in that area (see ICJ, Judgment, *North Sea Continental Shelf case* (Germany v Netherlands/Denmark), 1969, paragraph 73).

In general, States do not send persons who have been recognised as refugees back to their State of nationality, thereby respecting the *non-refoulement* provision. Often, conformity to the rule receives—understandably—a lot less attention than non-conformity, which might therefore be more difficult to track. Yet, as pointed out above, the ICJ held in the *Nicaragua* case that conformity to a rule has only to exist 'in general' and not all the time. Thus, the fact that some States might not conform to the *non-refoulement* rule at all times does not prevent the existence of sufficient State practice.

Moreover, as we have argued above, treaties can be a source of customary rules. After all, signing or ratifying a treaty is a positive act of a State, declaring thereby that it agrees to behave in conformity with the rules contained therein. If we thus accept the general idea that the acceptance of treaties containing *non-refoulement* rules is an expression of State practice as well, we can make reference to different international treaties as an additional element. According to the UNHCR, these treaties reflect a consistent practice of States in relation to the *non-refoulement* rule. A selection of such treaties includes the CAT (Article 3) and the ICCPR (Articles 6 and 7, as clarified by eg General Comment 20 of the Human Rights Committee), the Organisation of African Unity Convention Governing the Specific Aspects of Refugee Problems in Africa (Article II paragraph 3), and the Inter-American Convention on Human Rights (Article 22 paragraph 8). It should also be noted that the Cartagena Declaration stresses the importance of the *non-refoulement* principle in its Article III paragraph 5.

Furthermore, the principle of *non-refoulement* has also been reaffirmed in numerous conclusions of the UNHCR Executive Committee (ExCom). Even though admittedly conclusions by the ExCom are not formally legally binding, they are still of some weight in the interpretation and application of the Convention, since the ExCom is composed of 78 States. This represents a weighty voice. One criterion in order to be elected to the ExCom is to have a 'demonstrated interest in and devotion to the solution of refugee problems'. Therefore, we can say that those States are among 'most interested States'. This in turn fulfils the requirement posed by the ICJ in the *North Sea Continental Shelf* case, noted above, that we have to look at the practice of the States whose interests are especially affected. Consequently, if those States reaffirm the *non-refoulement* principle, this can be seen as contributing to the practice of States.

[*If you do not accept that the acceptance of treaties and certain statements can be seen as contributing to State practice, then you would leave out the last two elements treated above.*]

Thus, there seems to be a sufficient number of States generally acting in conformity with the principle of *non-refoulement*, and thus the element of State practice can be said to be fulfilled.

(b) Opinio juris

Opinio juris refers to the fact that in order to amount to a customary rule, States need to believe that they are acting in a particular way because it is the law.

According to the ICJ, *opinio juris* can 'with all due caution' be deduced from UN General Assembly resolutions (see ICJ, Judgment on the Merits, *Military and Paramilitary Activities in and against Nicaragua* (Nicaragua v United Sates of America), 1986, paragraph 188). Arguably, similar documents in the relevant field of law can thus also serve as helping to identify the *opinio juris*.

The UNHCR has reported that most States either tacitly accepted the principle or even expressly affirmed it (even when they were not party to the 1951 Convention), indicating that they believe it is the law to be followed.

It is true that the rule of *non-refoulement* is sometimes breached by States in practice. However, in these situations States usually try to find an excuse why *non-refoulement* in this case did not apply. For example, a State might argue that the persons concerned were not refugees but illegal aliens and therefore not protected by *non-refoulement* under Article 33 of the 1951 Convention (this was, for example, the line of argument used by Tanzania, when expelling refugees in the late 1990s) or the State claims that there was an exception (eg exclusion) which applied. Yet, when a State acts prima facie in violation of a particular rule, but at the same times offers justifications why this rule is not applicable in the case at hand (thus arguing that there is no violation), this can be taken as strengthening the rule rather than weakening it. It means, that the State actually believes in the legal rule just violated and tries to find a way not to have it breached by its actions.

There seems to be enough evidence to conclude that *opinio juris* too exists. Consequently, we can conclude that *non-refoulement* contained in Article 33 of the 1951 Convention is indeed a customary law provision, a conclusion that is widely supported by legal scholars as well. [*If you are able to, you could provide here a reference to a particular legal scholar or article. Remember that according to Article 38 paragraph 1(d) of the ICJ Statute, the writings of legal scholars are secondary sources of law. A possible reference here would for example include: E Lauterpacht and D Bethlehem, 'The Scope and Content of the Principle of* Non-refoulement*: Opinion' in E Feller, V Türk and F Nicholson (eds),* Refugee Protection in International Law: UNHCR's Global Consultation on International Protection *(Cambridge, Cambridge University Press, 2003) 87–179*].

3. What are the obligations of Naret under international law in relation to the Shasta?

The Shasta are recognised as refugees in Naret. Naret has not made this determination itself; it was done by the UNHCR to which Naret has given this power. It is not prohibited to outsource these refugee status determinations to the UNHCR. There are numerous reasons—such as limited financial and human resources—why States might prefer not to conduct these assessments themselves. As stated, Naret does recognise the decisions by the UNHCR, which is important to ensure the proper protection of refugees in the State in question. Consequently, the Shasta should benefit from all rights (and obligations) as refugees.

We have concluded above that *non-refoulement* contained in Article 33 of the 1951 Convention is part of customary law. Therefore, Naret is bound by it, regardless of the fact that it is not party to the 1951 Convention. This means that under customary international law, Naret has an obligation not to *refoule* the Shasta to Essa, where they might face torture or other inhuman or degrading treatment. It is true that Article 33 of the 1951 Convention contains in paragraph 2 some exceptions when refugees cannot profit from the protection against *refoulement*. However, nothing in the facts indicates that the Shasta are (or are seen) as a 'danger to the security' of Naret or its community. Therefore, we do not have to further analyse this point.

In addition [*or if you came to the conclusion that the obligation in Article 33 of the 1951 Convention is not customary*], it should be kept in mind that Naret also has obligations under human rights treaties. The Shasta are protected by human rights obligations since they are human beings (thus even if Naret would not recognise them as refugees they would be protected). For example, Article 4 CAT very clearly prohibits States from sending people back to States where they would face torture. In addition, the Human Rights Committee has interpreted Articles 6 and 7 ICCPR as containing *non-refoulement* obligations. Naret is a party to both of these instruments and is thus bound by these obligations. It should be noted that unlike Article 33 of the 1951 Convention, these provisions in the human rights treaties do not contain exceptions.

4. Conclusion

Having established that Naret is bound by the customary reflection of the principle of *non-refoulement* under the 1951 Convention and the relevant provisions in the two human rights instruments it is a party to (CAT and ICCPR), we can conclude that by sending the Shasta (recognised refugees) back to Essa, Naret is clearly violating its customary as well as conventional obligations under international law.

Suggested Solution—Case 8.6

Abbreviations used

CAT	=	UN Convention against Torture and other Cruel, Inhuman or Degrading Treatment or Punishment
1951 Convention	=	1951 Convention Relating to the Status of Refugees

1. Applicable law

Since Ometry is a party to the 1951 Convention Relating to the Status of Refugees (1951 Convention), we will first and foremost apply this convention. If necessary, we will also apply the UN Convention against Torture and other Cruel, Inhuman or Degrading Treatment or Punishment (CAT), to which Ometry is also a party.

2. Ending of refugee status under the 1951 Convention in general

We are asked to clarify in general under what circumstances refugee status can end under the 1951 Convention. First of all, it can clearly be said that Roberto Linea is wrong when he claims that refugee status can never be ended and that it is an unlimited status. On the contrary, refugee status is meant to be a *temporary* status for individuals who are, due to specific circumstances, currently without protection of their State of nationality. Thus, as soon as this international protection is no longer necessary, the refugee status granting this protection should also end.

In fact, the 1951 Convention itself provides in Article 1C for situations when the status of a refugee can be ended. Article 1C contains thus the so-called 'cessation clauses', which are exhaustive in the 1951 Convention.

Article 1C of the 1951 Convention contains two types of situations. Paragraphs 1–4 are based on voluntary acts by the refugee him/herself. Paragraphs 5 and 6, on the other hand, are based on fundamental changes in the circumstances in the home country.

Voluntary acts

These acts are regulated in paragraphs 1–4 of Article 1C. The important element concerning these cessation clauses is that the act in question (ie the reavailment of protection by the refugee's State of nationality) happens truly voluntarily. That is, no pressure—whether active or implicit—or other circumstances should have led the refugee to act in that particular manner. Furthermore, the refugee must really be able to enjoy protection from a State—be this his 'old' State of nationality or another one. Thus, just getting a new passport without a change in the attitude and situation at home would not suffice. As way of an example it should be noted that political refugees fleeing the Pinochet regime in Chile were able to get new passports from their embassies abroad, but would still have been without protection had they returned home. As to paragraph 4, it should be noted that it is generally accepted that visiting one's country does not count as 're-establishment'. Re-establishment in the sense of paragraph 4 needs to be permanent.

Ceased circumstances clauses

Article 1C paragraphs 5 and 6 are the so-called 'ceased circumstances clauses'. The situation under these clauses is such that there has been a change of circumstances. This change effectively ends the reason why the person previously had a well-founded fear of persecution on one of the convention grounds. These clauses can be more difficult to apply, since there is no voluntary act of the refugee involved, but it is the authorities of the country of asylum that decide whether or not the circumstances have changed sufficiently. Consequently, these clauses have given rise to more controversies and court cases. When assessing a situation under paragraphs 5 or 6 of Article 1C it is crucial to determine whether the circumstances in the country really *fundamentally* changed in a way as effectively to end persecution of the refugee in question. If the situation changed, but not for the refugee in question, then the ceased circumstances clauses would not be applicable. Consider, for example, a female refugee who is recognised on the basis that she feared female genital mutilation. If there is a new government but the practice of female genital mutilation is still widespread, it cannot be said that the circumstances have fundamentally changed for her.

Furthermore, the change needs to be *durable*. Thus, it has to be assessed whether the situation remains stable and is not just a brief period of relaxation. Generally, it is recommended to wait for 12–18 months when assessing the stability.

Again, it has to be shown that the State of nationality or origin can and is willing to protect the person in question. This could, for example, be assessed by determining whether the State guarantees protection for the most fundamental human rights.

It might be noted that there are exceptions contained in paragraphs 5 and 6 of Article 1C, in which cases the person concerned will not cease to be a refugee since international protection continues to remain necessary. [*Despite the limit in referring only to refugees under Article 1A paragraph 1, it is today generally accepted that the exceptions apply to all refugees*].

[*There is a further situation when refugee status can end, namely revocation. Revocation is not contained in the 1951 Convention as such, but is developed by State practice based on this Convention. Since the question is asked under the 1951 Convention it is thus not strictly necessary to mention revocation. For the sake of completeness, it should just be said that this is the situation when a recognised refugee commits a crime falling under Article 1F(a) or (c), after having been granted refugee status. The refugee status can thus be ended. Note that this is not a possible scenario for Article 1F(b), since this provision contains a geographical as well as temporal limitation.*]

It is important to point out that cessation of refugee status needs a formal decision. Refugee status will thus never cease automatically; the relevant authorities need to make the necessary determinations. During that formal decision-making process, procedural safeguards need to be in place and in addition every individual should have the possibility to challenge the decision concerning cessation.

3. Roberto Linea's situation

We have also been asked to assess the concrete situation of Roberto Linea.

There have been some radical changes in Calculu, the State of nationality of Roberto. A new democratic government is in place, in which all ethnic minorities are represented proportionally. New laws have been passed, including laws protecting human rights. The situation is now peaceful and stable. Roberto had been persecuted because he belonged to an ethnic minority.

Seeing that these minorities are now part of the government and that the situation is described as peaceful, it can be concluded that persecution on this ground no longer happens. Therefore, there has indeed been a fundamental change in the circumstances in relation to Roberto.

In addition, the new democratic government has been elected three years ago and the country has been peaceful and stable for about two years. This therefore seems also to be a durable change and not just a passing phase. We can thus conclude that there has indeed been a change in the circumstances which led Roberto to become a refugee in the first place. The government of Calculu, as far as we can tell from the facts, is making a genuine effort to protect its citizens, as can, for example, be inferred from the fact that they have passed laws protecting basic human rights. Nothing in the facts indicates, moreover, that Roberto has 'compelling reasons' to invoke a *previous* persecution (thus not the one whose circumstances have now ceased) in order to refuse to avail himself of the protection of Calculu. Thus, the exception is not applicable.

Consequently, we can argue that Article 1C paragraph 5 applies to Roberto.

In addition, we can also argue that Article 1C paragraph 2 applies to Roberto as well. He had previously lost his nationality of Calculu, but when he was offered the possibility to reacquire it, he did not hesitate. Nothing indicates that there was some pressure involved in his decision. As argued above, it seems furthermore that Calculu is genuinely able and willing to protect its citizens, thus the purpose of ceasing refugee protection (obtaining protection again from the State of nationality) would seem to be fulfilled.

However, the fact that Roberto has visited Calculu several times would not be enough to satisfy the requirement for voluntary re-establishment (Article 1C paragraph 4). As indicated above, voluntary re-establishment means permanent establishment and not visits.

Consequently, based on Article 1C paragraphs 2 and 5, Roberto Linea's refuge status indeed ceases.

4. Consequences of the end of refugee status

The consequence of cessation of refugee status is first of all the loss of refugee status as such. Connected to that, the person in question also loses all the rights and benefits attached to that status, as contained in the 1951 Convention.

5. Conclusion

Based on the reasoning above, we can conclude, first, that refugee status is a temporary status, which can cease in accordance with Article 1C of the 1951 Convention. Roberto Linea is thus wrong to claim that refugee status is an unlimited status, which can never end. Second, based on the fundamental and durable changes in Calculu—Roberto Linea's State of nationality—and Roberto Linea's own voluntary reacquisition of his former nationality, we can conclude that his refugee status in Ometry can cease. He is thus no longer a refugee. The process of cessation has to be notified to Roberto Linea in a formal decision and he has the right to challenge this decision.

SUGGESTED SOLUTIONS
International Humanitarian Law

Suggested Solution—Case 8.7

Abbreviations used

Additional Protocol I (AP I)	=	Additional Protocol I of 8 June 1977 to the Geneva Conventions of 12 August 1949, and Relating to the Protection of Victims of International Armed Conflicts
Additional Protocol II (AP II)	=	Additional Protocol II from 8 June 1977 to the Geneva Conventions from 12 August 1949, and Relating to the Protection of Victims of Non-International Armed Conflicts
DoL	=	Defenders of Liberty
Geneva Conventions (GCs)	=	Geneva Conventions from 12 August 1949
IAC	=	international armed conflict
ICJ	=	International Court of Justice
ICTY	=	International Criminal Tribunal for the former Yugoslavia
IHL	=	International Humanitarian Law
NIAC	=	non-international armed conflict
SRA	=	ILC Articles on Responsibility of States for Internationally Wrongful Acts 2001 (State Responsibility Articles)

1. Introduction

As stated in the facts, clashes have occurred between the government of Nounabe and the Defenders of Liberty (DoL) since 2010. In this question we are asked to determine the existence of an armed conflict between the different players. If an armed conflict exists, we are further asked to qualify its character. Since the applicable law largely depends on the existence and of the type of the armed conflict, we will not be able to make a general statement as to the applicable law beforehand, but will deal with it under each of the stages analysed.

In order to answer this question we have to divide the chronology of events into different parts. For our purposes, it is possible to establish five distinct stages: from the beginning of 2010 to November 2010; from November 2010 to February 2011; from March 2011 to end of May 2011; from beginning of June 2011 to 13 November 2011; and finally from 14 November 2011 to today.

2. From beginning 2010 to November 2010

During this time, a group—the DoL—decided to rebel and to destabilise the government of Nounabe. Therefore, the DoL launched several sporadic attacks, but did not succeed in destabilising the government in power.

Applicable law

From the facts we know that Nounabe is a party to the four Geneva Conventions from 12 August 1949 (Geneva Conventions, GCs). Nounabe is also a party to Additional Protocol II from 8 June 1977 to the Geneva Conventions from 12 August 1949, and Relating to the Protection of Victims of Non-International Armed Conflicts (Additional Protocol II, AP II). We will therefore base our analysis on these documents.

Common Article 3 of the GCs sets out that in order for a non-international armed conflict (NIAC) to exist in the sense of this Article, the rebels have to have a minimum of organisation and need to be placed under responsible command. Furthermore, a certain minimum level of violence is also necessary to determine the existence of a NIAC. This minimum level of violence can be deduced from different factors, such as the high number of victims or the involvement of the armed forces due to the fact that the police are no longer able to deal with the violent situation on its own.

Application of law to facts

During the period under consideration here, the rebel group DoL is confronting the government, as noted above. However, nothing in the facts indicates whether or not this group is sufficiently organised for the purposes of Common Article 3 of the GCs. There is no information as to the DoL's structure or if its members are under responsible command. Moreover, the facts only mention sporadic attacks, not able to destabilise the government of Nounabe.

Based on the available information it is not possible to conclude that the DoL is a structured armed group under responsible command. It is furthermore also not possible to conclude that the sporadic attacks carried out by the DoL represents a conflict of a minimum level of intensity.

Conclusion

In conclusion we can say that in the period from beginning 2010 to November 2010, no NIAC in the sense of Common Article 3 of the GCs exists between the DoL and the government of Nounabe. Consequently, the international humanitarian law (IHL) applicable to NIACs is not applicable. This includes both Common Article 3 of the four GCs and AP II. (The international humanitarian law applicable to international armed conflicts (IACs) is obviously not applicable either, since there is clearly no IAC going on in this period.)

In the present case, the situation could be qualified as one of internal troubles or tensions. To these situations international human rights is applicable, but not international humanitarian law.

3. From November 2010 to February 2011

From November 2010 onwards, the State of Gagea decided to support the DoL financially and by supplying it with various arms. Due to this support, the DoL developed into a very well-structured paramilitary group and took control over a part of the territory of Nounabe. Furthermore, the military clashes between the DoL and the regular army of Nounabe became much more serious.

Applicable law 1

First, we will ascertain whether a NIAC in the sense of Common Article 3 of the GCs exists. The same criteria as mentioned above apply. Furthermore, since Nounabe is a party to AP II, we also have to see whether a NIAC in the sense of Article 1 paragraph 1 of this instrument occurs. In order to find the existence of a NIAC based on the requirements of AP II, the conflict in question needs to occur on the territory of a High Contracting Party. Furthermore, it is necessary that the conflict opposes the regular armed forces of this High Contracting Party to either a dissident armed force or to an organised armed group. The dissident armed forces or organised group need to be placed under responsible command. Finally, this armed force or organised group needs to control a part of the territory of the High Contracting Party, so as to allow them to carry out sustained and concerted military operations.

As can be seen, the criteria found in Common Article 3 of the GCs and in Article 1 paragraph 1 of AP II are the same, with the exception that the latter requires control over a part of a territory. Consequently, the threshold of Article 1 paragraph 1 AP II is higher than the one of Common Article 3 of the GCs. Therefore, it seems more appropriate first to consider the existence of a NIAC in the sense of Common Article 3 of the GCs before dealing with the situation under Article 1 paragraph 1 of AP II.

Application of law to facts 1

Thanks to the material support provided by Gagea, the DoL was able to develop into a very well-structured armed group. From this fact—the structure—we can therefore deduct that the DoL is henceforth placed under a responsible command. Furthermore, seeing the growing intensity of the conflict between the armed forces of Nounabe and the DoL and the large number of victims—3,000 at the end of February 2011—we can confirm that the conflict has attained a sufficient level of violence in the sense of Common Article 3 of the GCs.

Consequently, we find that a NIAC in the sense of Common Article 3 of the GCs exists in this period.

We can further hold that the conflict in question opposes the armed forces of Nounabe and an armed group. Thus, in the conflict the armed forces of a High Contracting Party fight an organised armed group.

Furthermore, with the support of Gagea, the DoL was able to grow in importance and to take control over a part of the territory of Nounabe. Thus, we can say that the DoL controls a part of the territory of a High Contracting Party, allowing it to carry out sustained and concerted military operations. This is in fact exactly what it is doing in its fight against the Nounabian government.

Seeing these developments, we can thus conclude that a NIAC exists, satisfying both the criteria of Common Article 3 of the GCs and Article 1 paragraph 1 AP II.

Conclusion 1

During the period from November 2010 to February 2011 a NIAC exists on the territory of Nounabe, between its armed forces and the rebel group DoL.

Consequently, the applicable law is to be found in Common Article 3 of the four Geneva Conventions and AP II, both instruments to which Nounabe is a party. In addition, customary IHL relating to NIACs is also applicable.

Applicable law 2

During this period, it is also necessary to analyse Gagea's participation and role. From the facts, we know that Gagea financed and armed the DoL. Therefore, we have to ascertain whether this is enough to internationalise the ongoing NIAC. For this purpose, we first need to determine whether the acts carried out by the DoL are attributable to Gagea. In the present case, it is only possible to find attribution under Article 8 of the ILC Articles on Responsibility of States for Internationally Wrongful Acts 2001 (SRA). It is well established that these Articles are not a treaty, but that they reflect customary international law in matters of State responsibility. This has also been confirmed by the International Court of Justice (ICJ) in several cases, for example the *Gabčíkovo-Nagymaros* case (ICJ, Judgment, *Gabčíkovo-Nagymaros Project* (Hungary/Slovakia), 1997, paragraph 47), the *Iran Hostages* case (ICJ, Judgment, *United States Diplomatic and Consular Staff in Teheran* (United States of America v Iran), 1980, paragraphs 56–92) and most recently in the *Genocide* case from 2007 (ICJ, Judgment, *Application of the Convention on the Prevention and Punishment of the Crime of Genocide* (Bosnia and Herzegovina v Serbia and Montenegro), 2007, paragraph 401). Article 8 SRA provides that 'the conduct of a person or group of persons shall be considered an act of a State under international law if the person or group of persons is in fact acting on the instructions of, or under the direction or control of, that State in carrying out the conduct'.

The notion of 'direction or control' has been clarified in various cases. First, the ICJ held in its *Nicaragua* case that the control had to be effective control (ICJ, Judgment on the Merits, *Military and Paramilitary Activities in and against Nicaragua* (Nicaragua v United States of America), 1986, paragraphs 105–116). The ICJ determined that participating in the organisation, financing, training, supplying and equipping of a paramilitary group were insufficient to establish effective control (see paragraph 115 of the judgment cited above). It is necessary that the State exercises both vertical and horizontal control over the group. In other words, the State in question needs to properly control the group as such and for all its operations.

In 1999, the International Criminal Tribunal for the former Yugoslavia (ICTY) also dealt with the matter of 'direction and control' contained in Article 8 SRA. According to the ICTY, if the group is structured, overall control is sufficient to internationalise a NIAC (ICTY, Appeals Chamber, Judgment, *Tadić*, 1999 (Case No. IT-94-1-A) paragraphs 99–145, especially paragraph 131). In order to demonstrate this lower level of control, financing or simple military support is not enough (paragraph 127 of the judgment cited above). It needs to be shown that 'the State wields overall control over the group, not only by equipping and financing the group, but also by coordinating or helping in the general planning of its military activity' (ICTY, Appeals Chamber, Judgment, *Tadić*, 1999 (Case No. IT-94-1-A) paragraph 131).

However, in 2007 in the *Genocide* case, the ICJ reaffirmed its decision from the *Nicaragua* case and held that the relevant criterion in relation to Article 8 SRA was effective control (ICJ, Judgment, *Application of the Convention on the Prevention and Punishment of the Crime of Genocide* (Bosnia and Herzegovina v Serbia and Montenegro), 2007, paragraphs 396–407). According to the Court it was thus necessary that orders were given and actions controlled by the State for every operation and not just in general. However, at the same time the ICJ left the pertinence of its finding in relation to the question of the internationalisation of conflicts open. In fact, the ICJ held that '[i]nsofar as the "overall control" test is employed to determine whether or not an armed conflict is international, which was the sole question which the Appeals Chamber was called upon to decide, it may well be that the test is applicable and suitable' (ICJ, Judgment, *Application of the Convention on the Prevention and Punishment of the Crime of Genocide* (Bosnia and Herzegovina v Serbia and Montenegro), 2007, paragraph 404).

Consequently, in light of the jurisprudence cited above, the test to be applied to determine the internationalisation of a conflict is the overall control test developed by the ICTY in its *Tadić* decision.

Application of law to facts 2

In the period under consideration, Gagea only supports the DoL financially and logistically with arms. This is, however, not enough to fulfil the overall control test as explained in the applicable law part just above. Consequently, it is not possible to attribute the actions of the DoL to Gagea.

Conclusion 2

The intervention of Gagea is thus not sufficient to internationalise the NIAC between the army of Nounabe and the DoL. Therefore, the applicable law instruments remain those mentioned in conclusion 1 of this section, namely Common Article 3 of the four GCs and AP II, as well as customary IHL relating to NIACs.

4. From March 2011 to end of May 2011

From March 2011 onwards, Gagea decided to tighten its link with the DoL and gave it strategic military advice for certain operations.

Applicable law

As we have seen above, the involvement of a third power—a foreign State—in the operation of a paramilitary group can potentially internationalise a NIAC. For this to occur it is necessary to show that the paramilitary group is in fact acting under the control of this foreign State. Following the jurisprudence outlined above, the applicable test is the overall control test developed by the ICTY in the *Tadić* decision.

Application of law to facts

Gagea gives strategic military advice to the DoL for some of its operations. We can thus deduct that Gagea supports the DoL—a well-organised armed group—in their general planning of military operations, in addition to supporting it financially and with arms.

These elements, and especially Gagea's involvement in the planning of operations, thus allow us to conclude that Gagea exercises overall control over the DoL. However, Gagea's involvement does not satisfy the necessary requirements of effective control, as elaborated in the jurisprudence cited above.

Conclusion

Following our reasoning above, we can conclude that from March 2011 onwards the conflict between the armed forces of Nounabe and the paramilitary group DoL is internationalised due to the overall control exercised by Gagea over the DoL. Accordingly, IHL in relation to IACs is henceforth applicable, but only between the two States Gagea and Nounabe. As we have concluded above, Gagea does not exercise effective control over the DoL. Thus, the DoL cannot be considered as a de facto organ of this State in the sense of Article 8 SRA. Consequently, IHL in relation to NIACs remains applicable in the relation between DoL and Nounabe. This solution might—justly—appear as surprising and slightly worrying. It results from the different criteria that are applicable on one hand to the internationalisation of an armed conflict, and on the other to the attribution of acts of private persons or entities to a State by way of Article 8 SRA.

The four GCs are applicable. AP I is equally applicable, but only in relation to Gagea, which is the only State involved in the conflict that is a party to that instrument. Obviously, customary IHL in relation to IACs is applicable as well.

The relationship between the DoL and Nounabe remains governed by the law in relation to NIACs, as we have concluded above for the period of November 2010 to February 2011.

5. From June 2011 to 13 November 2011

During this period, officers and agents from the secret service of Gagea were actively engaged in the planning and execution of all military operations of the DoL.

Applicable law

It is not necessary to repeat here what has been said concerning the question of overall control. We will apply our legal analysis above to this period of the conflict.

Application of law to facts

Based on the facts provided we observe that the links between Gagea and the DoL have grown even tighter. In addition to financial and logistical support, Gagea participates in the planning and execution of all military operations of the DoL. Gagea thus exercises vertical control (planning and execution of military operations) as well as horizontal control, in the sense that it controls all military operations of the group. Thus, since June 2011 Gagea exercises even effective control over the DoL.

Conclusion

We have already concluded in the previous period that the conflict has been internationalised. This internationalisation has been affirmed during the period June 2011–13 November 2011. By applying the criterion of effective control, we can conclude that the acts of the DoL are attributable to Gagea. This group has thus to be considered as a de facto organ in the sense of Article 8 SRA. Consequently, the applicable IHL is only the law in relation to IACs, ie the four GCs and customary IHL. AP I is still only applicable to Gagea, since Nounabe is not a party to this instrument.

6. From 14 November 2011 to today

As from 14 November 2011 onwards, Gagea sends its own troops into the territory of Nounabe.

Applicable law

An IAC is defined in Common Article 2 to the four GCs. This is an armed conflict between two High Contracting Parties. The threshold to satisfy the conditions of an IAC is comparatively low. In fact, simple armed clashes are sufficient.

Application of law to facts

Since Gagea sent its own troops to fight the army of Nounabe in the latter's territory, there exist armed clashes between the armies of two High Contracting Parties, Gagea and Nounabe both being parties to the four GCs.

Conclusion

From 14 November 2011 onwards a 'classic' IAC between two States exists in the sense of Common Article 2 of the GCs between Nounabe and Gagea, on the former's territory.

The four GCs are thus applicable to the situation. Also AP I is applicable in virtue of its Article 1 paragraph 3, but it is only applicable to Gagea, since Nounabe is not a party to that instrument. In addition, the two States have to respect the customary rules of IHL applicable to IACs.

7. Overall conclusion

As we have seen in the development above, the question of the applicable law changes depending on the type of conflict, thus involving a determination of factual elements on the ground. The conflict in question was not an armed conflict under the definitions of IHL in the beginning, but rather amounted to internal tension. However, it then developed into a NIAC, which was later internationalised by Gagea's involvement. Finally, as soon as Gagea sent its own troops the conflict became a 'classical' IAC. The law applicable to NIACs can be found in Common Article 3 of the four GCs, in AP II (in our case only applicable to Nounabe) and customary IHL in relation to NIACs. IHL in relation to IACs is contained in the four GCs, protecting different categories of people, in AP I (which is here only applicable to Gagea) and also relevant customary IHL. As we have seen in our development, the law applicable to internationalised conflicts is—due to their international element—IHL in relation to IACs.

Suggested Solution—Case 8.8

Abbreviations used

Additional Protocol I (AP I)	= Additional Protocol I of 8 June 1977 to the Geneva Conventions of 12 August 1949, and Relating to the Protection of Victims of International Armed Conflicts
Additional Protocol II (AP II)	= Additional Protocol II from 8 June 1977 to the Geneva Conventions from 12 August 1949, and Relating to the Protection of Victims of Non-International Armed Conflicts
Geneva Conventions (GCs)	= Geneva Conventions from 12 August 1949
IAC	= international armed conflict
ICTY	= International Criminal Tribunal for the former Yugoslavia
IHL	= international humanitarian law
PoW	= prisoner of war
SRA	= ILC Articles on Responsibility of States for Internationally Wrongful Acts 2001 (State Responsibility Articles)

1. Applicable law

In order to determine whether the four Geneva Conventions from 12 August 1949 (Geneva Conventions, GCs) and their two additional protocols (AP I and AP II) are applicable, we have to classify the conflict taking place between Kurki and Kaolea.

In the facts it is indicated that since 1 June 2012 an armed conflict has taken place between these two States. Thus, clearly armed clashes between two States exist. Both States in question are parties to the four GCs and their additional protocols. Consequently, this situation can be qualified as an international armed conflict (IAC) in the sense of Common Article 2 paragraph 1 of the GCs. The four GCs are therefore applicable to the situation. In addition, according to Article 1 paragraph 3 of AP I, this protocol is also applicable here.

The conflict remains an IAC despite the intervention of the paramilitary group TousseKaos. This paramilitary group is acting under the command of the army of Kaolea. Acting under the instructions and control of this State, the TousseKaos are an organ de facto in the sense of Article 8 of the State Responsibility Articles (SRA). The acts of the TousseKaos are thus attributable to Kaolea. Consequently, the armed clashes between the TousseKaos and the army of Kurki are to be considered as being between the armies of Kaolea and Kurki. In short, the conflict remains an IAC between the two States, regardless of whether Kaolea acts through its regular army or the TousseKaos.

In order to answer the question, we have to distinguish between three categories of persons: (a) the 13 captured soldiers and the bomber crew from Kaolea's armed forces; (b) the captured members of the TousseKaos; and (c) the two journalists, Alex and Boris.

(a) The 13 captured soldiers and the bomber crew from Kaolea's armed forces

According to Article 4A paragraph 1 of the third Geneva Convention (GC III), members of the armed forces of a party to the conflict who have fallen into the power of the enemy are prisoners of war (PoWs).

The Kaolean bomber crew as well as ten soldiers and three officers have been captured by the armed forces of Kurki. These persons are all members of the armed forces of Kaolea. Having been captured by the army of Kurki, they find themselves thus in the power of the enemy.

Consequently, they all benefit from the status as PoWs and thus enjoy the protection accorded by the third GC III.

Furthermore, these soldiers, officers and bomber crew are also PoWs in the sense of Article 43 paragraph 1 and Article 44 paragraphs 1 and 3 of AP I. Even though the bomber crew and the soldiers from the ground forces belong to two different military units, all are members of the armed forces of Kaolea. Nothing in the facts indicates that they are not placed under a responsible command, which is normally the case in regular armed forces. In addition, nothing suggests that there is no regime ensuring internal discipline and especially the respect and application of the rules of international humanitarian law (IHL). And finally, nothing in the facts implies that the soldiers were not clearly distinguishable from the civilian population during the operation on 27 September 2012.

Thus, the bomber crew and the 13 soldiers and officers form the army of Kaolea are PoWs in the sense of Article 43 paragraph 1 and Article 44 paragraphs 1 and 3 AP I. Therefore, they benefit also under this aspect from the protection of GC III.

(b) The captured members of the TousseKaos

The TousseKaos—a paramilitary group—is independent of the army of Kaolea. It is hence not part of the regular armed forces in the sense of Article 4A paragraph 1 GC III. We have therefore to determine whether the members of this group can be combatants and can be PoWs in the sense of Article 4A paragraph 2 GC III.

The first condition to be fulfilled in order to benefit from this statute as PoWs under Article 4A paragraph 2 is that the group belongs to a party to the conflict. The International Criminal Tribunal for the former Yugoslavia (ICTY) has developed the criterion of 'belonging' to one party to the conflict in its *Tadić* decision. According to this case, this criterion requires a certain measure of control by the State party to the conflict over the group in question and a relation of dependence and allegiance from this group towards the State party. (See ICTY, Appeals Chamber, Judgment, *Tadić*, 1999 (Case No IT-94-1-A) paragraph 94).

In our case, the TousseKaos, despite being independent, is placed under the command of the army of Kaolea. We can thus deduce that this State—a party to the conflict—exercises control over this group. In addition, seeing that the TousseKaos fight together with the army of Kaolea, there appears to exist a relation of allegiance between the paramilitary group and the State. The question concerning the dependence, however, is more difficult to answer. We do not possess enough factual information to conclude with certitude that such dependence exists. For the sake of our analysis we will assume that such a relation of dependence exists and that thus the TousseKaos belong to Kaolea.

It does not matter whether the TousseKaos acts in or outside their territory (Kaolea). Thus, for the purpose of Article 4A paragraph 2 GC III it is irrelevant that the TousseKaos acts in the territory of Kurki. This condition contained in the Article just mentioned is thus satisfied.

Yet, all these elements are not enough to conclude that the captured members of the TousseKaos benefit from PoW status. In addition to the elements contained in the *chapeau* of Article 4A paragraph 2 GC III, the members of the TousseKaos have to fulfil the four conditions enumerated in letters (a)–(d) of this Article. Thus, they need to be commanded by a person responsible for his/her subordinates, have a fixed distinctive sign recognisable at a distance, carry their arms openly, and conduct their operations in accordance with IHL.

From the facts we know that the TousseKaos is very well structured. We can therefore conclude that this group has a well-established hierarchy and that thus there is a person in command who is responsible for his/her subordinates.

When fighting, members of the TousseKaos wear colourful brassards on both arms. In addition, they have their own characteristic sign embroidered highly visibly on their coats. Thus, the condition of having a fixed distinctive sign recognisable at distance is fulfilled.

We have no particular information as to the question whether the group carries its arms openly or not. As there is no contrary information on this crucial point, we can assume that it is fulfilled.

Finally, seeing that the TousseKaos is themselves very well structured and that it is placed under the command of the army of Kaolea we can presume that it adheres to the applicable rules and customs of IHL. The facts of the case do not indicate that it has violated these rules. We can thus consider this last condition as being fulfilled as well.

For the above reasons the members of the TousseKaos are thus combatants. Since they have been captured and are in the power of the enemy—Kurki—they are PoWs in accordance with Article 4A paragraph 2 GC III.

It remains to be seen whether they can also be considered as PoWs under Articles 43 and 44 AP I.

Article 43 paragraph 1 AP I contains an overview of the structure of the armed forces of a party to the conflict. In fact, it considers that 'all organized armed forces, groups and units which are under a command responsible to that Party for the conduct of its subordinates' are part of the armed forces. In addition, these armed forces have to be subjected to an internal disciplinary system, which among other things ensures the compliance with the rules of IHL.

It is possible to base our analysis here on the considerations made in relation the 'belonging' to a party to the conflict under Article 4A paragraph 2 GC III above. In fact, since the very well-structured TousseKaos is placed under the command of the army of Kaolea, we can conclude that it belongs to the latter's armed forces in the sense of Article 43 paragraph 1 AP I.

However, in order to benefit from the status as PoWs, the TousseKaos has also to fulfil the conditions in Article 44 paragraph 3 AP I. We have shown above that members of this group wear a distinctive sign every time they are engaged in fighting. Therefore, we can conclude that members of the TousseKaos distinguish themselves from the civilian population during combat operations.

Consequently, we can consider the TousseKaos as combatants also in the sense of Article 43 AP I. Those members of the TousseKaos that have been captured are thus PoWs.

In conclusion, we can say that the members of the TousseKaos too are PoWs when captured and are hence protected by GC III.

[*In relation to the status of the TousseKaos it would not be wrong to argue based on its members potential status as mercenaries. Yet, you should be aware that the conditions to fulfil such a status are extremely difficult to satisfy. Due to the scarcity of factual elements at our disposition in this regard, we have decided not to proceed with this analysis. However, if you have done so, this would clearly not be wrong.*]

(c) The two journalists, Alex and Boris

As a preliminary remark it should be noted that there are no 'black holes' in the categories of protected persons under IHL. This means that every person necessarily falls within one of the categories provided by IHL (see in this sense Article 4 paragraph 4 GC IV and Article 50 paragraph 1 AP I.).

Alex and Boris are both journalists and are not members of the armed forces of either of the two parties to the conflict. Nothing in the facts provided suggests otherwise. Furthermore, there is also no indication that the two journalists are war correspondents. On the contrary, it seems that they act independently and do not depend on either Kaolea or Kurki. Boris and Alex can thus clearly not be recognised as persons falling within the categories listed in Article 4 GC III. Furthermore, it is clear that they cannot be protected under GC I and GC II. Consequently, they can only be protected persons under GC IV.

Article 4 GC IV sets out which persons are protected under this Convention. In its first paragraph it is provided that in order to be a protected person under GC IV, this person has at any given moment and in whatever manner to find him/herself in the hands of a party to the conflict of which this person is not a national.

[*In order to facilitate the analysis we will deal with Alex and Boris at the same time, supposing that there are no differences between these two persons. However, in principle an analysis for each of them should be done.*]

According to the facts at our disposal, during the night of 3–4 October 2012, Alex and Boris have been captured by the army of Kurki and are detained in Paradisjail Prison. As we know, Kurki is a party to the conflict taking place with Kaolea. Consequently, the two journalists fell in the power of one of the parties to the conflict.

As far as the condition of having a different nationality to the party in whose power the persons finds itself is concerned, the facts do not give any clear indication as to the nationality of the journalists. However, in light of Article 4 paragraph 1 GC IV and the facts provided, it is enough to show that Boris and Alex are not nationals of Kurki. There is a small amount of information available in this regard. The facts mention that the two journalists have smuggled themselves across the border to Kurki. This allows us to deduce that they are not nationals of Kurki, since it is unclear why they should have undertaken this risk had they been nationals of this State.

We can hence conclude that Boris and Alex are indeed persons who have fallen into the power of a party to the conflict—Kurki—of which they are not nationals. They thus fulfil Article 4 paragraph 1 GC IV and are protected persons under the GC IV. However, we need to ascertain if the conditions in paragraph 2 of Article 4 GC IV are fulfilled. These are the conditions under which persons, even though satisfying the elements in paragraph 1, are not protected by GC IV.

Paragraph 2 of Article 4 GC IV names three situations in which protected persons lose their protection under GC IV: (a) nationals from a State not bound by GC IV; (b) nationals from a neutral State finding themselves in the territory of a belligerent State while their State of nationality has a normal diplomatic representation in the State in whose power they are; and (c) nationals from a co-belligerent State as long as their State of nationality has a normal diplomatic representation in the State in whose hands they are.

As we have no elements to determine conclusively the nationality of Boris and Alex, we cannot pronounce on the application of Article 4 paragraph 2 GC IV in the case at hand. For the purposes of the exercise we will consider that the journalists fall in none of the three categories mentioned above.

[*It would be possible to draw the opposite conclusion from this lack of facts and to deny them the status of protected persons under GC IV. They would, however, nevertheless not be without any protection, since they could ask for protection from their own State of nationality through one of its diplomatic representations. Furthermore, they would in any event remain protected by the applicable human rights instruments. It is now widely recognised that human rights law continues to apply also in times of armed conflict. However, since this question deals with the application of IHL, we have opted for the solution that allows us to apply GC IV itself.*]

In conclusion, we can hold that Alex and Boris are protected persons in the sense of Article 4 GC IV and are thus protected by this Convention.

Furthermore, as far as AP I is applicable as well, they will also be covered by the provisions protecting civilian persons contained in this instrument, as well as the special protection granted to journalists. This last point will be developed further below.

We know from the facts that during the 'torturous' interrogation, the two journalists have been subject to practices such as waterboarding, burns with cigarettes and other atrocities, all of which can be qualified as acts of torture. They have been accused of espionage and have been placed in detention for an undetermined time without the possibility to have the legality of their detention verified. We have consequently to determine whether these facts constitute violations of GC IV.

Acts of torture

According to Article 27 paragraph 1 GC IV, protected persons shall at all times be treated humanely. Article 31 GC IV provides that 'no moral or physical coercion shall be exercised against protected persons, in particular to obtain information from them'. Article 32 GC IV stipulates that parties to GC IV are prohibited from taking any measure that would cause physical suffering to the protected person in their power. This prohibition concerns acts of torture and other brutal acts, regardless of whether they are perpetrated by civilian or military agents.

Reading these provisions, it seems difficult to reconcile the obligation contained therein with the acts suffered by the two journalists. Certainly, waterboarding and burns with cigarettes are now recognised as acts of torture. If not considered as torture, these treatments would at least have to be considered as inhumane treatment, physical coercion and physical suffering. The prison guards of Paradisjail, agents of the State of Kurki, have perpetrated these acts. Seeing that the acts have been inflicted during interrogation sessions and that the army of Kurki was convinced that Alex and Boris were mercenaries engaged by Kaolea, it can be deduced that the acts were inflicted to obtain information from the two journalists.

We can henceforth conclude that Kurki has gravely violated its obligations under GC IV, especially in relation to Article 27 paragraph 1, Article 31 and Article 32, due to the acts of torture perpetrated against Alex and Boris. Following Articles 146 and 147, we can further hold that these violations can be considered as grave breaches of GC IV.

The acts of torture are also in violation of Article 75 paragraphs 1 and 2 AP I, concerning fundamental guarantees. In fact, these Articles also provide that all persons affected by an IAC who find themselves in the hands of a party to the conflict have to be treated humanely. Alex and Boris can be said to be affected by an IAC since they are in the territory of one of the belligerents. They are detained by Kurki and are thus clearly in the power of a party to the conflict. Boris and Alex thus have the right to be treated humanely, which was—as we have established above—not the case during the interrogations. Furthermore, paragraph 2 of Article 75 AP I expressly prohibits torture in all its forms. Basing ourselves on the development above, we can therefore conclude that Kurki has also violated its obligations under this provision of AP I.

Detention

The detention of protected persons outside of occupied territories is possible under Articles 42 and 43 GC IV. The treatment of these interned persons is regulated in Article 79 GC IV and following.

According to Article 42 paragraph 1 GC IV, the internment of protected persons can only be ordered if this measure is absolutely necessary for the security of the detaining

State. The wording of this provision places the bar to make interment or detention lawful quite high.

We need to discuss whether Kurki satisfied this requirement when it decided to detain Alex and Boris. They have been accused of espionage. It is true that espionage can potentially be very harmful for a State, in particular when it is involved in an armed conflict. Alex and Boris, who had illegally entered Kurki, were caught when taking pictures of a military prison. It could thus be argued that Kurki was justified in detaining Alex and Boris since Kurki feared for its security.

Article 43 paragraph 1 GC IV provides that every detained person is 'entitled to have such action reconsidered as soon as possible by an appropriate court or administrative board'.

By detaining Alex and Boris indeterminately without giving them the possibility to have the reasons for their detention reviewed by a competent body, the authorities of Kurki have consequently violated Article 43 paragraph 1 GC IV.

Article 75 paragraph 4 AP I sets out that it is not possible to condemn a person and to execute the attached sentence for a penal offence related to the armed conflict, except following a conviction by an impartial and regular court which respects the generally recognised principles of regular judicial procedure enumerated in letters (a)–(j).

In our case, Alex and Boris have been accused of espionage by the commander of the Paradisjail Prison. Based on this pronouncement they have been detained indeterminately. Yet, espionage normally amounts to a penal offence, especially in times of armed conflict. Even though we do not have any information concerning the penal legislation of Kurki, we can presume that it will follow the general rule and that espionage is thus a penal offence.

Consequently, Alex and Boris have the right to be tried by an impartial tribunal, presenting all the judicial guarantees listed in Article 75 paragraph 4 AP I. The commander of the prison, who has taken the decision to detain the two journalists indeterminately based on charges of espionage, can hardly be said to be an impartial tribunal in the sense of Article 75 paragraph 4 AP I.

Due to the fact that Boris and Alex did not benefit from the rights contained in Article 75 paragraph 4 AP I, we can conclude that Kurki has also violated its international obligations under this provision.

In conclusion we can point out that journalists are the subject of a specific provision in AP I, namely Article 79 of this instrument. According to Article 79 paragraph 1 AP I, journalists are to be considered as civilians within the meaning of Article 50 paragraph 1 AP I. Thus, under Article 79 paragraph 2 AP I they should be protected as civilians, provided that they do not engage in any action that adversely affects their status as civilians, eg taking up arms in order to participate actively in the armed conflict.

It is true that Boris and Alex took pictures of the military detention facility for PoWs in Kurki. This action was, however, undertaken in their function as journalists and for the purpose of writing and illustrating an article on the living conditions of PoWs in this prison. As far as we can judge from the facts, the two journalists have not engaged in any activity that would make them lose their status as civilians. Therefore, they remain civilians and are protected under that status as we have seen above.

Finally, we can point out that Alex and Boris probably do not possess specific identity cards as journalists as mentioned in Article 79 paragraph 3 AP I. Had they had such cards, they would most certainly have showed them after their arrest to bolster their claim that they are journalists, sparing them the serious consequences they suffered. Consequently, it is not necessary to consider this provision more in depth here.

[*It should be noted that Article 46 AP I on spies is not applicable in our case and does not need to be considered, since Alex and Boris are clearly not members of any armed forces, as argued above.*]

2. Conclusion

As we have established above, there clearly is an IAC, the applicable law thus being the GCs and AP I.

We have shown that all the captured soldiers from Kaolea as well as the members of the paramilitary group TousseKaos are to be considered as PoWs and are thus protected under GC III and the relevant provisions of AP I pointed out above.

As for Alex and Boris, they are protected as civilians, since they clearly do not fit in any other category. Furthermore, under AP I, journalists are expressly considered as civilians. We regret with respect to these two persons that our State—Kurki—has violated numerous rules applicable under IHL. Both the interrogation techniques (amounting to torture or at least degrading treatment) and the unlimited detention are not in conformity with international obligations that our State has signed up to when it became a member of the GCs and their additional protocols.

Suggested Solution—Case 8.9

Abbreviations used

Additional Protocol I (AP I)	=	Additional Protocol I of 8 June 1977 to the Geneva Conventions of 12 August 1949, and Relating to the Protection of Victims of International Armed Conflicts
Geneva Conventions (GCs)	=	Geneva Conventions from 12 August 1949
Hague Regulations	=	Regulations concerning the Laws and Customs of War on Land from 18 October 1907
IAC	=	international armed conflict
IHL	=	international humanitarian law

1. Applicable law

From the facts we know that an armed conflict is taking place on the territory of Mourna, between its army and the army of Pescade. The latter operates from its aircraft carriers located on the high seas. This is an armed conflict between two States, thus an international armed conflict (IAC) in the sense of Article 2 paragraph 1 of the Geneva Conventions from 12 August 1949 (GCs). It does not matter that Pescade is not present on Mourna's territory but makes its attacks from aircraft carriers on the high seas.

Both States are parties to the four GCs as well as the Additional Protocol I of 8 June 1977 to the Geneva Conventions of 12 August 1949, and Relating to the Protection of Victims of International Armed Conflicts (AP I). Consequently, we will apply the GCs and—based on Article 1 paragraph 3 AP I—also AP I.

We are asked to assess the legality of the attacks of two fighter planes from Pescade on 14 June 2012. The applicable legal framework is consequently the conduct of hostilities.

Article 49 and following of AP I set out rules in relation to the conduct of hostilities. These rules are recognised as reflecting customary international humanitarian law (IHL), but we recall that both States are parties to AP I, which can thus be directly applied.

In general, three broad principles exist in the matter of conduct of hostilities: the principle of distinction (Article 48 AP I), the principle of precautions against the effects of attacks (Article 58 AP I), and the principle of proportionality (Article 51 paragraph 5(b) and Article 57 paragraph 2(b) AP I).

As the name suggests, the *principle of distinction* requires belligerents always to distinguish between civilian and military persons as well as civilian and military objects. Military persons and objects can generally be attacked. Civilian persons and objects, however, benefit from certain immunity and cannot be the object of an attack (Article 51 paragraph 2 and Article 52 paragraph 1 AP I). Consequently, only military persons and objects can be targeted (Article 52 paragraph 2 AP I).

Under the *precautionary principle* the parties involved in the conflict need to take all possible means in order to limit the potential effects of an attack. The military character of the targeted object as well as the absence of any special protection of the object needs to be ascertained and the most appropriate method and means for the attack have to be selected. In addition, the attack needs to be cancelled if it is noticed that the targeted object is not a military one, the civilian population has to be warned if there is the risk that it will be affected by the attack and finally all precautionary measures against the effects of the attack need to be taken.

Finally, the *principle of proportionality* requires balancing the loss of civilian lives and damage to civilian objects to the concrete and direct military advantage anticipated. The former should not be excessive in relation to this advantage. In addition, it is crucial to note that based on its wording it is clear that this principle applies ex ante and not ex post facto.

2. Application of the law to the facts

Launching missiles from warplanes against a building in the territory of Mourna constitutes an act of violence against the adversary. This is consequently indeed a military attack in the sense of Article 49 AP I.

The object of attack was a building used by the army of Mourna to produce new types of weapons and ammunition. It is undeniable that the production of new types of weapons makes an effective contribution to military action. Consequently, by its use the building in question effectively contributes to the military action of Mourna. Its destruction would thus be a definite military advantage for Pescade. This building is therefore a military object in the sense of Article 52 paragraph 2 AP I.

During the attack the pilots of the fighter planes did not hit their target. Instead, they entirely destroyed a school and partially a hospital. In the latter, 40 people were killed when the missile hit a wing of the hospital.

The pilots did not target the school and hospital as such, but they intended to hit the building in which ammunition and weapons were produced. The attack was thus targeted at a military object. Consequently, it is difficult to establish a violation of the principle of distinction. Yet, the situation is far more problematic in light of the precautionary and proportionality principles.

The attack was aimed at a building in a residential neighbourhood in the capital of Mourna. Thus, there existed a very high risk of collateral damage. The army of Pescade was aware of this, as can be inferred from the fact that the planes were equipped with extremely precise missiles. Lacking more detailed information, we can thus argue that Pescade took the necessary precautions concerning the means and methods to carry out the attack.

Yet, in light of the very high risk of collateral damage, which sadly has become reality, the precautionary principle requires that the civilian population be warned, if possible, before the attack (as is provided in Article 57 paragraph 2(c) AP I). As far as we can see from the facts provided, no warning was given. It seems that moving a production facility of arms would require a certain amount of time. Consequently, it would have been possible to give advance warning to the civilian population, for example by using aircraft to drop information sheets into the city the evening before the attack. This would maybe have given the hospital the possibility to evacuate all or some of its patients. However, due to the scarcity of information on this point it is difficult to make a final determination in this regard.

The attack was carried out shortly after four o'clock in the morning. Thanks to the early hour of the attack, there were no victims in the destroyed school building. This was unfortunately not the case for the hospital. Hospitals obviously remain occupied and busy day and night. In addition, we can recall that the attack targeted buildings in a residential neighbourhood. At four o'clock in the morning most people will be at home, sleeping, thus robbing them of any possibility to face a surprise attack. Even though the missiles used were extremely precise, the pilots nevertheless missed their target. These considerations—the early hour, the use of fighter planes and the specific geographic situation of the target—strengthen the assumption that such an attack requires exceptional precautionary measures in order to limit the effects of the attack as much as possible. In our opinion, the precautionary measures adopted by Pescade are highly doubtful, which would thus lead to a violation of the precautionary principle. However, due to a lack of factual elements it remains difficult to make a final determination on this point.

We now have to analyse the last element, the proportionality principle. Two civilian objects, a school and a hospital, were (partly) destroyed in the attack. In addition, 40 persons have lost their lives.

As we have seen above, the proportionality principle needs to be analysed ex ante. Pescade could have foreseen that launching missiles into a residential neighbourhood could cause loss of civilian lives and objects, something which unfortunately indeed occurred. The resulting collateral damage to both civilian lives and objects was considerable. The expected military advantage was the destruction of a production facility for weapons and ammunition. Even though the destruction of such a production facility could certainly amount to a definite military advantage, it seems that the possible damage that could result from such an attack was excessive in relation to this advantage. Therefore, this attack should never have been carried out and constitutes a violation of the principle of proportionality.

3. Conclusion

As argued above, the attack was illegal at least in regard to the principle of proportionality. It is also possible that the precautionary principle was violated in this attack. However, as pointed out, due to a scarcity of factual information we cannot conclusively settle this point in relation to the precautionary principle. Nevertheless, we are of the opinion that a violation of the precautionary principle probably has occurred, since the specific circumstances in which the launch of the missiles took place called for the adoption of exceptional precautionary measures, which were not adopted.

SUGGESTED SOLUTIONS International Criminal Law

Suggested Solution—Case 8.10

Abbreviations used
ICC = International Criminal Court
ICC Statute = Rome Statute of the International Criminal Court

1. Applicable law

The question we are asked to answer here is whether Columbi can prosecute the responsible authors of the alleged international crimes, and if yes, how it can do so.

According to the facts presented, Columbi does not want to engage in discussions concerning State responsibility. We will thus focus our answer exclusively on individual criminal responsibility.

We can further note that Columbi is not willing to engage in domestic prosecution, claiming that it is short on financial resources. Instead, it asks for action under international law. Since Columbi is a party to the International Criminal Court (ICC) Rome Statute (ICC Statute), it might be an option to bring the issue to the ICC.

Columbi, as well as Falcon, are both parties to the ICC Statute. Thus, we will apply first and foremost this Statute.

2. Preconditions for ICC jurisdiction

Article 14 paragraph 1 ICC Statute indicates that State parties to the ICC Statute can indeed refer to the Prosecutor of the Court a situation in which one or several crimes within the jurisdiction of the Court have been committed. However, before actually looking at the Court's jurisdiction, there are a few preconditions that need to be looked at.

The ICC does not have universal jurisdiction. Article 12 ICC Statute clearly States that the ICC only has jurisdiction regarding a State party. As soon as a State is a party to the ICC Statute and if the ICC's jurisdiction is validly triggered, the ICC will be competent to deal with issues involving that State without any further consent. This is unlike, for example, the International Court of Justice, which always needs the consent of all States involved in the specific case.

In case the situation is brought to the ICC by a State party or the investigation is started *proprio motu* by the ICC Prosecutor (Article 13(a) and (c) ICC Statute), Article 12 of the ICC Statute provides that the State where the conduct potentially being a crime occurred (territorial State, paragraph 2, letter (a)) or the State of nationality of the potential offender (paragraph 2, letter (b)) need to be parties to the ICC Statute in order for the ICC to have jurisdiction. We will look at Article 13 in the next section.

Here, it is enough to State that Columbi and Falcon are both parties to the ICC Statute, while Tyton is not. Columbi and Falcon are both States of nationality of potential offenders, while Falcon is at the same time also the State on the territory of which some of the potential crimes were committed. Thus, the preconditions in Article 12 do not pose a problem as such

[*It should be noted that these requirements do not apply in case of a referral by the Security Council under Article 13(b) ICC Statute.*]

We can also appease the President's concern not to be involved in State responsibility issues. The ICC does not deal with State responsibility, but only with *individual* criminal responsibility. This is evident from Article 1 ICC Statute, which States that the ICC 'shall have the power to exercise its jurisdiction over *persons*' (emphasis added). Furthermore, Article 25 ICC Statute clearly speaks of *individual* criminal responsibility and in its paragraph 4 it is clarified that none of the provisions on individual criminal responsibility in the Statute will affect the question of State responsibility under international law. In other words, the question of State responsibility is not dealt with under the ICC Statute. Thus, by triggering the ICC's jurisdiction, Columbi would not raise any State responsibility issues as such.

3. Triggering of ICC jurisdiction

Jurisdiction has been conferred on the ICC under the ICC Statute. It needs, however, to be triggered by one of the mechanisms under Article 13 ICC Statute. For our purpose, the relevant provision is letter (a), since it is a State party to the Statute—Columbi—which seeks to take action (there is no information on any action by either the Security Council of the United Nations or the ICC Prosecutor). Letter (a) of Article 13 States that a *situation* can be brought to the ICC by a State party. It is important to stress the expression 'situation', since it means that the State party is not bringing a particular case on a potential crime only. Rather, the State party refers a larger geographical and temporal context, in which several crimes—as defined by the ICC Statute—might have been committed. It will then be up to the ICC Prosecution to identify the relevant and 'most serious' crimes that they will prosecute. The State party thus makes rather a general referral, not linked to a specific case. This is also clear from Article 14 ICC Statute, which has to be taken into account in the case of a referral by a State party.

The relevant situation involves the numerous atrocities committed during the conflict between Falcon and Tyton by soldiers of both of these States plus soldiers of foreign States such as Columbi. Columbi will refer this situation to the ICC. Columbi is indeed a State party to the ICC, thereby satisfying the requirements under Articles

13(a) and 14 ICC Statute. The alleged crimes involve crimes against humanity and war crimes, both clearly crimes within the jurisdiction of the ICC, according to Article 5 paragraph 1 ICC Statute. The jurisdiction of the ICC can therefore successfully be triggered by Columbi.

4. Admissibility

Even though the jurisdiction is triggered, admissibility also needs to be assessed. Admissibility is dealt with under Article 17 of the ICC Statute. The ICC operates under the so-called complementarity principle. This means that the ICC can only prosecute international crimes when no competent national court is able or willing to do it. We know from the statements made by Columbi that Columbi is not willing to start prosecutions. However, we do not know whether Falcon is able and willing to start proceedings for atrocities committed during the conflict. Since from the facts it seems that the conflict is still ongoing, it might be presumed that Falcon—being absorbed in other activities—is unable to conduct the proceedings, but we do not know whether—in order to satisfy the 'unable' requirement—the judicial system of Falcon (partly) has broken down. Neither do we know whether Falcon would be willing at all to start proceedings. Thus, the following conclusions are drawn based on the assumption that Falcon is not able or willing to start proceedings. This would, however, have to be carefully assessed by the ICC.

5. Conclusion

As seen above, Falcon and Columbi are both State parties to the ICC Statute, thereby fulfilling the preconditions mentioned in Article 12. The ICC jurisdiction will be triggered through the referral of the situation by Columbi in accordance with Article 13(a) and 14 ICC Statute. Since Falcon is also a State party, no further consent is necessary from its side in order to make the ICC competent to investigate crimes on its territory or by its nationals (see Article 12 ICC Statute). This is, however, in relation to Falcon only true under the reservation concerning admissibility mentioned above.

In conclusion, we can say that in this situation based on the articles discussed above, the ICC will be competent for the following crimes: all crimes committed by *nationals* of Colombi and Falcon, regardless of the territory where it was committed (thus also in the territory of Tyton) (Article 12 paragraph 2(b) ICC Statute) and all crimes committed on the *territory* of Falcon, regardless of the nationality of the offender (and thus involving also crimes committed by nationals of Tyton) (Article 12 paragraph 2(a) ICC Statute). However, the ICC will not be competent to deal with crimes committed by nationals of Tyton on the territory of Tyton, since Tyton is not a State party to the ICC Statute (see Article 12 ICC Statute).

Suggested Solution—Case 8.11

Abbreviations used
GC III = Third Geneva Convention form 1949 Relative to the Treatment of Prisoners of War
IHL = international humanitarian law
PoWs = prisoners of war

1. Applicable law

Both Neit and Painal are parties to the four Geneva Conventions (GCs) of 1949 (which are all also customary law). In order to conclude that the GCs are indeed applicable, we need to address briefly the question of the classification of conflict. This is due to the fact that the GCs are only applicable in international armed conflicts. Yet, the conflict at hand is clearly a conflict between two States (Painal and Neit) in the sense of Article 2 paragraph 1 of the GCs. It is thus an international armed conflict and the GCs are indeed applicable.

Since we are dealing here with alleged crimes committed against prisoners of war (PoWs), we will mainly apply the Third Geneva Convention from 1949 Relating to the Treatment of Prisoners of War (GC III). [*Since it is clearly stated in the facts that the persons are PoWs and there seems to be no doubt about this status, it is not necessary to analyse whether they really fall under the definition of a PoW contained in Article 4 GC III.*]

The allegations of Painal against Neit concern principally two sets of conduct, which need to be analysed separately. First of all there is the issue of the goods available at the camp kiosks in the PoWs camps in Neit (ie no tobacco, a range of other goods at prices higher than market prices). Second, there is the fact that Neit compels PoWs to fight in its army.

2. Definition of a war crime

In order to determine whether the activities mentioned above constitute war crimes, we first need to analyse what war crimes are.

In general, it can be said that a specific conduct amounts to a war crime if the following elements are fulfilled:

(a) There exists an armed conflict (an international or a non-international armed conflict; the classification of the conflict is important since not all war crimes exist in both sets of conflicts).
(b) The conduct in question amounts to a *serious* violation of a specific rule of international humanitarian law (IHL), whether this is a treaty or a customary rule. The violation is said to be 'serious' when the rule protects important values and the violation of this rule has serious consequences for the victim.
(c) A nexus (link) exists between the conduct in question and the armed conflict.
(d) In order to amount to a war crime, the specific violation of IHL must be criminalised under international law.
(e) And of course, all material and mental elements (*actus reus* and *mens rea*) regarding

that particular conduct (ie the criminal offence) need to be fulfilled as well, as is the case for every crime.

Generally, if one of these points listed above is not fulfilled (ie there was for example no armed conflict), then the conduct in question will not be a war crime (but potentially might amount to another (international) crime).

3. Application to the facts of the case: available goods at the kiosk

Article 28 CG III provides that '[c]anteens shall be installed in all camps, where prisoners of war may procure foodstuffs, soap and tobacco and ordinary articles in daily use. The tariff shall never be in excess of local market prices'. What the places where these goods can be procured are called (canteen instead of kiosk) is irrelevant, the important element is the function. It seems indeed that Article 28 is violated by Neit by the fact that many goods are sold at prices higher than market prices and that tobacco cannot be bought at all.

We will apply the schema established above in order to assess whether this amounts to a war crime.

(a) Existence of an armed conflict: indeed, we know from the facts that there is an international armed conflict taking place between Neit and Painal.
(b) Serious violation of a rule of IHL: Article 28 GC III clearly is an IHL treaty rule, in force for Neit. However, it has to be ascertained whether this is a *serious* violation, since only serious violations of rules of IHL amount to war crimes. However, this rule arguably does not protect 'important values' since it is a more technical rule ensuring comfort for PoWs rather than, for example, their survival. In addition—and maybe more importantly—its violation does not have serious consequences for the victims (the PoWs). They are not seriously harmed by the non-availability of tobacco and the fact that prices for some goods are slightly higher than market prices. The examples provided—newspapers and chocolate—are all not goods strictly necessary for survival.
[*Assessing the 'seriousness' of a violation is arguably often a somewhat subjective exercise and can thus potentially change depending on who is making the assessment.*]

As seen above, the points in the definition of a war crime need to be fulfilled cumulatively. Since regarding the violation of Article 28 CG III there was no serious violation, this breach does not constitute a war crime. However, this does not change the fact that it is a breach of IHL and a violation of a treaty obligation in force, for which Neit could thus incur State responsibility, potentially leading to compensation and/or satisfaction. Yet, regarding the violation of Article 28 GC III, Painal's allegation that this constitutes a *war crime* is not correct.

[*Since all points of the definition need to be fulfilled cumulatively, it is not necessary to continue with the analysis once one point is not fulfilled.*]

4. Application to the facts of the case: compelling PoWs to fight

Article 130 GC III clearly provides that compelling a PoW to fight in the forces of the enemy is a grave breach. Grave breaches are a specific class of war crimes in relation to the GCs, ie they are specifically established by the GCs as war crimes and have attached to it a system of repression (see eg Article 129 GC III). The general notion of war crimes is, however, far wider. Thus, regarding this conduct Painal is correct in calling it a war crime, since compelling PoWs to fight in the enemy's armed forces is a grave breach according to Article 130 GC III.

[*Seeing that Article 130 GC III labels the conduct in question—compelling PoWs to fight in the enemy's army—as a grave breach, it is not actually necessary to go through the steps defining a war crime as set out above. Regardless of your reasoning the result is that this is a war crime, a grave breach.*

Yet, for students who took the time to go through the steps, which is not wrong, we would like to deal briefly with the possible reasoning.

(a) Existence of an armed conflict: there is indeed an international armed conflict taking place between Neit and Painal. Thus, the first element is fulfilled.

(b) Serious violation of a rule of IHL: Article 130 GC III clearly States that compelling PoWs to fight is not allowed, thus any action contrary is a violation. (Furthermore, for example Article 50 and 52 GC III on types of work that PoWs can be requested to do, do not mention fighting or other similar dangerous activities at all.) Article 130 GC III is an IHL treaty rule in force for Neit. Additionally, it is a serious violation. The 'seriousness' is already hinted at by the fact that it is contained in the grave breaches provisions, thus per se qualifying as a war crime. Besides, it is inhumane to require PoWs to fight against their own country and their own comrades, thus it is violating fundamental values of humane treatment and humanity to force them to do it. Furthermore, it also has serious consequences for the PoWs, since they can be killed or wounded in the fighting, not to speak of potential psychological problems when having to fight against your own people and to kill your own nationals.

(c) Nexus to an armed conflict: in order to amount to a war crime, the conduct in question needs to have a link with the armed conflict. Usually, this link is said to exist—among other things—when protected persons under the GCs are involved, since they would not exist outside the context of an armed conflict (because the GCs apply only in case of armed conflict). This can be said to be satisfied as well here. The victims are PoWs, a special status existing under GC III in times of international armed conflict, and the alleged perpetrators are soldiers of the other camp (ie Neit). This constellation of PoWs and 'enemy soldiers' would not exist outside an armed conflict. There is thus a link between the acts allegedly amounting to war crimes and the armed conflict.

(d) Criminalisation: again, this is rather straightforward here, since the grave breaches are themselves criminalising the activities mentioned (see Article 129 GC III), thereby giving rise to individual criminal responsibility. If you would have to deal with a potential war crime not contained in the grave breaches provisions, you would need to find criminalisation elsewhere. It might be possible to find criminalization under customary international law (State practice and opinio juris*). As an inspiration, you can also look at the crimes listed in the statutes of international*

criminal courts and tribunals, but keep in mind that not necessarily all crimes listed there exist (yet) in customary law and that a specific criminalisation might thus exist only for the purpose of that particular court or tribunal.

(e) Actus reus *and* mens rea*: the material act (*actus reus*) contained in Article 130 GC III refers to the actual conduct. Thus, what is criminalised here is to compel PoWs to fight in the enemy's armed forces. This is exactly what the authorities and soldiers of Neit are doing: compelling PoWs from Painal to fight in Neit's armed forces. Thus, the material element of the crime is satisfied.* Mens rea *(the mental element) means the mental mind-set that is necessary in order for the conduct to be a crime. Most of the time, if nothing else is provided, intent is required in international criminal law. For example, Article 130 GC III speaks of 'wilful' or 'wilfully', thereby hinting at the fact that indeed criminal intent and not, for example, recklessness is required. In our case, the soldiers and authorities are perfectly aware of what they are doing and they are intentionally sending the PoWs to fight. Thus, this last element is also fulfilled.*

Seeing that all elements have been satisfied, we can conclude that compelling PoWs to fight in the enemy's armed forces is indeed a war crime. Thus, Painal's allegations in this regard are correct.]

5. Conclusion

As argued above, not selling tobacco and selling other goods at higher than market prices is not a war crime, even though it is a violation of a rule of IHL (Article 28 GC III). But it is not a serious violation. However, compelling PoWs from Painal to fight in Neit's armed forces is a grave breach (and thus a war crime). Painal is thus partly correct in its claims that war crimes were committed in Neit.

Suggested Solution—Case 8.12

Abbreviations used

ICC = International Criminal Court
ICC Statute = Rome Statute of the International Criminal Court
ICTY = International Criminal Tribunal for the Former Yugoslavia

1. Applicable law

We are asked to assess whether the acts mentioned in the facts amount to crimes against humanity. Centrostan has a definition of crimes against humanity in its national law, which is thus applicable. This definition copies word for word the definition of crimes against humanity found in the Rome Statute of the International Criminal Court (ICC Statute), in its Article 7. Thus, in the answer below, any mention of Article 7 ICC Statute should be read as referring to the applicable national law.

2. Definition of crimes against humanity

Article 7 ICC Statute—which has been incorporated into Centrostan's national law—provides in its chapeau that any of the acts listed in paragraph 1 amounts to a crime against humanity if it is committed 'as part of a widespread or systematic attack directed against any civilian population, with knowledge of the attack'. There are thus several elements in this definition that need brief consideration before we will apply them to the facts of the case. All these elements are part of the so-called chapeau, the context in which one of the underlying crimes (eg murder) needs to take place in order to amount to a crime against humanity.

[*Almost every one of the elements contained in the definition could give rise to a long and thorough analysis and discussion, especially since their definition is not always uncontroversial. It should thus be kept in mind that these elements can be defined differently. Since this is not the goal of the question—asking for an application to the facts of the case rather than a purely theoretical and extensive essay—the analysis of the different elements is held rather short on purpose. If students have time during an exam, it would certainly not be wrong to provide more information, especially also case law, which is highly important for the development of international criminal law.*]

'Widespread or systematic'

It is important to note at the outset that this requirement is disjunctive, so the attack only has to be widespread *or* systematic and not widespread *and* systematic.

Widespread: in general this refers to the large-scale nature of the attack and the large number of victims. (See eg the *Kunarac* case (ICTY, Trial Chamber, Judgment, *Prosecutor v Kunarac et al*, 2001 (Case No IT-96-23-T & IT-96-23/1-T) paragraph 428.)

Systematic: there have been various ways to define this criterion, but it generally refers to a high level of organisation, following a regular pattern or plan and also involving significant private or public resources. Often, it is also required that high-level authority is involved. (Compare eg *Akayesu* (ICTR, Trial Chamber, Judgement, *Prosecutor v Akayesu*, 1998 (Case No ICTR-96-4-T) paragraph 580) and *Blaškić* (ICTY, Trial Chamber, Judgment, *Prosecutor v Blaškić*, 2000 (Case No IT-95-14-T) paragraph 203).)

In relation to the widespread and systematic element it is important to point out that it is only the *attack* that needs to be widespread or systematic and not the individual act of the perpetrator. Thus, the widespread or systematic attack against any civilian population is the necessary context element in which an individual crime (one of the underlying acts) needs to be committed. Consequently, if the context element is present, one single act by a perpetrator can potentially amount to a crime against humanity.

'Attack'

As is pointed out in the ICC Elements of Crimes (we assume that it is reasonably possible to use them as inspiration since the national law definition of Centrostan is exactly the same as the one in the ICC Statute), an attack for the purpose of crimes against humanity does not necessarily have to involve an armed attack, but enacting discriminating laws leading to the commission of one of the underlying acts might, for example, qualify as an attack as well. There is a disagreement whether it is necessary to have a plan or policy in order to have an attack. The ICC requires this organisational element (see Article 7 paragraph 2(a) ICC Statute), but the ICTY held that this is not necessary under customary international law (ICTY, Appeals Chamber, Judgment, *Prosecutor v Kunarac et al*, 2002 (Case No T-96-23 & IT-96-23/1-A) paragraph 98). Yet, in any event it seems that should it be required, the policy or plan behind the attack does not need to be expressly defined, but can be inferred from, for example, political programs, speeches, propaganda and so on. (On this see ICC, Pre-Trial Chamber I, Decision on the confirmation of charges, *Prosecutor v Katanga and Ngudjolo Chui,* 2008 (Case NoICC-01/04-01/07-717) paragraph 396 and ICTY, Trial Chamber, Judgment, *Prosecutor v Blaškić*, 2000 (Case No IT-95-14-T) paragraphs 204, 205.)

'Directed against'

The civilian population has to be the primary object of the attack and not just 'collateral damage'. Thus, the civilian population is deliberately attacked and is intended to be the main target.

'Any'

The targeted civilian population is *any* civilian population. This small word is highly significant, since it means that unlike with war crimes the nationality or allegiance of the victim does not matter. Thus, also crimes of a State against its *own* nationals can amount to crimes against humanity.

'Civilian'

The term civilian is also surrounded by debate, especially in relation to the inclusion or not of soldiers *hors de combat*. In general it means, however, that the population has to be *predominantly* civilian (ie non-military). (See eg ICTY, Trial Chamber, Opinion and Judgment, *Prosecutor v Tadić*, 1997 (Case No IT-94-1-T) paragraph 638.) The presence of a few soldiers among the civilian population would thereby not deprive it of its predominantly civilian character. Yet, for example, an attack on a military barracks would not satisfy this element of 'civilian'.

'Population'

This element refers to the fact that a larger body of victims is targeted with the attack. It is, however, not necessary that the whole population of a town or country is the object of the attack. (See eg ICTY, Appeals Chamber, Judgment, *Prosecutor v Kunarac*, 2002 (Case No IT-96-23 & IT-96-23/1-A) paragraph 90.)

Yet, crimes against a limited and randomly selected number of individuals would not satisfy the requirement. (See ICTY, Trial Chamber, Judgment, *Prosecutor v Limaj*, 2005 (Case No IT-03-66-T) paragraph 218.) However, it has to be kept in mind that while the attack as such has to be directed against a population, it is of course necessary to have individual victims under the underlying acts.

Mental element

In addition to the mental element required by the particular offence (eg the intent to kill in case of murder), there is also a mental element attached to the context. This mental element requires—as is clear from the definition in the ICC Elements of Crimes cited above—that the alleged perpetrator must have known of the broader context in which his action occurred. That is, he must have known that he was acting within a widespread or systematic attack against any civilian population. (See eg ICTY, Appeals Chamber, Judgment, *Prosecutor v Tadić*, 1999 (Case No IT-94-1-A) paragraph 248.) Therefore, general knowledge is enough; he must not necessarily know all the details of the plan or all the characteristics of the attack.

Sum up

To sum up, we can say that there are three elements necessary in order for an act to qualify as a crime against humanity:

(a) the perpetrator must have committed one of the prohibited underlying acts (eg murder) with the necessary intent;
(b) the act objectively falls within the context of the broader attack (widespread or systematic attack against any civilian population); and
(c) the perpetrator knew about this broader context.

[*Whether students decide first to analyse the context element or the underlying act is not important.*]

3. Application of the law to the facts

Now we need to apply the theoretical considerations above to the facts of the case at hand.

Underlying act

The alleged perpetrators, soldiers from Centrostan, have captured five fleeing civilians, whom they burn, stab and subject to electric shocks. The five victims are according to the facts severely wounded in the process. Inflicting such severe physical but also mental pain arguably amounts to torture. Torture is one of the underlying acts of crimes against humanity (see Article 7 paragraph 1(f) ICC Statute). Under the legally non-binding ICC Elements of Crimes we can find some indications on when torture is seen as fulfilled for the purpose of the ICC. We do not know whether the same elements would be necessary for the national law of Centrostan, but since the definition of crimes against humanity is exactly the same, there is at least a reasonable possibility that they would gain some inspiration from the Elements of Crimes for the purpose of defining torture as a crime against humanity in their national law. The elements indicated in the Elements of Crimes are met in our case: the perpetrators did inflict severe physical and mental pain on the victims, as mentioned above, and this pain or suffering was not at all part of a lawful punishment. Furthermore, the five victims were in custody—or at least under control—of the soldiers, since they had been captured by them. [*Note that unlike the definition of torture in the United Nations Convention against Torture, Inhumane and Degrading Treatment, the definition of torture as a crime against humanity under the ICC Statute does not require the involvement of a public official and a purpose of why the torture was inflicted in the first place. This is also unlike the definition of torture as a war crime under the ICC Statute, which does require a purpose for torture, but no involvement of a public official.*]

Furthermore, the perpetrators acted with intent, that is they *wanted* to burn, stab and otherwise harm the five persons they had captured. It was not merely an accident but an active decision to 'amuse' themselves.

Hence, we can conclude that one of the underlying acts has indeed been committed with the necessary intent. Next, we need to look whether the necessary context element also exists.

Context

There is indeed an *attack* taking place: in our case it is an armed attack by the armed forces of Centrostan against Pomacan. Since the definition contained in Centrostan's national law is the same as under the ICC Statute, it is possible that Centrostan's law contains the same policy element as is necessary under the ICC Statute (see Article 7 paragraph 2(a) ICC Statute). Under the ICC Statute the attack has to be done 'pursuant to or in furtherance of a State or organizational policy'. In our case, the armed forces of Centrostan 'methodically and as a rule' attack undefended villages. Since these are the official armed forces of Centrostan (and thus organs of the State), the conclusion is warranted that there is indeed a State policy (or at least an army policy) behind the methodical attacks against villages. It is not just random violence against villages, but because it is methodical it seems to follow a certain organisational policy.

The attack needs to be *widespread or systematic*. Since as mentioned above the attacks are committed 'methodically and as a rule', the attack is indeed systematic (there seems to be a regular pattern). [*From the information we have it does not seem possible to determine whether the attack is widespread. However, remember that it is only necessary to proof one of the two elements.*]

The target of these attacks is the *civilian population*, since it is stated that the villages are undefended. Thus, the systematic attack is indeed *directed against* the civilian population. By targeting villages, the objects of the attack are a number of people, not just random individuals. Thus, the population element is also satisfied. Furthermore, if some soldiers would happen to be among the village inhabitants (which we do not know), this would not matter, since the population only needs to be predominantly civilian. In addition, the nationality of the civilians does not matter, since the civilian population under attack can be *any* civilian population. Thus, the fact that some of the civilians attacked by the army of Centrostan are nationals from Centrostan is irrelevant.

Mental element in relation to the context

As for the mental element in relation to the chapeau requirements we need to ascertain whether the alleged perpetrators knew that they were acting within this broader attack. They are soldiers who are actively involved in the attack at hand and who—as we can reasonably assume—have participated in other 'methodical' attacks on undefended villages. Therefore, they must have known that they were acting within the context of one of these systematic attacks against a civilian population. Any assertion to the contrary would seem to be implausible. This is even more so since the soldiers do not need to know every detail of the attacks, but since they follow orders and are actively engaged in the attacks as such, they are bound to know in which context they are acting.

We can thus hold that the necessary context element of crimes against humanity—ie a widespread or systematic attack against any civilian population—is fulfilled as well.

4. Conclusion

It has been clearly established that the underlying act of torture has been committed in the context of a systematic attack against the civilian population in Pomacan. This underlying act was part of the systematic attack, ie it was committed during and in relation to the attack in question. The soldiers took advantage of the specific situation to torture captured civilians.

Consequently, the crime against humanity of torture has indeed been committed by these soldiers from Centrostan.

SUGGESTED SOLUTIONS
International Environmental Law

Suggested Solution—Case 8.13

Abbreviations used

GHGs	=	greenhouse gases
ICJ	=	International Court of Justice
Kyoto Protocol	=	Kyoto Protocol to the United Nations Framework Convention on Climate Change
SRA	=	ILC Articles on Responsibility of States for Internationally Wrongful Acts 2001 (State Responsibility Articles)
UNFCCC	=	United Nations Framework Convention on Climate Change

1. Applicable law

We are asked to answer the question under the so-called State Responsibility Articles. These ILC Articles on Responsibility of States for Internationally Wrongful Acts from 2001 (SRA) are not an internationally binding treaty, but they are binding as customary international law. The ICJ has confirmed their customary nature in several cases, such as the *Iran Hostages* case (ICJ, Judgment, *United States Diplomatic and Consular Staff in Teheran* (United States of America v Iran), 1980, paragraphs 56–92), the *Gabčíkovo-Nagymaros* case (ICJ, Judgment, *Gabčíkovo-Nagymaros Project* (Hungary/Slovakia), 1997, paragraph 47) and most recently the *Genocide* case (ICJ, Judgment, *Application of the Convention on the Prevention and Punishment of the Crime of Genocide (Bosnia and Herzegovina v Serbia and Montenegro)*, 2007, paragraph 401).

According to the SRA, a State can be hold responsible under international law for an internationally wrongful act if this act is (a) attributable to it and (b) constitutes a violation of an international obligation of the State in question (Article 2 SRA).

2. Attribution

Ceotu alleges that the new factories are polluting the environment. We do not know from the facts, however, whether these factories are State owned. Assuming that such an important element would not be omitted in the facts, we should conclude that they are to be seen as privately owned factories, and thus are not organs of the State. [*In addition, even if you considered that the factories were State owned, attribution under the SRA seems not to be straightforward. State-owned enterprises are almost never considered to be organs of the State in virtue of Articles 4 or 5 SRA, since despite their public ownership they retain a distinct personality. Thus, while it is not impossible to find attribution under these Articles, it would require extensive justification.*]

Seeing that Othree has not done anything itself *directly*, we should analyse whether we are in the presence of a so-called catalysing fact, ie a violation which is revealed by another violation, whereby the first violation is not attributable to the State but shows that it has not acted in conformity with international law on some points revealed by this first violation (according to the ICJ's theory developed in the so-called *Iran Hostages* case (ICJ, Judgment, *United States Diplomatic and Consular Staff in Tehran*, 1980, especially paragraph 61)).

Othree could thus be reproached for being passive with regards to implementing or at least enforcing international environmental obligations at the national level, revealed by the fact that new factories were constructed and not obliged to reduce their harmful effects on the environment. Under this scenario, the violation would be attributable to Othree under Article 4 SRA, since it is clearly the legislative and/or executive organs of a State which are tasked to ensure proper application of international law at the national level.

Yet, as can be seen, this attribution would only work if these factories are actually found to be responsible for the increase in GHGs—a difficult issue to which we turn next.

[*Since the thorny issue in this question lies with finding a violation rather than attribution, it would be completely acceptable for students first to analyse the violation and only if such a violation is to be found to deal with attribution.*]

3. The difficulty of establishing a link

According to the SRA, in order to find a violation there must be an act that is not in conformity with a State's obligations under international law, regardless of the customary or treaty character of this obligation (Article 12 SRA). In addition, this obligation must be in force for the State in question at the time of the commission of the act (Article 13 SRA).

Othree is a party to the UNFCCC and the Kyoto Protocol. Being an Annex I country and party to the Kyoto Protocol, Othree has indeed committed itself to reducing greenhouse gas (GHG) emissions. It could thus be said that Othree is violating in particular Article 3 paragraph 1 of the Kyoto Protocol. The Kyoto Protocol entered into force on 16 February 2005 and is thus binding on Othree in 2010 (at the time when the increased GHG concentrations are discovered, which is nevertheless not necessarily the date when the 'violation' might have been committed).

However, in relation to our case it springs immediately to mind that it is very difficult in general, but also based on the facts we know, to show that Othree is actually committing a violation of an international obligation. Yet, in order to find an internationally wrongful act, it is crucial to prove a violation and to establish the necessary link between the harm and the violating behaviour. This is clear from the definition of an internationally wrongful act in Article 2 SRA.

The scientists were not able to give a reason for the increase in GHGs. The fact that Othree struggled with mainting environmental standards in the past cannot prove that this increase is due to any activity within its borders. In addition, also the fact that new factories were established in Othree's territory cannot serve as concluding proof, since we do not know anything about these factories or their GHG output. Concluding that factories are per se environmentally harmful would clearly go too far. We also know from the facts that the allegations by Ceotu that these factories are 'bad for the environment' are not supported by scientific facts.

Thus, it cannot clearly be established that Othree or its factories are responsible for the increase in GHGs. It could be due to the action of any other State or—what is more likely—the action of several States combined. It could also be due to the occurrence of a natural disaster such as large-scale burning of large areas of forests or volcanic eruptions. This difficulty in finding the responsible polluter illustrates a fundamental problem in relation to international environmental law, where it is notoriously difficult to establish conclusively the necessary links between an alleged polluter and harm resulting from pollution. While this might not be true for all areas of environmental law, it is certainly true for issues such as air pollution, the climate and often also sea pollution. A further problem is that a large number of States are polluter and victim at the same time, a situation that is not envisaged by the SRA.

Thus, it does not seem possible under the present circumstances and with the present information to bring a case against Othree under the SRA.

4. Hypothetical case

Necessity to be an injured State

If we assume that at least part of the increase in GHGs could conclusively be traced back to Othree's factories, and *if* we further assume that it could be clearly established that Othree has not passed the necessary laws and does not exercise the required controls in order to attain its reduction goals, then we might have a (weak) case under State responsibility. It would be a case of a catalysing act as seen above, since it is most likely not the government of Othree itself or any of its organs which pollute, but private individuals and companies (a further difficulty in international environmental law). Thus—as seen above—if Othree is violating its reduction goals under the Kyoto Protocol (mainly Article 3 Kyoto Protocol), it might be argued that it is violating an international obligation in force for it due to its failure to enact the necessary regulations and laws and to exercise appropriate controls (Articles 12 and 13 SRA). In addition, the omission could be said to be attributable to Othree, since it is the government of Othree which did not pass these laws (thereby satisfying Article 4 SRA, since the government clearly is an organ of the State).

Yet, the next difficulty under the SRA lies close at hand. According to Article 42 SRA, the responsibility of a State can be invoked by an injured State. While this normally does not pose any problems, it does not seem to be so obvious here. Certainly, Article 42(a) SRA is not possible, since the obligations under the Kyoto Protocol are not individually owed to Ceotu. Under Article 42(b)(i) SRA the injured State of an obligation owed to a group of States has to be 'specially affected'. However, an increase in GHGs is not limited to one State alone, but affects several if not all States in the world. Thus, Ceotu cannot be said to be a 'specially affected' State. Article 42(b)(ii) SRA then sets out the situation where the violation radically changes the position of the other States to which the obligation is owed concerning the further performance of this obligation. However, even if it could be clearly established that Othree was responsible for a breach of the Kyoto Protocol, this would not change the obligations of the other State parties under the Kyoto Protocol. The obligations specified in Article 3 Kyoto Protocol are calculated based on a 'base year', namely 1990 (ie the emission should be reduced by at least 5% under the 1990 levels). Thus, an increase in 2010 does not alter the parties' individual obligations in their own emission reduction. Therefore, it cannot convincingly be argued that Othree's hypothetical violation would alter the position of the other parties to the Kyoto Protocol. Consequently, Ceotu cannot be seen as an injured State in accordance with Article 42 SRA.

Options as a non-injured State

Article 48 SRA provides for the possibility that a non-injured State can invoke the responsibility of a State responsible for an internationally wrongful act. It should, however, be noted that it is not yet quite clear in practice how Article 48 SRA should be applied and there is quite some doctrinal debate and controversy surrounding this Article.

It can be argued that Article 48 paragraph 1(a) SRA is indeed fulfilled. The obligations under the Kyoto Protocol are owed to a group of States, including Ceotu, a party to the Kyoto Protocol. In addition, the emission reduction obligation is indeed established for the protection of a collective interest, namely the reduction of GHGs in the atmosphere and ultimately the fight against climate change—an issue affecting everyone.

[*Article 48 paragraph 1(b) would not be applicable since the obligation of reducing emissions is not owed to the whole international community but only to parties to the Kyoto Protocol. Even though everyone will ultimately profit from emission reductions, non-parties usually do not have rights and obligations under international treaties (see Article 34 Vienna Convention on the Law of Treaties), and thus this obligation cannot be owed to non-parties. Although a large majority of States are parties to the Kyoto Protocol, not all are, eg the USA. Thus, as long as not every State is party to a treaty or the rule is customary law, we cannot speak of a rule 'being owed to the whole international community'.*]

Yet, if we assume that Ceotu can indeed invoke Othree's State responsibility under

Article 48 paragraph 1(a) SRA, paragraph 1 of the same Article somewhat limits the possible consequences. Ceotu could ask Othree to cease the internationally wrongful act, ie to stop emitting more GHGs than allowed and to ask Othree for guarantees of non-repetition (letter (a)). Article 48 paragraph 2(b) SRA deals with the possibility of reparation, but again an injured State or a 'beneficiary of the obligation' is needed. However, as argued above, in this case none of the States can be said to be injured (following the argument made for Ceotu's case above). Therefore, asking for reparations would very likely not be possible.

5. Conclusion

We have seen above that it is not possible actually to bring a well-founded case against Othree in this situation. In the hypothetical case we have been asked to examine wherein Article 2 SRA is satisfied (ie violation and attribution has been established so that Othree is responsible for an internationally wrongful act), it has been shown that invoking State responsibility would still be hampered by the fact that arguably there exists no clearly identifiable 'injured State' as such. Other possibilities under the SRA such as Article 48 SRA are not well established and are surrounded by considerable doctrinal debate. Furthermore, the consequences of invoking Article 48 SRA are neither clear nor wholly satisfactory. As this case illustrates, State responsibility is not set up to play a crucial role in the environmental field and can only be successfully applied in a few well-defined cases where the link between environmental harm and the polluting or violating State in question can be clearly established.

Suggested Solution—Case 8.14

Abbreviations used

CFCs	= chlorofluorocarbons
ICJ	= International Court of Justice
Montreal Protocol	= Montreal Protocol on Substances that Deplete the Ozone Layer
NCP	= Non-Compliance Procedure
ODS	= ozone-depleting substances
VCLT	= Vienna Convention on the Law of Treaties

1. Applicable law

In order to solve this question we will first of all apply the Montreal Protocol on Substances that Deplete the Ozone Layer (Montreal Protocol). Argonia and Bismu are parties to this Protocol, and thus bound by it. Chloland is not a party to the Montreal Protocol, the consequences of which we will examine shortly.

In addition, we will also apply the Vienna Convention on the Law of Treaties (VCLT). Article 4 VCLT sets out the non-retroactivity principle contained in this convention. This means that the VCLT is not applicable to treaties, which have been concluded by States before all State parties to that treaty are also parties to the VCLT. Here, the three States in question are parties to the VCLT since its entry into force. The general entry into force of the VLCT—and thus also for Argonia, Bismu and Chloland—took place on 27 January 1980, in accordance with Article 84 paragraph 1 VCLT. The Montreal Protocol has been concluded in 1987, thus after the entry into force of the VCLT for all three States (only two of which are, however, parties to the Montreal Protocol). Therefore, the VCLT is in our case applicable to the Montreal Protocol.

[*The fact that the Montreal Protocol is called 'Protocol' and not treaty is irrelevant. As provided in Article 2 paragraph 1(a) VCLT, the name of such an expression of concurring wills of States under international law does not matter.*]

2. Situation of Chloland

Chloland is not a party to the Montreal Protocol. This means, however, that it is not bound by the provisions of this protocol either. The VCLT clearly provides in its Article 34 that treaties do not create obligations (or rights) for third States, without their consent. We do not know about any consent of Chloland to be bound by the obligations contained in the Montreal Protocol. Thus, the Montreal Protocol as such is not applicable to Chloland and consequently no action can be taken against this State under the Montreal Protocol.

Since the question is expressly limited to international treaty law, we do not have to deal with international customary law.

[*It should be noted that if the question would not be limited to international treaty law, an analysis of international customary obligations regarding the production and consumption of ozone-depleting substances (ODS) would be necessary. In doing so, the pedagogic split into State practice (positive actions, abstentions, but also behaviour at conferences and possibly statements) and* opinio juris *(the belief that something is 'the law') should be used, though keeping in mind that these two elements often overlap considerably. It is well established that treaty rules can become customary rules as well. Without going into too much detail, it seems that there could be a convincing case to claim that obligations to phase out ODS such as CFCs have become customary and thus also binding on Chloland. First of all, it could be pointed out that there is a general agreement among States as to the danger of ODS, thus demanding action. This was the general consensus at the conference adopting the Vienna Convention on Substances that Deplete the Ozone Layer and later on at the conference for the Montreal Protocol. Furthermore, these two instruments are among the most widely ratified treaties, each having—as of 31 August 2012—197 State parties. While this overwhelming participation is not necessarily an indication of the existence of an international customary rule in itself, it is one piece in the puzzle as well. We could further mention declarations such as the Stockholm Declaration where States recognised, apart from a general importance to limit dangerous levels of pollution, that there are limits to State sovereignty, which need to be balanced against the right of third States not to see their environment damaged (Principle 21). Other pieces in the line of evidence could be the* Trail Smelter *case, which recognised that States have a duty to protect other States from injuries emanating from actions of private individuals within its jurisdiction (Arbitral Tribunal, Award,* Trail Smelter Case *(USA, Canada), 1938, 1963). While the* Trail Smelter *case dealt with fumes, the analogy to the emission of ODS is relatively easy to see.*

It seems thus possible that the obligation generally to phase out ODS is indeed a customary obligation. Yet, contrary conclusions are also possible, based on different weighing of the above elements or the argument that it is very difficult to establish custom in presence of such a widely ratified treaty, since conforming behaviour will be due to treaty respect rather than the belief in opinio juris, *for example.*

In any event, it should be noted that in general procedural rules are not customary. Thus, any time limits contained in the Montreal Protocol for phasing out ODS would not directly apply to Chloland, but 'reasonable' time would have to be allowed. Furthermore, although Chloland might under customary law have the same obligations as parties to the Montreal Protocol, no action to induce Chloland to compliance can be taken under the Montreal Protocol or the Vienna Convention on Substances that Deplete the Ozone Layer. The Secretariat, responsible for these steps, is a body established by a treaty, which is not binding on Chloland. Since these are again procedural issues, there is no customary rule which allows Argonia to take action by involving this convention's Secretariat.]

3. Situation of Bismu

Unlike Chloland, Bismu is a party to the Montreal Protocol and is thus clearly bound by the conventional obligation to phase out ODS, including CFCs (see eg Article 2A of the Montreal Protocol specifically for CFCs). Article 26 VCLT clearly provides that parties to a treaty need to perform the obligations therein in good faith, thus they are binding on them. Hence, it seems indeed that Bismu is violating its obligations under the Montreal Protocol.

As a next step we need therefore to ascertain whether third States—such as Argonia—can take such actions as it has done under the Montreal Protocol.

Article 8 of the Montreal Protocol holds that the Meeting of the Parties shall establish procedures and institutions for dealing with non-compliance. The Meeting of the Parties indeed adopted a non-compliance procedure (NCP) for the Montreal Protocol (latest version in 1998, 10th meeting of the parties). According to paragraph 1 of this NCP, any State party can address its concern for the implementation of the Montreal Protocol by another party to the Secretariat of the Vienna Convention on Substances that Deplete the Ozone Layer. This communication has to be in writing and shall contain 'corroborating information'. The Minister for the Environment of Argonia has indeed sent a letter (thus information in writing) to the Secretariat. This letter also contains the latest scientific evidence (corroborating information). Consequently, the action taken by the Minister is perfectly legal under the Montreal Protocol.

4. Possible consequences

We are asked what the possible consequences of sending this letter might be. The Secretariat will now as a next step send the submission received from Argonia to Bismu, the concerned State party (paragraph 2 NCP). Bismu then has time to respond, but in accordance with paragraph 2, no later than six months after having received the submission, the Secretariat will forward all the information to the Implementation

Committee. This Implementation Committee is established based on paragraph 5 NCP, following the mandate given to the Meeting of the Parties in Article 8 of the Montreal Protocol to establish institutions. This Implementation Committee is composed of 10 State parties, elected by the Meeting of the Parties for two-year terms. The functions of this Implementation Committee are to be found in paragraph 7 NCP. Looking at these functions and subsequent paragraphs, it is very clear that this is not a court. The Committee under paragraph 7(d) NCP identifies facts and possible causes for non-compliance and then makes recommendations to the Meeting of the Parties. It is then the Meeting of the Parties which decides on what measures should be taken (paragraph 9 NCP). In paragraph 8 NCP it is stressed that the Implementation Committee shall try to achieve an 'amicable solution'. The desire to find such an amicable solution is also apparent from paragraph 9 NCP, talking about measures to 'assist' the party to achieve full compliance. At their fourth meeting, the Meeting of the Parties adopted an indicative list of measures that the Meeting of the Parties might take when facing non-compliance. These measures are mainly non-confrontational and aimed at helping the State to achieve compliance (appropriate technical, financial or other assistance such as technology and information transfers). The most 'punishing' decision the Meeting of the Parties could take is to suspend some specific rights and privileges under the Montreal Protocol, such as those related to trade, production and consumption, technology transfers and the financial mechanism.

5. Conclusion

In conclusion we can say that Argonia cannot take any action against Chloland under the Montreal Protocol, since Chloland is not a party to this Protocol and thus is not bound by its obligations. Concerning Bismu, however, Argonia acted in conformity with the Montreal Protocol and the NCP established based on Article 8 of the Montreal Protocol. Under this NCP, State parties can send well-supported information about non-compliance of other State parties to the Secretariat of the Vienna Convention on Substances that Deplete the Ozone Layer. The possible consequences recommended by the Implementation Committee and decided by the Meeting of the Parties are largely non-confrontational and aimed at helping the concerned State party to come back into compliance.

List of cases used—according to subject

(Some cases might appear in several subjects)

Note: this list is *not* exhaustive of all important case law, but only contains those cases used in the preceding exercises. In addition, it has been decided not to include the cases used in the exercises of Chapter 8, the specialised branches of international law, since these cases, and especially the subject to which they refer, are often very specific to this particular branch alone.

Subject	Case	Exercise book case where this case is quoted and/or used

Subjects of international law

States

Element of government (in definition of a State) also means that the State can control its territory to the exclusion other States (sovereignty).	→ Arbitral Tribunal, Award, *Island of Palmas case* (Netherlands, USA), 1928, 838	Case 1.1
Territorial sovereignty of States involves rights but as a corollary also a duty: to protect within its territory the rights of other States, eg in the form of the foreign State's nationals.	→ Arbitral Tribunal, Award, *Island of Palmas case* (Netherlands, USA), 1928, 839	Case 7.7
There is no prohibition of declarations of independence in international law and they are not generally seen as contrary to international law.	→ ICJ, Advisory Opinion, *Accordance with international law of the unilateral declaration of independence in respect of Kosovo*, 2010, paras 79–81	Case 7.11
Lotus principle: sovereign States may act in any way they wish so long as they do not contravene an explicit prohibition.	→ PCIJ, Judgment, *Lotus*, 1927, 18	Case 3.5

Principle of continuity of States (change in government is not important for the continuance of the State).	→ Arbitral Tribunal, Award, *Aguilar-Amory and Royal Bank of Canada claims* (*Tinoco case*) (Great Britain v Costa Rica), 1923, at 377, 378	Case 4.7; Case 7.3

International organisations

International legal personality of international organisations.	→ ICJ, Advisory Opinion, *Reparations of Injuries suffered in the Service of the United Nations*, 1949, 177–180	Case 1.2; Case 1.3
A vast majority of States can create an international organisation whose international personality also extends to non-parties.	→ ICJ, Advisory Opinion, *Reparations of Injuries suffered in the Service of the United Nations*, 1949, 185	Case 1.3

Diplomatic and functional protection

Diplomatic protection

ILC Draft Articles on Diplomatic Protection 2006 are a reflection of customary law.	→ ICJ, Judgment on Preliminary Objections, *Ahamdou Sadio Diallo* (Republic of Guinea v Democratic Republic of the Congo), 2007, para 39	Case 2.1; Case 2.2; Case 2.3; Case 2.4; Case 2.5 Case 7.7
Legal fiction: a State exercising diplomatic protection is in reality asserting its *own* right.	→PCIJ, Judgment on the Objection to the Jurisdiction of the Court, *The Mavrommatis Palestine Concessions*, 1924, 12	Case 7.7

The exercise of diplomatic protection is a discretionary right of the State.	→ ICJ, Judgment Second Phase, *Barcelona Traction, Light and Power Company Limited* (Belgium v Spain), 1970, paras 78, 79 → *Abbasi and Anor, R. v Secretary of State for Foreign and Commonwealth Affairs & Secretary of State for the Home Department*, 6th November 2002, [2002] EWCA Civ 1598, para 99	Case 7.7
The scope of *ratione materiae* of diplomatic protection has been extended and includes now all internationally guaranteed human rights (and no longer only the international minimum standard of treatment).	→ ICJ, Judgment on Preliminary Objections, *Ahamdou Sadio Diallo* (Republic of Guinea v Democratic Republic of the Congo), 2007, para 39	Case 7.7
The validity of the nationality is up to each State (reserved domain).	→ PCIJ, Advisory Opinion, *Nationality Decrees Issued in Tunis and Morocco*, 1923, 22–24	Case 2.1; Case 2.2; Case 2.3; Case 2.5 Case 7.7
Effective link requirement is set out.	→ ICJ, Judgment, *Nottebohm* (Liechtenstein v Guatemala), 1955, 22	Case 2.2; Case 2.3 Case 7.7
'Old' principle concerning double nationality in diplomatic protection (no protection possible against one of the two States of nationality).	→ ICJ, Advisory Opinion, *Reparations for Injuries Suffered in the Service of the United Nations*, 1949, 186	Case 7.7

'New' principle concerning double nationality in diplomatic protection (protection against State of nationality possible if there is an effective link of nationality).	→ Italian – United States Conciliation Commission, Decision No 55, *Mergé Case*, 1955, at 247 → Iran – United States Claims Tribunal, Award No 31-157-2, *Nasser Esphahanian (Claimant) v Bank Tejarat (Respondent)* (Case No. 157) 1983, reproduced in Iran–United States Claims Tribunal Reports, Vol 2, 1983 (I), Grotius Publications, Cambridge, 157, at 161–164	Case 7.7
In case of dual nationality and claim against a third State, no need to establish an effective link.	→ Arbitral Tribunal, Award, *Salem Case*, (Egypt v USA), 1932, 1188	Case 2.2 Case 7.7
Doubts whether need effective link requirement in all instances (case seems to say yes, need always an effective link).	→ ICJ, Judgment, *Nottebohm* (Liechtenstein v Guatemala), 1955, 21–23	Case 2.1; Case 2.5
Exhaustion of local remedies is a customary rule.	→ ICJ, Judgment on Preliminary Objections, *Interhandel* (Switzerland v United States of America), 1959, at 27 → ICJ, Judgment, *Elettronica Sicula SpA (ELSI)* (United States of America v Italy), 1989, para 50	Case 2.1; Case 2.2; Case 2.4; Case 2.5 Case 7.7

Functional protection

There is no hierarchy between functional and diplomatic protection, but the defendant State cannot be compelled to pay twice.	→ ICJ, Advisory Opinion, *Reparation for Injuries Suffered in the Service of the United Nations*, 1949, 185, 186	Case 2.5

Local courts have to be informed about findings of the UN Secretary General on immunity of UN agents. This creates a presumption of immunity, that can only be set aside by national courts for most compelling reasons.	→ ICJ, Advisory Opinion, *Difference Relating to Immunity from Legal Process of a Special Rapporteur of the Commission on Human Rights*, 1999, paras 60, 61	Case 2.5

Treaty law and customary international law

Treaty law

Lotus principle: sovereign States may act in any way they wish so long as they do not contravene an explicit prohibition.	→ PCIJ, Judgment, *Lotus*, 1927, 18	Case 3.5
The VCLT is a reflection of customary law.	→ ICJ, Judgment, *Gabčíkovo-Nagymaros Project* (Hungary/ Slovakia), 1997, para 46	Case 3.1; Case 3.4; Case 3.5; Case 3.6; Case 3.10 Case 7.1; Case 7.2; Case 7.3; Case 7.5; Case 7.8; Case 7.10
The denomination of a treaty does not matter.	→ ICJ, Judgment on Preliminary Objections, *South West Africa* (Liberia v South Africa and Ethiopia v South Africa), 1962, 331	Case 7.1; Case 7.3
A joint communiqué can be a treaty.	→ ICJ, Judgment on the Jurisdiction of the Court, *Aegean Sea Continental Shelf* (Greece v Turkey), 1978, para 96	Case 7.3
Minutes and exchange of letters can be a treaty.	→ ICJ, Judgment on Jurisdiction and Admissibility, *Maritime Delimitation and Territorial Questions between Qatar and Bahrain* (Qatar v Bahrain), 1994, paras 23–25	Case 7.3

The regime of reservations as contained in the VCLT is a reflection of customary international law.	→ ICJ, Judgment on the Jurisdiction of the Court and Admissibility of the Application, *Border and Transborder Armed Actions* (Nicaragua v Honduras), 1988, para 35	Case 7.5
Legal effects of reservations to a treaty and interpretative declarations.	→ ECtHR, *Belilos v Switzerland*, Judgment, Application No 10328/83, 29 April 1988, especially paras 38–60	Case 3.2; Case 3.3; Case 5.5; Case 7.1 Case 7.9
Consequence of invalidity of reservation to a treaty: also the consent to be bound is *invalid.*	→ ICJ, Judgment on Preliminary Objections, *Interhandel* (Switzerland v United States of America, 1959), Dissenting Opinion of Judge Lauterpacht, 116–119	Case 7.9
Consequence of invalidity of reservation to a treaty: invalid reservation is severable from the consent to be bound, which thus remains *valid.*	→ ICJ, Judgment on Preliminary Objections, *Interhandel* (Switzerland v United States of America), 1959, Dissenting Opinion of Judge Klaestad, 76–78	Case 7.9
Change of practice vis-à-vis reserving States: one acceptance by another contracting State is enough to make the reserving State a party to the convention (before: all States needed to accept to make the reserving State a party to the treaty).	→ ICJ, Advisory Opinion, *Reservations to the Convention on the Prevention and Punishment of the Crime of Genocide*, 1951, 21–26	Case 3.2 Case 7.1; Case 7.2; Case 7.5

International law prevails over domestic law (confirmation of Art 27 VCLT).	→ ICJ, Advisory Opinion, *Applicability of the Obligation to Arbitrate under Section 21 of the United Nations Headquarters Agreement of 26 June 1947*, 1988, para 57 → ICJ, Judgment, *Avena and other Mexican Nationals* (Mexico v United States of America), 2004, paras 111–113 → ICJ, Judgment, *LaGrand* (Germany v United States of America), 2001, paras 90, 91	Case 3.5
No obligation on States to know the internal law of other States and to keep themselves up to date about legislative and constitutional developments within other States.	→ ICJ, Judgment, *Land and Maritime Boundary between Cameroon and Nigeria* (Cameroon v Nigeria), 2002, para 266	Case 3.5
The Rule codified in Article 46 VCLT (provisions of internal law regarding competence to conclude treaties) is the same as in customary law.	→ Arbitral Tribunal, Award, *Case concerning the delimitation of maritime boundary between Guinea-Bissau and Senegal*, 1989, paras 54, 55	Case 7.10
Error (as then also later formulated in Art 48 VCLT) is a customary rule.	→ ICJ, Judgment, *Temple of Preah Vihear* (Cambodia v Thailand), 1962, 26	Case 3.6
VCLT rules on termination of a treaty on account of its breach (Article 60 VCLT) is a codification of customary law.	→ ICJ, Advisory Opinion, *Legal Consequences for States of the Continued Presence of South Africa in Namibia* (South West Africa) notwithstanding Security Council Resolution 276 (1970), 1971, para 94	Case 3.10

Material breach as a violation of a provision essential to the accomplishment of the object and purpose of the treaty (Article 60 para 3 VCLT, 2nd type of material breach).	→ Arbitral Tribunal, Award, *Case concerning the difference between New Zealand and France concerning the interpretation or application of two agreements, concluded on 9 July 1986 between the two States and which related to the problems arising from the Rainbow Warrior Affair*, 1990, para 100	Case 3.10
Fundamental change of circumstances (Article 62 VCLT) is customary international law	→ ICJ, Judgment on the Jurisdiction of the Court, *Fisheries Jurisdiction* (United Kingdom of Great Britain and Northern Ireland v Iceland), 1973, para 36	Case 7.3; Case 7.5
A fundamental change of circumstances 'must have been unforeseen' and Article 62 VCLT must be strictly construed.	→ ICJ, Judgment, *Gabčíkovo-Nagymaros Project* (Hungary/ Slovakia), 1997, para 104	Case 7.3; Case 7.5
The *State* is bound by treaties to which it has become a party (and thus continues to be bound even though government changes).	→ Arbitral Tribunal, Award, *Aguilar-Amory and Royal Bank of Canada claims* (Tinoco case) (Great Britain v Costa Rica), 1923, 377, 378	Case 7.4

Customary international law

Relationship treaty and customary international law in general: declaratory, crystallising and generating effect.	→ ICJ, Judgment, *North Sea Continental Shelf case*, (Germany v Netherlands/Denmark), 1969, paras 60–83	Case 8.5
Relationship treaty and customary international law: treaty and customary rules on the same subject exist independently from each other.	→ ICJ, Judgment on the Merits, *Military and Paramilitary Activities in and against Nicaragua* (Nicaragua v United Sates of America), 1986, paras 172–182	Case 8.5

Two element theory for the existence of a rule of customary international law: State practice and *opinio juris*.	→ ICJ, Judgment, *North Sea Continental Shelf case*, (Germany v Netherlands/Denmark), 1969, paras 70–79	Case 8.5
State practice for showing customary law: positive acts but also abstentions.	→ PCIJ, Judgment, *Lotus*, 1927, 28	Case 8.5
State practice only needs to be consistent 'in general'.	→ (ICJ, Judgment on the Merits, *Military and Paramilitary Activities in and against Nicaragua* (Nicaragua v United Sates of America), 1986, para 186	Case 8.5
State practice: need to look especially at the practice of States whose interests are specially affected.	→ ICJ, Judgment, *North Sea Continental Shelf case* (Germany v Netherlands/ Denmark), 1969, para 73	Case 8.5

State responsibility

The ILC Articles on State Responsibility are a reflection of customary law.	→ ICJ, Judgment, *United States Diplomatic and Consular Staff in Teheran* (United States of America v Iran), 1980, paras 56–92 → ICJ, Judgment, *Gabčíkovo-Nagymaros Project* (Hungary/ Slovakia), 1997, para 47 → ICJ, Judgment, *Application of the Convention on the Prevention and Punishment of the Crime of Genocide* (Bosnia and Herzegovina v Serbia and Montenegro), 2007, para 401	Case 4.1; Case 4.2; Case 4.3; Case 4.4; Case 4.5; Case 4.6; Case 4.7; Case 4.8; Case 4.9; Case 4.10 Case 6.1; Case 6.2 Case 7.1; Case 7.2; Case 7.3; Case 7.4; Case 7.5; Case 7.6; Case 7.7; Case 7.8; Case 7.9; Case 7.10; Case 7.11

'Complete dependence' test for attribution under State responsibility (Article 4 SRA).	→ ICJ, Judgment on the Merits, *Military and Paramilitary Activities in and against Nicaragua* (Nicaragua v United States of America), 1986, paras 109–112 → ICJ, Judgment, *Application of the Convention on the Prevention and Punishment of the Crime of Genocide* (Bosnia and Herzegovina v Serbia and Montenegro), 2007, paras 390–395	Case 4.2; Case 4.6 Case 7.1; Case 7.3; Case 7.8
Confirmation of rule that a State can be responsible for ultra vires acts of its organs (if they act in their official capacity) (Article 7 SRA).	→ Arbitral Tribunal, Award, *Thomas H. Youmans (USA) v United Mexican States*, 1926, paras 12–14	Case 4.3 Case 7.8
Effective control test for attribution under State responsibility (Article 8 SRA).	→ ICJ, Judgment on the Merits, *Military and Paramilitary Activities in and against Nicaragua* (Nicaragua v United States of America), 1986, paras 105–116 → ICJ, Judgment, *Application of the Convention on the Prevention and Punishment of the Crime of Genocide* (Bosnia and Herzegovina v Serbia and Montenegro), 2007, paras 396–407	Case 4.2; Case 4.4 Case 6.5 Case 7.1; Case 7.2; Case 7.3
Overall control test for attribution under State responsibility (Article 8 SRA).	→ ICTY, Appeals Chamber, Judgment, *Tadić* 1999, (Case No. IT-94-1-A), paras 99–145	Case 4.2; Case 4.4 Case 6.5 Case 7.1; Case 7.2; Case 7.3

Basis for Article 11 SRA.	→ ICJ, Judgment, *United States Diplomatic and Consular Staff in Teheran* (United States of America v Iran), 1980, especially paras 56–92	Case 4.6
Environmental protection as an essential interest of the State (Article 25 SRA, necessity).	→ ICJ, Judgment, *Gabčíkovo-Nagymaros Project* (Hungary/Slovakia), 1997 → Arbitral Tribunal, Award, *Award between the United States and the United Kingdom relating to the rights of jurisdiction of United States in the Bering's sea and the preservation of fur seals*, 1893	Case 4.9
Distress applied.	Arbitral Tribunal, Award, *Case concerning the difference between New Zealand and France concerning the interpretation or application of two agreements, concluded on 9 July 1986 between the two States and which related to the problems arising from the Rainbow Warrior Affair*, 1990, especially at paras 78–101	Case 7.10
The obligation to make reparation is customary law (a 'principle of international law').	→ PCIJ, Judgment, *Case concerning the Factory at Chorzów* (Claim for Indemnity), 1927, 21.	Case 4.1; Case 4.2; Case 4.3; Case 4.4; Case 4.5; Case 4.6; Case 6.2 Case 7.1; Case 7.2; Case 7.3; Case 7.4; Case 7.5; Case 7.6; Case 7.7; Case 7.8; Case 7.9

International dispute settlement—the International Court of Justice

Contentious cases

Definition of a dispute.	→ PCIJ, Judgment on the Objection to the Jurisdiction of the Court, *The Mavrommatis Palestine Concessions*, 1924, 11	Case 5.1; Case 5.3; Case 5.4; Case 5.5; Case 5.6; Case 5.7; Case 5.8; Case 5.9 Case 7.1; Case 7.2; Case 7.3; Case 7.4; Case 7.5; Case 7.6; Case 7.7; Case 7.8; Case 7.9; Case 7.10; Case 7.11
For the finding of the existence of a dispute, it has to be shown that the claims of the parties are positively opposed.	→ ICJ, Judgment on Preliminary Objections, *South West Africa* (Liberia v South Africa and Ethiopia v South Africa), 1962, 328	Case 7.2; Case 7.5; Case 7.7; Case 7.9; Case 7.10; Case 7.11
The presence of a dispute is an objective determination by the ICJ (what parties say does therefore not matter).	→ ICJ, Advisory Opinion, First Phase, *Interpretation of Peace Treaties with Bulgaria, Hungary and Romania*, 1950, 74 → ICJ, Judgment on Preliminary Objections, *Questions of Interpretation and Application of the 1971 Montreal Convention arising from the Aerial Incident at Lockerbie* (Libyan Arab Jamahiriya v United States of America), 1998, para 21	Case 5.3; Case 5.5; Case 5.6; Case 5.7; Case 5.8 Case 7.1; Case 7.2; Case 7.5; Case 7.6; Case 7.7; Case 7.8; Case 7.10; Case 7.11
Consent to the Court's jurisdiction is an essential principle.	→ ICJ, Judgment, *Monetary Gold Removed from Rome in 1943* (Italy v France, United Kingdom of Great Britain and Northern Ireland and United States of America), 1954, 3 → ICJ, Judgment, *Case concerning East Timor* (Portugal v Australia), 1995, para 26	Case 5.1; Case 5.3; Case 5.4; Case 5.5; Case 5.6; Case 5.7; Case 5.8; Case 5.9 Case 7.1; Case 7.2; Case 7.3; Case 7.4; Case 7.5; Case 7.6; Case 7.7; Case 7.8; Case 7.9; Case 7.10; Case 7.11

In order to make an optional clause declaration operational, transmission to the UN Secretary General is sufficient. It is not necessary that the other States have been informed about this new declaration before instituting proceedings at the ICJ based on this declaration.	→ ICJ, Judgment on Preliminary Objections, *Right of Passage over Indian Territory* (Portugal v India), 1957, 146, 147	Case 7.5
General principle of reciprocity of optional clause declarations (Article 36 para 2 ICJ Statute).	→ ICJ, Judgment, *Certain Norwegian Loans* (France v Norway), 1957, 23, 24	Case 5.7 Case 7.8
Principle of reciprocity of optional clause declarations: one party can also invoke the reservation to the optional clause declaration made by the other party.	→ ICJ, Judgment, *Certain Norwegian Loans* (France v Norway), 1957, 22–27 → ICJ, Judgment on Preliminary Objections, *Interhandel* (Switzerland v United States of America, 1959, 23	Case 5.3; Case 5.4 Case 7.8; Case 7.11
Jurisdiction of the Court under optional clause declarations (Article 36 para 2 ICJ Statute) is based on the smallest common basis.	→ ICJ, Judgment, *Anglo-Iranian Oil Co* (United Kingdom v Iran), 1952, 103	Case 5.3; Case 5.5 Case 7.1; Case 7.7; Case 7.8; Case 7.11
Invalidity of automatic reservations (self-judging reservations) to optional clause declarations: not dealt with by ICJ as such but confirmed by various separate and dissenting opinions in the *Interhandel* case (based mainly on two reasons: (1) with this type of reservation States do not assume any legal obligations; (2) incompatibility with Article 36 para 6 ICJ Statute.	→ ICJ, Judgment on Preliminary Objections, *Interhandel* (Switzerland v United States of America), 1959: —Separate Opinion of Judge Spender, 56,57; —Dissenting Opinion of President Klaestad, 76, 77; —Dissenting Opinion of Judge Lauterpacht, 115, 116; —Dissenting Opinion of Judge Armand-Ugon, 91–94	Case 5.5

Consequence of invalidity of reservation to optional clause declaration: also optional clause declaration is *invalid*. (The same reasoning is also applicable to invalid reservations to treaties.)	→ ICJ, Judgment on Preliminary Objections, *Interhandel* (Switzerland v United States of America), 1959, Dissenting Opinion of Judge Lauterpacht, at 116–119	Case 5.5
Consequence of invalidity of reservation to optional clause declaration: invalid reservation is severable from the optional clause declaration, which thus remains *valid*. (Same reasoning is also applicable to invalid reservations to treaties.)	→ ICJ, Judgment on Preliminary Objections, *Interhandel* (Switzerland v United States of America), 1959, Dissenting Opinion of Judge Klaestad, 76–78	Case 5.5
Confirmation of *forum prorogatum*.	→ ICJ, Judgment on Preliminary Objections, *Corfu Channel* (United Kingdom of Great Britain and Northern Ireland v Albania), 1948, 27, 28 → ICJ, Judgment, *Certain Questions of Mutual Assistance in Criminal Matters* (Djibouti v France), 2008, paras 60–95	Case 5.7 Case 7.2; Case 7.7; Case 7.8; Case 7.9
Continued validity of compromissory clauses in treaties, even if a party claims the treaty is invalid/terminated/suspended.	→ ICJ, Judgment on the Jurisdiction of the Court, *Fisheries Jurisdiction* (United Kingdom of Great Britain and Northern Ireland v Iceland), 1973, paras 43–45	Case 7.1; Case 7.4; Case 7.5; Case 7.6; Case 7.9; Case 7.10

Admissibility of cases before the ICJ: legal interest of a third State: needs to be the 'very subject-matter' and not 'only affected' by the decision.	→ ICJ, Judgment, *Monetary Gold Removed from Rome in 1943* (Italy v France, United Kingdom of Great Britain and Northern Ireland and United States of America), 1954, 32 → ICJ, Judgment on the Jurisdiction of the Court and the Admissibility of the Application, *Military and Paramilitary Activities in and against Nicaragua* (Nicaragua v United States of America), 1984, para 88 → ICJ, Judgment, *Case concerning East Timor* (Portugal v Australia), 1995, paras 28–29	Case 5.9 Case 7.4; Case 7.11

Advisory opinions

Advisory opinion: it is in the discretion of the Court to decide to answer even if jurisdiction is established (permissive formulation of Article 65 ICJ Statute).	→ ICJ, Advisory Opinion, *Reservations to the Convention on the Prevention and Punishment of the Crime of Genocide*, 1951, 19 →ICJ, Advisory Opinion, *Legality of the Use by a State of Nuclear Weapons in Armed Conflict*, 1996, para 14 → ICJ, Advisory Opinion, *Legal Consequences of the Construction of a Wall in the Occupied Palestinian Territory*, 2004, para 44	Case 5.10
Unless there are 'compelling reasons' ICJ should in principle (if it has jurisdiction) not refuse to give an advisory opinion.	→ ICJ, Advisory Opinion, *Certain Expenses of the United Nations (Article 17, paragraph 2, of the Charter)*, 1962, 155	Case 5.10

Use of force

The UN Charter in general is a reflection of customary international law, and both custom and treaty (Charter) continue to exist simultaneously.	→ ICJ, Judgment on the Merits, *Military and Paramilitary Activities in and against Nicaragua* (Nicaragua v United States of America), 1986, paras 172–179	Case 7.1; Case 7.11
Sovereign equality/rule of non-intervention is customary law (Article 2 para 1 UN Charter).	→ ICJ, Judgment on the Merits, *Military and Paramilitary Activities in and against Nicaragua* (Nicaragua v United States of America), 1986, paras 202–209	Case 4.7; Case 4.8; Case 4.10 Case 7.1; Case 7.6
Non-use of force is a customary law rule (Article 2 para 4 UN Charter).	→ ICJ, Judgment on the Merits, *Military and Paramilitary Activities in and against Nicaragua* (Nicaragua v United States of America), 1986, paras 187–192	Case 4.9; Case 4.10; Case 6.2 Case 6.4 Case 7.6; Case 7.10
Non-use of force is a rule of *jus cogens* (Article 2 para 4 UN Charter)	→ ICJ, Judgment on the Merits, *Military and Paramilitary Activities in and against Nicaragua* (Nicaragua v United States of America), 1986, paras 190	Case 6.3; Case 6.5; Case 6.7